Jukka Paastela

Finnish Communism under Soviet Totalitarianism

Oppositions within the Finnish Communist Party in Soviet Russia 1918–1935

Series B:27 Helsinki 2003

KIKIMORA PUBLICATIONS

Finnish Communism under Soviet Totalitarianism :
Oppositions within the Finnish Communist Party in Soviet Russia 1918–1935

ISBN 952-10-0755-9
ISSN 1455-4828

Graphic design of cover: Vesa Tuukkanen
Layout: Marita Alanko

Multiprint Oy
Helsinki 2003

Contents

Tables

List of Abbreviations

C.	Comrade
CC / C.C.	Central Committee
Cheka	Всероссийская чрезвычайная комиссия по борьбе с контрреволюцией, саботажем и спекуляцией (Чека) (All-Russian Extraordinary Commission for Combating Counterrevolution, Sabotage and Speculation, 1918–1922; predecessor of the GPU)
Chekist	An agent of Cheka. This term were also generally used after the organisation's name was changed.
Com.	Comrade
Comintern	Коммунистический интернационал (Communist International, known also as the Third International, 1919–1943)
CPSU	Communist Party of the Soviet Union
d.	Дело (file)
DF	Document folder
ed. hr.	Единица хранения (storage unit)
Ek-Valpo	Etsivä keskuspoliisi – Valtiollinen poliisi (Finnish Detective Central Police – Political Police)
f.	Фонд (collection)
GPU	Государственное политическое управление (State Political Administration [attached to the Council of People's Commissars of the Russian Soviet Federative Socialist Republic], 1922–1923; successor to Cheka, predecessor of the OGPU)
KA	Kansallisarkisto (National Archives)
Krestintern	Крестьянский интернационал (Peasants' International; known also as the International Peasant's Council, 1923–1933)

KtS!	*"Kallis toveri Stalin!" : Komintern ja Suomi* ("Precious Comrade Stalin!" : Comintern and Finland). For publication data, see Bibliography.
l.	Лист (page)
ll.	Листы (pages)
MCC	Minutes of the Central Committee of the SKP
MMC	Manner & Malm Correspondence. Kullervo Manner and Hanna Malm, *Rakas kallis toveri : Kullervo Mannerin ja Hanna Malmin kirjeenvaihtoa 1932–33.* (Dear Precious Comrade : Correspondence between Kullervo Manner and Hanna Malm in 1932–1933.) For publication data, see Bibliography.
MMFB	Minutes of the meeting of the Foreign Bureau of the SKP
MMP	Minutes of the meeting of the Politburo of the SKP
MOPR	Международная организация помощи борцам революции (International Organisation for Aid to Revolutionary Fighters, 1922–1947)
MPCC	Minutes of the Plenum of the Central Committee of the SKP
NEP	Новая экономическая политика (New Economic Politics)
NKVD	Народный комиссариат внутреннух дел (People's Commissariat for Internal Affairs, successor of the OGPU from 1934)
OGPU	Объединенное государственное политическое управление (State Political Administration [attached to the Council of People's Commissars of the Russian Soviet Federative Socialist Republic]), 1923–1934 , successor of the GPU, predecessor of the NKVD. During the OGPU period, the abreviation GPU was also commonly used.
op.	Opisx (inventory)
PF	Personal folder
Profintern	Красный интернационал профсоюзов (The Red International of Trade Unions, 1921–1937)
PSS	В. И. Ленин, *Полное собрание сочинений* (Lenin's Collected Works, fifth edition)
Rabkrin	Рабоче-крестьянская инспекция (Workers' and Peasants' Inspection)
RGASPI	Российский государственный архив социально-политической истории (Russian State Archive of Social and Political History), formerly Российский центр хранения и изучения документов новейшей истории (Russian Centre for the Preservation and Study of Documents of Contemporary History, RTsKhIDNI). – The page numbers in RGASPI documents of refer to the original page numbers of the documents and not to possible later page numbering made in the archives, unless otherwise stated.

RKP(b)	Российская коммунистическая патрия (большевиков) (Russian Communist Party (Bolsheviks)), the official name of the Party between the VIIth Congress in March 1918 and the XIVth Congress in December 1925.) Also referred to in the text as the "Bolshevik Party".
RSDRP	Российская социал-демократическая рабочая партия (Russian Social Democratic Labour Party, the official name of the Party from its Ist Congress in March 1898 to the VIth Congress in August 1917)
RSDRP(b)	Российская социал-демократическая рабочая партия (большевиков) (Russian Social Democratic Labour Party (Bolsheviks)), the official name of the Party between the VIth Congress in August 1917 and VIIth Congress in March 1918
RTsKhIDNI	See RGASPI
SDP	Suomen Sosialidemokraattinen Puolue (Finnish Social Democratic Party)
SKP	Suomen Kommunistinen Puolue (Finnish Communist Party)
SSTP	Suomen Sosialistinen Työväenpuolue (Finnish Socialist Workers' Party)
STV	*Suomen Tilastollinen Vuosikirja / Annuaire Statistique de Finlande*
TTA	*Työväenjärjestöjen Tiedonantaja*
VPK(b)	Всесоюзная коммунистическая партия (большевиков), (All-Union Communist Party (Bolsheviks), the official name of the Party between the XIVth Congress in December 1925 and the XIXth Congress in October 1952). Also referred to in the text as the "Bolshevik Party". (VKP was also an abbreviation used in Finnish. It meant "Venäjän kommunistinen puolue" or the Russian Communist Party.)
URSS	Union of Socialist Soviet Republics

They [the Bolshevik leaders] were not celebrating the triumph of the proletariat, but the triumph of the idea of the proletariat

MAX EASTMAN on the fifth anniversary of the Bolshevik revolution, 1922

Preface

I became interested in the history of the SKP in 1918–1935 in 1993, when the archives of the former Soviet Union became accessible to non-Communist foreign researchers. Since the SKP was an illegal party in Finland in 1918–1944, all its documents were in Moscow. I was able to work in the former Institute of Marxism-Leninism for ten months in 1994–1995. I am deeply grateful to Kirill Anderson, leader of the Russian Centre for the Preservation and Study of Documents of Contemporary History (RTsKhIDNI, later renamed the Russian State Archive of Social and Political History, RGASPI), and to the personnel of the institute for their patience with me. I read, or at least leafed through, the whole collection of papers of the SKP (*fond* 516) and in addition Finnish and Russian documents concerning the Finnish Party oppositions in other collections.

In the University of Tampere I have enjoyed rewarding discussions in the more or less informal Research Education Seminar. I have also given lectures to undergraduates on my subject and received much interesting feedback. Professor (emeritus) Olavi Borg, Professor Vilho Harle, Docent Jyrki Iivonen and Docent Mikko Lahtinen read the final draft of the manuscript and made valuable suggestions to improve the text. I am most grateful to them, as well as to those postgraduate students who commented in papers read in various seminars. An anonymous referee of the Kikimora Publications suggested valuable alterations and corrected some factual mistakes I had done. I want to thank him or her.

This work has been possible within the framework of the *CPSU and Finland* research project, funded by the Academy of Finland and led by Professor Ohto Manninen. Cooperation with him and other members of the team, Docent Hannu Rautkallio and Licentiate Konstantin Sorokin has been pleasant. I warmly thank them, as well as the Academy of Finland for the possibility to do the research.

I express my special thanks to my Russian teacher, Liisa Marchenko, who spared no efforts in hammering the language into my hard skull. I am deeply indebted to her, since without a knowledge of Russian the project might never have been completed. Robert MacGilleon corrected my numerous grammatical mistakes and made my clumsily worded and structured sentences readable. For this I am very grateful to him. In addition, I acknowledge my debt to Veikko Tarvainen, who helped me in the proof-reading and in compiling the index. We had many interesting discussions over this study. Thanks are also due to Marita Alanko for efficient editing. In the process of publication I was also ably aided by Elina Kahla, director of publication of the Kikimora publications. – In transliterating of Russian names I have used the standard US Library of Congress system.

The reader may wonder why I publish this volume only now in 2003. There have been two reasons for the deferment, teaching duties and another research project. After my return home from Russia in 1995, being now involved in problems of totalitarianism, authoritarianism, etc., I noted that most of the textbooks in Finnish universities dealt with democratic societies only. However, if one does not understand the alternatives to democracy, one perhaps does not understand democracy itself very well. I therefore wrote a textbook on autocracies, oligarchies, tyrannies, despotisms, dictatorships, military governments, theocracies, one-party governments and so on and about conceptions concerning non-democratic political systems, *Yksin- ja harvainvallasta : tutkimus muinaisista ja nykyisistä autokratioista ja oligarkioista sekä niistä esitetyistä käsityksistä*, which was published in two volumes at the end of 2000.

Tampere, January 1, 2003

Jukka Paastela

I Introduction

In 1922 Max Eastman, an American Communist (later disillusioned), made his pilgrimage to Russia and participated in the fifth anniversary celebrations of the Great Proletarian October Revolution in Moscow. He was surprised to see that the Red Square and its surroundings, including a public park, were hermetically sealed off from the toiling masses, the proletariat. There were guards "armed to the teeth with weapons of war" on horses ensuring that nobody without authorisation entered the closed *jubilée* area. For Eastman these guards "were not distinguishable from the Cossacks of infamous memory". Eastman was there with a friend, who knew Russia better; he smiled at Eastman's naïveté and remarked that they were in Russia, not in America.[1]

Another Communist, Eric Hobsbawn, in the title of his famous book on the political panorama of the XXth century, refers to as an *Age of Extremes.* Hobsbawn quotes Yehudi Menuhin, who said that this century "raised greatest hopes ever conceived by humanity and destroyed all illusions and ideals".[2] The great violinist no doubt had Communism and Russia in mind when he levelled this condemnation. His parents were émigrés from Imperial Russia and he knew the Soviet Union fairly well, having visited in the country in 1945 and several times later.[3]

Traditions associated with the famous "Russian soul" were not erased by the new leaders although they ruled in the name of the working class. The Finnish

---

1 Max Eastman, *Love and Revolution : My Journey Through an Epoch*, p. 328, quotation on p. 329.

2 Eric Hobsbawn, *Age of Extremes : the Short Twentieth Century 1914–1991*, p. 2.

3 Yehudi Menuhin, *Unfinished Journey*, pp. 245–253. One day in 1945, Menuhin succeeded in taking a walk in Moscow without his guide. He joined a queue for food and pondered: "Between the food lines and the state banquets the gulf seemed as pitiless as that in France before 1789". (*Ibid.*, p. 247.)

Reds, who had escaped to Russia after the Red defeat in the Civil War found much to wonder at. Nonetheless, the Finnish Red leaders who adopted the Bolshevik doctrine (not all did) very soon became adapted to the realities of the "Workers' State", including notably the privileges of those who held political and economic power. – There were contradictions, however. It was difficult to explain to rank-and-file Finns why they had to live in misery whilst the leaders, at least many of them, lived, relatively speaking, in luxury. Oppositions arose; not all of them were by any means "proletarian"; the struggle for power within the leadership of the Finnish Communist Party (*Suomen Kommunistinen Puolue*, SKP) was in some, if not most cases more important than the protests of ordinary members.

The study of Communism is no easy matter. If we speak of crimes committed under the rule of the Communist parties in various countries from Russia to Ethiopia, does this mean that we must brand all Communist parties as criminal organisations at least in countries where they have been or still are in power?[4] Can we use one term, totalitarianism, when we speak of so-called Socialist or Communist countries? Can we compare Nazism and Communism and use this term in pointing out possible similarities between them?

There have been "grand debates" on Communism and its relation to Nazism in France and Germany. In Finland, somewhat similar, fervent, even caustic debate took place around January 27, 1998, when eighty years had elapsed since the beginning of the Finnish Civil War. I shall revert to these debates at a later point. My interest here is to study how a party which claims to be that of the working-class, develops into a totalitarian one when it functions in a totalitarian state and society. The Finnish Communist Party, SKP (*Suomen kommunistinen puolue*) was founded in Soviet Russia in August 1918 after what was called the Finnish Revolution ended the defeat of the Reds. Perhaps as many as 20,000 Reds (the precise number is not known) escaped to Russia and the Party founded in Moscow was a party of refugees. A refugee, writes Harto Hakovirta, is one who has left her/his country in fear of persecution, mayhem, violence etc. in order to find protection against them. A refugee ceases to be an exile if she or he goes back to the country of origin or becomes self-supporting in the country of asylum,[5] especially if this person is granted citizenship of the host state.

The lot of the Finnish refugees was far from pleasant, Russia herself being in a state of chaos, but acceptable in that for the alternative in Finland could be facing a firing squad. Eventually some refugees returned to Finland, some even succeeded

---

4 The idea of "criminality" is not mine. On the dust cover of *Molotov Remembers : Inside Kremlin Politics : Conversations with Felix Chuev*, Woodford McClellan, Professor of Russian History in the University of Virginia, characterises the Communist Party of the Soviet Union as a "gigantic criminal organization".

5 Harto Hakovirta, *The World Refugee Problem*, p. 10.

in migrating to America; most, however, remained in Russia, especially in Russian Karelia. They were now émigrés, no longer refugees.

1. The Purpose of this Study

The main purpose of this present study is to elucidate the policy-making among the Finnish émigrés in Soviet Russia from one particular point of view, that of opposition formation. The rationale in investigating emigration politics is that emigration is from a political viewpoint a strange phenomenon. Friedrich Engels wrote to Karl Marx in a letter dated February 12, 1851 – roughly one and half years after their escape from Germany to England – that[6]

> [o]ne comes to realise more and more that emigration is an institution which inevitably turns a man into a fool, an ass and a base rascal unless he withdraws wholly therefrom and unless he is content to be an independent writer who doesn't give a tinker's curse for so-called revolutionary Party. It is a real school of scandal and meanness in which the hindmost donkey becomes the foremost saviour of his country.

Engels was indubitably familiar with the phenomenon of which he wrote. England was in the second half of the XIXth century a shelter for many kinds of refugees from the Continent. Russia under the Bolshevik rule was afar cry from Liberal England. For a Finnish Red who did not know Russian the SKP represented the only possibility of engaging in politics. For intellectuals the SKP was also some kind of a haven in which, especially in the 1920s, it was possible retain personal independence. Not independence, however, in the way Engels conceived it. One had to remain within the framework set by the Party. This framework was at the outset, 1918–1920, fairly expansive, but it was gradually tightened in the 1920s. In congresses, conferences and Central Committee plenums, debate was still reasonably open in the early 1930s; in the 1935 Congress, however, there were no dissidents. The Party had become, we may say, totalitarian.

One approach in assessing the internal democracy of a political party is to consider the freedom versus non-freedom of internal oppositions. Are they tolerated and if so, to what extent? Robert Michels, whose aim was to show how oligarchies impede any mode of political (or trade union, co-operative etc.) organisation, pictured extremely cynically (or rather realistically, depending on the point of view) the relation of Party leaders to internal oppositions. He wrote:[7]

---

6 Published in Karl Marx and Frederick Engels, *Collected Works*, vol. 38, p. 287.

7 Robert Michels, *Zur Soziologie des Parteiwesens in der modernen Demokratie : Untersuchungen über die oligarchischen Tendenzen des Gruppenlebens*, p. 215.

> It is sought to discredit every new oppositional current in the Party as demagogical [by the Party leaders]. When this current makes a direct appeal to the elements of the masses who are dissatisfied with the people who dominate the Party, it is explained as inexpedient, as a wicked attempt to split the Party and undermine the Party discipline without considering whether the motives of the opposition are heinous, or based on tactical conviction, or the most honorary and relevant grounds in the world and undoubtedly justified by the basic right of all democracy.

There may be a great deal of truth in these words, but a number of critical remarks may be appropriate. Firstly, we may ask whether it is impossible, that there may be an opposition which in reality consists of "vulgar intriguers"? Secondly, in multi-party democracies, Conservative and Liberal parties are usually organised on less stringent principles, so to speak, than parties of the Left. This remark, of course, is relevant only in a political system under which party formation is free. There is also a phenomenon – this is our third point – which gives internal oppositions a good deal of weight: let us call it "doctrinism". On the Left (and among the Greens, for that matter) the question of party doctrine has been much more important than in parties of the Right or Centre. Communism has perhaps been more doctrinal than any other party formation in known history; the doctrine has been, moreover, robustly utopian as to its ultimate aim.[8] For this reason internal conflicts in Communist parties also have been centred more on Party doctrine than in any other pattern (this also includes Fascist-type parties). From the point of view of party study, one has to take into account quarrels over doctrines in Communist parties much more seriously than is the case with, say, Conservative parties. This also means, of course, that a student of Communism must know the doctrine. The doctrine was also especially important in early phases of the Communist movement, when Communist parties in capitalist countries were clearly anti-system parties.[9] Communism also penetrated the everyday life of the members of the Party – in Soviet Russia as well as in capitalist countries where the movement was strong – more thoroughly than in other parties. The distinction between public and private life was, as Maurice Duverger wrote, non-existent, which meant that the Party was totalitarian.[10]

If a study of Communism, in its many variations – one should always keep in mind that there have been many versions of it –, demands a knowledge of the doctrine, a study of émigré Communism demands a knowledge and understanding of the "strange institution" of emigration. Especially in such a study as this, which is a study of elite(s), one must look at "external" aspects such as the knowl-

---

[8] I shall refer to this briefly in the context of V. I. Lenin's *State and Revolution* and in connection with the Workers' Opposition in Russia.

[9] See Giovanni Sartori, *Parties and Party systems : a framework for analysis*, vol. 1, p. 132.

[10] Maurice Duverger, *Les partis politiques*, p. 183.

edge of the Russian language possessed by political actors, in order to understand certain phenomena. There were ethnically Finnish people in Russia who were bilingual and there were those who could speak only a few words of Russian. Bilingual persons were mostly Finns who were born in St. Petersburg or in Ingermanland, that is the hinterland to the city,[11] or had migrated from Finland to Russia before the Finnish Civil War of 1918. Some Russo-Finns also knew Finland rather well because they had worked or studied there. A bilingual individual had many advantages compared with those who had studied Russian, a language very difficult for Finns, when they were already adults. It was easy to form connections with Russians; it was also easy to understand unwritten rules, for instance, what is considered polite and what is not in Russian society. Some intellectuals, for example Otto Wille (in Russia known as Otto Vil'gel'movich) Kuusinen, had already studied Russian in Finland and when, in Russia in 1918, he realised that without Russian political activity was impossible, he studied the language thoroughly. At the outset he could use German in discussions with the Bolshevik Party, because its leaders, Vladimir Il'ich Lenin, Lev Davidovich Trotskii, Grigorii Evseevich Zinov'ev, Nikolai Ivanovich Bukharin, Lev Borisovich Kamenev, Karl Berngardovich Radek and others were fluent in German and that language was the working language of the Comintern.[12] On the other hand there were those who did not study Russian. Many of them initially believed that it would be possible to return to Finland very soon, i.e. they were convinced that a new revolution would save the situation.

Are émigrés experts on the politics of their old homeland? This is not strictly speaking the subject of this study, but I would point out that researches have convinced me that they do not necessarily possess any expert knowledge of their old countries.[13] The level of their understanding may, however, vary considerably and even one individual may in one situation understand a political situation very badly and in another very well. A case in point in this regard is Kuusinen. In 1930 the prohibition of all Communist front-organisations in Finland came as a surprise to Kuusinen, who was sure that the Finnish workers would not submit to this, but would flock to the barricades. The second time the Finnish workers behaved in a way Kuusinen found incomprehensible was in the Winter War of 1939–1940. No

---

11 There were 140,000 ethnic Finns – called *chukhna* by the Russians – in Ingermanland in 1917 (Pekka Nevalainen, "Inkerinmaan levottomuudet ja Suomen rajarauha 1919–1920" in *Kahden Karjalan välillä : kahden Riikin riitamaalla*, p. 149.)

12 Коммунистический интернационал (Communist International)

13 Niccolò Machiavelli observed this perspicaciously. He wrote that refugees (now people who want to go back to their home countries but cannot do this for political reasons) "naturally believe much that is false and artfully add much more". "A ruler", Machiavelli warns, meaning a ruler of a host country, "should be slow to take up an enterprise because of what some exile has told him, for more often than not all he will get out of it is shame or most grievous harm". (Niccolò Machiavelli, *The Discourses* [*on the First Ten Books of Titus Livius*], book II, ch. 31.)

"resistance movement" emerged in Finland, no soviets were established by the workers and poor peasants in spite of Russian propaganda to the effect that this would be politically correct.[14] – On the other hand, in 1963 Kuusinen advised the Finnish Communist leaders to make a pact, albeit an informal one, with the Social Democratic Party and the Agrarian League in order to achieve sufficient acceptatability to rise to the status of a government Party. The SKP leaders behaved as Kuusinen had advised them and entered the government in 1966.[15] – Already in 1961, when the new programme for the Communist Party of the Soviet Union under construction, Kuusinen thought that the Communists could make in the West alliances with the Social Democrats.[16]

There were four oppositions, i.e. factions[17] within the Finnish Communist Party in Soviet Russia in the years 1918–1935, i) the Kuusinen Opposition (1919–1921), which consisted mainly of intellectuals; ii) the Murder Opposition (1919–1923), which comprised mainly workers; iii) the Rahja Opposition (1919– or 1921–1927), which also mainly consisted of workers and iv) the Manner and Malm Opposition (1928–1935), comprising mainly intellectuals. (See time scale on p. 138). The questions I seek answers to in this study are the following: i) under what conditions did an internal opposition grow up; ii) how did such an opposition work; iii) what sort of relationships were there between the opposition and the Party leadership; iv) what kind of doctrinal differences were there (if any), and v) what kind of international examples, especially Russian, influenced the Finnish oppositions. This last question is awkward in that there were analogous movements in various countries. This, however, does not prove that there were connections, or even influence between them. The Workers' Opposition and other similar oppositions in the Russian Communist Party (Bolsheviks), RKP(b)[18] in 1919–1923, probably had no influence on "workers' oppositions in Finnish colours"; it may nonetheless be appropriate here to glance at the Russian oppositions.

---

[14] No less a personage than L. D. Trotskii (in exile!) fully believed official Soviet propaganda that "Soviets of workers and poor peasants" were established in Finland. (Trotskii, "Bilan de l'expérience finlandaise", published in Léon Trotsky, *Défense du marxisme : U.R.S.S., marxisme et bureaucratie*, p. 257.)

[15] Jukka Paastela, *The Finnish Communist Party in the Finnish Political System 1963–1982*, pp. 57–58.

[16] Jukka Renkama, "Kuusinen ja neuvostovaltion käsitteen uudistaminen vuosina 1957–1961" in *O. W. Kuusinen neuvostoideologina* (forthcoming).

[17] The words *faction* and *fraction* are used here in different meanings. *Faction* is a more or less organised group or political tendency inside a political party. *Fraction* is a group inside a so-called mass organisation. If there is, for instance, a Communist group within a trade union, group is called a *fraction*.

[18] Российская коммунистическая партия (большевиков) (Russian Communist Party (Bolsheviks)) was the official name of the Party between the VIIth Congress in March 1918 and the XIVth Congress in December 1925.

2. On Sources and Former Studies

The most important archival source used in this study has been the archive of the Finnish Communist Party in the *Russian State Archive of Social and Political History* (RGASPI), the former *Russian Centre for the Preservation and Study of Documents of Contemporary History* (RTsKhIDNI), under the Soviet power *Institute of Marxism-Leninism.* Its *fond* or collection number is 516 and it consists of two *opisi* or inventories. In inventory 1 there are documents of the Finnish Social Democratic Party before summer 1918 and papers pertaining to Finnish Red's bodies in the summer of 1918, before the founding of the SKP in August 1918. There are also some casual papers of the SKP. Inventory 2 contains papers of the SKP.

A necessary question when we speak of the archives of the former Soviet Union is whether they have been "cleansed" or not. I assume that there might have been some purge of material like personal letters in the late 1930s. This is, however, only an impression which I cannot substantiate. Since then, I presume, there has been no "purge". One apparent lack is in papers on the "military line" of the SKP. There are some concerning work among Finnish soldiers in collection 516, but not much. They might have been destroyed, possibly already in the 1920s or 1930s. It is, however, also possible that in 1918–1921 no papers were written; the "military line" might have operated largely in a verbal basis. This limited my possibilities of obtaining an overall picture of the Rahja Opposition, because Eino Rahja was a leader of that line. As will be shown in the chapter VI, the Murder Opposition had something to do with the spying organisation(s) of the Red Army, but what exactly has been impossible to establish.

One obstacle, the seriousness of which is difficult to estimate, has been the fact that it was possible to get Comintern documents (collection 495) only very restrictedly. Documents of the Secretariat were declassified, but those of the Presidium were not. There were few documents of these organs in *fond* 516, however, but these were "accidentally" there.

Personal folders were an important means of power in the Communist movement. Sad to say, it has been quite impossible to get these folders. In Moscow, one needed the written permission of descendants or relatives of persons whose folders one sought. It was, however, possible to get the folders of persons if one could prove that they had no descendants. Malm and Manner had none; therefore, their folders were obtainable. Before the opening of Russian archives to researchers who had no mandate from any Communist Party, it was possible for such mandate-holders to obtain personal folders. In the *Kansallisarkisto* (the National Archives, former *Valtionarkisto*, the State Archives) in Helsinki, there are personal folders of the Finnish Detective Central Police (*Etsivä keskuspoliisi*, later *Valtiollinen Poliisi* or Political Police) and they are at the disposal of everyone up to the year 1948. When the Political Police was led by the Communists in 1945–1948 these folders were cleansed, but, fortunately, not very extensively. Nevertheless, O. W. Kuusinen's folder,[19] for instance, contains only a few insignificant documents. The professionalism of the Detective Central Police was low in the early years of independence and this had its consequences for archive material, but by about the mid-1920s expertise achieved a satisfactory level.[20] The aim of the Detective Central Police was to put as many Communists as possible behind bars, and this must of course be taken into account; in several cases, however, the material of the Detective Central Police corroborates that in Moscow.

There are some copies of collection 516 in *Kansan arkisto* (the People's Archives) in Helsinki. If one is studying the activities of the SKP and its front-organisations between 1918 and the 1930s in Finland, it is necessary to read the materials in this archive. – There are two primary source publications, apart from the publication of sources made by the SKP itself in the 1930s. The correspondence between Hanna Malm and Kullervo Manner from 1932 and 1933 when Hanna Malm was in exile in Ukhta (Kullervo Manner and Hanna Malm, *Rakas kallis toveri*), edited by Hannu Rautkallio and myself, was published in 1997. – *"Kallis toveri Stalin!" : Komintern ja Suomi* ("'Precious Comrade Stalin!' : Comintern and Finland"), edited by Natalia Lebedeva, Kimmo Rentola and Tauno Saarela, was published in 2002. The collection includes some, presumably only now declassified documents, which were new to me. Many documents, however, were the same as I had read in Moscow. I have not changed my original notes to archive materials which are not only in Finnish but also in Russian or in German (or in some cases also in English or in French), translated from Russian or German into Finnish for *"Kallis toveri Stalin!"*. If, however, a document has been published in this collection, I have added information on that book (abridged KtS!) to my notes. For material new to me now used, I have referred only to this collection; there are references to original sources. – There is one difficulty concerning archival *signums*. In *fond* 516 they have been changed in 2000. In 1995, collection 516 was exceptionally divided according to years. Now the numbering follows the usual *fond – opis' – delo* system. The editors of *"Kallis toveri Stalin!"* have had to use both the old and the new system. They state, however, that it is also possible to locate documents in the archive according to the old system[21] which I have been confined to.

There are also two important books of documents concerning Finnish-Russian relations, although not from the period of this study. The first is *Puna-armeija Stalinin tentissä : talvisodan jälkipuinti Kremlissä 14. – 17.4.1940* ("The Red Army in Stalin's examination : post-mortem of the Winter War in the Kremlin, April 14 – 17, 1940), edited by Ohto Manninen and Oleg A. Rzheshevski, published by Edita

---

19 Archival number 603.

20 See Matti Lackman and Tuulia Sirviö, "Etsivä keskuspoliisi : 'valkoisen Suomen' turvallisuuspoliisi (1919–1937" in *Isänmaan puolesta : Suojelupoliisi 50 vuotta*, pp. 22–23.

21 "Teknisiä selityksiä" in *"Kallis toveri Stalin!" : Komintern ja Suomi*, p. 91.

in Helsinki in 1997.[22] The second is *NKP ja Suomi 1953–1962* ("The CPSU and Finland 1953–1962), edited by Hannu Rautkallio, Mikhail Su. Prozumenschikov and Natalia G. Tomilina, published by Tampere University Press, 2001. There is also a Russian version of this book: *КПСС и Советско-финляндские отношения : сборник документов* 1953–1962. Составители: Н.Г. Томилина (ответственный редактор), Х. Рауткаллио, Л.А. Величанская, И.В. Казарина и М.Ю. Прозуменщиков, published by Tampere University Press, 2001. These two versions are not identical.

There are various earlier studies in which some aspects of the oppositions – especially the Murder Opposition – have been researched. The best English-language study as for the Comintern period of the Finnish Communist Party is still John H. Hodgson's *Communism in Finland*, published in 1967. It is based on abundant published material and interviews with Finnish Communist movement veterans. A. F. Upton's study "The Communist Party of Finland" (in A. F. Upton with contributions by Peter P. Rohde and A. Sparring, *Communism in Scandinavia and Finland: Politics of Opportunity*) is based on narrower sources than Hodgson's. The most famous memoir on the Communist movement in Finland 1918–1939 is that written by Arvo Tuominen, a secretary general of the SKP in the late 1930s. His several books are published only in Finnish, but there is a shortened version of them in English, *The Bells of the Kremlin : an Experience in Communism* (1983). There is a remarkable doctoral dissertation on all memoirs published by Finns who experienced the reality of the GULag, Erkki Vettenniemi's *Surviving the Soviet Meat Grinder : the Politics of Finnish Gulag Memoirs*. One book of memoirs about the GULag by Aino Kuusinen (Otto Wille Kuusinen's second wife), originally published in German (*Der Gott stürzt seine Engel*, Wien: Fritz Molden Verlag, 1973), has been translated into many languages, including English, Finnish, French and Swedish. Finally, there are two anthologies in English, *Communism National & International*, edited by Tauno Saarela and Kimmo Rentola (Helsinki: Suomen Historiallinen Seura, 1998), which contains seven articles on the SKP and Soviet Karelia, and *Rise and Fall of Soviet Karelia*, edited by Antti Laine and Mikko Ylikangas (Helsinki: Kikimora Publications, 2002). This anthology contains articles written by both Finnish and Russian scholars.

As to studies in Finnish, there are two outstanding doctoral dissertations on the history of the SKP: Tauno Saarela's *Suomalaisen kommunismin synty 1918–1923* (The Birth of Finnish Communism 1918–1923), published in 1996 and Kimmo Rentola's *Kenen joukoissa seisot? : Suomalainen kommunismi ja sota 1937–1945* (In

---

22 Bibliographical data are mentioned if a book is not used as a source in this study. If it is, the reader will find these data in the Bibliography.

Whose Ranks Do You Stand? : Finnish Communism and War 1937–1945) published in 1993. Very useful book is also a history of the Social Democratic Party, written by Hannu Soikkanen, *Kohti kansanvaltaa* (Toward People's Power), vol 1, *1899–1937 : Suomen Sosialidemokraattinen Puolue 75 vuotta* (the Social Democratic Party 75 years old). Panu Rajala and Hannu Rautkallio have published a biography on Arvo Tuominen, *Petturin tie : Arvo Poika Tuomisen todellinen elämä* (The Path of a Traitor : Arvo Poika Tuominen's Real Life) in 1994.

As to Soviet Karelia, there is Markku Kangaspuro's important dissertation *Neuvosto-Karjalan taistelu itsehallinnosta : nationalismi ja suomalaiset punaiset Neuvostoliiton vallankäytössä 1920–1939* (Soviet Karelia's Struggle over Autonomy : Nationalism and the Finnish Reds in the Soviet Wielding of Power), was published in 2000. There is an English summary, pp. 375–386. Juri Kilin's *Suurvallan rajamaa : Neuvosto-Karjala Neuvostovaltion politiikassa 1920–1941* (Borderland of a Great Power : Soviet Karelia in the Politics of the Soviet State, 1920–1941) was published in 2001 (original in Russian). There is an English summary, pp. 262–266. Hannu Rautkallio's *Suuri viha : Stalinin suomalaiset uhrit 1930-luvulla* (Great Hate : Stalin's Finnish Victims in the 1930s) was published in 1995, and Jukka Rislakki's and Eila Lahti-Argutina's *Meillä ei kotia täällä : suomalaisten joukkotuho Uralilla 1938* (We have no Home Here : the Mass Destruction of Finnish Defectors in the Ural 1938, Helsinki: Otava, 1997.) Finally, it should be mentioned that Eila Lahti-Argutina, a prominent member of the *Memorial* society in Petrozavodsk, has collected data on 8,000 Finns who were arrested and sent to labour camps in the 1930s, 1940s and early 1950s. As Lahti-Argutina emphasises, the catalogue is far from complete, because many more Finns suffered the fate of being condemned to labour camp or to be executed as "enemies of the people". The title of Lahti-Argutina's book is *Olimme joukko vieras vain : venäjänsuomalaiset vainouhrit Neuvostoliitossa 1930-luvun alusta 1950-luvun alkuun* (We Were Only an Alien Herd : the Russian-Finnish Victims of Persecution from the beginning of the 1930s to the beginning of the 1950s).

II Totalitarianism and Communism

The term "totalitarianism", although invented in the 1920s,[1] only attained common usage in Nazi-German and Soviet studies in the United States in the 1950s. There most important works on totalitarianism were Hannah Arendt's *The Origins of Totalitarianism* (1951), Merle Faisod's *How Russia Is Ruled* (1953) and Carl J. Friedrich's and Zbigniew K. Brzezinski's *Totalitarian Dictatorship and Autocracy* (1956). This was the era of the "Cold War" and "totalitarianism" as a concept acquired strong conservative (in the American sense of the word) overtones. The most enduring of these studies has, arguably, been that by Arendt. The questions raised by theoreticians of totalitarianism were, however, not entirely new. Aristotle's analysis of tyranny[2] comes in many ways close to the modern analysis of totalitarianism and Stalinism. For Aristotle tyranny is degenerated monarchy, i.e. the rule of one man over the *polis*.[3] In tyranny, there are two elements, extreme democratic and extreme oligarchic, of which it is a composite. The tyrant rises from the populace and presents himself as a friend of the people, who fights against the notables to prevent their abuse.[4] Plato considered it probable that the origin of tyranny was in a democratic regime where "the mightiest and most savage form of slavery results from pushing freedom to the extreme".[5] A tyrant leads a populace,

---

[1] About history of the concept, see Leonard Schapiro, *Totalitarism* and my *Yksin- ja harvainvallasta : tutkimus muinaisista ja nykyisistä autokratioista ja oligarkioista sekä niistä esitetyistä käsityksistä*, vol. 1, pp. 380–386.

[2] See Mario Turchetti, *Tyrannie et tyrannicide de l'Antiquite à nos jours*, pp. 83–95.

[3] *The Politics*, 1279b15–20.

[4] *Ibid.*, 1310b.

[5] *The Republic*, 564a

seizes power and does various deeds favourable to the people, he frees them from debt and distributes land. Once in power he begins to prepare war and tightens taxation. Probably some of those politicians who helped him in the take-over and share the power begin to disapprove of his policy. The bravest of them speak out, even to the tyrant himself. In order to stabilise his power the tyrant now purges all dissidents until not "a man of worth, friend or foe, remains".[6]

Aristotle examines tyranny from two viewpoints: first, how a tyrant should, in order to preserve his power, handle the people and second, as what kind of a man he must present himself. He must, paradoxically, prevent both collectivism and individualism among the populace. All individual, independent thinkers and men who distinguish themselves from the mass must be suppressed; collective associations and leisured discussion must not be permitted. The tyrant must know what is going on among the people; therefore he needs spies, "eavesdroppers" who are sent out to places where people meet and gather.[7] The tyrant must publicly behave as if he were a steward of the state, not a tyrant. He should honour those who prove good in some respect, but leave punishment to others, officials or courts. No single man, however, must be exalted in the proximity of the tyrant; there must always be several so that they will watch each other.[8]

Also oligarchy, a degenerate form of aristocracy, has explanatory power in the study of totalitarianism. Aristotle distinguished four forms of oligarchy, only one of which is pertinent here,[9] namely the type where power is in the hands of (possibly hereditary) officials.[10]

Many of the criteria of tyranny presented by Aristotle can also be seen in modern totalitarianism. Firstly, totalitarianism has a *popular and egalitarian basis.* In Bolshevism, this can be seen in the legitimation of the regime. This was effected by pleading that the regime realises the objective interests of the working-class and its "historical task", the building of Communism.[11] Secondly, a totalitarian system seeks to *mobilise* people in activities which are (at least seemingly) political, but under the tight control of Party authorities. Any independent political activity is

---

6 *Ibid.*, 565d–567c.

7 *The Politics*, 1313b1–25.

8 *Ibid.*, 1314b40–1315a15

9 Other forms are i) access to political office is restricted by a property qualification; ii) in addition to the property qualification the ruling oligarchy itself fill open posts; iii) positions among the oligarchy are hereditary. (*The Politics*, 1292a39–1292b5.)

10 *Ibid.*, 1292b5–10.

11 See e.g. Richard Kossolapow, "Zur Herausbildung des kommunistischen Charakters der Arbeit im realen Sozialismus", *Marx-Engels-Jahrbuch* 3, 1980, pp. 9–24 and Michail Mtschedlow, "Das Problem des Allgemeinmenschlichen und Klassenmäßigen im Marxismus-Leninismus", *Marx-Engels-Jahrbuch* 2, 1979, pp. 54–72.

forbidden. Thirdly, the political system is, in Aristotelian terms, *tyranny* or *oligarchy* or *a combination* of these. An elite, the vanguard in Leninist language, rules. Among the elite, there may be one revered leader, but the leadership can be also collective.

As Aristotle did not "know" the role of the vanguard Party in totalitarianism, we should add a fourth criterion to our list: in a totalitarian society, *one political Party holds all political power.* This criterion is further qualified by the following five appendages: i) the Party is responsible to nobody for its doings; ii) it is impossible to topple the Party from power by institutional means; iii) the Party maintains an official ideology by which it legitimates its power; iv) the ruling elite seeks to indoctrinate people at school, in the army and in various "mass" movements in such way that they adopt, more or less profoundly, that ideology; v) the Party leads all state organs and organisations of mass mobilisation. A totalitarian Party is, as Edgar Morin defines it, "a Party in which all spiritual and temporal powers are concentrated in the apparatus which governs, controls and administers".[12] – Finally, the fifth criterion of totalitarianism is that only if all the criteria mentioned above are present a society is a totalitarian one.[13]

All totalitarian regimes are authoritarian, but not vice versa. In a typical authoritarian regime, there is no elaborated ideology and no enduring extensive and intensive political mobilisation of people. There can be mobilisation for instance when a charismatic leader makes a coup d'état, but this mobilisation is relatively temporary. For authoritarian governments, like military dictators, the political passivity of their subjects presents no problem.[14]

1. Arendt and Associates on Totalitarianism

Hannah Arendt's *The Origins of Totalitarianism* appeared for the first time in 1951. In fact, only the third part of the book considers totalitarianism (the other two discuss antisemitism and imperialism).[15] Arendt's primary material is drawn mainly from Nazi Germany, and she often extrapolates her conclusions to the Soviet Union. Arendt saw totalitarianism as a fiction: totalitarian movements "conjure up",

---

[12] Edgar Morin, "The Anti-totalitarian Revolution" in *Between Totalitarianism and Postmodernity : a Thesis Eleven Reader*, pp. 88–89.

[13] Cf. Juan J. Linz, "Totalitarian and Authoritarian Regimes" in *Handbook of Political Science*, vol. III, pp. 188–192.

[14] *Ibid.*, pp. 179–180 and p. 264.

[15] For the background to Arendt's book, see David Watson, *Arendt*, pp. 36–41 ja Derwent May, *Hannah Arendt*, pp. 59–72. On commentaries, see Sylvie Courtine-Denamy, *Hannah Arendt*, pp. 213–249, Angnes Heller, "An Imaginary Preface to the 1984 Edition of Hannah Arendt's The Origins of Totalitarianism" in Ferenc Fehér ja Agnes Heller, *Eastern Left, Western Left*, pp. 243–259 and Stephen J. Whitfield, *Into the Dark : Hannah Arendt and Totalitarianism.*

before the seize power, "a lying world of consistency" which appears "more adequate to the needs of human mind than reality itself" and in which "uprooted masses can feel at home and are spared the never-ending shocks which real life and real experiences deal to human beings and their expectations".[16] In a totalitarian state lying may be consistent and its scale may be vast simply because people usually have no rival sources of information.[17] It is well known that the Soviet leaders made every effort to jam foreign radio station and succeeded fairly well; only in border areas, it seems, was the jamming not successful.

Some critics of Arendt have complained that the empirical basis of *The Origins of Totalitarianism* is too frail. Raymond Aron writes that Arendt replaces real history by "ironical and tragic history".[18] In addition, of course, she and her followers were accused of spreading "cold war hysteria". Totalitarianism was not a fiction, but Arendt's conceptions were fictive.[19] The problem in this kind of criticism is that Arendt's book is being taken for a historical tract which it is not. There cannot be a society which is identical with a theoretical model. It may be useful to use concepts similar to Feudalism and Capitalism, even if no "one hundred per cent Capitalism" has ever existed. It may be useful, for instance, when we wish to point out differences between capitalist and precapitalist modes of production.[20] Moreover, I would claim that the "best" examples of totalitarianism are closer to the model of totalitarianism (consider North Korea!) than some democratic societies to any "model" of democracy. Is the United States more a plutocracy than a democracy?

There has been extensive debate on totalitarianism and many counter-arguments have been presented. It has been said, for instance, that the concept of totalitarianism in fact excludes personalities, political leaders, because it is a "structuralist" theory. Richard C. Tucker criticises Hannah Arendt's claim that in totalitarian society leaders are not needed as human beings but as "functions"; only as such are they "indispensable" for a totalitarian movement.[21] According to Tucker, this kind of argumentation reveals the fundamental "flaw" of the theory of totalitarianism. The function of institutions in a totalitarian society may seem to be

---

16 Arendt, *The Origins of Totalitarianism*, p. 353.

17 *Ibid.*, p. 413.

18 Aron published his criticism in *Critique*, January 1954. (Courtine-Denamy, *Hannah Arendt*, p. 229.) One may ask whether it is possible to write about the Soviet Union, "the only country in the world with an unpredictable history", as a popular saying goes without considering tragic element. (Quoted by Scott Shane in his *Dismantling Utopia* : *How Information ended the Soviet Union*, p. 121.)

19 Robert Burrowes, "Totalitarianism : the Revised Standard Version", in *Between Totalitarianism and Pluralism*, p. 36 Burrowes' critique was written in 1969, when a new edition of *The Origins of Totalitarianism* appeared.

20 Leszek Kolakowski, "Totalitarianism and the Virtue of the Lie", in *1984 Revisited* : *Totalitarianism in Our Century*, p. 122.

21 Arendt, *The Origins of Totalitarianism*, p. 387.

depersonalised, but in the final analysis "radically evil behaviour" is always that of a human being, "a totalitarian dictator".[22] I deem this conception correct if it means that we should not exclude political leaders from history. An analysis of Stalinism would be curious indeed if the personality of I. V. Stalin were totally absent. However, what is essential is that political leaders always act in some institutions and are "part" of a political structure. The young Iosif Vissarionovich acted in circumstances of revolutionary agitation, provoking the working-class to action such as strikes. In other circumstances I. V. Dzhugashvili might well have ended his days as an Orthodox priest.

Many concepts have been devised to replace or to complement totalitarianism.[23] Martin Malia, in his analysis of Soviet society, uses such terms as "partocracy" and "ideocracy". He does not present them as alternatives to the concept of totalitarianism; by ideocracy and partocracy, he claims he makes a similar upturn as Marx did to dialectics of Hegel. In traditional Soviet studies, economic and societal factors have often been seen in Marxian fashion as basis, ideology and policy as superstructure. According to Malia, the situation is the contrary.[24] Ideocracy means "secular theology", in which "The Idea of Socialism" ruled (as in traditional theology God) through the vanguard Party. Partocracy means a society where everything has been submitted to the "political imperatives" of the all-powerful Party.[25] Undoubtedly Malia is right as to the role of ideology (and Party, of course) in Soviet society. There is propaganda in every society, but the Soviet Union was the first state of which we can say that it was propaganda-dominated. To Bolsheviks propaganda was part of education, the aim of which was no less than the creation of a new kind of human beings.[26] All possible means were used to this end: agita-

---

22 Tucker, "Does Big Brother Really Exist?" in *1984 Revisited : Totalitarianism in Our Century*, p. 92.

23 Linz mentions in his article "Totalitarian and Authoritarian Regimes" (p. 110) such concepts as "administrative totalism", "populist totalitarianism" and "totalitarianism without terror". It is difficult to see what real improvements such terms would mean. In addition, T. H. Rigby's "mono-organisational society" is similar in this regard. Applied to the former Soviet Union this means that political organisations have a dominating position over organisations like market and religion, but despite all centralisation, coercion and indoctrination, there are "cleavages" based on local, professional etc., interests, which are different. (T. H. Rigby, "Politics in the Mono-organizational Society" in *Between Totalitarianism and Pluralism*, pp. 196–209.) There have certainly been no societies without cleavages.

24 Martin Malia, *The Soviet Tragedy : a History of Socialism in Russia, 1917–1991*, p. 8. Claude Lefort represents a standpoint rather similar to Malia's. He, however, wonders why the non-Communist Left has not been eager to use the concept of totalitarianism. Lefort's explanation is that Socialists may be good politicians but they cannot usually understand society in political terms. (Claude Lefort, *The Political Forms of Modern Society : Bureaucracy, Democracy, Totalitarianism*, pp. 277–278.)

25 Malia, *The Soviet Tragedy*, pp. 137–138.

26 Cf. Peter Kenez, *The Birth of the Propaganda State : Soviet Methods of Mass Mobilization 1917–1929*, pp. 8–9.

tors, press, teaching in schools and universities and even in conservatories, where not only music but also Marxism-Leninism was taught.

There were placards and banderols everywhere. If we imagine how this might function if transformed to the West, we can picture banderols like the following: "Raise High the Banner of Tocqueville's Liberalism!" over the Champs Elysée in Paris, "Glory to the Stock Exchange!" over Wall Street in New York, or "We Build Together the People's Home!" over the Kungsgatan in Stockholm.[27]

The one-party system is one of the creations of the twentieth century,[28] although something resembling it existed in the XIIIth and XIVth centuries in Florence, when the Guelph Party was in power there.[29] A totalitarian society has always a one-party system, although not all such systems (for example many weak political systems of Africa) have been totalitarian.

What is the methodological significance of the conception of totalitarianism for research? It must be clear that it is not reasonable, or even possible, to describe day-to-day policy by this conception. I agree with Steven Paul Soper, who sees the purpose of the conception to be to identify the criteria of totalitarianism, to understand conceptually what kind of society we are dealing with.[30]

---

[27] Cf. Hedrick Smith, *The Russians*, p. 378. Ideological banderols did not entirely disappear in Russia with Communism. In July 1995 there was a banderol "For Civil Peace and Social Harmony!" over the Puskinskaia ulitsa in Moscow.

[28] There are also different opinions. Barrington Moore Jr. speaks of totalitarian features in Chinese premodern society. It consisted of three elements, a "welfare" system (granaries for times of shortage of grain), a system of mutual surveillance (*pao*, a chief of ten households reported upward on the conduct of members of the *pao*) and a system of popular indoctrination (compulsory lectures on Confucian ethics). (Barrington Moore Jr., *Social Origins of Dictatorship and Democracy : Lord and Peasant in the Making of the Modern World*, pp. 205–207). If we accept these kinds of phenomena as criteria for totalitarianism, we can label as totalitarian very old societies. According to Plutarch nobody in Sparta could live as he pleased, the Spartans "viewed themselves as part of their country, rather than as individuals". (Plutarch, *Lucurgus*, 24, in *Plutarch on Sparta*, p. 36. See also e.g. Oswyn Murray, *Early Greece*, pp. 160–161.) Prostration, "a symbol of total submission" (Karl A. Wittfogel, *Oriental Despotism : a Comparative Study of Total Power*, pp. 152–153) may be regarded as a symbol of totalitarianism. In addition, worship of rulers as Gods (see e.g. Rafael Karsten, *A Totalitarian State of the Past : the Civilization of the Inca Empire in Ancient Peru*, pp. 104–105) can be considered such a symbol etc. A totalitarian society as defined above, can, however, exist only in modern society.

[29] Max Weber (*Wirtschaft und Gesellschaft : Grundriss der verstehenden Soziologie*, p. 849) was perhaps the first to realise that the Bolshevik creation was not absolutely the first in the history of humankind. On this case, see Gene Brucker, *The Civic World of Early Renaissance Florence*, p. 15 and 41; *Gene Brucker, Florentine Politics and Society 1343–1378*, pp. 116–120, p. 125 and 132.

[30] Steven Paul Soper, *Totalitarianism: a Conceptual Approach*, p. 33.

2. The Communist Party

In the Party, we trust. In the Party, we see the reason, honour, and conscience of our epoch.

V. I. Lenin[31]

In totalitarianism the idea of political pluralism, democracy or struggles among political ideas are not countenanced even within the Party. The Bolsheviks, however, held more or less clearly, a belief according to which the democratic regime inside the Party could compensate for the lack of political pluralism in society. Thus the Communist Party could act as the trusted regulator which built the country according to the interests of what was seen as the "leading force" of society and its "ally", the peasantry.[32]

We may call Leninist concept of the Party a theory of substitution and reflection. V. I. Lenin identified the dictatorship of the Party with that of the proletariat. The Party, which is only a "drop in the ocean" of the whole people, can rule only if it "conveys correctly the consciousness of the people"; otherwise, it would not be able to rule and lead the proletariat "correctly" and the proletariat, in turn, would be unable to lead other "masses".[33] Substitution takes place when the Party, according to Lenin, "imbibes, if I may say so, the vanguard of the proletariat and this vanguard effectuates the dictatorship of the proletariat".[34]

The conception of the Party as supervisor of the masses was one of the most important doctrines of Leninism. According to Trotskii's *Terrorism and Communism* (1920) the dictatorship of the proletariat meant, "direct power of the revolutionary vanguard, which is based on the heavy strata of the workers; if needed, this vanguard compels those who remain rearward, to rise to the level of head".[35]

We can find the roots of this substitution and reflection in Russian radical thinking in the XIXth century, especially in the concept of the *intelligentsia*. This concept has, in its traditional Russian meaning, a paternalist connotation. The *intelligent* had a mission: he had to serve the people but at the same time patronise them, because the people did not know their own interests: these interests had therefore to be taught. Antonio Gramsci's concept of the intellectual and his division of

31 В. И. Ленин, "Политический шантаж", *Пролетарий*, Aug. 24 / Sept. 6, 1917. В. И. Ленин, *Полное собрание сочинений*, издание пятое (hereafter abridged as PSS), vol. 34, p. 261.

32 *Власть и оппозиция : российский политический процесс XX столетия*, p. 89.

33 В. И. Ленин, Политический отчет центрального комитета РКП(б) 27 марта, 1922. Speech in the XIth Congress of the RKP(b), March 27–April 2, 1922. PSS, vol. 45, p. 112.

34 В. И. Ленин, О профессиональных союзах, о текущем моменте и об ошибках т. Троцкого : речь на соединенном заседании делегатов VIII съезда советов, членов ВЦСПС и МГСПС – членов РКП(б) до декабря 1920 г. PSS, vol. 32, pp. 203–204.

35 Л. Троцкий, *Терроризм и коммунизм*, p. 104.

intellectuals into traditional and organic[36] are crucially different from the old Russian conception of the intelligentsia in that, for instance, Gramsci's traditional intellectuals, like priests – whose main function especially in the countryside was ritualistic and magic[37] – or those in high positions in the ranking system of Tsar, did not belong to the intelligentsia. Those who belonged to it formed a small minority of non-careerist educated Russians who came mainly from the nobility or the bourgeoisie.[38] They had a moral vision of a better society. There were various visions depending, for instance, on whether an intelligent was a Slavophile or a Westerniser, but here only the radical vision itself matters.[39] According to a Russian religious thinker, Nikolai Aleksandrovich Berdiaev, an intelligent is a fanatic because Russians tend to totalitarian thinking; scepticism is alien to them. If an intelligent adopts, say, Darwinism, this Darwinism is not a biological theory, subject to debate, but a dogma and a basis of syllogisms like "we descend from apes, therefore we must love each other". The soul of such an intelligent is thirst for the "Absolute" under which every phenomenon of life must be subjected. An intelligent cannot accept any particular, only the universal and the result is idolatry.[40]

Berdiaev's description is extremely harsh; the author clearly loathes the type of person he describes. It is nonetheless impossible, I think, to deny the basic validity of his description. We can speak of the intelligentsia in a broad and in a narrow sense. In the narrow sense an intelligent was, as already defined, a person who had a special moral vision;[41] in the broad sense, an intelligent was any politically liberal or radical-minded educated person. Narodniks were, of course, typically intelligents. Broadly speaking we may define as a Narodnik anyone, who aimed at some kind of revolution which would bring down Tsarism and the Orthodox Church and establish an ideal egalitarian and collectivist society. The peasantry had to be an agent of this revolution and therefore it was the task of the intelligents to "go to the masses" and agitate among them with their revolutionary doctrines.[42]

---

[36] Antonio Gramsci, *Selections from the Prison Notebooks*, pp. 14–16.

[37] Richard Pipes, *The Russian Revolution 1899–1919*, p. 110. Some clerics taught children to read and write, but many holy men – if not practically illiterate – had themselves difficulties in reading and writing and therefore had great trouble if they tried to teach.

[38] L. G. Churchward, *The Soviet Intelligentsia : an Essay on the social structure and roles of Soviet intellectuals during the 1960s*, pp. 1–2. Cf. also Richard Pipes, *Russia under the Old Regime*, pp. 251–253 and André Ropert, *La misère et la gloire : histoire culturelle du monde russe de l'an mil à nos jours*, pp. 258–260.

[39] Cf. Boris Kagarlitsky, *Thinking Reed : Intellectuals and the Soviet State : 1917 to the Present*, pp. 12–34.

[40] Nicolas Berdyaev, *The Origin of Russian Communism*, pp. 16–19.

[41] Cf. Pipes, *Russia under the Old Regime*, pp. 251–253.

[42] Cf. T. H. Rigby, *The Changing Soviet System : Mono-organisational Socialism from its Origins to Gorbachev's Restructuring*, pp. 27–28.

Of Narodniks the most important predecessor of Lenin as a Party theorist was Piotr Nikitich Tkatchev who formulated a doctrine of a small tightly organised and disciplined vanguard who alone can have higher consciousness and morale than ordinary people and therefore must stage a coup d'état and establish a dictatorship. This should not be left to any indefinite future, but immediately, right now![43] When the revolutionary vanguard was then in power, it must, in order to achieve Communism, organise a "collective dictatorship", eliminate "hostile elements", establish revolutionary tribunals and control the press and even family relations.[44] This was unmistakably a Blanquist doctrine. Lenin also thought that the masses, in this case industrial workers, could not form a "social democratic consciousness"; intelligents would form it and bring it to the workers.[45] The German National Socialists had a basically similar theory of a vanguard Party, although the "Aryan masses" had to fulfil their national task shown to them by the Nazi Party.[46] To be sure, there was an important difference between the Nazi and the Bolshevik theory of the Party. Adolf Hitler in his *Führerprinzip* openly despised the masses[47] whereas Lenin declared that the Party must have a "connection with the masses" because thereby the vanguard was able to educate, to enlighten the masses and "to guide *all* their activity toward a conscious class policy".[48]

We may illustrate this Party concept by the example of Andrei Andreevich Gromyko. Gromyko joined the Party in 1931. He relates that this was the fulfilment of his "dream":[49] "The members of the Party were at that time as always in the whole history of our state in the foremost front and carried out the most important and most difficult tasks." They agitated for collectivisation and on Saturdays and Sundays did "voluntary" work such as helping in unloading firewood from wagons.[50] This passage in his memoir adequately illustrates the experience of Party members; they felt they were in a special position – and they indeed were in a special position, they were even special creatures. Stalin said in his oration after Lenin's death the following:[51]

---

[43] Adam B. Ulam, *In the Name of People : Prophets and Conspirators in Prerevolutionary Russia*, p. 243; Franco Venturi, *Roots of Revolution : a History of Populist and Socialist Movements in Nineteenth Century Russia*, pp. 413–414 and p. 419.

[44] Albert L. Weeks, *The First Bolshevik : a Political Biography of Peter Tkatchev*, p. 97.

[45] В. И. Ленин, *Что делать? : наболевшие вопросы нашего движения*, pp. 38–39, PSS, vol. 6, pp. 38–39.

[46] Aureh I. Unger, *The Totalitarian Party : Party and People in Nazi Germany and Soviet Russia*, pp. 10–11.

[47] Adolf Hitler, *Mein Kampf*, vol. 1, *eine Abrechnung*, pp. 197–202.

[48] В. И. Ленин, "Как В. Засулич убивает ликвидаторство", *Просвещение*, September, 1913, PSS, vol. 19, p. 404.

[49] Andrej Gromyko, *Erinnerungen*, p. 34.

[50] *Ibid.*, p. 36

[51] И. В. Сталин, По поводу смерти Ленина : речь на II Всесоюзном съезде Советов, 26 января 1924 г. И. В. Сталин, *Сочинения*, vol. 6, p. 46.

> Comrades! We Communists are special creatures. We have been shaped in special matter. We are those who form the army of a great proletarian strategist, the army of Comrade Lenin. There is no higher honour than the honour to belong to this army. [...] Not everybody can be a member of such a Party. Not everybody can endure those hardships and storms that follow membership of such a Party. The sons of the working-class, the sons of indigence (*нужда*) and struggle, of unbelievable hardship and heroic efforts – precisely (*вот*) they, above all, must be members of such a Party.

The special position of Party members, described in militaristic and masculine terms, followed from the place of the Party in society, which remained immutable even though Lenin spoke against "Communist pomposity" or "compomposity" "to use similar great Russian language".[52] (The reader may decide whether Stalin's oration just quoted was or was not pompous.)

Although the principle of democratic centralism allowed, in principle, presentation of different opinions before resolutions, it was discipline which dominated life in the Party as the central element. I. V. Stalin cited Lenin, who during the Civil War had said that the Party could carry out its task only if it was organised "as centralistically as possible", only if there was "iron discipline close to military discipline". Stalin concluded that there must be this kind of discipline before the achievement of the dictatorship of the proletariat. When this dictatorship was then attained, there must be even harsher discipline.[53]

We may consider solidarity the opposite of discipline, at least of blind obedience of orders. When the Bolshevik leaders tried to impose their discipline on the workers, one of the "hindrances" was the solidarity felt by the workers. In the summer of 1923 there were strikes in several factories in Petrograd and Moscow. When the GPU[54] began to investigate the "origin" of these strikes, it found, after considerable efforts, that there was a "Workers" Group" (of which more later) and, espe-

---

[52] В. И. Ленин, Политический отчет центрального комитета РКП(б) 27 марта, 1922. Speech in the XIth Congress of the RKP(b), March 27–April 2, 1922. PSS, vol. 45, p. 261. In addition, Stalin attacked pomposity. He quoted Lenin (the same passus we cited) and defined pomposity as "sick belief in force of fiction and construction of ukases". (И. В. Сталин, *Об основах ленинизма : лекции читанные в Свердлосвском университете* (1924) in И. В. Сталин, *Сочинения*, vol. 6, p. 187.) Stalin declared that "Leninist style in work" means two things: "a) Russian revolutionary wing-spread (*размах*)" and b) American efficiency (*деловитость*)." (*Ibid.*, p. 186.) Later Stalin dropped out his "American efficiency". But still in the beginning of the 1930s his Finnish disciples might speak about "American efficiency" (*amerikkalainen asiakkuus*). (Kullervo Manner to Hanna Malm, Jan. 27, 1933. Published in Kullervo Manner and Hanna Malm, *Rakas kallis toveri : Kullervo Mannerin ja Hanna Malmin kirjeenvaihtoa 1932–1933*, (Dear Precious Comrade : Correspondence between Kullervo Manner and Hanna Malm 1932–1933), hereafter abridged as MMC, p. 188.)

[53] *Ibid.*, p. 182.

[54] Государственное Политическое Управление (State Political Administration).

cially, three leaders of it, who joined the Party before 1906. In the hearings Feliks Edmundovich Dzerzhinskii noted that also workers who were otherwise loyal to the Party leadership refused to witness against their comrades. Moreover, many old Bolsheviks at this time sought to dissociate themselves from that agency. As such they might have nothing against a political police; they might even have been working in its ranks faithfully and eagerly when they regarded their opponents as class enemies or heretics. Dzerzhinskii stated that only saints and scoundrels can serve the GPU and complained that the saints were disappearing and only scoundrels remained.[55] The ordinary working-class members of the Party were between "the devil and deep blue sea": they were educated in conspiracy, to obey without questioning, but the struggle against their own comrades, who, moreover, presented old demands of the Bolshevik Party itself, was a bitter pill to swallow.

A democratic party cannot be secret. Lenin wrote in 1902 that "probably" everyone agrees that the "principle of extensive democratism" involves two preconditions: "full publicity" and the election (not appointment) of leaders and functionaries.[56] Carl J. Friedrich, who cites these two criteria, adds a third; the free right to join the Party.[57] In normal conditions, there was usually only one obstacle to this free right to join: one should not belong to any other party. When Lenin stressed the compulsory secrecy of his Party, which did not respect the principle of "extensive democratism", he pleaded the peculiar conditions which existed in autocratic Russia.[58] The Bolshevik Party remained, however, closeted also when it was in power and secrecy was characteristic of the activities of the Comintern. Congresses, plenums etc., were, of course, at least partly public, but all other decision-making was privy.[59] There were different grades of secrecy: for instance the Secretariat of the Comintern had two different folders: ordinary and "special folders" *(Sondermappe)*. The rules laid down by the politburo of the All-Union Communist Party (Bolsheviks), VKP(b)[60] in 1929 for its own activity and that of its apparatus were extremely complicated.[61] One may explain the secrecy by the fact that the Party or-

---

[55] Isaac Deutscher, *The Prophet Unarmed* : *Trotsky: 1921–1929*, pp. 106–109.

[56] Ленин, *Что делать?*, PSS, vol. 6, p. 138.

[57] Carl Joachim Friedrich, *Man and His Government* : *an Empirical Theory of Politics*, p. 520.

[58] Ленин, *Что делать?*, PSS, vol. 6, pp. 139–140.

[59] See Vladimir Boukovsky, *Jugement à Moscou* : *un dissident dans les archives du Kremlin*, pp. 11–13; Michael P. Voslensky, *Das Geheime wird offenbar* : *Moskauer Archive erzählen 1917–1991*, pp. 12–16.

[60] Всесоюзная коммунистическая патрия (большевиков), (All-Union Communist Party (Bolsheviks) was the official name of the Party between the XIVth Congress in December 1925 and the XIXth Congress in October 1952.

[61] Постановление Политбюро о конспирации, May 16, 1929, in *Сталинское Политбюро в 30-е годы* : *сборник документов*, pp. 74–77.

gans were, in fact, state organs, and in no state are all of its activities public. However, as to the Bolshevik Party, the secrecy was very close: it was impossible even for members of the Party to know the real power relations between different organs. There was also the system of surveillance which made possible to the leaders of the Party (in various levels) to obtain knowledge of the political attitudes and private lives of members.[62]

It is important to note that secretiveness had always characterised traditional Russian governance and administration. The Bolsheviks were only continuing this tradition. The Marquis Astolphe de Custine, who travelled in Russia in 1839, wrote:[63]

> In Russia, secrecy prevails everywhere: in administration, politics and social life; there is useful and useless discretion, superfluous silence to ensure the necessary. Such are the inevitable consequences of the primitive character of these men, corroborated by the influence of their government.

One of foundation stones of Bolshevism, especially after Lenin was unable due to ailing health to act politically, was distrust in the human being, in free deliberation. After Stalin had guaranteed his absolute power by 1929, knowledge in Soviet society was carefully rationed. Every publication, even local newspapers, were censored by a representative of the Party.[64] For rulers this secrecy was advantageous because political turns could be made in a moment, without time-consuming preparation and public debate and, on the other hand, it was easy to launch an extensive "debate" on a matter of secondary importance such as the constitution of the country.

Secrecy in the Soviet Union did not mean that no scandals occurred. Excessive drinking, sexual orgies, bribery, corruption etc. among individuals in high position were now and then reported in the press. It was common, however, to argue that these degenerated elements were themselves kulaks, counter-revolutionaries and renegades, or at least that they had contacts with such. It was very difficult to know who were merely the victims of Bolshevik denigration and who really were guilty of criminal acts or at least drunkards.

---

[62] See Niels Erik Rosenfeldt, *Knowledge and Power : the Role of Stalin's Secret Chancellery in the Soviet System of Government*, p. 35 Already in the 1920s Stalin organised a possibility to listen secretly to the telephones of all other Bolshevik leaders.

[63] Marquis de Custine, *La Russie en 1839*, vol. 1, letter 29, p. 418.

[64] Hanna Malm, who in December 1932 edited a small 4-page newspaper *Punainen Uhtua* ("Red Ukhta") in Karelia, relates that she showed all of her writings to the "leader of mass work", nominated by the local Party committee. (Hanna Malm to Kullervo Manner, Dec. 18, 1932, MMC, p. 105.)

Hannah Arendt wrote that although the ordinary member of the National Socialist or Communist Party belonged to the surrounding society, i.e. professional or social relationships were not completely determined by Party membership – or by the official Party ideology – "in the case of conflict between Party allegiance and private life, the former [was] taken to be decisive".[65] We shall later see some examples of this kind of conflict. In the light of findings regarding the Finnish Communist Party, Arendt would seem to underestimate the role of ideology in Party life. She says that for "the intimate circle around the Leader", like the Bolshevik Politburo or the "entourage of Hitler" "ideological clichés are mere devices to organise the masses and they feel no compunction if only the organizing principle is kept intact".[66] This is an erroneous conclusion at least as to Communist parties; the "creative development" of ideology was considered extremely significant. This did not exclude "interrupting every existing class struggle with a sudden alliance with Capitalism"[67] as Arendt correctly points out, but this was not essential. All changes, including alliances with the class enemies, were justified by ideological arguments; all struggles for power were exonerated by ideological statements. "Ideological clichés" were by no means mere devices. The political education of the cadres and the indoctrination of the masses were of utmost importance.[68] Ideology in Soviet-type societies was more fully elaborated than in Nazi Germany, although petrified Marxism-Leninism in the Soviet Union was in the thirties so changed that the doctrine became more simplified and cultural life even more seriously hampered.[69]

The ideal role of a member of a totalitarian Party is fully dedicated. He must always be involved in Party work. In a Russian, Finnish-language "textbook for shortened Party schools in cities", "accepted by the scientific-political section of the committee of scholars of the state", published in 1926, it was advised to establish Party cells in every factory. These cells should make "initiatives" through fac-

---

[65] Hannah Arendt, *The Origins of Totalitarianism*, p. 367.

[66] *Ibid.*, p. 385.

[67] *Ibid.*, p. 386.

[68] Cf. Juan J. Linz, "Totalitarian and Authoritarian Regimes", pp. 192–193.

[69] See Dave Laing, *The Marxist Theory of Art*, pp. 36–44. Cf. *Stephen P. Cohen, "Bolshevism and Stalinism"* in *Stalinism : Essays in Historical Interpretation*, p. 16. – Nazi and Stalinist conceptions of art were often close to each other. (See a comparative study by Igor Golomstock in his article "Problems in the Study of Stalinist Culture" in *The Culture of the Stalin Period*, pp. 110–121.) There were also important differences, however. The cult of Richard Wagner's mystical heroism, so dear to Adolf Hitler – the *Führer* labelled the Bolshevik regime as "Alberichs-Herrschaft" (Joachim Köhler, *Wagners Hitler : der Prophet und sein Vollstrecker*, p. 104) – could not be imagined in the Soviet Union. Wagner's operas were even rarely performed there in the 1930s and afterwards. Performances of *Die Walküre* at the Bol'shoi theatre in 1940 – the first night was on November 21; the opera was conducted by V. Nebol'sin and directed by S. Eisenstein (В. Н. Зарубин. *Большой театр : первые постановки опер на русской сцене* 1825–1993, p. 251) – were an exception and obviously an outcome of the Ribbentrop-Molotov pact of 1939.

tory committees to "defend the material and cultural demands of the workers" and at the same time through the trade unions "show great consideration for questions of productivity and discipline in the factory".[70] When all social life was conducted, or at least was supposed to be, under the guidance of the Party, the Party became an end in itself, it was reified, i.e. changed from profane to sacred. It was in Durkheimian terms the object of a negative cult. A believer must never abandon the cult; he must not sever relations considered sacred. A negative cult consists of interdictions and they are, according to Émile Durkheim, "religious interdicts *par excellence*". Most important are prohibitions of contacts: the "profane should never touch the sacred".[71] Aleksandr Isaevich Solzhenitsyn tells of a citizen, a semi-literate stove-maker, who did not show respect to pictures of the leaders published in newspapers. He was in the habit of writing his name everywhere. If blank paper was not at his disposal, he wrote his name on newspapers. Once, unfortunately, his "pen-and-ink flourished across the countenance of the Father and Teacher". His neighbours found this in communal toilet and reported the matter to the authorities. The unfortunate stove-maker got ten years for "Anti-Soviet agitation".[72]

Lenin proclaimed that Marx's doctrine was omnipotent because it was correct. This political correctness was total, because "from this Marxist philosophy, cast from one piece of steel, one cannot remove any basic principle, no essential part, without disassociating oneself from objective truth, without falling into the bosom of the reactionary bourgeois lie".[73] In all human or even natural affairs there were wrong and right positions.[74] The right position was at the same time "partisan", (or preferably "Partyist", *parteilich* in German) and objective: there was a "main line" that should be followed "firmly and without faltering". One should fight on "two fronts", against Right and Left, against, as Finnish Communists in Russia expressed it, against all "side aspirations" and "inclinations".[75] "He who does not realise this [struggle]", a triumvirate of Finnish ideologists wrote in 1932, "turns from the battling Partyist line of the Marxist-Leninist theory to the position of [Eduard] Bernstein, [Karl] Kautsky, [Piotr Berngardovich] Struve [and] all bourgeois and Social Fascist ideologists in general".[76] Now, if no real world is absolutely

---

70 G. Abeshaus and Protasov, *Puoluetiedon kirja : oppikirja kaupunkien supistettuja puoluekouluja varten : valtion oppineiden komitean tieteellispoliittisen jaoston hyväksymä*, vol. 1, p. 16.

71 Émile Durkheim, *The Elementary Forms of the Religious Life*, p. 302.

72 Alexander Solzhenitsyn, *The Gulag Archipelago 1918–1956 : an Experiment in Literary Investigation*, vols. 1–2, p. 75.

73 В. И. Ленин, *Материализм и эмпириокритицизм : критические заметки об одной реакционной философии*, PSS, vol. 18, p. 346.

74 Cf. Jan Jaroslawski, *Soziologie der kommunistischen Partei*, p. 448.

75 The Finnish words used were *syrjäpyrinnöt*, *viistopyrinnöt* and *kallistumat*.

76 N. Jaakkola, P. Hyppönen and V. Takala, *Leniniläisen vaiheen puolesta (tov. I. Lassyn Marxismin perusteiden arvostelua)*, p. 17.

dualistic and absolute dualism is not rational, we face here sheer mysticism. The doctrine of a totalitarian Party was idealistic, paradoxically in the Marxist sense of this term. As Maurice Duverger wrote, the "material organisation of the entirety of man's activities does not take on a truly totalitarian sense if it is not accompanied by a spiritual organisation of the whole of his thought". Thus, "real totalitarianism" is spiritual.[77] The notorious "Balaton oranges" were consequences of "spiritual totalitarianism".[78]

It is impossible to define absolutely who was and who was not a Communist in certain situations in Finnish history, especially at the time when the Finnish Communist Party was illegal (1918–1944). The membership of the Party was very small throughout the period under research in this study. There were, for example, in the third quarter of the year 1924, 798 "active" members[79] and 398 candidate members.[80] The figures are questionable, but I think it is safe to say that the number of the members of the SKP did not exceed 2,000 before 1944. There were, however, many people in Finland who were not members of the SKP, but who considered themselves "Communists". In 1921 it was possible for a Member of Parliament, Hilda Hannunen, to speak about the "Communist section of the people" and to identify herself with this,[81] but later such public identification became dangerous, although in bourgeois and Social Democratic circles, members and voters of the Finnish Socialist Workers' Party (SSTP) and voters for the Electoral Organisation of Socialist Workers and Smallholders (1923–1930) were routinely called Communists. They might in some situations protest at the use of this word[82] and use the expression "Left-Wing working-people" or "Socialist working-people" instead.

---

77 Duverger, *Les partis politiques*, pp. 184–185.

78 Duverger gives as a motto of his *Les orangers du lac Balaton* (p. 5) the following story: "In the era of Stalinian [Matyas] Rakosi, the Hungarian leaders decided to cultivate oranges on the shores of the Lake Balaton. The lake is frozen every winter, although its mass of water alleviates the rigour of the continental climate and gives some meridional allure to banks sheltered from the Northern winds. The agronomist responsible for the enterprise courageously pointed out that it was chimerical. In vain. The Party, which interprets historical materialism which is scientific truth, could not err. Thus thousands of trees, imported with the little currency available, were planted. They died. Consequently, the agronomist was condemned for sabotage. Was he not evincing his wicked will from the beginning by criticising the decision of the Politburo?"

79 It is not clear what was meant by word "active" here.

80 These figures are from the Report on the activities of the Finnish Communist Party from August 1923 to November 1924. *Российский государственный архив социально-политической истории* (Russian State Archives of Social and Political History, RGASPI), *fond* (f.) 516, *opis* (op.) 2, 1924, *delo* (d.) 9, *list* (l.) 9. The *list* numbers in the documents of the RGASPI refer to the original page numbers of the documents and not to the possible later page numbering made in the archives, if not otherwise stated.

81 Hilda Hannunen in the *Eduskunta*, Dec. 2, 1921. Valtiopäivät 1921, pöytäkirjat, vol. 2, p. 1057.

82 E.g, "Paha omatunto", TTA, Dec. 17, 1926, leading article.

However, if we take a glimpse at newspapers which supported the SSTP and the Electoral Organisation of Socialist Workers and Smallholders, it is not difficult to see that they represented Communist standpoints. The articles published on Soviet Russia / the Soviet Union were uncritical. Although not all who had an uncritical attitude to the Soviet Union were Communists, I am of the opinion that it is possible to use the term Communist also when Finnish "Left-Wing working-people" are in question, even at the risk of being misleading in some contexts. Possible alternatives could be equally unappropriate. It was, for example, for a Social Democrat not impossible to consider that he belonged to the "Left-Wing working-people", but there were also people who were "in between", neither Communists nor Social Democrats.

The SSTP and Electoral Organisation of Socialist Workers and Smallholders were typical front-organisations. A front-organisation was an auxiliary association – a political party, trade union, peasant, youth, student, sport, cultural etc. society – which was, as one definition states, "under either open or disguised communist leadership whose purpose was to enrol non-communists and thus gain broader 'civic support' for communist aims and causes".[83] They could recruit "in between" workers as voters and, for example, as participants in demonstrations, which, however, were commonly, and correctly in most cases, understood as Communist by nature, because the organisers of the demonstrations were members of the SKP.

According to David Caute, the French *Clarté* group, founded by Henri Barbusse in Paris in 1919, was the "first front-organisation".[84] It was a typical organisation of "fellow-travelling" intellectuals.[85] In Finland the phenomenon of fellow-travelling intellectuals belongs mainly to the "popular front" period of the Comintern[86] and thus falls outside the period of this study. If, however, this term is understood

83 Witold S. Sworakowski, "International Communist Front Organizations" in *World Communism : a Handbook 1918–1965*, p. 210.

84 David Caute, *The Fellow-Travellers : a Postscript to the Enlightenment*, p. 55.

85 In the context of the Communist movement, this concept was already used by Lev Trotskii in 1924. He regarded as fellow-travellers writers who supported the Communist rule, but were hesitant, doubtful; they did not "grasp the Revolution as a whole", even "the Communist ideal" was "foreign" to them. In Trotskii's mind fellow-travellers were intellectuals, who were inclined to look hopefully at the peasant over the head of the worker". (Leon Trotsky, *Literature and Revolution*, p. 57.) In other words, they were people who had still some Narodnik rubbish in their brains and were therefore unreliable elements. "As regards a 'fellow-traveller'", Trotskii wrote, "the question always comes up – how far will he go"? (*Ibid.*, p. 58.)

86 See R. Palomeri (pseudonym of Raoul Palmgren), *30-luvun kuvat*, pp. 356–357 and *passim*. Palmgren, whose book was published in 1953, somewhat naively believed that the idea of a "popular front" originated in Paris (*ibid.*, p. 356). Palmgren's book is a *roman à clef*. – In Finland we find *Clarté* activities among the Left-Wing intellectuals in the mid-1930s. (Cay Sundström, "Barbusse ja 'ajatuksen internationaali'", *Kirjallisuuslehti*, July 15, 1935, pp. 222–225.)

more broadly, it is possible to consider as fellow-travellers people who were "in between" on the political map, in the case of Finland especially trade union activists. For the Finnish Communist leaders in Russia they were at the same time allies and enemies; allies in trade unions, enemies, in that they might try to build their own, non-Communist political identity; there was always the danger of a fellow-traveller, as well as a Communist, becoming a "renegade".[87]

[87] The most famous Communist renegade was Arvo Tuominen, the Secretary of the SKP, who was able to move from the Soviet Union to Sweden in 1937. (Panu Rajala and Hannu Rautkallio, *Petturin tie : Arvo Poika Tuomisen todellinen elämä*, pp. 128–131; this part is written by Rautkallio.) In 1940 Tuominen condemned the attack of the Soviet Union against Finland. Later he became a Social Democratic politician, he was an editor of a newspaper of this Party and an MP.

III Rebellion, Revolution and Civil War in Finland

1. The Finnish Workers' Movement in 1899–1917

Finland, originally comprising several of Sweden's provinces, became an autonomous state in 1809 after Russia had annexed the land in the Russian-Swedish War. The Emperor of Russia (called also Tsar), Alexander I, formed Finland as a Grand Duchy and added the expression "Grand Duke of Finland" to his list of titles. The Russian Tsar summoned the members of the Swedish Estates residing in Finland, now called the Finnish Estates (there were four of them: nobility, clergy, bourgeoisie and peasantry), to the small town of Porvoo, where the Diet pledged its allegiance to the Grand Duke and Alexander, in turn, ratified the existing basic (Swedish) laws. This was, however, no "pact" between the Tsar and the Estates; as Eino Jutikkala notes, what the Emperor promised to "his Finnish subjects", he pledged "out of his omnipotence". There was the Diet, but its meetings were convened by the Grand Duke and he had absolute executive power. On the other hand, the consent of the Diet was nonetheless required when new laws were enacted or old ones altered. Also new taxes could not be decreed without assent of the Diet.[1]

The first important modern party organisation in Finland, the Finnish Workers' Party, was founded in 1899. In 1903, the name was changed to the Social Democratic Party in Finland (*Sosialidemokratinen Puolue Suomessa,* later *Suomen Sosialidemokraattinen Puolue*, SDP) and a Marxist programme – Karl Kautsky's

---

[1] Eino Jutikkala, "Finland Becomes an Autonomous State" in Eino Jutikkala with Kauko Pirinen, *A History of Finland*, pp. 288–291.

version – was adopted. Because even the leaders of the Party knew relatively little about this Marxism, it was deemed advisable simply to translate the most recent European Socialist Party programme into Finnish. This programme happened to be that of the Social Democratic Party of Austria, accepted there in 1901. It was duly translated into Finnish and adopted at the 1903 Party Congress held in the small industrial town of Forssa. As the Austrian Party programme was a programme of principles, the reform demands were adopted from the 1891 Erfurt programme of the German Social Democratic Party.[2] One addition, unknown in other European Socialist parties, was however made: this was the demand for prohibition.

When the general strike broke out in Russia in October 1905, its revolutionary alacrity also spread to Finland, where likewise a general strike was organised in November. When the Russian police and gendarmerie collapsed, a Civil Guard (*kansalliskaarti*) was soon organised. This Civil Guard, in which both bourgeois Constitutionalists (Young Finns, opposite to Old Finns, supporters of "policy of concessions" as regards Russians), who had ardently opposed the Russification which had been the aim of Tsarist policy since 1899 and Social Democrats participated, was very soon divided into two Guards, the Protection Guard (*suojeluskaarti*) and the Red Guard (*punakaarti*). The abstract idea of a class struggle was concretised in the notion of revolutionary violence among some Finnish Social Democratic leaders, especially intellectuals who had joined in many cases the Party often in November, 1905, and who were usually called "Socialists of November". Many later heroes of our story, such personalities as Otto Wille Kuusinen (already in 1904), Yrjö Sirola and Kullervo Manner, made their debut in working-class politics at this time. In addition, Voitto Eloranta, Leo Laukki and Jukka Rahja participated in events in 1905 and 1906.

The question of revolutionary violence now emerged prominently on the agenda. Many if not most leaders who had become well known in the 1890s took a negative stand on any violence. The more or less official position of the Party, as represented for example Edvard Valpas, editor of *Työmies* (The Working Man) the Party newspaper in Helsinki was of the opinion that in a revolutionary situation violent acts may be necessary because the bourgeoisie might organise armed resistance to the otherwise peaceful action of the proletariat. The "Socialists of November", however, usually adopted a more straightforward attitude on the question. Having come to the movement from bourgeois circles (the fathers of both Manner and Sirola were priests) and being young and enthusiastic, they had to prove that they were not under the influence of any bourgeois ideas. They stressed that it was necessary to be ready to use all appropriate means in a revolutionary situation, armed strug-

---

[2] Olavi Borg, *Suomen puolueideologiat : periaateohjelmien sisältöanalyyttinen vertailu sekä katsaus niiden historialliseen taustaan ja syntyprosessiin*, pp. 63–65. The Forssa programme is published in Olavi Borg, *Suomen puolueet ja puolueohjelmat 1880–1964*, pp. 31–35.

gle included.[3] Not all intellectuals, however, behaved, in this way. There were also those who spoke mainly of immediate reform aims and "concrete questions". In many cases, they were deeply interested in the co-operative movement. Most of these intellectuals became leaders of the SDP when the workers' movement split after the Civil War in 1918. Väinö Tanner, who did not approve the rebellion in 1918, and re-established the Social Democratic Party in December 1918, is the best example of this kind of intellectual. However, in addition to the Left, Centre and Right (in embryonic form, of course, in 1906) in the Party itself, there were various anarchist groups and, above all in the ranks of the Red Guard, many enthusiastic young proletarians who saw the Guard as a main forum of action. Connections with various Russian Socialist currents[4] and rebellious Russian troops in Finland obviously increased support for violent means among them. The Red Guard comprised in the summer of 1906 about 25,000 members and from the point of view of the SDP leaders there was a serious danger that these Guards would form an independent political force. The Imperial ukase, which established a 200-member unicameral Parliament, the *Eduskunta,* elected by universal (also female) suffrage, seemed, however, to fulfil even the most radical democratic dreams of the Social Democrats. When the Senate (the Finnish government), after a failed mutiny of the Russian troops aided by Finnish Red Guards in the naval base of Viapori on an island just off Helsinki,[5] proclaimed the Red Guard dissolved, most "veteran" leaders of the SDP were more delighted than disappointed.[6]

The general strike and the first elections of the *Eduskunta* had an enormous mobilising effect among the industrial and rural workers, crofters (*torpparit*) and cottagers (*mäkitupalaiset*). The crofters were regionally concentrated in Southern

---

[3] Here the radicals could refer to the Forssa programme, in which it was stated: "To organise the proletariat and to raise it to understand its position and tasks, to render [the proletariat] mentally and materially able for struggle, is thus, the proper programme of the Social Democratic Party in Finland. In order to achieve this, it uses all means appropriate and responds to the natural sense of justice of the people." (*Sosialidemokratisen puolueen ohjelma.* Accepted in the Party Congress in Forssa, Aug. 17–20, 1903. Published in Olavi Borg, *Suomen puolueet ja puolueohjelmat 1880–1964*, p. 32.) Especially the last sentence quoted was dear to the "Socialists of November".

[4] Finland was in fact a sanctuary for many Russian Socialists, including the Socialist Revolutionaries, who had committed terrorist acts in Russia. (On Socialist Revolutionaries and Finland, see Antti Kujala, *Vallankumous ja kansallinen itsemääräämisoikeus : Venäjän sosialistiset puolueet ja suomalainen radikalismi vuosisadan alussa*, pp. 69–77 and 286–294. There is an English summary, *Revolution and the Right to National Self-Determination: Russian Socialist Parties and Finnish Radicalism at the Beginning of the Twentieth Century*, pp. 310–328.

[5] See Hella Wuolijoki, *Und ich war nicht Gefangene : Memoiren und Skizzen*, pp. 74–79. The official name of the base was Sveaborg: "Viapori" is a Fenicisation of this Swedish name, which means literally the "Swedish Castle".

[6] Hannu Soikkanen, *Sosialismin tulo Suomeen : ensimmäisiin yksikamarisen eduskunnan vaaleihin asti*, pp. 224–257.

and Middle Finland; in Ostrobothnia, Karelia and Northern Finland peasants were largely independent, although the sizes of farms were small among independent peasants as well as among crofters. Cottagers were agricultural workers who held only a small piece of land for cultivating vegetables, potatoes etc. Crofters usually paid their rents in the form of work for the patron on service days defined in their contract. A Congress of crofters, organised by the SDP, in 1906, decided that the demand of the Crofter Movement should be for a stable, hereditary right of rent, not ownership, a decision which showed that the movement was under the control of the SDP; the demand for ownership, namely, was understood as non-Socialist.[7] As Risto Alapuro has stated, it was typical of Finland that in contrast to other Eastern European countries, there was strong link between the rural and urban workers' movement despite the dissimilarity in class relations of crofters and agrarian workers and landowners on the one hand, and industrial workers and capitalists on the other.[8]

In the first elections in March 1907, the SDP received 37 per cent of votes and 80 seats in the *Eduskunta*. The problem was that in spite of its democratic character this body was powerless; reforms were in almost all cases impossible because the final decision was in the hands of the Emperor. When the situation calmed down, the process of Russification was resumed. When the *Eduskunta* made its protest, Grand Duke Nicholas II dissolved it and ordered new elections. This happened six times during 1907–1914. One cause of bitterness for the Social Democrats was that municipal administration remained oligarchic.

The Social Democrats were divided into two tendencies on the question of co-operation with bourgeois parties in common protest against Russification. What we may call a Nationalist tendency supported co-operation with bourgeois Constitutionalists because Russification meant, as they could argue, a unification of the Finns with a people (i.e. the Russians) on a lower level of development. The other, the above-mentioned Kautskyan tendency, became known as "Siltasaarism". The term came from a district (Siltasaari) in Helsinki where the redaction of the above-mentioned *Työmies* and the Party headquarters were located. Edvard Valpas was often called the "Pope" of the Party, for he was seen as the main representative of the orthodox, or "Centrist", Kautskyan line in the Party leadership. Valpas was against any co-operation with the "class enemy". In the *Eduskunta*, for instance, the Socialists had always to act independently and shun any policy of what could be construed as *khvostism*,[9] a term used by the Bolsheviks implying that the Communists are going "behind" the working-class in its instinctive struggle, instead of

---

7 Hannu Soikkanen, *Kohti kansanvaltaa*, vol. 1, *1899–1937*, p. 114.

8 Risto Alapuro, *State and Revolution in Finland*, p. 120.

9 The word comes from the Russian *хвост*, tail.

purposefully leading that struggle. – Early in the second decade, an open Revisionist tendency surfaced, although the word was usually used to denote something pejorative in the Party.[10] One important reason for this was that there was no democracy at municipal level. Nicholas II did not accept the new municipal laws decided on by the *Eduskunta* in 1908. Thus, local labour leaders had little possibility of participating in any decision-making. Hannu Soikkanen is of the opinion – correctly in my view – that because no municipal democracy prevailed it was usual for the "field", led by the local leaders, to be more radical than the leadership.[11] – During the First World War, the *Eduskunta* did not convene. Parliamentary elections were however held in 1916 and the SDP won 103 seats, i.e. the majority.

The downfall of Tsarism initiated in Finland a political process which led to the declaration of independence on December 6, 1917, and soon afterwards to the Red rebellion, revolution and the Civil War of 1918, which ended with the victory of the Whites and the flight of the Red leaders of the revolution to Russia.

The traumatic effect of the Civil War is reflected in the different names for it. The Whites called it the *vapaussota*, which can be translated into English as the "War of Liberation", or "War of Independence". The import of this term is to emphasise the fact that on the Red side some Russian troops also participated and Russia supplied the rebels with arms, although during the War most Russian combatants were in fact evacuated to Russia.[12] However, another speculative but important argument can be presented for the "War of Liberation" thesis: had the Reds won, would it have been possible to preserve Finland's independence? This is, of course, a difficult *if*-question. One may argue, however, that throughout the Old Russian Empire where it was militarily possible (in Armenia, Georgia etc.) the Bolsheviks reconquered these newly independent states and annexed them to their new Red Imperium.[13] A world revolution was the aim of the Bolsheviks, and al-

[10] Soikkanen, *Kohti kansanvaltaa*, vol. 1, pp. 110–157.

[11] Hannu Soikkanen, "Miksi revisionismi ei saanut kannatusta Suomen vanhassa työväenliikkeessä?" in *Oman ajan historia ja politiikan tutkimus*, p. 189.

[12] Turo Manninen, *Vapaustaistelu, kansalaissota ja kapina : taistelun luonne valkoisten sotapropagandassa vuonna 1918*, p. 179.

[13] Another aim of the Russian Bolsheviks was to ally with anti-colonialist and anti-imperialist forces in Western and Central Asia and Northern Africa etc. There was lively discussion of the liberation of colonial countries in the II[d] Congress of the Comintern and subsequently a large congress (about 2,000 delegates) convened in Baku in September, 1920. There were, however, two obstacles in rousing peoples to revolution. The first problem was the role of the "national bourgeoisie": was it possible to form a united front with leaders of this stratum? The second question was religion. In his opening address to the congress, G. E. Zinoviev sought to use Muslim vocabulary speaking of "holy war, in first place against English imperialism". (E. H. Carr, *The Bolshevik Revolution 1917–1923*, vol. 3, pp. 262–263.) In the late 1920s, O. W. Kuusinen became some kind of an expert on Indian and Chinese affairs.

though the revolutionary fervour of the Bolsheviks leaders gradually waned, they still believed in 1921 and even in 1923, when there were uprisings and disturbances in Germany, that it was Germany which would be the second country in the world revolutionary chain. When the Soviet Union was established in December 1922, the aim was to collect all earlier Russian possessions in that federative state. At the time, the Whites were in power in Finland and she was militarily relatively strong. There could therefore be no immediate aim to annex Finland and incorporate her in the "fraternal community of friendly peoples". On the contrary, before the peace treaty was agreed in Finnish-Russian negotiations in Tartu in October, 1920, the Finnish Whites sent various military expeditions to Russian East Karelia to "liberate" Finnish and/or Karelian people there. The commander of the Whites, General, Baron Carl Gustaf Emil Mannerheim, a former officer in the Tsar's army, refused to attack Petrograd as was hoped especially by a number of Russian generals who led various White troops in the Russian Civil War. These generals, however, were ready to accept Finnish independence.[14] This probably had some impact on Mannerheim's attitude.

It has also been asked what kind of independence Finland would have enjoyed *had* Germany won the WW I. German troops participated in the war on the White side, although this was not a decisive factor from the point of view of the outcome of the war. As General Mannerheim, an Anglophile rather than a Germanophile, notes in his memoirs, the White government on March 7, 1918 made a peace agreement with Germany in which there was a secret clause concerning German bases in Finland. According to this clause, the Germans had the right, as long as there were German troops on Finnish soil, to establish military bases wherever she wished. Mannerheim deplored this pro-German orientation, incarnated in Regent Pehr Evind Svinhufvud, as well as the election of a German Prince as King of Finland.[15] On October 9, 1918, the *Eduskunta*, where with one exception only Whites were present, elected the Prince of Hesse, Friedrich Karl, King of Finland.[16] The Prince began to learn the Finnish language, but when Germany lost the war there was no reason for the hapless "heir designate" to continue his studies.[17] Svinhufvud was replaced as Regent by Mannerheim.

If-questions are more or less futile in the social sciences; nonetheless I bring some such arguments up by way of demonstrating how they have been employed in the debate on the war in Finland and its causes. For ordinary working-class people the war long remained the "rebellion" (*kapina*) or the "Red rebellion"

---

14 See e.g. Hélène Carrère d'Encausse, *Lénine*, p. 450.

15 G. Mannerheim, *Muistelmat*, vol. 1, pp. 363–364.

16 Oiva Ketonen, *Kansakunta murroksessa : kesä 1918 ja sen taustaa*, pp. 22–23.

17 Vesa Vares, *Kuninkaan tekijät : suomalainen monarkia 1917–1919 : myytti ja todellisuus*, pp. 300–301.

(*punakapina*).[18] The Communists and some other leftists favoured the expression "class war" (*luokkasota*); this term, however, seems to be used mainly in "Red" studies of the war and in propaganda.[19]

A coup d'état as such is not a revolution. A Putsch may take place in a dictatorially ruled country among the ruling elite without much significance for the man in the street. By revolution, I do not mean these type of coup but more profound transformations in the economy (in the case of a social revolution) and in the political system (in the case of a political revolution) alike. Karl Marx and Friedrich Engels wrote of a coming "alteration", a necessary revolution, in which not only the "ruling class" would be "overthrown" but where also the rising class would "succeed in ridding itself of all the muck of ages and become fitted to found society anew".[20] This "society anew" can be, as examples in the XXth century show, such in which a new ruling elite takes power and begin to destroy society, even itself. Otherwise, Marx's and Engels' definition of revolution would seem satisfactory.

For Kautskyan Socialists in the late XIXth and early XXth century, the revolutionary symbols retained eschatological elements of Christianity, the redemption and the separation, in Augustinian manner, of the City of Man and the City of God.[21] The Russian revolutions of 1917 and 1991 can both be defined as revolutions of both political and social character. – The distinction between rebellion and revolution is not easy to define. Theda Skocpol says that rebellions, successful or not,

---

[18] I have seen no academic study on all this terminology. Turo Manninen's above cited study deals with the White propaganda only. My claim is based mainly on my own experiences. As a boy in the 1950s I lived in working-class quarters in Helsinki. The elderly, who had experienced the Civil War, always spoke of the "rebellion" (*kapina*). I remember also a term "red rebellion" (*punakapina*), but its use was rare. Professor Olavi Borg, who grew up in the countryside in Southern Finland, tells me that the expression used in his childhood was usually the "rebellion spring" (*kapinakevät*).

[19] After the Second World War, especially in the 1960s, when the first scientific studies of the war were published, a new terminology of "consensus" emerged. People began, also in official contexts, to speak of the "Citizen War", as the Finnish term *kansalaissota* is literally translated, or the "Internal War", as *sisällissota* is literally rendered. *Kansalaissota* is always translated into English as the Civil War. Some people tried to use still more "impartial" expressions like the "War of Reds and Whites", "War of 1918", or even "events of 1918". "Revolution" – let alone "counter-revolution" (by this is meant the victory of the Whites) – was a relatively rare term; these, especially "revolution", were sometimes used by the Communists. In addition, some scholars might use this word. (See *Suomen työväenliikkeen historia*, pp. 95–97.) There are still also researchers who use "War of Liberation". It is also possible to speak of both "War of Liberation" and "Citizen War". According to this interpretation, there were two elements in the confrontation, it began as a "War of Liberation" (against the Russians), but later became a "Citizen War".

[20] Karl Marx and Frederick Engels, *The German Ideology*, published in Marx and Engels, *Collected Works*, vol. 5, pp. 52–53. Cf. Jean-Yves Calvez, *La pensée de Karl Marx*, pp. 257–267.

[21] Cf. S. N. Eisenstadt, *Revolution and Transformation of Societies : a Comparative Study of Civilizations*, pp. 183–184.

"may involve the revolt of subordinate classes – but they do not eventuate in structural change".[22] The problem is that a rebellion may also be a non-successful revolution. As the rebellion in Finland did not lead to any breakthrough, we do not know whether it was an abortive revolution or only, if (too) crude language is allowed, the uproar and hullabaloo of scum. Many people on the Right were of the opinion that Finnish Socialism had nothing to do with any workers' movement properly speaking; it was only "a movement of anarchism and rebellion".[23]

2. The Preconditions of Revolution and the Finnish Situation in 1917

According to James DeFronzo, there are five elements in revolutionary political movements and in revolutions themselves: i) "mass frustration resulting in popular uprising"; ii) "a severe political crisis paralysing the administrative and coercive capabilities of the state"; iii) "dissident elite political movements"; iv) "unifying motivations" for revolution and v) "a permissive or tolerant world context".[24] I shall set out by discussing these elements on a theoretical level, and then in the context of the revolutionary situation as it emerged in Finland after the abdication of Nicholas II.

---

[22] Theda Skocpol, *States and Social Revolutions : a Comparative Analysis of France, Russia and China*, p. 4. When John Locke defended parliamentary representation, he tried to answer all manner of counter-arguments against his ideas. One was that popular representation "lays a *ferment* for frequent *Rebellion*". His answer to this argument is that although people in many situations did not oppose even "acknowledg'd Faults", the "People *generally ill treated*, and contrary to right, will be ready upon any occasion to alleviate themselves the burden that sits heavy upon them". Such developments were for Locke "*Revolutions*". He stressed that such revolutions do not happen "upon every little mismanagement in publick affairs. Even "many wrong and inconvenient Laws" and "*great mistakes*" can be made by the authorities "without mutiny or murmur". If, however, "a long train of Abuses, Prevarications, and Artifices, all tending the same way, make the design visible to the People, and they cannot but feel, what they lie under, and see, whither they are going; 'tis not to be wonder'd, that they should then rouse themselves, and endeavour to put the rule into such hands, which may secure to them the ends for which Government was at first erected". (John Locke, *Two Treatises of Government*, second treatise (original name: *An Essay Concerning the True Original, Extent, and End of Civil Government*), Book II, §§ 224–225.) Although the difference between rebellion and revolution is not clear in Locke, one may, I think, discern in rudimentary form a distinction between rebellion as a single act, so to speak and revolution as a chain of acts of rebellion.

[23] E.g. Pekka Ahmavaara in the *Eduskunta*, May 24, 1918. Toiset valtiopäivät 1917 : pöytäkirjat, vol. 2, p. 1143. Pekka Ahmavaara was a bank director. He represented the Young Finn Party; later in 1918, when the *Kansallinen Kokoomuspuolue* (National Coalition Party, i.e. Conservatives) was founded, he joined this Party.

[24] James DeFronzo, *Revolutions and Revolutionary Movements*, pp. 10–11.

(i) Skocpol notes that in February 1917 bad weather caused delays in the supply of comestibles to Petrograd, suffering already from shortages of necessities. The uprising of workers and soldiers was leaderless and spontaneous, although workers and soldiers formed vertical links between themselves. The Tsarist authority collapsed and the mutinous military rank-and-file nullified possible "upper-class resistance".[25] Obviously material difficulties of life as such do not breed revolts. In Finland, tens of thousands of people starved in the late 1860s due to exceptional climatic conditions, but no kind of mass movement evolved, even thought the authorities did not import grain until it was too late. DeFronzo speaks of relative deprivation. What is essential is not the level of living conditions as such but the gulf between the expectations of the masses as to what is possible, "right" and the capability of the system to satisfy these expectations. Of course, a sudden decline in living conditions due to such man-made factors as political and economic crisis, war etc. may result in a significant increase of mass frustration.[26] I would call this factor *the penury and unrest factor.*

(ii) Max Weber defined the modern state by territoriality and legitimacy of violence. The modern state is capable of monopolising all legitimate use of violence in its territory[27] in contrast to an aggregation of rival governments, warlords, guerrillas etc. As David Held puts it: "The state's web of agencies and institutions finds its ultimate sanction in the claim of monopoly of coercion". If this monopoly erodes, the political order is in crisis. When people no longer believe in the validity of the rule of the law, if they do not believe that the agencies conduct the affairs of state according to its own laws and legal principles, the position of officials who can normally expect to be obeyed simply because they hold these offices, become vulnerable.[28] In the XXth century, successful revolutions have often occurred as results of unsuccessful wars. People have perceived the loss of life in wars as futile and governments have lost their legitimacy.[29] I would term this factor *the legitimacy factor.*

(iii) Many revolutions have been outcomes of nationalism and popular hatred of dictatorship, domestic or foreign. Nationalism usually draws its symbols from the mythology and life of the peasants believed to be healthy and pristine. In non-independent countries, provinces etc. repression by an alien power has in Europe usually first been opposed by cultural means and then in many cases by violence.[30] In a nationalist movement, different classes may join forces. Especially this may

---

[25] Skocpol, *States and Social Revolutions*, p. 98.

[26] Cf. DeFronzo, *Revolutions and Revolutionary Movements*, pp. 10–11.

[27] Max Weber, *Wirtschaft und Gesellschaft : Grundriss der verstehenden Soziologie*, p. 520 and 822.

[28] David Held, *Models of Democracy*, pp. 164–165.

[29] DeFronzo, *Revolutions and Revolutionary Movements*, p. 16.

[30] Cf. Ernest Gellner, *Nations and Nationalism*, p. 57.

take place in a political revolution in which people sharing a language and other characteristics of a nation may unite regardless of class differences and ideological orientations.[31] I call this factor *the nationalism factor.*

(iv) The world context has often been decisive from the point of view of revolutionary movements. In 1918, the military forces of several states, Great Britain, France and Japan tried to help White forces in Russia to topple the Bolshevik regime. As we have seen, the Germans intruded into Finland in 1918 and Soviet Russian troops took part in the Civil War. These Powers, however, did not settle the outcome of that war. In this context, however, it is pertinent to note that in 1917 the presence of often restless and undisciplined Russian armed forces in Finland created many problems. I shall refer to this factor in this study *the Russian factor.*

(v) Revolutions are seldom, perhaps never, led by what Antonio Gramsci called organic intellectuals, i.e. intellectuals who rise to a political (counter-)elite from below. The usual situation is that traditional intellectuals take part in the formation of a revolutionary movement and an ideology.[32] Intellectuals from elite families form, or at least participate in forming, revolutionary ideologies which are used to proselytise the discontented masses into more or less conscious revolutionary activities and struggles.[33] From the point of view of revolution, what is significant is that competition between different elites and political forces may generally become fierce in a crisis. This may take place not only between political parties and movements, but also within these. This factor I would designate *the political factor.*

In the following presentation of the development leading to the Finnish confrontation, I shall follow the above classification.

i) The penury and unrest factor. Finland was not self-reliant as to corn: 60 per cent of grain consumed was imported from Russia. When this import ceased in the spring of 1917 rationing became urgent, but was realised only in May. In the summer of 1917, the situation was further aggravated and there was unrest in many towns. Especially stores of butter were looted by the mobs who were ironically branded "Masloviks" (from Russian *maslo,* butter). Because the summer of 1917 was unusually cold, the harvest was poor.[34] The farmers, furthermore, concealed a part of the yield and the black market flourished. Among urban workers there

---

31 DeFronzo, *Revolutions and Revolutionary Movements*, pp. 14–15.

32 Antonio Gramsci, *Selections from the Prison Notebooks*, pp. 5–9.

33 Skocpol, *States and Social Revolutions*, pp. 170–171. DeFronzo, *Revolutions and Revolutionary Movements*, p. 13.

34 See figures in *Finland and Russia 1808–1920 : from Autonomy to Independence : a Selection of Documents*, pp. 214–215.

were wild rumours of huge hidden reserves of grain and other food. – The trade union movement, which had grown during the World War – there were 60,000 members in the Finnish Trade Union Federation (*Suomen ammattijärjestö*) at the end of 1917 – sought in many instances to prevent the robbing and pillaging of the "Masloviks" more or less successfully. In October 1917, as unrest in the country grew, the Federation urged workers to found their own Order Guards.[35] They were soon called Red Guards. In autumn 1917, the shortage of food played an important part in the radicalisation of the workers.[36]

ii) The legitimacy factor. As Anthony Upton has pointed out, the first revolutionary elements in Finland were the Russian soldiers who forced police officials and other agents of the Old Russian authority to resign. They also opened the gates of prisons, for instance in three largest towns, Helsinki, Turku and Viipuri (Vyborg in Russian). The Russians gave the task of maintaining order to the Finnish militia. The members of this militia were in most case members of the Social Democratic Party, or at least were controlled by the Party. To be sure, this control was not particularly strict, and when unrest broke out in the summer of 1917, nobody checked the militia. The bourgeoisie desired a return to the normal police system because from their point of view the situation was dangerous: a coercion force they distrusted and the Russian troops remaining in the country.[37] In addition, the new Finnish Senate (of which more below) was not able to control the militia and thus the legitimacy crisis developed. Since local administration remained in the hands of the Right, the municipalities were far from eager to pay the costs of the militia as its leaders and members demanded.[38] In autumn 1917, the bourgeoisie began to establish their own guards. Workers' Order Guards and the militia often combined and the situation was soon such that there were two opposing guards, Whites and Reds. Pertti Haapala remarks that when the "state machine was paralysed" there was no force in civil society which could take the place of the state and retain the unity of political power.[39]

iii) The nationalism factor. The official language of Finland as of cultural life was Swedish in (roughly) the first half of the XIXth century. Finnish nationalism, the main aim of which was to develop Finnish as a cultural language and spread its use in administration and culture (opera, theatre, literature etc.) evolved in the second half of the century into an important social movement. This development was encouraged by the Russian authorities. However, when Finnish nationalist intellectuals began to teach nationalism to workers and peasants, they found that

---

[35] Pirjo Ala-Kapee and Marjaana Valkonen, *Yhdessä elämä turvalliseksi : SAK:laisen ammattiyhdistysliikkeen kehitys vuoteen 1930*, pp. 407–418.

[36] Alapuro, *State and Revolution in Finland*, pp. 163–164.

[37] Anthony Upton, *The Finnish Revolution 1917–1918*, pp. 31–33.

[38] *Ibid., 1917–1918*, p. 31.

[39] Pertti Haapala, *Kun yhteiskunta hajosi : Suomi 1914–1920*, p. 152.

the masses were by no means always ready to adopt their conception of the Fatherland.[40] A saying goes that the common people despise the lords but adore the Tsar. When Emperor Nicholas II, in 1899, promulgated the manifesto aiming at the Russification of Finland, Finnish nationalism entered a new phase in its development. Radical anti-Russian nationalists established a secret movement called the Activists. After 1905–1906, their activity ceased but during the World War a nationalist secret society of the same name was founded. Its members formed a separatist group, which aimed at the full independence of Finland, to be attained with the support of Germany.[41] The Germans were interested in this possibility of weakening its Russian enemy, and in 1915–1916 a *Jäger* battalion of 1,897 Finnish volunteers was established. After a period of (Prussian-style) military training in Germany, the battalion fought on the Russian front. In Finland, some Social Democrats were interested in this movement and recruits also included Social Democrats. Most of the members of the battalion, however, came from bourgeois circles.[42] – Some so-called Worker *Jägers* did not return to Finland in 1918 but went over to Soviet Russia.[43]

iv) **The Russian factor.** There had been Russian troops in Finland since 1809, but when the World War broke out, many more were brought in. In 1917, their total number was about 100,000. There were few problems with these Russian troops before 1917 as they were usually well disciplined. It seems that the gender question constituted a considerable problem especially in the countryside. Russian soldiers and young Finnish men competed for women, and because the Russians, who were in uniform, were often the more successful in this rivalry, this created envy. Some countryside municipalities imposed local curfews for women or women without male (Finnish, of course) company at nighttime. – After the February revolution, the situation in Finland worsened. *Svoboda* ("freedom") reigned: the soldiers often no longer obeyed orders issued by their officers and various forms of crime increased. Fears among Right-Wing circles were increased in the autumn 1917 when Russian soldiers murdered a number of officers of their own army.[44] The fact that the radical wing of the Social Democrats fraternised with Russian soldiers also had a most unfortunate effect. The fraternisation, moreover, took official forms, as on the First of May 1917, when Finnish workers and Russian soldiers marched

---

40 Osmo Jussila, *Nationalismi ja vallankumous venäläis-suomalaisissa suhteissa 1899–1914*, pp. 18–19.

41 Kari Immonen, *Ryssästä saa puhua : Neuvostoliitto suomalaisessa julkisuudessa ja kirjat julkisuuden muotona 1918–39*, p. 68.

42 See Matti Lackman, *Suomen vai Saksan puolesta? : jääkäriliikkeen ja jääkäripataljoona 27:n (1915–1918) synty, luonne, mielialojen vaihteluita sekä sisäisiä kriisejä sekä niiden heijastuksia itsenäisen Suomen ensi vuosiin saakka*, pp. 199–216.

43 Matti Lackman, "Mitalin toinen puoli" in Lackman, *Jääkärimuistelmia*, pp. 48–51 and *passim*.

44 Mikko Uola, *"Seinää vasten vain!" : poliittisen väkivallan motiivit Suomessa 1917–18*, pp. 99–112.

together in the traditional demonstrations in which a collection of money for Russian Social Democracy was also organised.[45]

The Finns knew little of the internal conflict in the Russian Social Democratic Labour Party. At the end of April 1917, a Social Democratic delegation was sent to Petrograd to clarify the stand of Russian comrades on the issue of Finnish autonomy and possible independence. The delegation met representatives of the Socialist Revolutionaries, Mensheviks, and Bolsheviks. The representatives of the two first-mentioned groups gave evasive answers explaining that such questions could only be solved when the Russian Constitutional Assembly was convened. The Bolsheviks promised full autonomy and even, if the Finns insisted, independence. The Bolsheviks had internal problems on this question, however, as there was a "Luxemburgist" faction represented by Georgi Leont'evich Piatakov and Feliks Edmundovich Dzerzhinskii who considered the right of self-determination a bourgeois idea and an obstacle to the realisation of international Socialism. In the VIIth Congress of the Bolshevik Party on April 24 / May 5, 1917[46] V. I. Lenin explained that if Finland were given "full freedom" the Finns would trust Russian "democracy" and when this "democracy" was realised in Russia the Finns would no longer wish to separate from Russia. This standpoint was adopted by the Congress by 56 votes for, 16 against, 18 delegates abstaining.[47] In June, Aleksandra Mikhailovna Kollontai, in the Congress of the SDP, declared that the Bolsheviks opposed the "domestic policy" of the Provisional Government, which oppressed small peoples in the Russian Imperium. The Bolsheviks demanded, moreover, that now, "when the revolutionary situation continues" the question of Finnish independence "must be solved" and they, the Bolsheviks, supported independence as far as to the separation of Finland from Russia. The independence of small countries could be attained if one "achieved complete victory over capitalist class and imperialist policy".[48] When Kullervo Manner, the chairman of the Congress, thanked Aleksandra Mikhailovna, he cordially remarked that for the Finns the matter of the policy of the Provisional Government concerning Finland was not a domestic but foreign-political question,[49] i.e. Finland was an independent political unit in

---

45 Eino Ketola, *Kansalliseen kansanvaltaan : Suomen itsenäisyys, sosialidemokraatit ja Venäjän vallankumous 1917*, pp. 90–91.

46 Until February 1, 1918, the calendar used in Russia (but not in Finland) was the Julian; after that date, the Gregorian calendar was in usage. In the XXth century, the Julian calendar was thirteen days behind the Gregorian. I give, in Russian contexts, dates in both calendars from the February revolution (which took place in March, according to the Gregorian calendar) until February 1, 1918.

47 Tuomo Polvinen, *Venäjän vallankumous ja Suomi 1917–1920*, vol. 1, *helmikuu 1917–toukokuu 1918*, pp. 62–66.

48 Suomen Sosialidemokratisen Puolueen yhdeksännen puoluekokouksen pöytäkirja : kokous pidetty Helsingissä kesäkuun 15–18 p:nä 1917 (minutes of the XIXth Congress of the SDP, Helsinki, June 15–18, 1917), p. 57.

49 *Ibid.*, p. 60.

regard to Russia, although not (as yet) an independent state. Whoever in the audience of the Party Congress grasped what Kollontai really said would have realised, as Eino Ketola points out, that the question of Finnish independence was not for the Bolsheviks any kind of juridical one.[50] Their aim was the World Revolution and they took their entire standpoint from this perspective. As to the Finns, perhaps only the Finnish-speaking Bolsheviks from Russia, Adolf Taimi, and Jukka Rahja, understood this mode of thinking.

v) The political factor. By a manifesto issued on March 7/20, 1917, the Russian Provisional Government assumed the sovereign prerogatives of the Grand Duke of Finland. However, "internal independence" was promised to the Grand Duchy. The Russians left the formation of the new Senate entirely to the Finns, which meant to them a new situation. The problem was that the Party holding the majority in the *Eduskunta*, the SDP – in the elections held in 1916, the Party, although it had less than 50 per cent of votes, returned 103 MPs –, was not willing, following the Kautskyan doctrine, to form or even to participate in the Senate. After a confusing debate in the Party executive council, those who supported participation won by a majority of ten votes against nine. Consequently a Senate (government) was formed, chaired by Oskari Tokoi, a Social Democrat. There were six Left-Wing and six Right-Wing senators; Tokoi had casting vote as chairman. The Social Democratic senators were not leaders of the Party and four of them were relatively young, reformism-oriented intellectuals.[51] Parties, especially the SDP, were not tied to the government as parties are in a "normal" parliamentary democracy. Moreover, there was no municipal democracy: every man (but not woman) who paid taxes was entitled to vote, but the amount of votes followed one's income. The Social Democrats usually boycotted municipal elections.[52]

Most, and in any case most radical, leaders of the SDP claimed that the Russian Provisional Government was not successor to the Tsar as to legal rights regarding Finland; these leaders insisted that the *Eduskunta* alone had these rights. In July, after complicated negotiations with various political groups in Russia, the SDP-led *Eduskunta* in a vote in which most bourgeois MPs voted against accepted on July 18, 1917, the so-called Law on Authority (*valtalaki*). According to this law, Finland had to have full internal autonomy; only military and foreign policy were left to the Russians.[53] The attitude of Conservative bourgeois politicians can be seen in the memoirs of the Finnish Minister State Secretary Carl Enckell, who

---

[50] Ketola, *Kansalliseen kansanvaltaan*, p. 137.

[51] Anthony Upton, *The Finnish Revolution 1917–1918*, pp. 28–29. The senators were Oskari Tokoi (a worker), Väinö Tanner (a lawyer), Väinö Voionmaa (already a famous historian), Wäinö Wuolijoki (a lawyer), Julius Ailio (an archaelogist) and Matti Paasivuori (a carpenter).

[52] Haapala, *Kun yhteiskunta hajosi*, pp. 32–34.

[53] See Alapuro, *State and Revolution in Finland*, p. 159.

presented Finnish affairs to the Provisional Government (previously the Minister State Secretary had presented Finnish affairs to the Emperor). For Enckell the Law on Authority could be characterised only as "a revolutionary incident" due to "Bolshevik agitation".[54] It is questionable whether Enckell at the time really thought the Law was passed in the *Eduskunta* because of Bolshevik agitation. Nevertheless, at the beginning of July there had been a mutiny in Petrograd and Kronstadt, led, after a spontaneous outbreak, rather unwillingly by the Bolsheviks.[55] The mutiny was crushed by troops loyal to the Provisional Government. Enckell, who obviously now saw a good opportunity to be rid of a Parliament in which the Social Democrats had the majority,[56] advised the Provisional Government to dissolve the *Eduskunta*.[57] This was realised and new elections were ordered, to be held at the beginning of October. The Social Democrats did not accept the dissolution but participated in the elections, where they lost their majority; the bourgeois parties now had 108 seats and the Social Democrats 92.

In the new *Eduskunta*, Kullervo Manner, chairman of the one dissolved, announced on November 8, 1917 that since the Provisional Government had no legal rights, "this assembly is not the legal Finnish *Eduskunta*".[58] It was not entirely logical for the Social Democrats to participate in new elections, which they considered illegal, and then work in the new *Eduskunta*, likewise considered illegal.

On November 1, 1917, the SDP issued a manifesto, *We Demand*. Its main demands were i) confiscation of all stores of foodstuff by the state and distribution of foods equally to all citizens; ii) aid to the unemployed; iii) democratisation of municipal councils as decided by the former *Eduskunta*; iv) expulsion of the Senate and all state officials who oppress the people; v) dissolution of the bourgeois Civil Guards (branded by the Social Democrats as "Slaughterer Guards" (*lahtarikaartit*); vi) an eight-hour working day; vii) proclamation of freedom to the crofters; viii) pensions for the elderly and health insurance; ix) progressive taxation; x) acceptance of the Law on Authority and, as a provisionally minimum measure, "the protection of the internal liberty of Finland by an agreement between Finland and Russia".[59] The manifesto implied a demand for the election of a constitutional assembly, which was unacceptable to the bourgeois parties.

---

[54] Carl Enckell, *Poliittiset muistelmani*, vol. 1, p. 91.

[55] See I. V. Stalin's account of the role of the Bolsheviks in the mutiny in the VIth Congress of the RSDRP(b), July 26–Aug. 3, 1917. I. B. Сталин, Отчетный доклад ЦК. 27 июля, 1917 г. in И. В. Сталин. *Сочинения*, vol. 3, pp. 161–166.

[56] Cf. Polvinen, *Venäjän vallankumous ja Suomi 1917–1920*, vol 1, p. 92.

[57] Enckell, *Poliittiset muistelmani*, vol. 1, p. 92.

[58] Toiset valtiopäivät 1917 : pöytäkirjat, vol. 1, p. 37.

[59] *Me vaadimme* programme, published in *Kansalaissota dokumentteina*, vol. 1. pp. 221–224.

3. The General Strike of November 1917

News of the Bolshevik coup d'état on November 7, 1917 immediately alerted the political communities in Helsinki. Bourgeois politicians decided to elect a Regent (the above-mentioned P. E. Svinhufvud), as was implied by the constitutional law of 1772 for the case of the demise of the ruling royal house – it was now, after the Bolshevik coup, deemed to be defunct. The Social Democrats established a Workers' Revolutionary Central Council, which consisted of the executive committee of the SDP and that of the Trade Union Federation, as well as nine representatives from the parliamentary group. The Social Democrats demanded that the old Manner *Eduskunta* should convene until a constituent assembly was elected. Local Bolsheviks in Helsinki together with Aleksandr Vasil'evich Shottman,[60] an emissary sent by Lenin, urged Finnish Social Democrats to stage a coup and promised arms as well as recognition of independence. O. W. Kuusinen and Karl Harald Wiik, the SDP leaders who negotiated with the Bolsheviks, hesitated not only because they could not be sure that such an operation would be successful, but also because they had little trust in the stability of the new Russian government. It was called among the Social Democrats at the time the "new Provisional Government". Finally, Kuusinen announced that the Social Democrats intended to seize power with weapons to be received from the Russians.[61] This did not materialise at this point but Lenin, when he met the delegation of the SDP on November 12, again urged the Finnish Social Democrats to act decisively and, first, to proclaim a general strike.[62]

Meanwhile in the *Eduskunta*, the Agrarians[63] brought up the notion of regency and were ready to revert to the Law on Authority so that the present *Eduskunta* would now accept it. Some moderate Social Democratic parliamentarians were ready to accept this compromise, but for the radical majority this was unacceptable, since it meant acknowledgement of the legality of the present *Eduskunta* with its bourgeois majority. Thereafter, on November 15, the Agrarians proposed that the *Eduskunta* itself take over supreme power in the country. This proposition was accepted and at the same time, the *Eduskunta* approved a law on an eight-hour

---

[60] The name was sometimes spelled Schottman or Schottmann.

[61] Polvinen, *Venäjän vallankumous ja Suomi 1917–1920*, vol. 1, pp. 120–121. Upton, *The Finnish Revolution* 1917–1918, pp. 140–141.

[62] Polvinen, *Venäjän vallankumous ja Suomi*, vol. 1, pp, 123–124.

[63] The Agrarians had 26 seats and the Social Democrats 92. Together the two parties would have formed a majority. – The Agrarian League (*Maalaisliitto*) was fairly conservative in political questions which implied morality or religion: the Agrarians, for example, strongly supported the system of a state church. They were, however, ardent Republicans, which after the rebellion was crushed, proved important because most Old Finns supported a monarchy.

working day and new municipal laws which extended democracy to the local level.[64] (No municipal elections were, however, organised before the Civil War.)

Being considered a revolutionary ultimatum by the Right-Wing forces, the manifesto *We Demand* was not presented officially to the *Eduskunta* as the Social Democrats and a Congress of the Trade Union Federation had demanded. The Workers' Revolutionary Central Council proclaimed a general strike on November 14. In demands issued by the Council, there were stipulations similar to those in the *We Demand* manifesto, but also the convocation of a constitutional assembly was now definitely demanded.[65] As Hannu Soikkanen has pointed out, the strategy of the Social Democrats before, during and after the general strike was ambiguous. For perhaps most Social Democratic leaders, especially the MPs, the outstanding issues were concrete reform in the *Eduskunta*. Their aim was, paradoxically, to strengthen the position of Parliament and protect it from outside pressure. On the other hand, the Russian Bolsheviks and the two ethnically Finnish Russian Bolsheviks in Helsinki, Adolf Taimi and Jukka Rahja, tried to use the general strike for their own revolutionary aims. Their pressure, however, hardly influenced even the leaders of the radical wing of the SDP.[66] On November 14, the Workers' Revolutionary Central Council issued for the Workers' Order Guards a list of assignments which included the arrest of people who were "observed to be engaged in dangerous undertakings against the workers" and "prevention of the distribution of all mendacious proclamations".[67] Two days later the Council demanded a revolution in the following manner: "The power has until now been used by the bourgeoisie only. Part of it must now pass into the hands of the working-class".[68] The Council also demanded that the railways, other vehicles and the telephone be taken over by the workers. "The obstruction of the bourgeoisie and armed opposition must be discouraged. Deprive the slaughterers of their arms!"[69]

A serious problem for the leaders of the general strike was the spontaneous action of the Workers' Order Guard in many parts of the country. During the strike (November 14–20, 1917), the Red Guards slew 16 people and during the week following its official end another nine persons. In addition, there were many unsuccessful attempts at assassination. There was also pillaging.[70] It was obvious that

---

[64] Polvinen, *Venäjän vallankumous ja Suomi 1917–1920*, vol. 1, p. 125.

[65] *Työväen Vallankumouksellisen Keskusneuvoston Tiedonantolehti*, Nov. 14, 1917, published in *Kansalaissota dokumentteina*, vol. 1, pp. 232–234.

[66] Hannu Soikkanen, "Johdanto suurlakkoa koskeviin asiakirjoihin" in *Kansalaissota dokumentteina*, vol. 1, p. 231.

[67] *Työväen Vallankumouksellisen Keskusneuvoston Tiedonantolehti*, Nov. 14, 1917, published in *Kansalaissota dokumentteina*, vol. 1, p. 237.

[68] *Työväen Vallankumouksellisen Keskusneuvoston Tiedonantolehti*, Nov. 16, 1917, published in *Kansalaissota dokumentteina*, vol. 1, p. 245.

[69] *Ibid.*

[70] Jaakko Paavolainen, *Poliittiset väkivaltaisuudet Suomessa*, vol. 1, '*Punainen terrori*', pp. 76–77.

the Social Democratic leaders were losing control of the Workers' Guard, whose members were usually relatively young and eager for "revolutionary action", which in some cases resembled more individual terrorism than anything which might be called disciplined action. In this situation, the Council decided, on November 17, to stop the strike. It announced that the "black undertakings of the bourgeoisie have now been crushed". The language used was extremely radical, but the radicalism could not cover the confusion which reigned among the Social Democratic leaders.[71] Especially O. W. Kuusinen argued for an ending to the strike. He was not ready to assume dictatorial powers for the Social Democrats because such an enterprise would endanger the existence of the Party organisation in the event of bourgeois forces organising resistance. He also feared that the Bolshevik government in Petrograd might be gnashed.[72] The decision to discontinue the strike met with infuriated protests by many members of the Workers' Order Guards. For instance, on November 18 an angry delegation of railwaymen in Helsinki came to the Workers' House and told Kullervo Manner: "You have betrayed the workers, the strike must go on until a Socialist government is established".[73] Emil Laiho (later Louhikko), chairman of the Metal Workers' Union, claims that in May 1918 Lenin had told him and Kustaa Rovio: "You did wrong when you ended the strike. You should have continued it until you got the power in your hands".[74] Anthony Upton seems to be of Lenin's opinion; his verdict is pitiless: "The Finnish revolutionaries were in general the most abject ones in history, behaving throughout akin to men contemplating their own funerals".[75]

This chagrin may explain the fact that although the SDP Party Committee and an *ad hoc* workers' Conference held in Helsinki on November 21 discussed a plan to form a Red government and ignore the *Eduskunta*, nothing like this transpired. One motive behind this plan was the poor discipline of the Workers' Guard; Manner, Kuusinen, Sirola, and other Party leaders wanted, above all, to control the Guards.[76]

When bourgeois newspapers again appeared after the strike, they devoted much space to descriptions of the murders and pillaging which took place during the strike and argued that the leaders of the SDP were responsible. Because the Workers' Order Guards had now received arms from the Russians and because Russian soldiers had participated in some of the violent disturbances, they were seen as "blood brothers" of the Finnish Reds. Social Democratic papers tried to prove that

---

[71] *Luokkataistelu ilman suurlakkoa : keskusneuvoston päätös ja julistus Suomen järjestyneelle työväelle*, published in *Kansalaissota dokumentteina*, vol. 1, p. 248.

[72] Polvinen, *Venäjän vallankumous ja Suomi 1917–1920*, vol. 1, p. 126.

[73] Quoted in Upton, *The Finnish Revolution 1917–1918*, p. 162.

[74] E. K. Louhikko, *Teimme vallankumousta*, p. 174.

[75] Upton, *The Finnish Revolution 1917–1918*, p. 150.

[76] *Ibid.*, p. 169.

those who were guilty of the violence were not class-conscious proletarians but people on a lower level of development or even *agents provocateurs*.[77]

The radical wing of the SDP, Manner, Kuusinen, Sirola etc. were by no means Bolsheviks. These leaders simply knew very little about the Bolshevik doctrines and were, above all, not aware of the most central doctrine of a disciplined Leninist Party of the "new type". On the other hand, Lenin behaved as if the Finnish radical leaders were Bolshevik revolutionaries and suggested they make a coup d'état. On November 24, 1917, Vladimir Il'ich sent the following letter to Manner, Sirola, Kuusinen, Valpas and Wiik:[78]

> Distinguished comrades! To my greatest pleasure, I have heard from my Finnish friends that you are at the head of the revolutionary wing of the Finnish Social Democratic Labour [*sic*] Party and are carrying on the struggle for a Socialist proletarian revolution. On behalf of the Russian revolutionary proletariat I can assure you that the great organising talents, high level of development and long political experience of the Finnish workers, gained in democratic institutions, will help them to realise successfully the Socialist rearrangement of Finland. We trust in the fraternal aid of the revolutionary Finnish Social Democrats.
>
> Long live the international Socialist revolution!
>
> Best regards,
>
> N. Lenin.

It seems that Lenin's letter had no impact on events. An extraordinary Congress of the SDP which met on November 25–27 discussed the question of a takeover. The proposition was finally supported by only a small group; the leaders were not ready for a coup for various reasons, one of them being the belief that Finland was not developed enough for a proletarian revolution. Among the delegates, however, the idea of a takeover found support. When the choice between parliamentary and revolutionary strategy was put to the vote, 59 delegates voted for parliamentary and 43 for revolutionary methods.[79] The vote took place before Iosif Vissarionovich Stalin, People's Commissar for National Affairs, presented the greetings of the Bolshevik Party to the Congress. In order to steer the Finns, (the Finns being for Iosif Vissarionovich one of "peoples of Russia") onto the revolutionary road he promised them full independence:[80]

---

77 Paavolainen, *Poliittiset väkivaltaisuudet Suomessa*, vol. 1, pp. 77–78.

78 PSS, vol. 35, p. 90.

79 Upton, *The Finnish Revolution 1917–1918*, pp. 172–178.

80 И. В. Сталин, Речь на съезде финляндской социал-демократической рабочей партии в Гельсингфорсе, 14 ноября 1917 г., *Правда*, Нож. 16, 1917. И. В. Сталин, *Сочинения*, vol. 4, pp. 3–4.

> I must say with categorical conviction that we should not be democrats (I do not speak at all about Socialism!) if we did not recognise the right of free self-determination (*самоопределение*) for the peoples of Russia. I say we should betray Socialism if we did not institute all measures to restore fraternal trust (*доверие*) between Finnish and Russian workers. [...] The voluntary alliance of the Finnish people with the people of Russia! No kind of patronage, no kind of control from above! [...] Only on the basis of such a policy, it is possible to realise in life the incorporation (*сплочение*) of peoples of Russia into one army. Only because of such incorporation, one can strengthen the victories of the October revolution and further the cause of the international Socialist revolution. [...] Comrades! We have found out that your country is affliction from similar shortage of power as Russia in the threshold of the October revolution. [...] Moreover, if you need our help, we help you and stretch to you fraternally our hand.

The general strike was a defeat for the workers' movement. No aims had been achieved. The trade union movement had not been able to control the devastation caused by both individuals and undisciplined Order Guard detachments. The SDP issued proclamations in which individual terrorism was declared to be in contradiction of Social Democratic principles. – The bourgeoisie were frightened by the violence. As Upton writes, the strike was an impulse to the previously divided bourgeois parties to unite their forces. In the workers' movement, the "more lasting damage" was "the crisis of confidence" between the militant rank-and-file "vanguard" and the hesitant leadership.[81] The effect of all this was subsequently to have important consequences among the Finnish Communists in Russia.

4. The Rebellion

One effect of the Bolshevik coup d'état in Russia was that all Finnish bourgeois parties now began to support the idea of full independence for Finland. In mid-November a bill by the transfer of sovereign power to the *Eduskunta* was accepted. Independence was proclaimed on December 6, and recognition of independence by Soviet Russian Council of People's Commissars was obtained on December 31. Prior to this, on December 27, a delegation of the SDP (Kullervo Manner, Edvard Gylling and K. H. Wiik) met V. I. Lenin and L. D. Trotskii in Petrograd. The delegation presented an address in which it was stated that recognition of independence was a precondition for the victory of the Finnish proletariat. It seems that once Lenin and Trotskii became convinced that from the point of view of the possibili-

[81] Upton, *The Finnish Revolution 1917–1918*, pp. 177–173.

[82] *Ibid.*, pp. 180–198.

ties of the Social Democrats' gaining state power recognition of independence was needed, they assented and the official (bourgeois) delegation of the Finnish government obtained acknowledgement of it.[82] The Bolsheviks were thorough highly critical of the Finnish Social Democrats. When Stalin presented the decision of the Council of People's Commissars to the Executive of the Congress of Soviets on January 4, 1918 for approval, he said, according to *Pravda*:[83]

> If we look deeper into how Finland gained independence, we note that the Council of People's Commissars did not give real freedom to the people, to the representatives of the Finnish proletariat, but to the Finnish bourgeoisie, who by a curious turn of events had taken over the power, and received the independence from the hands of Russian Socialists. The Finnish workers and Social Democrats had fallen into such a position that they had to receive freedom through the Finnish bourgeoisie and not directly from the hands of the Russian Socialists. Seeing here the tragedy of the proletariat of Finland, we cannot do this without remarking that it was only because of their irresolution and inexplicable cowardice that the Finnish Social Democrats did not take decisive measures to take the power in their own hands and wrench their independence from the hands of the bourgeoisie.

The Bolsheviks were deeply disappointed in the performance of the Finnish Social Democratic leaders. In mid-January 1918, Lenin told the Swedish Social Democrat Carl Lindhagen that if only the revolution in Finland could be realised, Finland and Russia would unite again and form a federation. When Lindhagen noted that the Finnish Social Democrats themselves had been for independence, Lenin answered: "The Finnish Social Democrats are traitors. They do not want to make a revolution although it is their duty [to make it]". Lindhagen doubted whether the Social Democrats were capable of this, but Lenin had no doubt: "They are able to if they only want to."[84] At roughly that time Lenin expressed a critical view of the delegation of the SDP he had met on December 27, 1917 to a delegation of the Finnish Bolsheviks of Petrograd. This delegation included Otto Palho (a member of the future "Murder Opposition"), Jukka Rahja, Eino Rahja and V. Kukkonen (a worker in Petrograd). Palho said in the second Congress of the SKP that Vladimir Il'ich's comment on the visit of the previous Wiik, Manner and Gylling delegation was to the effect that this delegation "haggled like *khalat* Tatars".[85]

---

[83] И. В. Сталин. О независимости Финляндии : доклад на заседании ВЦИК 22 декабря 1917 г. (Газетный отчет). *Правда*. Dec. 23, 1917. И. В. Сталин. *Сочинения*. vol. 4, pp. 23–24.

[84] Carl Lindhagen, *I revolutionsland*, p. 77. Excerpt published in *Kansalaissota dokumentteina*, vol. 2, p. 346. See also Polvinen, *Venäjän vallankumous ja Suomi 1917–1920*, vol. 1, pp. 192–193.

[85] Minutes of the II[d] Congress of the SKP, Aug. 31–Sept. 11, 1919. RGASPI, f. 516, op. 2, 1919, d. 4, l. 58. – The Russian word *халат* means oriental long rope.

On January 12, 1918, the *Eduskunta* authorised (the Social Democrats, of course, voting against) the government to create a "strong security force"[86] and on January 25, the White Civil Guards were declared to be the troops of the government. On 27 January the Whites began military action in Ostrobothnia, where the Civil Guards, led by C. G. E. Mannerheim, disarmed Russian troops without encountering significant resistance.[87]

The Red Guards, as they were now officially called, held a Congress on December 16–19, 1917, where a real military organisation was created. Of particular importance was that such Social Democratic leaders as O. W. Kuusinen, Yrjö Sirola and Kullervo Manner came out in support of a coup d'état.[88] In a meeting of the Extended Party Executive Committee[89] on January 23, 1918 Sirola presented a plan for creating a revolutionary organisation and the following day a plan of action. The organisation in question consisted of the Party Executive Committee into which five "additional members" were co-opted from the Red Guards. According to the plan of action, the members of the Senate and leading bourgeois politicians were to be arrested. In addition, Sirola suggested discussion of the nature of the coming revolution: was it to be "democratic" or "proletarian Communist"? Sirola noted that the majority of people did not support the revolution, but when the aims were explained to them, it would be possible to attain the support of the majority. The Executive Committee made the decision on a coup on January 26.[90] This took place in Helsinki without bloodshed on January 27 simply by lighting a red lantern in the tower of the Workers' House in Helsinki. The government succeeded in moving to Vaasa, in Ostrobothnia. The front between Whites and Reds was formed in February and the country was thus divided into two parts. As to the class composition of the Reds and Whites, civil servants and independent farmers formed

---

86 Paasivirta, *Suomi vuonna 1918*, p. 66.

87 See e.g., Alapuro, *The State and Revolution in Finland*, pp. 171–174.

88 Paavolainen, *Poliittiset väkivaltaisuudet Suomessa*, vol. 1, p. 80.

89 The Extended Executive Committee of the SDP was created on January 19, 1918 in the Party Council of the SDP. The Council rejected a suggestion to elect a special "Revolutionary Committee" which would act as a separate body in relation to the Executive Committee. In this situation Kuusinen, Sirola, Manner and Matti Turkia refused membership of the Executive Committee. The situation seemed to be a deadlock. Edvard Gylling then proposed that the Council elects to the Executive Committee "additional members" from leaders of the Red Guards. This was accepted and five additional members, among them Adolf Taimi, were elected. (Soikkanen, *Kohti kansanvaltaa*, vol. 1, pp. 263–265.)

90 *Ibid.*, pp. 262–270.

the core of the White army, whereas industrial workers, artisans and farm workers were strongly represented in the Red army.[91]

In the South a revolutionary government, called the People's Deputation (*Kansanvaltuuskunta*) was formed. In addition, there was a Workers' Central Council (*Työväen pääneuvosto*). This body, a "Parliament", consisted of 48 persons elected by the SDP, the Trade Union Federation, the Red Guards and a representative body of the workers of Helsinki. The Workers' Central Council had committees similar to a Parliament, but it was of little importance.[92] The People's Deputation had real power, although this body could not always control what was going on, especially in the final phase of the Civil War.

The People's Deputation (in actuality O. W Kuusinen) drafted a proposal for a constitution for Finland.[93] The obvious model for it was the Swiss. The highest state organ was to be the Finnish People's Parliament (*Suomen kansaneduskunta*) (§ 2), elected by the same electoral system as the *Eduskunta* for three years (§ 16). Parliamentary committees were to be elected by proportional vote (§ 20), which implied that what was envisaged was a multi-party system. Political parties were explicitly mentioned in the section on negotiations with foreign countries; Finnish delegations were to be so appointed that different parties were represented.

---

[91] This is seen in Table 1.

Table 1. The Statistics of Dead in the Civil War (per cent)

	whole population in 1920	dead Reds	dead Whites
Civil servants, people in leading positions (also students on the White side)	9.8	1.1	17.0
Farmers who owned their farms	27.6	5.4	45.4
Crofters	21.3	12.5	11.0
Farm workers without land, owned or hired	13.3	16.1	8.7
Industrial workers, artisans	19.9	62.8	14.2
Others	8.1	2.1	3.7

(Source: Rasila, *Kansalaissodan sosiaalinen tausta*, p. 43.)

In the White army, there were about 70,000 men, of whom not more than about 35,000 were at the front at the same time. The Red Army comprised 90,000 men, of whom not more than about 30,000 – 35,000 were at the front at the same time. (Jussi T. Lappalainen, *Itsenäisen Suomen synty*, p.151 and 154.)

[92] Osmo Rinta-Tassi, *Kansanvaltuuskunta punaisen Suomen hallituksena*, pp. 151–158.

[93] Suomen kansanvaltuuskunnan ehdotus Suomen valtiosäännöksi : esitetty pääneuvostolle tarkastettavaksi ja päätettäväksi yleistä kansanäänestystä varten.

Human rights were largely protected, for instance by the right to strike and by the right to form picket lines (§ 10). There was to be a referendum, firstly on the constitution and then on any alteration to it (§ 20). The most curious section concerned the people's right of uprising:

> If something so unbelievable were to happen, that the majority of the People's Parliament itself had the audacity to displace this whole constitution or obviously intentionally to break stipulations of this basic law in order to gain an oligarchic order in the country, let the people rise and dissolve this People's Parliament and assume that in three months new elections of members of Parliament would be organised as decreed in this constitution (§ 43).

What is meant by "people" in this section is unclear; it also remains vague who would decide that the stipulations of the constitution had been contravened.

There were complicated decrees regarding the people's initiative. The basic rule was that an initiative signed by at least 10,000 persons entitled to vote should be promptly discussed and voted on in the People's Parliament. If it was rejected, one third of the MPs or 5 per cent of the people entitled to vote could obtain a referendum (§ 45–48). This 5 per cent could also submit to referendum any decision of the People's Parliament, the People's Deputation, the administration, or the court (§ 51). The constitution did not acknowledge parliamentarism. The People's Deputation was to be nominated by the People's Parliament for three years. The chairman of the Deputation was to be the head of state, called "Chief (*esimies*) of the Republic of Finland". Being a member of the People's Deputation, he was elected, as well as the Vice-Chief, by the People's Parliament. He could not be elected for more than three years; the same member of the People's Deputation could not be elected Chief for more than two consecutive terms (§ 59).

The constitution contained no mention of the economic system of the country. The Chief of State was to be more of a prime minister than a president. There is no indication of an analogy with the Soviet system as decreed in the first constitution of Soviet Russia in 1918, let alone with the declared aim of the formation of a dictatorship of the proletariat. The difference between these two constitutions lies in the different conceptions of the state. The Bolshevik conception was totalitarian: the state had unlimited, absolute power. The individual citizen was not protected against the state; the constitution of Soviet Russia contained no safeguards for individuals against mistreatment by the government.[94] In the Finnish "Red" constitution there were such safeguards: it was decreed that anyone who thought that he or she had been a victim of abuse by the administration had the right to bring this cause to court (§ 56); there was also to be a procurator to whom a citizen

[94] See Edward Hallet Carr, *The Bolshevik Revolution 1917–1923*, vol. 1, pp. 150–151.

could make complaint and a special parliamentary body which was to monitor the lawfulness of the acts of all organs of the state (§ 72 & 73).

Although the planned constitution was fairly moderate, in other contexts the Red leaders presented much more radical plans, such as that only workers could influence the political affairs of the country and that the aim of the revolution was to be Socialism.[95]

The Bolsheviks began immediately after their own coup d'état to speak of a federation in which Russia was to be the centre. In a fervent speech on vistas of the World Revolution, held in the third all-Russian Congress of the deputies of the Soviets of workers, soldiers and peasants on January 31, 1918, Lenin declared: "I am deeply convinced that around revolutionary Russia will come together more and more different federations of free separate nations".[96] According to Lenin, this would take place "voluntarily", there would be no "divide and rule" policy as in ancient Rome, the Bolsheviks would only "rule", not "divide". As to Finland, Lenin congratulated the "unwavering resoluteness" of the Finnish "workers and peasants" to "go with us on the path of the International".[97] These words were uttered three days after the outbreak of the Finnish Civil War.

Some among the leaders of the Reds evinced positive attitudes to formation of such a federation. Oskari Tokoi, for instance, spoke favourably of it.[98] In the negotiations with Lenin on a Russian-Finnish agreement, the clause pertaining to citizenship was difficult. Lenin demanded that all Russians in Finland automatically obtain Finnish citizenship and vice versa. The Tsarist regime had used this kind of agreement on equality in the policy of Russification. Many if not most People's Deputies saw in this kind of agreement a good propaganda weapon from the point of view of the White government. After the negotiations Lenin agreed to the formulation that, on the one hand, Finland agreed "to offer [to the Russians] as easy conditions as possible" the granting of citizenship and, on the other that Finnish workers and peasants who were not salaried agricultural workers, would receive on demand full rights of citizenship in Russia. This agreement, signed on March 1, 1918, was celebrated as a world-historical event: it was the first agreement between "two Socialist states". This allusion to "Socialism" was Lenin's demand. When the negotiations began and the Finns presented their draft agreement, Lenin would not accept the formulation "the Republic of Finland" because, as he pointed out, it was possible for the Bolsheviks to establish a friendship only with countries where the workers were in power. The formulation was thus altered to the "Socialist Work-

---

95 Soikkanen, *Kohti kansanvaltaa*, vol. 1, pp. 275–276.

96 В. И. Ленин. Заключительное слово перед закрытием съезда 18 (31) января. PSS, vol. 35, p. 288.

97 *Ibid.*, pp. 287–289.

98 Polvinen, *Venäjän vallankumous ja Suomi 1917–1920*, vol 1, p. 241.

ers' Republic of Finland".[99] Lenin, however, was not at all satisfied. The Finns demanded that the area of Pechenga (in Finnish Petsamo) in the North of Russia, which would give the Finns access to the Arctic Ocean, be annexed to their republic. The grounds for this demand was a promise made by Tsar Alexander II. The area in question was given, but Lenin could not understand why revolutionaries could be interested in such bourgeois trivialities as boundaries between states. He doubted whether the Finnish Reds were really Socialists at all; they had behaved like bourgeois chauvinists.[100]

Meanwhile the military situation was worsening for the Reds. Perhaps the most important cause here were precisely the Finnish military personnel the Whites possessed, but the Reds not. The Whites had former Finnish officers of the Imperial Russian Army; some of them, like Mannerheim, did not even, in 1918, speak Finnish (his native language was Swedish). Some 1,000 *Jägers* came from Germany to Ostrobothnia at the end of February.[101] The Reds had some Russian officers in their service and they received weapons from the Russians, but only about 1,000–2,000 Russian voluntaries fought on the front[102] although altogether about 10,000 Russian soldiers participated in the Civil War for a while.[103] They had a major role in the Red artillery.[104] The great problem was the hostility of the Red soldiers to the Russians. The Finnish chiefs tried to stress in their propaganda that national prejudices and differences of language should not result in "disagreements and suspicions" between Finns and Russians.[105] Most of the Red soldiers had no military training, although there were some who had belonged to the Russian army or had even served in the old Finnish army at the end of the XIXth century. They were, however, simple soldiers and non-commissioned officers. Moreover, the Red troops formed a "democratic army": chiefs were elected by the men themselves, and this might be a slow process: in one case it took one month to elect the chief of a Red regiment. When the Red soldiers became dissatisfied with their chiefs they simply dismissed them and elected new ones.[106]

---

99 *Ibid.*, pp. 245–249. Yrjö Sirola, "Ulkoasiain valtuutettuna vallankumoushallituksessa : muistelmia ja mietteitä" in *Suomen luokkasota : historiaa ja muistelmia*, p. 50. The partners of the agreement were the "Soviet of People's Commissars of the Russian Federative Soviet Republic" and the "People's Deputation of the Finnish Workers' Republic". (*Kansalaissota dokumentteina*, vol. 2, p. 133)

100 Polvinen, *Venäjän vallankumous ja Suomi 1917–1920*, vol 1, pp. 247–248 and p. 251.

101 Juhani Paasivirta, *Suomi vuonna 1918*, p. 191.

102 Heikki Ylikangas, *Tie Tampereelle : dokumentoitu kuvaus Tampereen antautumiseen johtaneista sotatapahtumista Suomen sisällissodassa 1918*, p. 53.

103 Ohto Manninen, "Taistelevat osapuolet" in *Itsenäistymisen vuodet 1917–1920*, vol. 2, *Taistelu vallasta*, p. 73.

104 *Ibid.*, p. 141.

105 Ylikangas, *Tie Tampereelle*, p. 97.

106 Manninen, "Taistelevat osapuolet", pp. 162–163.

The decisive battle in the Civil War was that of Tampere. The Whites captured the town on April 6.[107] At the beginning of April, German troops (about 12,000)[108] landed in Southern Finland and took Helsinki on April 14. Before the conquest, the People's Deputation had escaped to Viipuri in spite of the opposition of the Red Guard.[109] In the night of April 10–11, 1918 an *ad hoc* meeting attended by members of the People's Deputation, members of the Workers' Central Council and officers of the Red Guard convened and decided to establish a dictatorship with Kullervo Manner as dictator with an eye to "restoring order and discipline in the army" and organising defence against the Whites. Only Adolf Taimi opposed dictatorship. Manner supported a dictatorship but opposed his own appointment as the dictator. He was, however, appointed as the first and (until now) only dictator of the country.[110]

Hereafter, on April 26, the People's Deputation escaped to Petrograd.[111] Ten days before Lenin, who obviously feared that the Germans might continue the war against Soviet Russia in spite of the Brest-Litovsk peace, had declared to the People's Deputies O. W. Kuusinen and Edvard Gylling in Petrograd that Finnish Reds would not be allowed to continue the war against the Whites from Russian soil. He even forbade Finnish Red Guards to enter Russia because there was a lack of food.[112] This threat was not actualised, however. Lenin urged the Reds to hold Eastern Finland for the duration, until the German revolution broke out; this was however rendered impossible by the military strength of the White army.[113]

The number of victims of the Red terror (i.e. victims not dead at the front) was about 1,650;[114] the portion of victims of the White terror during the war 1,200–1,300; after the war, the Whites executed about 5,600 Reds.[115] In the camps in which 82,000 people were incarcerated and where the inmates suffered serious undernutrition, about 12,500 people died.[116] In the actual fighting, about 4,000 Whites and about 6,000 Reds died.[117]

---

107 Paasivirta, *Suomi vuonna 1918*, p. 209.

108 Lappalainen, *Itsenäisen Suomen synty*, pp. 175–176.

109 Rinta-Tassi, *Kansanvaltuuskunta punaisen Suomen hallituksena*, pp. 468–470.

110 *Ibid.*, pp. 474–475.

111 Paasivirta, *Suomi vuonna 1918*, pp. 215–227.

112 Soikkanen, *Kohti kansanvaltaa*, vol. 1, p. 295.

113 Soikkanen, *Luovutetun Karjalan työväenliikkeen historia*, p. 321.

114 Paavolainen, *Poliittiset väkivaltaisuudet Suomessa*, vol. 1, p. 94.

115 *Ibid.*, vol. 2, '*Valkoinen terrori*', p. 193. This makes altogether 6,800 – 6,900 victims. According to Ohto Manninen ("Rauhantahtoa ja väkivaltaa" in *Itsenäistymisen vuodet*, vol. 2, *Taistelu vallasta*, p. 461) there were 8,380 victims of the White terror.

116 Jaakko Paavolainen, *Vankileirit Suomessa 1918*, p. 332.

117 Ylikangas, *Tie Tampereelle*, p. 47.

The total number of deaths and disappearances in the Finnish Civil War is presented in Table 2 and the total numbers of all war victims in Finland in the years 1914–1922 in Table 3.

Table 2. Death Toll of the Finnish Civil War[118]

Citizens of Finland	
1917 skirmishes	21
1918, Whites	5,305
1918, Reds[119]	28,008
1918 Civilians	240
1919[120]	121
Citizens of other countries	
Russians (about)	3,000
Germans	294
Swedes[121]	34
Total of all dead and disappeared	about 37,000

[118] Source: Jari Eerola and Jouni Eerola, *Henkilötappiot Suomen sisällissodassa 1918*, p. 159.
[119] Dead on the front; executed or died in camps.
[120] Executed or died in camps.
[121] Swedish volunteers on the side of the Whites.

Table 3. War Victims 1914–1922[122]

War action	Approximate numbers of war victims
People executed and killed by the Russian military officials in Finland, 1914–1917	50
Finns dead in the Russian and German armies during the First World War	50
Russian officers killed in Finland, 1917	100
Political atrocities in Finland in the autumn of 1917 and in January 1918	50
Civil War of 1918	about 35,000[123]
Russian military officials and civilians in Finland executed by the Finns, 1918	at least 1,000
East Karelian expeditions, 1918	100
Finnish Red Guard units in Soviet Russia, 1918–1922	1,500
Estonian expedition, 1919[124]	100
East Karelian expedition, 1919	400
Others	500
Total of all dead and disappeared	about 39,000

[122] Source: *The research project on War Victims in Finland 1914–1922 : a brief introduction*, p. 4. The source gives 38,000. The total given by a count of the numbers given is, however, 38,850.

[123] This number is 2,000 less than that given by Eerola and Eerola. The figures for Russians killed are markedly different and those given in the Table 3 are approximate. There is a research project on war victims in Finland 1914–1922, conducted by the Prime Minister's Office. When the database is completed, the numbers may change. Among the foreigners killed between 1914 and 1922, there were not only Germans, Russians and Swedes, but also the Chinese (*The research project on War Victims in Finland 1914–1922 : a brief introduction*).

[124] Finnish voluntaries who participated in the War against Soviet Russia in Estonia in 1919.

5. After the Civil War

After the Civil War, there was only one Social Democratic MP in the *Eduskunta*, Matti Paasivuori, who had been publicly and strongly opposed to the rebellion. When this "Rump Parliament" voted to elect a King, Paasivuori preferred to speak very briefly. He said: "I shall not participate in this political joke and I express my protest against the whole proceedings".[125] In addition, representatives of Agrarian League and some former members of the Young Finns declared their protests.[126]

After the Civil War a problem in Finno-Russian relations was the question of Eastern Karelia, i.e. the part of Karelia which belonged to Soviet Russia. There were disturbances in the area after the Bolshevik coup; some Finnish-speaking people there wanted their territory to be annexed by Finland. However, these elements were not important and their number was small. They were used, at least partly, as a smoke screen by Finnish nationalist intellectuals, who spoke of the "tribal question" (*heimokysymys*),[127] to launch "expeditions" to this area to seize East Karelian territories. From the present point of view what is important is that in confrontations with men of the "tribal idea", branded by the Finnish Reds in Russia as "slaughterers", involved recruits in the Red Officer School (also known "International War School") in Petrograd. These Finnish expeditions, however, were futile: no part of Soviet Karelia was annexed and the peace with the Russians agreed in the Tartu negotiations virtually put a stop to the expeditions, although local skirmishes also took place in the early 1920s.[128] As to the Social Democrats, they supported the annexation in principle, but were against any military action. The annexation, they said, must be realised by peaceful negotiations.[129]

The Civil War and the "monarchist venture" profoundly changed the Finnish party system. There were the following main parties: i) The National Coalition Party (*Kansallinen kokoomuspuolue*, or KOK). The prominent leaders of this Party were

---

[125] Matti Paasivuori in the *Eduskunta*, on October 5, 1918. Ylimääräiset valtiopäivät 1918 : pöytäkirjat, p. 16.

[126] Vares, *Kuninkaan tekijät*, p. 255. See also Anders Huldén, *Kuningasseikkailu Suomessa*, pp. 185–191.

[127] Toivo Nygård, *Suur-Suomi vai lähiheimolaisten auttaminen : aatteellinen heimotyö itsenäisessä Suomessa*, p. 19.

[128] Mauno Jääskeläinen, *Itä-Karjalan kysymys : kansallisen laajennusohjelman synty ja sen toteuttamisyritykset Suomen ulkopolitiikassa vuosina 1918–1920*, e.g. pp. 206–223 and passim. See also Markku Kangaspuro, "Russian Patriots and Red Fennomans" in *Rise and Fall of Soviet Karelia, : People and Power*, pp. 32–33 and V. M. Holodkovskij, *Suomi ja Neuvosto-Venäjä 1918–1920*.

[129] Kari Immonen, *Ryssästä saa puhua ...* , p. 119

monarchists of 1918 and by ideology the Party was conservative. ii) The Swedish People's Party (*Svenska Folkpartiet*, or SFP). This Party was a heterogeneous combination. Its main purpose was defensive; to preserve the Swedish language in conditions in which, due to mixed marriages, the natural basis of the Party was slowly eroding. iii) The Progressive Party (*Edistyspuolue*, or ED), a Republican and Liberal formation, was situated in the political centre. It was never a large Party, but its location in the centre gave it more power than its number of seats in the *Eduskunta* would as such have allowed. The first President of Finland, Kaarlo Juho Ståhlberg, was an esteemed leader of this party. iv) The Agrarian League (*Maalaisliitto*, or ML) was the Party of peasants, likewise located in the centre. The Party's electoral strongholds were Ostrobothnia and Karelia. Its support in Southern Finland was scanty and in towns minimal. The Agrarian League supported reforms, e.g. in the field of education, but the values of their leaders and supporters alike were strongly conservative.[130] v) The Social Democratic Party (SDP). vi) Front-organisations of the Communists (KOM, 1922–1930). vii) The Patriotic People's Movement (*Isänmaallinen kansanliike*, or IKL), founded in 1932 after the collapse of the Lapua movement. viii) Others. There was a small Christian Workers' League in the 1920s and in the 1930s there were two smallholders' parties. The parliamentary strength of these parties 1919–1936 can be seen in Table 4.

Finland had become a republic and a new constitution was endorsed in July 1919. In the early 1920s, there was a myriad of reform legislation. The aim was to enhance education; many bourgeois politicians thought that the rebellion had taken place because the level of mores and education among the lower classes was hopelessly insufficient. The result was a law on basic education; the minimum duration of schooling was decreed as six years. Elementary education now spread to the countryside, even, at least in principle, also to the most remote parts of the country in which in some cases there were not even roads, only paths. The constitution of 1919 guaranteed freedom of religion, press etc.[131] One vitally important step was also a land reform which liberated the crofters and produced some 100,000 new independent smallholders.[132]

The Social Democratic Party condemned violent action and in the Party Congress in December 1918 announced that the Party strategy will be centred in the *Eduskunta*, in which the Party will work for reforms which would enhance the

---

[130] One example, illuminative of this point, was that the Agrarian League in the *Eduskunta* opposed state aid to ballet and opera. Ballet was seen as morally disruptive. As to the opera, the problem was that some writers in the Party press did not know the difference between ballet and opera. (Hannu-Ilari Lampila, *Suomalainen ooppera*, 170–171.)

[131] See Paasivirta, *Finland and Europe*, p. 235.

[132] *Ibid.*, p. 236.

Table 4. Representation of Parties in the *Eduskunta*, 1919–1936 (Total of Seats: 200)

Year	SDP	ML	KOK	ED	SFP	KOM	IKL	Others
1919	80	42	28	26	22			2
1922	53	45	35	15	25	27		
1924	60	44	38	17	23	18		
1927	60	52	34	10	24	20		
1929	59	60	28	7	23	23		
1930	66	59	42	11	21			1
1933	78	53	18	11	21		14	1
1936	83	53	29	7	21		14	5

living conditions of the working-class and all poor people. Väinö Tanner, who during the rebellion had condemned this move, was elected chairman.[133]

The Communists in Finland tried at first what was later termed among the Trotskyites "entrism". The idea was simply to "enter" the Social Democratic Party organisation and take it out of the hands of the Social Democratic leaders. This strategy was however not successful. The Communists tried first to win a majority among the Social Democratic Party Congress delegates in 1919, but the move failed. The next move was to establish a front-organisation, the above-mentioned Finnish Socialist Workers' Party (*Suomen sosialistinen työväenpuolue*, or SSTP), founded in May 1920. The new Party was not, however, fully controlled by the Communists. Although the aim of the Party was defined in its programme as "council power", it was also stated that the SSTP[134]

> does not urge workers to anarchistic, violent acts, disorders, riots, or rebellions. On the contrary, our Party seeks by its enlightenmental and organisational activity to influence to the direction that the full victory of the working-class will be achieved in order, as calm and serious, as painless and rapid a way as only possible.

---

[133] See Eino Jutikkala, "Independent Finland" in Eino Jutikkala with Kauko Pirinen, *A History of Finland*, p. 414. – Tanner was chairman of the SDP 1918–1926.

[134] Suomen sosialistisen työväenpuolueen ohjelma (Programme of the Finnish Socialist Workers' Party, accepted in the foundation Congress of the Party in Helsinki, May 13 1920), published in Olavi Borg, *Suomen puolueet ja puolueohjelmat 1880–1964*, pp. 157–158, quotation p. 158.

To be sure, it was stated that the "ruthless violence and terror of the bourgeoisie" thwarts "in many countries" painless etc. realisation of the "Socialist revolution",[135] but stress on peacefulness did not in any case belong to the Communist vocabulary of the time. – When the delegates voted for joining the Comintern the police dispersed the meeting and arrested leaders and participants at random. Next month, the SSTP was again founded; this time the question of the Comintern was not raised.[136]

In the *Eduskunta* there were, in 1921, two MPs who were considered (and also considered themselves) Communists, Ville Vainio and Hilda Hannunen.[137] Although the Communists had proclaimed, in 1919, that they would boycott parliamentary elections, they had been elected from the list of the Social Democratic Party. Vainio and Hannunen made a parliamentary initiative on the promulgation of a new constitution. The draft was copied from the first constitution of Soviet Russia. According to the proposed constitution "Finland is proclaimed to be a sovereign Socialist Council Republic. All power in the area of the Finnish Socialist Council Republic belongs to the working-people of the country united by the Councils of towns and the country-side".[138]

In the 1922 parliamentary elections, Communists and their fellow-travellers obtained 27 mandates. There was now and then cooperation in the *Eduskunta* between the Parliamentary Group of the Working-people and Smallholders and the Social Democrats. Usually, however, relations between the two groups were cool, to put it mildly.

The relations between Communists and Social Democrats were reflected in the vocabulary used. As stated above, Social Democrats used the word "Communist" of people whom they considered to be on the Left in relation to themselves. The Communists tried not to use the word in public as an indication of self-identification, but they might do this indirectly. In 1927, *Työväenjärjestöjen Tiedonantaja*, the main newspaper of the "Socialist working-people and smallholders'" informed its readers that some newspapers of the National Coalition had published news on a "First of May Declaration", signed by Kullervo Manner, Yrjö Sirola and Kalle Lepola on behalf of the Central Committee of the SKP and O. V. Kuusinen, Bohumil Smeral (a Czechoslovakian) and J. S. Murphy (an Englishman) on behalf of the Executive Committee of the Comintern. In the declaration itself it was stated that if the "Finnish White bourgeoisie" launch a war against the Soviet Union, working

---

135 *Ibid.*, p. 158.

136 Tauno Saarela, *Suomalaisen kommunismin synty 1918–1923*, pp. 158–166.

137 Soikkanen, *Kohti kansanvaltaa*, vol. 1, p. 361.

138 Ville Vainio and Hilda Hannunen, Ehdotus laiksi Suomen hallitusmuodon perusteista, April 14, 1921. Valtiopäivät 1921, liitteet I–VIII, pp. 7–8.)

people must follow Lenin's advice, which is that in this kind of situation an "imperialist war must be transformed into a Civil War".[139] This was a clever means of preventing (or at least trying to prevent) arrest and imprisonment for treason: the paper only quoted a bourgeois paper, without any kind of comment.

"Noskean"[140] vocabulary concerning the Social Democrats mirrors the attitude of the Communists towards them. In the very first years of the 1920s the term was rare, but could be used, for example as follows:[141]

> The statement by the Noskean Boss [Väinö] Tanner to the representative of the workers, [Hilda] Hannunen, who demands the Noskeans to promote demands for the release of imprisoned workers, because they hold the trumps, is illustrative. The Socialist lord, the lawyer Tanner, answered cynically: "We do not need your advice". [...] Is there, after this, any longer anyone who considers himself an honest worker [and] who regards Noskean Bosses like Tanner as their own representatives? – It cannot be. If there is, shame on him, it is unanimous contempt of other workers.

By the mid-1920s "Noskean" expressions became customary. When the Social Democrats formed a minority government (1926–1927) and when its Prime Minister Väinö Tanner, in his capacity as acting President (President Lauri Kristian Relander was ill[142]) received in 1927 a parade of the Army and the Civil Guard on May 16, an official day of victory of the Whites in 1918, he was condemned by the

---

139 "Vartiopaikalta", *Työväenjärjestöjen Tiedonantaja* (hereafter abridged TTA), May 14, 1927.

140 Gustav Noske was a Social Democratic minister of defence in Germany 1919–1920. According to the Communists, Noske was responsible for the murders of Karl Liebknecht and Rosa Luxemburg. (Braunthal, *History of the International 1914–1943*, vol. 2, pp. 130–132.)

141 "Joko silmät avautuvat?", *Suomen Työläinen*, Dec. 14, 1921. – The background to this statement was a debate in the *Eduskunta* over an amnesty proposed by the government for two leaders of the Åland separatists, Carl Björkman and Julius Sundblom; their aim had been the annexion to Sweden of the Åland islands, (J. R. Danielson-Kalmari, *La question des îles d'Aland de 1914 à 1920*, pp. 123–126) where practically everyone spoke Swedish as their native language and most people even did not understand Finnish. In the *Eduskunta* Hilda Hannunen, a Communist MP, and Social Democratic leaders had had a quarrel over the question whether one should couple the amnesty of Björkman and Sundblom to that for Red prisoners who were behind bars because they had fought in the Civil War or participated in the activities of the SSTP. The Social Democrats refused to make this connection between two entirely distinct questions, and voted for acceptation of the governmental bill. Hilda Hannunen used the expression "you [the Social Democrats] have the trumps in your hand" in the *Eduskunta* on December 2, 1921. (Valtiopäivät 1921, pöytäkirjat, vol. 2, p. 1058.) See also Väinö Tanner, *Kahden maailmansodan välissä : muistelmia 20- ja 30-luvuilta*, pp. 15–19. – In point of fact it was not Tanner who said so in the *Eduskunta*, but another Social Democratic MP, Väinö Hakkila. (Valtiopäivät 1921, pöytäkirjat, vol. 2, p. 1060.)

142 Lauri Kristian Relander, *Presidentin päiväkirja*, vol. 1, *Lauri Kristian Relanderin muistiinpanot vuosilta 1925–1927*, p. 422.

Communists, and not only by them but also by many Social Democrats themselves.[143] In the Communist press, the *jubilée* was termed a "skull orgy"[144] and the organ of the SDP, *Suomen Sosialidemokraatti*, was labelled "head Noske".[145] Tanner became a symbol of treachery, squalidness etc. in Communist circles as far as the Social Democrats were concerned.

Under Social Democratic rule, it became possible for the Communists to send delegations of working-people on "conducted tours" in the Soviet Union. The Detective Central Police monitored these travels closely and names of the participants were recorded in its catalogues. It seems that in the most numerous delegation there were 137 "young workers and railwaymen".[146] In Beloostrov, the first railway station on the Russian side of the border, there were, according to a newspaper article, a brass band, which played the "International" (this piece was at the time also the national anthem of the Soviet Union), a large crowd, flags and banderols. One banderol held a text: "We hereby salute you, workers coming from Finland, and welcome you to the Union of the Soviet Socialist Republics".[147] The delegations visited museums, imperial palaces, children's homes and factories.[148] One delegation visited, probably later, a model prison. It was then reported that prisons in the Soviet Union were not "penal establishments in their principles" at all, but "reformatories", in which the prisoners have "self-administration".[149] The secretary of the Trade Union Federation, Arvo Tuominen, also visited a prison when enjoying his vacation in the Soviet Union. Tuominen, who pointed out that he was an expert on the Finnish prison system, compared the two prison systems saying rather like the Delphic Oracle: "Differences in life between them were really unbelievably great".[150]

During the whole period from 1920 to 1930, the Detective Central Police Force arrested leading Communists and their fellow-travellers. Initially the professional skills of the police were not high, but with experience their proficiency improved,

---

143 Only Tanner and Kaarle Heinonen, the Minister of Defence, were present. Other members of the government, notably Minister of Foreign Affairs Väinö Voionmaa (representatives of *corps diplomatique* followed the parade) were absent. (Tanner, *Kahden maailmansodan välissä*, p. 91.)

144 "Sosdem Tanner 'tervehti sotaväkeä, suojeluskuntajoukko-osastoja sekä paljastetuin päin niiden lippuja'", TTA, May 17, 1927.

145 Inkvisiittori, "No kaikkea niillä keltaisilla veljillä teetetään", TTA, May 17, 1927.

146 Report of the Terijoki Subdivision of the Detective Central Police to the Head Division of the Detective Central Police, April 21, 1927. Etsivä keskuspoliisi – valtiollinen poliisi I (hereafter abridged Ek-Valpo I), Document folder (hereafter abridged DF) II 6 1 b. Kansallisarkisto (National Archives, hereafter abridged KA), Helsinki.

147 "Helsingistä Leningradiin", *Liekki*, May 6, 1927.

148 "Huomioita metallimiesten Neuvostoliiton matkalta", TTA, July 4, 1927.

149 Jallu Rötkö, "Työläisen näkemyksiä Neuvostoliitossa", *Työ*, March 3, 1929.

150 "Suomen Ammattijärjestön sihteerin vaikutelmia matkalta työväen maassa", TTA, Aug. 4, 1927.

and in 1928, they were able to make an agreement with an organiser of the Party, Jalmari Rasi, who knew the whole organisation well. By this agreement, Rasi told the police everything. Subsequently a new identity was created for him and he and his family were sent to Australia.[151] Between the wars, there were altogether more than 4,000 political prisoners in Finland, mostly Communists.[152]

The Trade Union Federation was controlled by the Communists until 1930, when the authorities suppressed the organisation on the grounds that, being under Communist control. It organised often long strikes, supported financially by the Soviet Union, although Nordic fraternal unions, especially Swedish also donated money. These strikes were often dubbed political strikes and claimed to be ordered by the URSS in the bourgeois press. For example, a strike of harbour workers in 1928–1929, lasted 10 months. This succeeded in obstructing a large part of the export of timber, crucial to the Finnish economy. In addition, one strike in the metal industry in 1927 was long, seven months. One of the reasons for the strike was the plan of a metal firm to construct submarines for the army.[153] As a countermove, Right-Wing circles and employers created a blackleg organisation called "Export Peace". The Social Democrats participated in trades unions in spite of the fact that most of these were controlled by the Communists. In order to retain their support, the Federation did not join the Profintern[154] or, for that matter, the Amsterdam Union, the international body of Social Democratic trade unions.

One particularly important step in the way of developing the Social Democratic Party to a status presentable at court occurred in 1926–1927, when, after futile negotiations between bourgeois parties (governments, in the 1920s were generally ephemeral), an above mentioned Social Democratic minority government was formed with Väinö Tanner as Prime Minister. – The plight of the Communists and their front-organisations was growing after the relative thaw under this minority government. Arrests and prosecutions were normal life for them. In November 1929 the SKP leaders in Moscow ordered the Communist-led Trade Union Federation to proclaim a general strike showing solidarity with comrades in Tammisaari prison, where the inmates had gone on hunger strike.[155] The leaders in Finland were extremely sceptical as to this move – in particular because the Social Democrats, as expected, considered the general strike silly and imprudent –

151 Rasi arrived to Australia in February 1929. He died there in November 1935. (Finnish Consulate to the Ministry of Foreign Affairs, Jan. 22. 1935. Ek-Valpo I, personal folder (hereafter abridged PF) 2017, Jalmari Rasi, KA.) See also Matti Lackman, "Mihin katosi Jalmari Rasi", *Turun historiallinen arkisto* vol. 37.

152 Heikki Ylikangas, *Käännekohdat Suomen historiassa : pohdiskeluja kehityslinjoista ja niiden muutoksista uudella ajalla*, p. 176.

153 Juha Siltala, *Lapuan liike ja kyyditykset 1930*, p. 43.

154 Красный интернационал профсоюзов, Red International of Trade Unions.

155 John. H. Wuorinen, *A History of Finland*, p. 248.

but the Communists had to obey such a clear order issuing from the Muscovite headquarters. The strike was a fiasco. It served wonderfully the aims of the Detective Central Police in that now they knew who were under Communist discipline from the simple fact that mainly or even only the Communists and their sympathisers failed to appear at their workplaces when the "general strike" began.

The autumn of 1929 there emerged a Semi-Fascist, anti-Communist organisation called the Lapua movement, where the most important peasant leaders were responsible for its establishment in that Ostrobothnian municipality. When the Communist Youth in the autumn of 1929 organised a rally in Lapua, the rightist scum attacked them, tore their red shirts from them, and prevented their meeting. The government, headed at this time by Kyösti Kallio, did not punish the perpetrators guilty of the disturbances. The government received in the *Eduskunta* a vote of confidence by a large majority.[156]

Many of the activities of the Lapua movement were illegal, even terrorist. A Communist printing press was demolished in Vaasa (the main city in Ostrobothnia), some Communists were assassinated and many of them were forced into a car, then beaten up and carried to the Finnish-Soviet border and compelled to cross over to the Soviet Union. To be sure, these "forcible ejections", did not always lead to the frontier at all. When Communists only were the objects of these kidnappings, the bourgeois press and political leaders were not particularly eager to condemn them, but when the Social Democratic Speaker of Parliament, Väinö Hakkila, was cast out, and particularly when the Progressive ex-president K. J. Ståhlberg was ejected, attitudes among the moderate bourgeoisie changed.[157]

Meanwhile the legal activities of the Communist front-organisations were suppressed in the summer of 1930 when the government, under the pressure of the Lapua movement, sent to the *Eduskunta* a set of bills which aimed at a complete ban on any public Communist activities. This limitation of civic freedoms could not proceed through the *Eduskunta* according to normal procedure because the constitution guaranteed basic liberties to all citizens. Hence acceptance of the "laws of protection of the Republic", called also "Communist laws", required a two-thirds majority vote in two successive Parliaments or a five-sixths majority to be accepted in one Parliament. At this time a five-sixths majority was impossible to obtain due to the opposition of the Social Democrats and therefore the President dissolved the *Eduskunta*[158] and the Communist laws could be accepted at least formally in the correct way.

---

[156] Jutikkala, "Independent Finland", p. 420.

[157] L.A. Puntila, *Histoire politique de la Finlande de 1809 à 1955*, pp. 203–204.

[158] Jutikkala, "Independent Finland", pp. 420–421.

For many Social Democratic theoreticians, for example K. H. Wiik, Fascism was a reaction to Communism and therefore – by implication, this was not explicitly "booed off the stage" – it might be possible to prevent a Fascist coup by suppressing Communism.[159] Because the Lapuans did not always see much difference between Social Democrats and Communists the Social Democrats feared that the next step would be suppression of their own movement. Politicians on the extreme Right indeed were not satisfied with the banning only of Communist activities: they also demanded suppression of the Social Democratic Party. Moreover, a new plan for a coup d'état was afoot. In February 1932, some 500 men close to the Lapua movement gathered at Mäntsälä, a municipality not far from Helsinki. The coup was prevented mainly by a radio speech by President P. E. Svinhufvud: he declared that he had always advocated legality (for this he had before independence been deported by the Russian authorities to Siberia), and he announced that he would not tolerate any illegal action by the Lapua movement. Svinhufvud, a Conservative, had been a favourite of that movement in the previous presidential elections and his words lessened the tension. Some Mäntsälä men were condemned to prison. The Lapua movement ceased its activities and the extreme right formed a political party, the Patriotic People's Movement (*Isänmaallinen kansanliike*, or IKL). This movement was openly Fascist and derived its inspiration from Mussolini's Italy and, to a lesser extent, from Nazi Germany.[160]

One psychological factor during the interwar period was the rampant hatred of the Russians, especially the Soviets, an emotion which was exploited by the Lapua movement. This hatred was reflected in the pejorative word about Russia and Russians, *ryssä*, which is very difficult to translate; "Russky" has been used by some authors. Outi Karenmaa, who has studied this phenomenon, points out that the anti-Russian policy was beneficial especially to the Agrarians, who were also eager to promote this policy. However, all political parties (except, of course, the Communists and their front-organisations) were in fact more or less anti-Russian, including the Social Democrats, who sought to gain approval in society at large after the Civil War.[161]

---

[159] Cf. Soikkanen, *Kohti kansanvaltaa*, vol. 1, p. 492.

[160] Cf. Jutikkala, "Independent Finland", p. 422.

[161] Outi Karemaa, *Vihollisia, vainoojia, syöpäläisiä : venäläisviha Suomessa 1917–1923*. English summary: *Foes, Fiends and Vermin : Ethnic Hatred of Russians in Finland 1917–1923*, pp. 216–217 (this refers to the English summary).

6. How to Explain Revolution – and Communism?

I must immediately stress that in this section my intention is not to give an answer to the question posed in the heading, only to consider some problems in the light of both foreign and Finnish debates.

In France, fierce debate on Communism set in when a collective of eleven authors published, in 1998 a monumental book on the crimes of Communism, *Le livre noir du Communisme*.[162] Already before the publication, a quarrel broke out within the team over the title of the book. According to Jean-Louis Margolin (who wrote chapters on China, Vietnam, Laos and Cambodia) he and Nicolas Werth (who wrote a chapter on Russia) threatened to withdraw from the project if Stéphane Courtois (who wrote the introductory and summary chapters) "imposed" the title *Le livre des crimes Communistes*.[163] Immediately after publication, Werth and Margolin condemned the chapters written by Courtois for the following reasons. Firstly, the central place given to mass crime in the repressive practices of the Communist Parties in power; secondly, the identification of the Communist doctrine with the criminal practice of Communism; thirdly, the allegation of similarity of Nazism and Communism as to their criminal foundation; fourthly, the erroneous estimate of the numbers of victims of Communism.[164]

In his concluding article Courtois ponders the question why Lenin and Stalin exterminated their enemies (real or imagined), why not only "control and punish" them as rulers in a "normal" society do. His answer is that in terrorism a "double mutation" takes place: an adversary is firstly an enemy, then a criminal, finally a person excluded from society and not even only from society but also from humanity. By the same token, the "logic of exclusion" leads to an "eliminative ideology" and this to an exterminatory doctrine where human beings are no longer human beings but animals.[165] "At the end of this logic is crime against human-

---

[162] There was a debate in Finland concerning the crimes of Communism in the leading newspaper of the country, *Helsingin Sanomat*, when the book appeared in Finnish (*Kommunismin musta kirja*, Porvoo: WSOY, 2000). Finnish scholars on Communism did not participate in this debate. I published a review article ("Kommunismin musta kirja: historioitsijakiista à la française", *Historiallinen aikakauskirja* 4/1998, pp. 324–333) on *Le livre noir du Communisme* and its German translation *Schwarzbuch der Kommunismus* (there are two articles on East Germany, which do not appear in the French original).

[163] Jean-Louis Margolin, "'Historien, militant politique ou procureur?'" *Le Monde*, Nov. 9–10, 1997.

[164] Jean-Louis Margolin and Nicolas Werth, "Communisme : retour à l'histoire", *Le Monde*, Nov. 14, 1997.

[165] As Courtois points out, one characteristic of the Moscow trials was "animalisation" the of the accused. (Stéphane Courtois, "Pourquoi?" in Stéphane Courtois, Nicolas Werth, Jean-Louis Panné, Andrzej Paczkowski, Karle Bartosek and Jean-Louis Margolin in collaboration with Rémi Kauffer, Pierre Rigoulot, Pascal Fontaine, Yves Santamaria and Sylvain Boulougue, *Le livre noir du Communisme : crimes, terreur et répression*, p. 818.)

ity."[166] Such argumentation was presumably in the minds of Margolin and Werth when they accused Courtois of placing crime in the centre of the repressive practice of Communism. The second point, assimilation of doctrine and practice, may refer to Courtois' assertion that "in certain regards, the Terror was foreshadowed in the procedure (*démarche*) of the Bolsheviks: the manipulation of tensions by a Jacobinian faction, the exacerbation of ideological and political fanaticism, the launching of a war of extermination against the rebellious peasantry". Here Courtois notes the continuity between the French and Russian revolutions: "Robespierre incontestably laid the foundation to the path which later led Lenin towards terror".[167] The last two points are easy to identify in Courtois' text. He presents a table of deaths: the Soviet Union 20 million, China 65 million etc. and counts, roughly, a total toll of 100 million people.[168] He compares this figure to that of the victims of the Nazis: 25 million. Courtois concludes (and this is his opponents' third point) that this[169]

> must at least incite some comparative reflection as to the similarity between the regime, which has been considered since 1945 the most criminal of the century and a Communist system, which until 1991 conserved all its international legitimacy and which until our days is in power in certain countries and which retains its following all over the world. Moreover, even if many Communist Parties have tardily recognised the crimes of Stalinism, they have not, for the most part, abandoned the principles of Lenin and do not give much thought to their implication for the terrorist phenomenon.

This kind of text obviously has its political implications in France, desirable or not. Thus, it was soon pointed out that Monsieur Jean-Marie Le Pen has said that we are still attending a "Nuremberg of Communism". In addition, of course, the representatives of the *Parti Communiste français* denounced the thesis of a "similarity" between Nazism and Communism.[170] We must, of course, ask whether the possible political implications, the use or misuse of a scientific text for partisan political purposes, are sufficient reasons for a scientist not to publish a text she or he thinks adequate and right. I think not.

---

[166] Courtois, "Pourquoi?," pp. 816–817.

[167] *Ibid.*, p. 796. Here Courtois also makes an important point: the terror of the Jacobins did not particularly inspire the "principal revolutionary thinkers" in the XIXth century, like Karl Marx (*ibid*).

[168] Stéphane Courtois, "Les crimes du Communisme" in *Le livre noir du Communisme*, p. 14.

[169] *Ibid.*, p. 25.

[170] Patrick Jarreau, "Nouvelle controverse sur le caractère criminel du Communisme", *Le Monde*, Nov. 9–10, 1997.

Is comparison between Communism and Nazism reasonable? Many participants in the French debate sought to deny this. Annette Wiewiorka declared that Stéphane Courtois "proposes purely and simply to substitute Nazi criminality by Communist criminality in the memory of the peoples".[171] Lilly Marcou, a historian of the Cominform, used an "if argument": what would have happened if Adolf Hitler and not I. V. Stalin had won the Second World War?[172] Georges Mink and Jean-Charles Szurek argued that the fact that one finds many former Communists among the leaders of various East European ex-Communist states proves that Communism was different from Nazism. The origins as well as the goals of Nazism are entirely different. Why confuse them?[173]

Stéphane Courtois published a long answer to his critics in *Le Monde.* He argued that the fact that there are ex-Communists in responsible positions in the former Socialist countries is an "honour for democracy", not for Communism. He also described Lenin as "a counter-revolutionary putschist who must be considered one of the principal agents responsible of the Russian misfortune in the XXth century, who reintroduced thraldom among the peasantry as well as among the workers". For Courtois, the Bolshevik coup d'état was counter-revolutionary in relation to the February 1917 revolution which brought an emergent democratic institution to Russia after the overthrow of Tsarism.[174] Here we must note that Courtois does not deny the legitimation of a revolution as such.

From a comparative perspective we may ask what were the similar and what the unique traits in Nazism and Communism. In the German *Historikerstreit,* Ernst Nolte had denied the uniqueness of the German concentration camps. For Courtois both Nazism and Communism were guilty of mass murder, the uniqueness of Auschwitz was its "industrial method of murdering"; Russian camps were more chaotic. Courtois sees no basic ideological difference between Communism and Nazism: namely, that Communism could have been "an ideology of liberation", unlike Nazism with its *Führerprinzip*. Courtois declared that after the split within the Social Democratic movement during and after the First World War Communism in its Leninist form had nothing to do with any ideology of liberation.[175]

Up to this point the French debate had to a great extent resembled the German *Historikerstreit.* Courtois, however, does not claim that there was any causal connection, even a putative, between Communist and Nazi atrocities; he claims, on the contrary, that there was no "direct" causal relation between the Bolshevik take-

---

171 Annette Wieviorka, "Stéphane Courtois en un combat douteux", *Le Monde*, Nov. 27, 1997.

172 Lilly Marcou, "Tardive querelle d'Allemands", *Le Monde,* Nov. 14, 1997.

173 Georges Mink and Jean-Charles Szurek, "Pour une analyse complexe du Communisme", *Le Monde*, Nov. 27, 1997.

174 Stéphane Courtois, "Comprendre la tragédie Communiste", *Le Monde*, Dec. 20, 1997.

175 [Stéphane Courtois], "Der rote Holocaust : Interview mit dem französichen Historiker Stéphane Courtois, dem Herausgeber des 'Schwarzbuches'", *Die Zeit*, Nov. 21, 1997.

over and the emergence of Nazism, although the Bolsheviks might have inaugurated some "techniques of mass violence".[176]

Among historians one of the most controversial subjects was indeed this possible causal relation. According to Nolte the explanation for the Holocaust is not to be sought primarily in traditional German antisemitism; it was an example previously given by the Bolsheviks. Concentration camps and the mass murder of Jews were only a "copy" of this "original".[177] Although Nolte warns that it would be "a gross simplification" to see in the Nazi will to extermination only a reaction to the annihilations in Bolshevik Russia, he nevertheless assumes that the Russian revolution was the "most important precondition" for the Third Reich.[178] Auschwitz "was above all a reaction born out of the anxiety at devastating events in the Russian Revolution".[179] Nolte also asks whether "the National Socialists did an 'Asiatic' deed possible only because they saw themselves and their like as possible and real victims of an 'Asiatic' deed?"[180] Further: "Was the 'Archipelago GULag'[181] more original than Auschwitz? Was the 'class murder' of the Bolsheviks a logical and practical predecessor (*Prius*) of the 'race murder' of National Socialists?" Nolte proclaims that while one mass murder does not justify another, a study which "looks up" only one mass murder without paying attention to the other, although there is "probably a causal nexus" between them, is misleading.[182]

If one phenomenon resembling some other, earlier phenomenon emerges, this is not as such proof of a causal relationship. Concentration camps, these central institutions in both Bolshevik and Nazi rules, were inventions neither of the Russians nor of the Germans. It seems that the British have the honour to be the originators in this regard. The setting is South Africa under Boer War, 1898–1902. To counter the Boer guerrilla or "mobile commands", as an *Afrikaner* historian puts it,[183] the British enclosed 117,000 whites, mainly women and children suspected

---

[176] Courtois, "Les crimes du Communisme", p. 25.

[177] Ernst Nolte, "Between Myth and Revisionism? : the Third Reich in the Perspective of the 1980s" in *Aspects of the Third Reich*, pp. 35–36.

[178] *Ibid.*, p. 32. Nolte refers to traditional Right-Wing antisemitism, radical Malthusianism, Prussian militarism etc. (p. 33).

[179] *Ibid.*, p. 36.

[180] Ernst Nolte, "Vergangenheit, die nicht vergehen will : eine Rede, die geschrieben, aber nicht gehalten werden konnte", *Frankfurter Allgemeine Zeitung*, June 6, 1987, published in *"Historikerstreit" : Die Dokumentation der Kontroverse um die Einzigartigkeit der nationalsozialistischen Judenvernichtug*, p. 45. One apologist of Nolte, Rolf Kosiek, notes that Nolte is here only asking questions, not giving answers! (Rolf Kosiek, *Historikerstreit und Geschichtsrevision*, p. 49.)

[181] Главное управление лагерей.

[182] Nolte, "Vergangenheit", p. 46.

[183] W. J. de Kock, "The Anglo-Boer War, 1899–1902" in *Five Hundred Years : a History of South Africa*, p. 349.

of aiding the Boer guerrilla and 107,000 blacks living on Boer farms, in this case also men, in camps.[184] About 41,000 inmates perished in conditions equally typical of later camps: overcrowding, poor food rations and austere conditions. African inmates, unlike the Boers, were forced to labour and their mortality percentage was higher than that of whites.[185]

In the South African camps we may observe the main traits of concentration camps: they are internment centres for political prisoners or for national, racial or class groups. Their inmates were not treated as individuals and they were there without fair trial. American sites for the ethnic Japanese after Pearl Harbour[186] and Finnish encampments for East Karelian (mainly Russian) civilian population when parts of East Karelia were occupied by the Finnish troops in 1942–1944[187] also fulfil the criteria of concentration camps. These examples may serve to show that similar phenomena can exist in different places and times without any causal connections.

In Finland, most investigators of the years 1917–1918 have not been interested in theoretical conceptions concerning revolution. The sociologist Risto Alapuro has been an exception. However, although theoretical conceptions have not often been very clearly expressed, there have been studies in which not only the political process but also the social context of the rebellion has been researched. Viljo Rasila, for instance, has successfully explained the formation of the front line between Reds and Whites by factor analysis. Ostrobothnia was the stronghold of the White forces. The peasants there were mainly independent farmers and the electoral support for Social Democracy was inconsiderable if compared to other regions in Finland.[188] Supporters of the Reds were mostly industrial workers in Southern Finland reinforced by poor agricultural workers living there.[189]

Such "structuralist" explanations have not sufficed for some historians. In 1992, Jari Ehrnrooth published a doctoral dissertation on the Socialist revolutionary doctrines and their effect on the Finnish workers' movement 1905–1914. Ehrnrooth argued that in different historical interpretations there has been a common "effort

---

[184] Shula Marks, "Southern and Central Africa, 1852–1910" in *The Cambridge History of Africa*, vol. 6, from 1870 to 1905, p. 479. T. R. H. Davenport, *South Africa : a Modern History*, p. 200.

[185] According to Marks ("Southern and Central Africa, 1852–1910") the official figure for African camp dead was 14,315; Davenport (*South Africa : a Modern History*) states that the official figure was 14,154. According to Marks the true figure was "probably much higher".

[186] See e.g. Gary Okihito (essay) and Joan Myers (photographs), *Whispered Silences : Japanese Americans and World War II*, pp. 160–224.

[187] Antti Laine, *Suur-Suomen kahdet kasvot : Itä-Karjalan siviiliväestön asema suomalaisessa miehityshallinnossa 1941–1944*, pp. 122–124; Helge Seppälä, *Suomi miehittäjänä 1941–1944*, pp. 75–88.

[188] Viljo Rasila, *Kansalaissodan sosiaalinen tausta*, pp. 151–152.

[189] Juhani Piilonen, "Rintamien selustassa" in *Itsenäistymisen vuodet*, vol. 2, *Taistelu vallasta*, p. 616.

for a smoothing of class hatred". Ehrnrooth criticises the views of several scholars who, according to him, see the revolution as something which simply took place; the workers' movement was an "equality movement of the poor", which was "even a part of the emergent nation and not only its opposing force". This view involves for Ehrnrooth four problems: i) it is not possible to understand why the "moderate Kautskyan" workers' movement launched a war in the moment the situation made it feasible; ii) the view is "almost openly" sympathetic towards the movement; iii) it is excessively based on the official history-writing of the movement itself and iv) it does not analyse "popular mentality and collective emotion dynamics upon which the mass influence of the movement was based". There were in the movement not only "national genii of modern civilisation", enlightenment and *Bildung*, "but also bloodthirsty furies of archaic hatred, envy and vengeance".[190] Ehrnrooth suggests that this archaic hatred explains the "revolutionary spirit which emerged in the Red uprising of 1918".[191]

Did such hatred exist? There is no doubt that it did. Ehrnrooth gives abundant examples of extremely bloodthirsty texts; here one may suffice. In 1910, a local workers' paper wrote in somewhat clumsy language (which I have sought to preserve in the translation):[192]

> Tread you us under your feet, dash us to pieces, but remember when you are doing this: that once the downtrodden raises his head defiantly from his chains! [...] Woe to you then! Poor you, over you roars the voice of the horrifying sentence of the revenge of the people.

The other side of the coin was awareness of the life of the rich. The proletarian writer Ossian Suvanto wrote in 1915 that[193]

> O, why is the faithful and honest working-man so much tried in life, while the rich live in overeating surfeit and drunkenness. At the golden calf, they sacrifice their soul and body. In the end, they would want our flesh to roast and our blood to drink.

Note the Christian allusions in this passage.

---

190 Jari Ehrnrooth, *Sanan vallassa, vihan voimalla : sosialistiset vallankumousopit ja niiden vaikutus Suomen työväenliikkeessä 1905–1914*, pp. 22–24. There is an English summary, *Power of the Word, Force of Hatred : Socialist Revolutionary Doctrines and their Effect in the Finnish Workers' Movement.*

191 *Ibid.*, p. 576 (this refers to the English summary).

192 "Mielivalta miekkoineen", *Kuritus*. Handwritten paper published by the Workers' Society of Niinivedenpää, 1910. Cited in Ehrnrooth, *Sanan vallassa, vihan voimalla*, p. 390.)

193 Ossian Suvanto, *Kovan koulun käynyt*, cited in Raoul Palmgren, *Joukkosydän : vanhan työväenliikkeemme kaunokirjallisuus*, vol. II, p. 287.

Another cause of the revolt was, according to Ehrnrooth, agitation. He writes that the "collective consciousness" of the workers "was not constituted solely of a humble striving to understand rationally formulated Kautskyism"; there was also another, equally powerful factor, "a fanatical, agitated and excitable emotional affect". In the long run, it was not possible to suppress it and when an opportunity came, "the encapsulated hatred took over".[194]

Ehrnrooth's unquestionable merit is in his having drawn attention to handwritten papers, which were the lowest level of written articulation in the workers' movement. The question is how much does the fury of archaic hatred and agitation explain. There was already much debate over this in 1918 and subsequently, because the Whites usually saw the *only* (here unlike Ehrnrooth, to be sure) reason for the uprising in agitation and hatred. We find good examples of this in speeches delivered in the *Eduskunta* just before and after the Civil War and may cite some here. On January 11, 1918, Artur Wuorimaa, a Lutheran clergyman and an MP (the Agrarian League), who might argue in terms of the organic state theory,[195] declared in the *Eduskunta* that the "atrocities" of the Red Guards were in no way odd, since Social Democracy "had sown hatred", although "it is not possible to attain the birth of a better society by agitating class struggle and hatred".[196]

After the victory of the Whites, Wuorimaa on May 24, 1918, explained to the House his position in more straightforward terms:[197]

> The rebellion that now has raged in our country with unprecedented brutality is the result of constant agitation over a period of ten years. It has been developed by Marxist Socialism and is the fruit of the mendacious agitation sown by the Socialist Party here in this country during ten years. It created among the masses a hypnotic condition, which is no longer normal, but must be understood as a pathological psychosis, as an illness, which can be removed from the brains of the people only if the agitation is suppressed for so long that this hypnosis, so to speak, evaporates and disappears.

Many MPs agreed with Wuorimaa's arguments.[198]

---

[194] Ehrnrooth, *Sanan vallassa, vihan voimalla*, p. 375. On Ehrnrooth's "archaic hatred", see his English summary, pp. 574–579

[195] A professor who gives lectures works with his brains and is therefore a working-man as well as a ditcher who works by his hand, Wuorimaa taught. "Society is like a body, in which there are many kinds of organs. A man needs brains which put the organs of his body in motion. It is the same in the body of society. A man needs brains which put his organs in motion; he needs hands, which execute the orders of the brains." (Artur Wuorimaa in *Eduskunta* May 24, 1918, Toiset valtiopäivät 1917 : pöytäkirjat, vol. 2, p. 1142.)

[196] Toiset valtiopäivät 1917 : pöytäkirjat, vol. 1, p. 869.

[197] Toiset valtiopäivät 1917 : pöytäkirjat, vol. 2, p. 1141.

[198] This kind of argumentation was typical especially of MPs of the Agrarian League, men like Kalle Lohi (*ibid.*, p. 1144) and Santeri Alkio (*ibid.*, p. 1145).

Should there be a sixth factor, *the hatred factor*, added to the typologies presented above? Perhaps not, since in any popular uprising some kind of hatred is self-evident. We hear news of wrath breaking out in some part of the globe almost daily. At the time of writing (May 1998), there is serious unrest in Indonesia. It is evident that there is a legitimacy crisis in that country. Is it now essential to point out that those demonstrators and pillagers are under the emotional influence of hatred? Alternatively, may we perhaps look at the history of the Suharto dictatorship and the class, religious, regional etc. cleavages and try to find our explanatory factors there? Former Yugoslavia was and still is a much more complicated case than Indonesia. In our present case, moreover, we must also ask how much hatred there was on the other, the White side in Finland. It is not to be conceived that the peasants of Ostrobothnia or the bourgeois political and economic elite were free of all hatred for the workers' movement and for workers and crofters in general. However, I do not know any study treating of this aspect.

If we say that the root of the Civil War was "Bolshevik infection", agitation or the like, we imply that the workers (or possibly human beings in general) were people who were not able to think independently. As Oiva Ketonen writes, one must take one step further in the chain of cause and effect; one should study social and economic problems as well as the communication between classes,[199] which communication was often minimal beyond the sphere of work.[200]

In Ostrobothnia, the centre of White power, people regarded that power as legitimate more readily than elsewhere. Ostrobothnia had, as already pointed out, its own peculiarities and on the whole the country was divided into a rather static North and a dynamic South, with Helsinki as not only the political, but also cultural capital of the country. In the South the number of industrial proletarians was relatively high. There were also great manors, even estates. Cultural activities, the opera, a philharmonic orchestra, theatre, art gallery, good libraries etc. were centred in Helsinki, and, above all, the largest university in the country was there. At the same time, differences in income in the South were, as Heikki Ylikangas has pointed out, enormous. At the turn of century a farm labourer received 100 *markkas* a month, a teacher in high-school 4,000 *markkas*, and a judge in a Court of Appeal 10,000 *markkas* a month. In the North differences were not so striking. However, as Ylikangas notes, no mutinies break out when only "structural conditions" exist.[201] The Bolshevik revolution in Russia had its effects on Finland. Most Right-Wing politicians, who in the summer of 1917 had not Finland's full independence

[199] Oiva Ketonen, *Kansakunta murroksessa : kesä 1918 ja sen taustaa*, pp. 134–135. Cf. Heikki Ylikangas, "Vuoden 1918 vaikutus historiatieteessä" in *Vaikea totuus : vuosi 1918 ja kansallinen tiede*, pp. 98–99.

[200] Cf. Risto Alapuro, *Suomen synty paikallisena ilmiönä, 1890–1933*, p. 139.

[201] Heikki Ylikangas, "Miten sisällissodasta tehtiin vapaussota", *Helsingin Sanomat*, Jan. 27, 1998.

as an aim, began, as we have seen, immediately to support the idea. Among the working-class, this idea had matured after the Tsarism was overthrown. Ylikangas' thesis is that by speaking of a War of Liberation and not a Civil War, or some neutral term, the Whites sought to conceal the nature of the War. The Finnish Reds were seen by Ostrobothnian peasants as "Red Russkies" who supported the Russian army. In this way, says Ylikangas "a Civil War was, in words, transformed as a War of Liberation". Perhaps it is most paradoxical that the assistance of former soldiers of the Russian Imperial army, above all, of course, experienced officers, in Finland were of much more assistance to the Whites than to the Reds.[202] The Civil War was a national disaster. No-one, or no segment of society, was alone guilty for it. No biased explanation of its causes is satisfactory.

[202] *Ibid.*

IV "Proletarian" Oppositions within the Russian Communist Party (Bolsheviks) 1918–1923

Inside the Bolshevik Party there were in 1918–1923 several Left and/or proletarian oppositions, such as the Democratic Centralists, the Workers' Opposition in about 1920–1922, the Workers' Group and the Workers' Truth about 1923 and possibly later. These oppositions claimed that they were "proletarian" by nature, but there were intellectuals in their ranks; the Democratic Centralists Opposition was indeed led mainly by intellectuals. In this regard, it resembled the Kuusinen and the Malm and Manner Oppositions in the Finnish Communist Party. The Workers' Opposition was more markedly proletarian – despite the fact that its most famous leader, Aleksandra Mikhailovna Kollontai,[1] had an aristocratic background – reminiscent of the Murder Opposition and the Rahja Opposition among the Finns in Russia. – I am not however interested in factional struggles among the top leadership of the RKP(b), as it is difficult to see that any Finnish opposition could be analogous for example to the Trotskyite Opposition in the Bolshevik Party.

The ideas the different Left oppositions represented were something in the vein of what Lenin had written in his *State and Revolution* in summer 1917. There Lenin delineated a society where all workers – this is an important point – are armed;

[1] Kollontai's fame or notoriety was not based on her position in the Workers' Opposition, but on her role as a Social Democratic / Bolshevik feminist. Kollontai was from 1920 for two or three years leader of the *Zhenotdel*, the women's organisation of the Central Committee of the Party, subsequently a diplomat. In the 1930s, she belonged to those very few members of an ancient Party opposition who were not executed or lost in the dark confines of the GULag.

they learn to direct societal production and they do all the administrative work. To be sure, in this transitional society there will be bourgeois specialists, engineers, agronomists etc., but they will work in obedience to armed workers. "The whole society will be one office and one factory, in which equality will reign in work and salary." This is, however, only the first stage of Communism. It is only temporary, because when all have really acquired the skills to direct society, i.e., can read and write and know the four fundamental arithmetical operations, independently direct production and society in general, the "door" from the first stage of Communism to the second, higher stage will be "wide open" and the state will be dead.[2]

How seriously Lenin's utopian thoughts were taken among the Bolshevik Party cadres and members is impossible to know. However, when the Bolsheviks had seized power, Lenin's ideas of a "first stage" changed completely and the proletarian oppositions within the Party might reflect this change. In April 1918, Lenin said that it was necessary to pay high salaries to bourgeois specialists[3] it was necessary to adopt the so-called Taylor method in industrial work etc. This was for Lenin a step backward; it was a necessary compromise to raise the productivity of work.[4] Moreover, it was, according to Vladimir Il'ich, necessary to organise a "common will" in production "by submitting the will of thousands to one will". There must be "mass meetings" concerning work conditions, but in work itself, everybody must submit "absolutely to the will of a Soviet leader, a dictator".[5] Lenin proclaimed that individual dictatorship in production is only the necessary means to achieve the (utopian) end. Many Bolshevik leaders, especially in the trade union sector, had doubts about the compromise and the temporary nature of this conception. They obviously feared that the individual dictatorship would remain *in perpetuum*.

1. Democratic Centralists

The first significant protest movement within the RKP(b) was called the Left Opposition. It emerged in the spring of 1918. Originally it was a movement which opposed Lenin's policy in the negotiations on a peace treaty with the Germans at Brest-Litovsk. Its most prominent leader was N. I. Bukharin, who advocated a World

---

2 В. И. Ленин, *Государство и революция : учение марксизма о государстве и задачи пролетариата в революции*. PSS, vol. 33, pp. 100–102.

3 В. И. Ленин, "Очередные задачи советской власти", *Правда*, April 28, 1918. PSS, vol. 36, pp. 180–181. On growing inequalities, see Pipes, *Russia under the Bolshevik regime*, pp. 440–443; on the formation of the nomenclature, see Michael S. Voslensky, *Nomenklatura : die herrschende Klasse der Sowjetunion*, pp. 131–145.

4 В. И. Ленин, "Очередные задачи советской власти", *Правда*, April 28, 1918. PSS, vol. 36, pp. 187–190.

5 *Ibid*., pp. 200–203.

Revolution. For this Opposition the peace treaty with Germany was unacceptable and Bukharin's opposition found wide support in the Party. Bukharin's biographer, Stephen S. Cohen, claims that this grouping was "the largest and most powerful Bolshevik opposition in the history of Soviet Russia".[6] The Left Opposition also raised the question of the characteristics of the Party: a manifesto published in the first issue of the journal *Kommunist* declared that in consequence of the unprincipled peace treaty "there arises the strong possibility of a tendency towards deviation on the part of the majority of the Communist Party and the Soviet government [...] into the channel of *petty-bourgeois* politics of a new type".[7] What was interesting in this declaration was the conception that a majority can diverge from the Party line; usually it was said that only a minority could deviate. We may say that the Left Communism of 1918 was mainly a movement of intellectuals; people who later participated in the oppositions will be discussed below.

In the ninth Congress (March 1920) of the Party, there appeared an opposition which used the name of a most central Bolshevik doctrine, i.e. democratic centralism. The Democratic Centralists' Opposition,[8] led by N. Osinskii[9] (Valerian Valerianovich Obolenskii), candidate member of the Central Committee of the RKP(b) in 1921–1922 (and later 1925–1937) and T. V. Sapronov, drew its basic support from the trade unions, led by Mikhail Pavlovich Tomskii, who with other trade union leaders more or less tacitly supported this Opposition. Especially the doctrine of a one-man lead in industry and privileges of Party leaders[10] was anathema to them. The leaders, however, did not deny the fact that the country was in a chaotic condition, that there was dire economic exhaustion, hunger, war and disintegration of the proletariat.[11] One may even say that the Democratic Centralists

---

6 Stephen S. Cohen, *Bukharin and the Bolshevik Revolution : a Political Biography, 1888–1938*, pp. 61–63.

7 "The Left Communists on the Consequences of Peace Treaty with Germany", originally published in *Kommunist*, April 1918. Extracts published in *The Russian Revolution 1917–1921*, p. 194.

8 I have found no explanation for this name. In fact, the "Democratic Centralists" criticized democratic centralism, if they were not actually hostile to it.

9 Osinskii's book concerning the "building of Socialism", written in the summer of 1918 was published in Finnish in 1920, when the Opposition already existed. (N. Osinski, *Sosialismin rakentaminen : yleiset tehtävät : tuotannon järjestäminen.*)

10 T. V. Sapronov at the IXth Conference of the RKP(b) in September 1920 eloquently described a sanatorium in Samara, reserved for Party and state leaders. The sanatorium was like "its own state", fenced off by barbed wire, where the members of the nomenclature ate "sumptuous meals" at state expense. (Extracts from the speech of T. V. Sapronov in the IXth Conference of the RKP(b), September 1920, published in *The Russian Revolution 1917–1921*, p. 207.)

11 Disintegration of the proletariat meant migration of industrial workers from towns to countryside, usually to the villages from which workers or their parents had migrated to towns. By autumn 1920, Petrograd has lost 57.5 per cent of its population and Moscow 44.5 per cent, both in three years. This phenomenon was seen in all industrial centres. (E. H. Carr, *The Bolshevik Revolution 1917–1923*, vol. 2, pp. 194–200.)

aimed at creating order in the Party administration. The actual concrete suggestion, presented in the Party Conference in September 1920, was the establishment of a Control Commission institution. Control Commissions were to be established at all levels of the Party, including the Central Committee. Such an institution was created in the tenth Congress of the RKP(b) in 1921.[12] Even a "Kremlin Control Commission" was set up to examine the privileges of the Party leaders, which had created discontent among Party members. The Kremlin Control Commission was a temporary body, but the Control Commission system was not. It was decreed that a member of the Central Committee must not be a member of the Central Control Commission. This clause did not however concern the Cheka:[13] its leader, F. E. Dzerzhinskii, was elected as a member of this Commission when it was founded in March 1921.[14]

The Democratic Centralists criticized the Party leadership from within. The leaders of the Democratic Centralists Opposition were mainly Party functionaries who thought they were not sufficiently taken into account when some kind of a nomenclature was created. Although they could call the Central Committee of the Party only a "small handful of Party oligarchs", and although they might complain that functionaries evincing deviant views were banned, it seems that they thought primarily of their personal fate. Democratic Centralists were disappointed in what they called exile. They complained that comrades who even before a Congress make known deviant viewpoints, were exiled to such places as the Ukraine![15] Later the Democratic Centralists had contacts with other opposition movements. Most of their leaders were expelled from the Party in 1927[16] and were, like Osinskii, liquidated in the 1930s.[17]

---

[12] The original task of Control Commission was to prevent corruption and bureaucratism and also to control the behaviour of the Party members in their private life. Later the Commissions dealt with pure political affairs and revealed the "enemies of people". (J. Arch Getty, *Origins of Great Purges : the Soviet Communist Party Reconsidered, 1933–1938*, pp. 42–43.)

[13] Всероссийская чрезвычайная комиссия по борьбе с контрреволюцией, саботажем и спекуляцией (All-Russian Extraordinary Commission for Combating Counter-revolution, Sabotage and Speculation).

[14] *Ibid.*, vol. 1, pp. 202–203.

[15] Merle Faisod, *How Russia is Ruled*, pp. 142–143.

[16] Robert Vincent Daniels, *The Conscience of the Revolution : Communist Opposition in Soviet Russia*, p. 320.

[17] *Ibid.*, pp. 388–389.

2. Workers' Opposition

The most famous proletarian opposition in the first half of the 1920s was the Workers' Opposition. While the Democratic Centralists had no leaders well known outside the Party, the Workers' Opposition had. In addition to Kollontai, there were two trade union leaders, the former metal workers Aleksandr Gavrilovich Shliapnikov and Sergei Pavlovich Medvedev.[18] Kollontai wrote a kind of manifesto for the Workers' Opposition in 1921, before the tenth Congress of the RKP(b) in March 1921. In Russia 1,500 copies were printed for trade union activists and for delegates of the Congress. The manifesto was soon translated into English in both England and the United States, into German and into Finnish in the United States at the beginning of the 1920s.[19] How leaders of trade unions and a leader of a radical women's organisation in the Party, the *Zhenotdel*, could form a common Opposition, is not comprehensible.[20] The trade union leaders can hardly have been interested in questions like free sex.

The background of the Workers' Opposition lay in the disappointment of the workers, particularly trade union activists, in their state of affairs at work. They were not satisfied with the current policy of employing more and more "specialists" – *spetsy* in the Russian acronym – in responsible positions in industry. Workers complained that nothing was changed despite the nationalisation of industry in the summer of 1918. Working conditions were unaltered as was the subjection of the workers to the will of a *spetsy*. The state paid the *spetsy* comfortable salaries when compared to the wages of the workers and with time differences in income were tending to grow.[21]

By the autumn of 1920, the Civil War had ended, even if there were scattered pockets where military operations continued and some more formidable confrontations like the Soviet invasion of the independent state of Georgia in 1921 and, above all, the Kronstadt sailors' mutiny in March of the same year (The tenth Con-

---

[18] Shliapnikov was an important person – with Viacheslav Mikhailovich Molotov – in the Bolshevik underground organisation in Petrograd at the end of 1916 and the beginning of 1917, when more prominent leaders of the Party were either in exile or in Siberia. ([V. M. Molotov], *Molotov Remembers : Inside Kremlin Politics*, p. 87.)

[19] When Alix Holt edited a selection of Kollontai's works in her *Selected Writings of Alexandra Kollontai*, she stated that the original, *Рабочая оппозиция*, was not available. The text in the book is the 1921 English translation, published on the initiative by Sylvia Pankhurst. Holt ("Translator's Note", p. 7) says that this early English translation is "sometimes unclear and ambiguous".

[20] See Arkadi Vaksberg, *Alexandra Kollontaï*, pp. 224–225 and Sinowi Schejnis, *Alexandra Kollontai : das Leben einer ungewöhnlichen Frau : Biografie*, pp. 196–197.

[21] Beatrice Farnsworth, *Alexandra Kollontai : Socialism, Feminism and the Bolshevik Revolution*, pp. 214–215.

gress of the Party had its sessions simultaneous with the Kronstadt campaign.) The mutiny presented a very serious threat to Bolshevik power, because the mutineers were precisely those sailors who had in 1917 formed an important powerbase for the Bolsheviks. The sailors demanded equal rights for all citizens in elections, freedom of expression, of assembly, of travel, of move from one place of work to another, of forming workers' co-operatives; abolition of privileges for Communists, the closing down of the secret police and the elimination of "extreme punishment", i.e. the death penalty, "this vile institution of tyrants".[22] They also presented, from the Bolshevik point of view, the most dangerous slogans: "Power to the Soviets!" and "Soviets without Communists!".[23]

In 1920 and in January – February 1921 relatively free discussion of Party matters was still possible. In the ninth Party Conference, Democratic Centralists and Workers' Oppositionists called for reforms in the Party bureaucracy, which they considered too heavy. Kollontai demanded freedom of criticism, using an argument which may now seem bizarre:[24]

> Comrades! There should be a guarantee that if in fact we are going to criticize and criticize thoroughly, what is wrong with us, the one who criticizes should not be sent off to a nice sunny place to eat peaches. Now, comrades, this is not rare phenomenon. [...] Long live criticism. But without the necessity of eating peaches after it.

Kollontai was referring to another critical Communist, Angelica Balabanoff, and to G. E. Zinov'ev, who in his capacity as chairman of the Comintern had sent her to Turkestan to carry out agitation there, using a special propaganda train.[25] We remember that this practice, deportation, was also criticized by the Democratic Centralists.

Before the Xth Congress of the RKP(b), A. G. Shliapnikov published *Theses of the Workers' Opposition* in *Pravda* in January 1921. Shliapnikov demanded full independence for the trade unions.[26] It is not known how Kollontai became involved in this opposition movement of trade unionists. That she was entitled to write some kind of programme for the group is not curious; she was surely the most experienced writer in the faction. When we now proceed to look at the main points

---

[22] *The Demands of the Kronstadters*, published in *The Russian Revolution 1917–1921*, pp. 230–231.

[23] С. М. Смагина. "Советский политический режим в условиях нэпа : ликвидация небольшевистских партий и организаций" in *Политические партии России в контексте ее истории*, p. 219.

[24] KPSS; Deviataia konferentsiia RKP(b): Protokoly (Moscow: Politzadat, 1972), p. 188. Cited in Barbara Evans Clements, *Bolshevik Feminist : the Life of Alexandra Kollontai*, pp. 185–186.

[25] Farnsworth, *Alexandra Kollontai*, p. 213.

[26] *Ibid.*, pp. 218–219.

in this remarkable document, we must keep in mind that Kollontai naturally wrote within certain political limits. This is not to say that she might have written something which was against to her convictions. My impression is, for example, that she believed in the one-party system. Her viewpoints on the role of the Party in the Soviet Union might have been even more orthodox than Shliapnikov's and his comrades'. In addition, of course, the document was the political programme of a group and therefore the concrete demands had naturally been compiled by a group. We shall return to this question at a later point.

The background to Kollontai's writing was the so-called trade union debate before the tenth Congress. There were three main standpoints. L. D. Trotskii (and at one stage also N. I. Bukharin) represented an extreme position: Trotskii wished to integrate the unions in the machinery of government. Why, in a workers' state is an organisation needed, which defends worker's interests? Against whom? In Trotskii's opinion, the task of trade unions in a workers' state was to maintain discipline, even military discipline, in workplaces in order to raise productivity, although the unions may also educate the workers for the management of industry. The Workers' Opposition also represented an extreme position, in direct contradiction to Trotskii's conception. V. I. Lenin, L. B. Kamenev and G. E. Zinov'ev formed an intermediate position. They saw the unions as institutions which maintained discipline and educated workers to take responsibilities. Although the unions had to submit to the omnipotent Party, they were allowed some degree of autonomy so as to be capable of exerting some pressure on state administration and management of industry.[27] In fact, there were not many differences between Lenin and Trotskii. The Democratic Centralists considered the dispute as only an aspect of the crisis caused by extreme centralisation. They had little sympathy with the Workers' Opposition, although the two factions had similar aims.[28]

In order to understand Kollontai, we must note that her conception of human nature was collective. We submit ourselves under tyrants of various kinds only because they maintain the repressive mechanism under which upheaval is futile or even impossible. Aleksandra Mikhailovna was especially against one-man management, not only in factories, but also in all human institutions. "One-man management" was for Kollontai "a product of the individualist conception of the bourgeois class". Kollontai claimed that "rejection" of the principle of collective management was a "deviation from the class policy" originally intended to be only a "tactical compromise" in very harsh circumstances.[29]

---

[27] Isaac Deutscher, *The Prophet Armed : Trotsky: 1876–1921*, p. 507.

[28] Leonard Schapiro, *The Origin of the Communist Autocracy : Political Opposition in the Soviet State : First Phase 1917–1922*, p. 285.

[29] Aleksandra Kollontai, *Workers' Opposition*, published in *Selected Writings of Alexandra Kollontai*, pp. 160–163, citation in p. 160. I have slightly altered the English of the old translation I have had at my disposal.

Democracy held in central place on the agenda of the Opposition. This demand, first on a list of five, was formulated by Kollontai as follows:[30]

> In the name of Party regeneration and the elimination of bureaucracy from Soviet institutions, the Workers' Opposition, together with the responsible workers in Moscow, demand complete realisation of all democratic principles not only for the present period of respite, but also for times of internal and external tension. This is the first and basic condition for the Party's regeneration, for its return to the principles of its programme, from which it is more and more deviating in practice under the pressure of elements foreign to it.

The "foreign elements" mentioned were defined as "non-proletarian elements", elements which should be – this was the second demand – expelled from the Party. When Soviet power becomes stable and strong, persons of middle-class background "and even hostile elements" would try to join the Party. This development began immediately after the October revolution. The Party must be purged in such a way as to become a "workers' party". The Workers' Opposition suggested that all non-workers who had joined the Party since 1919 should be registered and expelled. After three months, they could be allowed to try to join the Party again. In other words, recent members of the Party had to submit to an experimental period in which they must demonstrate their usefulness to the Party. It was also necessary, Kollontai argued, to establish a "working status" for all those non-working-class elements which would try to join the Party. Every applicant must have had in his or her work history a "certain period of time at manual labour". Kollontai did not specify how long this probation period should be. – Thirdly, the Party administration. All committees of the Party, central, provincial, local or workplace, must be so "composed that workers closely acquainted with the conditions of the working masses should be in the preponderant majority therein". Fourthly, the Party must again adopt "the elective principle"; nominations, which were increasingly becoming general practice, should be permissible only in exceptional circumstances. In other words, Kollontai and the Workers' Opposition were against the nomenclature system, which was developing under their eyes. Fifthly, one should revert to the state of affairs where "all the cardinal questions of Party activity and Soviet policy" were to be submitted for discussion among regular members. As to freedom of criticism and discussion, there should be a "right of different factions freely to present their views at Party meetings". Kollontai proclaimed that these were no longer the demands of the Workers' Opposition, but the demands of the "masses".[31]

---

[30] *Ibid.*, p. 193.

[31] *Ibid.*, pp. 192–196.

The trade union question was the most controversial. According to Kollontai, the following formula was a "simple Marxist truth":[32]

> The Party task is to create the conditions – that is, give freedom to the working masses united by common economic industrial aims – for workers to become worker-creators, find new impulses for work, work out a new system to utilise labour power and discover how to distribute workers in order to reconstruct society and thus to create a new economic order of things founded on a Communist basis. *Only workers can generate in their minds new methods of organising labour as well as of running industry.*

The Workers' Opposition had several concrete demands: they wished, for instance to "form a body out of the workers – producers themselves – for administering the people's economy", they also sought to "strengthen the rank and file nucleus in the unions" and to prepare factory and shop committees for running the industries. Perhaps the most decisive demand was a "concentration of administration":[33]

> By means of concentrating in one body the entire administration of the public economy (without the existing dualism of the Supreme Council of the National Economy and the All-Russian Executive Committee of the trade unions) there must be created a singleness of will which will make it easy to carry out the plan and put life into the Communist system of production. Is this syndicalism? Is not this, on the contrary, the same as what is stated in our Party programme and are not the elements of principles signed by the rest of the comrades deviating from it?

At bottom, the Workers' Opposition represented the idea that the liberation of the working-class could be accomplished by the workers themselves. To criticism of syndicalism, Kollontai answered: "Who is right, the leaders or the working masses endowed with a healthy class instinct?"[34]

We shall meet the "class instinct" conception later; many kinds of oppositions in the Communist movement made political capital by pleading this instinct. For Lenin and his ilk the trades unions were "schools of Communism", and, according to Kollontai's interpretation, no more.[35]. Kollontai accused "all of them – Lenin,

---

32 *Ibid.*, p. 184. Italics in original.

33 *Ibid.*, pp. 188–189.

34 *Ibid.*, p. 162. The two main oppositions within a couple of years at the beginning of 1920s, the Democratic Centralists and the Workers' Opposition, had no good relations with each other. The "class instinct", however, was a phenomenon in which the Democratic Centralists also trusted. From the class instinct, one could proceed to "class initiative". (V. V. Osinskii in the journal *Kommunist*, April 1918, quoted by Daniels, *The Conscience of Revolution*, p. 87.)

35 Kollontai, *Workers' Opposition*, p. 182.

Trotskii, Zinov'ev and Bukharin –" of "distrust towards the working-class". "They do not believe", Kollontai thundered, "that by the rough hands of workers, technically untrained, can be created those foundations of economic forms which, in the course of time, shall develop into a harmonious system of Communist production".[36] This conception of workers may be called romantic or "ouvrierist"; workers can do everything themselves without any *spetsy*.

Kollontai's portrayal of the Party was gloomy: there reigned a "spirit of bureaucratism, an atmosphere of officialdom". If there is no longer any "comradeship" in the Party, it "exists only among the rank and file members". The Workers' Opposition had three "cardinal demands". They were the following:[37]

1. Return to the principle of election all along the line with the elimination of all bureaucracy, by making all responsible officials answerable to the masses.
2. Introduce wide publicity within the Party, both concerning general questions and where individuals are involved. Pay more attention to the voice of the rank and file [...]. Establish freedom of opinion and expression (giving the right not only to criticise freely during discussions, but to use funds for publication of literature proposed by different Party factions.)
3. Make the Party more a workers' Party. Limit the number of those who fill offices, both in the Party and at the same time in the Soviet institutions.

Kollontai considered the last demand particularly important. She said that the task of the Party was to "prepare and educate the masses for a prolonged period of struggle against world Capitalism".[38] She thought, akin to all Bolsheviks at the time, that a war against imperialism would materialise in some way or other. About the world revolution she did not speculate.

The Workers' Opposition stipulated a "separation of powers". The scheme had, however, nothing to do with that of Montesquieu. The powers in question should be the Party, the Soviets and the trade unions. They should separately assume responsibility in their own fields.[39] However, this was not all. Shliapnikov wanted the Communist fraction of the All-Russian Council of Trade Unions to be an independent centre which controlled the Party organisation in the trade unions.[40] This kind of dualism in organisation was probably thought as a means to support and underline the power of the trade union organisations. This was not in Kollontai's brochure, perhaps because she opposed it or considered it tactically unwise to present it. In any case, in the draft resolution of the Opposition pre-

---

36 *Ibid.*, p. 177.
37 *Ibid.*, p. 197.
38 *Ibid.*, pp. 197–198.
39 Daniels, *The Conscience of Revolution*, p. 125.
40 Farnsworth, *Alexandra Kollontai*, p. 217.

sented to the tenth Congress (1921), Kollontai wrote orthodoxically that all Party and political work in the unions must be subordinated to the respective Party organs.[41] On the other hand, there was nothing about feminism and women's affairs in the programme. This is, of course, odd; very likely it was a compromise. In the tenth Congress Kollontai's feminist writings were used against her.

The question arises of the kind of sources (not literally speaking) Kollontai had when she wrote the programme. Cosmopolitan as she was, she had travelled around Europe, and knew many currents and schools of Socialism, including the French revolutionary syndicalism and the English Guild Socialism. In the framework of this present study we cannot seek answers to this kind of questions.[42] Aleksandra Mikhailovna's proletarian romanticism, her "ouvrierism", was so extreme that perhaps the closest counterpart, namely Chairman Mao Zedong's Great Proletarian Cultural Revolution, was at the time still to come.

The Workers' Opposition was, of course, condemned in speeches and resolutions. I take two typical examples. Lev Trotskii:[43]

> The Workers' Opposition has come out with dangerous slogans. They have made a fetish of democratic principles. They have placed the workers' right to elect representatives above the party, as it were, as if the arty were not entitled to assert its dictatorship even if that dictatorship temporarily clashed with passing moods of the workers' democracy. [...] The party is obliged to maintain its dictatorship, regardless of temporary wavering in the spontaneous moods of the masses, regardless of the temporary vacillations even in the working class.

The resolution of the Xth Congress of the RKP(b) *On the Syndicalist and Anarchist Deviation in Our Party* declared[44]

> Marxism teaches [...] that only the political Party of the working-class, i.e., the Communist Party, is capable of unifying, teaching and organizing a vanguard of the proletariat and of the entire mass of working people, a vanguard capable of countering the inevitable petty-bourgeois waverings of this mass, of countering the traditions of and inevitable backsliding to, a narrow trade-unionism or trade union prejudices among the proletariat and of guiding all aspects of the proletarian movement or, in other words, all labouring masses. Without this, the dictatorship of the proletariat is unthinkable.

---

41 *Ibid.*, p. 219.

42 In England Sylvia Pankhurst was interested in Kollontai's ideas and wrote a document titled *Constitution for British Soviets, Points for a Communist Programme.* (See Mary Davis, *Sylvia Pankhurst : a Life in Radical Politics*, p. 91 and sources mentioned there.)

43 Desiatyi S"yezd RKP, p. 192. Cited in Deutscher, *The Prophet Armed*, pp. 508–509.

44 Published in *Resolutions and decisions of the Communist Party of the Soviet Union*, vol. 2, *The Early Soviet Period: 1917–1929*, p. 122.

In this case, it is not difficult to point to the source; it is Lenin's *What Is to Be Done*, published in 1902.

One may ask why the Bolshevik leaders, Lenin, Trotskii and others, considered the danger of the Workers' Opposition so serious, although it had little support in the Party as a whole, only some local strongholds, of which that in Moscow was undeniably important. First, an obvious reason is that such ideas might possibly prove pleasing to the masses who worked under specialists in those factories which still by some miracle functioned. If not suppressed, the notions of workers' self-management might gain support. Second, there were Lenin's writings, e.g. *The State and Revolution*. It was impossible to censure them, or indeed to explain why there were such obvious contradictions in Lenin's works. (This aspect, to be sure, was more important to the intellectuals of the Democratic Centralists than it was to the Workers' Oppositionists.) Third, the trade union leaders who led the Opposition (or tacitly accepted its activities) were usually so-called Old Bolsheviks. Shliapnikov had been a Party member since 1901.[45] Finally, it is crucial that Kollontai presented her arguments strictly in the framework of the Party and the Communists inside the Unions. The Opposition was not, for example, interested in the starving, oppressed peasants.[46] As to the industrial working-class, organised in unions, there were contradictory statements. We have seen that Shliapnikov, by insisting on the independence of the trade unions, was demanding a sort of "separation of powers". Nevertheless, in the Xth Congress Shliapnikov stated that in the unions delegates nominated and elected to various tasks in the control of industry at all levels should be accepted by the Communists. The election principle was now reduced broadly speaking to local level only. There the delegates of various organs must, according to Shliapnikov, be local workers experienced in grass-roots union work and known to the masses. They should not be nominated from the centre.[47]

In the Xth Congress, Lenin spoke callously, as could be excepted, against the "syndicalist" and "Semi-Anarchist" "deviation". He made much of not having read

---

[45] *Большой энциклопедический словарь*, vol. 2, p. 664.

[46] The peasant problem was, of course, the most crucial from the Bolshevik point of view. The Bolshevik leaders were city men, and for the difficulties of peasants they had little understanding. They were treated as a nuisance, harmful, but unavoidable elements in society, where the working-class, as was said, was in power. In the Xth Congress of the RKP(b), Lenin declared: "The peasant must starve a little so as to relieve the factories and towns from complete starvation. On the level of the state in general this is an entirely understandable thing, but we do not count on the exhausted, impoverished peasant-owner understanding it. And we know you cannot manage without compulsion, to which the devastated peasantry is reacting very strongly." (В. И. Ленин. Отчет о политической деятельности ЦК РКП(б) 8 марта [1921]. Speech in the Xth Congress of the RKP(b). PSS vol. 43, p. 29.)

[47] Schapiro, *The Origin of the Communist Autocracy*, p. 294.

all opposition pamphlets although it would have been his duty.[48] Shliapnikov, however, was elected to the Central Committee on Lenin's insistence.[49] Lenin stated that Shliapnikov and he himself had already known each other at the time when the Party was underground and when most Bolshevik leaders stayed in exile.[50] His tactic here was integration. It was successful, at least partly. Shliapnikov's presence in the Central Committee did not prevent the use of the nomination principle in the case of the unions; here the case of the Metal Workers' Union is illustrative. When the Union held its Congress in May 1921, the delegates were given a list of candidates for the leadership drawn up by the Central Committee of the Party. The delegates voted it down, but the Central Committee then simply nominated its leaders. Shliapnikov tried to resign from the Central Committee in protest, but his resignation was not accepted.[51]

3. Workers' Group and Workers' Truth

Despite the ban on factions in the tenth Congress and the successful suppression of the Democratic Centralists and the Workers' Opposition in 1922, troubles continued. Now, however, the organisations were clandestine after the illegalization of all independent labour organisations within the Party or outside it.[52] Best known of these were the Workers' Group and the Workers' Truth. The New Economic Politics (NEP) raised claims that there was a danger of "new exploitation of the proletariat". In July 1923, the Workers' Group issued a manifesto on this danger, the danger of the formation of a new "economic caste of oligarchy". The manifesto also proposed means of overcoming the danger: the administration of economy and production should be in the hands of Soviets at all levels, from local factory to All-Russian Executive Committee, which should be the sovereign governing body in the country. The trade unions should be independent "pure proletarian class organisations", with rights to control all governing bodies from factory to central, national level. If anyone feared this kind of role of the trade unions, he "fears the proletariat and has lost all contact with it".[53] Such demands may strike some as

---

48 В. И. Ленин, Отчет о политической деятельности ЦК РКП(б) 8 марта в 1921 г. Speech in the Xth Congress of the RKP(b)..PSS vol. 43, p. 17.

49 Leonard Schapiro, *The Communist Party of the Soviet Union*, pp. 214–215.

50 В. И. Ленин, Заключительное слово по отчету ЦК РКП(б) 9 марта [1921]. Speech in the Xth Congress of the RKP(b). PSS vol. 43, pp. 39–40.

51 Daniels, *The Conscience of Revolution*, p. 157.

52 John B. Hatch, "Labor Struggles in Moscow, 1921–1925" in *Russia in the Era of NEP : Explorations in Soviet Society and Culture*, pp. 66–67.

53 *Манифест Рабочей Группы Российской Коммунистической Партии (б) : издание Рабочей Группы Р.К.П. (б).* Moscow, July 1923. RGASPI, f. 17, op. 71, d. 4, ll. 101–102.

syndicalist. There were, however, already existing bodies which had rights to control, the above-mentioned Control Commissions inside the Party and the *Rabkrin*,[54] the Workers' and Peasants' Inspection outside it. What the Workers' Group really meant by its demands was the independence of proletarian class organisations from the Communist Party. The *Rabkrin* was headed by I. V. Stalin, and criticised by many Party leaders, including Lenin and Trotskii, as only a new bureaucratic organ without real power to control the administration of the economy.[55]

The existence of the Workers' Group and the Workers' Truth was no secret in spite of their underground nature. As we saw, one could read attacks against them in the newspapers, where long citations of opposition arguments were published. Their own manifestos could no longer be printed, but it was possible to spread leaflets made on duplication machines.[56]

The Workers' Truth was obviously a more radical faction than the Workers' Group. In its manifesto, titled *To the Russian Revolutionary Proletariat and to All Revolutionary Organs Faithful to the Struggling Proletariat*, the Workers' Truth declared that the "[s]ocial existence of the Communist Party necessarily defines a corresponding social consciousness, interest and ideals which are in conflict with the struggling proletariat".[57] This is a somewhat perplexing definition. My interpretation is that the said "social consciousness" *also* defines the negative interest and ideals from the point of view of the workers. It may be true that the participants in this faction were mainly workers, as John B. Hatch has claimed,[58] but then they belonged to a stratum which can be described as a worker aristocracy. They declared that the RKP(b) was now no longer a genuine workers' party, but a party of "organised intelligentsia". The financial position of bureaucrats in the Soviets, the Party and the trades unions, as well as those in state capitalism – this was an allusion to the so-called nepmen, men who were running small-size enterprises, owners of shops, carpenter firms etc. – were much better than the condition of the working-class. What is important is that the living conditions of the bureaucrats depended on the extent to which the bureaucrats could "exploit" workers. Here

---

54 Рабоче-Крестьянская Инспекция.

55 See Carr, *The Bolshevik Revolution 1917–1923*, vol. 1, pp. 231–232.

56 For instance, the manifesto of the Workers' Truth was written by hand on duplication waxes. A copy was stored in the Archives. Later, after the Second World War, it was typed by a clerk in the Institute of Marxism-Leninism. Both versions are kept in the RGASPI. It is easier to read the typed version and my references are to it. – It goes without saying that only the most reliable comrades had access to these dangerous papers.

57 *Обращение к революционному пролетариату России и всем революционным элементам. оставшихся верными борющемуся рабочему классу*. No date, probably written in November or December 1923. RGASPI, f. 17, op. 71, d. 81, l. 9.

58 Hatch, "Labor Struggles in Moscow, 1921–1925", p. 66.

exploitation means that the masses were obliged to serve the needs of dignitaries, not their own needs. The inevitable conclusion to be deduced from this argumentation was that there was inevitably a credibility gap between the Party and the working-class.[59]

According to the Marxist theory of exploitation, the workers are exploited by the capitalists. But now in Russia, although there were nepmen and some degree of capitalist exploitation, the nomenclature, above all, had become a stratum, or a class, which exploited the proletariat. If there was exploitation, it followed, according to Marxism, that there were antagonistic interests and that a class struggle was in progress in Russia. This interpretation was, of course, impossible to accept by the nomenclature leaders. Emelian Mikhailovich Iaroslavskii, secretary of the Central Committee of the Control Commission of the RKP(b) / VKP(b) 1923–1934,[60] wrote a plea against the Workers' Truth manifesto, published in *Pravda* in December 1923. He admitted that there had been harmful "non-proletarian elements" in the Party, but it had also organised a purge of troublesome petty-bourgeois etc., and "petty-bourgeois elements" had in fact been expelled from the Party. Thus, the Party itself had purged the Party.[61]

---

[59] *Ibid*., pp. 8–9.

[60] *Большой энциклопедический словарь*, vol. 2, p. 728.

[61] Е. М. Ярославский, "Что такое 'Рабочая Правда'", *Правда*, Dec. 19, 1923. The "purge" (*чистка*) was realised in 1921–1922 by a resolution of the Xth Party Congress. (Carr, *The Bolshevik Revolution 1917–1923*, p. 211.) Purge meant, in the 1920s, examination of Party members: had they fulfilled their Party duties in workplaces, trade unions, Soviets etc., but also followed the correct line without deviation. One should not confuse these purges, decided in the Politburo, with purges in which people were sent to forced labour or executed as in 1936–1938. A great purge took place in 1929, especially severe in the countryside. According to official figures, 80.8 per cent of Party members living in the country were examined and of these 15.7 per cent had been expelled from the Party. In Party cells in factories, the purge was not so radical; only eight per cent were expelled. The purge had thus class and ideological motivation. Iaroslavskii complained in a meeting of the Moscow Party organisation that many industrial workers still had ties with the countryside and thought of working in industry only as a means to improve their rural economy. (Edward Hallet Carr, *Foundations of a Planned Economy*, vol. 2, pp. 152–155.) This was obviously not politically correct behaviour because these workers also preserved, it was obviously thought by the Bolsheviks, attitudes of the rural petty-bourgeoisie. – Purges of oppositions also concerned the SKP because most of its leaders in Russia were also members of the Russian Party. As far as I know, no oppositional cadres in the SKP were purged in the sense of the Russian Party. However, opposition leaders like Kullervo Manner feared the purge that was carried out in 1933. (Kullervo Manner to Hanna Malm, June 3–4 (?) 1933, MCC, p. 388.) After that year (at least), in fact the word lost its original sense – cleansing, purification – and came to mean death penalty or deportation to the GULag. Purges – now again in the original sense of the word – directed against oppositions inside the SKP were carried out against the opposition leaders. On the other hand, however, the fact that they were members of the Russian Party in which purges were regular could not be without influence on life inside the Party.

The Workers' Group and the Workers' Truth were the last relatively well-known rank-and-file oppositions in the Bolshevik Party. As a Russian study of oppositions in the Soviet Union states, it was impossible for small (usually not more than 50 participants) "exhausted underground groupings" to fight seriously against "Party-state power" and its chirurgical instrument, the GPU.[62] Then there were, of course, various oppositions: Lenin's faction (at least in the XIth Congress of the Party in 1922),[63] Trotskii's faction, Stalin's faction, Bukharin's "Right-Wing" opposition and so on. These were, however, factions among the ruling elite.

[62] *Власть и оппозиция : российский политический процесс XX столетия*, pp. 114–115.

[63] According to V. M. Molotov's memoirs, Lenin assembled some twenty delegates in the XIth Congress in a separate meeting in order to organise common behaviour in the vote. Molotov says that Stalin, who was to be appointed general secretary of the Central Committee, "reproached Lenin for holding a secret or semisecret conference during the congress". Was it something other than just a faction, and factions were forbidden in the Xth Congress, in March 1921? According to Molotov, Lenin said to Stalin: "Comrade Stalin, you are an old, experienced factionist yourself! [...] I want everyone to be well prepared for the vote and comrades must be told that they are to vote firmly for the list without any amendments!" (*Molotov Remembers*, p. 104.)

V *Dramatis personae*

In this chapter I shall present the main actors in the drama, the Party and its opposition leaders. One important criterion is their possible political activity in the Social Democratic Party before 1918 and / or their participation in the Civil War, or, as in one case (Leo Laukki), activities in the American-Finnish workers' movement. Another essential criterion is, naturally, their role in the SKP leadership or in some Party opposition in Soviet Russia. They are classified as follows: first, the "main line" as represented by the Party leadership after the 1921 Party Congress; this means people who did not belong to any opposition within the Party after that year. They are Otto Wille Kuusinen, Yrjö Sirola, Johan Henrik Lumivuokko, Adolf Taimi and Toivo Antikainen. The second group comprises the leaders of the Murder Opposition: Voitto Eloranta and Väinö Pukka. The third group was formed by the leaders of the Rahja Opposition, later also known as the Beer Opposition: Jukka Rahja, Eino Rahja, Leo Laukki and Kustaa Mikko Evä. Finally, the fourth group of opposition leaders to be presented here are Hanna Malm and Kullervo Manner. The classification cannot in fact be very strict: Lumivuokko, for instance, seemed to have some sympathies with the Rahja opposition in 1923–1924. O. W. Kuusinen formed an opposition in 1919–1921. The order of presentation follows my own impression of the significance of the respective figures from the point of view of factional struggle in the Finnish Communist Party in Soviet Russia. It goes without saying that such a preference list is disputable, but I would ask the reader to bear in mind that the preferences are set from the standpoint of this study. For instance, leaders like Edvard Gylling and Arvo Tuominen were more important players than Lumivuokko or Taimi if we look at the history of the Finnish Communism "in general". Gylling was a leader of the Karelian Commune / Soviet Karelia in 1920–1935 and Tuominen an important leader in Finland, but only in the latter half of the 1930s did he emerge as an important figure in the leadership of the SKP in Russia. – The possibilities of obtaining information on the above-mentioned personages are disproportionate. At one end of the scale there is, of course, Kuusinen, on whom the available information is immense, while at the other end is August (Aku) Paasi, a member of the Murder Opposition, who in August 1920 shot participants in a Party meeting in the Kuusinen Club in Petrograd. He is not included in this chapter at all, but the reader may derive some impression of his personality in the Murder Opposition chapter. – I give the names also in Cyrillic because they were not always strict transliterations.

1. The Kuusinen Opposition/Group

Otto Wilhelm (Wille) Kuusinen

(Отто Вильгельмович Куусинен, 1881–1964)

O. W. Kuusinen is arguably the most successful Finnish-born politician who ever lived: no other ethnic Finn has been a member of an executive political organ of a superpower (at the time when there were two of them). Kuusinen was a member of the Politburo / the Presidium of the Communist Party of the Soviet Union in 1952–1953 and 1957–1964. He was also a leading ideologist of the Communist movement; he was elected to the Academy of Sciences of the Soviet Union in 1958, in 1961 he received the honorary title of "Hero of Socialist Labour". His mortal remains rest in the Wall of the Kremlin and there is in Moscow and in Petrozavodsk *ulitsa Kuusinena* (Kuusinen Street) and in Petrozavodsk also his statue. In spite of his high position in the Soviet nomenclature after World War II, he was always involved, albeit indirectly, in Finnish politics as a mentor of the SKP. His daughter, Hertta Kuusinen, was one of the most prominent Communist politicians after the Second World War up to 1970. In the 1970s, O. W. Kuusinen was an icon of the Finnish pro-Soviet student movement, the slogan of which was "forward on the lines laid down by O. W. Kuusinen!" This notwithstanding, Kuusinen could not visit Finland after the WW II in spite of his desire to do so. The Finnish authorities claimed that they could not guarantee his personal safety. He was hated by bourgeois and Social Democratic circles above all by reason of his role in the Winter War. In 1939 he was appointed by Stalin – who once said that Kuusinen is "good, but an academician"[1] – chairman of the "Finnish People's Government" and as the Commissar of Foreign Affairs in the said "government", better known as the Terijoki

---

1 Georgi Dimitrov quotes in his diary (dated April 7, 1934) Stalin's remark. Stalin, Molotov and Dimitrov discussed affairs of the Comintern in the Kremlin. (Georgi Dimitroff, *Tagebücher 1933–1943*, p. 99.)

government.[2] When a "bourgeois" publishing house issued a collection of scientific essays on his early years in Finland, a special, and most unusual preface was inserted by the publisher, in which it was explained, to justify the publishing such a book, that Kuusinen was a "national of note" at the beginning of the XXth century and therefore one should "put away one-sided, stiff attitudes" concerning him, that the essays were written by "young unprejudiced researchers", and that Kuusinen was not only a politician but also an aesthete etc.[3]

Kuusinen's background was humble. His father was a crofter and a tailor, but in spite of poverty, artisans not uncommonly enjoyed upward mobility in Finland as elsewhere in Europe. O. W. Kuusinen was educated: at school he showed talent, matriculated with high marks[4] and became a student of philosophy, aesthetics and the history of art in the Imperial Alexander University of Helsinki. Kuusinen joined the Social Democratic Party in 1904 and was one of the founders of the Social Democratic Association of Students in the following year with, among others, Yrjö Sirola and Edvard Gylling. He was such a devoted Kautskyist that he was nicknamed "little Kautsky". The general strike of November 1905 radicalised him as it did many others. "Socialists of November" believed in the use of violence, the Red Guards, and general strikes as forms of struggle for the formation of a constitutional assembly after the (forced) abdication of the Tsar.[5] (It is, however, difficult to say how ready they themselves were to use violence.) Their attitude by no means ruled out peaceful and parliamentary means in the struggle for Socialism. All possibilities were kept open.

As Tauno Saarela points out, leading Finnish Social Democrats in 1905–1906 thought that the possibilities of a Finnish revolution would depend on a revolution in Russia.[6] Thus began a tradition which was inherited by the leaders of the Finnish revolution after their escape to Russia. In 1906 Kuusinen became an expert of the Left-Wing of the Social Democratic Party on Finnish-Russian relations. He thought that the interests of the Finnish bourgeoisie and the Russian ruling class were in the last instance the same: the bourgeoisie, however, feared their historical task of realising "full democracy" and because, in spite of the existence of the democratically elected *Eduskunta*, ultimate power lay in the hands of the Grand Duke, it was possible for the Finnish bourgeoisie to hide behind the Russian authorities.[7]

---

2 Terijoki was a village on the old Finnish-Soviet border taken by the Soviet troops immediately upon the outbreak of the Winter War on November 30, 1939. It is nowadays the town of Zelenogorsk.

3 "Kustantajan alkusana" in *Nuori Otto Ville Kuusinen 1881–1920*, p. 10.

4 Martti Paakkanen, "Kyläräätälin poika" in *Nuori Otto Ville Kuusinen 1881–1920*, pp. 11–25.

5 Vesa Salminen, "Estetiikan opiskelijasta poliitikoksi vuosina 1900–1906" in *Nuori Otto Ville Kuusinen 1881–1920*, pp. 27–45.

6 Saarela, *Suomalaisen kommunismin synty*, p. 50.

7 Jouko Heikkilä, *Kansallista luokkapolitiikka : sosiaalidemokraatit ja Suomen autonomian puolustus 1905–1917*, p. 65. This position is, roughly speaking, similar to Marx's and Engels' political line

The Red Guards were officially dissolved in 1906, but there existed for about a year a secret organisation whose aim was the arming of workers for the coming Russian revolution, which was expected to spread to Finland. Kuusinen was the main ideologist of this organisation. The revolution for which these preparations were made was to be only a democratic one; a Socialist revolution in semi-feudal Russia was impossible and because Finland was tied to Russia, a proletarian revolution there was equally impossible.[8]

After 1906 Kuusinen was one of the editors of the main newspaper of the SDP, *Työmies*, and editor of the theoretical magazine, *Sosialistinen aikakauslehti*. In 1908, he was elected to the *Eduskunta* and there to the Committee on Constitutional Affairs, which at that time was particularly important from the point view of Finland's Russian policy. In 1911, Kuusinen was elected second chairman (the first was the reformist-oriented Matti Paasivuori) of the Party. He was becoming a leading figure of the Party alongside Kullervo Manner.[9]

After the February revolution in Russia, Kuusinen's role as a Party ideologist became of great consequence. A difficult ideological as well as political question was participation in the Senate. The orthodox Kautskyan position was that the participation of Socialists in a bourgeois government was permissible only as a temporary expedient in exceptional circumstances.[10] When the leaders of the SDP discussed possible participation in the Senate, they sought to follow this Kautskyan line. Kuusinen and Manner suggested that the Social Democrats and Agrarians put their men in the Senate and in addition, seek out five "wild" bourgeois senators. However, it proved impossible to find such "wild" representatives of the bourgeoisie, and this being the case Kuusinen and Manner announced that they opposed participation in the Senate formed by a Social Democrat Oskari Tokoi.[11]

Kuusinen's cautious political line and determinist conception of history was manifested in his ambiguous attitude toward dictatorship. When the possibility of revolution was discussed by the Party and trade union leaders on October 23, 1917, Kuusinen's opinion was that Social Democrats should by no means further the

---

during the German revolution of 1848–1849: they even advocated, in the summer 1848, a war with Russia, a war that would lead to the liberation of Poland from the Russian yoke and this, in turn, would lead to the establishment of a democratic Germany. (See my *Marx's and Engels' concepts of the parties and political organizations of the working-class*, p. 85.) It is not likely that Kuusinen knew the positions of Marx and Engels in all details, but as a Kautskyist he supported a conception of revolution which had its roots in Marx's and Engels' thought, formed at that time, on democratic revolution led by the bourgeoisie.

8 Antti Kujala, *Vallankumous ja kansallinen itsemääräämisoikeus : Venäjän sosialistiset puolueet ja suomalainen radikalismi vuosisadan alussa*, pp. 255–257.

9 Vesa Salminen, "Laillisuuden esitaistelija vai oman edun tavoittelija – Kuusinen ja toinen sortokausi" in *Nuori Otto Ville Kuusinen 1881–1920*, pp. 55–74.

10 Julius Braunthal, *History of the International 1864–1914*, vol. 1, pp. 272–273.

11 Väinö Tanner, *Kuinka se oikein tapahtui : vuosi 1918 esivaiheineen ja jälkiselvittelyineen*, pp. 22–23.

realisation of a dictatorship of the proletariat, but at the same time by no means oppose the creation of such a dictatorship.[12] This was, of course, a typically Kautskyan position. During the general strike (November 14–20, 1917) Kuusinen was against revolutionary action. The question of a coup d'état was raised in the Workers' Revolutionary Central Council on November 16. Kuusinen argued that if the general strike ended in time the organisations of the working-class would remain intact.[13] He soon changed his opinion: on November 21, 1917, Kuusinen was for a coup, although he was pessimistic, as to the prospects of proletarian revolutions in Western European countries, above all in Germany. In the Social Democratic Party Congress held November 25–27, 1917, Kuusinen did not take a stand on the question of a coup.[14] Subsequently, in the decisive meeting of the Party Committee of the SDP in January 1918, Kuusinen's opinion was that the question of a coup was now only a technical one.[15]

Kuusinen participated in the People's Deputation; his portfolio was that of education.[16] His main task, however, was to write a draft for the constitution discussed above. This second notable task was to lead a committee which was to draft an answer to an offer by the German government to mediate between the Whites and the Reds. This offer was made in mid-March; at the point when the People's Deputation became aware of an agreement between the White Senate and Germany on the intervention. The committee thought for nine days what to answer and a plan for a cessation of hostilities and arrangement of a referendum was drafted. The People's Deputation, however, decided not to give any answer to the Germans.[17] – In Russia Kuusinen was secretary general of the Comintern in 1921–1922 and afterwards a member of the powerful Secretariat of the Comintern, it seems until 1943, when the Comintern was terminated.

Many writers have more or less seriously deliberated the question of the composition of Kuusinen's brains, if such a crude expression be allowed. As Kimmo Rentola shows, Kuusinen's personality contained a strong visceral side: one of his maxims was "holy hate – it is holy love".[18] Love, hate and destruction are perpetual, incessant themes in folk poetry and it is perhaps no chance that Kuusinen was a life-long student of that poetry, especially the *Kalevala*.[19]

---

[12] Rinta-Tassi, "Kuusinen vallankumousvuosina" in *Nuori Otto Ville Kuusinen 1881–1920*, pp. 112–113.

[13] Polvinen, *Venäjän vallankumous ja Suomi 1917–1920*, pp. 125–126.

[14] John H. Hodgson, *Otto Wille Kuusinen : poliittinen elämäkerta*, pp. 46–47.

[15] Hodgson, *Otto Wille Kuusinen*, p. 49.

[16] Upton, *The Finnish Revolution 1917–1918*, p. 352.

[17] Juhani Paasivirta, *Suomi vuonna 1918*, pp. 94–96.

[18] Kimmo Rentola, *Kenen joukoissa seisot? : suomalainen kommunismi ja sota 1937–1945*, p. 48.

[19] See O. W Kuusinen, "Kalevala ja sen luojat" in *Kalevala : karjalais-suomalainen kansaneepos*, pp. vii–xxiii.

Kuusinen's speech to the new employees of the NKVD,[20] is indeed an interesting melting pot. Invited in his capacity of secretary of the Comintern perhaps by Nikolai Ivanovich Ezhov, People's Commissar for Internal Affairs, i.e. head of the NKVD (September 1936 – December 1938[21]) and member of the Executive Committee of the Comintern, his task was obviously to give theoretical and ideological instruction to new recruits of this institution, known as "four letters" (the GPU, was known as "three letters"). It is clear that this presentation was not from Kuusinen's point of view entirely safe; he was, of course, also under secret supervision by these "letters". For his lecture in the NKVD Kuusinen prepared a list to held him remember what he was to say.[22] The following notes are to be found in Kuusinen's papers:[23]

> – Where has one heard in cap. – or where is it even thinkable – that someone who had been in the hands (state's) sec. organs could feel afterwards thankfulness towards them, would feel that they have assist. him to a life which is of human value! Nowhere!
> – But in the Sov. Union there are thousands of such examples!

But if this is so, why hunt these people down? The answer is that there are always the most dangerous "terrorists" (i.e. dissidents, independent-minded people etc.) who in every totalitarian regime constitute a dire threat to the system. As for them, Kuusinen had only outright and severe condemnation:

> Not revenge (is bourg.)
> Not because has made mist., lapsed, fallen into crime.
> But for the reason that injur. and dangerous to soc.
> For this reason, must be shut away, punished, liquidated.

It is possible that during the great terror Kuusinen's personality changed somewhat.[24] Cruel times required cruelty. Deep down, Kuusinen was undoubtedly against the liquidation of, say, Bukharin, a personal friend of his.[25] However, like other personages concerned to preserve their own head, he kept silence.

---

[20] Народный комиссариат внутренних дел (People's Commissariat for Internal Affairs).

[21] Roy Medvedev, *Let History Judge : the Origins and Consequences of Stalinism*, p. 171 and 308.

[22] Among Kuusinen's papers there are all manner of notes and copies of important speeches by Ezhov and other leaders of the state of the working-class.

[23] Kuusinen's note, RGASPI, f. 522, op. 1, d. 114. There is no date. Taking account of its style the time is almost certainly that of the great terror, i.e. 1936–1938, when Ezhov headed the NKVD.

[24] Or perhaps Kuusinen's "love and hate" was inbuilt in him. Max Eastman (*Love and Revolution*, p. 337) writes, with Trotskii in mind, that the "somewhat ambivalent creature called Bolshevik [...] has faith, hope and charity in him at his best, but he has also the gift of hate and he has the disease of the doctrine in its most virulent form".

[25] To be sure, Kuusinen supported, in 1929, Stalin and opposed Bukharin as "Rightist". (O. W. Kuusinen, "Uusi kausi ja käänne Kominternin politiikassa (Tov. Stalinin 50-vuotispäivän johdosta

Yrjö Sirola

(Юрье[26] Сирола, 1876–1936)

Yrjö Sirola was a son of a curate who was said to be a traditionalist Lutheran Christian but tolerant towards his children. In the university, Sirola chose aesthetics as his main subject. He was to remain, however, an "eternal student". In 1903, he began to take up Socialist ideas and soon found himself an assistant editor in a Liberal (Young Finn) paper, *Kotkan Sanomat*, then as a translator.[27] In his tasks as writer and translator, Sirola was deeply engaged. One of first Socialist works he translated into Finnish was August Bebel's *Die Frau und der Sozialismus.*[28] We may guess that for the sensitive Sirola Bebel's utopian speculations envisaging, for instance, the replacing of private kitchens by "Communist", i.e. communal ones, equipped with the most modern machines to be invented, were no less than thrilling.

In 1905, Sirola spoke in mass meetings wearing a red ribbon. In the 1905 Congress of the Social Democratic Party he was elected to the Party Executive Committee and then as Party secretary. Sirola belonged, like Kuusinen, to the Siltasaari group. In the 1906 Congress he refused to continue in the post of Party secretary because the Congress of the German Social Democratic Party had just reached a decision that "gentlemen" should not be elected to leading posts in a workers' Party.[29] It is, of course, difficult to know whether this was Sirola's real motive, but nothing speaks against this possibility. Sirola was an idealist, if not in fact a romantic Socialist.

Sirola participated in the Copenhagen Congress of the Second International in 1910. From Copenhagen, he travelled to America, to the surprise of everyone at home. He wrote that he wanted to see the world outside Finland. Especially capitalist America was interesting because people spoke so much about its economic and democratic achievements. He also felt that the question of Revisionism and Marxism was not "clear" to him. Though he was not fond of Revisionism, Siltasaarian Marxism too seemed such a doctrine that although "principally correct it did not give a practical answer to the question what is to be done".[30]

---

kirjoitettu artikkeli)" in O. W. Kuusinen, *Kommunistisen internationalen ja sen osastojen tehtävistä : puheita ja kirjoituksia*, pp. 280–282.

26 Sirola's first name was in Russian also written as Ирье and Иурий.

27 Erkki Salomaa, "Yrjö Sirola" in *Tiennäyttäjät*, vol. 1, 166–175.

28 August Bebel, *Nainen ja sosialismi*. The first Finnish edition appeared in 1905.

29 Salomaa, "Yrjö Sirola", pp. 175–178.

30 *Työmies* (USA), Nov. 2, 1928, quoted in Erkki Salomaa, *Yrjö Sirola : sosialistinen humanisti*, pp. 149–151. There is no indication as to the time when this text was actually written, but it may have been when Sirola was in the United States: it reflects his always sceptical mind.

Sirola did not leave for America on his own initiative; he was invited to work as head in the Finnish Workers' College of Duluth. Sirola taught e.g. history, poetry, evolutionary theory, hygiene, the Finnish language and Socialist tactics. As to his conception of Socialism and its strategies, the following answer by one of his pupils in an examination is illustrative. To the question "what is Socialism", this pupil answered in somewhat clumsy language:[31]

> One calls Socialism the revolutionary rise of the modern industrial workers as a determining factor through ending of the governance of means of big production and distribution and wage slavery, being effected this by the compulsion of social-economic development and through it.

Sirola returned to Finland in December 1913. After the February Revolution, in May 1917, the SDP sent Sirola and K. H. Wiik to Stockholm to explore the opinions of Swedish and other Social Democratic leaders regarding Finland. At this time, Stockholm was a centre of various diplomacies because Sweden was neutral in the war. The so-called Zimmerwaldians prepared a third Conference of this anti-war movement in Stockholm. For the Finnish Social Democrats, the most important task was to gain support for the independence of Finland. Many Socialist leaders, however, had no sympathy for the Finnish case: Socialists in entente countries were against the decimation of Russia, their ally in the war. When Sirola met Karl Kautsky, the latter realised that Sirola did not at all understand the essence of capitalism and imperialism. It was against objective historical laws to try to create new small states. However, Sirola also met a representative of the Bolshevik Party, K. B. Radek, and was delighted to learn that the Bolsheviks supported Finnish independence without reservation. Sirola was a representative of the SDP in the third Zimmerwald meeting in Stockholm on September 5, 1917. There were delegates from only 11 countries, to whom Sirola delivered a speech on Finnish independence. Sirola also had contacts with the Finnish Activists.[32] In the summer of 1917 it was still possible for him to discuss matters more or less fraternally with the representatives of the *Jäger* movement.

Sirola returned to Finland in mid-October. He had been elected to the *Eduskunta* in the new elections and when the Workers' Revolutionary Central Council was formed on November 9, 1917, Sirola was appointed secretary.[33]

It seems that Sirola's position with regard to the Socialist coup d´état was as vacillating as that of Kuusinen. He was on November 15, 1918 against a coup,[34]

---

[31] Salomaa, *Yrjö Sirola*, pp. 155–156.

[32] *Ibid.*, pp. 170–203.

[33] *Ibid.*, pp. 204–206.

[34] *Ibid.*, p. 210.

but in the meeting of the Social Democratic parliamentary group on November 21, 1917, he suggested a coup and the election of a Red government. This proposal lost in the vote (36 votes for, 42 votes against).[35]

As we have seen, Sirola was – with Kuusinen and Manner – one of the main protagonists of revolution, although he was not sure of the "nature" of the revolution. The preparation of the coup evinced amateurish features. In the night of January 26–27, 1918, Kuusinen, Sirola and Manner drafted a proclamation to the "inhabitants of Helsinki" which was distributed around the city on January 27. The proclamation announced that members of the Senate had been arrested. Nobody, however, even tried to arrest the senators, who had their regular meeting before they went underground. When the real situation in respect of the senators became known, Sirola, on the day when the coup began (January 27), wrote the following letter to the Party Committee of the SDP:[36]

> Because I am seriously guilty of criminal incompetence, which must cause incalculable damage, I ask to be assigned some insignificant post of commissar in which I cannot commit such stupidities.

Sirola's resignation was, of course, not accepted; instead he was appointed People's Deputy of Foreign Affairs. The letter may seem foolish when we take into account the situation in which it was written. There is surely no doubt, however, as to the sincerity of his announcement. One of Sirola's problems was his continuous self-doubt.

On February 15, Sirola met Lenin in Petrograd. The Bolshevik leader told him that because Germany had recognised the Soviet government in Brest-Litovsk, it was not out of the question that Germany might recognise the Red government in Finland as well.[37]

Sirola was in Petrograd again in mid-April. His task was now to prepare for the coming of Finnish refugees to Russia. He asked the People's Deputation to acquire textbooks, dictionaries, scientific literature, as well as belles-lettres for the trains carrying the refugees, often to remote areas. As Rinta-Tassi remarks, it is illustrative of Sirola's personality that he made such requests in a situation in which both physical and mental pressures were high.[38]

For Sirola, the flight of the Red leaders to Russia was a complex and difficult moral question. Upon his arrival in Petrograd, he wrote a letter to the "Warriors of the Red Guard and all participants in the Finnish workers' revolution and to comrades who have had to suffer because of it". He deplored the poor preparation for

---

[35] Rinta-Tassi, *Kansanvaltuuskunta punaisen Suomen hallituksena*, p. 56.

[36] *Ibid.*, p. 98.

[37] Salomaa, *Yrjö Sirola*, pp. 240–241.

[38] Rinta-Tassi, *Kansanvaltuuskunta punaisen Suomen hallituksena*, p. 486.

the revolution and this not only in a material but also in a "spiritual" regard. He also deliberated whether the revolution was really needed or could have been prevented. The result was that "I leave it to be solved by objective historical writing". Of his own role Sirola wrote:[39]

> As to myself, I grievously confess that my conscience urged me to prepare [for the revolution], but I did not do so. I can, of course, make excuses in my defence, but at the same time I know that defence means confession of guilt.

I do not know whether this letter remained private; I have not seen it published. Sirola thought he was not guilty of the revolution, but of its poor preparation he confessed his error. What better preparation would actually have meant, remains open. As we shall see, this kind of self-castigation continued in Russia.

In Russia Sirola held a number of different posts. In 1919–1920 he was chairman of the SKP. In 1921 he worked as a journalist in Petrograd, a teacher in a rudimentary Party School in Lempaala (near Petrograd) and in Party and Comintern work in Moscow. In spring 1922, he worked in the service of the Comintern in Germany, and in the autumn of 1922 Sirola was a teacher of economy and head of the Communist University of Western Minority Nationalities[40] in Petrograd. In 1923, he worked in the service of the Comintern in Sweden. In late autumn Sirola returned to the above-mentioned university as a teacher of historical materialism. In 1925–1926, he worked for the Comintern in the United States and in 1926, again in the university and for some time in Karelia.[41] – This information derives from a letter to the members of the Politburo of the SKP in January 1927. I have not seen so detailed a *curriculum vitae* since. It seems that Sirola's life became somewhat more serene. He taught in the Lenin School[42] in Moscow and participated in Party and Comintern work.

One may ask whether as a young man Sirola made a sensible and rational decision when he engaged in politics. A career of, say, a social scientist, would possibly have been more apposite. – Sirola's death was natural. According to his biographer,

---

39 Yrjö Sirola, *Punasen Kaartin taistelijoille ja kaikille Suomen työväen vallankumoukseen osaaottaneille ja sen johdosta kärsimään joutuneille tovereille*. RGASPI, f. 525, op. 1, d. 3, ll. 2–3.)

40 Students participated in courses several years; according to Arvo Tuominen (*Kremlin kellot : muistelmia vuosilta 1933–1939*, p. 54) the "complete course" took four years. "Western minority nationalities" meant (at least) Estonians, Finns, Latvians, Lithuanians and Karelians.

41 Yrjö Sirola to the members of the Politburo of the SKP, Jan. 7, 1927. Published in *"Kallis toveri Stalin!" : Komintern ja Suomi* (hereafter abriged as KtS!), pp. 216–219.

42 Lenin School was important institute of political education. The Finnish "sector" was established in the late 1920s. The course took two years; previous studies e.g. in the Communist University of Western Minority Nationalities were, at least in principle, required. (Tuominen, *Kremlin kellot : muistelmia vuosilta 1933–1939*, pp. 56–65.)

Erkki Salomaa, charges were being collected against him while he was still living, but he died before arrest.[43]

Adolf Taimi

(Адольф Тайми, 1881–1954)

Of the persons presented here, Adolf Taimi is the only one to leave published memoirs.[44] The book appeared in Petrozavodsk in 1954. It covers Taimi's childhood in St. Petersburg, his work as an engraver in various metallurgical firms in Russia and Finland, his activities in the Russian Social Democratic Labour Party from 1902 and in the Finnish Social Democratic Party in 1917–1918. Taimi's memoirs do not cover his activities in the Finnish Communist Party except for his illegal work in Helsinki, his arrest and prison years in Finland 1928–1940. Taimi makes no mention of his brother or half-brother Aleksander Vasten, who like Taimi was a noteworthy Russian-Finnish Bolshevik,[45] but was not so deeply involved in the internal quarrels of the SKP as Taimi in the 1920s. The reason for this depersonalisation is Vasten's imprisonment in September 1937;[46] he was shot in Leningrad in January 1938.[47] Taimi himself was very probably saved from the same fate only because he was at the time in a secure Finnish prison in Riihimäki.

Taimi, who belonged to the Bolshevik faction of his Party, was arrested in 1906 and deported to the small town of Nikolski in the Northern Ural region. He escaped to St. Petersburg the following year and there met Nadezhda Konstantinovna Krupskaia, his Party contact, who, realising that Taimi spoke Finnish, sent him to Helsinki. There Taimi obtained work in a dock used by the Russian fleet and was involved in a "Military Committee" engaged in Bolshevik agitation in the Russian army. Taimi was also in contact with the mysterious "Struggle Group of Finnish Social Democrats". Regarding this group, Taimi tells us only that the Military Committee received money from it in the spring of 1907.[48]

---

[43] Salomaa, *Yrjö Sirola*, p. 345.

[44] A. Taimi, *Sivuja eletystä.*

[45] Taimi's original surname was Vasten; he officially changed his name in Finland in 1906 for conspirational reasons.

[46] Taimi's wife Liubov Taimi, who was probably in Moscow, wrote to Adolf Taimi in December, 1937: "I write nothing about your brother, but do not expect a letter from him". (Extract from Liubov Taimi's letter to Adolf Taimi; the letter arrived Dec. 13, 1937. Ek-Valpo I, PF 1279, Adolf Taimi, KA.)

[47] Eila Lahti-Argutina, *Olimme joukko vieras vaan : venäjänsuomalaiset vainouhrit Neuvostoliitossa 1930-luvun alusta 1950-luvun alkuun*, p. 560.

[48] Taimi, *Sivuja eletystä*, pp. 91–107 and 114–118. The "Group" may be simply the SDP. It may also have been some Activist group. (Cf. Kujala, *Vallankumous ja kansallinen itsemääräämisoikeus*, p. 264 and 272.) Taimi was well educated and followed the rules of conspirationism even some 50 years later: for instance, no names are mentioned.

Taimi was imprisoned in 1912 and deported to Siberia for four years. There, in Podkamennaia Tunguska, he studied Marxist literature, which could be borrowed from a library, formed of books belonging to earlier deportees. He also read *Pravda* and *Prosveshchenie*, a periodical which was in inexplicably far-sighted because it was, so Taimi announces, a "Leninist-Stalinist magazine". – The usual hobbies of the deportees were hunting and fishing.[49] The life of a political *éxilé* was not very hard in the Tsarist times.[50]

After the February revolution, Taimi returned from Siberia to Petrograd. In April 1917 he was again sent to Helsinki, where he worked as an engraver. His political task involved maintaining contacts between the Russian Bolshevik Helsinki Town Committee and the SDP.[51] In this capacity, Taimi participated in the June Congress of the Social Democratic Party [52] and in the extraordinary Congress on November 25–27, 1917, where he urged the Finns to make a revolution.[53] In a meeting of the Workers' Order Guards in Tampere on December 16–18, 1917, it was decreed that the Guards should take no independent political action, but had to submit to the Party Committee of the SDP. Taimi did not accept this and when, on December 20, he explained the situation to the Red Guard in Helsinki, the meeting proclaimed that the Guard would not obey the decisions of the Tampere meeting. Taimi operated in accordance with the Bolshevik-led Soviet of Helsinki, which consisted of Russian soldiers, but Osmo Rinta-Tassi doubts that he had any direct contacts with Petrograd.[54] In January, Taimi was among those who were elected to the Party Committee of the SDP as "external members".[55] During the rebellion, he became the second People's Deputy for Internal Affairs, which entailed maintaining relations with the Red Guards.[56] That office was one of the most important in the People's Deputation. Taimi's relations with the other Deputy, Eero Haapalainen, were not entirely comprehensible. Haapalainen was commander-in-chief of the Red Guard and Taimi something like a minister of war. Haapalainen, however, was unseated because of his excessive drinking.[57] In his stead, a triumvirate was ap-

---

[49] Taimi, *Sivuja eletystä*, pp. 176–177.

[50] Lenin's comfortable life in deportation has been described in many biographies. (See e.g. Dimitri Volgogonov, *Le vrai Lénine : d'après les archives secrètes soviétiques*, pp. 53–55.) Trotskii's case corroborates this impression. (See e.g. Dmitri Volgogonov, *Trotsky : the Eternal Revolutionary*, pp. 13–15 and also Trotskii's own record in Leon Trotsky, *My Life : an Attempt at an Autobiography*, pp. 129–137.)

[51] Taimi, *Sivuja eletystä*, pp. 176–177.

[52] Suomen Sosialidemokratisen Puolueen yhdeksännen puoluekokouksen pöytäkirja (minutes of the XIXth Congress of the SDP, Helsinki, June 15–18, 1917), p. 62.

[53] Soikkanen, *Kohti kansanvaltaa*, vol. 1, p. 248.

[54] Rinta-Tassi, *Kansanvaltuuskunta punaisen Suomen hallituksena*, pp. 66–67.

[55] *Ibid.*, p. 76. The other "extra members" were Eero Haapalainen, Antti Kiviranta, Lauri Letonmäki and Emil Elo.

[56] *Ibid.*, p. 104.

[57] *Ibid.*, pp. 179–181.

pointed; its members were Taimi, Eino Rahja and Evert Eloranta (People's Deputy for Agriculture) on March 20, 1918. As Jussi T. Lappalainen points out, it was notable that two Peterburgians (Taimi and Eino Rahja) were now at the head of military action.[58] Both were, moreover, Bolsheviks. This did not, however, save the disastrous military situation and the Collegium was in power only until April 10. Later, in the 1920s, Taimi entered Finland illegally – as he had already done in 1922–1923 – but was soon arrested and imprisoned. He was handed over after the Winter War in 1940, together with Toivo Antikainen, to the Soviet authorities on the demand of the government of the Soviet Union.

During the Winter War there were quarrels in Riihimäki prison, where the Communists were kept. The "Prison Council", a secret leadership formed by the Communists and comprising mainly a new generation of Communist leaders, most of them educated in Russia in the 1930s, sent to the Russian authorities a very negative report on Taimi's behaviour and political attitudes. They accused him of Rahjaism; Taimi criticised the Council for excessive prudence.[59] In the Soviet Union Taimi was sent to Soviet Karelia and he no longer participated in the activities of the SKP.

Johan Henrik Lumivuokko

(Ю. Г. Лумивуокко, 1884–1938)

J. H. Lumivuokko's background was in the trade union movement. He was chairman of the Timber Workers' Association in 1911–1916 and a member of the *Eduskunta* in 1914 and 1917–1918. In the SDP Lumivuokko was a vice-member of the Party Committee from 1911 and a full member from 1913.[60] When Oskari Tokoi's Senate was formed in March 1917, Tokoi resigned from the post of chairman of the Trade Union Federation; Lumivuokko was elected in his stead. He, in turn, resigned from the post of chairman of the parliamentary group of the SDP.[61] In 1917 the trade union leaders were usually more radical than the Party leaders. Lumivuokko proposed a coup d'état in the Revolutionary Central Council in November 16, 1917. When the majority did not follow the trade unionists, Lumivuokko is said to have remarked bitterly that whenever the trade unionists "give themselves up to politicians", they lose. When Lumivuokko was invited to join the revolutionary government, he reportedly did so without enthusiasm.[62]

---

58 Jussi T. Lappalainen, *Punakaartin sota*, vol. 1, pp. 128.

59 Rentola, *Kenen joukoissa seisot*, pp. 192–193. See also S. Hj. Rantanen, *Kuljin SKP:n tietä*, pp. 64–66.

60 Ala-Kapee & Valkonen, *Yhdessä elämä turvalliseksi*, p. 247.

61 *Ibid.*, pp. 391–392.

62 Rinta-Tassi, *Kansanvaltuuskunta punaisen Suomen hallituksena*, pp. 128–129.

In the People's Deputation Lumivuokko held the important post of People's Deputy for Labour. Under him, the administration of labour affairs was divided into five departments: commerce, industry, shipping and pilotage, public works and social affairs. Later a further eleven subdepartments were created along trade union lines; in point of fact, the most important unions were ordered to form these subdepartments and many of their leaders and functionaries (secretaries, rabble-rousers etc.) became state officials.[63] Had the revolution continued, some kind of corporatist structure might have been a result.

In Russia Lumivuokko was a member of the Politburo of the SKP. In 1927 he was invited to Soviet Karelia, where he held high posts; he was, e.g. chairman of the Radio Committee of Petrozavodsk. He also, however, participated in meetings of the leaders of the SKP in Moscow. In 1929 Lumivuokko expressed his "heavy feeling" and "pessimism" because now again an opposition, in this case Bukharin's Opposition in the VKP(b) had become a factor of internal struggle.[64] From 1935 or 1936, he worked for the MOPR.[65] Posts in the MOPR were some kind of dump for unreliable elements. Lumivuokko was arrested in January 1938 and shot in the February of that year.[66]

Toivo Antikainen

(Тойво Антикайнен, 1898–1941)

Toivo Antikainen was born to a working-class family in Helsinki. His father was an upholsterer. Although the family was large, eight children, and lived in one room, it clearly belonged to those (skilled) working-class families in which there was upward mobilisation. In the Antikainen family this meant, above all, education for the children. For this there was not enough money, but the eldest son, Väinö, was put to a (for a working-class family) relatively expensive secondary school; the others remained at primary school, Toivo Antikainen six years. All children were members of the *Ihanneliitto* ("Ideal League"), the child organisation of the Social

[63] *Ibid.*, pp. 231–233.

[64] Minutes of the Plenum of the Central Committee of the SKP (hereafter abridged to MPCC) in April 13–18, 1929, p. 142. (Page numbers of this documents are those added in the archive.) Kullervo Manner replied that "feelings must play no significant part in politics. [...] Beating is a political necessity". (*Ibid.*, p. 165.)

[65] Международная организация помощи борцам революции (International Organisation for Aid to Revolutionary Fighters). Lumivuokko's depression is reflected in an article he wrote to a local newspaper about the work of the MOPR. (J. Lumivuokko, "MOPR:n työstä Sovietti-Karjalassa", *Punainen Karjala*, Sept. 24, 1936.) Lumivuokko complained of the results of collection of money for the MOPR. Only the unit of the NKVD had done its duty in exemplary manner.

[66] Lahti-Argutina, *Olimme joukko vieras vain*, p. 313.

Democratic Party.[67] The cells of the *Ihanneliitto* were alternatives to Sunday Schools; it was usual for their meetings to be held on Sundays at the same time as these. There the children listened to short (10–15 minutes) lectures on subjects like "Why should workers have an eight-hour working day", "Why should one avoid and oppose alcoholic beverages", "Why is it not possible for worker children to have secondary and university education".[68]

In 1917, Antikainen participated in the formation of the Red Guard. In the Civil War, he was not sent to the front; he worked in the Helsinki Revolutionary Committee.[69] In April he escaped to Russia, where he sympathised with the Opposition, i.e. the later Murder Opposition, but in the spring of 1920 at the latest gave his support to the Central Committee led by Kullervo Manner. Antikainen took part in the first Red Officer Course, organised in Petrograd 1918–1919; he was *primus* in his course. He then fought in Soviet Karelia (at the time known as the "Karelian Commune") against Finnish military expeditions and local White Karelians. In 1920–1923, he continued his studies in the Petrograd International War School, being at the same time an instructor in machine-gun training and tactics. At the same time, at least until 1922, Antikainen fought again in Soviet Karelia. In 1922, his rank was that of *efreitor* or corporal, as can be seen in his uniform (plate B). Later, in 1935, Antikainen was prosecuted in Finland for the mysterious murder of a Finnish White soldier in Kiimasjärvi, in Soviet Karelia, in 1922. It was claimed that Antikainen and his comrades burned this soldier alive over a campfire.[70]

Antikainen was an officer in the Red army until 1925.[71] He then became one of most important leaders of the Party. He was made a member of the Politburo in 1923. In 1934, he was sent on illegal work in Finland, where he was soon arrested and condemned to life imprisonment for the murder (in Kiimasjärvi). In prison, Antikainen began to ask questions about imprisonments of Finnish Communists in Russia. After the Winter War, he was extradited, together with Adolf Taimi, to the Soviet Union. There he also gave evidence of an independent mind. He protested against writings about Finland in *Pravda*. There was false information about strikes and wages paid to workers there, and exaggerations; it was, for example, declared that because all workers had been sent to the front, there was no industrial production.[72] He died in a mysterious air crash in 1941. It is not known whether

[67] Uljas Vikström, *Toiska : kertomus Toivo Antikaisen elämästä*, pp.7–9.

[68] Aura Kiiskinen, *Vuosikymmenien takaa : muistelmia*, p. 63.

[69] Vikström, *Toiska*, p. 22.

[70] Ensio Hiitonen, *Vääryyttä oikeuden valekaavussa*, pp. 323–352. Antikainen's defense counsel, A. Rydling from Sweden, obtained a statement from the Swedish Crematorium Authorities, according to which the burning of a human being over a campfire, so that only bones are left, as it was argued, is not possible (*ibid.*, p. 343).

[71] This did not prevent his illegal work in 1924–1925.

[72] Toivo Antikainen to Georgi Dimitrov, Sept. 4, 1941. KtS!, pp. 463–464.

this accident was organised by the Russian authorities or was its cause a technical fault.

2. The Murder Opposition

Voitto Eloranta

(Виктор-Войто Элоранто, 1876–1923)

Voitto Eloranta is one of most mysterious and enigmatic personages among the leaders of the Murder Opposition. In Finland his wife, Elvira Willman-Eloranta, was perhaps more famous than her husband, but not due to her political activities: she was a playwright whose works were performed on the most prestigious stage among Finnish theatres, that of the Finnish National Theatre in Helsinki. Earlier on, Willman had participated in a variety of political activities; she belonged the Young Finn Party, and helped to organise a conscription strike at the beginning of the 1900s. She and Voitto Eloranta married in 1906. Eloranta was a primary school teacher by education, but at that time an editor of *Työmies*, the organ of the Social Democratic Party. In 1907, he was elected to the first *Eduskunta*, but later he failed to gain election to Parliament.

A little later, the Elorantas bought a farm in Leppävaara, close to Helsinki, and grew fruits and vegetables and raised pigs – a considerable number[73] –, which was an aggravating factor in the future court in Petrograd; was he not a kulak?[74]

During the Civil War Voitto Eloranta worked in the headquarters of the Red Guard in the small town of Kouvola. Willman-Eloranta and her son (born in 1907[75]) left for Russia when it became clear that the Whites would soon conquer Eastern Finland. Eloranta hid in Kouvola, or somewhere in Finland, after the Whites had conquered the whole country.[76] He escaped to Russia in the autumn, perhaps in September 1918. Later in Russia this hiding generated accusations that he was an agent of the "slaughterers". Eloranta was the only member of the Murder Opposition who was executed in the 1920s (in 1923). – Of Elvira Willman-Eloranta it is

---

[73] Martta Salmela-Järvinen, *Alas lyötiin vanha maailma : muistikuvia ja näkymiä vuosilta 1906–1918*, pp. 72–74. The Elorantas had a car, a rare means of transport in those days.

[74] An untitled document about the Finnish case, attached to the minutes of the Organisation bureau (Организационное бюро, or Orgbyro) of the CC of the RKP(b), Jan 16, 1921, § 26. RGASPI, f. 17, op. 112, d. 112.

[75] This son, Voitto Ilmari Eloranta published his memoirs in 2000 (*Poika vallankumouksen jaloissa*). He was able to return to Finland in early 1920s.

[76] Maarit Vallinharju, "Elvira Willman-Eloranta : ihanteellinen sosialisti" in *Tiennäyttäjät*, vol. 1, p. 379.

now known that she was a household servant in Moscow. She was arrested in July 1924 and executed in April 1925.[77]

Väinö Pukka

(Вяйнэ Пукке,[78] 1895–1935)

We know nothing of Pukka's background except that he was born in Sippola, near the town of Kotka in Southeast Finland. It is probable that Pukka attended school for some years. He went to Petrograd as a very young man because in 1918, when we have the first evidence of his activities in Russia. This was by no means uncommon; many ambitious Finns tried their luck in the Russian metropolis.[79] In 1913 Pukka studied at the Party School of the Finnish Social Democratic Party in Finland.[80] He was at this time only eighteen years old; it is possible that he went to Russia after completing that school.

We do not know where Pukka worked in Petrograd; it is possible that he had a job for some time in a laundry because in later battles he was to be elected to Congresses etc. as a representative of the Finnish co-operational laundry, the named *Taisto* (Struggle). Be this as may, one trait in Pukka's behaviour indicates that he was an ambitious man. In most cases, Finnish workers who came from Finland to Petrograd spoke only very little, or not at all, Russian. Pukka was an exception. By reason of his fluent Russian he was an interpreter on the Russian side in the first diplomatic contacts between the Russian and Finnish governments in Berlin in summer 1918.

During the Civil War, the People's Deputation appointed Jukka Rahja a representative of the "Republic of Finland" to Petrograd. His assistants were Pukka and Hugo Jalava.[81] Jukka Rahja, however, was soon wounded in a clash with Finnish Whites who tried to prevent the access of a train carrying arms and other war material to the Reds. Pukka now soon assumed his tasks as "ambassador".[82]

---

77 Lahti-Argutina, *Olimme joukko vieras vain*, p. 571.

78 The name was in Russian also spelled Пукка and sometimes Пуккэ.

79 There were, according to one study, 21,000 citizens of Finland in Russia in the 1910s before WW I, most of them in Petrograd and in the guberniia of Petrograd. (Pekka Nevalainen, *Punaisen myrskyn suomalaiset : suomalaisten paot ja paluumuutot idästä 1917–1939*, pp. 30–32 and p. 331, n. 36.)

80 Ehrnrooth, *Sanan vallassa, vihan voimalla*, p. 531.

81 Hugo Jalava is better known as an engine-driver than as a diplomat. On August 22 / September 4, 1917, he helped V. I. Lenin to escape from Russia to Finland, disguised as an engine-fireman. (Г. Э. Ялава, "'Кочегар' паровоза № 293" ин *Воспоминания о Владимире Ильиче Ленине*, vol. 1, pp. 532–533.)

82 Väinö Pukka, "an envoy of the Republic of Finland in Russia" to the People's Deputation of Finland, March 22, 1918. RGASPI, f. 516, op. 1, 1918, d. 138.

From Berlin Pukka sent a letter to the "Central Committee of the Foreign Organisation of the Finnish Social Democrats", which functioned before the founding Congress of the SKP. It was a surprise to Pukka that the Russian delegation knew, according to him, next to nothing about Finland and did not take into account the Manifesto of the Provisional Government concerning the rights of the Finnish people.[83] It seems that he felt he had been drawn into a contradictory situation. It is not known whether Pukka silently supported the demands of the Finnish delegation. According to them, Russia should cede to Finland the Murmansk area, the Kola Peninsula and the whole of East Karelia.[84]

Pukka had ambitious plans to write large books on various subjects in the social sciences. Some among the SKP considered these plans an indication of megalomania; however, he went to study in the Sverdlov Workers' University, and in the Far East, on the coast of the Pacific Ocean, where he was deported in 1923 or 1924. Pukka, "a red professor", became known as a proficient and industrious author: he wrote several small books, mainly on trade unions. These works are remarkably free of the jargon typical of Soviet books on the workers' movement. According to one book published in 1929, twelve of his books (or booklets) were translated into Chinese, three into Korean and two into Japanese.[85]

3. The Rahja Opposition

Jukka Rahja

(Иван Абрамович Рахья, 1887–1920)

Jukka Rahja was a smith, born in Kronstadt. His parents were immigrants from Ostrobothnia, Finland. Jukka Rahja was very young when he, in 1903 it is said, joined the Russian Social Democratic Labour Party.[86] In 1905, he participated in a revolt in Kronstadt; after this was quelled, he fled to Finland.[87] It is unfortunately not possible to form a coherent picture of Rahja's political activities in Finland

---

[83] Väinö Pukka (in Berlin), to the CC of the Foreign Organisation of Finnish Social Democrats. RGASPI, f. 516, op. 1, d. 288. The letter is not dated, but probably written in mid-August, 1918. – The Central Committee in question was an organisation of the Finnish Red refugees in Russia.

[84] Tuomo Polvinen, *Venäjän vallankumous ja Suomi 1917–1920*, vol. 2, p. 55.

[85] Вяйнэ Пукке, *Международные объединения профессиональных союзов : популярные ДВ краевой школы профдвижения ДКСПС во Владивостоке в мае месяце 1929 года*, pp. 32–35. – One book deals with the development of industry, or lack of industry, in Far Eastern countries, including India and trade unions in these countries. (Вяйнэ Пукке, *Тихокеанский секретариат профессиональный союзов*.)

[86] *Большой энциклопедический словарь*, vol. 2, p. 246.

[87] Marja-Leena Salkola, *Työväenkaartien synty ja kehitys punakaartiksi*, vol. 2, p. 253.

from 1906 to 1913, when he moved back to Russia.[88] In 1908, he is found in the small town of Kuopio in the province of Savo. He took part in the activities of the Social Democratic youth organisation there. In Kuopio there existed a clandestine organisation which advocated violent means and, according to Hannu Soikkanen, committed a few "revolutionary robberies".[89] It may well be that Jukka Rahja, a Bolshevik, had something to do with these robberies. At least he saw nothing wrong in terror if the "circumstances" demanded it.[90]

The next point in time for which I found information on Jukka Rahja is in 1912. He was still participating in the activities of the above-said youth organisation, e.g. as a speaker in its local groups.[91] He lived at that time in Adolf Taimi's flat in Helsinki. Taimi claims that he and his fellow conspirators found Jukka Rahja too "wavering" to be suitable for underground work and therefore Rahja knew nothing of Taimi's affairs.[92] This explanation is not at all credible.

When Jukka Rahja moved to Petrograd, he became an important personage, e.g. co-founder with his brother Eino Rahja of the Finnish Red Guard after the February revolution. Although information is only from 1917, i.e. four years are unaccounted for, it is not plausible that Jukka Rahja's political activity only began in 1917, when the Finnish Red Guards were formed. Before February, when no public political activities were permitted, there had been various forms of activities, such as the Finnish temperance societies, sports associations, amateur theatres and choirs. There were covers for political activities and the Finnish societies which had contacts with Russian Socialist organisations.[93] Taimi's information is obviously biased, because later he was one of the main opponents of the Rahja Opposition.

In May 1917, Jukka Rahja was elected a member of the Petrograd town committee of the Bolshevik Party.[94] He appeared at the Petrograd Conference of the Bolshevik Party in May and spoke there about the Finnish Social Democratic Party. He said:[95]

> The Finnish Party has always striven, in these two decades it has existed, for unity and this unity there in external forms also reigns. In fact, the situation is not at all

[88] Polvinen, *Venäjän vallankumous ja Suomi*, vol. 1, p. 71, n. 2.

[89] Soikkanen, *Sosialismin tulo Suomeen*, p. 240.

[90] Pöytäkirja Suomen Sosialidemokratisen Nuorisoliiton II:sta edustajakokouksesta Vaasassa 6–8 p. kesäk. 1908, p. 27.

[91] Aimo Kairamo, *Ponnistuksien kautta vapauteen : Sosialidemokraattisen nuorisoliikkeen historia*, vol. 1, *1906–1922*, p. 177.

[92] Taimi, *Sivuja eletystä*, p. 152.

[93] Arvid Luhtakanta, *Suomen punakaarti*, pp. 221–222

[94] Salkola, *Työväenkaartien synty ja kehitys punakaartiksi*, vol. 2, p. 253.

[95] Cited after Polvinen, *Venäjän vallankumous ja Suomi*, vol. 1, p. 117.

> so good. Only iron discipline conceals this. Strive to pay attention to what can be achieved at once instead of aims that are directed to the final solution, means to leave to the smooth road of opportunism.

Jukka Rahja, like Aleksandra Kollontai, participated as an "invited guest"[96] in the SDP Congress in June 1917 as a representative of the Bolshevik group of the Russian Social Democratic Labour Party. He behaved there like a *Besserwisser*, know-all, which brought him into conflict with O. W. Kuusinen and Kullervo Manner. The quarrel with Kuusinen concerned the question of the Party's international affiliation. A committee of the Congress presented a proposal on international affiliation in which no unambiguous standpoint was taken. The committee suggested founding a committee to study the matter and to make a proposal in the unspecified future. After this suggestion was presented to the Congress, Jukka Rahja, who, of course, wanted the Party to join the Zimmerwald International, declared that if the proposal of the committee was accepted by the Congress, the Party "would be manifesting its ignorance of the international political activity of workers".[97] O. W. Kuusinen reacted to the declaration saying that "these Zimmerwaldians, Scheidemanns, Thomases etc. are for us very dim concepts"; in principle, however, Kuusinen did not oppose membership in the Zimmerwald International.[98] When Aleksandra Kollontai also recommended joining the Zimmerwald, the Party did so. This was obviously a result of Kollontai's tactful behaviour,[99] not that of Jukka Rahja's agitation.

The second controversy concerned the Senate. A committee of the Congress recommended that the Congress accept the presence of the Social Democrats in the Senate because the circumstances were exceptional. Jukka Rahja now announced that when the Senate was formed – it was, we should remember, appointed by the Provisional Government – the Finnish Social Democrats negotiated in Petrograd with "all sorts of bourgeois". He concluded his speech saying, "when the Social

---

[96] This word (*kutsuvieras*) was used in the Congress. The SDP had sent an invitation to all "groups" of "Russian brother parties". (*Suomen Sosialidemokratisen Puolueen yhdeksännen puoluekokouksen pöytäkirja : kokous pidetty Helsingissä kesäkuun 15–18 p:nä 1917*, pp. 5–6.)

[97] *Ibid.*, pp. 82–83.

[98] *Ibid.*, pp. 86–87.

[99] She began her speech as follows: "As a guest I really should have no right to present to the meeting anything special, but considering that the question of belonging to international Social Democracy is very important not only to the Finnish Party but also extremely important to the Russian Social Democratic Party, I ask to express some ideas." Moreover, after presenting her arguments, which also were creamed with courteous remarks about the importance of the Finns, Kollontai finished her speech: "Let the Finnish Social Democratic Party express in this matter its clear and conscious word, so that it is not possible to interpret this word in one or other way. For it means much more than one can measure at the moment, if the strong and well organised Finnish Social Democratic Party has clearly stated its opinion in the question of the building of the new International." (*Ibid.*, pp. 83–885.)

Democratic Party accepts the proposal of the committee, the Party gives thereby twofold proof of its poor class consciousness". Here Manner, who was in chair, stated that it may be "understandable" if a "guest ran down a person he had invited" but if he lies about the Social Democratic delegation, it is not acceptable.[100]

I presume that the embryo of the future quarrels between Kuusinen and the Rahja brothers lay in this Congress. Jukka Rahja in his arrogance threatened Kuusinen's intellectual authority and dignity, something which for Kuusinen perhaps was more serious than official positions in the leadership.

Immediately after the Bolsheviks had seized power in Petrograd, the Bolshevik Oblast, or Area Committee of Finland, as the body was called, nominated one seaman, P. Shisko as Governor-General[101] of Finland and Jukka Rahja as his assistant. When the bourgeois Senate refused to accept them, Jukka Rahja threatened that the workers of Russia, like Rahja himself, would not remain outside when the struggle against the bourgeoisie took place. Jukka Rahja soon lost his official position in Finland when the Bolshevik government on December 4 nominated, the Area Committee as such as the representative body of Russia in Finland.[102] This, however, did not prevent Jukka Rahja from advocating, with Taimi, the establishment of the dictatorship of the proletariat in Finland.[103] In the meeting of the Council of the SDP on January 19–22, 1918, Jukka Rahja agitated against all parliamentary activities and for armed uprising.[104] After the meeting, he went to Petrograd and began to organise arms to be sent to Finland. A train carrying weapons, among them 10 field guns, left Petrograd for Finland on January 27, 1918. On the Finnish side of the border, the local Whites tried to stop the train.[105] In the following battle, Jukka Rahja was so badly injured in the leg that he lay in a Petrograd hospital until the decisive battles of the Civil War were over. His brother Eino Rahja was nominated chief of the train and it arrived in Tampere on February 2.[106] Jukka Rahja perished in the murders in the Kuusinen Club in Petrograd on August 31, 1920.

---

[100] Suomen Sosialidemokratisen Puolueen yhdeksännen puoluekokouksen pöytäkirja, p. 114.

[101] Under Tsarism, a Governor-General was the Grand Duke's highest representative in Finland and chairman of the Senate. Under the Provisional Government the post remained, but the Governor-General did not usually participate in the meetings of the Senate. On January 11, 1918, I. V. Stalin informed the Finnish (White) government in Helsinki that the Area Committee would remain an official Russian body in Finland until an agreement on diplomatic bodies of the respective Powers. (Ohto Manninen, "Sodanjohto ja strategia" in *Itsenäistymisen vuodet*, vol. 2, *Taistelu vallasta*, p. 44.)

[102] Polvinen, *Venäjän vallankumous ja Suomi*, vol. 1, pp. 121–122.

[103] Soikkanen, *Kohti kansanvaltaa*, vol. 1, p. 263.

[104] Excerpt from the minutes of the meeting of the Party Council of the SDP in *Kansalaissota dokumentteina*, vol. 2, p. 21.

[105] Jukka Rahja, "Kämärä" in *Punakaarti rintamalla : luokkasodan muistoja*, pp. 228–232.

[106] Jussi T. Lappalainen, *Punakaartin sota*, vol. 1, p. 58.

Eino Rahja

(Эйно Абрамович Рахья, 1885–1936)

It is difficult to obtain any reliable picture of Eino Rahja's political and other activities before 1917. He was not as well known as his brother. There is Nikolai Kondratiev's novel,[107] written according to the principles of Socialist Realism, and various data in the archives of the Finnish Detective Central Police. There must have been personal folders on him in various archives, because during his life he was a Chekist, an officer of the Red Army of Soviet Russia / the Soviet Union and an active member of the RKP(b) / VKP(b), as well as of the SKP; such material has not, however, been at my disposal.

Eino Rahja's background was similar to that of his brother Jukka. He was originally a metalworker, a turner. It is said that he joined, like his brother, the Bolshevik faction of the Russian Social Democratic Labour Party in 1903.[108] According to Kondratjev, Eino Rahja studied in a technical school in Helsinki, and was thereafter a foreman in various factories, probably also in an aircraft factory.[109] Rahja apparently participated in the World War and his subsequent rise in the Soviet military hierarchy was rocket-like. He might even have served as a pilot, because in the Finnish Civil War he was piloting, a rare phenomenon in that hapless war, an aeroplane. From his aircraft, Rahja even bombed the posts of the Whites, albeit without success.[110]

Eino Rahja's name became a legend in Soviet Russia because on several occasions in 1917 he helped V. I. Lenin to hide when the Provisional Government tried to arrest him.[111] Nor did his good services for the Lenin family end in the Bolshevik take-over: at the beginning of January 1918 he arranged the holiday trip of N. K. Krupskaia and Mariia Il'ichina Ul'ianova (Lenin's sister) to a sanatorium in East (Soviet) Karelia.[112]

In the Finnish Civil War Eino Rahja was a commander, often, in chaotic circumstances the only commander, who had some authority in Tampere, where the

---

[107] Nikolai Kondratjev, *Luotettava toveri*.

[108] At least so it is claimed in *Большой энциклопедический словарь*, vol. 2, p. 246.

[109] Kondratjev, *Luotettava toveri*, pp. 22–28.

[110] Ylikangas, *Tie Tampereelle*, p. 211.

[111] Polvinen, *Venäjän vallankumous ja Suomi*, vol. 1, p. 89; Robert Service, *Lenin : a Biography*, pp. 280–281). When Lenin returned to Russia, again with Eino Rahja, he was dressed as a Finnish Pastor of the Lutheran Church (*ibid.*, p. 303). Still on October 24, 1917, Lenin went from his hiding place to Smolna under the protection of Eino Rahja. According to Robert Service (*ibid.*, pp. 306–307), "Rahja's presence was crucial since he had no fear when confronted by inquisitive, boisterous soldiers."

[112] Rinta-Tassi, *Kansanvaltuuskunta punaisen Suomen hallituksena*, p. 83.

bitterest battles of the war were fought,[113] although even to him the rebellious Red troops shouted "go yourself" when he tried to send them to the front in a critical moment.[114] When Tampere was already encircled by the Whites, the Red troops under Rahja tried, at the end of March and the beginning of April, to open the way from and to Tampere with an armoured train. He was not successful, although the Reds in this operation fought with unusual dexterity and courage.[115] As we saw above, he was a member of the "triumvirate" established on March 20, 1918. Among other Red leaders, he escaped to Russia at the end of the war. There Eino Rahja joined the Workers' and Peasants' Red Army in July 1918. In the said army he was raised to the rank of *komkor*, commander of army corps (in 1940 the earlier rank of commander of an army corps was the same as that of major-general). In his collar badge there were three diamonds (four was the maximum) and he wore two medals of the Red Flag. He was decorated with this medal for the first time in 1922. (See Plate A.) It is not known when this picture was taken, but the military uniform he is wearing came into use in 1924.[116] According to the very brief obituary published in *Vapaus*, Eino Rahja retired in 1933.[117] When he was on pension, he dictated, according to Leo Laukki, his memoirs to a shorthand writer of *Ispart* in Leningrad.[118] It is not known where these memoirs are.

Among the Finnish Red refugees, the behaviour of the Rahja brothers created bitterness, as we shall see. Often the brothers were not distinguished from each other in wild rumours about their extravagant and depraved life. According to one story, the brothers lived in "some former palace of a Grand Duke with many women". There were funny and bitter anecdotes; it was said, for instance, that a "new Grigorii Efimovich Rasputin" (this probably meant Eino) had appeared in Russia.[119]

---

113 Ylikangas, *Tie Tampereelle*, p. 174.

114 *Ibid.*, p. 165.

115 *Ibid.*, pp. 368–389.

116 I thank professor Ohto Manninen for explaining Rahja's military rank.

117 "Eino Abramovitsh Rahja", *Vapaus*, April 24, 1936.

118 Leo Laukki to O. W. Kuusinen, Feb. 14, 1937. KtS!, p. 363.

119 Helena Hartikainen's examination record in the Finnish Detective Central Police, Jan. 9, 1920. PF 1064, Eino Rahja, KA. – A Rahja appears in the memoirs of famous Russian opera singer Fiodor Ivanovich Shaliapin. He relates that one evening there was at his home a Red entourage, including a "Finnish Communist Rahja". Shaliapin had Estonian potato vodka and everything went smoothly until someone began to speak about the theatre and actors. According to Shaliapin, Rahja announced that all people like Shaliapin should be executed because – Shaliapin quotes Rahja – "nobody must have advantages in relation to another". (Fjodor Šaljapin, *Šaljapin* in Maxim Gorki & Fjodor Šaljapin, *Šaljapin*; the reference is to memoirs written by Shaliapin himself, ch. 71, p. 457; the Russian original is titled *Маска и душа*.) It is impossible to say whether this Rahja was Jukka or Eino. It is probable that the party took place in 1918 or in 1919.

Kustaa Mikko Evä

(К. М. Евя, 1878/9–1927)

Our information on K. M. Evä is scanty. As a young man, he was for some time a dragoon in the Russian Army. He had thus some military experience badly needed on the Red side in the Civil War. After the army, Evä worked as a railway stationmaster in Tampere. In 1905, he joined the Social Democratic Party and in 1910, became a "reporter"[120] for *Kansan Lehti*, a Social Democratic newspaper published in Tampere; in 1916 he became a director of the cooperative fire insurance company *Turva*.[121]

In the Civil War, Kustaa Mikko Evä acted as a commander in Tampere. One of his tasks was to enrol men into the Red Guards, not only Finns, also Russians. With Russians there were many problems. Evä later complained, writing of the Finnish Civil War in the Soviet Union, that most officers were not interested in the Finnish Civil War at all, although they had to act as if they were sympathetic to the revolution. Among the ranks, there reigned a similar indifference. According to Evä, only a small minority were conscious of their duty to help the revolution. He also complained that the Finnish Reds hated or at least had an extremely negative attitude to the Russians. They were not, for instance, willing to fight under a Russian officer.[122]

At the beginning of March, Evä and four other commanders of the Reds, hemmed in Tampere by the Whites, took Finnish and Russian money from a bank, divided the haul, and escaped by a lake which was still frozen.[123] In mid-March Evä was able to get to Russia.[124] The People's Deputation founded at the end of March the Petrograd Department of the Maintenance Office of Finnish Workers, whose task was to enrol men into the Red Guard in Finland. This was directed by Evä. There were large staffs in this office, but how many, the sources do not state. A serious problem was the excessive drinking of the staff.[125] After the founding of the SKP, Evä became its secretary (second in the hierarchy). He was injured in the Kuusinen Club on August 31, 1920. In the Party Congress in 1921, he was not elected to the Central Committee. He became an editor of the Finnish-language daily in Petrograd, *Vapaus*. His injuries probably contributed to his death as a relatively young man.

---

[120] The word was new at the time. (Minutes of the board of directors of Tampereen Työväen Sanomalehti Oy [the publisher of the paper], Feb. 21, 1910. Työväen arkisto (Workers' Archives).)

[121] "Mikko Evä kuollut", *Suomen Sosialidemokraatti*, April 19, 1927.

[122] K. M. Evä, "Luokkasodan taistelutoimet luoteisella (pohjoisella) rintamalla" in *Punakaarti rintamalla : luokkasodan muistoja*, pp. 37–39.

[123] Ylikangas, *Tie Tampereelle*, pp. 463–466.

[124] K. L. Kulo, "Puolustimme Tamperetta" in *Luokkasodan muisto*, p. 116.

[125] Rinta-Tassi, *Kansanvaltuuskunta punaisen Suomen hallituksena*, p. 477.

Leo Laukki

(Лео Лаукки, 1880–1938)

Leo Laukki[126] was one of most colourful personages in the Finnish workers' movement. His background was modest: his father was a trumpeter in the Finnish Guard and his mother a washerwoman. In spite of economic hardship, Leo Laukki was able to attend lower secondary school for five years. During his eventful life, Laukki learnt at least five foreign languages.[127] After school, he went to Russia and studied in the South Russian Cavalry School. It seems that he graduated from that institute in the spring of 1905 as a lieutenant. He is also claimed to have deserted, but we know next to nothing about Laukki's sojourn in Russia. He did, however, return to Finland in 1905 and it was not at the time very wise to proclaim one's Russian military education. He had contacts with Russian revolutionaries, mainly, it seems with the Socialist Revolutionaries. It was said that Laukki educated himself in Russia by reading Socialist books.[128]

Laukki arrived in Helsinki in time to participate in the general strike in November 1905. He got in touch with the above-mentioned Activists. This group had contacts with the Russian soldiers, who, for the most part, were at the Viapori base. The Activists were by no means Socialists, but were anti-Russian and many, if not most of them, supported Socialists who demanded universal suffrage. During the general strike, Laukki participated in a few military manoeuvres with some mutinous Russian sailors who were often Bolsheviks or at least supporters of them. After the strike had ended, Laukki participated in an obscure armed group known as the "Power League" (*Voimaliitto*). The League was masked as a sports society, which had, for instance, printed rules for "Skiing Competitions"; he contributed in drafting to the rules for such veiled military exercises.[129] Laukki had also contacts with the Bolsheviks. He was present as a representative of the Finnish Social Democrats in the famous Conference of the Russian Social Democratic Labour Party in Tampere[130] (Tammerfors[131]) in December 1905, where V. I. Lenin and a youngster from Georgia, I. V. Dzhugashvili, met for the first time. It is typical,

[126] Also known in Russia as Leo Tiura and Leo Laukki-Tiura. Tiura was his mother's maiden name. Laukki's own full and original name was Leonard Leopold Lindquist. In Russia he used also the surname Kurutin. (Lahti-Argutina, *Olimme joukko vieras vain*, p. 286.)

[127] Swedish, Russian, German, English and French.

[128] Tero Ahola, *Leo Laukki Amerikan suomalaisessa työväenliikkeessä*, pp. 1–3.

[129] Eino I. Parmanen, *Taistelujen kirja : kuvauksia itsenäisyystaistelumme vaiheista sortovuosina*, vol. IV, *Suurlakko ja sitä lähinnä seurannut aika*, p. 567. There is a facsimile of the "Competition Rules".

[130] Ahola, *Leo Laukki Amerikan suomalaisessa työväenliikkeessä*, p. 13.

[131] Tammerfors is Tampere in Swedish. It was usual for Swedish names of towns and areas to be used in foreign languages if such names existed. For example Helsinki (in Swedish Helsingfors) was in Russian at that time Хельсингфорс or Гельсингфорс.

however, that Laukki also helped to organise a Conference of the Socialist Revolutionaries.[132] – Authorities soon set eyes on above-said "sports society" and suppressed it.[133] Laukki thought it wise to emigrate to the United States.

There Laukki had a brilliant career. He arrived in America at an opportune moment in March 1907. Finnish Socialist workers had in August 1906 established an organisation, which was to join together all Finnish-speaking Socialists. The English name of this organisation was the Finnish Socialist Federation.[134] Laukki was a teacher in a boarding school (*Työväen-opisto*) for Finnish-speaking Socialist activists and wrote extensively to Finnish newspapers in America. – There were a number of disputes among the Finns. The most moderate group was usually called by their opponents "yellows". These opponents were in many cases Kautskyite, but after 1910 Laukki like many radicals, joined the Industrial Workers of the World (IWW), known among the Finns as *tuplajuulaiset* (literally "double W-ists", i.e. Wobblies). Laukki now began to support revolutionary syndicalism and he wrote about possible forms of sabotage, e.g. how to hammer nails into timber so that sawing would be impossible or at least very difficult and how to put sand on axles etc. Perhaps for "security reasons" Laukki urged people not to commit any sabotage acts.[135]

Laukki wrote three books in the United States. The first, published in 1912, was on the struggles of slaves in Antiquity; the second on industrial society and the third on the Russian revolution. When we look at his slavery book, we note that Laukki knew his subject very well, but he had a tendency to extend to the remote past concepts which were adequate in his own time, but very questionable when we speak about Antiquity. Laukki argued, for instance, that there were "workers' societies" and "trade unions" in Athens.[136]

Laukki's second book (1917) on industrial society, had its starting-point in even more remote history than in his slavery book, namely in the formation of the "ape human being". When Laukki reached his present day after some 500 pages, he condemned the Kautskyan Socialism based on Robert Michels' book *Zur Soziologie des Parteiwesens in der Modernen Demokratie*. He considered the work "abstract", but otherwise accepted its analysis.[137] It seems that Laukki did not understand – or did not heed – Michels' central argument, according to which *all* human organisa-

[132] Ahola, *Leo Laukki Amerikan suomalaisessa työväenliikkeessä*, p. 14.

[133] Erkki Salomaa, *Viaporin kapina : 60 tuntia vallankumousta*, p. 30.

[134] Elis Sulkanen, *Amerikan Työväenliikkeen historia*, p. 91. The Finnish name of the organisation was *Yhteinen Suomalainen Sosialistijärjestö*, usually abbreviated to "*S. S. Järjestö*".

[135] Sakari Sariola, *Amerikan kultalaan : amerikansuomalaisten siirtolaisten sosiaalihistoriaa*, p. 213.

[136] Leo Laukki, *Suuret orjataistelut : piirteitä vanhan-ajan työväenliikkeestä*, pp. 51–52.

[137] Leo Laukki, *Teolliseen yhteiskuntaan*, pp. 549–550.

tions are, or at least will become, oligarchic by some kind of natural law. Laukki's ideal was what he called "industrial unionism". His prognosis was the following:[138]

> If there is progress in the workers' movement in all countries, industrial unionism will be the final organisational form of that movement into which it will logically develop.

The new workers' society would be strictly egalitarian. Working men and women would govern simply because they form the majority of people. There would be no relationship "from above downwards" or "from down upwards" (quotation marks by Laukki), because supervision of work as it is known in capitalism will simply disappear.[139]

The starting-point of Laukki's book on Soviet Russia (1919) was the Russian people's settlement of what was later called Russia. His information on post-October Russia was derived from a propaganda magazine, *Soviet Russia*. According to Laukki, lack of foodstuffs in Russia is no longer a serious problem; pregnant women are by the "direction of the People's Commissar Kollonat" (*sic*) freed from work"; operas, concerts, theatres, art galleries flourished, no longer as luxury of rich people, but as a source of happiness for the common people. Finally, Laukki notes that the IWW has been called to participate in a Congress of the Comintern.[140] It seems that Laukki did not realise that the principles of Bolshevism and Wobblian industrial unionism were contradicted each other.

---

[138] *Ibid.*, p. 551.

[139] *Ibid.*, pp. 556–557.

[140] Leo Laukki, *Venäjän vallankumous, bolshevismi ja soviettitasavalta*, pp. 292–294. According to the incomplete Preliminary List of Delegates, published in *Workers of the World and Oppressed Peoples, Unite! : Proceedings and Documents of the Second Congress [of the Comintern]*, 1920, vol. 2. p. 843, there was no delegate from the IWW. Although the Wobblies were called "revolutionaries" (Appeal to the IWW, published in *ibid.*, p. 921), they were criticised because they, like the "revolutionary syndicalist and Industrialists" did not know how to fight against "the dictatorship of the bourgeoisie": "They do not realize that the working-class without a political Party of its own is a body without a head". (G. Zinov'ev, *Report on the role and structure of the Communist Party*, in *ibid.*, 1920, vol 1, p. 147.) However, Nikolai Bukharin (*Report on Parliamentarism*, in *ibid.*, p. 427) accused the IWW of confusing "political struggle with parliamentary activity". It was also declared that propaganda against the independent political party by revolutionary syndicalists (the IWW included), "served and serves only to support the bourgeoisie and the counterrevolutionary Social Democrats". (Theses on the role and structure of the Communist Party before and after the taking of power by the proletariat [drafted by Zinov'ev], *ibid.*, vol. 1, p. 191.) However, the Congress also published an Appeal to the IWW, which stressed that the dictatorship of the proletariat was "only temporary"; when "all class divisions will do away", "then the proletarian dictatorship, the state, [will] automatically disappear – to make way for an industrial administrative body which will be something like a General Executive Board of the IWW". (*Ibid.*, vol. 2, p. 926.) It seems that the Russians were trying to use to the IWW as cane and carrot at the same time.

The IWW firmly opposed war and condemned the engagement of the United States in the First World War. The American authorities, who already before the war considered the IWW a threat to legal order, opponents of private property etc. arrested, in the spring 1918, 166 Wobblies (the famous "166 case") whom they regarded as the most dangerous revolutionaries.[141] Laukki was among them and he was condemned to prison for twenty years. Because Laukki appealed to a higher court, he was released on bail of the huge sum of $ 10,000. The money for guarantee was collected from American Finns sympathetic to the IWW. Laukki, however, escaped to Russia in 1921, which meant that those people who had gone security for him, lost their money. In many cases, this caused serious financial difficulties to the contributors. Ironically, in 1923 President Warren Harding granted an amnesty to all Wobblies still imprisoned.[142]

In Russia Laukki did not right away put aside his Wobblian sympathies,[143] but he was a member of the Central Committee of the SKP in the 1920s. Because he belonged to the Rahja Opposition, he was not re-elected to the Central Committee in 1925. Afterwards he held various posts: he was, for instance, a teacher in the Sverdlov University, and a journalist in Persia (three years). It seems that his career ended in a professorship of philosophy in the Institute of Railway Traffic Engineers in Dnepropetrovsk. In 1937, Laukki wrote a bitter but also appealing letter to O. W. Kuusinen. Kuusinen had made a negative statement on Laukki to Mariia Frumkina, rector of the Communist University of Western Minority Nationalities. Kuusinen had told Frumkina that Laukki was not "politically trustworthy" because he had been "in relations with Eino Rahja, an enemy of the people". Therefore, Laukki was dismissed from the Party Committee of his Institute.[144] Laukki's appeal to Kuusinen did not save his life; he was arrested and shot in 1938.[145]

---

[141] Hans R. Wasastjerna, *Minnesotan suomalaisten historia*, pp. 301–302.

[142] Ahola, *Leo Laukki Amerikan suomalaisessa työväenliikkeessä*, pp. 98–118.

[143] According to Arvo Tuominen, Laukki acted as an interpreter of two Finnish worker delegates at the founding Congress of the Profintern (Красный интернационал профсоюзов, or the Red International of Trade Unions), in July 1921. There Laukki advised these Finnish representatives to vote for the acceptance of certain anarcho-syndicalist organisations (Italian, Spanish, French) as members of the Profintern. This caused an uneasy situation for Kuusinen, and the Finnish delegation had to announce that it cancelled its vote in favour of the anarcho-syndicalist organisations. (Interview of Arvo Tuominen by V. O. Veilahti on February 20–21, 1954. Unpublished manuscript, pp. 2–3. Workers' Archives, Helsinki). Arvo Tuominen was vice-chairman of the Finnish Trade Union Federation (*Suomen Ammattijärjestö*) and acted, as he himself said, as an "assistant" and as a *politruk* in the Congress of the Profintern.

[144] Leo Laukki to O. W. Kuusinen, Feb. 14, 1937. KtS!, pp. 360–366.

[145] Lahti-Argutina, *Olimme joukko vieras vaan*, p. 286.

4. The Malm and Manner Opposition

Hanna Malm

(Галина[146] Даниловна Мальм, 1887–1938)

Hanna Malm, the most famous female Finnish Communist politician in Russia, was born to a working-class family in Helsinki. Her career as a full-time politician began in Ostrobothnia in 1909. She was an agitator and secretary of the Pietarsaari Social Democratic District. Characteristic of her temperament was her enormous activity: in Ostrobothnia she not only did her work of a Party organiser, she also participated in female, children's, trade union, sports and cultural work within the Social Democratic movement.[147] When the Civil War broke out Malm was appointed secretary in the Department of Domestic Affairs of the People's Deputation.[148] There she received orders directly from the Commander-in-Chief Eero Haapalainen and found herself in an awkward position with the People's Deputy of Foreign Affairs, Yrjö Sirola. In 1932, Malm described this conflict as follows:[149]

> I had to fight against a gang of counter-revolutionary intellectuals who were trying to get out of the country. Com. Haapalainen had given me an unconditional order not to let anybody go. Com. Sirola and I were constantly at odds over this. Often gentlewomen came to my office. They appealed tearfully to civilised Sirola, who treats them humanly and would let them go, but I, who am a workwoman, not.

It is clear that Malm very well remembered these occurrences because she spoke of them 14 years later when, to be sure, Sirola was her political enemy. In 1918, she perhaps felt some inferiority complex in relation to Sirola, whose conduct was indeed particularly refined.

From Haapalainen's Secretariat Malm moved to Tampere, where she was an agitator and a front reporter for the local Social Democratic paper, *Kansan Lehti*. At the time when the Whites were already capturing Tampere, Malm, in a market square speech, urged the Reds to terrorist acts. After the war the Whites prosecuted another female politician, Emmi Murto, for this speech simply because these two women had a similar appearance. Murto was condemned to death, but the sentence was commuted to a long prison term. Malm remained in the town when the Whites took it and she managed not only to hide but also to pass through control

---

146 Also Ханна, Ханны, Ганна and Анна were used.

147 Jukka Paastela and Hannu Rautkallio, "Johdanto : Hanna Malmin ja Kullervo Mannerin elämä ja toiminta" in Kullervo Manner and Hanna Malm, *Rakas kallis toveri : Kullervo Mannerin ja Hanna Malmin kirjeenvaihtoa 1932–33*, p. 11–12.

148 Rinta-Tassi, *Kansanvaltuuskunta punaisen Suomen hallituksena*, p. 182.

149 MPCC, July 8–24, 1932. RGASPI, f. 516, op. 2, 1932, d. 3, l. 225.

posts of the Whites to Sweden.[150] This journey must have been extremely dangerous and she was very fortunate to reach her destination.

In Sweden Malm joined the Stockholm Committee of the SKP, but she was there only some months: she was already back in Helsinki on illegal assignments in November or December 1918.[151] In 1921, Malm worked in the clandestine Finnish Bureau of the SKP. Her legal forum was the Finnish Socialist Workers' Party (SSTP). Malm wrote articles for the papers of the SSTP using the pen name *Mutteri* (the Nut); it was, of course, impossible for her, due to her illegal status, to use her own name. *Mutteri* demanded the destruction of the state machine by a revolution which would occur as a result of "mass action" by the workers. Mutteri criticised especially the Communist leaders of the Finnish Trade Union Federation for their reformism.[152] Revolution and the realisation of the dictatorship of the proletariat were to be furthered by calling all workers – not only those who already supported that dictatorship and the "council (or soviet) idea" – to the "struggle for the realisation of the control of *production* in industry".[153] Here Malm referred to German factory councils as examples. Factory councils should take over the power in workplaces. Finally, when there are enough of such councils, some kind of conglomerate of them must be formed and this conglomeration must take over state power.[154] For obvious tactical reasons, Malm did not mention the Communist Party here, but she presented a definition of it:[155]

> The most forward, most conscious and most self-sacrificing part of the working-class goes ahead and leads the struggle between the classes, which manifests itself in the struggle of this leading proletarian Party against other [*sic*] bourgeois parties".

---

150 Arvo Tuominen, *Maan päällä ja alla : muistelmia vuosilta 1921–1933*, pp. 20–21.

151 Saarela, *Suomalaisen kommunismin synty*, p. 139.

152 Mutteri, "Mitä työmiesten ja työläisnaisten tulee tehdä työttömyyden lieventämiseksi : II Suomen Ammattijärjestön johto ei ole selvillä siitä onko maailman vallankumouksen kehitysprosessi vai eikö", *Suomen Työmies*, June 17, 1921.

153 Mutteri, "Mitä työmiesten ja työläisnaisten tulee tehdä työttömyyden lieventämiseksi : IV S. Ammattijärjestön johto tarjoaa työttömille 'valistamista' ja 'järjestäytymistä'!", *Suomen Työmies*, June 22, 1921 and "V Tunnuslauseeksemme: Työttömille työtä tuotannon kontrollin kautta", *Suomen Työmies*, June 24, 1921.

154 In Germany there were many models of council democracy, one of them that presented by Rosa Luxemburg. It is likely that Malm knew it. (See Rosa Luxemburg, *Unser Programm und die politische Situation*; speech given in the founding Congress of the German Communist Party, Dec. 31, 1918 in *Die Gründung der KPD : Protokoll und Materialen des Gründungsparteitages der Kommunistischen Partei Deutschlands 1918/1919*, pp. 182–183 and 196–200. See also Horst Dähn, *Rätedemokratische Modelle : Studien zur Rätediskussion in Deutschland 1918–1919*, pp. 192–207.)

155 Mutteri, "Mitä työmiesten ja työläisnaisten tulee tehdä työttömyyden lieventämiseksi : V Tunnuslauseeksemme: Työttömille työtä tuotannon kontrollin kautta", *Suomen Työmies*, June 24, 1921.

There was an obvious slip of the pen, but even without it, the definition was far from lucid to the common worker. Malm's articles nevertheless created a phenomenon called "Mutteri-ism". This meant vigorous revolutionary phraseology and sharp criticism of reformist trade unionism. "Mutteri-ism" had a negative connotation and was later used apart from Malm's personage, as a symbol of futile extremism.[156]

Another slip of Malm's pen caused a scandal in February 1922. She wrote a secret letter to the underground district Party workers about the objectives of Party work in Finland, in which she urged members of the SKP to "steal" (the quotation marks were in the original letter) tools and materials to be transported to Russia in aid of the destitute Russian people. By a typist's mistake in the Finnish Bureau of the SKP, the Social Democrats got their hands on this letter. The main organ of the Social Democratic Party published the letter *in extenso* under the somewhat clumsy title "The Tactics of the Communist Leadership as Presented by its Party Leadership" and commented: "Workers, let's steal. [...] 'Down with honesty'. This is the new Communists' slogan".[157] It was not immediately known that the author was Malm. At first, the Communists said that the document was a Social Democrat forgery. Then it was proved that the typewriter belonged to a Communist office cleric, who announced having written the document.[158] Among the Communist cadres, the real author soon became known and in Petrograd Malm was reprimanded for the scandal.[159] Malm remained thereafter in Soviet Russia, except for some clandestine trips to Sweden.

Kullervo Manner

(Кулерво Густавович Маннер, 1880–1939)

Kullervo Akilles Manner was, like Sirola, a son of a pastor of the Lutheran Church. Manner had the usual upper-class education and passed the matriculation in 1900. He did not, however, continue his studies in university; his was to be the career of a newspaper editor. Manner obtained a post on the radical bourgeois paper *Uusimaa*. This radicalism meant endorsement of universal suffrage, social reforms etc. When Manner embraced Socialist ideas, he began to present them in the paper. He joined the Social Democratic Party in 1905 simultaneously through the

---

156 Pauli Kettunen, *Poliittinen liike ja sosiaalinen kollektiivisuus : tutkimus sosialidemokratiasta ja ammattiyhdistysliikkeestä Suomessa 1918–1930*, p. 361.

157 "Kommunistisen puolueen taktiikka sen puoluejohdon esittämänä", *Suomen Sosialidemokraatti*, March 4, 1922.

158 *Suomen Työmies*, March 20, 1922.

159 Minutes of the meeting of the Extended Party Leadership of the SKP, Aug. 9–16, 1922. RGASPI, f. 516, op. 2, d. 6, ll. 53–54.

Porvoo Workers' Association and through the Social Democratic Association of Students in Helsinki. The Porvoo association was a "normal" society of working men and women. Here Manner developed his skills as a rabble-rouser. The students' association was intellectually important for Manner. There he adopted a Siltasaarian line similar to Sirola and Kuusinen.[160] Manner was all his life a very good orator, but his written texts were rather dull and often extremely propagandist. This can be seen in the newspaper *Työläinen* (The Worker), founded in 1907 by the Workers' Association of Porvoo, which Manner edited practically alone. In this paper a bourgeois party was qualified as a "herd"; the programmes of these parties were "swindling" and "sham", the bourgeois newspapers were "sleeping papers" etc.[161] It is possible that Manner covered his own doubts and hesitations under this kind of vocabulary, although, of course, such language was not uncommon in the workers' movement at that time. Manner's problem was that typical of a *déclassé*. He had always to prove he was not an "alien intellectual", but "worth" an (imaginary) worker.

Manner was elected to the *Eduskunta* in 1910. On the platform of Parliament he was in his own element. His language, however, proved an obstacle. For example, when the Social Democratic group, in 1911, presented its suggestion of protest, written by Manner, to the Grand Duke about the illegal actions of the Russian authorities, the Speaker refused to take the proposition into consideration because it contained such words as "strangling", governmental policy of "strangulation", "economic fleecing" and so on. Manner was at this point put in prison for some months for lese-majesty.[162]

In 1917, Kullervo Manner was elected Speaker of the *Eduskunta*, where the Social Democrats held the majority. As Speaker Manner was in a difficult position: when the Provisional Government dissolved the *Eduskunta* after it had accepted the above-described Law on Authority.[163] Manner did not read the Dissolution Manifesto decreed by the Provisional Government in the House because the Social Democrats considered the Manifesto illegal. Instead Manner said that the next plenary session would be announced "in due time".[164] Manner indeed convened the *Eduskunta* two times without success.[165] Most bourgeois politicians consid-

---

[160] Olavi Aaltonen, "Kullervo Akilles Manner" in *Tiennäyttäjät: Suomen työväenliikkeen merkkimiehiä Ursinista Tanneriin*, vol. 2, pp. 411–515.

[161] Soikkanen, *Sosialismin tulo Suomeen*, pp. 327–328.

[162] Aaltonen, "Kullervo Akilles Manner", p. 422.

[163] Manifesti Eduskunnan hajoittamisesta heinäkuun 18/31 päivänä 1917 ja uusien vaalien toimittamisesta, Suomen Suuriruhtinaanmaan Asetuskokoelma N:o 50, 1917. Published in *Suomen kansanedustuslaitoksen historia*, vol XII, pp. 210–211.

[164] Jan-Magnus Jansson, "Eduskunnan hajoitukset", in *Suomen kansanedustuslaitoksen historia*, vol. XII, p. 212.

[165] *Ibid.*, p. 178. Soikkanen, *Kohti kansanvaltaa*, vol. 1, p. 234.

ered the dissolution legal. We may conclude that Manner did not show himself as a strong leader, though, to be sure, the situation was difficult.

In the revolutionary regime, Manner was chairman of the People's Deputation.[166] His role was significant, perhaps even crucial in the last weeks and days of the Civil War. There were, as we have seen, various attempts to conclude an armistice or even peace at the time when it became obvious that the Reds would lose. By an armistice, it would be possible to spare human lives and perhaps even avoid the devastation of towns.[167] It seems that Manner opposed any attempts at contact with the Whites or the Germans. Later, in Petrograd, (on April 29) Manner reportedly had a heated discussion with G. E. Zinov'ev, who suggested negotiations with the Whites. Allegedly, L. D. Trotskii had supported Zinov'ev. Manner declared that the two men were "traitors to the revolution and the proletariat".[168] In any case, any negotiations at that time were out of the question because the Whites and the Germans controlled almost the whole country.

Before the hegira of the People's Deputies to Russia, Kullervo Manner was, as stated above, elected, on April 11 dictator of Finland.[169] The dictator had not much to do except to prepare for evacuation. The final question was whether to try to negotiate on surrender, fight to the end, or escape. Dictator Manner ruled out the first alternative. He and the members of the People's Deputation escaped, with the exception of Edvard Gylling who remained in Viipuri. He succeeded in hiding and getting out of out the town. Immediately after the capture of the town the Whites executed everyone they considered leaders of the rebellion.[170]

---

166 Rinta-Tassi, *Kansanvaltuuskunta punaisen Suomen hallituksena*, p. 104.

167 See various documents on attempts at armistice, made both by bourgeois and Social Democratic politicians in *Kansalaissota dokumentteina.*, vol. 2, pp. 154–159.

168 Jukka Nevakivi, *Muurmannin legioona : suomalaiset ja liittoutuneiden interventio Pohjois-Venäjälle 1918–1919* , p. 60.

169 Rinta-Tassi, *Kansanvaltuuskunta punaisen Suomen hallituksena*, p. 474.

170 *Ibid.*, pp. 489–493.

Time Scale of Oppositios and Persons

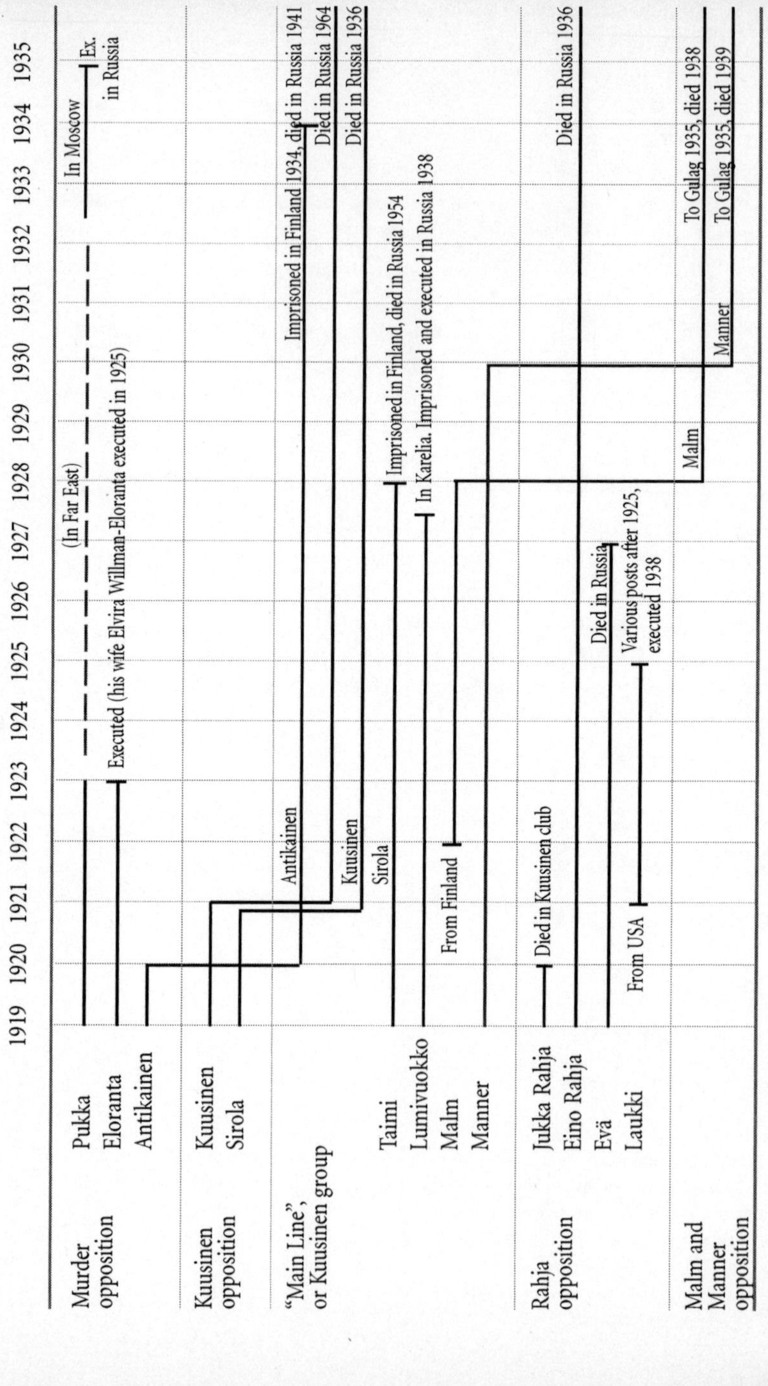

VI The Murder Opposition (1920–1923)

After the members of People's Deputation had fled to Russia, they experienced an "emigrant psychosis" as Juhani Paasivirta[1] has characterised this phenomenon of agony and empty expectations. N. I. Bukharin, who knew political emigration as intimately as one of his apostles, Friedrich Engels, depicted emigration as isolation from "living political work", plotting, mutual accusations and "constant squabbling".[2] The emigrant leaders did have alternatives. There were plans to establish utopian communes in remote areas;[3] some tried to persevere with the old Kautskyan conviction; a clear majority of the leaders adopted Bolshevism. They were called (also by themselves) "sloughers".

The leaders of Finnish Social Democracy did not know the Bolshevik doctrine. For instance Yrjö Sirola said that all the Finnish leaders knew about the Bolsheviks was their promise to allow Finland independence.[4] This sounds perhaps odd, for

---

1 Juhani Paasivirta, *Suomi vuonna 1918*, pp. 307–308.

2 N. Buharin, "Lahtarien provokatsiooni ja murhenäytelmä suomalaisten kommunistien keskuudessa", *Wapaus*, Sept. 11, 1920.

3 One example here was Oskari Tokoi's plan to establish a base in Murmansk for future military operations in Finland. In Murmansk Tokoi had contacts with the English navy which the newly founded SKP saw as perfidious and therefore condemned him and his two comrades to death. "The execution of the judgement is the duty of every revolutionary worker", the Central Committee of the SKP proclaimed. (*Suomalaisille työläisille Muurmannilla ja muualla : Oskari Tokoi, E. Elo ja K. Hämäläinen kavaltajina*. Printed leaflet. RGASPI, f. 516, op. 2, 1918, d. 63. See also *Wapaus*, Sept. 25, 1918.) On the complicated history of the Murnmansk legion, see Nevakivi, *Murmannin legioona*.

4 [Yrjö Sirola], *Kunnia Lokakuun Vallankumouksen Sankareille! : Puhe, jonka tov. YRJÖ SIROLA piti Pietarin Suomalaisten työläisten vallankumousjuhlassa 8 p:nä marrask. 1918*, p. 10. See also Juhani Piilonen, "Yhteinen vihollinen yhdistää 1908–1917" in *Lenin ja Suomi*, vol. 1, pp. 312–313.

there had been influential Bolsheviks in Finland, namely the Rahja brothers and Adolf Taimi. The explanation is obviously that these Bolsheviks were little interested in ideological questions: they were workers, men of "practice". One obstacle too was the language barrier. At least Manner and Sirola could not even read Russian fluently. The language of their own cultural background was German. Russian Bolsheviks leaders usually also spoke German, but, of course, almost all of their theoretical writings were at the time available only in Russian.

It was natural for the "sloughers" to try to cut the ties with the Social Democratic past as decisively and sharply as possible. In the meeting of the "Finnish Social Democrats in Russia" held in the Moscow House of the Ecclesiastical Seminar on August 25–29, 1918, O. W. Kuusinen declared that the meeting was still gripped "in Trinity" but this "Trinity" now ends.[5] By "Trinity" Kuusinen obviously meant Bolshevism, Kautskyanism and Revisionism. Bolshevism had to triumph, other currents had to be cast into the wastebasket of history. Kuusinen expected his triumph to take place very soon: "One should convey the word from cottage to cottage. The new Revolution can break out. It can save."[6] The most important doctrinal reform concerned democracy and dictatorship.

In this chapter, we firstly examine the Ultraleftist ideas that were influential amongst the Finnish refugees in Russia. One can understand the Murder Opposition only if one knows the circumstances in which it was conceived. Secondly, we investigate more specifically the conditions in the Petrograd Red Officer School, corruption and espionage. Thirdly, we describe in detail the development that led to the murders and the final consequences of them.

1. Ultraleftism in the Finnish Communist Party, 1918–1921

We may argue that Ultraleftism was indeed a result of the destruction of the traditional "Trinity" of the Finnish workers' movement. It can be seen in at least seven doctrinal changes: i) dictatorship, ii) terrorism, iii) intellectuals and workers, iv) masses and leaders, v) trade unions, vi) Parliament and vii) the Party.

In Finland, the workers' movement had always demanded democracy: democracy at state level (which implied the destruction of the Tsarist autocracy), democracy in local administration and even some kind of democracy in production. Dictatorship as an aim was not comprehensible to the Finnish Social Democratic lead-

5 Minutes of the meeting of the Finnish Social Democrats in Russia, Aug. 25–29, 1918. RGASPI, f. 516, op. 1, d. 269, l. 38.

6 *Ibid.*, p. 35.

ers, let alone the masses, except for some individuals, Bolsheviks like the Rahja Brothers and Adolf Taimi. In this phase, democracy and dictatorship were clearly opposites. The Orwellian explanations that the dictatorship of the proletariat was 100 times more democratic than the bourgeois parliamentary institution, or that the best possible form of democracy is a democratic dictatorship etc., were not used by the Finnish Communists before 1921. The terror was a concept similar to dictatorship. Again, some individuals had more or less worked out ideas about revolutionary terror. We may define these two phenomena as typical of the Ultraleftist political position. Then there was talk, or even quarrelling, about the role of the intellectuals in the workers' movement. This was by no means a new topic. Nevertheless, in the new circumstances, it acquired new overtones when a kind of Workers' Opposition was born. At first, this was vague and its rhetoric did not differ very clearly from the dominant style. We may say that in the second Congress of the SKP there was an embryo of this Opposition. Its activities led to an attempt to murder the leaders of the SKP on August 31, 1920. The grouping was therefore commonly called the Murder Opposition, sometimes also the Revolver Opposition or the Workers' Opposition.

As to the title "Workers' Opposition", it was used but seldom. In 1926, O. W. Kuusinen wrote an article on the Murder Opposition, which he labelled "Fascist" by nature[7] (in 1919–1920, i.e. the "Fascists" in question hardly had heard anything about Benito Mussolini's Fascism).[8] According to Kuusinen it was Väinö Pukka who while in prison labelled the Opposition the "Workers' Opposition" to "cover" its "Fascist" character. For Kuusinen, interestingly, the Russian Workers' Opposition was "proletarian" by nature, although, of course, erroneous, while the Finnish one was not "proletarian".[9] There were analogous features in the Workers' Opposition in Russia and the Murder Opposition among the Finns, but the Finnish Opposition was contemporaneous with, if not earlier than Shliapnikov's and Kollontai's Workers Opposition. I have found no sign of direct influence between the Russian and the Finnish Workers' Oppositions. Nevertheless, it is of course more than likely that Pukka knew some documents concerning the Russian Workers' Opposition.

---

[7] This was so although, according to Kuusinen, the Fascist movement was a "curious (*omalaatuinen*) [movement], stirred up and organised among the revolutionary refugees in Soviet Russia, led ultimately by the Okhrana of the slaughterers". (O. V. Kuusinen, "Fasistiliikettä suomalaisten vallankumouspakolaisten keskuudessa Neuvosto-Venäjällä" in *Elokuun kommunaardit : kommunaardien muistojulkaisu : kommunismin puolesta kaatuneille elokuun 31 p:nä 1920 veriteon uhrien muistolle omistaa tämän julkaisun Suomen kommunistinen puolue*, p. 2.)

[8] Cf. e.g. Nicos Poulantzas, *Fascism and Dictatorship : the Third International and the Problem of Fascism*, pp. 131–132.

[9] *Ibid.*, p. 23.

Dictatorship

In his opening address to the meeting of the Finnish Social Democrats in Russia, its chairman Kullervo Manner declared that the aim of the coming Finnish revolution must be the "dictatorship of the working people" (*työväki*). He said that in the recent revolution a good deal of "unclearness" was caused by "clinging to democracy", although the revolution was to be a proletarian, Socialist revolution and not at all any kind of "democratic" revolution.[10]

The meeting discussed two proposals for its programme and for the SKP, which was founded immediately after the meeting by those who accepted the programme. In memoirs as well as in studies, writers have usually accepted the argument that in this meeting and in the foundation Congress of the SKP there were already two tendencies, one led by O. W. Kuusinen and the other by Jukka Rahja and Kullervo Manner. According to this interpretation, Kuusinen's theses were accepted.[11] This was not the case. There was, however, some altercation between the Rahja brothers and Kuusinen. Kuusinen remarked that *Wapaus*, Finnish émigrés' newspaper, had advised people to read good books. He continued:[12]

> Here are among us e.g. two brothers, one of whom [Jukka Rahja] already in the first days of the revolution had to read for several months good books when the slaughterers shot him in the leg. [...] The other brother [Eino Rahja], again, has not to my knowledge for a long time read neither a good nor even a bad book. Nevertheless, he did his work in the revolution with such a force that about it others could afterwards, let us say – write good books.

Kuusinen's remark about the Rahja brothers and especially about Eino (who remembered this long time), was an obvious insult, but as to the political theses, this had no influence. Jukka Rahja proposed the theses,[13] as we shall soon see.

---

[10] Minutes of the meeting of the Finnish Social Democrats in Russia, Aug. 25–29, 1918. RGASPI, f. 516, op. 1, d. 269, l. 5.

[11] John H. Hodgson *Communism in Finland : a History and Interpretation*, p. 84, n. 11. Rinta-Tassi, "Kuusinen vallankumousvuosina" in *Nuori Otto Ville Kuusinen 1881–1920*, p. 138. Uljas Vikström, *Toiska : kertomus Toivo Antikaisen elämästä*, p. 30. E. K. Louhikko, *Teimme vallankumousta*, p. 187. Arvo Tuominen, *Sirpin ja vasaran tie : muistelmia*, p. 106.

[12] "Suomalaisten sosialidemokratien neuvottelukokous Moskovassa 25–29 p. [elokuuta] 1918" in *Mitä tahtoo Suomalainen kommunistinen puolue? : selostuksia Moskovan neuvottelukokouksista elok. 25 p.–syysk. 5 p. 1918*, p. 15.

[13] Markku Salomaa (*Punaupseerit*, p. 391, n. 101) has observed this on the basis of the intelligence reports of the Finnish Detective Central Police and Tauno Saarela (*Suomalaisen kommunismin synty*, p. 42) on the basis on primary material.

There were in the meeting two propositions for the programme, one presented by Kullervo Manner on behalf of the Muscovites,[14] the other by Jalo Kohonen on behalf of the Petrograders. The Petrograd programme was the more moderate of the two. The Petrograders did demand that it must be "explained" to the masses that reforms do not lead to Socialism and that the "fundamental improvement of the conditions" of the workers is possible only if a "class dictatorship of the working people" is established by a "proletarian revolution", but they also demanded an traditional series of reforms: health insurance, nationalisation of the means of production already under capitalism (not, of course, a Bolshevik demand at all) and even civil liberties.[15] In the Moscow programme the dictatorship statement was presented in the form that the "revolution of the working people means, above all, the establishment of class power of the poor people, the dictatorship", that is, the "state form" of the transitional period until the "people have been transformed wholly into a working society which will under no condition abandon its Socialist order". This transitional state form cannot be democracy, but only a "republic of Soviets", i.e. "mainly such a form of state which has been realised by the great revolution of the Russian poor people".[16] There were, however, some reservations and alleviations. One should not try to bring about a revolution in the Blanquist way, i.e. to "launch a revolution inopportunely and light-heartedly"; the "conditions"

---

[14] Arvo Tuominen (*Sirpin ja vasaran tie*, p. 106) extends the later dispute between Kuusinen and Manner to August 1918 and argues that Manner was a "Petrograder", which he clearly was not. (Report of the activities of the Petrograd committee of the Foreign Organisation of the Finnish Social Democrats after the move to Russia. RGASPI, f. 516, op. 1, 1918, d. 279.)

[15] A proposal for the programme of the Communist Workers' Party of Finland. Minutes of the meeting of the Finnish Social Democrats in Russia, Aug. 25–29, 1918. RGASPI, f. 516, op. 1, 1918, d. 269, ll. 22–24. There are several problems of translation in the Finnish terminology. Of the workers as a whole the following terms were used:

työväki,
köyhälistö,
proletariaatti
työväenluokka.

The two latter terms do not cause problems: *proletariaatti* is an international term and *työväenluokka* is the working-class. The problem is with *työväki* and *köyhälistö*. Both of them can in fact be translated by *proletariat*. In this case, however, the words lose some nuances. *Työ* is "work" and *väki* is a now old-fashioned word for "people". I have used "working people" for *työväki*. *Köyhälistö* comes from *köyhä*, "poor" and the suffix *-stö* is similar to the suffix "-iat" in "proletariat". *Köyhälistö* was the usual translation for "proletariat", often used only because the word was Finnish. However, *köyhälistö* may sometimes have a connotation like *Lumpenproletariat* in German. I have translated *köyhälistö* by "poor people".

[16] A proposal for the programme of the Finnish Communist Party (*Suomalainen Kommunistinen Puolue*) by the Muscovite Central Committee of the Finnish Social Democrats. Published in *Mitä tahtoo Suomalainen Kommunistinen Puolue? Selostuksia Moskovan neuvottelukokouksista elok. 25 p.–syysk. 5. p. 1918*, p. 39.

must always be taken into account and it depends on "conditions" how much the working people should use in advance "lighter means" like general strikes, or parliamentary, trade union and co-operative activities.[17] Co-operatives were indeed a typical form of "lighter means". Manner, who after all knew his Pappenheinmians, articulated this by saying that in a co-operative shop one should peddle not only coffee and sugar but also Communism.[18]

O. W. Kuusinen strongly criticised the reform programme of the Petrograders, comparing them with slaves who demand the mitigation of slavery.[19] Jukka Rahja joined Kuusinen: the "Social Democratic time of minimum and maximum demands" is over.[20] He declared that in the event of his being elected to the *Eduskunta* – an extremely hypothetical prospect – he could not, as a Communist, "do parliamentary errands", but "present over the heads of the MPs the demands of the Communists to the workers". He proposed that the meeting vote on five theses. Of these the third concerned the dictatorship and ran as follows:[21]

> Through revolution all power must be taken into the hands of the working-class themselves and an iron dictatorship has to be established; – one must, thus, aim at the destruction of the bourgeois state and not at all at democracy (*kansanvalta*), either before or after the revolution.

Rahja was seconded by Kuusinen, who at the same time withdrew the proposition of the Muscovites for the programme.[22] The decisive vote took place based on Jukka Rahja's theses on August 29, 1918. The result of the vote was 76 for the theses and 16 against. Those who voted for, continued the meeting, which now was transformed into the founding Congress of the Finnish Communist Party. Those who voted against were mostly men with a strong background in the trade union movement.[23] Johan Henrik Lumivuokko was among them, but he soon changed his mind and became one of the leaders of the Party.

There were differences of degree in the dictatorship discourse among the most important leaders of the SKP. Three types can be distinguished: i) non-voluntarist, ii) voluntarist and iii) extreme voluntarist. The first mentioned was presented in the formula of necessity; the cause for what has been done and what is done is the absence of alternatives. Yrjö Sirola was a typical representative of the non-voluntarist

---

17 *Ibid.*, p. 38.

18 Minutes of the meeting of the Finnish Social Democrats in Russia, Aug. 25–29, 1918. RGASPI, f. 516, op. 1, d. 269, l. 7.

19 *Ibid.*, l. 38.

20 *Ibid.*, l. 41.

21 *Ibid.*, ll. 70–71.

22 *Ibid.*, l. 75.

23 Saarela, *Suomalaisen kommunismin synty*, pp. 45–46.

type of argumentation. He presented the dictatorship as being necessary in Russia, and, by implication, everywhere:[24]

> More and more honest observers have already admitted that Russia has not had the choice between the Bolshevik "minority dictatorship" and some imaginary "democracy"; there is either the Soviet power of the workers or therewith black reaction.

In the voluntarist mode of argumentation the basis is, of course, that there are alternatives and the Communists (now) know these alternatives and may therefore have chosen a correct (or even scientific) political course. O. W. Kuusinen was a typical representative of this type of approach. He estimated that in the autumn of 1918 the "relative weakness" of the bourgeoisie was such as to "instigate" the Social Democrats to a misapprehension i.e. caused them to strive for Socialism through a "democratic representative institution",[25] and because the conscious intent of the People's Deputation was not the dictatorship of the proletariat, the Deputation gave to the bourgeoisie ample "liberty of plotting" and tried to "calm down" and "induce" the petty-bourgeoisie and the peasantry by "democracy and humanist proceeding".[26] The new rebellion will not proceed in this way. In the founding Congress Kuusinen announced that the aim of the future revolution was that the "bourgeoisie be wholly annihilated". By this annihilation Kuusinen meant that those bourgeois people who did not die in the new Civil War would be transformed into "working men", not, to be sure, as "ragamuffins", but as people who "do useful work". Thus, the worker could be elevated to the "position of a free gentleman". Kuusinen hypothesised on the expansion of the suffrage. In Soviet Russia, there were a number of groups who had not the right to vote: priests, kulaks, members of the nobility etc. Kuusinen planned the vote not only to salaried workers but also to certain other categories of people, whom, he did not say, but presented one reservation: to all poor people the suffrage will not be extended.[27] Presumably, Kuusinen meant here the peasantry or some sections of it.

At the time, Kuusinen did not publicly present these fairly precise plans for the future of the bourgeoisie. Kustaa Mikko Evä, however, presented very concrete plans for the coming dictatorship, intended to be realised immediately after the victory in the new rebellion. We may say that Evä represented those embittered workers who wanted the recognition as soon as possible. Evä's "programme" was

---

[24] Sirola, *Kunnia Lokakuun Vallankumouksen Sankareille!*, p. 14.

[25] O. W. Kuusinen, *The Finnish Revolution : a Self-Criticism*, p. 22.

[26] *Ibid.*, pp. 48–49.

[27] Minutes of the founding Congress of the Finnish Communist Party in the apartment of the Ecclesialstical Seminar in Moscow, on Aug. 29–31 and Sept. 1–5, 1918. RGASPI, f. 512, op. 1, 1918, d. 288. l. 34.

extremely voluntarist: by a victorious revolution the proletariat would take revenge on the bourgeoisie for all their wrongdoings. In contrast to Kuusinen's quite sophisticated rhetoric, or Sirola's sublime pathos in which he readily included references to the history of the French revolution,[28] Evä's "proletarian" rhetoric was straightforward and coarse. In a seminar for new agitators in autumn 1918, Evä explained that in the future battle one part of the bourgeoisie would be destroyed (i.e. the same theme as in Kuusinen) "as an unconditional result of the premonition of vindictiveness roused by the bestiality of the bourgeoisie". However,[29]

> there would remain opponents who must later be forced to submit and to serve when the new society of work is created. The working people must with iron hand and without pity subject the bourgeoisie under its class dictatorship. As cruelly as the bourgeoisie when it tortured the workers, the working people cannot treat the capitalists even in vengeance. But it has learnt, nonetheless, to understand that the enemy must be destroyed, or put under such rigid dictatorship that it will never have the possibility to bare its talons again.

Terrorism

K. M. Evä's visions of the subjection of the bourgeoisie to an iron hand under an unswerving dictatorship raise the question of means: how to realise this vision?

Russian radical political movements had a strong Jacobinian and terrorist tradition. The roots of this tradition can be traced as far back in history as to the Decembrists of 1825.[30] The Bolsheviks continued this tradition, although in principle they did not accept individual terrorism. Nonetheless, the cult of violence is obvious in their rhetoric. Thus, N. I. Bukharin praised violence against the oppressors of the "millions" as "holy".[31] What is important, however, was not the oratory alone, but also the deed. In the period under study, V. I. Lenin did not – as far as I know – publicly urge his supporters to commit terrorist acts. There were nevertheless such acts and Lenin was behind them. When we consider the situa-

---

[28] In June 1918, Sirola cultivated e.g. the following phraseology: "Russia is awakening. Her sons are gathering under the red banners. At the sounds of the International they march against the foe, and, as in France, drive them beyond the borders and bring the emancipating message of Socialism to other countries – as once the French revolutionary armies brought the word of freedom." (Yrjö Sirola, *"Isänmaa on vaarassa – aseisiin!" Puhe pidetty suomalaisille puna-armeijalaisille Moskovassa heinäkuulla 1918*, p. 4.)

[29] [K. M. Evä], *Työväen luokkadiktatuuri Suomeen! Tov. K. M. Evän luento työväen diktatuurin hallituskoneistosta Kommunistisilla agitaattorikursseilla Pietarissa 30 p. marrask. 1918*, p. 7. See also [K. M. Evä], *"Kosto Suomen köyhälistön pyöveleille"*, pp. 10–11.

[30] E.g. В. О. Ключевский, *Русская история : полный курс лекций в трех книгах*, vol. 3, pp. 412–413.

[31] Н. Бухарин, *Программа коммунистов (большевиков)*, p. 12

tion from the point of view of the Finnish emigrants, not only the words the Bolsheviks uttered but also what happened in the state under their control was influential.

In June 1918 V. Volodarskii (Moisei Markovich Goldstein), a member of the Presidium of the Petrograd Soviet was murdered. In a letter to Zinov'ev Lenin expressed his protests at the instructions given by the Petrograd Central Committee of the RKP(b) in respect of the murder. According to Lenin, the Committee did not allow the workers of the city to "answer the murder by mass terror". Lenin considered terror as a "*wholly* acceptable enterprising disposition of the workers".[32]

Theoretically the most important of Lenin's doctrines from the point view of terror was his definition of the workers' dictatorship: "The dictatorship of the revolutionary proletariat is power, attained by violence used by the proletariat against the bourgeois power, which is not tied to any laws".[33] The non-adherence to laws was also practice in Lenin's Russia: when the chief of the Petrograd Cheka, Moisei Solomovich Uritskii, was murdered in August 1918, 512 "counter-revolutionaries and members White Guards" were, according to the Petrograd *Izvestia,* shot in reprisal.[34] A Finn, E. K. Louhikko (before 1920 Emil Laiho), claims in his memoirs that he organised a boat manned by Finnish sailors on which the aristocrats, 200 in number, were transported to Kronstadt to be executed.[35]

The Bolsheviks did not exclude terror turned against their own cadres provided these had been found to be enemies. In this discourse they stressed, however, that terror against those in power is out of the question. In 1919 Zinov'ev elucidated this imperative in the following popular formula:[36]

---

32 Lenin to Zinov'ev, June 26, 1918. PSS, vol. 50, p. 106.

33 В. И. Ленин. *Пролетарская революция и ренегат Каутский*. PSS, vol. 37, p. 245.

34 E. H. Carr, *The Bolshevik Revolution,* vol. 1, p. 176. See also William Henry Chamberlin, *The Russian Revolution 1917–1921*, vol. 2, p. 66; Marcel Liebman, *Le Léninisme sous Lénine,* vol. 2, *l'épreuve du pouvoir,* p. 159; I. N. Steinberg, *In the Workshop of the Revolution,* p. 147.

35 E. K. Louhikko, *Teimme vallankumousta*, pp. 181–182. Louhikko is not always a very reliable memoirist. He claims, for instance, that Eino Rahja was condemned to death but died before execution. (*Ibid.*, p. 220.) This claim is not corroborated by any sources I know. – Another act of terror the Finns witnessed took place on the Estonian front. According to assistant political Commissar Jalmari Kotiranta, Trotskii came to the front and ordered 120 commanders and commissars to be shot because they had retreated. Kotiranta's comment on the executions was: "Whether the judgments were right or not, it is not my business now [to say], any more than then". (Jalm. Kotiranta to the CC, June 26, 1922. RGASPI, f. 516, op. 2, 1922, d. 15, l. 36.). Kotiranta does not state when this happened. It is probable that the time was N.N. Iudenich's second attempt to capture Petrograd from his base in Estonia, October–November 1919. Trotskii was in command of the Bolshevik troops. (Deutscher, *The Prophet Armed*, pp. 443–445; Toivo U. Raun, *Estonia and the Estonians*, p. 110.)

36 Г. Зиновьев. *Беспартийный или коммунист : речь т. Зиновьева на собранини. в театре Речкина на Московскои заставои*, p. 25.

> As to the thieves and scoundrels, who have successfully pretended to be not only "Communists", but also commissars, I have already compared them, with your permission, to bugs. If it so happens that there are bugs in a hut, we, to get rid of the parasites, resort to the effect of turpentine or some powder which exterminates insects. However, no one burns his house.

A vital force inspiring the founding Congress of the SKP was the hope and belief that the proletarian revolution, which had so promisingly begun in Russia, would prove to be permanent, to use Trotskii's word and would eventually, perhaps very soon, also be extended to Finland. It might not be surprising that one of the main motives in Finnish terror discourse was revenge for the White terror. In popular form, a newspaper article under a pen name, the White terror itself was described for instance in the following way:[37]

> Dying imperialism uses its last weapon, the slaughterer dictatorship, with Neroan cruelty. In this Caligulian absurdity there are heard only dull thumps of the slaughterer's axe; bullets sound in the ear as they speed towards the noblest breasts of the heroes of the revolution. The slaughterers wade in blood to their neck and elbow.

In the revenge motif one might first pose a rhetorical question, say, "should we [...] stand dumb, motionless statutes on the great burial mound of our comrades". The answer was grandiose and, what is interesting, had strong religious overtones: a revolutionary proletarian "does not remain idle, he strikes with greater vigour" in revenge and in thus exacting vengeance, he becomes "the Saviour, Creator and Lord of the world".[38]

There was much more concrete discussion of the Red terror behind the scenes. We may read of it from protocols of the meetings and letters. In the second Congress of the SKP in 1919 so-called forced mobilisation was debated. This involved the question whether in the areas the Russian Reds controlled recruiting should be compulsory or not. K. M. Evä advocated a procedure whereby gives an order to all men to be mobilised to be at a certain place at a certain time, and those who failed to attend were to be shot without further enquiries.[39]

Toivo Antikainen, *primus* on the first Finnish Red Officer Course in the Petrograd International War School,[40] with whom we shall become more closely acquainted

---

[37] Väkivasara, "Punasen luokkasoturin olemus", *Wapaus*, April 24, 1920.

[38] *Ibid*. The terms with religious overtones are in Finnish *maailmanvapahtaja, maailmanluoja* and *maailmanherra.*

[39] Minutes of the II[d] Party Congress of the SKP, Petrograd, Aug. 31–Sept. 11, 1919. RGASPI, f. 516, op. 2, 1919, d. 4, ll. 110–111.

[40] The political Commissar of the War School, Jukka Rahja, considered Antikainen the best pupil on the first course of Red Chiefs. (*Ibid*., s. 130.) Antikainen graduated as a Red Chief on April 25, 1919

below, saw the essence of terror in its randomness: "Injurious elements" of the bourgeoisie must be killed, he declared in the second Congress of the SKP in 1919. Someone had obviously spoken against desultoriness, because Antikainen remarked: "Certain people try to obstruct the protection measure just mentioned [i.e. killing], but we have means to make these attempts futile, for the people arrested became 'tired in journeys or drowned'".[41] Coercive measures must be used particularly towards the peasants:[42]

> The bourgeois state is profitable for the peasants, for they might carry on kulak commerce there. They do not understand what is advantageous to them and what is the aim of the Soviet power. This stuff must be coerced, they must be put to trench work, and the whip must be used. And good work will be forced out by a prick of the bayonet in the buttocks. It is said that this would provoke the disgust of the inhabitants against us, although the slaughterers use the same means on their own side.

In the coming Finnish revolution, must bourgeois officers be killed in order to avoid the Russian institution of political commissars, because this brings a most inconvenient double command.[43] As to the slaughter of officers Antikainen said:[44]

> While understanding well what social and economic value attaches to every educated officer, who thus represents social property, my opinion is nonetheless that all higher slaughterer officers in the Finnish army must be killed off. They should be killed in any case, be they as good they may; I do not speak here of professional envy (general hilarity).

The randomness in Antikainen's terrorist plans was what the delegates at the Congress opposed. Voitto Eloranta asked who was to be killed and who not. He obviously spoke on the basis of experience when he said that it may happen that in a village the Red Army captures, some worker comes and tells the Reds that some big boss is a gruesome bourgeois, because he hid grain although the accuser was starving, and must therefore be killed. When the Reds ask other people in the vil-

---

(Henkilötietoja punapäälliköistä kansainvälisestä sotakoulusta : I kansainvälisestä sotakoulusta päässeet. [Data on Red Chefs graduating from the First International War School.] RGASPI, f. 516, op. 2, 1919, d. 196.)

41 Minutes of the II^d Congress of the SKP, Petrograd, Aug. 31–Sept. 11, 1919. RGASPI, f. 516, op. 2, 1919, d. 4, l. 115.

42 *Ibid.*

43 *Ibid.* The Russian principle was that the political Commissars should not be involved in military affairs. (Charles Bettelheim, *Les luttes des classes en URSS : première période 1917–1923*, p. 247.)

44 Minutes of the II^d Congress of the SKP, Petrograd, Aug. 31–Sept. 11, 1919. RGASPI, f. 516, op. 2, 1919, d. 4, ll. 115–116.

lage about this lord, they may receive contradictory information.[45] Eino Rahja proclaimed that he had never opposed killings, but if one without any sense "shoots right and left" he may cause "much damage". Eino Rahja warned that such conceptions of "haphazard shooting" must not be allowed to spread among the soldiers of the Red Army.[46]

In the background of the Finnish terror rhetoric was, of course, the Civil War and not only the White terror, but also the Red terror. Heikki Ylikangas, who made a particular study of the war and capture of Tampere, says that the Reds were "gnawed" by doubts that they were committing crimes and not effecting an "acceptable revolution".[47]

Intellectuals and Workers

According to Karl Marx's and Friedrich Engels' assertions the proletarians are destined to overturn human history, and when the proletarians behaved in a most unproletarian way they faced a dilemma: who better know the interests of the proletariat, the proletarians themselves or the intellectuals, who know the world-wide task ascribed to the working-class. Marx and Engels had no straightforward answer to this quandary.[48] Lenin's answer is well known; in the light of it, it was interesting that those old working-class members of the Bolshevik Party; men like Eino Rahja, Adolf Taimi, or Aleksander Vasten were obviously not very familiar with the doctrine (but Jukka Rahja was).

In the argumentation on the theme of intellectuals, it was typical that front lines were often purely tactical. It was typical that workers accused intellectuals of not understanding their living conditions and experiences. However, if we look at the circumstances in which these accusations were presented, we may note that in the "dock" are *some* intellectuals who happen to be on the wrong side in some squabble. It was also possible that workers accused other workers of not being workers any more but intellectuals. In the second Congress of the SKP in Moscow

---

[45] *Ibid.*, s. 118.

[46] *Ibid.*, s. 120.

[47] Ylikangas, *Tie Tampereelle*, p. 524.

[48] The intellectuals could have positive role in the working-class movement if they adopted "without reservation the proletarian outlook" (*Anschauungsweise*) and brought with them to the workers' movement "real educational elements". (Karl Marx and Friedrich Engels, Letter to August Bebel, Wilhelm Liebknecht, Wilhelm Bracke etc. Sept. 17–18, 1879, published in Karl Marx and Friedrich Engels, *Werke*, vol. 34, pp. 402–403.) On the other hand, sometimes workers already had a very strong proletarian outlook (Friedrich Engels, Letter to Eduard Bernstein, Feb. 27–March 1, 1883, published in Karl Marx and Friedrich Engels, *Werke*, vol. 35, p. 443); sometimes, again workers were so deeply "demoralised" that no hint of a "proletarian" outlook was seen. (Karl Marx, Letter to Wilhelm Liebknecht, Feb. 11, 1878, published in Karl Marx and Friedrich Engels, *Werke*, vol. 34, p. 320.)

in September 1919, J. H. Lumivuokko, who had not accepted the founding of the SKP, but after the founding Congress joined the Party, accused Kuusinen of a lack of understanding of historical materialism. According to Lumivuokko, Kuusinen had stated that Eino Rahja provided two thirds of the arms of the Red Guard. This reflected for Lumivuokko typically bourgeois thinking, because everybody understood that one man could not carry out such a titanic task. Thus:[49]

> When Kuusinen says this, it is due to the bourgeois leaven of which he still has a great deal, and which always wells up when he forgets the doctrine. But we, who were sold into care by auction, while the gentlemen sat on the school bench, we are conscious that the class struggle is the only infallible teacher in the workers' movement.

Now Jukka Rahja, not the greatest of Kuusinen's friends (although it was Eino Rahja who was Kuusinen's worst enemy among Rahja camp), defended the highly learned Kuusinen against the workman Lumivuokko: it did not go without saying that a man who had had occasion to study enough to be regarded as a "scholar" was therefore "untrustworthy".[50] In fact, Rahja was here not defending Kuusinen but attacking Lumivuokko and thus accomplished a kind of dialectical trick by which he managed to brand Lumivuokko himself as a doubtful intellectual:[51]

> To this kind of argument [of Lumivuokko] one could answer that Jukka Rahja is not a learned man nor a gentleman, only a common smith, but he does what he can, being no less trustworthy or untrustworthy because he does physical labour. And in Lumivuokko one can see the bureaucracy of the workers, the aristocracy of workers so much that one can consider him as a person grown up among gentlefolk at least with as good reason as Kuusinen.

Masses and Leaders

The question of intellectuals and workers is somewhat akin to that of leaders and the masses. Although there had probably always been more or less tension between workers and leaders in the Finnish workers' movement, this was stressed in

---

[49] Minutes of the II[d] Congress of the SKP, Petrograd, Aug. 31–Sept. 11, 1919. RGASPI, f. 516, op. 2, 1919, d. 4., ll. 123–124. – The words "we, who were sold into care by auction" refer to the practice in the Finnish countryside where orphans, or children whose parents were unable to maintain them, were publicly "sold" to someone who pledged to take care of them. They received a payment for this from the municipality. In the auction the person who offered to do this at the lowest costs "won" the child.

[50] Minutes of the II[d] Congress of the SKP in Petrograd, Aug. 31–Sept. 11. RGASPI, f. 516, op. 2, 1919, d. 4, ll. 123–124.

[51] *Ibid.*, pp. 128–129.

the Civil War; many rank-and-file Red Guardists did not trust the leaders. This phenomenon has not, as far as I know, been systematically studied. It seems that there was tension in the relation between politicians and military leaders, and between the Guardists and their officers (we should remember that the Red Guard was a "democratic" army where the soldiers elected at least some of their officers).[52] Some examples are to be found of these contradictions. Hugo Salmela, who was (before his death on March 30, 1918[53]) commander on the Tampere front, was highly dissatisfied with the activities of the People's Deputation: he did not see any sense in law-making before the whole country was ruled by the Reds. He wrote letters to the main headquarters in Helsinki in which he demanded that the law-makers be sent to the front.[54] The same phenomenon troubled Kustaa Salminen, commander of the Pori front, who wrote in not very polished language (the translation mimics the original as to spelling mistakes):[55]

> I hope, that tere these law jurists would come here amonsg this suffering and blood-spattered gang to learn to give orders corresponding a little bit to preset time and not to judge accoring old paragraphphs accoring the rumours spread by the bourgeois.

One front commander, Evert Karjalainen, gave vent to his anger after futile battles in a telephone discussion with commander-in-chief Eero Haapalainen (this was heard by the White intelligence and is therefore recorded):[56]

> **Haapalainen:** Karjalainen, I appointed you leading commander 4 weeks ago at Korkeakoski, and all this time you have rested on a sofa and admired your beautiful boots, if you are tomorrow not in Vilppula [i.e. if the attack of the Reds is not successful], I dismiss you. [...]
> **Karjalainen:** Do it. I swear by Satan it is true I have done what a human being, God damn it, can do and I leave immediately even to Heaven, by God, when, God damn it, Haapalainen comes to Lyly [to the front], I leave even to Hell, God damn it, if I yet exist in the morning. [...] Sat[an], God damn it, I have been awake 3–4 nights, there is not here a sofa for anybody to rest, Satan, Fiend, by God, this kind of talk is too much even in Hell.

---

52 See e.g. "Komppania valitsi päällikön" in *Aatteet ja aseet*, pp. 107–108

53 Ylikangas, *Tie Tampereelle*, p. 351.

54 Luhtakanta, *Suomen luokkasota*, p. 104.

55 Kustaa Salminen to the Procurator of the People's Deputation, March 16, 1918, cited in Rinta-Tassi, *Kansanvaltuuskunta punaisen Suomen hallituksena*, p. 331.

56 There is no date about this telephone discussion. (*Kansalaissota dokummentteina*, vol. 2, pp. 227–228.) May I mention that this extremely uncouth language is very difficult to render into English.

This altercation reveals that in difficult situations there was little respect for the chiefs (and that the clergy had not been successful in its attempts to purge the language of the masses from curses). On the other hand, some chiefs of the Red Guard tried to calm the frantic mood among the troops. In Tampere, the commander Hugo Salmela issued a proclamation in March in which he denied that the leaders had betrayed the people.[57]

At the end of the war the bitterness increased – in Viipuri especially after the People's Deputation had fled to Russia. The idea of betrayal came easily to the minds of tired guardists; the leaders were then branded as cowards and poltroons, who with all their money and property escaped and were now enjoying life and playing cards in the best restaurants in Petrograd. One printed leaflet, dated April 8, 1918, conveying such notions was distributed in Viipuri, although stamped in Petrograd, written by "Thinking Socialists"; its origin is not known. The leaflet ended as follows (spelling mistakes again follow the original):[58]

> Comrades!
>
> It is time to call our chiefs to account. Jf the destruction comes, let them take responsibility for our bledding. Let them not scurryoff like cowards with the money they collected when in power now leaving us who sacrifice our lihes in danger. Comrades! Should we always carry the heaviest burden.
>
> Thinking Socialists.
>
> Petrograd 8–IV–18

Voitto Eloranta interpreted this phenomenon in an ouvrierist way: in the rebellion only the "lowest masses" really supported the revolution, whereas the leaders began the rebellion "repulsively" and tried to "hinder" the revolutionary activities of the masses. In Russia, many "rightists" had to confess their sins and obtain pardon from the "masses", but in the leadership of the SKP, the "rightists" have not done this. Eloranta announced in the Second Congress of the SKP, that there had now emerged "something" which had not satisfied the "masses".[59] This argumentation is so vague, that it is difficult to say what was the substance of the quarrel. In this phase, September 1919, the Opposition in the SKP was not yet transparently formed.

---

[57] Ylikangas, *Tie Tampereelle*, p. 226.

[58] *Kansalaissota dokummentteina*, vol. 2, pp. 248–249, quotation on p. 249. Hannu Soikkanen, the editor of this collection of documents, says it cannot be ascertained whether the Reds or Whites wrote this leaflet. I think that even if the Whites wrote it, they then knew what kind of mood reigned among the Reds and thus this does not lessen the evidentiary value of the document.

[59] Minutes of the II^{d} Congress of the SKP in Petrograd, Aug. 31–Sept. 11, 1919, pp. 53–55. RGASPI, f. 516, op. 2, 1919, d. 4., ll. 53–55.

Robert Michels notes that the leaders of internal oppositions and protest movements in the workers' parties often posit a "proletarian" standpoint against the leaders, who are branded as intellectuals. This does not necessarily mean that the opposition leaders themselves were not intellectuals.[60] This applies to the Murder Opposition. Voitto Eloranta was an intellectual; Väinö Pukka was becoming one. The rhetoric of Opposition was, however, ouvrierist, as can be seen in the wording of a kind of manifesto the Opposition published in the spring of 1920:[61]

> In the broadest strata of Finnish workers has become the conception established that the former Right-Wing leaders of the Finnish workers' movement, even after the "revolutionarising" that has taken place in them, do not enjoy the trust among the revolutionary soldiers and workers, be they now in Russia or possibly in Finland, that is necessary for the preparation of the new revolution.

Trade Unions

If compared to Western European countries the trade unions played no significant part either in the Finnish or the Russian workers' movement before 1917. As we saw above, the Finnish trade unions became important political actors only in 1917. One feature of the Ultraleftism in the SKP was enmity pure and simple against all trade unions. This attitude was obviously a particular problem for J. H. Lumivuokko, a former trade union leader, after he had joined the SKP.

In the trade union debate, especially Jukka Rahja and K. M. Evä opposed the unions. In January 1919, Jukka Rahja attacked Lumivuokko as "counter-revolutionary", because he had defended the right of existence of unions; it is not clear where and in what context. For Rahja the unions were useful before the "age of imperialism" only.[62] It is not certain, however, whether Rahja's view really was so extreme as to hold that the trade unions under capitalism were harmful. He spoke mostly, but not only, about the present situation in Russia and in general about post-revolutionary societies. K. M. Evä thought that the trade unions were superfluous when workers are both employers and employees;[63] here, of course, a post-

---

[60] Michels, *Zur Soziologie des Partieiwesens in der modernen Demokratie*, pp. 262–263.

[61] Aku Paasi, Otto Palho, A. V. Matikainen, Voitto Eloranta and Väinö Pukka, "Suomalaisten työläiskommunistien provoseerausta vastaan!", *Wapaus*, March 27, 1920.

[62] Minutes of the discussion in the Finnish Communist Club, Jan. 15, 1919. RGASPI, f. 516, op. 2, 1918, d. 73. The Club was founded on August 5, 1918 in Petrograd. (Minutes of the foundation meeting of Finnish Workers' Communist Club, Aug. 5, 1918. RGASPI, f. 516, op. 2, 1918, d. 73.) The Club organised mainly debates. In March 1919 the Club, however, arranged, on the demand of the military organisation of the SKP, exercises in the use of "hand bombs"; 213 members reportedly participated in these exercises. (Report of the activities of the Finnish Communist Club of Petrograd, Jan. 1.–April 25, 1919. RGASPI, f. 516, op. 2, 1918, d. 73.)

[63] Minutes of the discussion in the Finnish Communist Club, Jan. 31, 1919. RGASPI, f. 516, op. 2, 1918, d. 73.

revolutionary society is in question. For capitalist countries, Evä recommended a double organisation: closed and public. In every factory and workplace there must be a secret council which prepares the takeover of the factory in question. In addition, there should be public committees in workplaces instead of centralised unions.[64]

In the Extraordinary Conference of the SKP in January–February 1919 the general mood was that the new rebellion in Finland must be launched soon. According to Jukka Rahja, Finland was bound to "blow up" soon; "until April we cannot live without a solution".[65] Rahja prophesied that the Finnish economy would fall into the hands of the Communists in so a depraved condition that the workers would "grumble" about wages and the length of the workday, which cannot be improved. In these circumstances the trade union movement was "the best weapon" of the counter-revolution and therefore dangerous to the "working people". It must be destroyed and the "broad masses" should be convinced of the superiority of the Soviet model.[66]

J. H. Lumivuokko was proselytised into Communism, obviously in the first part of the year 1919.[67] As to the usual activities of the trade unions in a capitalist society, Lumivuokko's position was now crystal-clear: even if all wage workers are organised in the trade unions, be their programme as radical as it is "permissible and possible", the trade unions necessarily play second fiddle, because the capitalists are always stronger than the workers economically, and are, moreover, supported by the state with its armed forces.[68] After the take-over, the trade unions may be useful, provided they adapt themselves to the dictatorship of the proletariat and organise the socialisation of the means of production and production itself. Apart from the Soviets, no "struggle organisations" which "encumber" the progress of the revolution will be allowed. However, even the Soviet power, "especially in the dawning of the dictatorship of the proletariat", may come athwart some group of workers, who have "special interests". In this case, Lumivuokko argues, one might think that there would be a role for the trade unions as contestants against these special interests and arbitrators. However, this possibility of contradiction was, according to Lumivuokko, so small that a special organisation is not needed.[69]

---

64 Saarela, *Suomalaisen kommunismin synty*, p. 140.

65 Minutes of the extraordinary Conference of the SKP, Jan. 27.–Feb. 5, 1919. RGASPI, f. 516, 1919, d. 6, l. 12. (The minutes of this Conference are rather sporadic.)

66 *Ibid.*, l. 9.

67 In January 1919 he was still considered by Jukka Rahja a "counter-revolutionary", but in the same year he published two booklets which show that he had been converted. (J. Lumivuokko, *Teollisen tuotannon järjestämisestä Työväen diktatuurin ensi asteilla Suomessa* and J. Lumivuokko, *Laillinen ammattiyhdistysliike vaiko vallankumous?*)

68 J. Lumivuokko, *Laillinen ammattiyhdistysliike vaiko vallankumous?*, pp. 49–50.

69 *Ibid.*, pp. 51–55.

Although Lumivuokko's conclusion is in its context "orthodox", it is interesting that he formulates for the trade unions in "Socialism" the role they actually had in "really existing" Socialism, namely that of formal arbitrators of disputes and, above all, etatist machines of the imposition of discipline upon the workers. Lumivuokko was very much ahead of his time!

Parliament

The Finnish Communist Party was, similar to other Communist parties in this epoch, strictly antiparliamentary. In Finland, the first parliamentary elections after the Civil War were held in 1919. Before the elections, the political *paysage* in Finland underwent profound alterations, as we have seen. Interesting in this regard is the change in the Social Democratic Party. Some Social Democrats who had refused to accept any tasks from the People's Deputation published – already in April 1918 – an appeal to the Reds to surrender. In their proclamation, the attempt at revolution was condemned as unorthodox and heretical in the light of Marxist tradition. The "oligarchic" leadership of the SDP on the one hand and Bolshevism on the other were branded as guilty of the misadventure. Bolshevism, it was explained, was a phenomenon typical of a country in which level of culture is low. Important stress was placed on independence and those who have been or still were tools of foreign Powers were condemned.[70]

New general elections were arranged in May 1919. The Social Democrats were able to participate in these, the Communists not. For the elections the SKP presented a "Communist Ballot", written by O. W. Kuusinen, dated "in Petrograd on February 5, in the revolutionary year 1919". It was signed by 66 personages, most of them émigrés. The tone of the proclamation was strictly anti-parliamentarist. It is not possible to defeat the bourgeoisie by voting because the bourgeois fight for their "loot with rifles and cannons". This has been experienced in Finland: when the electoral activities of the workers began to take a dubious direction from the point of view of the "class dominance of the bourgeoisie", this bourgeoisie "went for the throat of the workers".[71] Here the answer to the question "who began..." was opposite to that of the leaders of the new SDP in Finland. The Communists considered the former *Eduskunta* only as a means of defence; it was, thus, needed as "some kind of self-protective activity". In some degree "the lust for gore" of the bourgeoisie" could be curbed. It offered conditions in which it was possible for the

---

[70] Soikkanen, *Kohti kansanvaltaa*, vol. 1, pp. 310–312.

[71] *Kommunistinen vaalilippu : Suomen köyhälistölle, maan raatajille ja herravallan sortoa vihaaville sotilaille*. Published in *Suomen Kommunistinen Puolue : puoluekokousten, konferenssien ja Keskuskomitean pleenumien päätöksiä : ensimmäinen kokoelma*, pp. 20–21. – As far as I know this important source publication is not available in any public library in Finland, but is to be found in the reading room of *Kansan arkisto* (People's Archive), Helsinki.

workers to strengthen their forces. However, universal suffrage was not a means to acquire power.[72]

This epoch was, the declaration expounded, an epoch of proletarian revolution: history had now furnished the opportunity to "obliterate" the bourgeois state and transform it into a "workers' state". There existed a "class instinct" among the workers and therefore they understood "this clear matter" more readily than the leaders of the old workers' movement, who "have sunk into the slough of doubt" and cannot imagine a world without "the machinery of bourgeois oppression". Now there are only two alternatives and two front lines, Red and White. The Social Democratic voters were warned about the "path of the abject scheidemanns" ("Noske" was not yet in use). The aim was to establish a "Finnish Socialist Soviet State" which will unite with the Soviet Republics of other states, so that the outcome will be the "unity of International Socialist Soviet Republics".[73]

The message of the *Communist Ballot* was the boycottage of elections, although this was not clearly stated in the document. In any case, the message had no effect at all. In the first post-Civil War elections Finnish workers, crofters and agricultural workers voted for the SDP; the Party received 356,046 votes (in 1917 444,670) or 38 per cent of votes and obtained 80 seats. This was remarkable in that 38,000 people either were in camps or had been released from camps: these people had no right to vote.[74]

The Party

One of the cornerstones of the Bolshevik doctrine was the centralisation of all political power to the Party. In Finland, this idea was completely alien to the so-called old workers' movement, i.e. the undivided movement before the Civil War. It was a mass Party, not a cadre Party, as according to Lenin's doctrine a Communist Party should be. It seems that O. W. Kuusinen had, at least vaguely, grasped this idea in the summer of 1918.

According to Kuusinen the most important condition for a Communist Party was that because in Finland the Party must be secret, the Party leadership must have all the power. This did not mean that there must be a one-man dictatorship, but that the centralised leadership must be "similar to a dictatorship of the working people". This was the principle, Kuusinen declared, on which none can disagree. Different opinions may be held only as to the manner in which it will be

---

[72] *Ibid.*, p. 20.

[73] *Ibid.*, pp. 22–24.

[74] For the first time the voting percentage among women, 70.0 per cent, was higher than that of men, 64.8 per cent. Although there were also women's camps, most prisoners were men. (Soikkanen, *Kohti kansanvaltaa*, vol. 1, pp. 355–358.)

formed in practice. However, eventually the Communist Party should transform itself as a "mass movement". In some kind of transition period there may be both a cadre Party and a mass movement, but the development will finally lead to the formation "of a great Communist Party".[75] Jukka Rahja advocated a Communist Party which in the next revolution would take all power in "its own hands. At that time we shall not give power to people whose class conceptions vacillate".[76] It seems that the role of a Communist Party, as Lenin had formulated it in his *What has to be done*, was not known to the delegates of the founding Congress. Rahja's and Kuusinen's conceptions of the Party were not identical.

In so-called proletarian Communist tendencies and factions, "pure" Soviet power and the dictatorship of the Communist Party were seen to be in contradiction with each other. The rebels of Kronstadt, for instance, demanded an end to the Party dictatorship and the realisation of Soviet democracy.[77] Similar lines of thought were also present in the formation phase of the future Murder Opposition of the SKP in autumn 1919. In the second Congress of the Party August Paasi, who represented the collective of the International War School, suggested that the Central Committee of the SKP be replaced by a "Finnish Workers' and Soldiers' Soviet". This Soviet would function "completely under the control of Russian Soviets, following Soviet principles in all of its undertakings". In this way the Finns could be trained in practical work in the Soviets. The Finnish Soviets would also be responsible for all service work still needed to feed and shelter the Red refugees; this work was at the time to be passed over to Russian governmental agencies. Paasi's suggestion had also the purpose of keeping this activity in Finnish hands. On this point, however, Paasi had to stress that in spite of this idea, his proposal had nothing to do with any kind of "patriotism".[78] Paasi's proposition did not enjoy support among the SKP leaders. Jukka Rahja demanded that the Congress takes no account at all of the proposal because it "leads the workers' movement astray". Kullervo Manner, chairman of the Congress, did not allow any debate on Paasi's proposal. In protest at this procedure, eleven delegates abstained. They comprised future members and sympathisers of the opposition, but Toivo Antikainen was also among those delegates who abstained. – Rahja's proposal was accepted by 24–1.[79]

---

[75] Minutes of the founding Congress of the Finnish Communist Party, Aug. 29–Sept. 5, 1918. RGASPI, f. 516, op. 1, d. 291, ll. 8–9.

[76] *Ibid.*, l. 34.

[77] Israel Getzler, *Kronstadt 1917–1921 : the Fate of A Soviet Democracy*, pp. 233–236.

[78] Minutes of the II[d] Congress of the SKP, Petrograd, Aug. 31–Sept. 11, 1919. RGASPI, f. 516, op. 2, 1919, d. 4, appendix 11.

[79] *Ibid.*, pp. 92–93.

2. The Military and Corruption

In conditions of extreme hardship, it is perhaps inevitable that various form of corruption should thrive. Petrograd was in a special position in this regard, because the Finnish border was so close to the metropolis, and the guard on the border so weak that smuggling soon became a flourishing business. Although Finland was devastated by the Civil War, its economy was nevertheless not so badly undermined as the Russian economy was. There was also corruption among the military and in the Red Officer School in Petrograd, a school in which the Finns were trained for the new rebellion.

The Red Officer School

One special factor in the internal struggles of the SKP was the military organisation of the Party. The Petrograd Finnish Red Officer School appears to have been loosely attached to this military organisation, usually referred to as "the military line". The military line was founded at the turn of October–November 1918. In November, the Officer School, a subdivision of the International War School, was also established. It was also known as the Third Officer Course of the Infantry. The designation "third" is curious, since there was no "first" or "second" course. The Commander of the School was Aleksander Inno, an Estonian professional soldier. The first political Commissar was Eino Rahja, then, in spring 1919, O. W. Kuusinen was for some months Commissar and after Kuusinen had left – secretly, of course – for Finland, Jukka Rahja replaced him.[80]

The life of the War School soon became troubled for various reasons. In January 1919, recruit (*kursant*) August Paasi made a complaint to the Inspection Committee of the School that the staff were stealing potatoes.[81] In extreme hardship, a matter like potatoes may indeed be very important, but there were deeper reasons for dissatisfaction. The recruits were especially dissatisfied with Commissar Eino Rahja and a delegation headed by Otto Palho, a member of the future Murder Opposition, went to meet the supreme Commissar Zickia to complain of Rahja's

---

[80] Kullervo Manner, Report on activities of the Soldier Organisation of the SKP, Aug. 8, 1919. RGASPI, f. 516, op. 2, 1919, d. 80, ll. 1–2. Kuusinen relates that he left for Finland without formal dismissal from his appointment as Commissar. (O. W. Kuusinen, "Suomen porvariston johtajille", *Viesti*, March 24, 1920 in Otto V. Kuusinen and Yrjö Sirola, *Suomen työväen tulikoe* : *kirjoitelmia Suomen luokkasodan jälkeisiltä ajoilta*, p. 47.) Kuusinen crossed the Russian-Finnish border on May 27, 1919. (Erkki Salomaa, "Usko Sotamies – O. W. Kuusinen" in *Tiennäyttäjät, Suomen työväenliikkeen merkkimiehiä Ursinista Tanneriin*, vol. 3, p. 371.)

[81] Minutes of the Inspection Committee of the IIIth Finnish Infantry Officer Course in Petrograd, Jan. 9. 1919. RGASPI, f. 516, op. 2, 1919, d. 171. See also "Pietarin suomalaisesta upseerikoulusta ja oloista siellä", *Helsingin Sanomat*, July 13, 1919.

behaviour and various defects in the School. The recruits did not follow the chain of command in doing this and Eino Rahja therefore declared that they were rebels and the fate of rebels might be similar as that of the rebelling workers in the Putilov factory in Tsarist times.[82]

In the second Congress of the SKP in August–September 1919, the problems of the Red Officer School were presented in various speeches. For example Toivo Antikainen said that the Central Committee of the SKP wished to withdraw the rights guaranteed by the "constitution of Soviet Power" to all, also to the recruits of the War School. "In practice the Rahjas' claim, supposedly on the basis of responsibilities given them by the Party, meant that their individual dictatorship was real Communism".[83] As a counterstroke, Commander Inno complained that there was much "indiscipline" in the School and demanded that the Congress delve into the matter. The Congress made a decision to establish a special committee to do so.[84]

The committee looked into to the matter carefully. It requested and received a long statement from the recruits, in which was a long list of grievances, the most serious being the poor food and hunger. It was also complained that among the men there were backward people and people mentally unfitted for military training, even criminals. The committee, it seems, largely appreciated the complaints, and proposed that the Commissar Jukka Rahja must devote more time to his recruits, and be more interested in their political and other education.[85] Among the means of education Jukka Rahja used were threats of execution of recruits who kept up the forbidden hobby of card playing.[86]

After receiving the report, the Central Committee established a new investigation committee (Jalo Kohonen and Kullervo Manner), which had a series of hearings in the School. Every recruit had to sign his protocol of the hearing, which undoubtedly prevented many from presenting complaints. Moreover, Jukka Rahja

---

82 Minutes of the general meeting of the Union of Comrades of the Finnish Detachment of the third Infantry Officer Course of the Soviets of Petrograd, March 31, 1919. RGASPI, f. 516, op. 2, 1919, d. 205. The chairman of the meeting was Voitto Eloranta.

83 Minutes of the II[d] Congress of the SKP, Petrograd, Aug. 31–Sept. 11, 1919. RGASPI, f. 516, op. 2, 1919, d. 4, ll. 38–39.

84 *Ibid.*, l. 82. The members of the committee were Jaakko Mäki, Mikko Kokko (later replaced by Juho Latukka) and J. H. Lumivuokko. The intention was that the committee would make its report to the Congress within a few days. Almost immediately the committee declared that the matter is very broad and asked that it can make its report to the Central Committee. So it was decided. (*Ibid.*, l. 84. See also f. 516, op. 2, 1919, d. 5, appendix 9.)

85 The report of the committee, set by the II[d] Congress of the SKP, on the indiscipline in the War School to the CC, Feb. 25, 1920. RGASPI, f. 516, op. 2, 1919, d. 201.

86 The presidium of the Communist collective of the third Infantry Officer Course of the Soviet of Petrograd to the District Committee of Vasiliostrova of the Russian Communist Party. No date, probably in the end of 1919. RGASPI, f. 516, op. 2, 1920, d. 125.

announced that when a man had confirmed his statement by signature it was no longer possible to annul the statement. The Commissar had possibility to put men who have made false statements in the dock.[87] Despite this threat, there were numerous men who described the shock they experienced when they came to the School. One, Aleksi Toivola, said, according to his hearing record:[88]

> When the new beginner has decided to enter the course, he has drawn up his account with himself and his life in one way and another. He has also himself created a picture of life here. About the Commander and the Commissar he has special concepts, that they are people who are able to go deeply into the spiritual and physical life of those on the course and that they treat their pupils with love and understanding, spending warm and comradely moments with them.

Aleksi Toivola experienced nothing like this. Instead, he found himself subjected to all manner of troubles. He did not understand the orders because they were given in Russian. They were, moreover, confusing and contradictory: it happened, for example, that one should be in two different places at the same time. There were no clean underclothes and therefore there were lice everywhere. In the stores of the School, there were, it was said, both clothes and food, but they were not given to the recruits (this was a common complaint). Worst of all was the behaviour of Jukka Rahja: he was always accusing his men of being "counter-revolutionaries and rebels",[89] a most horrendous charge against men who thought they were soldiers of the proletarian revolution, even on a world scale.

Racketeering

The Finnish refugees in Russia were suffering not only from lack of adequate nourishment; they were also distressed by the uncertainty of their own future and the fate of their families and relatives.[90] The Red Guardists were still in May and June paid wages out of the money the Reds had taken from the Bank of Finland or printed in Finland themselves,[91] but because not all pay sheets could be taken with the refugees, many men drew the wages several times, which aroused anger among

---

[87] Appendix to the minutes of the meeting of the Collective of the Finnish Red Officer Course, March 4, 1920. RGASPI, f. 516, op. 2, 1920, d. 152, l. 3.

[88] Väärinkäytöksistä ja virheellisyyksistä 3:nen neuvoston [*sic*] Pietarin suomalaisen jalkaväen päällikkökurssien koululla (On Malpractices and Faultinesses in the Third Soviet [*sic*] of the School of Commander Courses of Finnish Infantry), no date, spring 1920. RGASPI, f. 516, op. 2, 1920, d. 152, l. [I/] 2–3. – The title indicates how vacillating was the terminology regarding the War School.

[89] *Ibid.*, l. [I/] 10.

[90] М. М. Коронен, *В. И. Ленин и Финляндия*, pp. 258–260.

[91] Hjalmar Font, *Kremlin kiertolaisia : muistelmia monivaiheisen elämän varrelta*, p. 18. This Finnish money was in the summer 1918 convertible in Russia.

the leaders and personnel of the former People's Deputation. The indignation, however, was mutual. Väinö Pukka, who was in charge of Red refugees in Moscow, complained to O. W. Kuusinen in June 1918 that the refugees were accusing the former People's Deputation as an "arbitrary money-grabbing gang". Pukka suggested that a "clarification" must be published about "several million [*markkas*] everybody claims exist".[92] In fact, the SKP had at first a great deal of money because a great number of workers' organisations, whose leaders had escaped to Russia, brought the money of their organisations with them. This money was, however, not enough to meet colossal expenses of the Party and in 1920 at last, the Party began to receive some money from the RKP(b) and from the Comintern, and not only money but also diamonds and other jewels. The Party became dependent on the money it received from the Russians.[93]

Much dissatisfaction among the refugees arose by reason of various business activities in which the SKP was involved. The purpose of this activity was to obtain workplaces for the refugees. The SKP bought metal workshops and sawmills, but the enterprise was not successful,[94] at least partly because the companies given to the Finns were in extremely deleterious condition. It was therefore decided that the industrial activity was to be "liquidated"; this meant the transfer of the companies to the Russian state. From the autumn of 1918 to the autumn of 1919, the huge bureaucracy arising around this messy business cost the leaders of the SKP an unconscionable amount of time. In spite of the financial losses of this business, the SKP leaders did have much money available, as already noted. In addition, there was "spivvery"[95] on a vast scale: smuggling, black marketing and speculation. How much of this money was transferred to the funds of the SKP and how much Jukka and Eino Rahja put into their own pockets is unknown. The fact is, however, that the brothers became notorious for their swindling and extravagant life. In the second Congress of the SKP, 1919, many delegates delivered agitated speeches about the corruption of the leaders and spivvery of the Rahja brothers.

In the second Congress one delegate, Onni Tuomi, said that the Central Committee was receiving from "Russian funds" too much money, which has had two negative effects: the activities of the Party have been too extensive in consequence

---

92 Väinö Pukka to O. W. Kuusinen, June 27, 1918. RGASPI, f. 516, op. 2, 1918, d. 118.

93 Tauno Saarela, "Tuhatmarkkasia, miljoonia ruplia, dollareita : SKP:n tilinpäätös 1920-luvulta" in *...vaikka voissa paistais? : Venäjän rooli Suomessa*, pp. 276–278. Saarela's article has also been published in Danish: "Tusindmarksedler, millioner af rubler, dollars... : FKP's regnskap i 1920'erne" in *Guldet fra Moskva : Finansieringen af de nordiske kommunistpartier 1917–1990*, pp. 206–210.

94 Report of the activities of the Industrial Committee of the SKP, Jan. 1.–Aug. 28, 1919. RGASPI, f. 516, op. 2, 1919, d. 7.

95 The Finnish word *kulasseeraus* is translated by "spivvery" and "racketeering". It seems that this rare dialectal Finnish word was used only, or at least mainly, in Finnish spoken in Russia and in Karelian Isthmus.

of all manner of business and it has been possible to live "flauntingly" and not moderately as in the old Social Democratic Party, which had always lacked money.[96] Also, Matti Turkia complained of the substantial role of the business side and he calculated that for "educational" purposes only 10 per cent of all money was spent.[97] In addition, the auditor of the Party, Juho Viitasaari, complained of the "huge" sums of money swallowed up by the business. He thought that a better way to use the money would be in "furthering military, or in general revolutionary activities in Finland".[98] Turkia did not understand for what purposes the military organisation of the Party (led by the Rahjas) needed four expensive automobiles. He had been told by the chauffeurs that the brothers were driven home by them in the evenings.[99] According to Emil Laiho, there are no wagons for carrying wounded soldiers, but in Petrograd stand automobiles "worth millions" "at the gates of palaces" used "for other purposes":[100]

> A man transported one hundred and ten versts on bad road on wooden stretchers, his wounds insufficiently bound, will in a crystal-clear way recognize the difference between two days and nights of suffering and pain for the Communist world revolution and luxurious life and reckless driving.

The future Murder Opposition was in the process of formation at the time of the second Congress. It was represented e.g. by the engine-driver Henrik Puukko, who worked on the railway from Petrograd to Beloostrov (in Finnish Valkeasaari), the last railway station before the Finnish border. He knew that in the military organisation some odd smuggling was going on:[101]

> We know that from the Finnish border are transported products in whose acquisition the Central Committee as a whole cannot be involved [added by an unknown

---

96 Minutes of the II^d Congress of the SKP, Petrograd, Aug. 31 – Sept. 11, 1919. RGASPI, f. 516, op. 2, 1919, d. 4, ll. 31–32.

97 *Ibid.*, l. 13. Educational activities of the SKP in 1918–1921 were numerous. Courses were given and, above all, the Party published three papers: newspaper *Wapaus* in Petrograd, theoretical paper *Kumous* and a paper *Viesti* in Sweden. The Party had a publication series in which about 100 books and booklets were published. Twelve books on military matters were published for soldiers. In addition two booklets were published for Communist youth. (Saarela, *Suomalaisen kommunismin synty*, pp .488–490. See also M. M. Коронен, *Финские интернационалисты в борьбе за власть советов*, pp. 116–117.

98 Minutes of the II^d Congress of the SKP, Petrograd, Aug. 31–Sept. 11, 1919. RGASPI, f. 516, op. 2, 1919, d. 4., ll. 33–34.

99 *Ibid.*, p. 14 and p. 17. See also Helena Hartikainen's examination record, Jan. 9, 1920. Ek-Valpo I, examination report of the main department, 12/1920, box 1050. KA.

100 Minutes of the II^d Congress of the SKP, Petrograd, Aug. 31–Sept. 11, 1919. RGASPI, f. 516, op. 2, 1919, d. 4, l. 6.

101 *Ibid.*, l. 21.

> hand: "why cannot!?"]. It cannot be explicable with even the best will that spirits, liquor, women's fine shoes and men's alike are imported for the requirements of the military organisation; they remain for private purposes.

It is impossible to get a precise picture of the extent of the smuggling. Not only Finns but also Russians were practising it. The military organisation of the SKP had a tariff according to which smuggled goods were paid for to smugglers operating on the Finnish side of the frontier. According to Jalmari Kotiranta, who was responsible for illegal border activities, the Finns could not compete with the Russians because the latter had much more money. Kotiranta argued that the Russian "horse swindlers" (*hevoskulassit*) had bribed the Finnish frontier guards and because the transport of horses was therefore safe, the smugglers made "thousands of *markkas* in one day".[102] It is probable that Kotiranta underrated his ability to pay and exaggerated the sums the Russians actually paid, because it was in his interests to get more money for smuggling.[103]

The behaviour of the Rahja brothers, which included plentiful use of alcohol – in Finland the workers' movement has traditionally demanded prohibition – and the authoritarian bragging, menacing with a "Browning" etc., were grist to the mill for the emerging opposition. Jukka Rahja answered the charge of drinking that in Russia drinking on "private time" is not forbidden; he added that now in Russia he had, unfortunately, not been able to obtain two litres of vodka, the amount that for him was "necessary" to get drunk.[104] – Chairman Kullervo Manner said that he could not deny the truthfulness of the accusations of the opposition against the Rahja brothers.[105]

---

[102] Jalmari Kotiranta in Beloostrov to the military organisation of the SKP, Nov. 4, 1919. RGASPI, f. 516, op. 2, 1919, d. 81.

[103] Armas Koivuranta and Eetu Tietäväinen (two SKP "border men") to Jalmari Kotiranta Nov. 4, 1919 and Jalmari Kotiranta to the military organisation of the SKP, Nov. 5, 1919. RGASPI, f. 516, op. 2, 1919, d. 81. The "traffic" on the border was quite brisk and dangerous. Not all Finnish border guarders were bribed and armed exchanges between Finnish and Russian border guard detachments were not unusual. (Jalmari Kotiranta to the military organisation of the SKP, Nov. 4, 1919. RGASPI, f. 516, op. 2, 1919, d. 80.) On the Finnish side of the border, even whole villages were involved in smuggling. One of the reasons for the smuggling was simply the independence of Finland; before independence, the legal commerce over the border had been extensive and profitable for the Finns. (Pekka Nevalainen, *Rautaa Inkerin rajoilla : Inkerin kansalliset kamppailut ja Suomi 1918–1920*, pp. 178–179.) Then in 1919–1920 there were white Ingermanlanders (i.e. Finnish-speaking) "liberation" forces and battles between Bolsheviks and these forces. (There is a résumé in Russian in Nevalainen's book, pp. 273–278.)

[104] Minutes of the meeting held in the Finnish Red Officer School, March 4, 1920. RGASPI, f. 516, op. 2, 1920, d. 152, appendix, l. 10

[105] Minutes of the III[d] Congress of the SKP, Aug. 13–21, 1920. RGASPI, f. 516, op. 2, 1920, d. 2, l. 67.

The bitterness caused by racketeering was quite natural when we take into account the extremely harsh living conditions in Petrograd in the winter of 1919–1920. So-called War Communism meant the breakdown of both agricultural and industrial production. On the European side of Russia, only 15,000 versts of railways out of a total of 70,000 versts were fit to carry traffic.[106] Inflation made Russian money worthless.[107] The inhabitants of the towns escaped to the countryside, where food was better available: in autumn 1920 Petrograd had lost, according to the official statistics, 57.5 per cent of its inhabitants and Moscow 44.5 per cent in comparison with the year 1917.[108] The black market flourished: estimations of the percentage of foodstuff sales in cities varied from 60 per cent to 80 per cent.[109] Stealing and robbing of food was usual.[110] In Petrograd, people starved and shivered with cold.

Espionage

A special feature in the development of the Murder Opposition was its connections with military espionage. In the sources used, the information on relations between the Finnish Communists and Russian intelligence organs in 1919 and 1920 is fragmentary and no certain inferences may be drawn. It would appear that in 1918 the SKP established a special spying department which followed the activities of the Finnish "counter-revolutionaries" in Russia. Its efforts were hardly successful and in the second Party Congress, in August–September 1919, Kullervo Manner announced that this department would be transformed to a Russian "office" of the counter-revolutionary agency with which an agreement had already been made.[111] This Russian espionage agency was obviously the Cheka, but the agency with which the Opposition had contacts was that of the army, Register Administration (*Регистрправление*), usually abbreviated to Registrup.[112] (In addition, there were intelligence of the navy and intelligence of the military dis-

---

[106] E. H. Carr, *The Bolshevik Revolution 1917–1923*, vol. 2, p. 195.

[107] Maurice Dobb, *Soviet Economic Development since 1917*, p. 100.

[108] Carr, *The Bolshevik Revolution 1917–1923*, vol. 2, p. 198.

[109] *Ibid.*, pp. 242–243.

[110] Dobb, *Soviet Economic Development since 1917*, pp. 112–113.

[111] Minutes of the II[d] Congress of the SKP, Petrograd, Aug. 31–Sept. 11, 1919, l. 9. RGASPI, f. 516, op. 2, 1919, d. 4.

[112] George Leggett (*The Cheka: Lenin's Political Police : the All-Russian Extraordinary Commission for Combating Counter-Revolution and Sabotage (December 1917 to February 1922)*, s. 301) says that regarding the origin and early activities of this intelligence agency almost nothing is known. The institution was founded in November 1918. (Приказ по регистрационному управлению уполномоченным республики, Nov. 8, 1918. Центральный Государственный Архив Красной Армии (Central State Archives of the Red Army), Moscow, f. 6, op. 3, d. 1.)

trict of Petrograd. These different organisations had a number of coordinating problems.[113])

In November or December 1919 the Central Committee of the SKP became aware that Voitto Eloranta, his wife Elvira Willman-Eloranta, Valter Railo-Rissanen and Väinö Pukka had had "secret negotiations" with a representative of the Registrup. For this the Central Committee summoned Eloranta to be heard, but in the hearing on December 12, 1919, Eloranta refused to say anything because, according to him, a "Russian organ" takes precedence over the Finnish Central Committee. The Central Committee obliged Eloranta to write a report on the matter and threatened that if Eloranta in due form did not hand in the report he would not graduate as a Red officer.[114] Eloranta gave the report but said nothing more in it than in the hearing.[115]

K. M. Evä, the secretary of the Party, wrote to the Cheka – obviously after these futile attempts – demanding that the Elorantas and Railo-Rissanen be arrested and condemned for false accusations. According to Evä, Voitto Eloranta had accused Jukka and Eino Rahja and Aleksander Inno of "stealing or causing to be stolen" (*varastaminen tai varastuttaminen*) foodstuffs. Elvira Willman-Eloranta had accused the Central Committee of protecting the murderers of V. Volodarskii, and Railo-Rissanen had joined all these accusations and in addition accused Eino Rahja of smuggling and criminal "opening or causing to be opened" (*avaaminen tai avauttaminen*) letters.[116]

The claim that the Elorantas had accused the Central Committee of the SKP or the people working for it of protecting the murderer of V. Volodarskii,[117] the Commissar of the Press, Propaganda and Agitation of the Petrograd Commune, a Left Socialist Revolutionary Sergeev (who acted without sanction of the Central Committee of the Socialist Revolutionaries[118]), recurs in the sources. The Collective of the Red Officer School discussed the Eloranta case on February 9, 1920. Jukka Rahja demanded that Eloranta say whether it was correct to accuse people working for the Central Committee of involvement in the murder of Volodarskii. What Eloranta said to this is not known, because the protocol of the meeting is incomplete. Kullervo Manner argued that Eloranta's accusations were criminal and the case must therefore be given to the Cheka for investigation. Many recruits defended

---

[113] Juri Kilin, *Suurvallan rajamaa: Neuvosto-Karjala Neuvostoliiton politiikassa 1920–1941*, p. 56.

[114] The hearing of recruit Eloranta in the CC, Dec. 12, 1919. RGASPI, f. 516, op. 2, 1919, d. 287.

[115] Voitto Eloranta to the CC of the SKP, Petrograd, Dec. 13, 1919. RGASPI, f. 516, op. 2, 1919, d. 287.

[116] The CC to the Petrograd Special Committee. No date and signature. The handwriting is Evä's. RGASPI, f. 516, op. 2, 1920, d. 152.

[117] V. Volodarskii (Moisei Markovich Goldstein) was murderd on June 20, 1918. (Georges Haupt and Jean-Jacques Marie, *Les bolchéviks par eux-mêmes*, p. 381.)

[118] Pipes, *The Russian Revolution*, p. 810.

Eloranta; it was said, for instance, that if Eloranta had done something wrong it was only a "mistake" and the matter must not be given to the Cheka.[119]

Manner's and Kohonen's committee also investigated the Eloranta case.[120] Väinö Pukka was asked what he had told the Russians. Pukka was obviously not willing to tell the committee about his contacts with the Russian spying agencies. Pukka said he had told them something about the military organisation of the SKP and about the Rahja Brothers. "A Russian", who had presented the membership book of the Russian Communist Party, had spoken of combining the spying activities of the SKP and Russian espionage in Finland, led by Railo-Rissanen. This "Russian" had further said that in Moscow a decision on the combination of these activities had been made but the "staff" had refused to be employed in the new institution because Jukka Rahja's character was "intolerable". It seems that here Kullervo Manner lost his temper: he proclaimed to Pukka that before a member of the SKP gave information to "governmental bodies of a foreign country", in this case to a representative of the "Registburo" (obviously the Registrup), Rosnanskii[121] regarding the activities of the Party, be he even "mistaken", he must make the Central Committee aware of it, at least immediately afterwards.[122]

In addition to Pukka, Manner and Kohonen questioned two other of Railo-Rissanen's, companions Kauko Tamminen and Oskar Sundman. Tamminen, who was Railo-Rissanen's brother-in-law, told them that Railo-Rissanen has "quite a large organisation" in Finland.[123] Rosnanskii had been in Railo-Rissanen's flat on the evening of the "28th day" (obviously December 28, 1919). Rosnanskii had explained that his task was to combine Railo-Rissanen's activities with those of the military organisation of the SKP, but then the task had been changed by telegram order from Moscow "otherwise". Tamminen had received from Railo-Rissanen's talk the impression that the assignment was to create a "new organisation" which

---

[119] Minutes of the meeting of the collective of the Finnish Officer Course, Feb. 9, 1920. RGASPI, f. 516, op. 2, 1920, d. 125. Report of activities of the SKP to the III^{d} Congress in July 1921. RGASPI, f. 516, op. 2, 1920. There is no number in the *delo*. – In this document it is stated that the opposition began to accuse the members of the Central Committee "under the leadership of a representative of the Finnish slaughterers in Peters' intelligence agency [perhaps the Registrup in this context], an officer of Tsar", for the protection of Volodarskii's assassins and conspirators at [Nikolai Nikolaevich] Iudenich's time".

[120] The examination records of the Eloranta case have not been preserved completely. Two first pages and some other pages are missing. In the table of content of the *delo*, written in German, the title is "Verhörsprotokolle verschiedener Personen in der Sache Eloranta". RGASPI, f. 516, op. 2, 1920, d. 152. There are no dates.

[121] I have not succeeded in discovering any information about this Rosnanskii. It is possible that the name is wrongly written. In Finnish documents, it was quite usual for Russian names, especially these of people not known to the public, to be written incorrectly.

[122] The examination records of the Eloranta case. RGASPI, f. 516, op. 2, 1920, d. 125, l. [III/]19–22.

[123] *Ibid.*, l. [III/] 31.

would not concentrate only on spying but would also prepare the "revolution which soon would erupt in Finland".[124] According to Oskar Sundman, Railo-Rissanen had in writing expressed his unwillingness to close down the spying detachment he was leading. To Manner's question what "was basically possessing in this matter", Sundman answered that he could not even guess.[125]

Unfortunately, it remains unclear what "basically was possessing him in this matter". Juho Kovanen, a Red refugee, who came to Finland in 1922 and was examined by the Finnish Detective Central Police, explained that the wrangle was over smuggling. The "boutique" led by Eino Rahja and handled by Jalmari Kotiranta became a rival of the political department of the Russian Seventh Army, which also practised smuggling.[126] It is possible that the political department of the Seventh Army had some connections with the Registrup; perhaps they were even one and same institution. It is not sufficient, however, to explain the problem away by smuggling. One substantial question remains: who was Valter Railo-Rissanen.

According to Kyösti Wilkuna, who was imprisoned by the Russians in 1916 due to his connections with the *Jäger* movement, relates in his memoirs, published in 1917, that in the Shpalernaia prison in Petrograd there was a prisoner named Heino Voldemar Rissanen. He wore the *Jäger* uniform and disclosed everything he knew about the *Jägers* to the Russian authorities. Wilkuna tells that Rissanen escaped to Russian side when the Finnish *Jäger* battalion was on the Riga front in Latvia in the spring of 1916.[127] The Finnish Detective Central Police knew "Oskar Valter Railo or Rissanen", who in 1919 sent "bombs" from Russia to Finland. He headed a spying organisation which employed a staff of 200. He disappeared at the end of 1920 and was executed later in the 1920s after having confessed that in 1918–1919 he was an agent of the British intelligence.[128]

According to Eino Rahja's report to the fourth Congress of the SKP in 1921, Railo-Rissanen organised Russian espionage in Finland and was assisted in this work by the Elorantas, Pukka, and other "such people". He was paid for this by the Petrograd organisation of the Registrup, led by a man who used the name Pedder.[129] At the end of 1919, Pedder's organisation was shut down by the Moscow headquarters of the Registrup because it was found "untrustworthy". Thereafter the Elorantas and others began to "expose" people (to whom, it is not clear) and the

[124] *Ibid.*, ll. [III/] 31–32.

[125] *Ibid.* l. [III/] 34.

[126] Juho Kovanen's examination record, March 6, 1922, p. 6. Ek-Valpo I, PF 3699, August Paasi, KA.

[127] Kyösti Wilkuna, *Kahdeksan kuukautta Shpalernajassa*, pp. 285–296. Matti Lauerma, *Kuninkaallinen Preussin jääkäripataljoona 27*, pp. 367–368.

[128] Valter Oskar Rissanen's personal card. Ek-Valpo I. KA.

[129] Unfortunately, I have found no information on this Pedder.

Registrup had hired Jukka Rahja to "liquidate" the spying on Finland and he had arrested 50 people who were involved in spying.[130]

These are assertions which can scarcely be anything but exaggeration. It may be true that Railo-Rissanen organised espionage in Finland, but the claim that he had a staff of 200 people must be overstated. It is possible that Railo-Rissanen sent bombs to Finland, but certainly not in great numbers. It may be true that he confessed being a British agent, but the story itself is hardly true. In 1918–1919, the easiest way to establish contact with the English was in the Murmansk area, but no source I know about the Finns there at the time, has any mention of a Railo-Rissanen. There is again no source other than Eino Rahja's report about Jukka Rahja's role in the Registrup. If he had a role, the employment must have taken place relatively late. Railo-Rissanen, Eloranta, Pukka and others involved in the Opposition were cleared in Manner's and Kohonen's report: they had connections with Pedder's agency, which was found to be counter-revolutionary and criminal, but they had acted in good faith.

At the beginning of April 1920, the Cheka arrested Railo-Rissanen and several others found in his flat. They were, however, soon freed and the Central Committee publicly announced that it had nothing to do with the arrests.[131] It is probable that the Cheka made the arrests but that when it emerged that the arrested persons were working for Registrup, they were freed.[132]

It is apparent that the leaders of the SKP became frightened by the Opposition's Registrup connection. It is, however, difficult to see why they were so apprehensive. Perhaps they feared revelation of the smuggling and speculation in Eino Rahja's "boutique". It is not entirely impossible that they sought to protect certain Finns who had something to do with the assassination of Volodarskii, as Eloranta claimed. In June 1918, Left Socialist Revolutionaries, who believed in terrorist tactics, raised a revolt in Moscow. Iakov Khristoforovich Peters, who was vice-director of F. E. Dzerzhinskii's Cheka, says that at the time they had control of Finns who did not speak any Russian.[133] These were Red refugees and they actually participated in

---

130 Eino Rahja, To the Finnish Communist Party, the Executive Committee of the Communist International and to the Central Committee of the Russian Communist Party. Report on the conclusions of investigations concerning the murder of the members of the SKP. Minutes of the IV[d] Congress of the SKP. RGASPI, f. 516, op. 2, 1920, unnumbered *delo*, appendix 4, l. 3.

131 K. M., "Eräs vangitsemisjuttu", *Wapaus*, April 9, 1920.

132 According to the Cheka, the reason for the arrest was a letter, written in cipher, which was found among the goods of one Tyyne Viden. It was thought that the letter had information used for spying in Soviet Russia. When the letter was deciphered, it was found that it had nothing to do with espionage, and all those arrested were freed. (Cheka's certification to the CC of the SKP regarding the reasons for the arrest of Rissanen and 19 other people. RGASPI, f. 516, op. 2, 1920, d. 24.) This explanation do not hold water.

133 Peters, "Воспоминания о работе в ВЧК в первый год революции", *Пролетарская революция*, 10 (33), October 1924, pp. 18–19.

the failed coup d'état led by Left Socialist Revolutionaries.[134] Later the Murder Opposition claimed that they had courage enough – in contrast to the fearful and petrified Social Democratic leaders, Kuusinen, Sirola, Manner and others, living in their "luxurious flats" – to join these "Red Guard masses" and to speak *raison* to them, and with success, "as Com. Dzerzhinskii correctly remembers".[135] It is difficult to assess the reliability of the document from the leaders of the Murder Opposition, written in prison shortly after the murders. The trouble itself is well known and there is no doubt that Finnish refugees participated in the coup without knowledge of what was really happening. On the other hand the role of the future Opposition leaders in this episode may, of course, be exaggerated. Nevertheless, they might have resorted to Dzerzhinskii's memory; without cause, they could not do it.

Dzerzhinskii's Cheka, however, was not the same organisation as the Registrup. The Opposition also, it seems, had contacts with the political department of the Seventh Army Corps before and after the murders. One repentant subsequently claimed that the Opposition received a "hint" from this Army intimating a "purge".[136] The motive of this unit would have been to exclude its rival, the military organisation of the SKP, and especially the Cheka, from military espionage in Finland. However, I doubt this explanation because it is based on hearsay. It is difficult to say how effectively the espionage in Finland was organised at that time. It seems that the Russians well knew the disposition of Finnish troops and the armaments of the Finnish Army.[137] One possibility is that the Russians knew their locations because the Finns used the same bases as the Russians had before independence.[138] There was, however, also information obtained by espionage. One problem I have not succeeded in solving is *how* this information was received.

---

[134] On the attempted coup, see e.g. Pipes, *The Russian Revolution, 1899–1919*, p. 805.

[135] The Committee (Väinö O. C. [?] Pukka, A. Paasi, Otto Palho, E. A. Matikainen and F. Kääriäinen in the Cheka prison in Moscow) of the majority of the Finnish Communist organisations to chairman of the CC of the RKP(b), Com. Lenin, Nov. 11, 1920. RGASPI, f. 17, op. 84, ed. hr. 105, l. 36. Probably written by Pukka because the document is in Russian.

[136] Matti Halonen's report on his activities in Russia, March 25, 1923. RGASPI, f. 516, op. 2, 1922, d. 34.

[137] Summary of espionage no. 29, until April 16, 1919. Field headquarters of the Register Administration in Revolutionary War Soviet of the Republic. Центральный Государственный Архив Красной Армии (Central State Archives of the Red Army), Moscow, f. 6, op. 10, d. 54.

[138] When the Russian officers and I. V. Stalin discussed problems they had faced in the Winter War of 1939–1940 against Finland, some officers deplored the lack of effective espionage. Brigade Commander of the air force, Ivan Ivanovich Kopech said (on April 16, 1940) that intelligence reports from the staff of the air force of the Leningrad military district were from 1917, although some accounts were from 1930. (*Puna-armeija Stalinin tentissä*, p. 194. See also p. 258.)

3. The Opposition becomes the Murder Opposition

The second Party Congress of the SKP in August–September 1919 constituted an important step in the formation of the Opposition. The first quarrel in the Congress flared up at the very beginning, over credentials. The question was who represented the Communist collective of the Red Officer School. There were two candidates, Otto Palho and R. Tamminen. Palho had the credentials, Tamminen had not. Jukka Rahja announced that Palho was a representative of a small group. Tamminen had no credentials because there had not been time enough to give information about him to the recruits. According to Jukka Rahja, Palho represented five men, Tamminen 3,500 "electoral proletarians". When the Congress gave Tamminen the only right of speech, the Rahja brothers marched out. Jukka Rahja's protest is written in the minutes of the Congress as follows:[139]

> When [he] notes that there is in the meeting still the parliamentary leaven and the meeting does not thus represent the real revolutionary mass, he does not consider it possible to belong to these, but wishes to join those who represent the proletarian mass and are without credentials.

The Rahja brothers called a group meeting in which it became clear that Kullervo Manner supported their policy. Toivo Antikainen said that the differences were only tactical, not of principle. Manner disagreed: the criticism was only adventitiously tactical. Lumivuokko dissociated himself from all other speakers: he claimed the criticism of the Central Committee to be no more than "justified".[140]

The quarrels culminated in the election of the Central Committee. Jukka Rahja presented a list of candidates: O. W. Kuusinen, Lauri Letonmäki, Yrjö Sirola, Eino Rahja, Kullervo Manner, K. M. Evä, Väinö Jokinen and Mandi Sirola (Yrjö Sirola's wife). Kuusinen and Letonmäki, who were in Finland, were elected unanimously. Then several candidates were presented. In the vote, Lumivuokko and Kustaa Rovio received more votes than two candidates on Rahja's list, Jalo Kohonen and Mandi Sirola. Jukka Rahja then announced that his list was "fixed", i.e. unchangeable, and therefore his candidates could not take part in the Central Committee. Also, Lumivuokko and Rovio announced their refusal to participate in the Central Committee. Now the situation was that all elected (except Kuusinen and Letonmäki, who

---

[139] Minutes of the II^{d} Congress of the SKP, Petrograd, Aug. 31–Sept. 11, 1919. RGASPI, f. 516, op. 2, 1919, d. 4, ll. 2–5, quotation l. 5. Minutes of this Congress are especially for the two–three final days incomplete. The inspectors of minutes were August Paasi and Otto Vilmi. Paasi stated that the minutes correspond "poorly and incompletely" to what happened in the meeting. Vilmi expressed no reservations. (*Ibid.*, l. 184.)

[140] Minutes of the group meeting held during the 1919 Congress. RGASPI, f. 516, op. 2, 1919, d. 4.

were absent) had refused membership![141] Several delegates commented on the procedure. Toivo Antikainen said he now realised how the future posts of the People's Commissars in Finland would be distributed. Arvo Närhi accused the elected and rejected members of "contempt of the masses"; for him this policy was "Mannerheimian", done behind the scenes.[142] August Paasi suggested that the result of the vote remain unchanged. This was repudiated by eleven votes for, five against. Sirola then suggested that Rovio be not elected. This was accepted by eight votes, none against. Sirola further suggested that Kohonen be elected – again accepted by eleven votes for, none against.[143] These votes took place in the last day of the Congress. It is not known how many of the original 43 delegates were present. It is obvious, however, that most of them did not take part in the last three votes.

We can see a division into three groupings in the Congress. The main speakers for the opposition were Eloranta and Paasi, but "ouvrierist" criticism was very common. Some of the representatives of this line, for example Matti Turkia, left Russia and rejoined the SDP in the 1920s. Jukka Rahja was the spokesman of the "Central Committee line", but his arrogance aroused anger also among delegates who did not endorse the "ouvrierist" line. Lumivuokko had a "middle" position. He soon left Russia to engage in illegal activities in Finland. Sirola undertook to conciliate and was at least superficially successful in this. Among the Opposition, however, his doings were not liked and later, as we shall see, the Opposition argued that the election of the Central Committee had not been honest.

After Eloranta's confrontations with the Central Committee, he was arrested by Jukka Rahja with the consent of the Central Committee. This only exacerbated the situation in the Red Officer School; his supporters were elected to the leadership of the Collective (i.e. students' union) of the School.[144] In order to settle the conflict between the Red Officer School Collective and the Central Committee, a "meeting of clearance" was arranged on February 9, 1920. Eloranta was brought to the meeting from jail. In his speech in the meeting, Jukka Rahja stated his readiness to

---

[141] Minutes of the II[d] Congress of the SKP, Petrograd, Aug. 31–Sept. 11, 1919. RGASPI, f. 516, op. 2, 1919, d. 4, ll. 177–181.

[142] *Ibid.*, l. 182.

[143] *Ibid.*, l. 183.

[144] Yrjö Sirola to G. E. Zinov'ev March 13, 1920. RGASPI, f. 516, op. 2, 1920, d. 2. Minutes of the joint meeting of the members etc. of the third Officer Course of Petrograd Soviet, Dec. 18, 1919. RGASPI, f. 516, op. 2, 1920, d. 152. In the meeting recruit Toikka proposed that Eloranta be given a diploma for his merits as a "revolutionary soldier". Kullervo Manner, a representative of the Central Committee, announced that the Committee intended to have an "investigation" of the Eloranta case and suggested that the meeting await the results of the investigation. Because Manner was seconded by nobody, there was no vote and Toikka's proposition was accepted unanimously. It had meaning, however, only as a protest.

shoot Eloranta, which according to the minutes of the meeting, raised "a terrible hubbub". Many recruits gave detailed accounts of foodstuffs stolen and of corruption. Eloranta himself accused the members of the Central Committee of being the "crumbs of old Social Democracy". The meeting ended in a vote, in which 115 recruits voted against the Central Committee, 15 for and 13 abstained.[145] They then began to demand Eloranta's release and a Conference to settle matters with the Central Committee was organised.[146]

From the point of view of the Central Committee, the situation was alarming. It was also becoming complicated and perplexing in that at the same time the Committee itself was divided into two factions, Eino Rahja's, Evä's and Kohonen's on the one hand and Sirola's, Manner's and Jokinen's on the other. It cannot be said that the political differences between these factions were great; they were tactical. The Rahja brothers wished to call a secret Conference where quarrels in the Party could be settled. Manner opposed a secret Conference and suggested instead a public one.[147] Because Manner was chairman of the Party his vote would be decisive if the votes were divided 3–3. A means to solve differences already tried was to resign from posts of responsibility. First, Jalo Kohonen resigned from the Central Committee.[148] Second, Eino Rahja claimed that he has been expelled from the Committee and asked therefore to be relieved of the chairmanship of the military organisation of the Party.[149] Third, Jukka Rahja (who was not at that time a member of the Central Committee) announced that because the internal situation was unresolved he could no longer hold the post of political Commissar of the Red Officer School.[150] Because of this general confusion, a Conference of Finnish Communists in the RKP(b) was called.

The Conference was held on March 18–19, 1920. It began with a quarrel over the credentials of Väinö Pukka. It emerged that Pukka had been expelled from the

[145] Minutes of the Finnish Collective of the Officer Course, Feb. 9, 1920. RGASPI, f. 516, op. 2, 1920, d. 125. It seems that many recruits had left the meeting before the vote.

[146] Juho Kovanen's examination record made by the Finnish Detective Central Police, March 6, 1922, p. 5. Juho Kovanen was a sympathiser of the Opposition. His hearing was organised on his return to Finland from Russia. (Ek-Valpo I, PF 3699, August Paasi, KA.)

[147] Kullervo Manner's memorandum on a possible secret Conference. Manner complained that the Rahja brothers tried "systematically" to discomfit Sirola and to "harass" Manner, himself. (RGASPI, f. 516, op. 2, 1920, d. 25.)

[148] Jalo Kohonen to the CC. MCC of the SKP, Feb. 26, 1920. RGASPI, f. 516, op. 2, 1920, d. 2.

[149] MCC of the SKP, Feb. 29, 1920. RGASPI, f. 516, op. 2, 1920, d. 2. It cannot be seen from the minutes whether Eino Rahja was allowed to resign from the chairmanship or not. Nor is it clear how he could consider himself expelled from the Central Committee. The Committee did not even, at least theoretically, have power to expel its members, although the co-opting of new members was possible. In his letter to the Central Committee, dated Feb. 26, 1920, Rahja said that he "was leaving" the Central Committee. (KtS!, p. 103.)

[150] MCC of the SKP, March. 1, 1920. RGASPI, f. 516, op. 2, 1920, d. 2.

Petrograd Finnish Committee of the RKP(b), but the Collective of Laundry and Clothiers *Taisto* had appointed him an honorary member of this body! Pukka presented the statement of the secretary of the Petrograd Committee of the RKP(b), S. S. Zorin,[151] in which Zorin affirmed that such a drastic move as rejection of credentials should not be used.[152] This is an interesting point because it proves that the Opposition had support among leading Bolshevik circles in Petrograd.[153] – The Central Committee accused the representatives of the Opposition of various infringements and vice versa. Also talk of shooting was again to be heard: when the Opposition was accused of using all measures possible to get a Conference advantageous to itself, Eloranta, who was freed before the Conference, noted that all measures were by no means being used since the members of the Central Committee had "not yet been shot".[154] August Paasi[155] proclaimed that the Central Committee had been elected by fraud, which was too much for Sirola, the conciliator in the second Congress of the SKP (1919) where the Central Committee was elected. He demanded that the Conference condemns Paasi's statement.[156] When the Conference did not do so, the members of the Central Committee marched out.[157] The rival factions immediately held their own meetings. The Opposition elected a Committee of nine, among them Eloranta, Pukka, Paasi and Palho.[158] In the meeting of the supporters of the Central Committee Kullervo Manner stated that the Opposition did have cause for disappointment, namely the business activities of the SKP and the "emigrant circumstances in general".[159] He, however,

---

[151] Zorin was the secretary of either the Petrograd Provincial Committee or the Petrograd City Committee of the RKP(b), or a secretary of both organisations. In any case, he was a very influential leader, because Zinov'ev, veritable "Emperor" of Petrograd, was often not in the city. (Robert Service, *The Bolshevik Party in Revolution : a Study in Organisational Change 1917–1923*, p. 146 and 173.)

[152] Minutes of the Conference of the representatives of the collectives of the Finnish Communists in the Russian Communist Party, March 18–19, 1920. RGASPI, f. 516, op. 2, 1920, d. 9.

[153] It seems that Eloranta remained a member of the Petrograd Soviet in spite of the appeal of the SKP to expel him. The Collective of the Red Officer School did not accede to recall him if it did not receive a written certificate from the RKP(b) that Eloranta was not a Communist. (The Presidium of the Collective of the third Infantry Officer Course of the Petrograd Soviet to the CC of the SKP, Jan. 1, 1920. RGASPI, f. 516, op. 2, 1920, d. 152.)

[154] K., "Äskeinen suomalaisten järjestöjen konferenssi. Selostus siitä", *Wapaus,* April 23, 1920.

[155] Paasi was a pseudonym. His original surname was Pyy.

[156] Minutes of the Conference of the representatives of the collectives of the Finnish Communists in the Russian Communist Party, March 18–19, 1920. RGASPI, f. 516, op. 2, 1920, d. 9, l. 7.

[157] *Ibid.*, pp. 11–12.

[158] Eino Rahja to the Congress of the SKP, the Executive Committee of the Communist International and the CC of the Russian Communist Party. A report on the results of the investigation into the murder of the members of the SKP, June 20, 1921. RGASPI, f. 516, op. 2, 1920, unnumbered *delo*, appendix 4. I have found no minutes of the meetings of the Opposition and its Committee.

[159] Minutes of the negotiation meeting invited by the CC of the SKP, March 22–25, 1920. RGASPI, op. 2, 1920, d. 9, l. 2.

condemned Opposition's "scouting, anarchism-like, and hooliganism-like attitudes".[160]

In February 1920 Yrjö Sirola sent a letter to Zinov'ev in which he sought to explain the situation in the SKP. He stated e.g. that during the one and half years that the Party had existed, several complaints had been made against Jukka Rahja's "despotic behaviour". According to Sirola, the Rahjas had a tendency to treat the members of the Central Committee as despised intellectuals. As usual, Sirola found himself more than anyone else responsible for the chaotic situation. In his letter Sirola wrote:[161]

> I deeply regret that for the most part due to my own inattentiveness and lack of skill, being as I am in the responsible position, a state of affairs which I consider very worrying and which I see we cannot ourselves clear, has been brought about.

After the March Conference, the Central Committee again began holding meetings. The disappointed Sirola, however, did not attend the meetings and by this behaviour gave his opponents, in this case Jukka Rahja, reason to accuse him of deception. Jukka Rahja demanded that all trust be denied Sirola: "The purge of the Party must begin from its most responsible members".[162]

The demands of the Opposition were the summoning of a Congress of the SKP, the readmission of Eloranta and Pukka to the Party and nomination by the Comintern of a new Central Committee already before the Congress; its task would be preparation of plans for the revolution in Finland for the Congress.[163] The Comintern did in fact nominate a new Provisional Central Committee,[164] but this took place based on the list which consisted of Kullervo Manner, Eino and Jukka Rahja, Väinö Jokinen, Jalo Kohonen, Otto Wille Kuusinen, Johan Henrik Lumivuokko, Lauri Letonmäki and Jaakko Mäki. When the list was presented to Zinov'ev, he inquired why Sirola was not included in it. Sirola was added to the list;[165] nobody from the Opposition, however, was included. Sirola left Petrograd for Stockholm in June 1920.

---

160 Minutes of the negotiation meeting invited by the Cenral Committee of the SKP, March 22–25, 1920. RGASPI, op. 2, 1920, d. 9, l. 2.

161 Yrjö Sirola to G. E. Zinov'ev, Feb. 26, 1920. RGASPI, f. 515, op. 2, 1920, d. 2. Also KtS!, pp. 103–108.

162 Jukka Rahja to the CC of the SKP, April 14, 1920. RGASPI, f. 516, op. 2, 1920, d. 9.

163 The Committee of Finnish Communist Organisations to the CC, May 23, 1920. Signed by Voitto Eloranta, A. Paasi, Otto Palho, J. Kääriäinen, H. Puukko and W. Sormunen. RGASPI, f. 516, op. 2, 1920, d. 148.

164 Extract from the minutes of the Office of the Executive Committee of the Communist International, April 24, 1920. (Also the Russian text.) RGASPI, f. 516, op. 2, 1920, d 25. See also "Suomalaisille kommunisteille", *Wapaus*, May 15, 1920.

165 K. M. Evä's report on the opposition in Russia. Minutes of the III[d] Congress of the SKP, Aug. 13–21, 1920. RGASPI, f. 516, op. 2, 1920, d. 2. According to Evä, Zinov'ev had answered that Sirola

In June several members of the Opposition were expelled from the Party, among them Eloranta and Pukka, although they had already been expelled in 1919.[166] The idea of the "liquidation" of the Central Committee seems to have been presented for the first time in May; August Paasi suggested in a letter to an unknown recipient use of a "perforation knife and scalpel".[167] The appeals to Zorin and Zinov'ev in the summer of 1920[168] had no results. With the new Central Committee, the Opposition had at least one negotiation,[169] without outcome. In addition, the Petrograd Committee of the RKP(b) tried in some way to calm the situation,[170] but in vain. The Opposition claimed that 90 per cent of Finnish Communists in Russia supported it.[171]

In August, the third Congress of the Party was held in secret. It seems that for the Opposition this Congress was the last straw, because the Opposition had also demanded a Congress, hoping, of course, that it could replace the Central Committee there. The Congress did not remain secret for the Opposition.[172] On the contrary, drastic measures were planned for it: the problem was that the members of the Opposition were still members of the RKP(b) and this situation had to be ended.[173] – The Party Congress brought a dramatic turn when it became known that there was one supporter of the Opposition, Emil Vartiainen, a recruit. He presented to the Congress a letter in which he stated that the Congress was not legal because it represented only 6 or 7 per cent of the Finnish Communists in Russia. The remaining 94 per cent, Vartiainen argued, "do not suffer from child's disease in Communism"; they represented "as pure Communism" as the Central Committee. The latter had, however, committed "great offences" and therefore the "propaganda work for the world revolution had greatly suffered". Therefore these[174]

---

could be added to the list; if he was not willing to participate in the work of the Central Committee in Russia, he could be sent to Scandinavia.

166 "Puolueesta eroitettu", *Wapaus*, June 9, 1920. Also *Punasotilas*, July 10, 1920.

167 Paasi to an unknown recipient, May 17, 1920. RGASPI, f. 516, op. 2, 1920, d. 149.

168 A copy of A. Paasi's memorandum book. RGASPI, f. 516, op. 2, 1920, d. 149.

169 K. M. Evä's report on the Opposition in Russia. Minutes of the III[d] Congress of the SKP, Aug. 13–21, 1920. RGASPI, f. 516, op. 2, 1920, d. 2.

170 "Suomalaisten kollektiivien kokous kommunistitovereiden murhan johdosta : Pietarin Komitean sihteerin, tov. Sorinin puhe", *Wapaus*, Sept. 26, 1920.

171 Saarela, *Suomalaisen kommunismin synty*, p. 96.

172 One participant, August Marttinen, related that Otto Palho had demanded of him whether he knew anything about the Congress. Marttinen had said he knew nothing. He suggested that the Congress must have been transferred to "some basement". (Minutes of the III[d] Congress of the SKP, Aug. 13–21, 1920. RGASPI, f. 516, op. 2, 1920, d. 2, l. 78.) A copy of A. Paasi's memorandum book. RGASPI, f. 516, op. 2, 1920, d. 150.

173 Saarela, *Suomalaisen kommunismin synty*, p. 97.

174 Emil Vartiainen to the Congress of the SKP. No date. RGASPI, f. 516, op. 2, 1919, d. 287.

> 94 per cent of the Communists have demanded the liquidation of the Party, hoping that Finnish Communist organisations in Russia and individual members can merge into one entity to struggle for the world revolution.

When it became known that the letter was a copy, Jukka Rahja asked who had made the copy. Vartiainen said that he himself made it. Rahja then declared that a revolutionary did not take copies of a letter to a secret Congress. According to the minutes, there were cries of "traitor" and "informant" and Jukka Rahja "announced that in the name of the Executive Committee of the III^{d} International he was arresting Vartiainen for the time being".[175]

It seems that Vartiainen's arrest was the ultimate reason for the murders. In the autumn August Paasi sent a letter to his brother; this letter, however, was confiscated and sent on by the Russian authorities and reached the office of the SKP. In this letter, Paasi wrote that "one worker" had succeeded in entering the Congress and this worker had been arrested. Unspecified "workers' organisations" demanded his release by appeals to the Russian authorities. These proving futile, the Opposition decided to take the arms.[176] On August 30, the day before the murders, Paasi wrote a kind of ode to his lover, "little Olga", who "consciously or unconsciously" loved "spiritual force, which is capable of deeds – heroic deeds".[177]

On the day of the murders, but before the event, August Paasi also sent a letter to leaders of the Russian revolution in which he strongly condemned the old Social Democratic leaders and motivated the murders. He wrote:[178]

> In Finland, [before the rebellion] these miserable (*kurjat*) Soc. Dem. leaders concealed from us the development of the Russian revolutionary movement. They taught us to despise "Russkies". Here we have learnt the Communist doctrine and *fighting methods*. At the nose (*nokka*) of the same Communist doctrine have been put to the horror of the Finns, those miserable Social Democratic lords, and the criminal (*rikokselliset*) Rahjas, who are hated by everybody. [...] The thought of all Finnish worker and soldier Communists has already long been that it is possible to

---

[175] Minutes of the III^{d} Congresss, hold in Petrograd, Aug. 13–21, 1920. RGASPI, f. 516, op. 2, 1920, d 2 ll. 34–35.

[176] August Paasi to his brother (unnamed in the document), Sept. 9, 1921. RGASPI, f. 516, op. 2, 1921, d. 115. In addition, Juho Kovanen presented this argument, in the hearing of the Finnish Detective Central Police, March 6, 1922, pp. 8–9. (Ek-Valpo I, PF 3699, August Paasi, KA.) Cf. Jukka Paastela, "Miten poliittinen teko on selitettävissä? – Kuusisen klubin murhiin johtaneista tekijöistä" in *Vaalit, valta ja vaikuttaminen*, p. 265. My inference in that article was more cautious regarding the Vartiainen case as the final reason for the murders. I did not know Paasi's letter when I wrote that article in 1994–95.

[177] A copy of A. Paasi's memorandum book. RGASPI, f. 516, op. 2, 1920, d. 140.

[178] Aku (August) Paasi to the leaders of the Russian Revolution, Com. Lenin, Zinov'ev etc. etc. KtS!, pp. 127–128

get rid of these lords only by killing. [...] We go to death with a smile on the lips, since we have a firm belief that we have done a great service to Communism and the revolution.
Long live the revolution!
Long live the Communist workers' dictatorship!
Long live the best arm of them, the Red terror!

4. Crime and Punishment

In the Kuusinen Club,[179] there was on August 31, 1920, a meeting on the situation on various fronts in the Russian Civil War. In the protocol of the meeting there is a laconic comment about what took place:[180]

> 4 § When the meeting moved to the following point in the agenda, announcements, several men, led by Red Officer Paasi, rushed in and already in the vestibule began the shooting, aiming the first shots at comrade Jukka Rahja, who was smoking in the vestibule; he died immediately.

Jukka Rahja was shot by Allan Hägglund.[181] In addition to him, seven people were murdered. They were the following: Väinö Jokinen, a scientist and translator of Socialist books into Finnish, member of the Central Committee until the third Congress; Tuomas Hyrskymurto, a Red Commander in the Finnish Civil War, then an organiser in the service of the Central Committee of the SKP; Konstantin (Konsta) Lindquist, an engine-driver, member of the People's Deputation in 1918 (Depute of Transportation), in Russia on various assignments, at the time of his death an organiser of the Soldiers' Organisation of the SKP; Ferdinand (Fetka) Kettunen, a Peterburg worker, reportedly an active participant in Bolshevik underground activities in Russia from 1906; Juho (Jukka) Theodor Viitasaari, a baker, trade union activist, chief of the tramways in Helsinki during the Civil War; Liisa

---

[179] The meeting place of Finnish Communists in Petrograd was named after Kuusinen at the time when there was false news in the Finnish newspapers that an agent of the Central Detective Police had killed Kuusinen when he was escaping to Sweden by the Gulf of Bothnia. The name of the Club was not changed after it became known that the report was untrue. Afterwards the name was changed into "Club of the August Communards".

[180] Minutes of the meeting held in the Kuusinen's Club, Aug. 31, 1920. RGASPI, op. 2, 1920, d. 139. See also Olga Manner, "Verilöylyssä" in *Elokuun kommunaardit : kommunaardien muistojulkaisu : kommunismin puolesta kaatuneille elokuun 31 p:nä 1920 veriteon uhrien muistolle omistaa tämän julkaisun Suomen kommunistinen puolue*, pp. 59–63.

[181] According to the statement by Matthias Leander Krokfors and Lauri Sulander in the hearings of the Detective Central Police in Terijoki in 1926. Report by the Terijoki subdepartment of the Detective Central Police, Sept. 9, 1926, p. 4. Ek-Valpo I, DF XXXV A 1, KA.

Savolainen (born in St. Petersburg in 1897), a clerk in the service of the SKP; and Juho Sainio, a baker, recruit, and a sympathiser of the Opposition. Nine people were injured, among them K. M. Evä, the secretary of the Central Committee of the SKP and Jaakko Rahja, the "third" of the Rahja brothers, politically relatively unknown.[182]

According to Matti Halonen, a "repentant" member of the Opposition, also Eino Rahja, Jalmari Kotiranta (the leader of "border activity", i.e. smuggling), Aleksandr Inno and Kullervo Manner were to be murdered. Halonen explained that the people who were ordered to kill these leaders simply did not dare carry them out.[183] Halonen is not a very reliable witness because by presenting himself a penitent he tried to avoid deportation to the Far East (in the coast of the Pacific Ocean). He even offered his "help" to erase Pukka, Paasi and others from the "stage of history".[184] On the other hand, Halonen's story is not necessarily a product of the imagination, because the aim of the Murder Opposition really was to kill the leaders of the SKP.[185] – If we consider the list of dead and injured, one thing is definite: people died and were injured by chance, the shooting was indiscriminate.

The assassins did not try to escape; on the contrary, they immediately gave themselves to the militia. After their arrest, Väinö Pukka and some other members of the Opposition began to write addresses to various Russian authorities. Among these was a large appeal (about 50 typed pages) to the "chairman of the Central Committee of the Russian Communist Party, Com. Lenin". The Opposition stated as the basis of its arguments, that it in fact represented a majority, about ninety per cent of all Finnish Communists in Russia. The starting point for the activities of the Opposition was the March Conference, which was "dissolved" by the Central Committee (this claim, of course, was much exaggerated). The murders were said to be in their "audacity " comparable only to Tsarist times.[186] The racketeering of the members of the Central Committee was presented as a principal cause for the breakdown of Party discipline. They were accused of "systematic theft of the money of the people for the purposes of prostitutes, for agents of the White Guards and

---

182 See "Kaatuneet kommunaardit" in *ibid.*, pp. 66–76.

183 Matti Halonen to Eino Rahja, Aug. 10, 1922. RGASPI, f. 516, op. 2, 1922, d. 34.

184 Matti Halonen to Toivo Alavirta, chairman of the Central Bureau of the Finnish organisations in the RKP(b), July 24, 1922. RGASPI, f. 516, op. 2, 1922, d. 34.

185 Cf. Saarela, *Suomalaisen kommunismin synty*, p. 97. Not until one week had passed, did *Wapaus* inform its readers of the murders. The headline was "Slaughterers effected a gruesome bloodbath in the Kuusinen Club". ("Lahtarit toimeenpanneet kamalan verilöylyn Kuusisen klubilla", *Wapaus*, Sept. 6, 1920.)

186 Väinö Pukka, August Paasi, Otto Palho, E. Martikainen and Felix Kääriäinen (in a Cheka prison) in the name of "the Committee of the Majority of the Finnish Communist Organs" to V. I. Lenin, Nov. 19, 1920 (in Russian). RGASPI, f. 17, op. 84, ed. hr. 105, l. 27.

their fellows".[187] We see that the charge of cooperation with the "class enemy" was not the privilege of the SKP leaders only.

The Opposition presented eight demands to settle the "conflict". They were: i) in the war tribunal the "fact" must be recognised that the terrorist act was a result of a mistaken policy of the Central Committee; ii) in the near future a Congress of the SKP should be organised; iii) a provisional Central Committee should be elected composed of representatives of the Executive Committee of the Comintern, the Central Committee and the Opposition; this provisional Committee should lead the Party until the Congress; iv) all repressive measures against the Opposition must be stopped; v) the Finnish collectives in the RKP(b) should be given the right to convene a Conference to organise Finnish members of the Russian Party; vi) the organising of the Conference should be given to the "majority" (i.e. the Opposition); vii) all people imprisoned for their "conviction" and who participated in the terrorist act should be immediately freed; viii) the members of the Central Committee remaining (i.e. not murdered), who had committed a crime in not furthering eagerly enough the new Finnish revolution and who by their errant activities had "partly" betrayed Soviet Russia, must not be allowed to participate in the renovation of the SKP.[188]

This document, written in Russian and thus almost certainly by Pukka, is in its trust in the moral correctness of the murders rather childish: it proves that Pukka and others had little sense of reality. Or should we interpret this address as not seriously written? I should not doubt the seriousness of the Opposition or perhaps in this context especially of Pukka. He undoubtedly believed that by means of the murders it would be possible to make a kind of "new start" for the "purged" SKP. We may also think that the document is proof of the extreme naivety of its signatories and the Opposition in general. However, the Opposition was in some way or other encouraged by the Russians, as we shall see. A perhaps more interesting question then arises: why did the Russians feel sympathy for the members of the Murder Opposition?

The attitude of the Cheka and other Russian authorities was much harsher in the case of Voitto Eloranta than of other members of the Opposition. Eloranta was accused of two of his "sins" committed in Finland. The first was his position in the "rebellion" in 1906. Eloranta was "assistant" to Captain Johan Kock, a leader of the National Guard, then of the Red Guard.[189] Kock had to go underground, while Eloranta was elected to the *Eduskunta* in 1907 and the Tsarist police was not at all

[187] *Ibid.*, p. 36.

[188] *Ibid.*, pp.43–44.

[189] On Captain Kock see Kujala, *Vallankumous ja kansallinen itsemääräämisoikeus*, pp. 145–148 and 179–180 and Soikkanen, *Sosialismin tulo Suomeen*, pp. 241–247.

interested in him.[190] It was thus implied that Eloranta had some traitorous relation with the police. However, no Finns who did not participate in the rebellion in Viapori fortress were searched by the police. If this were a proof of betrayal, the Cheka must have been interested in Eero Haapalainen, whose role as assistant to Kock was much more important than that of Eloranta.[191] Thus, this particular charge against Eloranta seems to be fabricated. In other words, the accusation was typical of a secret police, which follows a totalitarian logic. The accusation was publicly presented to the Finns in the Petrograd Finnish-language newspaper *Wapaus*.[192] A great number of them, at least people who were in politics in 1906, must have known the hollowness of this allegation.

Eloranta's second "sin" was that he owned pigs in Finland.[193] In *Wapaus*, this charge was presented in detail, though probably the figures were exaggerated: Eloranta had owned 400 swine and as many as 20 workers had been working in his piggery.[194]

Other accusations against Eloranta were more credible if Eloranta indeed spoke in the hearings as reported by the Cheka. According to the Cheka, Eloranta told his investigators that he knew nothing about the murders. When the members of the Opposition, who planned the assassinations, met at Eloranta's home, he was in the kitchen and the plotters were in other room. Cheka argued that i) Eloranta was a "nucleus" of the Opposition; ii) the slayers met in Eloranta's flat on the day of the murder; iii) it is impossible that Eloranta did not know, as he himself claimed, what was said in his small flat. Moreover, Eloranta was, according to the Cheka, an "inspirer" of the murderers, giving them advice as to what to do. – The Cheka also claimed that it had found a letter to the Finnish workers signed by Paasi and Eloranta, written some hours before the murders, in which the murders were described as an accomplished fact and in which the accusations of the Opposition against the leaders of the SKP were repeated. The conclusion on the culpability of the various actors in the murder illustrates the Bolshevik conception of justice at the time. The murderer, August Paasi, is described, together with Palho, Allan Hägglund, etc. as "effusive, honest revolutionaries" who were "blind tools" in the hands of the experienced and old "provocateur" Eloranta, and a smuggler, an "agent

---

190 An untitled document of the Cheka pertaining to the murders, an appendix to the minutes of the Orgburo of the RKP(b), Jan. 16, 1921, § 26. RGASPI, f. 17, op. 112, ed. hr. 112.

191 I thank Antti Kujala, a specialist on relations between Russian revolutionaries and the Finns at the beginning of the XXth century, who confirmed my suspicions that this point of the accusation against Eloranta was a fabrication.

192 "S. K. P:n jäsenten murha Pietarissa. Suomen lahtarien provokatsiooni paljastumassa. – Voitto Eloranta ja [Kaarlo] Tuomainen olleet ohranan palveluksessa", *Wapaus*, Dec. 9, 1920.

193 An untitled document of the Cheka about the murders, an appendix to the minutes of the Orgburo of the RKP(b), Jan. 16, 1921, § 26. RGASPI, f. 17, op. 112, ed. hr. 112.

194 "S. K. P:n jäsenten murha Pietarissa", *Wapaus*, Dec. 9, 1920.

of the White Guard", Kaarlo Tuomainen.[195] It was perhaps self-evident that *Wapaus* wrote nothing about the said effusive and honest revolutionaries. It should be noted that there is nothing in Cheka's document about anyone's connections with British intelligence. Väinö Pukka's name is not mentioned.

The case of Tuomainen is interesting here, because he was a smuggler, but to say that he was an "agent of the White Guard" is not necessarily true. He was, with other smugglers,[196] arrested after the murders. They smuggled arms and horses from Finland to Russia. It seems that the highest contractor of the smuggling was L. D. Trotskii. On September 11, 1920, one M. Cheskis wrote to "Com." Sklianskii(?), obviously a Chekist, a letter in which he regretted that after the "event" in the SKP most of his agents were arrested, among them he mentioned Juho(?) Arvelo, Mikko Susi and Tuomainen, who were in Moscow at "Com. Dzerzhinskii's order". Cheskis informed Sklianski that the commission for buying arms given by Trotskii had been fulfilled and promised to send him the following day "150 horses and a batch of Mausers". Cheskis explained that the arrested agents were for him necessary: if they were not freed his buying would be discontinued.[197] Tuomainen succeeded from prison in establishing liaison with Finnish diplomatic representatives in Russia by buying over the prison staff. In the autumn of 1923 he wrote to the Finnish consul in Petrograd that from 1919 he "acted on commercial tasks of a Special Board on the Finnish border".[198] In another, earlier letter, he qualified the organisation as a "Russian commercial commission for the Scandinavian countries".[199] Tuomainen, however, complained that the Central Committee of the SKP had begun to "harass" him because, as it was explained to him, his "buyings of goods" from Finland, "disturbed propaganda work in Finland". According to Tuomainen's letter, he then "obtained by plots an ostensible work place in a Russian military organisation".[200] It is probable that "Special Board" and "a Russian military organisation" means the Registrup or some other army intelligence. M. Cheskis was perhaps a representative of the Registrup. This agency and the Cheka were rivals. Tuomainen, however, could understandably not reveal to the Finnish consul or

---

[195] An untitled document of the Cheka about the murders, an appendix to the minutes of the Orgburo of the RKP(b), Jan. 16, 1921, § 26. RGASPI, f. 17, op. 112, ed. hr. 112.

[196] According to Tuomainen, there were eight prisoners (himself included), who were not "men of action"; the other Finnish inmates in a Moscow prison were these "men of action". (Kaarlo Tuomainen to the Finnish ambassador, Knorring, Sept. 21, 1921. Ek-Valpo I, DF XXXV A 1, KA.)

[197] M. Cheskis to Com. Sklianski, Sept. 11, 1920. RGASPI, f. 17, op. 112, ed. hr. 112.

[198] Kaarlo Tuomainen to "the esteemed Consul of the Republic of Finland", Oct. 17, 1923. Ek-Valpo I, DF XXXV A 1, KA.

[199] Tuomainen to the Finnish ambassador, Knorring, Sept. 28, 1921. Ek-Valpo I, DF XXXV A 1, KA.

[200] Tuomainen to "the esteemed Consul of the Republic of Finland", Oct. 17, 1923. Ek-Valpo I, DF XXXV A 1, KA.

ambassador that he was an agent of a Russian military intelligence. He had two motives for contacting Finnish diplomats, first, the food in prison was gravely inadequate and second, he had hopes to be extradited to Finland.

But why was Tuomainen in prison? His explanation was that he had a Finnish typewriter and in August 31, 1920 at 10 o'clock he gave permission for two Finns to use this typewriter for four hours. They had then explained to him that the document must be signed by Paasi and Eloranta, but there was not time enough to obtain the signatures, so they asked Tuomainen to forge Paasi's and Eloranta's signatures, which Tuomainen did. He claimed that he was not allowed to see the text of the document.[201] That Tuomainen forged the signatures of Paasi and Eloranta to a document he did not know, is, of course, highly unlikely. The document in question was very probably the letter Paasi and Eloranta had prepared to send to Finnish workers, a letter in which the murders were presented as a *fait accompli*. Tuomainen was arrested immediately after the murders, on September 1, 1920, freed after two weeks and then, on September 21, again arrested as he was preparing for a journey to Murmansk. The Chekists found on him a forged Finnish passport manufactured by the "institution" he served.[202] It seems that this passport was a decisive proof against Tuomainen. He was set free in spring 1922, but arrested again and condemned to three years in a concentration camp in the ancient monastery to Solovetsk.[203] It seems that he was released after his term and finally became head of fur farm in Karelia. He was executed in 1937.[204]

Smuggling was, as already stated, a very profitable business. It was not limited to Finland; goods were also smuggled to Russia from Norway and the Finnish professional smugglers also had a part in this business. Who were the partners in furnishing goods for Russia in Finland, remains unclear. I have seen no mentions of Finnish partners. Probably they were private businessmen or leaders of cooperative firms. The smuggling business was so profitable that the temptation to make relatively easy money by it may have been so great that perhaps otherwise honest businessmen could not resist the lure.

Eloranta received first an execution sentence, which was transmuted to a five-year prison sentence; then again an execution sentence. It seems that of the Opposition luminaries only Voitto Eloranta and later his wife Elvira Willman-Eloranta were

---

201 Tuomainen to the Finnish ambassador, Knorring, Sept. 28, 1921. Ek-Valpo I, DF XXXV A 1, KA.

202 Tuomainen to the Finnish ambassador, Knorring, Sept. 21, 1921. Ek-Valpo I, DF XXXV A 1, KA.

203 Tuomainen to "the esteemed Consul of the Republic of Finland", Oct. 17, 1923. Ek-Valpo I, DF XXXV A 1, KA.

204 Lahti-Argutina, *Olimme joukko vieras vaan*, p. 538. Lahti-Argutina writes the first name of Tuomainen as Kaarle, but in all probability he is Kaarlo Tuomainen, because he was, according to Lahti-Argutina's documentation, from the municipality of Leppävirta. In his letters Tuomainen said he was from this municipality.

executed. The Cheka had evidently to find a scapegoat and Eloranta was picked on because of his age, kulak past and political experience.[205] According to the testimony of Lauri Sulander and Matias (or Matthias) Leander Krokfors, members of the Opposition who in 1926 returned illegally to Finland, it was Willman-Eloranta who in hearings before the Cheka, spoke of connections of the Opposition with British intelligence and the Finnish "Okhrana". Sulander and Krokfors stated that Eloranta was made a central figure in the murder affair as a result of this "nonsense" of "Eloranta's muddle-headed wife".[206] This may or may not be true.

The process in the war tribunal was very slow in the eyes of the leading members of the SKP, and of Eino Rahja in particular. According to Rahja, "Comrade" Tarasov, a Chekist, who organised the hearings of the Opposition, did not organise the hearings of most of the members of the Opposition at all.[207] Instead of hearings, many arrested members were already released from prison in January 1921.[208] In the Orgburo of the RKP(b) the protest was simply recorded in the minutes.[209] For Rahja the most difficult matter was that scores of real or imagined Opposition members were involved in the smuggling on the Finnish border, organised by "Registrarm 7" (this probably means the political department of the Seventh Army Corps,[210] which, again probably, was more or less same institution as the Registrup) and by the Cheka. For Rahja this was a "curious chance".[211] In April 1921, the Cen-

---

205 An untitled document in the context of the meeting of the Orgburo of the CC of the RKP(b), Jan. 16, 1921; minutes of the said meeting, § 26. RGASPI, f. 17, op. 112, ed. hr. 112. A curious point in a document of the Cheka on the Eloranta case was that it was stated he had been a member of the Finnish Senate, which was not true.

206 Report by the Terijoki subdepartment of the Detective Central Police, Sept. 9, 1926. Ek-Valpo I I, DF XXXV A 1, KA.

207 Eino Rahja to the CC of the RKP(b), a copy to Com. Dzerzhinskii, May 21, 1921. RGASPI, f. 17, op. 84, d. 106, l. 1.

208 The CC of the SKP to the CC of the RKP(b), Jan. 14, 1921. RGASPI, f. 17, op. 84, d. 106.

209 Minutes of the meeting of the Orgbyro of the CC of the RKP(b), Jan. 16, 1921, § 26. RGASPI, f. 17, op. 112, ed. hr. 112.

210 Matti Halonen mentioned in his report on his activities in Russia (written in March 25, 1923), that this army corps protected and even employed members of the Opposition. (RGASPI, f. 516, op. 2, 1922, d. 34, l. III/2.)

211 Eino Rahja to the CC of the RKP(b), a copy to Com. Dzerzhinskii, May 21, 1921. RGASPI, f. 17, op. 84, d. 106, l. 1. Manuil Karjalainen, Mikhail Karjalainen, Ivan Suikkanen and Semyon Suikkanen had confessed to Tarasov that being on border work, they became agents of the Finnish Secret Police. In a copy of Tarasov's statement (dated May 13, 1920), he explains that the Suikkanen and Karjalainen brothers were arrested on the border on October 8, 1920 and they said they were agents of the Finnish Detective Central Police. According to Rahja, at least Mikhail Karjalainen belonged to the Opposition. (RGASPI, f. 17, op. 84, d. 106.) I have not seen any mention of these brothers in other sources. Overall, it is difficult to form a clear conception of the way the smuggling was organised in the border, because there were so many involved in this activity: different agencies of Workers' and Peasants' Red Army, Cheka, SKP, the Rahjas and obviously numerous individual businessmen.

tral Committee of the SKP demanded that the process in the tribunal be soon furthered.[212] On February 7, 1922, the All-Russian Central Executive Committee of Soviets gave its verdicts, according to which most of the accused were freed.[213] In reaction to this, Eino Rahja announced to G. E. Zinov'ev that the condemnation of the murderers was only a "delusion" and threatened to kill a murderer or murderers if he were to meet them.[214]

After several demands by the SKP leaders,[215] Väinö Pukka and several other members of the Opposition were again arrested, now by the decision of the Politburo of the RKP(b) on August 17, 1922, which considered their release "illegal".[216] Pukka had been admitted early in 1922, to Sverdlov University, where so-called Red Professors were educated. When the extended Plenum held in August 1922 discussed the matter, Adolf Taimi remarked that Pukka had good relations with, among others, N. I. Bukharin. Taimi assumed that Pukka had adopted the label "Workers' Opposition" by recommendation of his Russian friends. The key organisation in the matter was, after the Tribunal, the Central Control Commission[217] of the RKP(b). Its influential chairman was A. Solts, who negotiated with Kuusinen, Taimi, Rahja etc., but without result from the point of view of the Cen-

---

212 CC of the SKP to the CC of the RKP(b), April 18, 1921. RGASPI, f. 616, op. 2, 1921, d. 2, l. 1.

213 Приговор. Именен Российской Социалистической Федеративной Советской Республики Верховный Суд при Всероссийском Центральном Исполнительном Комитете Советов в открытом судебном заседании своем от 7-го февраля 1922 года в составе Председателя тов. Карклина и членов тов. Межкна и тов. Немцова. RGASPI, f. 516, op. 2, 1922, d. 34. The accused were divided into five categories (ages of the condemned are in parentheses):

1. Voitto Eloranta (45), sentence: execution, which was transmuted to five years in prison, "strictly incommunicado".

2. August Paasi (24), Allan Höglund [Hägglund] (25), Juho Joronen (26), Lauri Sulander (27), Matti Halonen (24) and Leander Krokfors (24), five years, but taking into consideration time already spent in jail and the general amnesty in honour of the October revolution, all freed.

3. Otto Palho (35), Feliks Kääriäinen (27), Juho Pylkkänen (age not mentioned), Jalmar Forsman (32), Emil Hällström (25), three years, but taking into consideration time already spent in jail and the general amnesty in honour of the October revolution, all freed.

4. Elvira Willman-Eloranta (45), Kaarlo Tuomainen (29), Mikko Susi (28) Juho Kovanen (51), Emil Toikkanen (25) Juho Hyvönen (31), Armas Pokkinen (25), all freed.

5. Henrik Puukko (28), Väinö Sormunen (30), in hiding, to be sentenced when captured.

214 Eino Rahja to the "chairman of III^{d} Communist [*sic*] International, Comrade Zinov'ev". KtS!, pp. 159–160.

215 E.g. K. Manner, O. W. Kuusinen, Eino Rahja and A Taimi to the representatives of the CC of the RKP(b). KtS!, pp. 161–167.

216 KtS!, p. 160. The Politburo ordered Dzerzhinskii to "investigate" the circumstances in which the Finns were released.

217 The Control Commission institution was important from the point of view of the leaders of the Finnish Communist Party. Most leaders of the SKP were members of the RKP(b) / VKP(b). The Finnish Politburo / Foreign Bureau in Moscow had to give a statement about persons who had been members of the SKP, but were expelled from it when they tried to join the Russian Party. The

tral Committee. Manner stated that if a change of attitude of the Russians could not be implemented, "we must work and suffer".[218] Pukka, Paasi and other leaders were finally deported to the Far East, where Pukka had, as mentioned above, a remarkable career.

According to Pukka and his friends the act in the Kuusinen Club was terrorist by nature.[219] This was presented as a great merit because a terrorist act should be explained by causes and motives and when they are found to be noble, terrorism is virtuous. For the Russians this account was difficult because they could not deny the virtuous nature of Red terrorism. It was thus necessary to explain that the act was not a terrorist one. Zinov'ev declared that it was "incomprehensible" that "Red terror" should have been directed against "comrades", not the bourgeoisie and, above all, "mannerheims". They did not even try to eliminate General C. G. E. Mannerheim, enemy number one.[220] Zinov'ev stressed especially that Jukka Rahja was arrested in July 1917, he was an outstandingly courageous Bolshevik, who jeered, when brought to court that the "Kerenskian judge was not fit even to clean Lenin's boots".[221] The prosecutor in the murder case, Nikolai Vasil'evich Krylenko, stated in his speech in the tribunal regarding the nature of the act:[222]

---

question was constantly on the agenda of the Finnish Politburo / Foreign Bureau, later especially because former participants in the Murder Opposition eagerly sought membership in the Bolshevik Party. – The Central Control Commission and local control commissions were created, on Lenin's proposal, in the IXth Conference of the RKP(b) in September, 1920. Their tasks were, for example, to "fight encroaching bureaucatism, careerism, the abuse of their Party and Soviet positions by Party members [...] the spread of unfounded and unverified rumours and insinuations [...] that damage the Party's unity and authority". (Medvedev, *Let History Judge*, pp. 425–426. The quotation is from *KPSS v rezoliutsiiakh*, I (1953), p. 533.)

218 MCC of the SKP, Aug. 9–16, 1922. RGASPI, f. 516, op. 2, 1922, d. 6, ll. 120–137, Manner's statement on l. 137.

219 A letter written by Pukka, signed by A. Paasi, Sulander, I. Joronen, Otto Palho, M. Halonen, Kääriäinen and (the text is illisible), to Feliks Dzerzhinskii, Nov. 1920. RGASPI, f. 17, op. 84. ed. hr. 106, l. 15.

220 G. Sinovjev, "Mielettömyyttä ja rikosta", a speech held in the common meeting of Finnish Party organisations, Sept. 17, 1920, published in *Elokuun kommunaardit : kommunaardien muistojulkaisu : kommunismin puolesta kaatuneille elokuun 31 p:nä 1920 veriteon uhrien muistolle omistaa tämän julkaisun Suomen kommunistinen puolue*, pp. 14.

221 *Ibid.*, p. 13.

222 Extracts of Krylenko's speech is published under the title "Mitä vallankumouksellisen proletariaatin oikeus veriteosta sanoi" (What did the court of the revolutionary proletariat say about the bold deed) in *Elokuun kommunaardit : kommunaardien muistojulkaisu : kommunismin puolesta kaatuneille elokuun 31 p:nä 1920 veriteon uhrien muistolle omistaa tämän julkaisun Suomen kommunistinen puolue*, p. 78.

> This is a politically unprincipled deed. It is the same as if I wanted to murder someone, but murdered someone else only because by chance met this someone else. If you like to name this deed terrorist and parallel with the method of struggle used in the fight against Tsarist power, let us allow you the pleasure.

This is, of course, a very different conception of terrorism than that usually meant by the terms terror and terrorism. Although it is difficult to give a universal definition of terrorism, one form of terrorism is a deed which involves indiscriminate violence against individuals, not necessarily personally guilty of anything.[223] According to this conception, the act in the Kuusinen Club was, of course, terrorist by nature.

[223] Cf. Walter Laqueur, *Terrorism*, pp. 5–6.

VII The Kuusinen Opposition (1919–1921)

In February 1921, K. M. Evä wrote a memorandum on the wrangles in the SKP. His starting-point was the extremely harsh circumstances among the emigrants in Russia in the spring of 1921. In such circumstances the leaders had only two alternatives, either to give everyone what he wants until there is nothing to be given and then to state: "Let us die, the Lord has abandoned us",[1] or to behave like the Rahja brothers. This was the duty of a revolutionary:[2]

> to stand firmly and unwaveringly at one's post, to give justice and orders without mercy – as cold, cruel and rough as the circumstances among which one must stand and struggle – according to the best understanding of events and contingencies one can at any time, on the basis of honest deliberation, form [and] dare to do something, although one cannot be sure about the possibility of error.

Evä continued that in this very difficult situation the duty of Yrjö Sirola and O. W. Kuusinen, who were far from approving the doings of the Rahja brothers, would have been to say: get out, we can do better. That they did not do; instead Kuusinen had thought that the one to blame for difficulties on the Red Officer Course had been Commissar Eino Rahja, who spent too little time in this school. Indeed, Kuusinen had proposed in the Central Committee that Eino Rahja should be obliged to live in the school.[3] This proposition had been put to the vote: only Sirola voted

---

1 K. M. Evä, Tilapäisiä erimielisyyksiä vaiko menettelytapa-periaatteellista ristiriitaa : huomioita S.K.P:n olemassaolon ajoilta. Feb. 9, 1921. RGASPI, f. 516, op. 2, 1921, d. 114, l. 8.

2 *Ibid.*

3 *Ibid.*, l. 89.

for.[4] Later, in February, 1920, Eino Rahja had stated in the Central Committee that the grounds for Kuusinen's departure for Finland was the controversy over the policy of the Party. Sirola had denied this, but stated that before Kuusinen had left Russia for Finland (May 1919, illegally, of course) he had said that there were two tendencies in the Central Committee, that of Rahja and Kohonen and that of Manner and Sirola.[5] – As we saw in the preceding chapter, there were such factions in the Central Committee, but the division did not last very long.

According to Evä, Kuusinen had declared that the question of Eino Rahja's residence must be one of confidence in the next Congress, and played by the "bourgeois minister method".[6] It is difficult to say who was right; Evä, who held that the reason for Kuusinen's departure was quarrels with the Rahja brothers, or Sirola, who denied this. I think that when we take into account Kuusinen's deep antipathy towards the Rahja brothers and Sirola's tendency to avoid any quarrels, Evä's explanation may be closer to the truth. Kuusinen's later undertakings seem to confirm this explanation.

1. The Formation of the Kuusinen Opposition

In Finland Kuusinen's task was to create small secret cells for the new rebellion. It soon became known to the police that Kuusinen was in the country and the government promised a huge sum for his head. In February 1920 an agent of the Detective Central Police announced that he had killed Kuusinen on the ice of the Gulf of Bothnia when the latter had tried to escape by skiing from Finland to Sweden. In fact, Kuusinen was living in a secret flat in Helsinki and reading his own obituaries published especially in Social Democratic newspapers. They stressed his important role in the Social Democratic Party before the rebellion: "He was the most talented man in the Party", wrote the main organ of the SDP and the executive committee of the Party decided to bury him at Party expense.[7] Meetings in his memory were held both in Finland and in Russia. Kuusinen himself used the situation for his conspiratorial purposes and organised an "interview" as if it were given in Stockholm, to be published in a Left-Wing paper in Sweden.[8]

Kuusinen gradually changed his political stand as to a rebellion in Finland. Although he speculated about Russian military aid for a new uprising in a letter he

---

4 Yrjö Sirola to G. Zinov'ev, Feb. 26, 1920, RGASPI, f. 516, op. 2, 1920, d. 2.

5 Minutes of the Central Committee of the SKP (hereafter abridged MCC), Feb. 2, 1920. RGASPI, op. 2, 1920, d. 9.

6 K. M. Evä, Tilapäisiä erimielisyyksiä vaiko menettelytapa-periaatteellista ristiriitaa : huomioita S.K.P:n olemassaolon ajoilta. Feb. 9, 1921. RGASPI, f. 516, op. 2, 1921, d. 114, l. 9.

7 Rinta-Tassi, "Kuusinen vallankumousvuosina", pp. 140–141.

8 John Hodgson, *Otto Wille Kuusinen : poliittinen elämäkerta*, p. 64.

sent to the Central Committee as late as March 1920,[9] it is obvious that he had now realised the hopelessness of an immediate rebellion. His change of attitude can be read in his articles published in *Sosialistinen Aikakauslehti* (Socialist Review). In his first article in August 1919, he attacked the new Finnish constitution, accepted in July 1919. One of his "ultraleftist" points here was the suffrage. Kuusinen criticised the Social Democrats for having accepted universal suffrage. According to Kuusinen they should have demanded suffrage only to "working people" and opposed suffrage for "high-ups, injurious to the society".[10] In October 1919, Kuusinen defended the boycott of parliamentary elections. He saw Parliament and workers' councils as mutually exclusive and referred to Germany, where the coexistence of Parliament and councils had produced "amorphous and treacherous mongrels". Kuusinen's conclusion was that it would have been better if "the proletariat had left to the bourgeoisie the whole Diet".[11] In April 1920 Kuusinen no longer advocated, at least explicitly, a boycott in the elections, although he severely criticised the very basis of parliamentarism. He declared that under universal suffrage people might believe that the state power was divided equally among everyone. Under capitalism, Kuusinen wrote, it is the capitalists and state officials who have real power. In Soviet Russia, on the contrary, officials can be removed if they are not worthy of trust. White-collar workers "generally" are not paid higher wages than blue-collar workers, although this principle had not been possible to realise in the extremely harsh conditions; some technicians, Kuusinen said, had been paid even too high salaries.[12]

---

[9] Kuusinen stated that there was a need to maintain troops ready to invade Finland when a revolution broke out. Finnish troops in Russia are not enough; therefore Russian troops must also be used. Kuusinen suggested that there should be in Russia a strong cavalry company which can penetrate immediately after the beginning of hostilities to the rear of the "slaughterers" and cut their railway connections. Kuusinen pointed out, however, that nothing should be based on "vague rumours" from Finland. (O. W. Kuusinen to the CC of the SKP, March 20, 1920. RGASPI, f. 516, op. 2, 1920, d. 25. – There is no mention of the year in the letter, but if the date March 20 is correct no other year is possible.) Also Sirola made similar speculations in a document titled "On the immediate tasks of the Finnish Communist Party", dated January 2, 1920. He wrote: "If circumstances as is possible, demand that one should attack Finland to disperse counter-revolutionary forces without certainty that the revolutionary situation is mature there, a situation in which one should temporarily organise the administration of the rear, would arise." This would, according to Sirola, be difficult, because "conscious helping people" are not in the area between the Russian border and Viipuri. (RGASPI, f. 516, op. 2, 1920, d. 22, l. 2.) At the time Sirola wrote this, he was in Russia, unlike Kuusinen.

[10] Usko Sotamies (Kuusinen), "Valkoinen hallitusmuoto", *Sosialistinen Aikakauslehti*, Aug. 1, 1919, p. 3.

[11] Usko Sotamies (Kuusinen); "Kirje vasemmistososialismista ja kommunismista", *Sosialistinen Aikakauslehti*, Oct. 10, 1919, p. 84.

[12] O. W. K[uusinen], "Suomen sosialidemokratian johtajille", *Sosialistinen Aikakauslehti*, April 16, 1920, pp. 100–102.

In Finland Kuusinen and his comrades gained quite remarkable victories in the struggle with the Social Democrats about workers' organisations. The Communists were able to ally with vague Left-Wingers in the Social Democratic movement. First, in September 1919, they took over, the Social Democratic Youth League,[13] then the Social Democratic municipal organisation of Helsinki, and then several trade unions. Next was to be the Social Democratic Party in December 1919, but this failed.[14] Kuusinen then "helped" to establish the Finnish Socialist Workers' Party, in May 1920.

Kuusinen left Finland for Sweden in June 1920. His immediate purpose was to organise in Stockholm courses for cadres from Finland who would, in turn, organise the activities of the Finnish Socialist Workers' Party. About twenty "pupils" who attended the course came to Stockholm from Finland. Kuusinen, Sirola and Lumivuokko lectured, and, according to Arvo Tuominen, secretary general of the SKP in the late thirties, some kind of Party Conference was held. Everyone opposed, Tuominen says, secret operations of the SKP, which aimed at founding a new Red Guard and rebellion. In Stockholm, it was decided to concentrate Left-Wing activities in public organisations; the SKP was not needed and therefore must be dissolved.[15]

Kuusinen's, Sirola's and Lumivuokko's positions were, considered in the light of the letters they dispatched from Stockholm to Petrograd, more knotty than this "liquidationist" stand. Nevertheless, it is true that Kuusinen planned a complete reorganisation of the movement to the Left of the SDP. In 1920–1921, he presented several models for this purpose. The common point in all was some change in the role of the SKP. The first model was – indeed – liquidationist. In a letter from Kuusinen and Lumivuokko to the Executive Committee of the Comintern and the Central Committee of the SKP, written probably at the end of June or the beginning of July 1920,[16] they foretold that a Left-Wing Party more radical than the SDP would be permitted in Finland as soon as the "White Social Democrats" were taken into the government. Then a Socialist Workers' Party could undertake the tasks of the Communist Party and thus the latter would no longer be needed. Until the legalisation, however, there must be two illegal organisations, Socialist

[13] Kairamo, *Ponnistuksien kautta vapauteen*, vol. 1, 1906–1922, pp. 309–327.

[14] Soikkanen, *Kohti kansanvaltaa*, vol. 1, pp. 363–371.

[15] Arvo Tuominen, *Sirpin ja vasaran tie : muistelmia*, p. 173, pp. 177–178 and 195–198.

[16] There is a date only in a postscript written by Sirola, in which he announces that he supports the ideas presented in the letter. This date is July 15, 1920. O. W. Kuusinen, J. H. Lumivuokko and V. Ojanen to the Executive Committee of the Comintern and the "Central Committee of the Finnish Communist Party" set up by it, July 15, 1920, Sirola announced (July 18) at the end of the letter that he agreed to it. (The quotation marks are in the letter; RGASPI, f. 516, op. 2, 1920, d. 2 Also KtS!, pp. 114–124.)

and Communist. Both could belong to the Comintern because in fact these two parties would be one. Kuusinen argued that the SKP had existed only in Russia. He saw only one important task for Finnish Communists in Russia, namely military education and participation in the Red Army. However, for that no Party was needed, some Finnish Communists organisations, i.e. organisations "lighter" than a party, would be enough. These organisations could also maintain agitation among Finns in Russia. The logical conclusion from these arguments was that the SKP should be liquidated and a new Party established. Kuusinen and Lumivuokko called a meeting, obviously a founding Congress for a new Party, to be held in Stockholm, September 1920. – There were several arguments for these suggestions. According to Kuusinen and Lumivuokko the workers were already in conspicuous ways themselves organised in several legal organisations, above all the trade unions. Firstly, "negative opposition" to them was not in accordance with the "Marxist method"; secondly, comrades whom Kuusinen had contacted when he was in Finland, were of the opinion that there should be a common "front" of all revolutionaries; thirdly, there was a substantial minority in the Congress of the SDP and after the Congress there emerged a "mass withdrawal movement"; fourthly, in the founding Congress of the Finnish Socialist Workers' Party in May 1920 people "went as clearly along the lines of the Communist Party as they deemed it [possible] to present in face of a police state"; fifthly, in many trade union organisations in Helsinki workers joined the new Party and when the SDP founded its cells there, only "two or three men and a fistful of underdeveloped women" came to the founding meetings. [17]

Kuusinen's speculation on the Social Democrats entering the government was obviously based on the attitude of that Party to participation after the 1919 general elections. Most members of the Social Democratic parliamentary group favoured participation at least in negotiations on the new government, although a great proportion of them did not believe that an agreement with the bourgeois parties in the political Centre, i.e. the Progressives and Agrarians, could be reached. The Progressives favoured, at least in principle, Social Democratic participation. They did not, however, accept the minimum programme presented by the Social Democrats, which notably included an amnesty for Red prisoners.[18]

It seems that in the year Kuusinen was in Russia (April 1918–May 1919), although he studied the writings of Lenin, he did not adopt the Leninist doctrine on the Party. Is it possible that Kuusinen simply did not know it? I think it is. Although it is not credible that Kuusinen was unaware of the quarrels between the Mensheviks and Bolsheviks over the nature of the workers' Party needed in Russia, he probably did not know Lenin's *What is to be done,* a rather outdated work (pub-

---

[17] *Ibid.*

[18] Soikkanen, *Kohti kansanvaltaa*, vol. 1, pp. 338–340.

lished in 1902) in the situation which had changed so rapidly after the downfall of Tsarism. Kuusinen also wrote before the second Congress of the Comintern which began on July 19, 1920. It was decreed in the *Theses* on the Communist Parties that all Parties were obliged to follow the example of the RKP(b).[19] Since Kuusinen was not in Russia in the spring of 1920, he could not know the preparations for the Congress, which were not public. Presumably, no Finn participated in these preparations. In the report of the Executive Committee of the Comintern to the second Congress, only one Finn was mentioned. This was Sirola, who was said to have been a "permanent representative" on the Executive Committee.[20] I assume that his role in the Comintern was not particularly important because he had a good deal of work in the SKP in 1919–1920. In the third Party Congress of the SKP, Jukka Rahja bragged that in the second Comintern Congress the SKP had had seven votes; this proved, according to him, that the SKP was an internationally esteemed Party, not a "small clique", unknown in Finland.[21] The role of the SKP was, however, rather meagre in the Congress itself. Kullervo Manner spoke only briefly on the Finnish situation.[22] No Finnish delegate participated in the commissions of the Congress, unlike, for instance, an Estonian and a Lithuanian delegate.[23] The amount of seven votes put the Finnish Party in the second category of countries with Austria, Hungary and Poland.[24]

From the standpoint of the internal quarrels of the SKP, there were two important points in the Comintern *Theses* on the Communist Parties. It was proclaimed that Communists should not "abstain" from workers' organisations even if they had "a distinctly reactionary character". "In certain situations" a Communist may participate in "Yellow unions, Christian unions, and so forth" in order to "carry on" propaganda there.[25] This was contrary to the "Ultraleft" orientation of the

---

19 See Theses on the role and structure of the Communist Party before and after the taking of power by the proletariat, in *Workers of the World and Oppressed Peoples, Unite! : Proceedings and Documents of the Second Congress [of the Comintern], [July 19–August 7], 1920*, vol. 1, pp. 190–200. Thereafter cited by subtitle only.

20 Report of the Executive Committee, July 6, 1920 in *Proceedings and Documents of the Second Congress*, vol. 1, p. 74. In this report the intervention of the Executive Council in the affairs of the Finnish Party in spring 1920 is somewhat briefly reported. (*Ibid.*, pp. 82–83.)

21 Minutes of the III^d Congress of the SKP, Aug. 13–21, 1920. RGASPI, f. 516, op. 2, 1920, d. 2, l. 8.

22 *Proceedings and Documents of the Second Congress*, vol. 2, pp. 781–78. It is astonishing that Manner spoke in Finnish and not in German. His speech was interpreted into Russian by Jukka Rahja. This tells something of Manner's incertainty.

23 Composition of Presiding Committee and commissions in *Proceedings and Documents of the Second Congress*, vol. 2, pp. 844–845.

24 Preliminary list of delegates in *Proceedings and Documents of the Second Congress*, vol. 2, pp. 839–843. The first category (10 votes) was formed by Britain, France, Germany, Italy, Russia and the United States.

25 Theses on the role and structure of the Communist Party before and after the taking of power by the proletariat, point 7 in *Proceedings and Documents of the Second Congress*, vol. 1, p. 195.

SKP and in accordance with Kuusinen's policy. However, the role of the Communist Parties in relation to mass movements of workers was defined unambiguously: the Communist Party must lead all mass organisations. The workers' movement was "classified" into three parts, i) Party, ii) Soviet, iii) production association (trade union). The "vanguard of the working-class", "*must direct* the struggle of the entire working class"; it "must be the living spirit not only of the production associations and workers' councils but all other forms of proletarian organisation as well".[26] This was, of course, against Kuusinen's thesis about the possible liquidation of the SKP.

Kuusinen eventually abandoned this thesis. The development which led up to this is difficult to reconstruct in such a way as to bring all details into the right chronological order, because many of the letters from Stockholm to Petrograd according to which inferences must be made, are not dated. One event, the murders in the Kuusinen Club, helps to date some of them, but only in as far as they were written before or after news of the murders had reached Stockholm. One letter, however, is dated. On September 1, 1920, Kuusinen, Sirola and Lumivuokko wrote to Petrograd and asked the opinion of the Central Committee on the foundation of a new Party in Finland. They declared that the present situation was miserable: Finland was devoid of a Communist Party and the Communist Party was devoid of a working-class. The writers stated, however, that as to the foundation of a new Party there should be a general agreement: it was better to postpone the affair than have two quarrelling parties. Nevertheless, Kuusinen and his companions by no means dropped their plan pertaining to the possible liquidation of the SKP. They predicted that it would be possible to launch a public Communist Party already "this autumn", or it might be possible that the Socialist Workers' Party developed into a Party in which "all of us" can join, or – the third "alternative" – the Socialist Workers' Party could "slide" into the hands of the "opportunists"; then the Communists must provoke a split and secure a "large share" of this Party. Kuusinen and his comrades also announced that G. E. Zinov'ev had sent a letter to Sirola, in which he had stated that "our suggestion" would be "worth serious consideration" but, in the same breath, had warned about a split. Kuusinen, Sirola and Lumivuokko asserted that their aim was by no means a split; at the same time they complained that they had not received any serious answers to their suggestions and no delegates from Russia had been sent to their Party Congress in Stockholm.[27] Kuusinen

---

[26] *Ibid.*, point 8, pp. 195–196.

[27] O. W. Kuusinen, Yrjö Sirola and J. H. Lumivuokko to Petrograd, Sept.1, 1920, RGASPI, f. 516, op. 2, 1920, d. 2. To whom the letter is addressed is not stated, but obviously it is the Central Committee. It is possible that the receiver was deliberately not stated because the senders did not wish to recognise the Central Committee as a Central Committee.

and other comrades did not know of a decision to send a delegation consisting of Jukka Rahja and Iikka Luoma to Stockholm to discipline Kuusinen and other rebels. (Jukka Rahja was actually preparing his departure for Stockholm on September 1, 1920, but he was murdered one day prior to this.)

The third Party Congress in August 1920 heard Jukka Rahja's introductory address on the liquidation of the Party. In his opinion, the proletarian masses in Finland were now conscious of the courageous struggle of the Comintern and SKP for them. According to Jukka Rahja, Kuusinen was a theoretician who knew little about the propensities and inclinations of the Finnish masses and his suggestion in fact meant support for the existing "dictatorship of the bourgeoisie" in Finland.[28] Jukka Rahja told his audience that he had opposed the decision to send Kuusinen to Finland precisely because his ignorance of the "moods" of the workers.[29] Several speakers agreed with Jukka Rahja and it was solemnly decided that the Party would not be liquidated.[30]

The murders in the Kuusinen Club had two important consequences regarding the Kuusinen Opposition and its relation to Petrograd. As to the first, Jukka Rahja's death was obviously the most dramatic of these outcomes, because Jukka Rahja had been the "soul" of Rahjaism. Although his mode of behaviour was not cultivated, he was more intelligent than his brother Eino. Jukka Rahja's death changed the balance of forces between Rahja's and Kuusinen's tendencies in the Party.

The second consequence of the murders was that it gave a weapon into to Kuusinen's hands. He was now able to demonstrate what he saw as the bankruptcy of the line followed by the Central Committee. Of the murders he wrote:[31]

> The horrible murders of comrades there have incited us here to consider thoroughly, how there *could* develop such infinite hatred among the Finnish refugees of revolution. Have you not found any other explanation for it than the instigation of slaughterer provocateurs? But how might slaughterer provocation be so successful, that among the Red Officer Course participants and other refugees of the revolution, who hate the slaughterers' power, could also spread hatred against the Central Committee of our Party?

---

[28] Minutes of the III[d] Congress of the SKP, Aug. 13–21. 1920, RGASPI, f. 516, op. 2, 1920, d. 2, ll. 43–44.

[29] *Ibid.*, l. 23.

[30] *Ibid.*, ll. 44–48 and l. 55. See also Saarela, *Suomalaisen kommunismin synty*, pp. 212–214.

[31] The letter, addressed to the Central Committee, is without date and signature. The writer was undoubtedly Kuusinen because he refers to himself as the originator of the suggestion in the Central Committee in the spring of 1919, that Eino Rahja, the Commissar of the Red Officer School, should himself live there. RGASPI, f. 516, op. 2, 1920, d. 25, l. 1. It is illustrative to compare this estimation with Kuusinen's estimation made in 1926 of the "Fascist nature" of the Murder Opposition. (See p. 141.)

After the murders, Kuusinen no longer suggested a Party Congress in Stockholm.[32] He announced that he himself and other comrades were ready to come to Russia, "at least for a short time" on the condition that comrades in Petrograd become familiar with Kuusinen's suggestions and at least mainly agree with them.[33] Kuusinen with Lumivuokko, Sirola and Ville Ojanen, also presented theses on the situation in the Party. They accused the Central Committee of "some kind of children's disease of revolutionarism, falling into one-sided conspirationism and sectarianism". The action of the Central Committee must be based on "comradely trust and comradely discipline". Such was not the case, Kuusinen and his comrades wrote, in the Party or in its leadership; the situation could be changed only in "a real Congress". They suggested that such delegates who were not necessarily members of the SKP could also participate in the Congress.[34] If this kind of Congress could not be organised, "we cannot work in the present Party", the writers asserted. At this point, someone, probably Manner, wrote in the margin "ultimatum". Kuusinen was even ready to accept members of the Murder Opposition who had not been involved in violence for "conciliatory and equal cooperation".[35]

In a letter to "Dear Comrades" Kuusinen accused the Central Committee of "erroneous copying of the justified centralist method of the Russian comrades". In the Russian Party Kuusinen saw no problems because Congresses of the Party and the Soviets were "real representative assemblies"; they ensureded the maintenance of an "organic relationship" between leaders and masses.[36] Kuusinen cited in his letter various points of Lenin's *Infantile Disease of "Leftism" in Communism*, which he was translating into Finnish.[37] In this way he sought to point out that Manner, Evä and Eino Rahja represented precisely such "Leftism" which Lenin criticised in his book.[38]

---

[32] *Ibid.*, p. 3.

[33] O. W. Kuusinen to the CC, no date, probably in Oct. 1920. RGASPI, f. 512, op. 2, 1920, d. 25.

[34] The number of members was small. According to Evä, the registered membership was 350, but not all districts in Finland had sent membership forms. In Russia there were about 100 members; in Sweden a "very small" figure. Overall, there were about 500 members. (Minutes of the organisational committee of the SKP, May 18, 1921. RGASPI, f 516, op. 2, d. 114.)

[35] Theses written by O. W. Kuusinen, Yrjö Sirola, J. H. Lumivuokko and Ville Ojanen, no date, probably in October 1920. RGASPI, f. 512, op. 2, 1920, d. 25.

[36] O. W. Kuusinen to Dear Comrades, no date. RGASPI, f. 512, op. 2, 1921, d. 84, l. 1.

[37] Kuusinen titled his translation *Penikkatauti*, literally "Distemper".

[38] A dispute over the municipal policy of the Communists in Finland may illustrate this "Leftism". Lauri Letonmäki suggested in a programme for employment and municipal policy that the Communists and their allies should demand in municipal councils a "housing norm", a maximum space per person. Flats and rooms which exceeded the maximum should be given people without flats and people who live in cramped quarters. (Letonmäki's suggestion, no date. RGASPI, f. 516, op. 2, 1921, d. 114.) Evä wrote a counter-proposition in which Eino Rahja joined. Communists should demand in municipal councils that the living space of all houses in the municipality should be measured and then divided among all inhabitants equally so that everyone received the same

In yet another letter Kuusinen proposed that the Socialist Workers' Party should be purged of opportunists in order to fulfil the preconditions laid down by the Comintern as far as was possible without taking the risk of the Finnish government suppressing this Party. Its resolutions should be given to the Executive Committee of the Comintern asking whether it was possible for Communists to cooperate with this Party and if so, in what kind of cooperation.[39] In the same letter, Kuusinen outlined the relationship between the SKP and the Socialist Workers' Party. The Central Committee of the SKP should be divided into two parts, one being in Helsinki and another in Petrograd. Clandestine activities in Finland must be led by that part of the Central Committee which was in Helsinki, in cooperation with the Communists in the Socialist Workers' Party. In the case of conflicting interests, an appeal should be made to the Executive Committee of the Comintern. Its decisions should then be followed.[40]

One of Kuusinen's suggestions was that the Central Committee should publicly resign. The Executive Committee of the Comintern would then summon "a free general Congress" for all Communists, whether members of the SKP, RKP(b) or not members of any organisation at all. Only the members of the Opposition who were guilty of the murder of comrades or who had agitated for it should be excluded.[41]

It may not be all that surprising that the suggestions found no support in Petrograd. Manner and Evä stated in April 1921 that the suggestion regarding the resignation of the Central Committee was a "declaration of bankruptcy" and it was rejected because its "bases" were "profoundly in error".[42]

Since Jukka Rahja had died in the murders, Iikka Luoma, a future chief of the smuggling of the SKP, was sent with Jalo Kohonen to Stockholm. Their task was to get Kuusinen to Petrograd. In Stockholm Kohonen and Luoma considered their efforts were futile and on October 24, 1920, they wrote a letter to the Comintern in which they suggested that the Comintern would once again summon Kuusinen, Sirola and Lumivuokko to Russia.[43] It seems that Kuusinen and his comrades in Stockholm were simply teasing the delegation, because Kuusinen had already promised the chairman of the Comintern, Zinov'ev, that he would come to Petrograd.

space. Municipalities should also issue their own money, stop paying debts, stop paying salaries to high officials etc. The aim was to cause chaotic conditions in the administrative machinery of the bourgeois state in the municipalities and to "expose" the Social Democrats.

39 O. W. Kuusinen to Petrograd, no date. RGASPI, f. 512, op. 2, 1921, d. 84, l. 3.

40 *Ibid.*, ll. 6–7.

41 *Ibid.*, l. 5. O. W. Kuusinen to Dear Comrades, no date. RGASPI, f. 512, op. 2, 1921, d. 84, l. 1.

42 Manner's and Evä's memorandum, April 20, 1921. RGASPI, f. 516, op. 2, 1921, d. 114.

43 Jalo Kohonen and Iikka Luoma in Stockholm to the Executive Committee of the Comintern, Oct. 24, 1920. RGASPI, f. 516, op. 2, 1921, d. 114.

2. Kuusinen "Boils in the Bolshevik Pot"

O. W. Kuusinen wrote to G. E. Zinov'ev, probably in August 1920, in an attempt to convince the chairman of the Comintern that his aim was the "reorganisation" of the SKP, which was not possible without the "consent" of Finnish Communists in Russia and the Executive Committee of the Comintern.[44] On October 5, 1920, Kuusinen wrote another letter to Zinov'ev, an answer to a letter written by Zinov'ev, probably in September, summoning him to Petrograd to participate in the second Congress of the Comintern. Now Kuusinen informed Zinov'ev that he "self-evidently" was "ready" to leave Sweden for Russia. Kuusinen wrote of the murders more or less as he had written to the Central Committee. He asserted that everything that might render a reconciliation more difficult must be avoided. Nevertheless, blind obedience must be replaced by "Communist discipline", i.e. "proletarian-revolutionary confidence".[45]

Before Kuusinen came to Russia (January or February 1921), he received support from two members of the Central Committee in Petrograd, Heino Rautio and Lauri Letonmäki. In a letter to the Central Committee in December 1920, they had suggested that the SKP must be coupled with the public workers' movement: "The SKP must strive to change [itself] as soon as possible and be essentially the same [thing] as the Party organisation in Finland." Letonmäki and Rautio also complained that the Central Committee was in weak condition. Of its nine members one (Jukka Rahja) had been murdered, one was in Sweden (Iikka Luoma), two were in Karelia (Edvard Gylling and Jaakko Mäki), one was involved in the murder case (Eino Rahja). Only four members were left, Kullervo Manner and K. M. Evä, and in addition Letonmäki and Rautio themselves.[46] Letonmäki and Rautio also criticised the smuggling activity because those who benefited from it were organisers of the Central Committee and people "close" to it. They demanded that foodstuffs in stores be used for people who are in need. Clothes and leathers in stores must be "liquidated" in cooperation with the Russian authorities.[47] In spring 1921, before April 20, Letonmäki, Rautio and Gylling resigned from the Central Committee because they thought that their justified demand had not been taken in the consideration.[48]

Support from within the Central Committee was obviously necessary to Kuusinen when he came to Russia. It seems that Kuusinen's "laundering" began in

---

[44] O. W. Kuusinen to G. E. Zinov'ev, no date, probably in August 1920 (in German). RGASPI, f. 516, op. 2, 1924, d. 3. Also KtS!, pp. 129–131.

[45] O. W. Kuusinen to G. Zinov'ev, Oct. 5, 1920 (in German). RGASPI, f. 516, op. 2, 1924, d. 3.

[46] Lauri Letonmäki and Heino Rautio to the CC of the SKP, Dec. 4, 1920. RGASPI, f. 516, op. 2, 1921, d. 114.

[47] *Ibid.*

[48] Kullervo Manner and Eino Rahja to the CC on the meetings in the Comintern, May 3, 1921. See also Saarela, *Suomalaisen kommunismin synty*, pp. 222–223.

Petrograd in April 1921. He wrote a letter to Zinov'ev in which he argued that "decisive measures" on the part of RKP(b) and the Comintern would in the near future be necessary in order to avoid aggravation of the crisis into "general tumult".[49] In April Zinov'ev decreed that until the next Congress, which must be held within two months, a representative of the "Kuusinen group" should be nominated to the Central Committee, the meetings of which should be chaired by a representative of the Comintern. Zinov'ev also ordered the establishment of an Organisational Committee, in which both "groups" should have equal representation and which was to be chaired by a representative of the Comintern. Zinov'ev also referred to the possibility of inviting a representative of the Opposition, i.e. the Murder Opposition, to this Committee, if "suitable" people could be found. Finally, Zinov'ev declared that the proposal made by the majority of the Central Committee, that an "account" of Kuusinen by the Cheka would be accepted.[50]

Kuusinen became a member of the Central Committee and an Orgburo was established. Zinov'ev's suggestion as to searching for a "suitable" member of the Murder Opposition must have been a shock to most members of the Central Committee, particularly Eino Rahja and K. M. Evä. The suggestion sounds indeed so odd that we must ask whether it was presented seriously. The "elucidation" regarding Kuusinen probably had something to do with the Tuomainen case. When Kuusinen went to Finland in May 1919, Tuomainen was at the frontier helping him to cross over safely. Tuomainen had related in his hearings in the Cheka that Kuusinen gave him advice on how build a network of agents in Finland. Kuusinen said in his letter to the chairman of the Central Committee of the RKP(b), i.e. Lenin, that this talk of advice was a product of the imagination. He did not know Tuomainen in 1919 and he doubted whether Tuomainen knew him.[51]

In the Executive Committee of the Comintern Karl Radek suggested that a special Committee be formed for the Finnish case, because the members of the Executive Committee did not know the language and because the case involved "emigrant muddles" and other "complicated affairs".[52] The Committee consisted of three assemblages. Eino Rahja, Kullervo Manner, Edvard Gylling and O. W. Kuusinen represented the SKP; K. B. Radek, I. V. Stalin and Mikhail Pavlovich Tomskii represented the Central Committee of the RKP(b); G. E. Zinov'ev, Karl Steinhardt (secretary general of the Austrian Communist Party), Endre Rudnyánszky (member

[49] O. W. Kuusinen to G. E. Zinov'ev (in German), April 3, 1921. RGASPI, f. 516, op. 2, 1921, d. 2.

[50] G. E. Zinov'ev's suggestion of a Party Congress of the SKP (in Russian), f. 516, op. 2, 1921, d. 114.

[51] O. W. Kuusinen to chairman of the CC. of the RKP(b) on arrested Finns (in Russian), no date, after April 20, 1921. RGASPI, f. 516, op. 2, 1921, d. 114.

[52] Kullervo Manner and Eino Rahja to the CC, May 3, 1921. The document is a report on the meeting of the Plenum of the Executive Committee of the Comintern, April 20–21, 1921 and the meeting of the Committee for Finnish affairs set up by the Executive Committee, May 2, 1921. RGASPI, f. 516, op. 2, 1921, d. 114, l. 1.

of the Executive Committee 1920–1921[53]), M. Kobetski and Georgi Dimitrov represented the Executive Council of the Comintern. – The affair was introduced by Zinov'ev, who said that the quarrel was not very serious but because three members of the Central Committee had resigned, there was a danger that "the rest of the Central Committee would also leave". Kuusinen affirmed that the quarrel was deep: the crisis in the Party was "severe". Kuusinen suggested that the Executive Committee of the Comintern set up a new Central Committee, whereafter the Finns in the RKP(b) should convene, and then the Congress of the SKP should be held. Eino Rahja broadened the conflict into an international context. He, however, belittled the affair: there was no "other conflict than the one represented by Kuusinen", he accused Kuusinen of "Martovism" and "Levism". "Martovism" meant the position that the gates of the Party must be opened to all "revolutionaries"; "Levism" rejection of public condemnation of the murders.[54]

Rahja's "Martovism" referred to the dispute between L. Martov[55] and V. I. Lenin in the second Congress of the Russian Social Democratic Labour Party in 1903. This dispute, in which the Party was divided into Bolsheviks and Mensheviks, formally concerned qualification for Party membership in the statutes. According to Lenin's text a member of the Party is one who "supports it both materially and by personal participation in one of its organisations"; Martov suggested that a member is one who supports the Party "both materially and by regular cooperation under the leadership of one of its organisations".[56] In the Congress much more was of course at stake than these formulations, which were not far from each other. Here it is interesting that Rahja should allude to this quarrel over the nature of the Party; it is, as far as I know, presented for the first time in the documents of the SKP. – "Levism" is a much more complicated question than "Martovism". Paul Levi was co-chairman of the German Communist Party after its merger with the Left of the United Social Democratic Party in December 1920.[57] He may be qualified as a Luxemburgist; in the second Congress of the Comintern he spoke against too narrow a conception of the organisation: "For us the central question is to find the road to the masses and in my opinion any road that leads to the masses must be tried", he said.[58]

---

53 Rudnyánszky disappeared from Russia with a large sum of money belonging to the Comintern in 1921. ("Glossary" in *Workers of the World and Oppressed Peoples, Unite! : Proceedings and Documents of the Second Congress [of the Comintern]*, [July 19–August 7], 1920, vol. 2, p. 1029.)

54 Kullervo Manner and Eino Rahja to the CC, May 3, 1921, pp. 1–2. Also KtS!, pp. 138–139.

55 Iulii Osipovich Tsederbaum, also known as Julius or Yuli Martov.

56 Edward Hallet Carr, *The Bolshevik Revolution 1917–1923*, vol. 1, p. 41.

57 Julius Braunthal, *History of the International*, vol. 2, 1914–1943, p. 224.

58 *Proceedings and Documents of the Second Congress [of the Comintern]*, [July 19–Aug. 7], 1920, vol. 1. p. 165. On Levi's relations with Zinov'ev, see Pierre Broué, *Histoire de l'Internationale Communiste 1919–1943*, p. 208.

In the debate concerning the SKP, Georgi Dimitrov said, according to the somewhat sporadic Central Committee minutes that it was impossible for every "honest revolutionary" to be a delegate in the Party Congress. Stalin seemed to defend Kuusinen: he said that the quarrel in the SKP was different from that of Lenin and Martov in 1903. Manner now showed Stalin Kuusinen's thesis, according to which Communists who are not members of the SKP or the RKP(b) can be delegates. When Stalin had read the text, he declared that Kuusinen was in error. Kuusinen tried to defend himself by saying that he no longer adhered to his letter sent from Stockholm. Rahja suggested that the minutes should show that Kuusinen had taken back his suggestions. Zinov'ev declared there were two kinds of Communists in the SKP: Rahja was a "Russian Communist" and Kuusinen a "Western Communist". He remarked that not very long ago (i.e. in spring 1920) Rahja and Manner were fighting against each other; now "Kuusinen boils in the same pot until he also becomes ripe".[59]

Zinov'ev's point was prophetic. Kuusinen was indeed "boiling" and in the fourth Congress of the SKP he was to become "mature" for the purposes of the Russians, i.e. flattering whoever happened to be in power there. Now, before the Congress, however, he still tried to kick over the traces. However, Kuusinen was perhaps already ripe on the Comintern level because Lenin accepted a document written by him, *Theses on the Structure of Communist Parties and on the Methods and Content of their Work*, adopted by the third Congress of the Comintern on July 12, 1921.[60]

3. The 1921 Congress of the SKP

Immediately prior to the fourth Congress Kuusinen wrote a letter to Lenin in which he stated that the "central leadership" should be divided between Helsinki and Petrograd so that the majority of the members of the Central Committee would be in Helsinki and the minority in Petrograd. In Petrograd an editorial board should be established for mainly propaganda purposes and the members of the Central Committee should work in this organisation. It might be a consultative organ in relation to the Central Committee. Regarding the "maintenance of an extensive apparatus" for "the furnishing of provisions", i.e. smuggling on the Finnish-Russian border, Kuusinen wrote that it should at least be reduced as far as the lead of the Petrograd organisation deemed "desirable". On personal matters, Kuusinen wrote without inhibition. He asserted that Eino Rahja, K. M. Evä and Jaakko Mäki

---

59 Kullervo Manner and Eino Rahja (who quote Zinov'ev's saying) to the CC, May 3, 1921. RGASPI, f. 516, op. 2, 1921, d. 114, ll. 3–4. Also KtS!, pp. 139–141.

60 See Extracts of The Theses on the Structure of Communist Parties and on the Methods and Content of their Work. Published in *The Communist International 1919–1943 : Documents*, vol. I, *1919–1922*, pp. 257–271.

should not be elected to the Central Committee. Eino Rahja and Evä had in "too sharply conspicuous a manner" participated in the struggle with the "Opposition", i.e. the Murder Opposition. Rahja had, Kuusinen stated, ample merit in the posts he had occupied, but in the leadership of the Party he was a "*desorganisator*". The Finnish workers, Kuusinen wrote, "understood" that it was not correct to "retain" him. – Of Manner Kuusinen stated that he was "one of the best Communists of the faction of the former majority" in the Central Committee. He should be either in the Central Committee or, at least, in the editorial board. Kuusinen promised that he would try to "talk him over". He asked that in the event of Zinov'ev's not being able to attend the Congress of the SKP, Bukharin could do so. In the end, Kuusinen declared that his "closest comrades", Yrjö Sirola, J. H. Lumivuokko, Edvard Gylling and Arvo Tuominen had taken "small steps on the way Your Party lead has shown to us".[61]

One may firstly note that the Finnish workers did not presumably know much about Eino Rahja's activities after the Civil War. Secondly, the letter was openly partisan; it was a letter of a leader of a faction to the "Big Boss". This is interesting considering that the Bolshevik Party had just forbidden all factions whilst in the Finnish case the Executive Committee of the Comintern had recognised the Kuusinen group as a faction. The Comintern forbade the Kuusinen faction to present their viewpoints publicly, but decreed that they had the right of appeal to Zinov'ev on decisions of the Central Committee.[62] It seems that Kuusinen for the first time did not announce his opinion of Eino Rahja to Lenin. The problem is, of course, that we cannot know everything that had been discussed or even what had been written. My thesis is that Kuusinen, an intellectual, might hope that another of his kind would support him in a quarrel with a non-intellectual. It is clear, however, that Lenin had not time to waste on problems of a Party of secondary importance. Moreover, the head in the Comintern fief was actually not Lenin but Zinov'ev. This meant difficulties for Kuusinen, at least as to the affairs of the SKP, for several years to come.

In the fourth Congress of the SKP there were more delegates from Finland than in the two previous Congresses (1919 and 1920): 45 delegates out of a total of 92.[63]

[61] O. W. Kuusinen to "Dear Comrade Lenin", in July 1921. The letter is dated August 17, 1921, but it cannot have been written after the Congress of the SKP. The Congress began on July 25, 1921. (RGASPI, f. 5, op. 3, d. 163.) The letter is written (by hand) in German. There is also a Russian translation. – It may be interesting to note in passing that in a letter of March 16, 1921, O. W. Kuusinen wrote to his "Distinguished Comrade and Teacher" and informed Lenin that he had bought a "Parlograph (Dictaphone)" for him. Kuusinen wrote that he knew many writers who, when familiarised with the machine, no longer wished to write by hand. (RGASPI, f. 5, op. 3, d. 163.)

[62] Heino Rautio to the Executive Committee of the Comintern, June 1921. RGASPI, f. 516, op. 2, 1921, d. 2.

Their impact was not, however, very strong in the Congress; many seem to have been rather surprised and indignant at the leaders when they quarrelled with each other. From the present standpoint the Congress is particularly important in that here and here only were all factions and tendencies present. To be sure, there was nobody from the Murder Opposition, but this Opposition was in an important way present at the debates of the Congress. Then there was O. W. Kuusinen and his "Levism". Manner was his opponent and although the quarrel between Kullervo Manner and Kuusinen was settled, there were elements especially in Manner's brutally worded attacks on Kuusinen, which adumbrated the future quarrels between them. The Kuusinen Opposition, however, withered away very soon after the Congress, or perhaps we can say that it withered away already in the Congress. Kuusinen and Manner were able to bring about a reconciliation between them. The serious dispute between Eino Rahja and Kuusinen, in contrast, only became more sharpened. When the representative of the Comintern, K. B. Radek, intervened, Kuusinen had to accept Rahja's membership in the Central Committee. Radek was not perhaps the best possible representative from Kuusinen's point of view or possibly anybody's. According to Ruth Fischer, a German Communist, Radek was a "born cynic",[64] who, if we can trust Arvo Tuominen's statement in his memoirs, enjoyed following the quarrelling in the Congress.[65] The fact that Kuusinen had been elected to the important post of secretary of the Comintern, (one of three secretaries in the organisation until December 1921, when he was appointed secretary general[66]), was not seen as important by the delegates of the Congress.

It is perhaps of some interest that Kuusinen's opponents accused him of Ultraleftism. This was due to the fact that Kuusinen had written most important Party documents from the foundation of the Party until the 1919 election document (in which boycott of the election was – in veiled words – urged). Although Kullervo Manner did not claim that Kuusinen only was guilty of all deviations, he declared that in the foundation of the SKP one could discern Blanquism, Bakuninism and "small germs of conspiracy and sectarianism". Because most leaders had grown up in the spirit of Kautskyism, it was simply a "psychological necessity" to go to the opposite extreme.[67] Here Manner was using concepts which the young delegates from Finland could not possibly fully understand.

---

63 Saarela, *Suomalaisen kommunismin synty*, pp. 226–228 and p. 499. The figure of 92 included full delegates with voting right (52) and people who had the right of speak only (40). Many luminaries, like Sirola and Lumivuokko were among the second category.

64 According to Ruth Fischer, Radek had a "sense of irony" but with his "enormous head", "his ears stick out", his "horn-rimmed spectacles" and his pipe, he was a "grotesque apostle of Bolshevism". (Ruth Fischer, *Stalin und die deutsche Kommunismus*, vol. 1, *Von der Entstehung des deutschen Kommunismus bis 1924*, p. 261.)

65 Arvo Tuominen, *Sirpin ja vasaran tie*, p. 298.

66 Broué, *Histoire de l'Internationale Communiste 1919–1943*, p. 1031.

67 Minutes of the Congress of the SKP, July 25–Aug. 10, 1921. RGASPI, f. 516, op. 2, 1921, d. 17, l. 112.

As to the location of the Central Committee, Manner spoke for Russia because there the members of that body were close to "core" of Bolshevism. According to Manner, renunciation of Ultrabolshevism began in the Central Committee in the summer of 1919.[68] Here Manner was implicitly saying that positive development in the Party had started immediately after Kuusinen had left for Finland. If we remember the feverish second Party Congress in 1919 and especially the third Party Congress in 1920, his statement is not very convincing. More credible is Manner's observation that once in Finland Kuusinen began to abandon his Ultraleftist positions. Manner was satisfied with his development but he was not satisfied with the letters of Kuusinen and colleagues from Stockholm, in which they accused the Central Committee of "sectarian infantile disease" and "conspiratism". This was "self-praise" and "self-preening".[69] When Kuusinen and his comrades fought against Ultraleftism in Petrograd, they fought, according to Manner, against "the dead past" and when "corpses" were "laid hands on", a "hellish smell and stench" was produced. Moreover, some of Kuusinen's minions, people who had no will of their own, went after him and as they were digging, they sullied themselves "with the decay".[70] In Stockholm, their "petty-bourgeois elementarism" was strengthened when they read Western literature and were not controlled by Eastern Communism. This elementarism was seen in two ways: Kuusinen did not condemn the murders and opposed the "Prussian command".[71] When Manner still referred to Kuusinen's "Levism", Kuusinen shouted that he had abandoned his theses. Manner rejoined that this was indeed the case: "We Rahjaites" have abandoned "our Ultracommunism", so one can record that there are "no disagreements" on political principles.[72]

In several speeches Kuusinen's "indiscipline" was condemned, an indication that Kuusinen's position in the Comintern did not yet carry much weight at this time. Toivo Antikainen criticised Kuusinen for remaining in Sweden although the Central Committee had commanded him to return to Russia. How can the leaders demand discipline, if they themselves are not disciplined, he asked.[73] Kalle Lepola, a former MP, denounced the pseudonym "Father" Kuusinen had used in publications in Finland. Kuusinen was no "father", but a "child who has been spoiled in Party activities".[74]

Several delegates who had come from Finland were utterly disgusted. One unidentified delegate said the conflict between Manner and Kuusinen was a "cock-

[68] *Ibid.*, l. 110.
[69] *Ibid.*, ll. 119–121.
[70] *Ibid.*, ll. 131–132, l. 137 and 140.
[71] *Ibid.*, l. 140.
[72] *Ibid.*, l. 135.
[73] *Ibid.*, ll. 75–76.
[74] *Ibid.*, l. 106.

fight", and because the quarrelling leaders had been such "bovines", they had failed in their obligations in Finland. Now a "big black line must be drawn over these affairs".[75] Kalle Summanen declared that the Congress was not a "meeting of old men", but a "babbling of crones".[76] The delegates who had come from Finland did not understand the quarrels and were little interested in them, but a division between supporters of the Manner–Rahja faction and the Kuusinen faction was a disturbing development.

Kuusinen maintained a low profile. He described in detail what had happened after he had left Petrograd for Helsinki. He said that comrades in Stockholm were not aware of the doctrinal quarrel between the Central Committee and the Murder Opposition, because information received in Stockholm was "indefinite". Had the Congress been held in Stockholm and the lead of the Party transferred to Finland, the (future) Murder Opposition could not do anything but "to grasp at for empty air".[77] Here Kuusinen was not entirely honest. By July 15, 1920, Sirola had come to Stockholm and he had knowledge of the Opposition which was not "indefinite". Nobody, of course, could predict that the activities of the Opposition would lead to murder. Kuusinen said that it was his mistake to suggest that people who are not members of the SKP would also participate in the Congress. Its purpose, however, was only to "calm" people.[78] Manner's mistake, by contrast, was that he suggested to Zinov'ev a composition of the Central Committee "such as it was". Kuusinen thought that probably, but only probably, the murders could have been prevented by a different policy. He said that among the Opposition, "primitive anarchic factors" had a grip, but it would be possible to "paralyse" them by "strict policy".[79] Kuusinen did not say what this "strict policy" would have been, but it seems that this implied that representatives of the Opposition be taken onto the Central Committee in the spring of 1920. Manner, for his part, explained that the situation in which the leaders lived better than the masses generated dissatisfaction. Nothing could be done about this because "practical life points out that the purposes of the proletarian revolution demand for the time being such a difference".[80]

---

75 *Ibid.*, l. 159.

76 *Ibid.*, l. 172.

77 *Ibid.*, l. 53.

78 *Ibid.*, l. 54.

79 *Ibid.*, l. 71.

80 *Ibid.*, p. 141. According to a statistic from November 1–November 15, the SKP employed 36 "responsible functionaries" and 44 members of staff. The members of the Central Committee received the best monthly salary (all amounts are monthlies); it was 165,000 rubles. The "exporter", i.e. head of smuggling, received 132,000 rubles and the head of horsemen 111,000 rubles. He was counted as a "responsible functionary" and his salary was the smallest in this category. Salaries of the staff were much inferior. Two coders and a draughtsman (probably of maps for spying) received the highest pay, 70,000 rubles. The salary of typists varied between 32,000 and 48,000 ru-

Sirola tried in his way to conciliate. He declared:[81]

> I take an example from the Bible. We can say, as did the Christians in the early days, that we are the light of the world and the salt of the earth. Our light is in our propaganda; it illuminates all things rightly, puts them in their place. In addition, salt the Communists are through their organisation, by it they prevent the depravity of the capitalist class in the working-class. In addition, still by a biblical example, we are the leaven, which leavens the dough. We are, even as a little bacillus, the centres of social fermentation, which spreads activity around it.

The most serious conflict in the Congress was that between O. W. Kuusinen and Eino Rahja. The following quotation from Kuusinen's speech and Rahja's interjections is illustrative:[82]

> Before the Congress of the International, I wrote a principal writing, which was branded as opportunist by Eino. (Eino Rahja shouts: I said it is shit!) These principles were confirmed by the decision of the International. (Eino Rahja: It was us who suggested them!) Well, now you see that factional struggles are certainly ending. I thought that Lenin had given the thought to this writing, not Eino.

Kuusinen tried to discredit Rahja by the declaration that Rahja was "one of the best originators and arrangers in Russian offices", but he was a "soldier" who did not read very much and was not suitable for the position of a leader. There had been about 20 Red officers in Finland, sent by Rahja, who had acted as agents of the "Okhrana" (Finnish Detective Central Police). It was necessary to send Finland "serious-minded and trusted" men, who did not show their money and tell everyone that they had "special mandates from 'Rahja's boutique'", Kuusinen said. Following this there is in the minutes a remark: "At this point a heated exchange of words broke out between Comrades Rahja and Kuusinen".[83] K. M. Evä said that only one man out of all the men sent to Finland for espionage and other military

---

bles; drivers of cars received 63,000 rubles, horsemen 37,000 rubles, cleaners 25,800 rubles and errand boys and girls 18,000 rubles. (RGASPI, f. 516, op. 2, 1921, d. 84.) – The SKP received in 1921 from the RKP(b) about 146,200,000 rubles and other currencies worth 4,340,000 million Finnish *markkas*. In addition, the Comintern dispatched directly to the Finnish Socialist Workers' Party 1,500,000 Finnish *markkas*. In 1921 the SKP spent 163,000,000 rubles and other currencies worth 5,393,000 Finnish *markkas*. The SKP also transmitted money and jewels to the West. In December 1921, the Central Committee complained that there was a shortage of money. Later, however, the sums, decreased considerably and the SKP had to reduce its activities. (Saarela, "Tuhatmarkkasia, miljoonia ruplia, dollareita", pp. 278–281.)

81 Minutes of the Congress of the SKP, July 25–Aug. 10, 1921. RGASPI, f. 516, op. 2, 1921, d. 17, l. 262.

82 *Ibid.*, l. 53.

83 *Ibid.*, l. 187.

work had changed side.[84] Kuusinen had to announce that he was mistaken when he said that many men were agents of the Okhrana.[85]

In the final phase of the Congress Kuusinen experienced several defeats. The first concerned the location of the Central Committee. Kuusinen suggested that the Central Committee be transferred to Finland.[86] K. B. Radek stated that it should be in Russia because only there were its activities possible without fear of imprisonment.[87] Kuusinen then changed his opinion.[88] Secondly, Manner moved a statement according to which there had been "traces of Social Democracy" in the activities of Kuusinen and colleagues in Stockholm. The motion was passed by 24 votes for and 22 against.[89] Kuusinen then tried to prevent Eino Rahja's election to the Central Committee.[90] Manner stated that in this case he was not a candidate;[91] Kuusinen stated that if Rahja became member of the Central Committee, he would resign.[92] Adolf Taimi, who was chairman of the Organisational Committee of the Congress, which committee presented a list of persons to be elected members of the Central Committee, said that there were numerous "matters", i.e. espionage and military work, in the Central Committee, which were in Rahja's domain and therefore it was "essential" that Rahja be a member.[93] Taimi himself, as we shall see, was not the greatest friend of Rahja. The list of the Organisational Committee consisted of Kullervo Manner, O. W. Kuusinen, J. H. Lumivuokko, Leo Laukki, Adolf Taimi, Eino Rahja and Kalle Lepola.[94] In a secret vote, they were elected.[95]

My impression of Kuusinen is that he enjoyed intellectual work; this was for Kuusinen a value in itself and perhaps a motive to be in the Communist movement as well. Allan Wallenius, a Finnish Communist who claimed he lived a short time in the same room or flat as Kuusinen, described, in an adulatory article published in 1920, his ability to sit by his desk all days and nights, coffee and tobacco as his only material joy.[96] It was not very important what was the subject of the work. It could be Indian politics or the *Kalevala* as well as Finnish politics. Thus, although Kuusinen had suffered defeats in the Congress, he knew that he would

---

84 *Ibid.*, ll. 187–188.
85 *Ibid.*, l. 333.
86 *Ibid.*, l. 305.
87 *Ibid.*, l. 340.
88 *Ibid.*, l. 342.
89 *Ibid.*, ll. 350–356.
90 *Ibid.*, l. 361.
91 *Ibid.*, l. 362.
92 *Ibid.*, l. 363.
93 *Ibid.*, l. 370.
94 *Ibid.*, l. 361.
95 *Ibid.*, l. 382. See also Saarela, *Suomalaisen kommunismin synty*, pp. 238–240.
96 Allan Wallenius, "O. W. Kuusinen", *Sosialistinen Aikakauslehti*, March 1, 1920, p. 3.

have much interesting work in the Comintern. At the same time, however, the defeat was, if not humiliating, at least smarting. His appeal to Lenin to exclude Rahja had not been successful. He obviously could not forget everything that happened in the IVth Congress.

4. Excursion: Kuusinen (and Others) and the Russians

In order to understand Kuusinen's exceptional rise in the Comintern hierarchy, some remarks on his attitude to the Russians may be helpful. We have already noted that Kuusinen was able to impress Lenin by his ability to write theses for the organisation.[97] He had intellectual powers which were useful to the Bolsheviks. What about his Finnishness? Was it from the point of view of Kuusinen's career an advantage, or an obstacle, or was his nationality of only secondary importance? It is impossible to give any definite answer to this question. I think that it is reasonable to examine the question of the independence of Finland and Kuusinen's attitude to it in this context. However, it is not only Kuusinen's outlook which is interesting; also other Finnish Communist leaders, in addition to the Party as a whole, adopted standpoints concerning the independence of Finland, and in one case also that of Estonia.

When the Russian Empire disintegrated during and after World War I, numerous provinces became independent states, and were recognised as such by the Bolshevik government. These included the Ukraine, Azerbaijan, Armenia, Georgia, Khiva, Bukhara, Lithuania, Latvia and Estonia, Poland and Finland. By March 1921 (annexation of Georgia)[98] the Empire was reconstituted, apart from Finland, Poland and the Baltic states.[99] In his famous self-criticism concerning the Finnish revolution, written in the summer of 1918, O. W. Kuusinen adopted Lenin's view of the Social Democrats who failed to do their historical duty after the Bolshevik coup d'état in Petrograd. Kuusinen expressed this in the following poetic words:[100]

---

[97] As to the theses on organisation Lenin later, in the IVth Congress of the Comintern, gave a negative assessment of them. He said that they were excessively influenced by the Russian example. (В. И. Ленин, *Пять лет российской революции и перспективы мировой революции*, PSS, vol. 43, pp. 292–293.)

[98] Robert Parsons, "Georgians" in *The Nationalities Question in the Soviet Union*, p. 182. Osmo Jussila, *Terijoen hallitus 1939–1940*, pp. 90–124.

[99] Hélène Carrère d'Enchausse, *Victorieuse Russie*, pp. 61–63. Of Finland Carrère d'Enchausse writes: "[A]près [l'independance] avoir accordée en 1918 à la Finlande, Lénine avait tenté, par des soulevements révolutionnaires, de la remettre en cause." (*Ibid.*, pp. 61–62.) This is, of course, an oversimplification of the Finnish case.

[100] O. W. Kuusinen, *The Finnish Revolution : a Self-Criticism*, p. 6.

> Amongst us, too, the genius of revolt passed over the country. We did not mount upon its wings, but bowed our heads and let it fly above us. In this way, November [1917] was for us but a festival to commemorate our capitulation!

Kuusinen argued that revolution would have been possible in November, but this does not mean that "the revolution of the proletariat" would not have succeeded in gaining "the victory directly as in Russia".[101] This was because the Finnish Social Democrats saw a "Democratic State" as a "bridge" and a "passage from Capitalism to Socialism". Kuusinen declared that "it can now be seen that the idea of the Democratic State, with which the People's Commissariat [*kansanvaltuuskunta,* translated in this book as People's Deputation] deluded itself, was *historically false*". The "course" of the Finnish Social Democrats "could not agree with the true postulates of history", Socialist revolution and the "historical necessity" of the dictatorship of the proletariat.[102]

Although, as we have seen, Kuusinen had to be boiled in the Bolshevik pot, the Russian Bolsheviks were for him a paragon to be followed in other countries. As to Finland, the simplest way was to wed it to Soviet Russia. In 1920 Kuusinen wrote from Stockholm to Zinov'ev:[103]

> I am firmly convinced that after the victory in Finland no "independence" of Finland can come into question, at least not in foreign policy and in the highest military leadership. Only the foreign policy of Communist Russia can exist for the Communist Finland, is it not so?

Kimmo Rentola writes that there were "perhaps" "Old Finn remnants in Kuusinen's attitude towards those in power in Moscow".[104] This may be an accurate appraisal, although Kuusinen was by no means the only Communist politician who saw the future of Finland as a part of Russia. Leo Laukki, who ardently speculated on future state formations, stated in 1921 that the "Georgian way", i.e. barefaced invasion, was not appropriate in the Border States. There agitation must first create an "ideological basis" for unification, in the Finnish case that of Soviet Finland to Soviet Russia with Russian aid.[105] In 1922, Laukki pondered what would happen if

---

101 *Ibid.*

102 *Ibid.*, pp. 16–17.

103 O. W. Kuusinen to G. E. Zinov'ev, no date, probably in August 1920, in German. RGASPI, f. 516, op. 2, 1924, d. 3.) In the same letter, Kuusinen informed Zinov'ev that in April he had sent a letter to Prime Minister Rafael Erich of Finland, who was Kuusinen's classmate at school. In the letter, Kuusinen urged that "governmental people" should make peace with Russia.

104 Kimmo Rentola, "Finnish Communism, O. W. Kuusinen, and Their Two Native Countries" in *Communism National & International*, p. 161.

105 Leo Laukki to the Politburo of the SKP, date unclear, obviously after the Soviet invasion to Georgia, February 1921. RGASPI, f. 516, op. 2, 1921, d. 84.

the Red Army were "forced" to attack Finland. In this case Soviet Finland should give "aid" to South-West Russia and vice versa. The precondition for this would be the unification of Soviet Karelia with Soviet Finland. In agitation, this should be taken into account.[106] Sirola and Manner were not very interested in this kind of agitation; they said that this unification was only a theoretical possibility.[107] This concerned only agitation. Sirola thought that unification of Soviet Karelia with Soviet Finland would mean the unification of both Soviet Karelia and Soviet Finland with the Soviet Union.[108]

It seems that there were also plans – how serious, it is difficult to say – to invade Finland at some time in the early 1920s. Mauno Heimo, an official of the Comintern, noted in a letter to the Central Committee of the SKP on December 12, 1921 that he had met Lauri Letonmäki in Berlin. Letonmäki's task, given by the Central Committee, was to travel as soon as possible to Sweden to organise Finnish Red refugees into a military organisation if a "war from Soviet Russia against Finland was to break out on "February 1", 1920(?)[109] until which date the mobilisation of the Finnish revolutionary forces in Russia was to be completed". Heimo noted that he had no information about this attack when he left Russia (it is not clear at what time), but he had no reason to doubt it because he had been in Russia in a meeting with Jukka Rahja, Letonmäki and Zinov'ev where this question as well as invasions of Estonia and Latvia had been discussed.[110]

In addition, the Finnish Communists prepared a new Finnish rebellion on Swedish soil. They had in, 1919–1921, a military organisation known as "The Swedish Battalion of the Finnish Red Guard". The intention was to use this battalion not only in Finland, but also in Sweden and Norway, if there were prospects of the creation of a Scandinavian Soviet Republic. The leaders of the battalion included Heimo and Herman Hurmevaara, a former MP (more about him below), and a *Jäger* Heikki Repo. Some 200 men participated in military exercises held in Sweden and Norway. The Swedish police, however, succeeded in exposing parts of this organisation and in Stockholm in 1921 several people were condemned to prison. Many, however, were able to escape, for example Heimo and Repo.[111]

---

106 Minutes of the meeting of the enlarged Party leadership of the SKP, Aug. 9–16, 1922. RGASPI, f. 516, op. 2, 1922, d. 6, l. 23.

107 *Ibid.*, ll. 25–26 and 28–30.

108 Kilin, *Suurvallan rajamaa*, p. 84.

109 The year is not clear. See next note.

110 Mauno Heimo to the CC of the SKP, Dec. 20, 1921. RGASPI, f. 516, op. 2, 1921, d. 114. It is difficult to say when Heimo had met Letonmäki in Berlin. The reference to Jukka Rahja points out that the discussion had taken place before it became known that Jukka Rahja was murdered, i.e. early September 1920 at the latest.

111 Matti Lackman, *Kommunistiesn salainen toiminta Tornionjokilaaksossa 1918–1939*, pp. 23–36.

In 1923, there were again discussions about the unification of (Soviet) Finland and Soviet Karelia. The background was now the slogan "United States of Socialist Europe" cast by Trotskii. In Trotskii's view, an American blockade was to be expected if a Socialist revolution came about in Western Europe. Therefore, the countries there must be united. This was also because the United States of Socialist Europe and the Soviet Union together would have a "tremendous magnetic attraction for the peoples of Asia".[112] Sirola's explanation of the slogan was that it meant a transitional "democratic" period in the West and was not same as the "Union of Soviet Powers" (*Neuvostovaltain liitto*). The problem for Finland was whether the country would join Europe or Russia. Sirola's answer was Russia because in Finland the workers "understand" this and the "peasants and many middle strata people are not very much against Russia". Sirola stressed that "as Communists we should understand" that the independence of small Powers was "a passing phenomenon". Thus, Sirola continued, Finland "belongs in close affiliation with Russia". To join Karelia would be an "intermediate phase"[113] In this explanation it is interesting that democracy and the dictatorship of the proletariat, i.e. the Soviet Union, are sharply differentiated. Sirola's argument implies that the Soviet Union was not a democracy. It is also interesting that the Finns in Russia still rated Trotskii as an eminent personage worth noting in ideological debate. To be sure, Trotskii's star was still high in Russian Bolshevik circles and the struggle for power between Stalin and Trotskii was at this stage only beginning; for instance Kuusinen, who was always careful, no longer spoke of Trotskii's "greatness", as still in 1922, or at least I have not found any eulogy of Trotskii after 1922. – Important from our point of view is naturally Sirola's Russophilia: Finland should be integrated with Russia, not the West.

There was a slogan "Karelia-Finland". According to Manner, it was presented in order to stress that "Russia has no intention of oppressing the Finnish workers". There were also discussions with Stalin on this question. When the Finns asked what was to be done with Karelian Russians, Stalin suggested, laughing: "Drive them out". Manner stressed that this – ethnic cleansing we would today say – was no "definition of standpoint".[114] The idea of "Karelia-Finland" meant annexation of Finland to Soviet Karelia.

Kuusinen's position on the independence of Finland remained the same through the decades. In 1934, he declared that the foremost task of the SKP was to make it clear to "starving workers and peasants, that now salvation from the present situa-

---

[112] Deutscher, *The Prophet Unarmed*, p. 216.

[113] Minutes of the enlarged meeting of the CC of the SKP, Aug. 24 and Aug. 29 – Sept. 1, 1923. RGASPI, f. 516, op. 2, 1923, d. 4, ll. 64–65.

[114] *Ibid.*, l. 70.

tion, revolution, was near. The unification slogan (*yhdistämisloosunki*) of Soviet Karelia and Finland is today's slogan".[115] In the Supreme Soviet session of the VKP in 1940, Kuusinen wholeheartedly supported the liberation of Estonian working men and women, who from 1918 had had to endure capitalist exploitation which was like a "vampire, who sucked even the last marrow out of the assiduous Estonians in chained bodies". Kuusinen solemnly proposed that the "assiduous, wise and manly" Estonian people be accepted as a new member of the Soviet Union. He ended his *éxposé*, by raising hurrahs for Estonia, the Soviet Union, Viacheslav Mikhailovich Molotov, the Bolshevik Party, and of course, the immortal Comrade Stalin.[116]

In his theoretical writings in the Comintern periodical, Kuusinen was one of the most enthusiastic eulogists of Soviet Russia and the Bolshevik Party. In an article "In the Lead of Russia", published in 1924, Kuusinen defined the role and aptness of the RKP(b) in the world revolution. According to Kuusinen the "leading role" of the RKP(b) was not based only on the "prestige" of the Russian revolution, but also on the "prestige of the RKP(b) itself", and, furthermore, on the "qualifications" of the "leading Old Guard in that Party" to lead the whole "international movement", by merit of the "revolutionary past of its members", its "abundance of experience", its "heroic durability" etc.[117] Kuusinen also saw Russia as "bridge" between East and West: the Russian proletariat "connects" the "proletarian revolution of the West and the people's liberation movement of the East". Moreover, the Russian proletariat can show how it is possible to "win". Therefore, the Russian proletariat has the "hegemony" in the international workers' movement as far as it is needful to "carry out a giant historical task in the proletarian world revolution".[118]

One part of the eulogy was to write this kind of slogans. Another, by no means less important part, was to attack the internal oppositions of the Bolshevik Party. In the mid-1920s Kuusinen reviled especially the Trotskyite Opposition. Before going this matter, it would be interesting to see how Kuusinen judged the members of the presidium of the Comintern in 1922. Boris Suvarin (Souvarine in France) was "an overall strict and sharp man", Klara Zetkin was such a personage that "we have not been given many such people", she was "a good propagandist", her knowledge was vast and her speeches and articles were "strong and fiery". N. I. Bukharin had "immensely strong logic"; one may receive from his articles the impression

---

[115] Minutes of the meeting of the members of the CC convoked by the Foreign Bureau of the CC, l. 38 (the pagination of this document has been done in the archives). RGASPI, f. 516, op. 2, 1934, d. 3.

[116] Rentola, *Kenen joukoissa seisot?*, pp. 248–249.

[117] O. W. Kuusinen, "Venäjän johdolla" in O. W. Kuusinen, *Valitut teokset (1918–1964)*, p. 59; published originally in *Kommunistische International*, 1/1924.

[118] *Ibid.*, p. 73.

that he was "dogmatic", but in discussions he could give valuable advice to Western Europeans. In addition, G. E. Zinov'ev's articles were compiled in such a way that one did not "note his tactical proficiency". K. B. Radek had "an abundance of new thoughts and initiatives" and he advocated them with "force and vigour". As to L. D. Trotskii, Kuusinen declared, "nobody wants to deny Trotskii's greatness. He is a fighter, but one-sided. [He is] a good organiser, but in the field of international tactics Zinov'ev is stronger than him."[119] Here it is interesting, of course, how Kuusinen selected the people he estimated to be worth judging. As to Russians, Zinov'ev, Radek and Bukharin were members of the presidium of the Comintern. Trotskii, however, was not, but of course also participated in the activities of the Comintern. Trotskii was the only Russian politician of whom Kuusinen had something negative to say. More significant, however, is that Stalin was not mentioned at all. Although his role in the Finnish movement had not been negligible, in the international Communist movement he was not worth mentioning.

Two years later, the situation had changed. In 1923, Trotskii published a series of articles, known as *The New Course*, in which he criticised the economic policy of the NEP. He feared that private capital was able to interpose itself "increasingly between the workers' state and the peasantry" and by doing this, it was "acquiring an economic and therefore political influence over the latter". This constituted, according to Trotskii, "a grave danger for the proletarian revolution, and a symptom of the possibility of the triumph of the counter-revolution".[120] Bureaucracy was, as is well known, the main target of Trotskii's attack. For Trotskii bureaucratism was a "social phenomenon", "the profound causes" of which lay in "the heterogeneity of society", "the difference between the daily life and the fundamental interests of various groups of the population". The bureaucratisation of the apparatus threatened to "separate the Party from the masses".[121] As to the Party, Trotskii did not question its power monopoly under the dictatorship.[122] He feared the degeneration of the "Old Guard" and stated that the Party was living on "two storeys: the upper storey, where things are decided, and the lower storey", where all one does is learn of the decisions.[123] Trotskii saw a possible cure in youth and students: Lev Davidovich argued that Lenin proposed to "draw largely upon the students in order to combat bureaucratism", for "studying youth [...] endeavours to explain and to generalize".[124]

---

[119] Minutes of the extended meeting of the Party leadership of the SKP, Aug. 9–16, 1922. RGASPI, f. 516, op. 2, 1922, d. 6, ll. 93–94.

[120] Leon Trotsky, *The New Course*, p. 41.

[121] *Ibid.*, p. 45.

[122] *Ibid.*, p. 27.

[123] *Ibid.*, p. 13.

[124] *Ibid.*, p. 23.

In 1924, Kuusinen determinedly attacked the oppositions, especially Trotskii and the Democratic Centralists. Trotskii, however, was the main object. Taking into account Kuusinen's eulogy of the Bolshevik Old Guard, which eulogy itself can perhaps be understood in the context of the struggle against Trotskii, it was not surprising that Kuusinen saw Trotskii's criticism as a sacrilege, a blasphemy. As to the Party in general, Kuusinen accused Trotskii's Opposition of demanding democratic elections inside the Party. For Kuusinen this meant replacement of the "traditional Bolshevik iron discipline" by formal democracy. Kuusinen argued that for Lenin the Communist Party was "organically homogeneous, strongly structured, an absolutely uniformly functioning *machine*".[125]

Here we must ask whether Kuusinen was being more papal than the Pope himself. In Lenin's "democratic centralism", there was also a "democratic" component, namely the election of leaders in meetings at every level. This practice was changed to the nomination of the leaders from above, but in theory there existed an elective principle in the RKP(b).[126] – Kuusinen admitted, albeit indirectly, that there was indeed bureaucracy in the state apparatus of the Soviet Union. He declared that the Central Committee and the Central Control Commission had opposed bureaucratism by simplifying the state machine, replacing "petty-bourgeois officials by Communists and non-Party workers, and especially increasing control over the state apparatus. He saw this as a remedy for bureaucratism, not a cause of it.[127] This point was perhaps the most essential one. For Kuusinen the Party had become a holy institution, which could not make mistakes, or at least not serious ones. The Social Democratic parties were bureaucratised because they were Social Democratic parties; Communist parties, or at least the RKP(b), could not be bureaucratised because they were Communist parties. One of Trotskii's blasphemies, perhaps the most horrifying, was that he dared compare the German Social Democracy in 1914 to the Russian Communist Party in 1923.[128]

This kind of argumentation was, of course, welcome to Stalin and his entourage. It was used when Stalin suppressed the last oppositions in the VKP(b) at the beginning of the 1930s. We may see, perhaps, a connection with Kuusinen's fate in the late 1930s. Of course, eulogies of the Bolshevik Party and Stalin did not save numerous people from the firing squad or concentration camp, but it could possibly not influence in a negative way.

---

[125] O. W. Kuusinen, "Yhteenvedot VKP:ssa esiintyneestä oppositiosta" in O. W. Kuusinen, *Valitut teokset (1918–1964)*, p. 77; published originally in *Kommunistische International*, 7/1924.

[126] Cf. E. H. Carr, *The Bolshevik Revolution*, vol. 1, p. 208.

[127] Kuusinen, "Yhteenvedot VKP:ssa esiintyneestä oppositiosta", p. 78.

[128] On Trotskii's view, see E. H. Carr, *The Interregnum 1923–1924*, p. 318.

In 1925, the Congress of the vanguard of the Finnish working-class accepted the resolution "Political Situation in Finland and the Tasks of the SKP" (*Valtiollinen tila Suomessa ja SKP:n tehtävät*). It was urged that the Party and its front-organisations propagate in Finland the agrarian policy of the Soviet Union in order to "dispel" all fears and doubts among the peasants concerning Soviet Russia. In this regard, one should not "by agitation for the affiliation of Finland to Russia push the peasants at a critical moment into the camp of the chauvinists". Therefore:[129]

> One should engage in an effective struggle against infamous imposture and the stirring up of the vast peasant and poor masses by the bourgeoisie and Soc. Dem. leading nabobs based on independence and national questions. One should very much more widely and effectively than formerly make clear to these masses, and get them convinced, that the Communists are in earnest for the independence of Finland, and that also the Union of the Soviet Socialist Republics absolutely and unconditionally recognises the full right of self-determination to every people and nationality. Soviet Russia and the Finnish Communists have not the least intention of violating these rights of the Finnish people, [they have] not the purpose to force Finnish people to give up anything of their national right of self-determination.

The choice of expressions in this *passus* is equivocal. On one hand "independence" is assured, while on the other the phrase "national right of self-determination" is used. It was possible to explain that all republics in the Soviet Union enjoyed the "national right of self-determination". One must, of course, take into account that this resolution was intended for domestic consumption. It was beyond question, at least for most of the participants in the 1925 Congress, that the aim was to annex Finland to the Soviet Union. In that Congress Emil Järvisalo, who was the "first permanent, responsible secretary of the Regional Committee of Karelia of the RKP(b)" declared that the aim of the work they did in Northwest Russia was the creation of a "Finnish Soviet Republic" by transferring the Russian border to the Gulf of Bothnia.[130]

Worthy of note is the discussion of what was known as the Estonian rebellion. This rebellion was actually an attempt at a coup d'état on December 1, 1924: the Communists, led by Jaan Anvelt,[131] tried to seize power in Tallinn. For a while the conspirators took control of strategic locations such as communication and military installations. The background of the attempted Putsch was growing support

---

[129] RGASPI, f. 516, op. 2, 1925, d. 12.

[130] Minutes of the Vth Congress of the SKP, July 30–Aug. 16, 1925. RGASPI, f. 516, op. 2, 1925, d. 17, ll. 103–104

[131] In Russian Ян Янович Анвельт, born in 1884, died in Stalin's terror in 1937. (*Большой Энциклопедический словарь*, vol. 1, p. 52.)

of the Communists in Estonia and the economic crisis in that country. The purpose was to recruit several thousand men to the rebel forces, and, after the rebellion had been started, raise the main working masses into revolution. Only about 300 men, however, were under arms when the operation began, and the masses did not support the rebels at all. The rebellion was easily suppressed.[132] The Russian (and at least also Finnish) soldiers who waited behind the border, were withdrawn.[133] It was G. E. Zinov'ev[134] who drafted the plan after the Estonian government had, at the end of November, arrested several hundred Communists in Tallinn. I. V. Stalin, of course, accepted the plan, but when it failed, Zinov'ev was held guilty. For Zinov'ev's opponents and Stalin's supporters the Estonian failure was welcome. There were also many leaders who were anxious to restore economic and diplomatic relations with the rest of the world; they saw, as Ruth Fischer points out, Comintern-led incidents here and there as only an unnecessary nuisance and a burden.[135]

These views did not yet influence the Comintern, at least in any decisive way. According to Yrjö Sirola's memorandum on a "negotiation meeting of the participants[136] in the Tallinn rebellion of December 1", Zinov'ev regretted that only "the vanguard of the vanguard" fought and the workers only with strained attention

---

[132] Andres Kasekamp, *The Radical Right in Interwar Estonia*, p. 16.

[133] The Communist Party of Estonia was illegal and its best-known leader, Viktor Kingisepp, (a Bolshevik from 1906) was executed in 1922, but, as in Finland, the Communist Party was capable of maintaining a front organisation, which was represented in Parliament (*Riigikogu*). The Communists had five MPs (out of 100) in 1920–1923, ten in 1923–1926 and six in 1926–1932. In 1923–1924 there was economic hardship in Estonia; politically Estonia was suffering from an excess of political parties and, due (at least partly) to this plethora, governments were short-lived; their average term was eight months and twenty days in 1919–1933. (Raun, *Estonia and Estonians*, pp. 113–115.)

[134] It seems that G. E. Zinov'ev had hopes of a revolution in border states, and eventually in Germany, longer than other top Bolshevik leaders generally. (Г. Е. Зиновьев, *Новая волна мировой революции*, speech in the all-Russian Conference on enlightenment of the workers, Nov. 27, 1923, pp. 1–2. RGASPI, f. 324, op. 4, d. 42.) – Zinov'ev's revolutionary fever had somewhat abated, however, if we compare this statement with his pronouncements in 1918. At that time he declared in an international meeting: the armed Russian proletariat has taught the peoples of all countries two "magical" Russian words, which were unknown earlier on, but which have now "electric (*begeisternd*) influence" everywhere: they are "Soviet" and "Bolshevism". (G. Sinowjew, *Sowjet-Russland und die Wölker der Welt : Reden auf der internationalen Versammlung in Petrograd am 19. Dezember 1918*, p. 10. RGASPI, f. 501, op. 1, d. 14.)

[135] Ruth Fischer, *Stalin und die deutsche Kommunismus*, vol. 2, *Die Bolschewisierung des deutschen Kommunismus ab 1925*, pp. 101–102.

[136] Whether Sirola himself was in Estonia, is not known; probably he was not there. Also, Toivo Antikainen had something to do with the rebellion. He later regretted that the Central Committee organised instruction in street fighting, only just before the departure to Estonia. (Minutes of the closed meeting of Finnish-speaking members of the VKP(b) in Petrozavodsk, Jan. 9, 1926. RGASPI, f. 516, op. 2, 1924, d. 34.)

followed what would happen. Zinov'ev defended Anvelt, accusations of his "Trotskyism" were not justified, and Estonian comrades acted with "appropriate permission". Anvelt himself announced that because the Estonian Communist Party had the support of the majority of the workers, its act was not Blanquist, only "forces were wrongly calculated", which was a "mistake".[137]

The Politburo of the SKP drafted precise orders for the Finnish Bureau – although it is not clear whether the orders were ever sent to Finland[138] – on November 26, 1924: the moment the rebellion began in Estonia, the Bureau should organise strikes and sabotage in workplaces in which goods for export to Estonia were produced, and in transportation. The Finnish Bureau should immediately report what tools it needed: dynamite, arms, typewriters, paper etc. As to Estonia itself, the Bureau was told that Communists will probably not, for tactical reasons, immediately devise a "Soviet system on the Russian model" and unite Estonia to the Soviet Union, but first create "some kind of parliamentary government system", the "Estonian People's Republic" (this expression is interesting in 1924!), as a "temporary phase" before the founding of Soviet Estonia and its incorporation in the Soviet Union.[139]

For Finnish emigrant leaders the rebellion in Estonia proved troublesome because in Finland the Communist press did not write in orthodox fashion about the incident. In Helsinki, *Työväenjärjestöjen Tiedonantaja* wrote in its leading article on December 4, 1924 that the rebellion was a "desperate attempt, condemned to end to defeat". The paper told its readers that Communists always oppose the assassination of private personages.[140] In Kuopio, *Savon Työ* complained that there was no free press and civil rights in Estonia, but at the same time the paper qualified the rebellion as a "sad upsurge" and announced that in Finland the workers' movement had no desire to engage in "hopeless adventures wanted by shady ringleaders". The address was obvious: emigrant leaders, both Finnish and Estonian, although the paper tried to soften its standpoint by speculating that perhaps the whole affair was a provocation of the bourgeoisie.[141] In the fifth Congress of the SKP in 1925 Jalmari Salminen (Hjalmar Eklund) expressed his astonishment at

---

137 Sirola sent his memorandum to Manner on March 21, 1925; the meeting had taken place some days earlier. (RGASPI, f. 516, op. 2, 1925, d. 45.)

138 Political Situation in Estonia and the tasks of the SKP. The directives of the Politburo of the CC to the Finnish Bureau, Nov. 26, 1924. RGASPI, f. 516, op. 2, 1924, d. 30. The memorandum was "absolutely secret, there are only two copies of this". In the *delo* there are these two copies.

139 *Ibid.*

140 "Luokkataistelun nykyinen aste Virossa", TTA, Dec. 4, 1924.

141 "'Pätevää silmäin aukaisua': 'Viron kommunistikapinan johdosta': Ja missä tarkoituksessa täkäläinen monarkistilehti 'Savo' siitä kirjoittelee" ("'Effective opening of eyes': 'on account of the Communist rebellion in Estonia': and with what purpose is the local Monarchist newspaper 'Savo' writing about it"), *Savon Työ*, Dec. 4, 1924. The first two headlines were quotations from titles of an article published in *Savo*.

this kind of writing. His argumentation was strictly logical: if the rebellion had been impossible had there been rights and newspapers, it follows that in "free" countries a proletarian revolution is impossible. To say that the rebellion was arranged by the Soviet administrative organs is "ugly".[142] Here Salminen did not articulate the conclusion, which is, of course, that the Soviet administrative organs had a perfect right to arrange rebellions anywhere they considered them appropriate. There was again the predicament of emigrant policy: in the closed gatherings of the SKP, almost anything was possible: the aim of annexing of Finland to Russia was no secret. In Finland, there were restrictions. The Detective Central Police watched the press and many editors were imprisoned for their writings. Nevertheless, this was not the only reason for the relatively moderate tone. Among people who voted for Communist candidates, the prospect of a new rebellion was not at all popular. In addition, most of the editors of the legal Communist-oriented press were hardly the hard-core men the Muscovite leaders wanted them to be. They hesitated. This, too, was a problem.

[142] Minutes of the Vth Congress of the SKP, July 30–Aug. 16, 1925. RGASPI, f. 516, op. 2, 1925, d. 14, ll. 29–30.

VIII The Rahja Opposition (1921–1927)

Smuggling, black marketing and other forms of corruption in the border "traffic" remained a difficult problem for the SKP. Eino Rahja was, as earlier, involved in the smuggling. He also directed one of the oddest ventures in the 1920s, the production of forged Finnish money. Rahja also had several other activities. In December 1921, he was appointed leader of a Cheka group of 13 people whose task was to obtain information on all "moods", "aspirations" and "movements" and especially possible counter-revolutionary plans and activities among non-Party people.[1] (I do not know how long Rahja served the Cheka.) Rahja also had a high military rank; in the collar badge of his Red Army uniform he had three diamonds and he also received two "Red Flag" medals, the first as early as 1922. His last military rank was *komkor*, commander of an army corps, which was the second highest military rank in the Soviet Union before 1935[2] (see plate A).

Although Rahja and his Opposition were perhaps less "political" than the others in the SKP, there were characteristics of ouvrierism in his political discourse. – It seems that until 1923 Rahja's activities in the Central Committee were his main work. He did, however, receive the normal salary of a Central Committee member until 1927 when he was ousted from that body.

There were several changes in the top organisation of the SKP in 1921–1927. After the fourth Congress in 1921, the Central Committee was divided into two bureaus: the Politburo (Kuusinen, Manner and Taimi) and the Orgburo (Rahja,

---

1 Nomination of Eino Rahja to the Intelligence Service Group, Dec. 22, 1921. RGASPI, f. 516, op. 2, 1921, d. 111.

2 I thank professor Ohto Manninen, who explained Rahja's military rank to me.

Lumivuokko and Kalle Lepola). Leo Laukki was the secretary of both of them.[3] In 1922 the Central Committee co-opted Jalmari Salminen and Hanna Malm as members; Malm became secretary of the Central Committee. Kuusinen did not take part in its work; Manner, however, informed Kuusinen of what was going on and in some votes Kuusinen voted by letter. In 1922, the aid from the RKP(b) diminished and the staff of the Central Committee was reduced to 50.[4] – The division of the Central Committee into two different bureaus was practically abolished in January 1923 in consequence of perpetual difficulties with money matters.[5] In October 1923, both bureaus were officially replaced by the Political Department (Politburo), the Military Department – i.e. work within the Finnish army and the Civil Guard (*suojeluskunta*)[6] –, and the "Liaison and Economic Department".[7] This bizarre usage obviously referred to smuggling. Eino Rahja wanted to be leader of this department, but was not elected.[8] – In November 1923, the Politburo of the RKP(b) ordered Aleksander Vasten and Toivo Antikainen to be co-opted as members of the Central Committee (more of which below). At the same time, Rahja and Taimi were ordered to be at the disposal of the RKP(b). Lumivuokko was appointed to a post in the Profintern[9] in autumn 1924 and Manner worked in the Krestintern[10] and in the Comintern. In January 1925, the Politburo, consisting then of Kuusinen, Laukki, Lumivuokko, Malm and Manner (chairman), was transferred from Leningrad to Moscow; in Leningrad, an "Administrative Bureau" was formed. Its members were Aleksander Vasten, Yrjö Sirola and Otto Vilmi.[11]

---

3 Report of activities of the CC of the SKP, Aug. 1921–Feb. 1922. RGASPI, f. 516, op. 2, 1922, d. 6, appendix 1.

4 Report of the activities of the CC of the SKP, Feb.–Aug. 1922. This number (50) included smugglers on the border. RGASPI, f. 516, op. 2, 1922, d. 6, appendix 1.

5 MCC, Jan. 18, 1923, § 15. RGASPI, f. 516, op. 2, 1923, d. 6.

6 Because the Civil Guard was formed after the Civil War mostly of White Army units, it was only theoretically possible that the SKP did any kind of "work" there. This option, however, was included in Manner's proposal on the reorganisation of the work of the Central Committee. Manner's suggestion was accepted in the vote by 3–3; for chairman Manner's proposal voted Taimi and Malm; Laukki, Rahja and Vilmi voted against. The quarrel did not, however, concern the Civil Guard. (MCC, Oct. 7, 1923, § 1 and appendix 1, l. 1. RGASPI, f. 516, op. 2, 1923, d. 6.)

7 "Yhteys ja talousjaosto". (MCC, Oct. 7, 1923, § 1 and appendix 1, l. 1. RGASPI, f. 516, op. 2, 1923, d. 6.)

8 Kullervo Manner to the Presidium of the Executive Committee of the Comintern. A copy to chairman Zinov'ev, Oct. 24, 1923. RGASPI, f. 516, op. 2, 1923, d. 5.

9 Красный интернационал профсоюзов. (Red International of the Trade Unions).

10 Крестьянский интернационал (Peasants' International). A small underground publication was issued in Finnish, when the Krestintern was founded. Instead of usual slogan "proletarians of all countries, unite!" in the title page, there was a new one: "Working-people and peasants of all countries, unite!". (*Ensimmäinen kansainvälinen talonpoikain kokous : pidetty Moskovassa 1923 : selostuksia ja päätöksiä.*)

11 Report of the activities of the CC of the SKP from Nov. 1924 to June 1925. RGASPI, f. 516, op. 2, 1924, d. 9, ll. 36–37.

From 1921, the SKP had a Finnish Bureau as an official section. In theory, this Finnish Bureau led all Communist activities (including those of the Finnish Socialist Workers' Party). Military work caused problems for the Finnish Bureau. Vilmi, who reported in the autumn of 1922 on the doings of the Finnish Bureau, complained that there were people unknown to the Bureau, who were engaged in spying and agitation among the soldiers in the army. Vilmi expostulated that these unknown spies had much of money and used it with little restriction, and "babbled" about confidential affairs. Vilmi declared that because the Finnish "Okhrana" also tried to organise its "cells" in army units in order to disclose the Communist agents there, it was difficult to know whether the agents in Finland represented Russian military espionage or were agents of the "Okhrana".[12] It seems that the "military line", as the Military Department was also called, headed by Eino Rahja, was not functioning very effectively.

1. Corruption and Fabrication of Money

First Act

The SKP had three farms close to the Finnish border, in Lempaala and in Beloostrov (in Finnish Valkeasaari). The more important of them from the point of view of smuggling was the farm of Konnunselkä in the Beloostrov *volost*. As farms proper, i.e. production units for crops and cattle, the ranches were burdens to the SKP because they were not profitable. In January 1922, Adolf Taimi discussed the farms with G. E. Zinov'ev. Grigorii Evseevich was not at all willing to abolish them or to transfer them to Soviet organs. He suggested that the SKP take a loan in order to continue its activities on the farms.[13] Obviously the axis Zinov'ev – Rahja was still functioning.[14]

There were two kinds of smuggling. Human beings and goods were purveyed and there was a so-called "light post". This consisted of letters and propaganda material to Finland, letters and newspapers from Finland. (All important Finnish newspapers were at the disposal of all in the Communist University of Western Minority Nationalities at least until 1929[15] and at least until December 1932, the

[12] Otto Vilmi, Report on the activities of the Finnish Bureau from Nov. 1, 1921 to Aug. 1, 1922. RGASPI, f. 516, op. 2, 1922, appendix 2, ll. 3–4.

[13] MCC, Jan. 4, 1922, § 2 and Jan. 2, 1922, § 1. RGASPI, f. 516, op. 2, 1922, d. 5.

[14] One indicator of that was Zinov'ev's vacation in 1923. He was SKP's guest in a villa in Lempaala not far from Petrograd, which was in Party use. Eino Rahja was responsible for security arrangements with the GPU. (MCC, May. 30, 1923, § 10. RGASPI, f. 516, op. 2, 1923, d. 6.

[15] Ernst Vikstedt's examination record, 22.7–13.8 ja 20.8–15.9.34. Ek-Valpo I, PF 1064, Eino Rahja, KA.

District Committee of the VKP(b) in Ukhta received Finnish newspapers.[16]) The postal facility was important because post sent from Russia to Finland or from Finland to Russia in the usual way was opened in a Finnish police office and often even typewritten there. If the post was addressed to private people and nothing illegal was found, it was possible that the letters might eventually be handed to their addressees. As to Communist prisoners in Finland, only the official way to send them post was possible. For example articles meant to be published in the legal pro-Communist press could not be sent by official post except in 1926–1927 when there was a Social Democrat minority government in Finland; at this time the Communist had more room for their activities in Finland than under bourgeois governments.[17]

The situation on the frontier was complicated because the SKP by no means had a monopoly of smuggling there; Russian smugglers were also active. Some departments, other perhaps than the Registrup, of the Red Army were involved[18] and apparently the Registrup itself participated in illegal traffic on the border[19] as before.

At least until 1923, Eino Rahja was in charge of all Finnish border activities in which the SKP was involved. Without him, nothing important could be resolved. For instance, when in February 1922 the Cheka asked a representative of the Central Committee for negotiations on border activities, the Orgburo stated that it could not decide anything because Rahja was not in Petrograd.[20] Rahja ruled his fief through a manager. Until 1922, this was Jalmari Kotiranta, after him Iikka Luoma. Luoma complained in the meeting of the Central Committee in January 1923 that he had not received the funds of the former manager.[21]

The Cheka / GPU tried to impose some limits on racketeering on the border – and this institution obviously wanted a slice of the cake for itself. After laborious negotiations, the Central Committee and the GPU reached an agreement on the smuggling. According to this agreement smuggling of goods such as coffee and sugar was permitted as a cover.[22] Speculation and smuggling for profit was "strictly forbidden".[23] The GPU was, however, not satisfied with the practice on the border, and accused the SKP of "outrageous" violations of the agreement. The GPU demanded that crossings of the border with large amounts of material must be de-

---

16 Hanna Malm in Ukhta to Kullervo Manner in Moscow, Dec. 2, 1932, MMC, p. 70.

17 Kullervo Manner's statement in the enlarged plenum of the CC on July 28, 1927. (Minutes of the Enlarged Plenum of the CC of the SKP, July 28–Aug. 8, 1927. RGASPI, f. 516, op. 2, 1927, d. 2, l. 1.)

18 MCC, March 14, 1922, § 11. RGASPI, f. 516, op. 2, 1922, d. 5.

19 MCC, March 16, 1922, § 4. RGASPI, f. 516, op. 2, 1922, d. 5.

20 Minutes of the Orgburo of the SKP, Feb. 28, 1922. RGASPI, f. 516, op. 2, 1922, d. 18.

21 MCC, Jan. 18, 1923, § 15. RGASPI, f. 516, op. 2, 1923, d. 6.

22 MCC, May 4, 1923, § 9. RGASPI, f. 516, op. 2, 1923, d. 6.

23 MCC, Oct. 7, 1923, § 1 and appendix 1, l. 4. RGASPI, f. 516, op. 2, 1923, d. 6.

clared to the agency. The Finns considered this impossible; the crossing the frontier had, of course, to be done at the best possible time.[24] It seems that the officials of the GPU did not take into account that the activities of the SKP were criminal on the other side of the border.

On March 22, 1923 § 12 of the minutes of the Central Committee of the SKP read:[25]

> Especial secret matter. All members of the CC unanimously accepted the work and the purpose for which it had been started. An announcement at a suitable time on the matter to people concerned was left to the Secretariat.

On May 4, we have further information, written in the same "official" manner as the previous text:[26]

> The especial secret matter and the attitude of Com. O. W. Kuusinen to it, which [the relation], as announced by K. Manner, is negative, considering it dangerous and creating confusion and [considering] it bad that no announcement about it had been made earlier on to Com. Zinov'ev.

This especial secret matter was the fabrication of forged Finnish money, notes of 1,000 *markkas*. As we see, Kuusinen was not at all enthusiastic about the idea. Zinov'ev, for his part, accepted the plan, but urged the Central Committee to be "extremely careful" with such money.[27] According to Jalmari Rasi, the Russians forbade the distribution of forged money in Russia and recommended distribution "perhaps" in the Scandinavian countries and in Germany.[28]

It is not clear who was the initiator of this manufacture. If the impulse came from members of the Central Committee, possible candidates are Rahja, Laukki, Vilmi and Lumivuokko. The Central Committee nominated Lumivuokko to lead the enterprise with the powers of a "dictator", as Manner later explained to Kuusinen. The Central Committee forbade the dissemination of the notes in Russia.[29]

---

24 Minutes of the negations on the relations between the organs of the GPU and the SKP on the Karelian isthmus, April 12, 1923. RGASPI, f. 516, op. 2, 1923, d. 14. The participants were A. Kaul and Khropov representing the GPU, J. H. Lumivuokko and Eino Rahja representing the Central Committee of the SKP and Uuno Peltola and Iikka Luoma, managers of smuggling.

25 RGASPI, f. 516, op. 2, 1923, d. 6. Members present were J. H. Lumivuokko, Hanna Malm, Jalmari Salminen, Yrjö Sirola and Otto Vilmi.

26 MCC, May. 4, 1923, § 5. RGASPI, f. 516, op. 2, 1923, d. 6. Members present were Leo Laukki, J. H. Lumivuokko, Hanna Malm, Kullervo Manner, Eino Rahja, Jalmari Salminen and Otto Vilmi.

27 MCC, May. 30, 1923, § 1. RGASPI, f. 516, op. 2, 1923, d. 6.

28 Jalmari Rasi's confession (so-called *Siikasen kertomus*), Jan. 18, 1928, original typed version. Ek-Valpo I, DF III A 3, p. 181. KA.

29 Kullervo Manner to O. W. Kuusinen, Dec. 29, 1923. RGASPI, f. 522, op. 1, d. 123.

Lumivuokko, however, travelled abroad early autumn 1923, and delegated his powers to Vilmi. In practice, nevertheless, the leader of the endeavour was Eino Rahja. When a large batch of notes was ready, three fabricators Iikka Luoma, "masters" Jääskeläinen and Järvimäki could not hide such a fortune, but changed the notes in the consulate of Finland in Petrograd and in the stock exchange. The notes were not, however, very well falsified. The militia arrested Luoma and Jääskeläinen, but Eino Rahja soon arranged their release. Notes were later also spread in Germany, albeit not very successfully; some were also sent to Finland by post,[30] and fees for smuggling on the Finnish-Soviet border were paid in them. The director of the stock exchange demanded that the "millionaires" should pay back the roubles they received for the fake 900,000 *markkas*[31] they sold.[32] It seems that the Russian authorities officially informed their Finnish colleagues and in Finland, the press reported on the affair in Petrograd,[33] but at the time it did not become publicly known that it was the SKP who had fabricated the money.[34] In February 1924 Manner wrote nervously to Kuusinen: "I now only wait when the Finnish 'Okhrana' plays its trump".[35] Manner was also alarmed at what might happen if the leaders of the Murder Opposition, recently deported to the Far East, got an inkling of the affair.[36]

The police did not play their trump, although the Finnish consul in Leningrad, P. J. Hynninen, reported to the Foreign Ministry on January 21, 1924, that he presumed the involvement of Communists in the affair.[37] In 1927 an informer told the police, although not entirely accurately, about affairs in Petrograd in December 1923[38] and in 1928, at last, the police had all the facts when Jalmari Rasi, an

---

30 Manner to Kuusinen, Dec. 29, 1923 and Jan. 3, 1924. RGASPI, f. 522, op. 1, d. 123.

31 Some indication of the sum can be seen when compared to salaries of agricultural workers at the time. In the Viipuri district a male agricultural worker who did not receive food from his employers, received, in 1923, an annual average salary of 7,709 *markkas*, while a female agricultural worker received 4,454 *markkas*. These sums were close to the average of the whole country, 7,508 and 4,803 *markkas* respectively. ("Maanviljelystyöväen keskimääräiset palkat vuosina 1914–1923 / Salaires moyens d'ouvriers agricoles 1914–1923" in STV 1924, p. 237.)

32 Manner to Kuusinen, Jan. 3, 1924. RGASPI, f. 522, op. 1, d. 123.

33 The newspaper *Iltalehti* wrote that in the offices of the Bank of Finland there had been found 109 fake banknotes ("Setelien suurväärennös", *Iltalehti*, Dec. 31, 1924). Later the paper quoted an article published in a Soviet newspaper *Krasnaia Gazeta*. *Krasnaia Gazeta* had written that some sellers had been arrested in Russia, but the fabricators of the notes are probably in Sweden! ("Väärät 1,000 markan setelit", *Iltalehti*, Jan. 11, 1924.)

34 Saarela, "Tuhatmarkkasia, miljoonia ruplia, dollareita", pp. 276–277.

35 Manner to Kuusinen, Feb. 23, 1924. RGASPI, f. 522, op. 1, d. 123.

36 Manner to Kuusinen, March 19, 1924. RGASPI, f. 516, op. 2, 1924, d. 14. It seems that the members of the Murder Opposition had no hint of the fake money affair.

37 Finnish Consulate General in Leningrad to the Foreign Ministry of Finland (signed by P. J. Hynninen), Jan. 21, 1924. Ek-Valpo I, DF XXXIII 4 a, KA.

38 Arvo Kangashauta (a police officer), Report, Oct. 20, 1927. Ek-Valpo I, PF 1064, Eino Rahja. The informer is named only by initials A. R.

organiser who participated in a committee of the Central Committee Plenum in 1927 which investigated the case, made a full confession to the Finnish Detective Central Police. The reason for this silence remains, in my view, a mystery. For all Finnish political parties from Social Democrats to the Conservatives news of fake money manufactured in a secret villa near the border by the SKP would have been eminently welcome for propaganda purposes. – As far as I know, Rahja's, Luoma's and others' role was made public by someone who did not reveal his name in a pamphlet against the Trade Union Federation in 1929.[39] The Detective Central Police were still investigating the affair (or some branch of it) in 1935.[40]

One question remains: for what purposes was money fabricated? The first explanation that may come to mind is a grandiose plan to shake the entire Finnish money system and thus to further the revolution. This explanation is, however, too ostentatious. There was obviously no clear plan. More credible is simply the need of money of Rahja's *phalanstère* in Beloostrov. Manner referred to this aspect in a letter to Kuusinen, saying that when the "label" of the Party is removed, the farm, which wastes vast sums of money, there will be a desperate need for new sources of wealth.[41] When the plan was presented to Manner, at a juncture when preparations for manufacture were obviously complete, he hesitated, but was not strong enough to "raise a dispute".[42]

The money affair was undoubtedly one reason for Manner, Kuusinen and their colleagues to try to dismiss Rahja from the Central Committee and to put him to "Russian work". It seems that it was Manner who first tried to effect this. In September 1923 he wrote to Kuusinen telling him that on his own initiative he had discussed Rahja with Zinov'ev and suggested Rahja's transfer entirely to "Russian work". Manner wrote that Zinov'ev agreed to arrange the transfer, but he "went back on his word, and thus the plan to implant Eino in a new order and establish a new command in the house came to nothing".[43]

A new endeavour was made by Manner, Kuusinen and Taimi in a letter to Zinov'ev, Stalin and Bukharin in October 1923. In this rather long letter, Manner, Kuusinen and Taimi complained that Rahja in truth did not do enough Party work, but led the smuggling and speculation on the border, the result of which was complaints from the GPU against the SKP. Manner, Kuusinen and Taimi accused Rahja of forming a faction with Laukki and Vilmi in the Central Committee; they feared that some kind of factional struggle might spread from Russia to Finland. At the same time, somewhat contradictorily they stressed that Rahja had not very much

---

39 Asiantuntija ("Expert"), *Kommunismi ja Suomen Ammattijärjestö*, pp. 20–21.
40 "Väärän rahan kaupittelusta tuomittu", *Helsingin Sanomat*, Oct. 8, 1935.
41 Manner to Kuusinen, Jan. 3, 1924. RGASPI, f. 522, op. 1, d. 123.
42 Manner to Kuusinen, May 7, 1923. RGASPI, f. 516, op. 2, 1923, d. 15.
43 Manner to Kuusinen, Sept. 19, 1923. RGASPI, f. 522, op. 1, d. 123.

to do with Finnish affairs and did not even know Finland very well, because he had worked in the "Finnish movement" only 2–3 months during the rebellion. Because "experience" of work with Rahja made it manifest that he was such an "autocrat" that there was always "friction" with him, Manner, Kuusinen and Taimi suggested recalling him from the Finnish Central Committee and placing him in "Soviet work under the control of Russian Party organs". – Manner, Kuusinen and Taimi then stated that they had discussed the Rahja case with Zinov'ev, but Zinov'ev had not agreed with them. He had two arguments: firstly, Rahja was necessary from the point of view of the military work of the SKP, and, secondly, Rahja had "many supporters" in the SKP, so that his recall would give rise to a crisis inside the Party. Evidently, Rahja also had "many supporters" in the RKP(b). Manner, Kuusinen and Taimi argued that Rahja was by no means a good, on the contrary a bad organiser, and among "revolutionary Red Finnish commanders", one could find several men better than him. They also said that because Rahja was not known in Finland, he could not have many supporters there. In Russia he has supporters, but also enemies. Here Manner, Kuusinen and Taimi referred to the old wrangles in the War School. Manner, Kuusinen and Taimi announced that they could work together with Laukki and Vilmi if they ceased all factional activities. Finally, they threatened to leave the Central Committee themselves if Rahja remained there.[44]

Rahja, Laukki and Vilmi soon sent their own letter, this time to the Presidium of the Executive Committee of the Comintern. For them the suggestion made by Manner that Rahja must be transferred to some "Soviet work", meant a lack of "trustful cooperation". They declared that they felt that some members of the Central Committee "have taken as their task to follow and dog every word, deed or step, seeking from them a point they could seize upon and attack them". Moreover, the members, who were eager in this "warding", were those who had no "character" based on theoretical and political "revolutionary experience" and were thus incapable of solving problems "independently and authoritatively". These members were Adolf Taimi and Hanna Malm. Taimi was an old opponent of Rahja; there may have been disputes between them in Russian Party work, in which both of them participated. I have found no references to such quarrels, however. – Rahja, Laukki and Vilmi declared that Manner enjoyed their trust, but warned that if Manner "is fixedly connected especially to some members of the C.C.", he "isolates himself" and "by showing untruthfulness alienates [himself] from others", and this would easily lead others to "exercise group politics".[45] The words "fixedly con-

[44] K. Manner, O. V. Kuusinen and A. Taimi to Comrades Zinov'ev, Stalin and Bukharin, Oct. 4, 1923. RGASPI, f. 516, op. 2, 1923, d. 5. In Russian. Also KtS!, pp. 177–181.

[45] Eino Rahja, Leo Laukki and Otto Vilmi to the Presidium of the Executive Committee of the Comintern, no date, obviously soon after a meeting of the Central Committee on Oct. 22, 1923. RGASPI, f. 516, op. 2, 1923, d. 47. The letter is also in Russian. See also E. A. Rahja, Leo Laukki and O. Vilmi to G. E. Zinov'ev I. V. Stalin, N. I. Bukharin and O. A. Piatnitski, Nov. 21, 1923, KtS!, pp. 181–183.

nected" undoubtedly meant Hanna Malm, who now lived with Manner in a "Soviet marriage" as the Finnish police called marriages without the blessing of the Church in Russia.

A number of dramatic incidents followed. Rahja, Laukki, Taimi and Manner were invited to Moscow in the name of the Executive Committee of the Comintern and the Central Committee of the RKP(b). When the Russians did not immediately produce a solution, Rahja, Laukki and Vilmi returned to Petrograd,[46] proclaimed themselves the Central Committee, held a gathering in which Vilmi was chairman,[47] and sent a letter to the Finnish Bureau in Helsinki in the name of the Central Committee. Hanna Malm sent in the same "light" post a letter in which she stated that the Central Committee "is factually split and thus an interregnum had come into existence".[48]

The Politburo of the RKP(b) made its decision on the "conflict" in the Central Committee of the SKP. (There are two texts, which I refer to as A and B. They are slightly different. I follow text A and indicate one important difference from text B.) The main points of the decision were the following. i) The Politburo considered invalid the announcement by Hanna Malm to the Finnish Bureau that the Central Committee was "dissolute". ii) The Politburo condemned the meeting of the group of "Chekists", Rahja, Laukki and Vilmi, as a gathering in the name of the Central Committee. iii) The Politburo declared Rahja and Taimi the "most intransigent factionists" and ordered them to be sent for some time to "other work", i.e. Russian work. Rahja and Taimi had the right to participate in the plenums of the Central Committee, but in no other work of the Central Committee. iv) Aleksander Vasten and Toivo Antikainen were co-opted as members of the Central Committee. Here the texts diverge. In text B there is an additional clause to the effect that the question of co-optation of K. M. Evä to the Central Committee would be decided at the proposition of Sergei Ivanovich Syrtsov, the representative of the Comintern in the Central Committee of the SKP, within a month.[49] v) The Politburo dismissed Hanna Malm, whose "decision"[50] it was to send the letter to Fin-

[46] Kullervo Manner to the Soviet ambassador in Finland, Com. Chernyh, Dec. 8, 1923. RGASPI, f. 516, op. 2, 1923, d. 47.

[47] Minutes of the meeting of the CC, consisted of Rahja, Laukki and Vilmi. RGASPI, f. 516, op. 2, 1923, d. 47.

[48] "KK on faktillisesti hajalla sekä siten on syntynyt välitila." Hanna Malm to the Finnish Bureau of the SKP, Nov. 24, 1923. RGASPI, f. 516, op. 2, 1923, d. 47.

[49] This suggestion was presented by Rahja, Laukki and Vilmi in the form that Evä would be appointed secretary of the Central Committee, which would have strengthened the Rahja Opposition. This was, of course, opposed by Manner and Kuusinen. (Manner to Kuusinen, Dec, 29, 1923. RGASPI, f. 522, op. 1, d. 123, l. 1.) It never materialized.

[50] Kuusinen pointed out in his letter to Zinov'ev and Stalin that there was "keine Beschlüsse". (O. W. Kuusinen to G. E. Zinov'ev and I. V. Stalin, no date, on the back of the paper: "sent on Nov. 28, 1923", in German. RGASPI, f. 516, op. 2, 1923, d. 47.) Kuusinen wanted to amend this clause in the resolution.

land, from the position of secretary of the Central Committee and ordered Vasten, "who had not participated in this factional struggle" to replace her. vi) The Politburo ordered the Central Committee to send a circular to Finland in which it was announced that the conflict was terminated. All discussions regarding the "former struggle" were declared forbidden. vii) Kullervo Manner was "appointed" (*назначить*) chairman of the Central Committee of the SKP. viii) The Politburo considered that the "interest of the Finnish proletariat demanded absolute unity of the Party" and therefore declared that anyone guilty of undermining the "authority" of the Party will be expelled.[51]

This decision calls for no comment. If the Finns had not known who was the "Boss", they now knew. The episode also shows that in a serious situation it was not the Comintern which made decisions, although the organisation was formally above all its "sections" in different countries.

Second Act

The Central Committee resolved to terminate the money affair. It decided to compensate the losses incurred to the Soviet institutions, but refused compensation to any other possible debtor. After the decision had been made, all documents, including the paper on which the decision itself was written, were destroyed.[52] The affair was not over, however, there was a second act.

Of the second act, we gain a better picture than of the first, because at this time it had not been decided to destroy the documents.[53] The reason for this was obviously that now the enterprise was led by Eino Rahja alone, i.e. without the blessing of the Central Committee, and no forged notes were spread before the Central Committee received information about what was going on[54] and forbade the en-

---

[51] Appendix to § 5 of the minutes of the PB [Politburo of the RKP(b)] number 49, Nov. 29, 1923. The decision is signed by Zinov'ev and Stalin. RGASPI, f. 516, op. 2, 1923, d. 11. Also KtS!, pp. 184–185. It seems that the translation into Finnish has been made from text "B".

[52] Manner to Kuusinen, March 19, 1924. RGASPI, f. 516, op. 2, 1924, d. 14. Jalmari Rasi's confession (so-called *Siikasen kertomus*), Jan. 18, 1928, original typed version. Ek-Valpo I, DF III A 3, p. 181. KA.

[53] In the meeting of the Central Committee of the SKP, Feb. 8–10, 1927 Rahja moved (§ 8) that all documents of the new "affairs" be destructed. This was not agreed. The decision was that the Politburo must take care of the documents "following the most severe demands of the requirements of the conspiracy and if there is no certainty of their absolute preservation, they must be destroyed". (RGASPI, f. 516, op. 2, 1927, d. 7.)

[54] This probably happened in summer 1926. On September 1, 1926, there is a hint of the new affair in the minutes of the Politburo of the SKP (§ 8). Adolf Taimi had met Meer Abranovich Trillisser, a representative of the OGPU and discussed with him the confiscation of "some machines" and possibly of "certain products". It was decided to send Taimi immediately to Leningrad. On October 9, 1926, the Politburo heard Taimi's report (§ 7) about the "destruction" of "some products" in Eino Rahja's and I. Luoma's possession. According to the minutes of the Politburo on October 16,

terprise. A special committee was appointed in the Plenum of the Central Committee in August 1927 to investigate the affair. Jalmari Rasi, a future "traitor", was a member of this committee.

Eino Rahja, Iikka Luoma and Leo Laukki launched a new undertaking in 1924. In addition, J. H. Lumivuokko, Otto Vilmi and Aleksander Vasten participated in some way or other in the venture, but other members of the Central Committee were not informed. According to Rahja, Manner was not informed because "not everyone can keep this kind of thing to themselves".[55] Laukki bought a sample of paper needed for the printing in the summer 1924 in Stockholm and then, probably in the spring 1925,[56] when Lumivuokko was in Stockholm as a representative of the Profintern, he bought two lots and sent them by boat to Leningrad. Vasten arranged for the paper to pass customs and sent it on to Rahja and Luoma in Beloostrov.[57] Vasten, however, told a member of the Politburo, obviously one outside the Rahja faction, that a new venture was under way, and it was stopped.[58]

The affair was to be funded probably in two ways: by stealing a motorboat and by speculation with horses. At the time in Finland prohibition was in force and alcohol was being smuggled to Finland mainly from Estonia. Smuggling was a profitable business and hence the smugglers were able to convey spirits by fast and effective motorboats. Rahja planned to "blow" a motorboat. The boat to be stolen was owned by notorious smugglers, known as the Fast brothers, who were so-called "spirits kings" of Finland until after an exchange of fire, they were arrested in November 1924 and the precious speedboat was confiscated by the police.[59] Rahja with the consent of Laukki and Vilmi recruited two Finnish refugees and sent them to Finland to steal the boat, but the police were ahead of them.[60] The

---

1926, Taimi and Manner also discussed the matter with V. M. Molotov, secretary of the Central Committee of the VKP(b). (RGASPI, f. 516, op. 2, 1926, d. 26.)

[55] Eino Rahja in the hearings of the Committee of the enlarged Plenum of the CC of the SKP, Nov. 5, 1927 in Hotel Lux. Examination record. RGASPI, f. 516, op. 2, 1927, d. 10, l. 4.)

[56] Fredrik Hansson in Stockholm to Kullervo Manner, Oct. 13, 1926. RGASPI, f. 516, op. 2, 1926, d. 16. Herman Hurmevaara in Stockholm to Kullervo Manner, Sept. 2, 1926. See also "Pupil" [Hurmevaara] to "Teacher" [Manner], April. 29, 1926. (RGASPI, f. 516, op. 2, 1926, d. 27.)

[57] Eino Rahja in the hearings of the Committee of the enlarged Plenum of the CC of the SKP, Nov. 5, 1927 in Hotel Lux. Examination record. RGASPI, f. 516, op. 2, 1927, d. 10. ll. 4–5.

[58] According to the "absolutely secret" decision of the Secretariat on the "affair attempt", February 8, 1927, Vasten informed a member of the Secretariat of the Politburo only six months after he himself received knowledge of the attempt. Who was this "member" is not stated in the decision of the Secretariat. (RGASPI, f. 516, op. 2, 1927, d. 10.)

[59] Reijo Ahtokari, *Pirtua, pirtua.... : kieltolaki Suomessa 1.6.1919 – 5.4.1932*, p. 64 and picture.

[60] Iikka Luoma to the Politburo of the SKP, Nov. 4, 1925. RGASPI, f. 516, op. 2, 1927, d. 10. According to Eino Rahja also "other members" of the Central Committee knew of the affair. (Eino Rahja in the hearings of the Committee of the enlarged Plenum of the CC of the SKP, Nov. 5, 1927 in Hotel Lux. Examination record. RGASPI, f. 516, op. 2, 1927, d. 10, l. 8.)

purpose in stealing the boat was probably connected with money forgery was facing: by peddling the expensive boat, money would have been obtained to fund the purchase of paper and other material needed in printing money.

The horse trade case was a more serious matter than that of the motorboat. The director of the Vaasa Workers' Cooperative Retail Society, and one of the most prominent Communists in the cooperative movement, Jussi Lähdesniemi, visited Leningrad in March 1925. There he met Rahja and Luoma, who asked for a loan of 60,000 *markkas*. Rahja and Luoma intended to buy horses in Finland and sell them in Russia. According to Lähdesniemi, he had been told that the Central Committee would guarantee the loan.[61] Lähdesniemi was evidently not told that purpose of the profit to be gained from this horse-trading was the purchase of paper and dyes for the manufacturing of money.[62] As can be guessed, the two men were unable to repay the money. Lähdesniemi faced with awkward position because at the beginning of 1927 the audit of the accounts was coming up and there was a deficit of 43,000 *markkas* in the books of the aforementioned Society. In order to avoid charges of default he contacted the leaders of the Finnish Bureau of the SKP and argued that he must have his money back from the SKP because he had the impression that it was the Central Committee which had taken the loan.[63] Because the Central Committee had no such money at its disposal, it turned to the Comintern, explained the situation, and received the 43,000 *markkas* that were missing from the accounts of Lähdesniemi's cooperative.[64] It is not clear where Rahja and Luoma get the 17,000 *markkas* they paid to Lähdesniemi; possibly horses were smuggled from Finland and sold in Russia.

Because Lähdesniemi was an important personage, the Central Committee arranged it that he personally did not suffer as a victim of deception. The fate of one "common" smuggler, Esa Hölttä, who was also a victim, was strikingly different. Hölttä lived in the Finnish border village of Kivennapa on the Karelian Isthmus. He participated in the "border work" for some years, firstly for Jalmari Kotiranta, then for Iikka Luoma. Hölttä smuggled letters, people and goods. According to

---

61 Jussi Lähdesniemi to the Politburo of the SKP, no date, received August 28, 1926. In his letter to the Politburo of the SKP on October 21, 1926, Eino Rahja denied that he had taken or guaranteed a loan in the name of the Central Committee. According to Rahja, Luoma took the loan in a meeting where Rahja was only present and he, Rahja, warned the two men that the agreement in no way bound the Central Committee. (RGASPI, f. 516, op. 2, 1927, d. 10.).

62 Eino Rahja in the hearings of the Committee of the enlarged Plenum of the CC of the SKP, Nov. 5, 1927 in Hotel Lux. Examination record. RGASPI, f. 516, op. 2, 1927, d. 10, l. 4.

63 Aleksander Vasten to the Politburo, Aug. 16 and 18, 1926. (RGASPI, f. 516, op. 2, 1926, d. 27. The decision of the Politburo concerning the purchase of horses, Feb. 10. 1927. RGASPI, f. 516, op. 2, 1927, d. 7.)

64 In his letter to "Dear Comrades" (the Politburo) on January 30, 1927 Lähdesniemi thanked them for the decision to pay him the sum of 43,000 *markkas*. The audit was coming up on February 15, 1927. (RGASPI, f. 516, op. 2, 1927, d. 10.)

him, he did not always receive all the money promised to him, but was assured many times by Luoma that the payments were on their way. On November 3, 1923, Hölttä was arrested on the Russian side of the border when nobody came to pick up the goods he had brought from Finland. He was two weeks in the gaol of the GPU waiting for Luoma to come and put matters in order. When Luoma did not come, Hölttä escaped from the jail, and managed to reach the Finnish side of the border. On December 26, 1923, he was pleasantly surprised when a messenger from Russia brought him 15 notes of 1,000 *markkas*. Hölttä, in turn, paid his debt to the local cooperative shop in Kivennapa, but was soon thereafter arrested for spreading fake money and imprisoned for 14 months. Hölttä claimed he did not know that the notes he had received were not genuine, which is undoubtedly true. After his release from prison, he wrote a letter to the "Finnish Central Committee of the Soviet" and demanded compensation. He complained that after his release Luoma had sent him "word" that he wished to hear no more about the affair.[65] Hölttä wrote:[66]

> Having thus suffered the most unbelievable fraud, I herewith turn to the C.C. complaining of the unscrupulous treatment that the comrades there exercise towards us who are on this side of the border, in spite of the fact that I also have already suffered in the cubby-holes of the Okhrana for the earlier errand boy activities, and now finally for these fake notes, of which I believe the senders were aware [that they were fake].

It seems that Hölttä received no compensation. One Tyyne Kaukoranta brought the above letter to the GPU in November 1926.[67] She was questioned by GPU men who, after the hearings, asked her to be silent and wait. When nothing happened in six months, she asked the Central Committee whether Hölttä would be paid compensation or was the matter to be hushed up. Kaukoranta declared in her letter to the Central Committee: "I know that he [Hölttä] is not the only person who has come to suffer on account of the border policy at the time, and I cannot help wondering whether the C.C. knew about them [consequences of the border policies] and nevertheless allowed them happened."[68]

---

[65] Iikka Luoma explained in his letter to the CC of the SKP on September 11, 1926, that he had nothing to do with Hölttä's "candy papers". (RGASPI, f. 516, op. 2, 1927, d. 10.) This does not sound plausible.

[66] Lammela [Esa Hölttä], Letter of complaint to the "Finnish Central Committee of the Soviet", no date, received Nov. 3, 1926. RGASPI, f. 516, op. 2, 1927, d. 10.

[67] Kullervo Manner or J. K. Lehtinen in Moscow to Adolf Taimi in Leningrad, Nov. 5, 1926. RGASPI, f. 516, op. 2, 1927, d. 20.) It is unclear why Kaukoranta left the letter to the GPU.

[68] Tyyne Kaukoranta in Leningrad to the CC, July 16, 1927. RGASPI, f. 516, op. 2, 1927, d. 10.

A holding of Hölttä's father was mortgaged for the debt on the Kivennapa cooperative shop. Manner told Rasi in Moscow that a "peasant in Rajajoki" (the border river) lost his house due to the fake money affair.[69] The peasant in question was probably Hölttä. Iikka Luoma complained that the "technical" staffs recruited from Finland to print the money were now in a very difficult position. One family of five members were begging in the streets of Leningrad.[70] Although Luoma is one of the most unreliable sources in this affair, this story may well be true. As to Hölttä, the Secretariat of the Central Committee of the SKP decided in January 1928 that the Party was not responsible for the debts of Kotiranta and Luoma, the managers of the Beloostrov farm.[71]

The most plausible conclusion to be drawn regarding the recompense is that the SKP paid compensations for all the diverse "affairs" only to the Russians and to Lähdesniemi, to the latter because it was the only means to prevent a scandal in Finland. For smaller actors, the Party took no responsibility.

The result of the second affair was that Rahja was, in 1927, evicted from the Central Committee. Laukki, Lumivuokko, Luoma, Vasten and Vilmi received various reprimands and cautions.[72] Luoma protested at his "severe admonition and warning" because his actions were directed by three members of the Central Committee, Rahja, Lumivuokko and Vasten. Luoma especially stressed that in this group there were members from both factions of the Central Committee.[73] He also felt he had received a very severe punishment, since he was only a workingman.[74] Salient, however, was Rahja's punishment: he was ousted from the Central Committee. Our next step is to investigate whether there were also political disagreements behind this decision, and what other skirmishes there were inside the Central Committee during the period 1921–1927.

2. Was "Rahjaism" a Kind of Workers' Opposition?

In 1923, Eino Rahja, Leo Laukki and Otto Vilmi wrote a tactics paper in which they considered the possibilities of a revolution in Finland in the near future. Their starting-point was that only in "the most extreme case" would the Finnish workers now – we should remember that the period discussed was so-called "united front"

---

69 Jalmari Rasi's confession (so-called *Siikasen kertomus*), Jan. 18, 1928, original typed version. Ek-Valpo I, DF III A 3, p. 182. KA.

70 Iikka Luoma to the CC of the SKP, July 25, 1927. RGASPI, f. 516, op. 2, 1927, d. 10.

71 Minutes of the meeting of the Secretariat of the CC of the SKP, Jan 3, 1928. RGASPI, f. 516, op. 2, 1928, d. 18.

72 The decision of the Secretariat of the Politburo, Feb. 8, 1927. RGASPI, f. 516, op. 2, 1927, d. 10. Minutes of the meeting of the CC, Feb. 8–10, 1927. RGASPI, f. 516, op. 2, 1927, d. 7.

73 Iikka Luoma to the Politburo of the SKP, April 2, 1927. RGASPI, f. 516, op. 2, 1927, d. 10.

74 Iikka Luoma to the enlarged Plenum of the CC, Aug. 4, 1927. RGASPI, f. 516, op. 2, 1927, d. 10.

phase of the Comintern – rise to "open armed struggle". This did not mean that there were no possibilities. One possibility was a crisis at international level, an *élan* of revolution which would hit Finland so drastically that her trade with other countries would be cut, and a severe economic crisis might follow. The second, obviously more probable alternative was war between Finland and the Soviet Union, by assault of either Finland or the Soviet Union. Rahja, Laukki and Vilmi were obviously more interested in the latter possibility. They speculated that a "serious uprising" of Finnish workers and peasants might take place only when the "Finnish White Army" had been catastrophically defeated and "demoralised". Before such a demise arising was highly unlikely because the "peasant masses and workers of Soc. Dem. opinion can be easily agitated and mobilised [by the bourgeoisie] using national leanings and prejudices against Soviet Russia". – There was, however, one exception in this rather bleak picture: forest labourers and log floaters in Northern Finland. These about 15,000 – 20,000 men, who worked on lumber sites (*savotta*), apart from their families, might more readily than other workers give the Red Army "unstinted aid" provided they were armed in advance.[75]

The "Fat Rebellion" 1922

The background to this speculation on the mobilisation of forest labourers was apparently the so-called "meat box" or "fat rebellion". (The Finnish nickname, *läskikapina*, in fact refers to fatty meat.) On February 1, 1922, a group of men led by Red Officer Jahvetti Moilanen (pseudonym of Frans Johan (Janne) Myyryläinen) captured a lumber camp in Värriö, a very remote small village in Northeast Lapland. Moilanen, standing on an empty meat box (hence the name of the venture) read a proclamation in the name of the SKP. He declared that the revolution has begun and urged all workers to join the "Red Guerrilla Battalion of the North" which was going to launch a "decisive assault" on the capitalists. About 250 men joined the Battalion in Värriö, which, after commandeering cash and food, went on to rob some other lumber sites – where more men joined the Battalion –, and a border guard detachment. The Battalion then, on February 7, crossed the Russian border with its "impedimenta", including arms and a herd of reindeer! At this stage, the Battalion consisted of 243 men.[76] The "Red Power" thus reigned for only one week. The stolen arms were hidden in Russia for the next rebellion.[77] Plans for any fur-

---

[75] Eino Rahja, Leo Laukki and Otto Vilmi to the CC of the SKP, no date, probably 1923. RGASPI, f. 516, op. 2, 1923, d. 13.

[76] Matti Lackman, *Jahvetti Moilanen. – Läskikapinan johtaja : poliittinen elämäkerta (1881–1938)*, pp. 41–74; Ilkka Hakalehto, *Suomen kommunistinen puolue ja sen vaikutus poliittiseen ja ammatilliseen työväenliikkeeseen 1918–1928*, pp. 89–93.

[77] Matti Lackman, "Kommunistien salainen toiminta Kainuussa (1918–1944)" in Reijo Heikkinen and Matti Lackman, *Korpikansan kintereillä : Kainuun työväenliikkeen historia*, p. 317.

ther rebellion did not materialise, however, and maps showing the hiding places of the arms were given to the GPU, probably in 1925 or 1926.[78]

Arvo Tuominen claims that the "real head-organiser [of the fat rebellion] was the notorious Eino Rahja".[79] He adds the following remark on Rahja: "As far as I heard later, this was a very special Rahja *jubilée* rebellion, for it was this kind of hassle he took an interest in".[80] Particularly in Northern Finland agitation for rebellion was calculated to be easy.[81]

Markku Kangaspuro, who studied the archives of the RKP(b) connected to the fat rebellion, suggests that Eino Rahja's role in the preparation of the "uprising" was important, but that the Central Committee probably did not bless his adventure. Not the SKP but the Cheka – we should remember that Rahja was a Chekist – was behind the revolt. It also had Russian approval: the affair was presented to the Secretariat of the RKP(b) and V. M. Molotov sent the plan to the chairman of the Revolutionary War Soviet, L. D. Trotskii on December 16, 1921. Lev Davidovich decided that the army should make all necessary preparations. The Red Army was mobilised and a small group of Russian soldiers crossed the border in two places on January 31, 1922. These crossings were, however, no more than demonstrations connected to Russian diplomacy. Officially, the Russians denied any association with the crossings of borders and the fat rebellion.[82]

Eino Rahja was present at the meeting of the Central Committee in Petrograd on January 24, 1922. In this meeting, the Central Committee decided to go *in corpore* to Moscow to follow the trial of the members of the Murder Opposition.[83] Rahja, let alone the rest of the Central Committee, hardly expected the revolution to break out in Finland while they were in Moscow watching the trial. (A cynic, however, might say that Eino Rahja was more interested in the trial than in the revolution.) – In Finland, the fat rebellion was one piece of evidence on the basis of which the Finnish Socialist Workers' Party was suppressed in August 1923.[84]

---

78 Hanna Malm to Kullervo Manner, May 5, 1933, MMC, p. 351. – Myyryläinen, using another pseudonym, Juuso Matero, held later different posts in forest industry in Soviet Karelia. Condemned for espionage and distribution of counter-revolutionary propaganda, he was executed in 1938. (Ek-Valpo I, PF 802, Janne Myyryläinen, KA. Lahti-Argutina, *Olimme joukko vieras vain*, p. 327.)

79 Arvo Tuominen, *Maan päällä ja alla : muistelmia vuosilta 1921–1933*, pp. 105–106.

80 *Ibid.*, p. 109.

81 Cf. Lauri Järvinen, *Kalajoen työväenliikkeen historia*, pp. 179–180.

82 Markku Kangaspuro, "Läskikapina – SKP:n vallankumousyritys 1922", *Historiallinen aikakauskirja* 4/1998, pp. 346–352.

83 MCC, Jan. 24, 1922, § 11. RGASPI, f. 516, op. 2, 1922, d. 5.

84 Saarela, *Suomalaisen kommunismin synty*, pp. 353–356. The official suppression took place by decision of the Turku Court of Appeal in June 1924.

Political Differences between the Rahja Opposition and the Kuusinen Group

The strategic "plan" of the Rahjaites did not differ markedly from a plan drafted by O. W. Kuusinen in October 1923. Kuusinen – like all Comintern leaders – placed his hopes in Germany; he assumed that there would be within weeks a "great collision" and therefore comrades in Finland must be assured that also there the Communists must prepare themselves for the struggle by organising arms.[85] Kuusinen urged the Central Committee to plan, for instance, how the leading "rogues" of the Okhrana and Civil Guard could "right from the start be got out of the way". He even recommended suicide strikes.[86] His plan also included "revolutionary sabotage" against printing houses, electricity and gas plants and "probably" also waterworks.[87] As to the opening of the revolution by an attack of the Red Army, Kuusinen was not as graphic as the Rahja faction.

A real difference between the rival tendencies may have lain in their relation to the so-called united front. The slogan itself was officially coined by the Comintern in 1921. In its proclamation of January 1, 1922, it was explained that the Communists were ready to march with "patience and fraternity" with even those proletarians who still believed in "capitalist democracy".[88] The slogan caused considerable difficulties among the Communists, who were educated "in the spirit of a thoroughgoing breach with the reformist 'traitors'", as Fernando Claudin puts it.[89] It was not very easy to convince the cadres that now some common fronts must be built with these traitors.

O. W. Kuusinen defined the united front "briefly" as the "accomplishment of the united mass activity of workers, in which the Social Democratic leadership would be exposed as a traitor to the workers' demand".[90] The Central Committee and the Finnish Bureau had various disagreements about the Social Democrats. The Finnish Bureau, for example, did not always unambiguously oppose the idea of the Communists supporting the participation of the SDP in the government. For the Central Committee this was a heresy, because Communists should not further an alliance of the "bourgeois and the Noskes", but call even the Social Demo-

---

85 O. W. Kuusinen to the CC, Oct. 16, 1923. RGASPI, f. 516, op. 2, 1923, d. 15. ll. 2–3.

86 "It is necessary to get some vigorous men even to sacrifice themselves for this" (i.e, for eliminating leaders of the Okhrana and Civil Guard). (*Ibid.*, ll. 14–15.)

87 *Ibid.* Already on September 2, 1923, after the suppression of the Finnish Socialist Workers' Party, the Central Committee urged the Finnish Bureau to begin "vigorous activity" in preparation for the revolution. (RGASPI, f. 516, op. 2, 1923, d. 22.)

88 Broué, *Histoire de l'Internationale Communiste*, p. 251.

89 Fernando Claudin, *The Communist Movement : From Comintern to Cominform*, p. 110.

90 O. W. Kuusinen, Yhteisrintamasta (On United Front), no date, probably before August 1923. RGASPI, f. 516, op. 2, 1923, d. 7, l. 1.

cratic leaders to "the struggle against the slaughterer command" in which these leaders would then be exposed as allies of the bourgeoisie, traitors etc.[91]

There is a document signed by "L. – A." and addressed to the Central Committee in March 1923. It is clearly written from the oppositional point of view and the writer uses the plural "we". In view of the abundant use of such terms as "post festum", "teleological", "conditio super ultra", "sic!", "prognosis" etc., the writer cannot be anyone else but Leo Laukki. The writer declared that the definition of the united front given by the Central Committee was "unhappy". It must be "broader", which meant the following: i) the masses who followed the Communists must be mobilised; ii) one must establish contact with the Social Democratic masses and try patiently to draw them to the side of the Communists; iii) a split within the SDP must be effected; iv) unorganised workers must be made to "prick up their ears" at the propaganda of the Communists and be brought in this way under their leadership; v) the bourgeoisie must be provoked to pressure the Social Democratic leaders so that they would "angrily seize the Social Democratic Left by the hair"; vi) "and finally in all this the Soc. Dem. lead would be exposed as a traitor to work[ers'] dem[ands] etc." One should no longer only accuse, blame and expose the Social Democratic leaders. This has been done for two years without result.[92]

One may well ask where are the differences between the tactics of the Rahja Opposition and the majority of the Central Committee based on the documents described above. The final conclusion in Laukki's paper is also that the purpose of the united front should be the "exposure" of the Social Democratic leaders in front of the masses. In Communist parlance, the distinctions are often extremely subtle. Here we can take point (v) as an example. From this kind of definition, the conclusion that one may expect the Social Democrats to enter the government with the bourgeois parties may well be plausible. In a situation in which the Social Democrats sat in a coalition government, an internal opposition against the over-moderate policy of the government could be imagined to be highly possible. In this way, the bourgeoisie would be provoked to pressure the Social Democratic leaders and the outcome would be a split. This is, of course, an interpretation of extraordinarily subtle texts, but I think not at all an impossible interpretation.

Ouvrierist argumentation was typical to the Rahja Opposition. One of the best examples of this is a speech Laukki gave at an evening entertainment in Petrograd, perhaps in the War School. Unfortunately we have not Laukki's own text at our disposal. There are, however, three descriptions of the speech which are sufficiently similar for us to be satisfactorily, but as to details we cannot be entirely sure of

[91] Report of the activities of the SKP from Aug. 1922 to Aug. 1923. RGASPI, f. 516, op. 2, 1923, d. 3, l. 3.

[92] L. – A. to the CC, March 13, 1923. RGASPI, f. 516, op. 2, 1923, d. 22, l. 1.

what Laukki said. The first is a report of the speech, given on November 24, 1923 by Kustaa Rovio. After Kullervo Manner received his report, Hanna Malm asked for statements from two other people who attended the occasion, Toivo Antikainen and Vilfred Perttilä. According to Rovio, Laukki spoke about Germany, where conditions for the revolution were ripe but where no revolutionary leadership existed (later, by the way, a common Trotskyite argument); it did not exist because the Communist leaders were former Social Democrats and as such not revolutionary enough. In Finland, the masses started the revolution in 1918 and drew in the leaders who "sat on high, soft chairs and sucked their thumbs". Of the leaders of the Finnish Socialist Workers' Party Laukki said that in the Turku Appeal Court they denied Communism as Peter denied Christ.[93] As to the leaders of the SKP, he said nothing, but gave the impression that they were similar to those in 1918.[94] As a final climax Laukki said (literally, Rovio claimed): "The Finnish Revolution will be made by Russian bayonets and machine guns".[95]

In the Plenum of the Central Committee on January 30–31, 1924, the parties avoided confrontation. Rahja on behalf of Laukki, Vilmi and he himself presented the paper on tactics described above. It was decided that the paper was to be left as a basis for the work of the Politburo.[96] O. W. Kuusinen especially demanded an implacable and unappeasable attitude to the Social Democrats. In the coming parliamentary elections in Finland, the Central Committee urged the Communists and their supporters to proclaim the Social Democratic leaders to be "henchmen of Fascism". The "attacks and warnings" had to be directed especially against the leaders of the Left-Wing of Social Democracy, who "shun to rise in honest struggle against their Party leadership, but use the call to a united front of the workers as their mask".[97] All electoral alliances were ruled out.[98]

By jailing all Communist MPs in August 1923, the *Eduskunta* became incomplete, whereupon President K. J. Ståhlberg dissolved it in January 1924. This act was by no means uncontroversial, since the Right saw nothing dubious in an incomplete *Eduskunta*. For the Social Democrats, who had loudly demanded the dissolution, this was a victory. The Communists created for the elections an Elec-

---

93 This was an erroneous judgement. See e.g. Upton, "The Communist Party of Finland", pp. 152–153. It is true, however, that the SKP leaders were often dissatisfied with the behaviour of the accused in the court.

94 On this point, Perttilä's report is slightly different. According to him, Laukki said that although the leaders of the SKP were former Social Democrats, they were here under the control of the Russians. (Vilfred Perttilä to Hanna Malm, Nov. 26, 1923. RGASPI, f. 516, op. 2, 1923, d. 47.)

95 Kustaa Rovio to Kullervo Manner, Nov, 25, 1923. Toivo Antikainen to Hanna Malm, Nov. 26, 1923. Vilfred Perttilä to Hanna Malm, 26, 1923. RGASPI, f. 516, op. 2, 1923, d. 47.

96 MPCC, Jan. 30–31, 1924, § 4e. RGASPI, f. 516, op. 2, 1924, d. 5.

97 *Ibid.*, § 4c.

98 *Ibid.*, § 4e.

toral Association of Workers and Smallholders. In their campaign the Communists in Finland acted contrary to all directives from Russia. The propaganda was aimed much *less* at the Social Democrats than before the suppression, and the Electoral Association of Workers and Smallholders expressed its willingness to conclude an electoral alliance with the SDP. Specific Finnish circumstances were stressed, which meant that the orders of the SKP, originating in circumstances alien to the Finnish reality, must be forgotten. – The behaviour of the Electoral Association of Workers and Smallholders was duly condemned by the SKP.[99]

Now Eino Rahja reacted, after being advised by Zinov'ev, as he later claimed.[100] He sent the Central Committee a letter in which he unambiguously criticised its tactics in the elections. He declared that there were no "clearly definite tactics" for the SDP and its Left – this was an odd accusation because there was such a tactic, namely to have nothing to do with this Left –, there were too few cells and only little "enlightenment work" among the Social Democratic masses etc. Moreover – and this was an important point – a united front with the Social Democrats was ruled out by the SKP in the Plenum of January 1924. This was wrong; Rahja wrote that he did not oppose Kuusinen's line here, as he should have done, because he, Rahja, believed that Kuusinen's suggestion came from the Comintern. Now he realised that it had not, but was Kuusinen's private thinking. According to Rahja, the tactics of the Central Committee in relation to the masses has been "basically wrong throughout" and the result of this was that the underground Party in Finland was "weak both organisationally and ideologically". Rahja explained that the tactics decided upon in the Party Congress were correct but the Central Committee had not adopted them; here he did not say where the contradiction was. There was also a plain ouvrierist point in the letter. Rahja said that when paid organisers were appointed for clandestine work, the main criterion had been that they were well known; rank-and-file members were therefore not appointed. This was erroneous: "In my opinion the C.C. must round off the apparatus by placing more working men in posts and removing from the membership register such people whose stand has shown them to be Social Democrats and who do not acknowledge Party discipline".[101]

---

[99] Report of the activities of the SKP from Aug. 1923 to Nov. 1924. RGASPI, f. 516, op. 2, 1924, d. 9, l. 5.

[100] Minutes of the Vth Congress of the SKP, July 30–Aug. 16, 1925. RGASPI, f. 516, op. 2, 1925, d. 17, l. 107 (list numbers marked in the Archives).

[101] Eino Rahja to the CC, May 14, 1924. RGASPI, f. 516, op. 2, 1924, d. 12. According to the Report on the activities of the SKP from Aug. 1923 to Nov. 1924 (l. 9), there were in the third quarter of 1924, 798 "active members" and 398 candidates (RGASPI, f. 516, op. 2, 1924, d. 9.) The statistics do not indicate how many of them were Social Democrats in the Rahjaite sense, but in any case it was not possible to remove many from the register if a zero result was to be avoided.

The Kuusinen & Manner group naturally declared that Rahja's line was of "opportunist inclination" and that the cause of the defeat in the elections (see p. 73) was not the decision not to clinch an electoral alliance with the Social Democrats.[102] Manner made a statement in which he definitely contested all Rahja's arguments. There had only been some "lapses".[103] Manner argued that although in the elections figures have some meaning, one should not estimate elections according to these numbers. They should be assessed taking into account the influence of the elections on the "relations of the classes" and the "mood" of the masses. In the 1924 elections, the bourgeoisie and the Social Democrats had one and the same main target: the "exclusion" of the Communists from the *Eduskunta* and the "destruction" of the Communists. In this situation, the workers had, "for the first time" (?), a choice: against or for the Communists.[104] According to Manner, "the united front with the Soc. Dem. leaders, recommended by Com. Rahja, was in practice objectively transformed into the most naked opportunism which boded great danger to the Party and the whole movement".[105]

This debate was unavailing and scholastic in that there was, due to the attitude of the Social Democrats, no possibility of an electoral alliance with them. The debaters – ironically enough – had a kind of common starting-point: the course of the Central Committee in Finland had been either right or wrong, but there had been a course. However, in Finland the course of the Central Committee had been relatively insignificant. One may draw the conclusion that this debate was a typical example of emigrant policy, which frequently has nothing to do with the realities of the home country.[106] In Finland, the course had to be implemented in political realities and these realities were not dictated by the Communists alone.

---

[102] Report of the activities of the SKP from Aug. 1923 to Nov. 1924. RGASPI, f. 516, op. 2, 1924, d. 9, l. 12.

[103] Minutes of the meeting of the Politburo (hereafter abriged as MMP), June 12, 1924, § 2. RGASPI, f. 516, op. 2, 1924, d. 29.

[104] MMP, June 10, 1924, § 6. RGASPI, f. 516, op. 2, 1924, d. 29.

[105] MMP of the SKP, June 16, 1924. RGASPI, f. 516, op. 2, 1924, d. 29, appendix 4.

[106] One further example of this was the order that the Communists in Finland must proclaim O. W. Kuusinen a candidate in the 1925 presidential elections. In Finland, however, the Communists put up Matti Väisänen, a trade union leader who was in prison, as a presidential candidate. Furthermore, the Central Committee ruled that the slogan in the elections should be "power union of workers and peasants". The Communists in Finland, however, demanded freeing of political prisoners and the "cessation of persecution". Moreover, in Uusimaa province (Helsinki and surroundings) there "appeared such a 'self-made' slogan as 'Peace and reconciliation with foreign countries', which slogan reeked quite strongly of opportunism". (Report on the activities of the CC of the SKP from Nov. 1924 to June 1925. RGASPI, f. 516, op. 2, 1924, d. 9, ll. 18–21.) On the presidential elections, see Paavo Hirvikallio, *Tasavallan presidentin vaalit Suomessa 1919–1950*, pp. 27–28 and p. 42.

Eino Rahja in the Light of Memoirs

When we try to decide whether Rahjaism was a kind of workers' opposition, some memoirs by Finnish workers in Russia who held no important leading position, may furnish clues. We have stories by (at least) three workers, Väinö Salmi, Hjalmar Front and Ernst Vikstedt. There is also Arvo Tuominen's description of Eino Rahja.

Väinö Salmi came to the Soviet Union after his release from Tammisaari prison. He then came to know Eino Rahja. "I knew him as a calm and helpful comrade", Salmi writes. Salmi listened, in 1927, to Rahja's speech at the funerals of K. M. Evä (of which more below), and says that the speech was "pertinent, rhetorically beautiful"; he did not at all try to pick a quarrel. Salmi says that he also met Rahja personally many times afterwards, and that he was as "comradely as before".[107] He did not see in him anything "objectionable" or "obscene". Rahja helped several young Finnish Communists in their careers.[108] Hjalmar Front says he knew Rahja very well and evidently did know him better than Salmi. His description is less adulating than Salmi's, but basically positive. Front writes that "'cultivated' people who met Rahja occasionally" have described him as "unpleasant being". According to Front, Rahja enjoyed "trust", which would have brought him an important position in the world Communist movement. But he was not "a great politician, let alone a theoretician", characteristics essential to an independent political leader.[109]

The most interesting description we have is that of Ernst Vikstedt, who told about Rahja to the Detective Central Police. There was an agreement between Vikstedt and the police: Vikstedt related what he knew and the Detective Central Police arranged things so that Vikstedt would not be prosecuted. In the hearings, Vikstedt stressed that he was still a Communist and a follower of the Rahja faction. Vikstedt's depiction is biased, but here it is his account of the Rahja Opposition which is worthy of note, not its objectivity. Vikstedt, a worker in a brick factory, went to Russia in 1927 and studied four and half years in the Communist University of Western Minority Nationalities. In 1932–1934, he worked as a Party organiser in Leningrad and Kondopoga (in Finnish Kontupohja). He then escaped to Finland, his motives being, as he himself explained them, "misery" in Russia and the "oppression" of the proletariat by Stalin and his henchmen. Vikstedt doubted whether the Russian rulers had any intention of realising Communism. For Stalin, Vikstedt explained, Leninism was a "phrase" which was not followed at all, whereas Trotskii was a "genius". "Tyranny" in the Soviet Union, of which the liquidation of

---

107 Väinö Salmi, *Punaisen sirpin Karjala : suomalaisten kommunistien kohtaloita Neuvostoliitossa : muistelmia ja vastamuistelmia suomalaisten kommunistien kohtaloista Neuvosto-Karjalassa*, pp. 52–53.

108 Väinö Salmi, *Pakolaisena Itä-Karjalassa eli Neljätoista vuotta sosialismia rakentamassa : muistelmien II osa vuosilta 1927–1929*, pp. 49–40.

109 Hjalmar Front, *Kremlin kiertolaisia*, p. 169.

kulaks was the worst point, was a "shame to the world proletariat", because the "killing of millions of Ukrainian and Caucasian peasants" was not "useful to the revolution" at all.[110] Vikstedt also said that when in 1933 he travelled to Abhasia by an "international train" (this means first class, reserved for the high Party leaders and other notables), he saw in towns where the train stopped people starving to death and already dead, whom the militia had not yet removed. There, he said, he lost all his confidence in Stalin and Stalinism and decided to leave the country.[111]

According to Vikstedt, Rahja's attainments were substantial. In the Russian Civil War, he defended "Leningrad" against the attacks of Nikolai Nikolaevich Iudenich, then, in the second half of the 1920s, he "suppressed" Zinov'ev's "rebellion" in Leningrad.[112] (It is true that Rahja turned against his former mentor, Zinov'ev, but Zinov'ev was not, of course, "suppressed" by Rahja.) Vikstedt continued that Rahja's "authority among the common people" was "unfaltering", which "perhaps much irritates" Kuusinen. For Rahja the SKP were only a "handful of chinovniks". In Finland, the proletariat could attain to power only by war, because Finland is a country where agriculture is the dominant means of livelihood. For Vikstedt, however, the situation in Germany was similar due to the credibility gap between the masses and the leaders. In Germany, "working men said that they were making a revolution, but not so long as Telman [Ernst Thälmann] was in the lead." Rahja, however, could not replace Kuusinen, because Stalin would prevent such an alternative. As to the leaders in general, Vikstedt was of the opinion that when the revolution broke out, the "proletariat would find its leaders".[113]

Vikstedt did not mention Rahja's alcoholism, although, according to Edvard Malcolm Moberg, a Swedish engineer who worked in Karelia, he was many years in the 1930s in such "physical and especially mental condition" that he could not lead any opposition. When he went to Karelia (where he stayed in Kondopoga), as he frequently did, he was, Moberg told to police, so "blotto that reasonable discussion with him was impossible".[114]

Arvo Tuominen met Rahja for the first time in 1921. Tuominen says Rahja was "precisely" similar to his "preconceived picture" of him, "a revolting creature"; "Rahja" was "instinctively" transformed to "*rähjä*", "disgusting".[115] For Tuominen

---

110 Ernst Vikstedt's examination record, Aug. 20–Sept. 15, 1934, pp. 2–5. Ek-Valpo I, PF 3361, Ernst Vikstedt, KA.

111 Ernst Vikstedt, "Mietteittäni 'bolshevismivaarasta' Europan maissa", written in the custody of the Detective Central Police, dated Aug. 6, 1934, pp. 2–3. Ek-Valpo I, PF 3361, Ernst Vikstedt, KA. This refers to the original text. There is also a typewritten version in which, however, the language is corrected in such a way that it now and then alters the meaning of the original.

112 *Ibid.*, pp. 3–4.

113 *Ibid.*, pp. 3–5.

114 *Ibid.*

115 Arvo Tuominen, *Sirpin ja vasaran tie*, p. 250.

"Rahja was the essence of such 'elemental proletarianism'" of which Manner often opined. Tuominen writes that "a more foul-mouthed person has probably never appeared anywhere in politics. Presumably he was unable to say anything decently without threats."[116]

Tuominen did not know Rahja particularly well, having spent several years in prison in Tammisaari in the 1920s. He was, moreover, an ardent supporter of Kuusinen and thus an enemy of Rahja, who of course knew it; Rahja had no reason to be kindly disposed to Tuominen. All this must influence Tuominen's judgements. As to Salmi, his books contain strong anti-Tuominen overtones which obviously affected his judgements. He also writes much about things he knew only by rumour. Salmi claims, for instance, that Rahja was among the first men who demanded for the members of the Murder Opposition "complete forgiveness".[117] The truth is that Rahja never forgave them, obviously because his brother Jukka Rahja was slain. However, Salmi's, as well as Vikstedt's description of Rahja as some kind of People's Tribune may well be correct from the point of view of Rahja's supporters, and this is what counts here. His supporters evidently considered Rahja leader of a kind of workers' opposition. Moreover, of course, Rahja's own proclamations often had ouvrierist overtones.

In his own way, Kullervo Manner confirmed this conclusion in a letter to Yrjö Sirola in 1925. He wrote of an article about the Civil War written by Rahja and meant to be published in *Kommunisti*. In his article, Rahja qualified the leaders of the Finnish revolution as "students", and "academicians" (*maisterit*). Manner informed (in part mistakenly) Sirola that four members of the Murder Opposition,[118] including notably Elvira Willman-Eloranta, were to be shot, if they had not already been shot. Manner wrote:[119]

---

[116] Arvo Tuominen, *The Bells of the Kremlin : an Experience in Communism*, p. 39. In Finnish, *Sirpin ja vasaran tie*, p. 303.

[117] Salmi, *Punaisen sirpin Karjala*, p. 52.

[118] The other three names were Oskar[i] Pylkkänen, Otto Pylkkänen and "Kopponen". (Kullervo Manner to Yrjö Sirola, April 15, 1925. RGASPI, f. 525, op. 1, 131.) According to the Detective Central Police, Otto Pylkkänen was imprisoned in Russia, but freed in 1941 (Ek-Valpo I, PF 3896, Otto Pylkkänen). Of Oskari Pylkkänen, the police knew that he had been imprisoned and later (in the late 1930s) might again have been imprisoned. (Ek-Valpo I, PF 3895, Oskari Pylkkänen). Oskari Pylkkänen was executed in 1938. (Lahti-Argutina, *Olimme joukko vieras vain*, p. 426.) It seems that Manner erred when he wrote about the execution and the Pylkkänen brothers. I have not been able to find out what kind of connection, if any, they had with the Murder Opposition. One Kopponen is mentioned in a letter written by Juuso Matero (pseudonym of Janne Myyryläinen) in Ukhta to the CC of the SKP on May 22, 1924. The name appears in Matero's list of "former oppositionists" in Ukhta. (RGASPI, f. 516, op. 2, 1924, d. 18.)

[119] Kullervo Manner to Yrjö Sirola, April 15, 1925. RGASPI, f. 525, op. 1, 131.

It is an irony of fate that at the same time as one spiritual supplier and ideological leader [Willman-Eloranta] of the gang, who murdered the late Jukka Rahja, kicks her last kick, in the hands of the proletarian revolutionary class discipline, Jukka Rahja's brother, who has loudly sworn revenge for the murders of his brother, the slaughterers of Communist workers, who with great pathos has proclaimed those representatives of the Murder Opposition also ideologically petty-bourgeois, – writes an article that with its ideological background in many regards verges on the political arguments of the Murder Opposition.

3. Factional Struggles in the 1925 Congress and after

The Mother Party, RKP(b), as we saw above, forbade all factional quarrels in the SKP and demanded, in the name of the Finnish proletariat, "absolute unity of the Party". As can be expected, the quarrelling did not stop; on the contrary, it only accelerated. The warring parties nursed thoughts of revenge. Eino Rahja was not completely out of stock; he still had important friends in the Mother Party, G. E. Zinov'ev, above all. We should remember that the star of Zinov'ev was still high. Before 1926/1927, Stalin's target was still Trotskii; Zinov'ev was still in the queue awaiting his turn. On November 27, 1924, one of the Leningrad Finnish collectives of the RKP(b) declared:[120]

> We salute the leader of the World Communist Party, Com. Zinov'ev, expressing our full trust in the leadership of the RKP and the Comintern in its work of sanitation of Lenin's line and of Bolshevisation in the world workers' movement, for only under this mark can the working peoples attain their liberation in all countries. Away with attempts to fob Leninism off! Long live Communism-Leninism and its representatives, the RKP and the Communist International!

Why did Zinov'ev – in spite of the fact that he and Kuusinen cooperated closely in the Comintern[121] – support Rahja? At least three explanations can be proposed. Firstly, as a leader of the Comintern Zinov'ev wished to keep the reins in his hands and as a politician of long experience of factional struggles among the émigrés; he perfectly well knew that *divide et impera* is a very, if not the most, effective method to keep emigrant groups under the thumb. Secondly, Eino Rahja had done many services to Zinov'ev to maintain his well-being in the difficult years of the War Communism (1918–1921), and thirdly, it was said that Zinov'ev was a rather coarse

[120] Declaration "Agaist Trotskyism", accepted "unanimously" in the meeting of the "Finnish Collective of Petrograd side of Leningrad". According to the declaration there were about 150 Party member, also from other Finnish "collectives". (RGASPI, f. 516, op. 2, 1924, d. 48.)

[121] See E. H. Carr, *Socialism in one Country 1924–1926*, p. 33.

man;[122] in this regard, Rahja would be a congenial soul. Rahja was also active in keeping up the relationship[123] until he realised that the bell was tolling for Zinov'ev.

We should also keep in mind that at doctrinal level Kuusinen's and Manner's group, although it behaved arrogantly – Kuusinen, of course, deeply scorned Rahja, whom he considered a dull ignoramus –, was also in a defensive position. The united front policy Kuusinen's and Manner's group sought to impose on Finland could always be criticised, because the policy as outlined in the documents of the Comintern was anything but unequivocal, and because it was always possible to criticise the behaviour of the Communists in Finland. Kuusinen had during the Congress humbly to listen to the lecture given by Zinov'ev about Right and Left deviations in Finland.

Personal Characteristics and Quarrels

The SKP was a profoundly masculine Party; present-day feminists might justly describe it as a phallocratic organisation. Few women occupied any important positions in the Finnish Communist movement before the Party became legal in 1944. The most important exception was Hanna Malm. Although she was certainly no Amazon without feminine abilities to entice men, her behaviour in politics put her in positions in which she easily made enemies among both men and women.

Eino Rahja claimed in the Vth Congress of the SKP that Hanna Malm was the originator, or at least with Yrjö Sirola[124] one of the originators of his troubles in the Central Committee: "Hanna intruded into all affairs", also with Manner there

---

[122] Ruth Fischer, leader of a German opposition group, writes: "Among the members of the Russian Politburo, Zinov'ev was extremely hesitant, less passionate and equivocal in the carrying out of the National Bolshevik policy". (Ruth Fischer, *Stalin und die deutsche Kommunismus*, vol. 1, p. 351.) Edward Hallet Carr writes that in the period 1924–1926 no other Bolshevik leaders "incurred so much adverse personal criticism as Zinov'ev, or appears to have been so widely disliked". He considers Zinov'ev's intellect "nimble", but he was "politically unschooled". (Carr, *Socialism in one country*, vol 1, p. 171.) One may ask how such a fellow could have been raised to the posts of chairman of the Comintern and the Party boss of Leningrad.

[123] Rahja, for instance, informed Zinov'ev of what was considered a defeat of the Communists in the Finnish presidential elections. As a result, Zinov'ev invited Kuusinen and Manner to meet him. There they confessed all the sins of the Communists in Finland. (Kullervo Manner to Aatu, probably Adolf Taimi March 4, 1925. RGASPI, f. 516, op. 2, 1925, d. 48, ll. 2–3.)

[124] The quarrel between Rahja and Sirola originated in 1922, when Lumivuokko, head of the Administrative Bureau, was sent to Sweden. Lumivuokko suggested Rahja in his stead. Sirola announced that he did not second the motion. Rahja asked why not? Sirola declined to answer. In the Congress he said: "It was a leading position in the C.C. and in my view Com. R. has not the qualifications needed for it. This was the whole affair". (Minutes of the Vth Congress of the SKP, July 30–Aug. 16, 1925 (list numbers refer to those made in the archive). RGASPI, f. 516, op. 2, 1925, d. 17, l. 96 and 113).

was "friction", but when "Hanna was not in the C.C., no quarrel emanated".[125] Leo Laukki agreed with Rahja as to Malm: "Behind one's back she lurked and snooped after others' every step, searching after searching for mistakes in their deeds and writings etc., to be underlined with a red pen" – as indeed she did, many letters and documents in the archives are underlined in this way – "in order to prepare a basis for an attack on another member of the C.C." and thus create a "group controversy".[126] Malm found few defenders, Adolf Taimi declared that it was a question of power, the opposition wanted to get rid of Malm without any "real accusation".[127] Malm herself stated that the cause of her "angularity" had "also" been that "I have personally been defamed", which is "not a Communist method" for a comrade who "represents another political standpoint".[128]

Other personal characterisations included Rahja's portrayal of Jaakko Kivi (known as "Moses"), former leader of the Finnish Socialist Workers' Party, and follower of the Kuusinen group, and Laukki's description of Rahja's character. The Kivi case arose when Rahja tried to prove that there were "*chinovniki*" in the SKP, people who did "shoemaker's work" instead of "revolutionary work":[129]

> Let us take such a chinovnik as Moses as an example. He is such a great duffer that the like has never been seen. In every place he is hanging at the ass of the leaders. In the last Plenum, Moses tried to laud the Party like an official giving good reports of his [own] work.

Laukki told the Congress that Manner had announced he wanted to take a "headlock" of Rahja. However, [130]

> [e]veryone who knows Com. Rahja comprehends that by such holds one gets nowhere [...]. Instead, if one takes up a comradely and honest attitude towards him, it is well known that one will hardly find a more alacritous and easily pliable [person], than Com. Rahja.

Of his own future role Rahja told the Congress: "The Finnish revolution is coming [and] I shall take part in it, I have prepared for it. But before that I shall look that the rear is secured".[131]

---

[125] Minutes of the Vth Congress of the SKP, July 30–Aug. 16, 1925. RGASPI, f. 516, op. 2, 1925, d. 17, l. 96 and 98.
[126] *Ibid.*, l. 111.
[127] *Ibid.*, l. 122.
[128] *Ibid.*, ll. 131–132.
[129] *Ibid.*, l. 107.
[130] *Ibid.*, l. 112.
[131] *Ibid.*, l. 107.

In his attack on Rahja, Kullervo Manner argued that there were characteristics which "smack of Trotskyism".[132] Like Trotskii, Manner proclaimed, Rahja did not "recognise" that he had also made mistakes himself.[133] Although Manner was able to some extent to belittle, even to taunt the Rahja opposition – he caused laughter in the Congress when he told the audience that in a discussion with Zinov'ev and Bukharin, Laukki expressed *in French* his conviction that "we have there in the CC a woman who is the object of the quarrel"[134] – he was in trouble over the united

---

[132] In 1928 the SKP, however, decided that there had been no supporters of Trotskii in its ranks. (Decision of the Plenum of the CC about the opposition of the VKP(b), no date, 1928. RGASPI, f. 512, op. 2, 1928, d. 13.)

[133] Minutes of the Vth Congress of the SKP, July 30–Aug. 16, 1925. RGASPI, f. 516, op. 2, 1925, d. 17, l. 77. Trotskii was difficult problem for some members of the Finnish Politburo; for Vasten and Lumivuokko, for instance, it was hard to claim that Trotskii was a creature of the petty-bourgeoisie. The matter became actual before the XIIIth Congress of the RKP(b) (May 1924). Kuusinen urged the Finnish Politburo to make a declaration on the Trotskyite opposition. Manner also demanded a declaration because thereby the Party would also fight against "petty-bourgeois elementariness" in its own ranks, an obvious hint at Rahja. Malm, of course, seconded: "oppositional phenomena" are international. Laukki announced that he completely accepted the position of the Central Committee of the RKP(b) in the matter. However, he considered it inappropriate to criticise Trotskii "flagrantly", because he thought Trotskii would be needed in perhaps "very important revolutionary situations" in Finland, for he would be one of the "leading comrades" in the RKP(b). The result was that the SKP issued a short statement in which it was said that the Party supported the majority of the Central Committee of the RKP(b) and its "old guard", i.e. Stalin. (Manner's memorandum on the debate on Trotskii in the Politburo, no date. RGASPI, f. 516, op. 2, 1924, d. 29.) Kuusinen sent Stalin for inspection a long article he wrote on Trotskii for the use the Comintern. (O. W. Kuusinen, *Rückblick auf die Opposition in der K.P. Russlands*. The Stalin investigation emerges in the enclosed letter to Stalin, July 7, 1924 (in Russian). RGASPI, f. 522, op. 1, d. 74.) Kuusinen had no reservations in the matter. – Later, on September 27, 1927, Kuusinen chaired a joint session of the Presidium of the Executive Committee and the International Control Commission of the Comintern in which Trotskii was expelled from the Executive Committee. Kuusinen accused Trotskii and his supporters about "conducting a remorseless factional struggle". He said: "They call themselves 'Bolshevik Leninist", but what does their behaviour have in common with Bolshevism and Leninism?" Trotsky interrupted Kuusinen and said: "The hero of the Finnish revolution is teaching me Bolshevism and Leninism"; Kuusinen answered: "When you have the floor, you can tell your tales. Personal insinuations have always been your way. You use them even against the best Russian revolutionary leaders, so I regard it as an honour to be slandered by you [...]. The leadership of the Comintern must intervene and expel the Trotskyists from their midst." (Quoted by Dmitri Volgogonov in his *Trotsky : the Eternal Revolutionary*, p. 291.) In 1927 Kuusinen also attacked "Trotskii and Zinov'ev Opposition" in a pamphlet. Its title was "Zinov'ev's historical lie". He wrote e.g. that "'mad' Trotskyism is for Com. Zinov'ev – heavenly manna and even 'original Leninism-Bolshevism'". (O. W. Kuusinen, *Sinovjevin historiallinen valhe (Trotskiin-Sinovjevin oppositiota vastaan 1927 kirjoitettu kirjanen)*, published in O. W. Kuusinen, *Kommunistisen internationalen ja sen osastojen tehtävistä : puheita ja kirjoituksia*, p. 88.)

[134] Minutes of the Vth Congress of the SKP, July 30 – Aug. 16, 1925. RGASPI, f. 516, op. 2, 1925, d. 14, l. 52.

front affair. Rahja said that now Manner and Kuusinen did not deny the possibility of a united front with the Social Democratic leaders, but he, Rahja, knew that this was the correct position already in 1924! Thus, Rahja exclaimed, "if a working man sometimes talks politics, you must learn to listen".[135] Manner defended his position explaining, "when one offers a united front, one must have tools, with which to carry out the exposition of the leaders before the masses". In 1924, there were no such tools, only one small paper.[136] Here Manner escaped behind "objective circumstances", something that was later strongly condemned.

Why this change to the benefit of Rahja? If we look into what occurred in the Comintern at the time, we will hardly find an answer. In the fifth Congress of the Comintern, in June 1924, social-democracy was explained as "becoming one wing of the bourgeoisie, in places even a wing of fascism". Therefore "it is historically incorrect to speak of 'a victory of fascism over social-democracy'", for "so far as their leading strata are concerned, fascism and social-democracy are the right and left hands of modern capitalism"[137] A "political alliance of communists with social-democracy" was condemned: "[F]or the Comintern the main purpose of the united front tactics consists in the struggle *against* the leaders of counter-revolution and in emancipating social-democratic workers from their influence". Negotiations with the Social Democratic leaders were not, however, ruled out, provided that there was "unity from below", that the Communist parties maintained their "independence" and the negotiations were conducted publicly.[138] In the fifth enlarged Plenum of the Executive Committee of the Comintern, in April 1925, a "policy of Communist 'coalition' with counter-revolutionary social-democracy", which had been plaguing independent Communist activity in a number of countries, was condemned and the "Bolshevisation" of non-Russian Communist parties was demanded.[139] The Trotskyites had quarrelled between themselves over the question whether the course of the Comintern in 1925 could be defined as "Rightist" or not.[140] One reason for this seems to be the slogan "workers' and peasants' government", raised, if not coined, by Zinov'ev.[141] It purported to be, the Fifth Congress in June 1924 declared, the "slogan of the dictatorship of the proletariat

[135] Minutes of the Vth Congress of the SKP, July 30 – Aug. 16, 1925. RGASPI, f. 516, op. 2, 1925, d. 11, l. 445.

[136] *Ibid.*, ll. 456–457.

[137] Extracts of the Theses of the Tactics Adopted by the Fifth Comintern Congress. Published in *The Communist International 1919–1943: Documents*, vol. II, *1923–1928*, p. 147.

[138] *Ibid.*, p. 151.

[139] Extracts of the Theses on the Bolshevization of Communist Parties : adopted at the Fifth ECCI Plenum, April 1925. Published in *The Communist International 1919–1943 : Documents*, vol. II, p. 189.

[140] Broué, *Histoire de l'Internationale Communiste*, pp. 386–387.

[141] *Ibid.*, p. 405.

translated into popular language",[142] evidently because the demand for dictatorship was not particularly popular among the workers. It was stressed that the slogan did not imply a political alliance with Social Democracy or a government in "bourgeois-democratic framework".[143] – These endless explanations and condemnations gave weapons for representatives of every nuance, and, in fact, could obscure important disagreements. In the Finnish case the relation to the Social Democrats was not, I would argue, finally an important question at all in the factional quarrel (although in disagreements with the emigrant leaders and leaders in Finland it emerged as such).[144] The source of the victory of Rahja – it was a victory for him that Kuusinen and Manner failed to drop him from the Central Committee – was Zinov'ev's intervention.

On the fourteenth day of the Congress (August 14) which met in Leningrad, N. I. Bukharin attended its "political committee". He suggested that the Central Committee would not be elected yet, but that the Congress would instead elect representatives, who would travel to Moscow to negotiate on the composition of this body with the leaders of the Comintern. The presidium of the Congress therefore moved that a delegation, consisting of four representatives from Finland plus Kuusinen, Manner and Vilmi, proceed immediately to the Moscow train. After the inevitable squabbles over the delegation – should Rahja be included or not – the suggested delegation went to Moscow.[145] Rahja also travelled, but not as a member of the delegation.[146]

The *rendez-vous* with Bukharin and Zinov'ev took place in the Kremlin. According to the report of the encounter, Zinov'ev warned the delegation about the "Right danger" and "sectarianism". The Finns should take the results of the 1924 parliamentary elections as a "warning". Of the trade union movement, Zinov'ev said that it was in bad condition because the "Centrist leaders" of it could ally with "our Right flank".[147] Of Rahja Zinov'ev said that "we shall conserve C. Rahja, he

---

[142] Extracts of the Theses of the Tactics Adopted by the Fifth Comintern Congress. Published in *The Communist International 1919–1943 : Documents*, vol. II, p. 152.

[143] *Ibid.*

[144] Because the comrades in Finland had failed to "try to expose the counter-revolutionary lead of Social Democracy before the working masses", the Congress condemned, for example, negotiations with the Social Democrats about the common work in the *Eduskunta* on the question of amnesty for the prisoners condemned for participation in the Civil War. (The Political Situation and the Tasks of the SKP. RGASPI, f. 516, op. 2, 1925, d. 12, ll. 6–7.) To many Communist politicians in Finland, to say nothing of the "masses", this standpoint was surely incomprehensible.

[145] Minutes of the Vth Congress of the SKP, July 30–Aug. 16, 1925. RGASPI, f. 516, op. 2, 1925, d. 14, ll. 51–61.

[146] *Ibid.* l. 93.

[147] After the suppression of the Finnish Socialist Workers' Party in 1923, there was also a danger of the suppression of the Federation of the Trade Unions (which was Communist-led but in which the Social Democrats also participated) and several unions. In 1924 the chairman of the Federation,

will be put in naphthalene, so that he will be kept uninjured until you need him". In addition, Zinov'ev commanded that the Congress delegates from Finland be ordered to be silent regarding the internal struggles among the emigrant leadership on Finland.[148] This order did not, of course, prevent the spread of rumours in Finland.

The election of the Central Committee gave rise to a long discussion. The Congress was told that based on an agreement with the Executive Committee of the Comintern Rahja should be elected to the Central Committee, but he would remain at disposal of the RKP(b) and could take part in the work of the Central Committee when he was specially invited. Laukki was not on the list of candidates presented to the Congress and therefore Rahja asked that his own name be removed too. Laukki, on his part, announced that Zinov'ev insisted on Rahja's election because "when the time for struggles comes, Comrade Rahja will lead the revolutionary Red Guards as a Red Marshal". After the election of the Central Committee, the Congress was presented a list of candidates for the Politburo: Kuusinen, Manner, Sirola, Lumivuokko, Salminen, Antikainen and Malm. The name of Malm caused animosity. Aleksander Vasten said that Malm was also to blame for the quarrels. Moreover, Nadezhda Konstantinovna Krupskaia was never a member of the Central Committee of the RSDRP / RSDRP(b)[149] / RKP(b) "although she is a developed human being and has done a great deal of work which Hanna Malm would never be able to do". In addition, some delegates from Finland opposed Malm, but the people on the list were elected. At this time, a delegate from Finland protested because Malm was a candidate without vote although her candidacy was opposed. In other words, it was demanded that her candidacy should have been voted! At this time – it was 5.15 a. m. – in a very confused situation, chairman Manner announced a pause for negotiations. When the Congress met at 7.30, Manner suggested that after a test vote on Malm, a delegation would be sent to Moscow to ask the opinion of the Comintern leaders. Adolf Taimi and J. K. Lehtinen (Juho Kustaa, also known as "Jeesus Kristus Lehtinen") were suggested in Malm's

---

Edvard Huttunen, who was an MP, separated from the parliamentary group of the Socialist Workers and Smallholders. (Ala-Kapee and Valkonen, *Yhdessä elämä paremmaksi*, pp. 678–681.) He became a leading "Centrist", "Centre" being, from the point of view of the SKP leaders, between Social Democrats and Communists. As Centrists we may also regard three other members of the Executive Committee of the Federation who might vote with the Social Democrats. What the "Right flank" meant is difficult to say, probably all other Communist trade union leaders in Finland.

148 Minutes of the Vth Congress of the SKP, July 30–Aug. 16, 1925. RGASPI, f. 516, op. 2, 1925, d. 14, appendix 1. Also KtS!, pp. 203–208.

149 Российская социал-демократическая рабочая партия (Russian Social Democratic Labour Party) existed under that name from 1898 to 1917. In August 1917 "большевиков" (Bolsheviks) was added to the name, written Российская социал-демократическая рабочая партия (большевиков), which, however, was used only until March 1918.

stead. Taimi received 16 votes and Lehtinen 2. It was then announced that Moscow suggested Lehtinen's election. After a very long discussion (13 typed sheets in the minutes) the matter was transferred to the Central Committee.[150] There J. K. Lehtinen was elected as a full member and Adolf Taimi as a vice member of the Politburo.[151]

Subsequent Skirmishes

The struggle between Zinov'ev and Stalin in the RKP(b) / VKP(b) was also of some importance from the point of view of the Rahja Opposition. It seems that the first public quarrel took place in 1924; one of its symptoms was the wrangle between Stalin and Zinov'ev over the expression "dictatorship of the Party". It was coined in the Bolshevik context by Zinov'ev and Stalin opposed it because, as he argued, some Party members erroneously believed that there was a dictatorship of the Party but not one of the proletariat. On this question, Stalin even lost one vote in the Central Committee and asked to resign, but the Central Committee did not permit his resignation.[152] The struggle continued and Stalin soon succeeded in isolating Zinov'ev and his supporters in Leningrad.[153] Before the XIVth Congress of the VKP(b), in late December 1925, Stalin offered Zinov'ev a "compromise" which would have meant the submission of the Leningrad Party to the Central Committee, i.e. Stalin.[154]

In the Party Congress itself, Zinov'ev's ally in all situations, L. B. Kamenev, expressed his conviction that I. V. Stalin was not a person to unite the "Bolshevik general staff".[155] Zinov'ev suggested a very liberal compromise: all the forces of earlier oppositions should be offered a possibility to work in the Party, under the Central Committee, to be sure.[156] Zinov'ev and Kamenev, however, formed a clear minority in the Congress. A resolution denouncing the Leningrad leaders and calling the Leningrad Party to order was opposed by only 36 delegates from Leningrad.[157] Zinov'ev remained, however, a member of the Politburo; Kamenev was demoted as a candidate. Zinov'ev was recalled from his post of chairman of the Comintern.

---

150 Minutes of the Vth Congress of the SKP, July 30–Aug. 16, 1925. RGASPI, f. 516, op. 2, 1925, d. 14, ll. 84–118.

151 MCC, Aug. 18, 1925. RGASPI, f. 516, op. 2, 1925, d. 28.

152 Medvedev, *Let History Judge*, pp. 144–145.

153 *Власть и оппозиция*, pp. 126–127.

154 See Stalin's (and Kalinin's, Molotov's, Dzerzhinskii's etc.) proposal for a compromise, published in И. В. Сталин. Заключительное слово по политическому отчету центрального комитета. 23 декабря. XIXth Congress of the VKP(b), Dec. 18–31, 1925. И. В. Сталин. *Сочинения*, vol. 7, pp. 388–389.

155 Carr, *Socialism in one country*, vol. 2, p. 153.

156 *Ibid.*, p. 157.

157 *Ibid.*, p. 162.

At the same time, the post itself was abolished and replaced by a Secretariat. Bukharin became its head.[158]

O. W. Kuusinen duly condemned the "dictatorship of the Party". He argued that Lenin never stressed "a dictatorial relation of the Party to the proletariat".[159] In addition, Eino Rahja severed his ties to Zinov'ev. This did not prevent Manner from trying to assure the Comintern that the Rahja Opposition was supported in Leningrad by the Zinov'evite Opposition and there was supposedly a connection between the Rahja Opposition and illegal Communist associations in Finland, although withouth much to show for it.[160]

One purpose of Manner's intervention was to get Leo Laukki expelled from the post of rector of the Leningrad Department of the University of the Western Minority Nationalities, which he had occupied since the summer of 1925, and to replace him by Yrjö Sirola.[161] This operation was successful, although Sirola himself was not at all contented with his own fate. He had also been offered the post earlier, but had managed to refuse.[162] He wrote to Manner that he was "unprepared" for the work and, moreover, he had not the same qualifications as Laukki, especially as to languages.[163] Sirola spoke (at least) five languages but perhaps he thought not well enough. – In Laukki, the Party lost an able intellectual. It seems that he was, like Sirola, an inspiring lecturer. In his last lecture, the students cheered him and tossed him in air.[164] Laukki's weak point – considering that he lived in a totalitarian society – was his independent and adventure-loving character. This, perhaps, is an explanation for his curious alliance with Eino Rahja.

Eino Rahja was ousted, as we have seen, from the Central Committee for the second fake money affair. When the last salary was paid him, he wrote the following quittance:[165]

---

158 Medvedev, *Let History Judge*, p. 155.

159 Kuusinen's speech in the Plenum of the Comintern in Nov. 28 – Dec. 16, 1926, p. 4. RGASPI, f. 516, op. 2, 1926, d. 1. Kuusinen's claim is not true. Let us cite for the second time Lenin's declaration, according to which the "Party absorbs, so to speak, the vanguard (*авангард*) of the proletariat and this vanguard realises the dictatorship of the proletariat". (В. И. Ленин, О профессиональных союзах, о текущем моменте и об ошибках т. Троцкого : речь на соединенном заседании делегатов VIII съезда советов, членов ВЦСПС и МГСПС – членов РКП(б) до декабря 1920 г. PSS, vol. 32, pp. 203–204.) Moreover, "the dictatorship of the proletariat is possible only when it is realised by the Communist Party". (В. И. Ленин, Заключительное слово по отчету ЦК РКП(б) 9 марта ш1921щ. Speech in the Xth Congress of the RKP(b). PSS vol. 43, p. 42.)

160 Kullervo Manner to the Small Commission of the Secretariat of the Executive Committee of the Comintern, Dec. 29, 1926 (in Russian). RGASPI, f. 516, op. 2, 1926, d. 3. Also KtS!, pp. 211–213.

161 *Ibid.*

162 Yrjö Sirola to Kullervo Manner, Jan. 20, 1927. RGASPI, f. 516, op. 2, 1927, d. 14.

163 Sirola to Manner, Jan. 30, 1927. RGASPI, f. 516, op. 2, 1927, d. 14.

164 *Ibid.*

165 RGASPI, f. 516, op. 2, 1927, d. 7.

> Receipt
> I have received the payoff for eight years' service from the C.C. of the SKP, fifty roubles, which I promise to pay back in Finland – if in my lifetime some revolution is born, of which, well, I am not sure.
> 6/VIII 27.
> Eino Rahja

One incident between Rahja and the Mannerite Central Committee took place after Rahja's speech at K. M. Evä's funeral. The Central Committee condemned it as an "outrageous factional appearance".[166] For the Plenum of the Central Committee Rahja wrote a memorandum of his speech. It was quite a long history of the factional struggles in the SKP. For listeners who did not know this history some parts of the speech must have been incomprehensible because Rahja, in a certain Communist style, spoke of struggles but mentioned names sparsely; this was the case when, for instance, Rahja spoke of the Kuusinen opposition. Evä's name was naturally mentioned. Rahja reminded his hearers that in 1921, Evä was not elected to the Central Committee and in 1923 Kuusinen and Manner prevented his co-optation to that body. The climax of the speech was typically ouvrierist. There can be intellectuals in the leadership of a Communist party, but they must be selected carefully because "experience" indicates that even the best of them, like Trotskii, Zinov'ev and Kamenev, "cannot ultimately advocate the issue of the proletariat". Therefore the leadership should consist of workers who cannot be "led", for only "when *working men* themselves take the reins in their hands", "will our Party become such a force" that is able to lead the masses in the "struggle against the capitalists".[167]

---

[166] MCC, April 25–27, 1927, § 12. RGASPI, f. 516, op. 2, 1927, d. 7.
[167] Eino Rahja "in the camp of the Red Army" to the CC of the SKP, June 25, 1927. RGASPI, f. 516, op. 2, 1927, d. 10.

IX The Malm and Manner Opposition (1928–1935)

In the late 1920s, the official oratory of the Soviet Union and the Comintern became increasingly impetuous; one might also say sectarian or Ultraleftist. A turning-point can be seen in the VIth Congress of the Comintern. According to François Fejtö, the slogan adopted at the time, "class against class", comprised two postulates.[1] Firstly, the absolute priority of the defence of the Soviet Union was proclaimed. I. V. Stalin declared in the joint Plenum of the Central Committee and the Central Control Commission in 1927 that there was now, now when war threatens the Soviet Union, no "third position" concerning the Soviet Union. Stalin said:[2]

> He is a **revolutionary**, who without any reservations, absolutely, openly, and honestly, without secret military negotiations, is ready to protect the USSR [...]. He is an **internationalist**, who without reservation, without vacillation, without prerequisites is ready to defend the USSR because the USSR is the base of the world revolutionary movement and it is not possible to protect and to move forwards without defending the Soviet Union.

Secondly, in the West it was necessary to define Social Democracy as the main enemy.[3] Social Democrats were called Social Fascists; Social Democracy and Fascism were not "antipodes", but "twins". This theory was elaborated by Stalin as

---

1 François Fejtö, *L'Héritage de Lénine : introduction à l'histoire du Communisme mondial*, pp. 209–210.

2 И. В. Сталин, Международное положение и оборона СССР : речь 1 августа. И. В. Сталин, *Сочнения*, vol. 10, p. 51. Stalin's speech in the joint Plenum of the CC and the Central Control Commission of the VKP(b), July 29–Aug. 9, 1927.

3 Fejtö, *L'Héritage de Lénine*, p. 210.

early as 1924.[4] The VIth Congress of the Comintern declared, "[i]n foreign affairs the social-democratic and reformist trade union leaders in the imperialist countries are the most consistent representatives of bourgeois State interests".[5]

All this was in one way or another connected with intra-Party dealings of the VKP(b) in which a factional struggle was in progress as usual.[6] Also within most of the "sections" of the Comintern, oppositional groups and currents burgeoned and mushroomed.[7] In our context, perhaps the German Communist Party is the

---

[4] In his article "On the International Situation", Stalin also declared: "Fascism is such a fighting organisation of the bourgeoisie that relies on the active support of Social Democracy. Social Democracy is objectively a moderate wing of Fascism. There is no reason to suppose that a fighting organisation of the bourgeoisie can attain decisive success in struggles without support of the Social Democracy. No less reason there is to suppose that Social Democracy can attain decisive success in struggles or in governing a country without decisive struggle, without active support of a fighting organisation of the bourgeoisie. These organisations do not negate but supplement each other. They are not antipodes but twins. Fascism is an informal political block of these two chief organisations. This block arose in the circumstances of the post-war crisis of imperialism; its purpose is combating the proletarian revolution". (И. В. Сталин, "К международному положению". *Большевик*, Sept. 20, 1924. И. В. Сталин, *Сочинения*, vol. 6, p. 182. See also Mikko Majander, "The Soviet view on Social Democracy : from Lenin to the End of the Stalin Era", in *Communism : National & International*, pp. 61–104.)

[5] Extracts of the Theses of the sixth Comintern Congress on the international situation and the tasks of the Communist International : from the Protocol of the Congress, August 29, 1928. Published in *The Communist International 1919–1943 : Documents*, vol. II, *1923–1928*, p. 459. – Kimmo Rentola has pointed out that among the Finnish Communists leaders there was a conception that the Finnish Social Democracy was, as Rentola puts it, "especially morbid" compared with Social Democracy in other countries. Kuusinen wrote in 1940–1941, before the German attack to the Soviet Union, a brochure (that was never published), titled "The path of the Social Democracy and the path of the Communist Party" (*Sosialidemokratian tie ja kommunistisen puolueen tie*). According to Kuusinen, the Finnish Social Democratic Party was in the autumn of 1939 "main crusher of nationalist people's betrayal". It was a betrayal of the Finnish people (especially the working-class) not to defend the Soviet Union during the Winter War of 1939–1940. Rentola claims that this was the first time in the Communist parlance when such a conception is used. (Rentola, *Kenen joukoissa seisot?*, p. 319) It was not the first time. On June 7, 1931 a letter was sent from the Moscow leading body (at this time called Foreign Bureau) to the leading body (Politburo) in Finland in which it was stated that compared with Social Democratic Parties in other countries, Finnish Social Democracy had "especially clear" role, being "main supporter and aide of Capitalism and Fascist dictatorship". (RGASPI, f. 516, op. 2, 1931, d. 13, l. 4.) – As to the betrayal itself, the 1939 betrayal was the second betrayal. The first one happened in June 1930 (the above letter is a reflection of this first betrayal). The idea of a working-class, which betrays the Communist leaders, is not non-existent in Communist chatting. One may remember Bertold Brecht's famous poem *Solution* about this kind of betrayal, written in 1953 in which he stated that people had lost the confidence of the government and might have this confidence back only by doubling its work contribution.

[6] See e.g. Joint Plenum of the CC and the Central Control Commission, 16–23 April, 1929. Published in *Resolutions and decisions of the Communist Party of the Soviet Union*, vol 2, *The Early Soviet Period: 1917–1929*, pp. 324–349.

[7] See e.g. Broué, *Histoire de l'Internationale Communiste 1919–1943*, pp. 492–673.

most important, because it was still considered pivotal for the coming world revolution. Nevertheless, the Party there was very, or perhaps most sinisterly torn apart by numerous factions. According to Ruth Fischer, there were at the time of the Congress of the German Communist Party in 1927 no less than ten factions, partly inside, partly outside the Party *père*.[8] At the famous Hotel Lux, in which foreign Communist émigrés, including Malm and Manner, had their residence, they were living among continuous factional struggles of Communist parties which were illegal or semi-illegal in their own countries. There was no end of them.

Manner was also given some incidental international tasks. He was a member of the Executive Committee of Comintern and there he had tasks in the Scandinavian secretariat (Finland was considered in the Comintern a Baltic country and its affairs were consequently managed in the Polish-Baltic secretariat). In addition, Manner worked, as already noted, in the Peasants' International. This was to remain a somewhat insignificant organisation.[9]

Although both Manner and Gylling guessed in the Enlarged Plenum of the Central Committee, held in Moscow, that the Finnish Capitalism would "stabilise" (Manner) or that there would be "economic difficulties but not crisis" (Gylling), there had been, according to Manner, "severe attacks by the bourgeoisie and noskes" and it was now our task "to mobilise our Party masses to the defensive struggle".[10] What is important here is that there were no specifications as to changes, turning-points, attacks etc. It seems that the delegates from Finland in the Central Committee Plenum did not actually know what was going on in the VIth Congress of the Comintern at the same time.

In fact, the Politburo was in difficulties. In Finland, the clandestine organisation was more or less obliterated after the Rasi affair. There was also another threat. There had been negotiations in Copenhagen between the trade union federations of the Soviet Union, Norway and Finland over the agreement on friendship and cooperation. In February 1928, the agreement was signed, but it was decided by

---

8 For a catalogue, see Ruth Fischer, *Stalin und der deutsche Kommunismus*, pp. 267–268. As Hermann Weber (*Die Wandlung des deutschen Kommunismus : die Stalinisierung der KPD in der Weimarer Republik*, vol. 1, p. 8) notices, all parties had "variations" due to their "different character". There were, according to Weber, "Right" opposition, "Left" (or Workers') opposition (led, among others, by R. Fischer), "Ultraleft" opposition and the "Middle" group, known also as *die Versöhnlehr*, or "reconcilers". Different factions had ties to Russian factions and personages; the Left to Zinov'ev, the Middle to Buharin etc. (*Ibid*., pp. 16–19.) Comparison between Finnish and German oppositions would not be very fruitful because the German Party was, until 1933, legal, whereas in Finland only more or less ephemeral "front" organisations existed until, as we have seen, they were illegalised in 1930. About factional struggles inside the KPD, see also Ben Fowkes, *Communism in Germany under the Weimar Republic*, pp. 110–144 and *passim*.

9 Matti Lackman, *Taistelu talonpojasta : Suomen Kommunistisen Puolueen suhde talonpoikaiskysymykseen ja talonpoikaisliikkeeseen 1918–1939*, pp. 53–55.

10 Minutes of the enlarged Plenum of the CC of the SKP, Aug. 20–23, 1928. RGASPI, f. 516, op. 2, 1928, d. 5, ll. 2–6.

the Finnish Trade Union Federation not to ratify it in August 1928. The Soviets demanded a clause according to which trade unions in Norway and Finland must, in the case of war, urge workers to refuse to join an army of a capitalist country. There was probably more than one version of this agreement. Kuusinen told the Central Committee Plenum in 1928 that he had seen a draft for an agreement in Norwegian. According to this version, the Finnish Trade Union Federation should be, if a war broke out, ready to fight against the Finnish army.[11] Still in June 1929 the Politsecretariat of the Comintern demanded that the Trade Union Federation be ratified; the Politsecretariat argued that the "overwhelming majority" of the members of the Federation was "resolutely" for ratification.[12] It is questionable how many leaders (excluding the top Communist leaders) really knew what was agreed in the accord, to say nothing of members. Had the agreement been signed, the Social Democrats would have left the Federation, and presumably would have established their own trade union federation. To the Detective Central Police the publication of an agreement with this kind of clause would be a most welcome present. Kuusinen considered it impossible simply to leave the agreement not ratified. His strategy was to explain to the Russians the state of affairs: they should comprehend that this agreement was for the Finns impossible. However, we know only partly what happened behind the scenes. In August Sirola wrote a letter addressed to the Politburo of the VKP(b) in which he defended a "tactical retreat".[13] For Kuusinen the question was not for the "peace-loving" Soviet Union any kind of principle. He proclaimed in a Party Conference in October 1929:[14]

> The Soviet Union is now a peace-loving country and it is wise to be such. But it is a completely different thing when it will fortify. Can it, as a strengthened [state] be so patient e.g. in its relation to irritations from the border countries as it nowadays is? The exacerbation of the threat of war is unavoidable. The deep contradiction between the Socialist world and the Capitalist world cannot be solved by other means than war.

It seems that at least in public nobody expressed any dissenting opinion.

Relations between Manner and Kuusinen seemed to remain friendly or at least correct until the winter of 1928–1929. Then came the so-called "suitcase affair" and a squabble over a historical article written by Sirola in 1928.

---

[11] Kuusinen according to the minutes of the enlarged Plenum of the CC of the SKP, Aug. 20–23, 1928. RGASPI, f. 516, op. 2, 1928, d. 5, l. 41.

[12] Resolution of the Politsecretariat of the Comintern on the work of the SKP in the trade union movement, June 28, 1929. KtS!, p. 248.

[13] RGASPI, f. 525, op. 1, d. 121. We cannot know whether this letter was sent or not.

[14] Minutes of the Conference of the SKP, Oct. 10–15, 1929. RGASPI, f. 516, op. 2, 1929, d. 7, l. 67.

1. The Unfolding of Enmities (1928–1931)

The SKP soon adopted the "class against class" line. In the Party Conference held on August / September 1930 Manner declared that the Party had thought that the transition to Fascism would take place gradually. Manner told the Conference that in 1927 he had declared that under the White order in Finland the Communists were already in the process of "decomposition to legality". That was a "misjudgement" and a more correct statement was promulgated in 1929, in which Manner had explicated Finland as "Semi-Fascist", "Semi-", because the "workers" (i.e. the Communists and their supporters) there still had some civil rights. In addition, there had been many campaigns, but they were carried out only "routinely".[15] All this demonstrated that there had been a serious "lack of Bolshevik resolve" in the Party. In Finland, the Left (i.e. those in leftist position compared with the Social Democrats) proved their "decomposition" by suggesting in the Trade Union Federation a united front with Social Democracy against Fascism. The proposal was – again a very serious mistake – public, published on June 10, 1930 in *Työväenjärjestöjen Tiedonantaja*. According to Manner, it was reckless to spread such an "illusion". Finally, there was not enough conspirationism and here Manner himself and Malm were guilty of "gross negligence".[16]

The Suitcase Affair (Stockholm 1929)

In 1929 Malm and Manner were ordered to go to Stockholm illegally on certain conspiratorial business. They travelled to Sweden through Germany and reached Stockholm at the end of July 1929. There were serious problems in Communist legal work in Finland. The Trade Union Federation was not so disciplined as it might have been. There was a group of "vacillators" who sought to keep the Federation unified so that the Social Democrats would not leave the organisation. This, however, took place in 1929 and was applauded at least in some circles in the SKP leadership because it was thought a mistake to that of join forces with the "Social Democratic lords" – an expression often used. A concrete matter was the Copenhagen agreement and the International Labour Organisation (ILO): whether

---

[15] What Manner did not say was that these campaigns were ordered by the Comintern. They were indeed numerous. For example, in March 1929 the Politburo of the SKP commanded to organise the following campaigns : March 4 (Comintern's foundation day), March 8 (international women's day), March 9 and 10 (a Conference against Fascism, organised by the Comintern), March 15 (the day of the downfall of Tsarism) and March 18 (a day of the reminiscence of the Paris Commune). It was decreed that, in addition, "the connecting of above-said campaigns necessitates a strictly systematic method in agitation and propaganda work. One should organise continuous transition from one campaign to another." (Politburo of the SKP to the Finnish Bureau, Feb. 10, 1929. RGASPI, f. 516, op. 2, 1929, d. 18.)

[16] Minutes of the Conference of the SKP, Oct. 10–15, 1929. RGASPI, f. 516, op. 2, 1929, d. 7, ll. 26–34.

to send a delegate to its conference or not. For the Communists the ILO was an institution of class concord. Malm's and Manner's task was to discipline the Communists in Finland and force them to take the Federation under tighter control.

One reason for Malm's and Manner's journey to Stockholm was the new possibilities of travel between the Nordic countries since a passport was no longer be compulsory in travels between them. One had only to have a travel card, which was easy to obtain. It was now quite convenient to travel from Finland to Sweden legally, although the Communists decided to preserve the old illegal route from Ostrobothnia across the Gulf of Bothnia to Sweden. Nobody could guarantee that the legal system would last long and for people sought by the police the legal route was, of course, closed.[17]

Sweden was for the Finnish Communists a highly significant country, because the Swedish Communist Party was legal. This, however, did not mean that Finnish Communists were absolutely safe in Sweden. The Swedish and Finnish secret police collaborated in political matters involving Communists and, at least behind the scenes, the Swedish police was ready to give a helping hand to the Finns. That was also the case in the "suitcase affair". Manner's and Malm's problem was where to put a suitcase containing the names and addresses of Finnish Communists, the code names they were using and several copies of letters by various persons.[18] One leading Finnish clandestine worker was Herman Hurmevaara – officially a commercial representative of Soviet Karelia in Stockholm – with whom Malm and Manner discussed the problem. The suitcase was placed in an apartment, occupied by other illegal Finns, but was now under the control of the Swedish secret police. A police agent obviously saw that something suspicious was going on, but nobody was in the flat when police arrived to arrest the suspects. There was, however, the suitcase. The police confiscated it and sent Manner's notebook containing all names, addresses, secret names etc., to the Finnish Detective Central Police. The police had at first some trouble with it because Manner's handwriting was notoriously unclear, but in any case it was relatively easy for the police to arrest important Communist cadres. At least eleven people were taken into custody and subsequently condemned to prison.[19] Most fatal from the point of view of the clandestine organisation was the capture of Ville Honkanen,[20] of whom it was rumoured that his task was to organise work among conscripts in the army (which

[17] Ilkka Hakalehto, "Suomen kommunistisen puolueen kriisi 1928–30" in *Oman ajan historia ja politiikan tutkimus*, pp. 244–235.

[18] Kullervo Mannerilta Tukholmassa takavarikoituja kirjeiden jäljennöksiä, valokuvia muistiinpanoista, nimiluetteloja suomalaista kommunisteista v. 1929. (Copies of letters, photographs of memoranda, name lists of Finnish Communists, confiscated from Kullervo Manner in Stockholm, 1929.) Ek-Valpo I, DF III A 3, KA.

[19] Matti Lackman, "Mikä kaatoi Kullervo Mannerin?", *Historiallinen Aikakauskirja* 3/1981, pp. 209–210.

[20] "Yksitoista kommunistien johtajaa oikeuden edessä", *Suomen Sosialidemokraatti*, Feb. 12, 1930.

might well be true) and stir up a new rebellion[21] (which might possibly not be true; a rebellion could only be a long-term target).

Back home, Manner stressed to the Party Conference of 1929 that he was responsible for the mishap. Or can we speak of an unfortunate accident because the ABC of underground political work of course dictated that such a notebook as Manner's should not exist at all and at least it should always be hidden or otherwise in a safe place.[22] From Malm's point of view, it was Hurmevaara who was to blame for the catastrophe because he did not get the suitcase out from the apartment, which was known not to be completely secure. She argued that she had ordered Hurmevaara to get the suitcase out of there. Of her own role, Malm averred that the affair was also on her part "a severe mistake".[23]

Hurmevaara denied being the "main culprit" in the case. He declared that Malm was not telling the truth when she spoke of an order she had given him. He had received no such order.[24] It is impossible to know what really happened in Stockholm, but from the point view of our study what is important is that by accusing others, in this case Hurmevaara, Malm did not win the sympathies of the Conference delegates; on the contrary, she also in this case (others will be discussed below), weakened her own position.[25] The suggestions for punishment were presented to the Conference by O. W. Kuusinen. Kuusinen stressed that by writing down secret Party names, addresses etc., Manner and Malm were guilty of breaking the elementary rules of conspiracy. Considering his position in the Party, Manner had the "ultimate responsibility". In Malm's papers in the suitcase there were many "unconspirational" notes. Considering that both Malm and Manner had confessed their culpability, Kuusinen proposed in his capacity of member of the Executive Committee of the Comintern, that both should be given a "serious reprimand".

Malm and Manner had escaped Sweden soon enough to avoid arrest. Hurmevaara was arrested and ordered to leave the country in view of material which connected him to something which could be interpreted as illegal. However, Hurmevaara – although he was a Russian citizen – was accustomed to Swedish welfare and was far from pleased at the prospect of moving to Russia, where life would surely be less easy than in Sweden. To prevent his deportation, he wrote a letter to no less a personage than the King Gustav V of Sweden asking not to be

[21] See "Onko kommunistiemme keskuuteen ilmaantunut uusi n.s. Rasi?", *Suomen Sosialidemokraatti*, Jan. 24, 1930.

[22] Minutes of the Conference of the SKP, Oct. 10–15, 1929. RGASPI, f. 516, op. 2, 1929, d. 7, ll. 203–206.

[23] *Ibid.*, l. 118

[24] *Ibid.*, l. 203

[25] *Ibid.*, l. 135. Jalo Lepola's speech.

deported.[26] This did not prevent his expatriation and in Russia the Politburo of the SKP already before the Conference gave him "a most serious reprimand". – As to Malm and Manner, the Conference approved Kuusinen's proposal.[27]

The Controversy over the Year 1921

The formal starting-point of the controversy over the Party Congress in 1921 was Sirola's article "The Finnish Communist Party". Its original purpose was to give the Russian reading public a general acount of the history of the Finnish workers' movement, not only of the SKP, in spite of the title of the article. Sirola directed attention to what we have called in this study emigrant psychosis. History shows, he wrote, that life in a foreign country after the trauma of a revolution in the home country easily leads to quarrels among émigrés. According to Sirola, life as an emigrant offers superior and fruitful "soil" to all kind of petty bickering and mutual accusations. It is typical of émigrés to create grim contradictions in simply wording their texts. The case of Finland was even worse compared to other former states in the Russian empire, because the leaders in the new Party were often personages who had been in the lead in the Finnish revolution and every one of them was in his/hers different manner a participant in the "mistakes" committed by the revolutionary leaders. Hereafter comes a paragraph in which Sirola analyses the quarrel of 1921, which merits a long quotation because the core of the dispute is here expressed as in a nutshell:[28]

> At the same time as the above-mentioned émigré opposition [i.e. the Murder Opposition] developed, a crisis also faced the SKP leadership. Its rationale lay partly in disagreements over the émigrés, but also in the question of the Party's activities in Finland. A part of the members of the C.C. were becoming apt to bow to the instincts of to a certain extent the non-proletarian "masses". They proposed actions (like a Congress elected on a broad basis etc.), against what they saw as too tight centralisation, which, if realised, would have placed the very bases of a Communist party in danger. A debate on these questions between the members of the C.C., a part of which was outside the Soviet Union, finally brought the Party to sectarianism so that there was a danger of a split. In fact, there were already two factions:

---

26 MMP, April 20, 1930, § 1. RGASPI, f. 516, op. 2, 1930, d. 28.

27 Minutes of the Conference of the SKP, Oct. 10–15, 1929. RGASPI, f. 516, op. 2, 1929, d. 7, ll. 466–467 and ll. 487–489. The main argument in the letter was the following: "I am still a Finnish refugee, nothing else. Soviet Russia is alien to me and to my family. We do not know the language; we are not related to anyone who can give us work and livelihood [in Russia]. [...] To be a subject of Russia was for me the only possibility to get a passport in order to do my work as a commercial delegate in Stockholm and in Karelia." (Hurmevaara to King Gustav V, Dec. 11, 1929, copy. RGASPI, f. 512, op. 2, 1929, d. 37.)

28 Yrjö Sirola, "Suomen Kommunistinen Puolue", *Kommunisti*, July 1928, p. 299.

> they had their own meetings etc. By the leadership of the Comintern, however, the Party, evaded its crisis, although not without great complications. At late winter 1921, a parity Central Committee and the Organisation Committee was set up under leadership of the C[ommunist] I[nternational]. In the spring, after the III^{d} Congress of the Comintern, the crisis was cleared up in the Party Congress [of the SKP].

Now, it flies in the face of the philosophy of the phenomenon called the "Communist Party" to claim that there might be two factions in this Party. According to the Leninist-Stalinist doctrine of the Communist Party, there is always, if disagreements arise, a correct Party course, represented by a special body similar to the Party, the Central Committee, or some such organ. As to who is right in a situation of disagreement, it is not necessarily the majority, arithmetically speaking; a majority is a political, not a mathematical factor. All intra-Party oppositions in the 1920s and later were "anti-Party groups" as announced in the famous (or notorious) *Short Course* of the history of the Bolshevik Party, published in 1938.[29] In line with this clause, Malm declared in the 1930 Party Conference that in 1921 Kuusinen's and Sirola's faction was in actual fact a "Rightist Group", which "arose against our Party". In the same context, Malm also presented the kind of criticism she felt should now be adopted. She stated that "[w]e have 100 % cow-towed to stinking bourgeois democracy [and] our whole action betrays that we have been ill, suffering from the stinking wrecks of Social Democracy". Now, fortunately, the bourgeoisie have taught the Communists that they, instead of being only an "excrescence" (*kasvannainen*) inside the legal movement, must begin their activities from a completely different basis.[30] Malm did not explicitly define what this new basis should be. There were in Finland at the time Communist workers in Lapland who demanded arms in order to start a new "fat rebellion" and in Lahti (Southern Finland) pleas for permission to derail trains came to the Finnish Bureau of the

---

[29] *Ibid.*, p. 268. On factions and their explanation as illegitimate if not illegal in 1921, see, Graeme Gill, *The Origins of the Stalinist Political System*, pp. 93–100 and Roy A. Medvedev, *On Socialist Democracy*, p. 65. An example of the style in the *Short Course* can be seen in the conclusion concerning the victims, called "spies", "wreckers" and "traitors". It was said that Trotskii, Zinov'ev, Kamenev, Bukharin and Aleksei Ivanovich Rykov planned to "destroy" the Party and the Soviet state and "give up" the Coast of the Pacific to Japan, Byelorussia to Poland, and the Ukraine to Germany. "These White Guard midgets (*козявки*) forgot that the boss (*хозяин*) of Soviet land is the Soviet people, and Messrs rykov, bukharin, zinov'ev, kamenev are in all only temporarily in the service of the state, who may at any moment be thrown out of its bureaus as superfluous trash (*хлам*)." (*История всесоюзной коммунистической партии (большевиков) : краткий курс*, p. 332.)

[30] Minutes of the Conference of the SKP held in Moscow, Aug. 28 – Sept. 15, 1930. RGASPI, f. 516, op. 2, 1930, d. 7, ll. 115–119.

SKP in the spring of 1930. However, only truncheons and ash bags[31] to be used in the struggle against the police were promised.[32]

As to Malm's defamation of Sirola's article, one must say that the criticism constituted extreme hair-splitting because the main objects of Sirola's own criticism was himself and the Kuusinen opposition in 1921. Malm's target in her accusations, we must assert, was not Sirola but Kuusinen. At the time Sirola seriously doubted his own mental health and Malm was – quite surely because Sirola wrote of his situation to Manner[33] – aware of Sirola's state.

O. W. Kuusinen was more than nervous about the year 1921. He was worried that the debate would pass on to historical questions, and, of course, to questions which he would find far from welcome. He declared in the 1930 Party Conference:[34]

> The year 1921. In my opinion there is no reason to go into secondary matters, but if in the one side were liquidators [presumably someone, possibly Malm, had used this ideologically onerous word, although it does not appear in the minutes of the Conference], the matter would not have been solved as it was. There were rather a Right opportunist deviation on the one side and a Leftist sharp divergence. The Rightists who founded the STP [Socialist Workers' Party in 1920] were not full liquidators. [...] Now after nine years this case is dug out and one tries to seek cause [for the catastrophe of the SKP] in the fact that [in the Congress of 1921] the liquidators, Sirola and others, had a part.

Manner's assesment of the year 1921 was not so straightforward as Malm's. On the basic question concerning liquidation and tactical measures Manner agreed with Kuusinen: there were Rightist and Leftist divergences. Only Eino Rahja was a liquidator – Manner did not say when and where –, but for Manner, the 1921 resolution was "a showpiece (*näyte*) of eclecticism" and the "decomposition" had begun in 1921, because in this resolution mistakes were not "bolshevistically revealed". For Manner, it was necessary to return to the good old times, which meant that the Party should embark upon "vigorous" training for an armed revolution.[35] As to what this would have concretely meant, Manner said nothing. He was be-

---

31 This was presumably a large paper bag filled with ashes; a policeman struck over the head with it would be temporarily blinded as ashes covered his face on bursting.

32 *Ibid.*, l. 113b. The information came from Pentti (Lund), who worked at the time of the "Fascist Coup" in the Finnish Bureau.

33 Sirola to Manner, Jan. 9, 1929. RGASPI, f. 516, op. 2, 1929, d. 16. Later, on May 4, 1930, Sirola wrote to Kuusinen that he was indeed at the time he wrote the article "insane". (RGASPI, f. 525, op. 1, d. 121.)

34 Minutes of the Conference of the SKP held in Moscow, Aug. 28–Sept. 15, 1930. RGASPI, f. 516, op. 2, 1930, d. 7, ll. 233–234.

35 Minutes of the Conference of the SKP held in Moscow, Aug. 28–Sept. 15, 1930. RGASPI, f. 516, op. 2, 1930, d. 8, l.l. 386–387.

tween two fires: on the one hand, there was his friend Sirola (Sirola had friendly relations with almost everybody) and on the other, there was his fiery wife.[36] Manner himself, like Sirola,[37] obviously had some mental problems. Manner was disposed to obsessive feelings of guilt and depression. He did not value himself; on the contrary, he sought "errors" and "mistakes" in his own activities. (Examples of these phenomena are given below.)

Malm was in this regard different. She sought errors in the doings of others and was extremely reluctant to confess her own sins except under severe pressure. In the case of the Sirola article Malm accused the editors of the journal *Kommunisti* of the fateful mistake of publishing an erroneous article by Sirola. In the 1930 Party Conference, Jukka Lehtosaari, an editor of *Kommunisti*, pointed out that it was impossible to edit the journal before publication if all articles should be discussed and accepted in the Politburo. In addition, Malm's standpoint was not necessarily that of the Party leadership, not always even of Manner's.[38] Lehtosaari muttered, moreover, that "every wrong formulation is not a deviation (*ukłooni*)" and the article had been published under Sirola's name and it was Sirola who was responsible for it. Sirola agreed with Lehtosaari but said it was Malm's "mistake" that she did not bring about a decision of the "Politsecretariat" to prevent the publication of his incorrect article.[39] All in all the debate over 1921 was somewhat caustic and adumbrated, we can say now, a gloomy future.

The Debate on the "Fascist Coup d'état" in Finland (1930)

There were in Finland two kinds of opposition within or close to the Communist movement: the so-called "vacillators" (*hoipertelijat*) at the Right and the "Red Warriors" (*punaiset rintamamiehet*) at the Left. The *primus motor* of the "vacillators" was Niilo Wälläri, originally a seaman, who had been in the United States and had had contacts there with representatives of revolutionary syndicalism. When he returned to Finland at the beginning of the 1920s, he became involved in Communist activities and was thrown into Tammisaari prison. There he did not like

[36] To Sirola Manner wrote a compliant letter about Sirola's article. (It is quoted in Hannu Rautkallio and Jukka Paastela, "Johdanto : Hanna Malmin ja Kullervo Mannerin elämä ja toiminta" in Kullervo Manner and Hanna Malm, *Rakas kallis toveri*, p. 36.)

[37] In 1929 Sirola stated in a letter to Manner that he suffered from "mental aberration" (*mielenhäiriö*). He said he could behave "decently" only "by habit, by training (*treenaus*) so to say". Sirola also feared that he was "abnormal". (Sirola to Manner, Jan. 9, 1929. RGASPI, op. 516, op. 2, 1929, d. 16.)

[38] This is an obvious allusion to a letter Malm sent to Lehtosaari. In this letter she stated that Lehtosaari, because he has not the status in which he can solve political matters and advised him to "listen Manner's recommendation" about the affair. According to Malm, Manner was against the publication of the article. (Malm to Lehtosaari, Feb. 28, 1930. RGASPI, f. 516, op. 2, 1930, d. 27.)

[39] Minutes of the Conference held in Moscow, Aug. 28–Sept. 15, 1930. RGASPI, f. 516, op. 2, 1930, d. 7, l. 181

the "sub-discipline" of the prison Communist Party hierarchy, which when possible, took orders from the Party. Wälläri succeeded in gathering in prison a group around him, mostly trade union activists, who were also frustrated that in the trade union work in which they had been forced to follow orders coming from the clandestine movement. The group produced, in 1925, a letter the title of which was telling: *Irti emigranteista* (Let us be free of the emigrants).[40] Many members of this group were released in the late 1920s and continued their dissident policy mainly inside the Trade Union Federation. They also, in 1929, formed a grouping, called the "Left Group of the Finnish Workers".[41] Their hold was not very strong; they had followers in the main industrial centres of Southern Finland. Nevertheless, on the ideological plane, they formed a vanguard; they condemned the "class against class" course drawn up by the Comintern; they thought that Finnish workers should not take orders from any foreign country and unity in the trade unions should be maintained even if this meant concessions to the Social Democrats.[42] For the Communists the vacillators were "neonoskeans, i.e. opportunists"[43] and "renegades";[44] of the Communists, the vacillators used the word *huitojat*, which describes them as "gestigulating" or "beating the air". – The "Red Warriors" formed, after public activities had been forbidden, a clandestine organisation known as the Finnish League of Red Warriors (*Suomen punaisten rintamamiesten liitto*). These Warriors were not so depressed and unhappy over the "Fascist coup". The new situation, in which legal action was no longer possible, opened up for them new possibilities of illegal action.[45]

Meanwhile the continuous violent acts against the Communists (kidnappings) and against the property of the movement (destruction of printing presses and workers' houses), inspired the main legal Communist newspaper, *Työväenjärjestöjen Tiedonantaja* to print a poetic text on June 5, 1930: "The scorn of the Finnish bourgeois law and justice by the bourgeoisie itself, has lately marched forward in seven-league boots".[46] The newspaper appealed to Social Democratic workers to "recognise the crimes of their leaders" and in the same breath condemned the attempts of the "Social Fascists" to seek allies in the circles of "democratic bour-

---

40 Arvo Tuominen wrote a long memorandum about the dissidents in Tammisaari, "Lyhyt selostus niistä erimielisyyksistä joita Tammisaaren pakkotyölaitoksella olevain toverien keskuudessa on ilmennyt eräissä puoluettamme läheisesti koskevissa kysymyksissä", RGASPI, f. 516, op. 2, 1926, d. 22.

41 Upton, "The Communist Party of Finland", pp. 185–186.

42 Hodgson, *Communism in Finland*, pp. 132–133.

43 "Raukkamaista", TTA, March 1, 1930.

44 Rupla (pseudonym), "Me marttyyrit", TTA, March 15, 1930.

45 Tauno Tietäväinen, Selostus osallisuudestani Rintamamiesliittoon (Report on my participation in the Warrior League), no date but written after July 1930 when the author was freed from Tammisaari prison. RGASPI, f. 516, op 2, 1930, d. 30.)

46 "Suomen porvarillisen lain ja oikeuden halveksiminen itsensä porvariston taholta on viimeaikoina marssinut eteenpäin seitsemän penikulman saappailla." ("Rikollisten triumfi", TTA, June 5. 1930.)

geoisie".[47] There were demonstrations, but in general Communist workers submitted to the destruction of their legal organisations, press, houses etc. without resistance. In June 1930, the government decreed that from June 14 all Communist publications were prohibited. Thus, the last issue of *Työväenjärjestöjen Tiedonantaja* was published on June 13. The title of the leader of this copy was: "Thou hast won, Lapuan!" The paper commented on the Lapuan victory as follows:[48]

> This victory achieved by the Lapuans was easier than anyone could conceive of. We had not even the slightest misapprehension of bourgeois "democracy" (*kansanvalta*), so that we could believe that this democracy might be able to offer serious resistance to Fascism. Nevertheless, we confess we were mistaken in regard of some self-esteem of the government, which self-respect could give some bearing in front of the Fascist hoodlums (*fascistihulinoitsijat*). We did not believe that "democracy" was so utterly miserable, as it is now proved to be.

The next step, beginning in July, was to arrest and imprison all Communist MPs.

From the present point of view it is useful to compare the Mannerian political line to that of Kuusinen and his supporters, of which the most notable representative was Toivo Antikainen. We have two documents, a draft, dated August 30, 1930, written by Kullervo Manner for the Comintern as "open letter to the SKP",[49] and what is presumably likewise a draft, dated July 27, 1930, written by Toivo Antikainen as his presentation on the "Fascist upheaval" (*mullistus*) in the meeting of the Polish-Baltic Secretariat of the Comintern. Both leaders understandably tried to point out where the mistakes lay, both in the leadership in Finland and in that in Russia. For Manner, the basic confusion was caused by the characterisation of the pre-coup regime as "Semi-Fascist". This definition was bound to obscure the real situation, i.e. the possibility of the Putsch. His language was extremely complicated: Manner wrote that "unclarity" as to the "domination" of the bourgeoisie, as not yet a "dictatorial regime" was the cause of confusion and mistakes. One "covered opportunistically through this unclearness the possibility of an attempt at a coup and the prospect of building a Fascist dictatorship".[50] For Antikainen the analysis of the expression "Semi-Fascist" had been "mainly" correct. For Manner it was a mistake to prevent workers who were ready to fight, to derail trains, by the pretext that now "was not the time for the final struggle" and saying that using derailing

---

47 "Porvarillisen 'kansanvallan' harhakuviin vastattava kestävällä luokkarintamalla", TTA, June 5. 1930.

48 "Sinä olet voittanut, lapualainen!", TTA, June 13, 1930.

49 This may sound odd, but it was not exceptional that Party leaders wrote Comintern letters to themselves. This, to be sure, did not mean that the Comintern automatically accepted all "drafts" distributed to the diverse organs of this hideous organisation.

50 Draft by Kullervo Manner as an open letter of the Comintern to the SKP, Aug. 30, 1930. RGASPI, f. 516, op. 2, 1930, d. 3, l. 5.

"the terror of the slaughterers would only increase".[51] For Antikainen this was not a pretext. He said that terrorist acts directed against the railways would increase "terror" against Communists sitting in prison.[52] Manner condemned all attempts to defend democracy against the Fascists as futile.[53] Antikainen had nothing against a struggle of defence. He complained that the struggle had been not active enough; on the contrary, people had retreated and then been destroyed. This was a dreadful moral defeat. The situation would have been better had there been some "serious" attempt at battle and "trounce" the enemy.[54]

The basic difference between Manner and Antikainen was in the conception of Fascism. For Antikainen the situation was unambiguous: before the coup there had been a Semi-Fascist regime, after the coup the regime was Fascist. Manner's standpoint was confounded, or, to use Communist language, sectarian. On the other hand, one can point out that there were among the Moscow leadership still what later came to be called "legalist illusions". It was proclaimed, for instance, in the name of the Politsecretariat of the Comintern that in the coming parliamentary elections in the autumn of 1930, one should put up as candidates "known revolutionaries". The document also stressed that all "Social Democratic remnants" should be cleaned out.[55] The author of this document was no one but O. W. Kuusinen.[56]

---

51 *Ibid.*, l. 7.

52 Toivo Antikainen, *Fasistimullistus Suomessa ja siihen johtavia tekijöitä : alustus Baltian sihteeristön kokouksessa*. (On the Fascist upheaval in Finland and factors which led to this upheaval : *exposé* in the meeting in [Polish-]Baltic Secretariat), July 29, 1930.) RGASPI, f. 516, op. 2, 1930, d. 3, l. 22.

53 Draft by Kullervo Manner as an open letter of the Comintern to the SKP, Aug. 30, 1930. RGASPI, f. 516, op. 2, 1930, d. 3, l. 7.

54 Toivo Antikainen, *Fasistimullistus Suomessa ja siihen johtavia tekijöitä*, July 29, 1930. RGASPI, f. 516, op. 2, 1930, d. 3, l. 22.

55 SKP:n lähimmistä tehtävistä : Kommunistisen internationaalin päätös. (On the immediate tasks of the SKP : resolution of the Communist International.) July 16, 1930. RGASPI, f. 516, op. 2, 1930, d. 2, ll. 2–6. – In the minutes of the Politsecretariat of the Comintern, signed June 16, 1930 and declared "secret", there is the following mention: "In temporary directions of the SKP one must head for the development of a political mass strike". (KtS!, p. 259.) The directive is very odd in the light of the experiment in a "general strike" in the autumn of 1930. In the meeting of the Politsecretariat, Kuusinen was the *referent*; also Antikainen spoke in this reunion. It seems that the final, "secret" resolution was accepted on July 23, 1929. In this decree, there is no mention of "Social Democratic leavings". However, it was considered necessary to "reveal to the very end the vile role of the leaders of the Social Democracy as assistants of the Fascist system, from which they gain for themselves all kinds of advantages". The "vacillators" are named "opportunist renegades", whose "betrayal" must also be "revealed". The Communists should also "clear it up" that talks of a "return to the bourgeois democracy are just a sham, which serves the interests of the Fascist dictatorship". There is "only one way out for the proletariat, abolition of the Fascist dictatorship and a proletarian revolution". (KtS!, pp. 267–268.) In yet another "secret" resolution on "ineffectuality of the SKP against Fascism", November 28, 1930, the Politsecretariat condemned the resolutions of the SKP before the Putsch, because the Party had "mistakenly" affirmed that the "whole Finnish political system was Fascist", that there was already a "Fascist dictatorship", although, to be sure,

One may question whether the drafts for presentations to an official body, in this case a draft for a letter and a draft for a speech, are sources from which we can draw conclusions as to different persons' opinions. I think it is undoubtedly true that such letters are not necessarily indications of what the writers "really" thought. Then we must also say that we can never know what a person "really" thought. We can, however, try to explain what we read in sources. The interesting point here is what Manner and Antikainen thought they could present to the Comintern. There were certain differences between the two men, although both made an effort to present what was in accordance with the prevailing policy of the Comintern. That Manner's planned presentation was more orthodox than Antikainen's probably reflected both the temperament and situation of our two theoreticians. Manner's claustrophobic fear of mistakes played a part as well as his situation, which was not particularly assured after the suitcase affair and Malm's interventions, which formed the roots of numerous problems among the leadership of the SKP. Antikainen had no "cases" behind him in the recent past and he had not a wife like Malm. He also had Kuusinen's support, perhaps even guidance. Manner's relationship with Kuusinen was more complicated, especially since Kuusinen's attitude to Malm was, to put it mildly, critical. Manner, as pointed out above, had certain obsessions: he, for instance, imagined he was guilty of various errors. In 1925 he announced to the Vth Congress of the SKP that he had been guilty for thinking that it might be possible that a united front could also be useful with Left-Wing Social Democratic leaders, not only with the Social Democratic masses. Referring to that Manner declared:[57]

> The Soc. Dem. dross will be scrubbed off us through long experience and often through extremely grave errors. This is very tracigal, but it is a fact. [...] One often feels that before us there is total darkness. [...] It is the source of pessimism, hesitation, and despair.

In 1930, Manner's views were in a way proven correct by the resolution (discussed above) by the Comintern, or, in fact, by Kuusinen. In the 1930 Party Conference, Manner avowed that the reason for "our fecklessness" were the "Social Democratic remnants". That was the main cause of "paralysis and passivity, which still prevails both in the Party and in the masses" supposed to be lead by the Party to the strug-

---

there were "Fascist elements" in Finland. This "erroneous outlook" "weakened the mobilisation of the masses against gradually rising Fascisitation of state power and overrode the whole question of a struggle against the maturing Fascist coup d'état". (KtS!, p. 279.)

[56] This is proved by Direktiven an die K. P. : erster Entwurf von Kuusinen. July 13, 1930. RGASPI, f. 516, op. 2, 1930, d. 3.

[57] Minutes of the Vth Congress of the SKP, July 30–Aug. 16, 1930. RGASPI, f. 516, op. 2, 1925, pp. 75–76. Quotation on l. 76. (List numbers of this document have been made later by a filing clerk.)

gle.[58] There was, according to Manner, defeatism among the Communists in Finland. One paper, for instance, wrote that because the bourgeoisie could not fight against Fascism and defend bourgeois democracy, it was the task of the Communists to defend the said democracy. This was a fatal legalist error because it prevented the struggle against the "Fascist dictatorship". Manner also expressed self-criticism: he had in 1927 written that the "dominating White rule" was already a "Fascist dictatorship". Furthermore, he had written in 1929 that the rule was Semi-Fascist because there were "democratic elements". This, Manner continued, did not prove "Bolshevik solidity" because there were two different estimations of the same phenomenon but no explanation why there was a change in the estimations.[59] Manner stressed that "a turning point" was necessary to make the SKP a "real Bolshevik Party".[60]

The 1930 Party Conference decided to transfer the Politburo to Finland. It was considered erroneous that the Finnish Bureau had to wait instructions from the Politburo in Moscow in order to act. The Finnish Bureau was abolished and a new organ, the Foreign Bureau, was created. Manner's main duty was, so said Kuusinen, henceforth to direct this Foreign Bureau.[61] The new arrangement did not change the power relations in the Finnish Communist movement: the power in the Party remained in Moscow.

2. The Florescence of Hostilities (1931–1935)

Behind the burgeoning of hostilities between the Malm and Manner Opposition and Kuusinen's "correct line" was a frustrating falling-off of the Communist movement in Finland. At least from the point of view of Moscow this decline had already become alarming by the end of the 1920s. Although, for example, on the "Red Day" (first of August, 1929) imposed by the Comintern on all its sections, there were in Finland demonstrations – forbidden by the Ministry of the Interior[62] – in many towns[63] as well as clashes between demonstrators and the po-

---

[58] Minutes of the Conference of the SKP, Aug. 29–Sept. 15, 1930. RGASPI, f. 516, op 2, d. 7, 1930, l. 4.

[59] *Ibid.*, l. 30.

[60] *Ibid.*, l. 36.

[61] Minutes of the Conference of the SKP held in Moscow, Aug. 29 – Sept. 15, 1930. RGASPI, f. 516, op. 2, 1930, d. 8, l. 417.

[62] This was reported by the Communist press on the Red Day itself. ("Sisäministeriö on kieltänyt elok. 1 p. mielenosoitukset", *Työ*, Aug. 1, 1929.)

[63] It is difficult to say how many people participated in demonstrations. A Communist newspaper *Työn Ääni* ("Kiihdyttäviä piiskaniskuja", Aug, 7, 1929) claimed that "tens of thousands of workers marched". According to the organ of the National Coalition, *Uusi Suomi* ("'Punainen päivä' kului koko maassa rauhallisesti", Aug. 2, 1929) those who participated in "attempts at demonstrations" were "mainly known Communists and hooligans, whereas soberer working people kept aloof".

lice,[64] an interpellation in the *Eduskunta*,[65] and so on, this was not enough for Moscow headquarters. The leaders especially of the Trade Union Federation were accused of being passive, even hostile to this day. At local level, many leaders were so scared and petrified that they were not able to organise the workers in a demonstration.[66] The case of the anniversary of the October revolution was similar. It was even announced – which especially annoyed leaders in Russia – to the police that on this day demonstrations and meetings would be held.[67]

There were meetings in workers' houses, criticised by the Moscow leaders on the grounds that the workers behaved as earlier, they went after work to their homes, washed themselves and changed clothes. According to instructions from the Comintern, the workers should go to demonstrations wearied in their working clothes.[68] The Moscow centre gave copious instructions about the mobilisation of the masses in Finland. One document on mobilisation contained the following advice:[69]

> By organising special collective shock brigades of gymnasts, actors, orators, orator groups, singers, musicians and speakers etc. electoral propagandists can get good results by a well rehearsed and organised programme in accord with major election slogans. [...] Such a shock brigade goes into a yard of some house, alarms the inhabitants by song, harps, horns, drums, or accordions let us say in a yard and at windows and presents its programme vigorously.

This kind of instruction of course shows how far removed the émigré leaders in Moscow were from realities of Finland.

---

[64] In Helsinki in the place of demonstration even the fire brigade with its fire-engine was present, reportedly by the order of the Mayor of Helsinki. No water was, however, used, much baton instead. Police brutality caused protests not only in the Communist but also in the Social Democratic press. The police behaved "in a state of unrestrained herd instinct and rage". ("Helsingin poliisi käyttäytyi eilen raakalaismaisesti", *Suomen Sosialidemokraatti*, Aug. 2, 1929.)

[65] The first signer of the interpellation, discussed on August 8, 1929, was Asser Salo, a member of the "Parliamentary group of Socialist working people and smallholders". Toiset valtiopäivät 1929 : pöytäkirjat, vol. 2, p. 54.

[66] Yhteenveto punaisen päivän vietosta ja tuloksista. (Summary account of the Red Day in Finland and its consequences.) A document without indication of the writer or decision-maker. The document bears the marking: "Sent to the IKKI and the Baltic Secretariat". RGASPI, f. 516, op. 2, 1929, d. 9, l. 3.

[67] "Poliisi- ja suojeluskuntajoukot olleet liikkellä eilen eri puolilla maata", TTA, Nov. 11, 1929.

[68] Lokakuun vallankumouksen XII-vuotispäivän kamppailut Suomessa. (On struggles on the XIIth anniversary of the October revolution in Finland) RGASPI, f. 516, op. 2, 1929, d. 9, ll. 12–13. There is also a Russian translation of the document. The document bears no indication of the writer or the decision-maker.

[69] KL [Kalle Lepola?], *Vaalipropagandametodeista*. RGASPI, f. 516, op. 2, 1928, d. 13, ll. 6–7.) By harps in this context are probably meant mouth harps, harmonicas.

The same may be said of instructions concerning the elections. In the municipal elections there was some co-operation with the Social Democrats in about 50 municipalities, which was condemned by the Politburo of the SKP on the grounds that the Social Democrats were not effectively "exposed", the preparation of the bourgeoisie and Social Democrats for the war between Finland and the Soviet Union was not stressed etc. There were also incorrect slogans like "class domination should be completely overthrown" as if there could be "partial" conquering of class domination etc.[70] According to the Politsecretariat of the Comintern, there were even such illusory demands as that the "police should no longer lead and order state power" and "involvement in municipal affairs should be ended". The Communist must "explain to the masses" that such demands were "utopian" and enlighten the masses that the involvement of the state in municipal affair is "necessary" under the dictatorship of the bourgeoisie.[71] In the 1930 parliamentary elections as well as in the 1931 presidential elections[72] there was, according to Toivo Antikainen, much "illusion". Communists voted for Social Democrats, which proved that the Fascist nature of Social Democracy had not been effectively enough "disclosed". In the presidential elections there were "illusions of legality". On the other hand, there were among the Communist workers, ideas about "election strikes" which revealed "opportunism and passivity, covered up by blustering word-mongering".[73] There were some Communist candidates in the elections.

In Finland, there appeared – as mentioned above – an Ultraleft opposition called the "Red Warriors".[74] This gave rise to nervous reflections in Moscow, but, never-

---

70 Vaalitaistelun opetuksista kunnallisvaaleissa (On lessons drawn from the municipal elections), decision of the Politburo of the SKP, no date, obviously accepted in the autumn 1928. RGASPI, f. 516, op. 2, 1929, d. 18, ll. 10–14. One might wonder what kind of impact this kind of hair-splitting had among the comrades who were acting in very difficult conditions in Finland.

71 Resolution of the Politsecretariat of the Comintern on municipal elections in Finland, May 25, 1929. KtS!, p. 245.

72 In the 1931 presidential elections Pehr Evind Svinhufvud, also supported by Righ-Wing radicals, was elected President. His contestant was K. J. Ståhlberg, the first President of the Republic (1919–1925), a candidate of the Progressive Party supported notably by the Social Democrats. Svinhufvud was elected in the Electoral College by 149–151. (Jaakko Nousiainen, *Suomen presidentit valtiollisina johtajina K. J. Ståhlbergista Mauno Koivistoon*, pp. 110–111.) Under the electoral system of that time people voted for a candidate to the Electoral College (300 members), which, in turn, elected the President.

73 Minutes of the Conference of the SKP, Aug. 28.–Sept. 15, 1931. RGASPI, f. 516, op. 2, 1931, d. 2, l. 34.

74 "Red Warriors" is not a literal translation of *Punaiset rintamamiehet*; literally it should be "Red Front Men". – The Red Warriors consisted of workers. It seems that there were no intellectuals in the ranks of the group because the documents were written in grammatically poor Finnish. In its *Basic programme and statutes* the "Finnish League of Red Warriors" stated that the aim of the League was "by all means" to precipitate the collapse of Capitalism and found the dictatorship of the proletariat. It was declared that the League endeavoured to cooperate internationally with the "proletarian revolution armies" of other countries, but above all with the Soviet Union. In its

theless, in Moscow problems were focused on the person of Hanna Malm. Before we scrutinise the factional struggle between the Malm and Manner Opposition and Kuusinen's "main line", it is convenient to examine the question whether Hanna Malm was a Luxemburgist. She was more or less clearly accused of this in the process of the formation of the Manner and Malm Opposition. Before we go into the question about Malm's possible Luxemburgism, it seems appropriate to look at the debate over Rosa Luxemburg and Luxemburgism in Russia. In addition, possible "Luxemburgist" vocabulary used by the Finnish Communist is worth a glance.

Instinct, Spontaneity etc. Vocabulary among the Finnish Communists in Russia

Rosa Luxemburg figured during the 1920s as a god in the Communist Pantheon, but then, in 1931, I. V. Stalin published an article titled "On Some Questions of the History of Bolshevism". It was an attack on a certain A. Slutskii, a historian who in a journal called *Proletarskaia Revolutsiia* had dared to question Lenin's policy towards German Left-Wing Social Democrats, Rosa Luxemburg above all, in the period 1910–1914.

Rosa Luxemburg had cooperated with Lenin in the 1907 Congress of the Second International,[75] but she had also published, in *Iskra* and in *Die Neue Zeit,* a

work, the League would act according to decisions of the Comintern. The activity of the League, it was elucidated, was "wholly illegal". A section was reserved for punishments; the punishment for a "provocateur", agent of "Okhrana" and "denouncer" was "unconditional death". The highest decisive power belonged to the "Red Staff". (*Suomen Punaisen Rintamamiesten liiton perusohjelma ja säännöt.* There is no date, but in Moscow it was written for duplication "received 26.1.", i.e. Jan. 26, 1931. (RGASPI, f. 516, op. 2, 1931, d. 9.) In the organ of the League, *Toveri* ("Comrade") was given an explanation for the founding of the organisation. The main reason was that during the period 1920–1928 the leaders of workers' organisations (this means obviously organisations dominated by the Communists, trade unions especially) were "scoundrels, cowards and seekers of their own happiness". After the "Lapuan upheaval", the workers "sighed and stood like Hamlet, wondering whether to be or not to be". (*Toveri*, 4, 1930, RGASPI, f. 516, op. 2, 1931, d. 9.) There were plans for various sabotage acts and a demonstration for December 25, 1930. According to Tauno Tietäväinen, who participated in the League and later described its plans and activities to the SKP, nothing came of the sabotage and there were only a few demonstrators in the Senate Square in Helsinki. (Tauno Tietäväinen, Selostus osallistumisestani Rintamamiesliittoon. RGASPI, f. 516, op. 2, 1931, d. 9.) In the SKP, the League provoked, of course, hostile reactions. The Foreign Bureau and, what is interesting, the Polish-Baltic Secretariat of the Comintern, suggested that the representatives of the League should be invited to come for negotiations in Leningrad. In the Conference of the SKP Toivo Antikainen said that this invitation would have meant a recognition of the legitimacy of the League; therefore he opposed the invitation. It is not clear whether there was such an invitation, but I have not found any trace of negotiations in Leningrad. (RGASPI, f. 516, op. 2, 1931, d. 2, ll. 54–55.)

[75] Annelies Laschitza and Günter Radczun, *Rosa Luxemburg : Ihr Wirken in der deutschen Arbeiterbewegung*, pp. 194–200.

critique of Lenin's "Jacobinism" and "Blanquism" as far back as 1904.[76] This was at the time when the rest of the European workers' movement was not particularly interested in the internal quarrels of the Russian Social Democrats, often considered incomprehensible. Karl Kautsky, the editor of *Die Neue Zeit,* refused to publish Lenin's answer to Luxemburg on the grounds that German readers of the journal would not at all understand the dispute between the Bolsheviks and the Mensheviks.[77]

Slutskii's point was that before 1914 Lenin, like most Marxist Socialists at the time,[78] accepted the authority of Kautsky as a leading theoretician of Marxism. An embarrassing fact from Stalin's point of view was that Luxemburg already broke with Kautsky in 1910 and Kautsky's so-called Centre began to be formed. The dividing issue between Kautsky and Luxemburg was the mass strike. In her famous (or notorious, depending on the standpoint) essay on the Russian revolution of 1905, Luxemburg had declared that the use of mass strikes in this revolution had opened new horizons not only for the Russian workers' movement, but also for the labour movement in the West.[79] Kautsky argued that if the uprising in Russia, where the ruling class was much more feeble than in Germany, had not achieved its objectives, how would a mass political strike succeed in Germany, where the government and army were the strongest in the world.[80] In 1910, Luxemburg envisaged using a mass strike to end the *Dreiklassenwahlrecht*, still used in Prussian elections. Kautsky was against and August Bebel's opinion was that it is not wise to discuss the theme in the press at all.[81]

Slutskii wished to defend Luxemburg's position and declared that from 1910, when Kautsky's "reactionary and obstructive role" began to be evident, Luxemburg

---

76 Rosa Luxemburg,, "Organisationsfragen der russischen Sozialdemokratie", *Neue Zeit* 1904. Published in Rosa Luxemburg, *Gesammelte Werke*, vol. 1, part 2, pp. 427–428.

77 Claudie Weill, *Marxistes russes et social-démocratie allemande 1898–1904*, p. 139. Kautsky wrote to Lenin that he had published Luxemburg's article not because its subject was the Russian Party but in spite of this. According to Kautsky, Luxemburg's article dealt theoretically with the question of organisation, while Lenin concentrated precisely on quarrels. He added that a theoretical article on the question of organisation by Lenin would be welcomed. (*Ibid.*) See also Bernhard von Mutius, *Die Rosa Luxemburg-Legende*, vol. 1, pp. 175–197.

78 Norman Geras notes (*The Legacy of Rosa Luxemburg*, pp. 70–71) that in 1906–1909 Lenin tried desperately to prove that his views on strategic perspectives concerning Russia, including the concept "revolutionary-democratic dictatorship of the proletariat and the peasantry", were in accordance with Kautsky's positions.

79 Rosa Luxemburg, *Massenstreik, Partei und Gewerskchaften* (1906). Published in Rosa Luxemburg, *Ausgewählte politische Schriften in drei Bänden*, vol. 2, pp. 28–29.

80 Massimo Salvadori, *Karl Kautsky and the Socialist Revolution 1880–1938*, pp. 136–137. See also Peter Nettl, *Rosa Luxemburg*, p. 276.

81 Virve Manninen, *Sozialismus oder Barbarei?. Der revolutionäre Sozialismus von Rosa Luxemburg 1899–1919*, pp. 78–87. On personal aspects of the conflict, see Elzbieta Ettinger, *Rosa Luxemburg : a Life*, pp. 172–173. This author claims it is "possible" that Luxemburg's "vitriolic attacks" caused the nervous breakdown Kautsky suffered in August 1910.

"put the problem sharply",[82] whereas Lenin's "position" was "restrained" and "waiting"; he did not publicly criticise Kautsky and Bebel in the period from 1911 up to the outbreak of the war.[83]

For Stalin this meant nothing less than a questioning of Lenin's Bolshevism before 1914. He accused the editors of *Proletarskaia Revolutsiia* of publishing the Slutskii's article instead of branding "anti-Party and Semi-Trotskyite Slutskii" as a "slanderer and falsifier". No arguing about Lenin' s policy should be allowed because it is "well-known to everyone" that "Leninism was born, grew and was consolidated in the pitiless struggle against all sorts of opportunism, including Centrism in the West (Kautsky) [and] in our country (Trotskii and others)". This kind of permissiveness was "rotten Liberalism" and "curious Liberalism" and counter to the "vital interests of Bolshevism". According to Stalin, every Bolshevik knew that Lenin "in about 1903–1904" "took a line towards the split" both in "Russian Social Democracy in our country and in the II^{d} International, among others in German Social Democracy".[84] Here Stalin said nothing as to who were the enemies in Germany at the time, except that they were "opportunists". That the split did not take place, however, was not Lenin's fault, for it "cannot be demanded" that "Lenin and the Bolsheviks must from Russia [?] arrange a schism in the Western parties". The cause was the "organisational and ideological weakness" of Left-Wing Social Democrats. Here Stalin jumped from 1903–1904 straight into 1916; his example was Lenin's article on the Junius pamphlet, in which Lenin speaks of [85]

> "the weakness of all German Leftists, who are in every respect enmeshed in the disgusting net of Kautskyite dissimulation, pedantry, 'friendliness' towards opportunists", in which he says that "Junius has not be freed from German 'circles', even those of Left-Wing Social Democrats, who fear the split, who fear to follow revolutionary slogans to the very end."

Stalin further accused Luxemburg of inventing, with Parvus, (pseudonym of Aleksandr L'vovich Gelfand; Helphand in Germany), a "utopian and Semi-Menshevik scheme of permanent revolution", "seized upon" later by Trotskii and "partly" by L. Martov and "turned into a weapon of struggle against Leninism".[86]

---

[82] А. Слуцкий, "Большевики о германской с.-д. в период ее предвоенного кризиса", *Пролетарская Революция*, 6, July 1930, p. 41.

[83] *Ibid.*, p. 62.

[84] И. В. Сталин, "О некоторых вопросах истории большевизма : письмо в редакцию 'Пролетарская Революция'", *Пролетарская Революция*, 6/1931. И. В. Сталин, *Сочинения*, vol. 13, pp. 84–86.

[85] *Ibid.*, p. 87.

[86] И. В. Сталин, "О некоторых вопросах истории большевизма : письмо в редакцию 'Пролетарская Революция'", *Пролетарская Революция*, 6/1931. И. В. Сталин, *Сочинения*, vol. 13, p. 91.

The controversy continued in another theoretical journal, *Bolshevik*, in 1931–1932. A "comrade" called Aristov (Slutskii was not a "comrade") had noted a contradiction in Stalin's writings: in his preface to the book *On the Path to October* Stalin had claimed that Parvus and Trotskii, not Luxemburg, "put forward" the theory of a permanent revolution.[87] Stalin denied that there was a contradiction. He had claimed that Parvus and Trotskii "put forward" the theory; in the *Proletarskaia Revoliutsiia* article, he had said that Luxemburg and Parvus "concocted" the theory. As to Rosa Luxemburg, she had preferred, according to Stalin, to hide in the coulisses and abstain from "active struggle against Lenin" when Parvus and Trotskii "put forward" the theory. Later, Stalin claimed, also Luxemburg began to fight actively against "Lenin's revolutionary scheme". However, this was after 1905.[88]

Trotskii participated in the controversy by ridiculing the same contradiction Aristov had pointed out[89] (the two men could not possibly have any connection; Trotskii was at the time in exile in Turkey) and in fact defending Slutskii's thesis. According to Trotskii, Lenin did not participate in the "fight" between Luxemburg and Kautsky: "In Lenin's eyes Bebel and Kautsky stood immeasurably higher as revolutionists than they did in the eyes of Rosa Luxemburg".[90]

The question who coined and who presented the theory of permanent revolution is of secondary importance here.[91] Stalin's attack on Luxemburg, in contrast, is most crucial. Although its primary context was Stalin's intention to stop all free debate on the history of the Bolshevik Party,[92] the article also had implications in other Comintern parties, the German and Polish especially. It was difficult for them to swallow the wholesale condemnation of "Luxemburgism" as a variant of Trotskyism.[93]

---

87 И. В. Сталин. *Октябрьская революция и тактика русских коммунистов : предисловие к книге "На путях к Октябрю"*. И. В. Сталин. *Сочинения*, vol. 6, pp. 379–380.

88 И. В Сталин. "Ответ Олехновичу и Аристову : по поводу письма о редакцию журнала 'Пролетарская Революция' 'О некоторых вопросах истории большевизма'". *Большевик*, 16, Aug. 30, 1932 (the answer is dated Jan. 25, 1932), И. В. Сталин. *Сочинения*, vol. 13, pp. 131–132.

89 Leon Trotsky, "Hands off Rosa Luxemburg", *The Militant*, Aug. 6 and 13, 1932. Published in [Lev Trotskii], *Writings of Leon Trotsky* [1932], pp. 139–140.

90 *Ibid.*, p. 133.

91 Baruch Knei-Paz writes (*The Social and Political Thought of Leon Trotsky*, p. 161, n. 162), that when Luxemburg, Kautsky and Franz Mehring spoke in 1905 of a permanent revolution in Russia, they meant the bringing of the bourgeois-democratic revolution to completion in Russia, i.e. not stopping at some compromise with the Tsarist autocracy.

92 Cf. Михаил Геллер & Александр Некрич. *Утопия у власти : история Советского Союза с 1917 гὸда до наших дней в 3-х книгах*, vol. 1, p. 281.

93 E. H. Carr, *The Twilight of Comintern*, 1930–1935, pp. 428–432. Cf. Medvedev, *Let History Judge*, p. 312.

The names of Rosa Luxemburg and Karl Liebknecht were fairly well-known to Finnish Left-Wing militants and after 1918 to the Social Democrats as well as to the Communists. In 1919 the SKP published a booklet on *Spartakus Bund,* which included documents of the League and some last speeches and articles by Rosa Luxemburg and Karl Liebknecht.[94] Subsequently there were articles on Liebknecht and Luxemburg, including a critique of Luxemburg's *Russian Revolution* as early as 1922 and Lenin – Liebknecht – Luxemburg week was celebrated from 1925 up to 1934.[95]

Kommunisti, a political-economic monthly published by the district committees of the VKP(b) of Leningrad and Karelia, published Stalin's letter in November 1931.[96] It was commented on by Yrjö Sirola in *Kommunisti* in January 1932. His curious article bore a long title: "The lead of the Finnish workers' revolution of 1918 as a Luxemburgian critic of Bolshevism – in practice". Its opening was strictly orthodox. Sirola stated, for example:[97]

> In addition to the struggle going on against the manifestations of the infiltrations of counter-revolutionary Trotskyism, an important role in the purging work nowadays is also the struggle against other anti-Leninist and un-Leninist manifestations of theory and practice. Among such [manifestations] are, for example, relics of Luxemburgism in the literature of the German Comparty.

After this conventional "introit", Sirola very soon came to his theme: it was Luxemburg's *Russian Revolution.* Why this particular subject? Sirola stated that the inducement to present "Rosa Luxemburg's mistaken criticism" was that the lead of the old Finnish Social Democracy, i.e. pre-Communist, undivided Social Democracy, produced similar criticism of Bolshevism, not in theory, i.e. in written form, but in practice. In short, it did not follow the example of Bolshevism; it was not even Luxemburgist, but Kautskyist. Sirola presented two "concrete proofs" of this critique of Bolshevism in practice. The first was his meeting as People's Deputy of Foreign Affairs with a "leading" Russian Socialist Revolutionary. Sirola told him about the Reds' draft for the constitution. "He nodded his head with complacency:

---

[94] *Saksan Spartacus : omistettu Karl Liebknechtin ja Rosa Luxemburgin muistolle.* Liebknecht was better known to the Finnish Socialist public than Luxemburg. The Social Democratic Youth League published Liebknecht's book on militarism in 1910. (T:ri Karl Liebknecht, *Militarismi ja antimilitarismi erikoisesti kansainvälistä nuorisoliikettä silmälläpitäen.*)

[95] On the reception of Luxemburg and Liebknecht in Finland, see Heikki Marjomäki, "Translated Communism : Remarks on 'Politics Translated' in the Finnish Communist Movement during the 1920s and 1930s" in *Communism National & International,* pp. 267–272.

[96] J. V. Stalin, "Muutamista bolshevismin historian kysymyksistä", *Kommunisti,* Nov. 1931, pp. 536–544.

[97] Y[rjö] S[irola], "Suomen työväen v:n 1918 vallankumouksen johto bolshevikkien luxemburgilaisena arvostelijana – käytännössä", *Kommunisti,* Jan. 1932, p. 1.

'Quite correct!'" This was the first proof. The second was a little longer. Sirola wrote that he had just found this proof, an article in a "Centrist" publication "Novaja Shisnij" (*sic*), in which the anonymous author wrote in February 1918 that the revolution in Finland differed "essentially" from the Russian "coup": "In the Finnish workers' revolution there are no screaming promises of extravagant Socialism; there is no warring 'implacability' that the rulers of the soldier souls in Smolna so willingly flaunt".[98]

The problem of how to judge the role of Social Democratic, "Centrist", "Kautskyan" leaders, i.e. their own role, was unsolved for the Finnish Communist leaders in exile, although they of course claimed that it had been well settled. Sirola, for example, declared that it had already been solved in Kuusinen's "self-criticism" in summer 1918.[99] For us it is important to note that Stalin's condemnation of "Luxemburgism" was transformed in the leading Communist theoretical journal into criticism of the role of the Social Democratic leaders in the Finnish revolution *via* criticism of Luxemburg's criticism of the Russian revolution![100]

Now, neither Stalin nor Sirola, in the articles cited above, considered Luxemburgism as spontaneous or elementarist, or Rosa Luxemburg as an exponent of instinctiveness. When Hanna Malm spoke of instincts, she was branded as a Luxemburgist. Our task is to chart the path that led to this conclusion.

There have been different opinions about Rosa Luxemburg's spontanism.[101] However, she did indeed use "spontaneous" terminology. In her *Massenstreik, Partei*

---

[98] *Ibid.*, p. 8.

[99] O. W. Kuusinen, *The Finnish Revolution : a Self-Criticism.*

[100] One suspects that Sirola might ultimately not entirely disagree with Luxemburg concerning her judgements of the Russian revolution.

[101] Georg Lukács (*History and Class Consciousness : Studies in Marxist Dialectics*, p. 279) asserts that although Luxemburg "had no illusions about the inevitable relapses, corrective measures and errors of the revolutionary period", she had a "tendency to overestimate the organic element in history". To be sure, this emerges only in her "dogmatic" "conviction that history produces 'along with any real social need the means to its satisfaction, along with the task simultaneously the solution'". For Lukács, however, this was a fatal error, in that she reproached Lenin and Trotskii for their attitude to the Russian Constituent Assembly in 1918. Her attitude to it was "determined" by her "*overestimation of the spontaneous, elemental forces of the Revolution*" (italics in the original). Paul Frölich (*Rosa Luxemburg : Ideas in Action*, p. 143) claims that Luxemburg "perhaps" "overestimated the elementary activity of the masses". Peter Nettl (*Rosa Luxemburg*, p. 156) writes that it is a "fact" that Luxemburg "deliberately over-emphasised the element of the spontaneous" in her *Massenstreik* in the hope of persuading German Social Democrats to accept her analysis. Lelio Basso (*Rosa Luxemburg : a Reappraisal*, p. 105) states that Luxemburg understood "the importance of the unorganized masses in the revolutionary process" and, "substantially" "on the theoretical level no strong objections" can be raised to Luxemburg's conception of mass action, but "in practice she was occasionally inclined to overestimate the spontaneous element". According to Stephen Eric Bronner (*Rosa Luxemburg : a Revolutionary for Our Times*, p. 40), Luxemburg was not a "narrow spontaneist". Richard Abraham (*Rosa Luxemburg : a Life for the International*, p. 68) says that

und Gewerkschaften (1906), Luxemburg wrote, for example, that in the first mass strike in Russia in January 1905 "the demonstrative element" which was not "intentional", but appeared "more in an instinctive, spontaneous form", "still played a great part" (but later, when the Social Democrats called workers to a mass strike to demonstrate for the dissolved Duma, they were not willing to engage "in weak half actions and mere demonstrations").[102] Luxemburg deplored that in German theoretical debate the "spontaneous, elementary character" of the mass strike in Russia had been explained by the "political backwardness" of Russia, the necessity of "overthrowing Oriental despotism" etc.[103] Luxemburg, on the contrary, asserted that also in Germany there would be "a whole period of elementary economic struggles", from which a political struggle would derive; there is a "reciprocity between economic and political struggle".[104] Amongst the Finnish Communists in Russia, the question of elementariness was in some way dealt with at least from 1921. I do not claim that pronouncements on the subject were influenced by Rosa Luxemburg. Nevertheless, the fact is that Hanna Malm was branded as a Luxemburgist.

We need firstly a conceptual clarification: how were the "Luxemburgist" concepts used in the Finnish Communist Party? No less than nine concepts, identical or closely related, were used:

i) elementariness, elemental (*elemen(t)taarisuus, element(t)aarinen*);
ii) instinctiveness, instinctive (*vaisto(n)varaisuus, vaisto(n)varainen*);
iii) primordial might, primordially mighty (*alkuvoima, alkuvoimainen*);
iv) naturalness, natural, or more literally: natural might, invested with natural force (*luonnonvoimaisuus, luonnonvoimainen*);
v) natural instinct, naturally instinctive (*luonnonvaisto, luonnonvaistoinen*);
vi) instinct for life (*elämisen vaisto*);
vii) class instinct (*luokkavaisto*);
viii) spontaneity, spontaneous (*spontanisuus, spontaani*);
ix) self-streaming (*itsevirtauksellinen*).

Luxemburg in 1902 regarded spontaneous general strikes in Belgium in 1891 and 1893 as more successful than the organised one in 1902, and this was the first time she showed an interest in the "concept of 'spontaneity', with which her name has become, somewhat misleadingly, associated by some of her admirers".

[102] Rosa Luxemburg, *Massenstreik, Partei und Gewerskchaften*. Published in Rosa Luxemburg, *Ausgewählte politische Schriften in drei Bänden*, vol. 2, pp. 59–61.

[103] *Ibid*., pp. 64–67.

[104] *Ibid*., p. 73. It should be noted that Luxemburg was at least no exponent of fatalism. She wrote, for instance: "Social Democracy is the most enlightened, most class-conscious vanguard of the proletariat. It cannot and must not wait in fatalist fashion, with crossed arms for the arising of the "revolutionary situation", expecting a spontaneous people's movement to fall from the sky." (*Ibid*., p. 79.)

These words were not in day-to-day use; amongst the Communists they were used, at least mostly, as ideological concepts. In addition, the word *vaisto* (instinct) was used in Luxemburgist contexts, but it was not, of course, a construct similar to the other words.[105]

In the following section I shall present some examples of these terms as used by the Finnish Communists. Of all terms, I use the English translations given above. There are six examples.

i. The first example is from Party chairman Kullervo Manner's speech in the IVth Congress of the SKP in 1921. As pointed out above, in this Congress two factions, one led by Kullervo Manner and Eino Rahja and the other by O. W. Kuusinen, cleared up relations between them. Manner probably felt he had been encouraged by Zinov'ev to regard Kuusinen as a Western Communist and himself as a "Eastern Communist" endowed with superior awareness. He could thus declare (italics on all examples mine):[106]

> The Kuusinenites acquired their petty-bourgeois *elementariness* when they were in Stockholm, where they were acquainted with Western literature and were actually not under the Communist control of the East.

One of the manifestations of this "elementariness" was, according to Manner, the fact that Kuusinen sought to "strongly" oppose "Prussian discipline" in the Party.[107]

In 1924, the SKP had to condemn Trotskii. Manner suggested that in the declaration of the Party Trotskii be branded as a "petty-bourgeois". In the Central Committee, this move was opposed on various grounds. After Manner had explained – and announced that Zinov'ev demanded a decision – that by this statement the SKP sought to counter "petty-bourgeois *elementariness* in our country and our Party", the statement in which the SKP condemned Trotskii was unanimously accepted.[108] Who it was who represented this elementariness in the SKP was not said, but apparently it was the Murder Opposition.

ii. There is a similar statement by Sirola in an article he wrote in 1928, already cited above. Sirola, who, as noted, had a tendency to be exceedingly self-critical, wrote an article on the history of the SKP for some kind of anthology to be pub-

---

[105] The Russian word Lenin and Stalin usually used for "instinct" was *stikhiia.* In 1931 Yrjö Sirola suggested *vaistonvaraisuus* as a consistent Finnish translation. (Manner to Malm, Dec. 30, 1932, MMC, pp. 119–120.)

[106] Minutes of the IVth Congress of the SKP, July 25 – Aug. 10, 1921. RGASPI, f. 516, op. 2, 1921, d. 2, l. 136.

[107] *Ibid.*, l. 140.

[108] Manner's memorandum about the (probably unofficial) meeting of the CC, three days before the beginning of the XIIIth Conference of the VKP(b), i.e. January 13, 1924. RGASPI, f. 516, op. 2, 1924, d. 29.

lished in Russian. Writing about events and ideological developments before the fourth Party Congress (1921), he stated:[109]

> Some comrades, who were mainly abroad [i.e. in Finland or Sweden], who had an intention to remedy the crisis [in the Party], proposed such "democratic" measures that they had to bow to *instinctiveness,* to vagueness and instability of the non-proletarian "mass".

In the two first examples, "elementariness" and "instinctiveness" are in no way connected with the working masses, or non-educated Party leaders. Sirola's "mass" refers to his own petty-bourgeois surroundings. It is also interesting to note what Sirola meant by instinctiveness. It was comparable with "vagueness and instability".

When the Finnish organisation of the VKP(b) protested the release of the members of the Murder Opposition, it stated that the release "in our opinion tends hazardously to shake the morale of the masses and can also be a seed for different impulses and eruptions of *instinctiveness*".[110]

iii. The following example considers the leaders in Finland. In 1930 the Party Conference accused the leaders of the Finnish Trade Union Federation of a general strike, which was complete fiasco, as we have seen. The Conference proclaimed:[111]

> When the opportunists [i.e. the leaders of the Trade Union Federation] declared a general strike, they on the one hand, bowed before the *primordially mighty* pressure of the masses and, on the other, consciously sought to isolate our Party from the masses, calculating that if the general strike was successful, it had taken place under *their* leadership. If it failed, they could accuse our Party of "Ultraleftist" agitation.

Here we note a phenomenon described above as *khvostism*, going along with the working masses without leading them. The explanation given by the emigrant lead of the SKP meant, in other words, that the unorganised masses were dissatisfied and sought – in vain – revolutionary leadership. It is not clear, however, why they were dissatisfied, why there was this "*primordially mighty* pressure". Were the workers really dissatisfied because the Communist prisoners were on a hunger strike? We

---

[109] Yrjö Sirola, "Suomen Kommunistinen Puolue", a manuscript for an article to be published by "Moskovskij Pabotshij" (*sic*). Written after December 1, 1928. RGASPI, f. 525, op. 1, d. 23, l. 10.

[110] The Central Office of the Finnish Associations of the VKP(b) to the CC of the VKP, no date, not before March 1922. RGASPI, f. 516, op. 2, 1922, d. 14, l. 2.)

[111] The Economic Political Situation of Finland and the main tasks of the SKP. Accepted in the Conference of the SKP, Aug. 29–Sept. 15, 1930. RGASPI, f. 516, op. 2, 1930, d. 13, l. 10. See also Manner to Malm, Dec. 6–8, 1932, MMC, pp. 74–75.

may think that from the point of view of the Communist leaders the masses had to be dissatisfied with such a state of affairs.

iv. In November 1932 Hanna Malm wrote a letter to Kullervo Manner in which she referred to "Letter to Comrades" written by Lenin in October 1917. In her letter, Malm noted that in a Finnish translation of Lenin's letter, "instinctive" is expressed by the word "naturally mighty".[112] Lenin's letter is a polemic against L. B. Kamenev and G. E. Zinov'ev, who voted against the coup d'état in the Central Committee of the Bolshevik Party. Lenin explained that the rebellion was at the time on the agenda because the Soviets in Petrograd and Moscow were in the hands of the Bolsheviks. This had not been so in some earlier cases in 1917. Of them Lenin wrote (the quotation is from the Finnish translation Malm used):[113]

> The [present] situation is not such as it was before April 20–21, June 9, [and] July 3, because in those cases it was *naturally mighty* (*stikhiinyj*)[114] *excitement*, of which we, as a Party, did not take consideration (April 20–21) or direct to a normal peaceful demonstration (June 9 and July 3).

Lenin's original Russian word was *stikhiinyj*, "elemental", "spontaneous", "unbridled".

v–viii. When Malm once wrote to Manner about instinctiveness and explained that in some struggles of the workers in Finland the Communists had not prepared for them, she used different concepts in the following way:[115]

> They have been born down with *primordial might* of the masses, their instinctiveness; they have bowed to it and gone with it as long as the course of *instinctiveness* sufficed. Moreover, in this meaning economic strikes are *primordially mighty*, caused by the *instinct* of life of the workers – the movements took place because there was lack of bread.

Manner answered by quoting a letter by Yrjö Sirola, in which Sirola referred to the concepts "instinctiveness, "spontaneity", "primordial might" and "natural might". Sirola suggested that there should be a "fixed" word; his recommendation was "instinctiveness". According to Sirola, this meant a "popular movement" (*kansanliike*) impelled by the "class instinct", not by "natural instinct" or by "primordial might" (*alkuvoima*). It seems that Manner agreed with Sirola: he stated that "instinct for life" is included with "class instinct". He pointed out that Lenin

---

112 Malm to Manner, Nov. 25, 1932. MMC, p. 66.

113 V. I. Lenin, "Kirje tovereille", *Kommunisti*, Oct. 15, 1932, p. 897.

114 В. И Ленин, "Письмо к товарищам", *Рабочий Путь*, Oct. 19, 20 and 21 (Nov. 1, 2 and 3). PSS, vol. 34, p. 412.

115 Malm to Manner, Dec. 16–17, 1932. MMC, p. 97–98, quotation on p. 98.

and Stalin used the words "*stikhiia*" and "*stikhiinost*'"; they meant, according to Manner, "natural might" and "primordial might", but that "probably" did not mean, for Lenin and Stalin that there was no "class instinct".[116] – Malm had been in trouble with her concept of "*instinct* for the preservation of life". We shall have a look at Malm's difficulties at a later point.

ix. The concept "self-streaming" (*itsevirtauksellinen*) and the noun *itsevirtauksellisuus* were rare. They were probably used only in the Finnish spoken in Russian East Karelia. In a letter to Manner Malm referred to the extremely "bestial" treatment of horses by the new kolkhoz peasants in Ukhta and the lack of fodder for horses. She criticized the District Committee of the VKP(b) in Ukhta for not taking into account what happens in the kolkhozes in regard to feeding animals. The mistake was that the District Committee had allowed everything to proceed under its own weight, "self-streamedly".[117]

The role of the Communist Party in the struggles of workers in capitalist countries and its role in the Soviet Union were what was ultimately at stake. At the beginning of the 1930s the problem was acute, because all legal organisations were decimated by the authorities. Underground organisations of the SKP were weak and they – therefore, I should like to say – trusted in a spontaneous struggle of the workers. A certain "Martti" told the Plenum of the Central Committee of the SKP in July 1932 that the Tampere underground District Committee had issued a declaration in which, referring to a strike in an airplane factory there, it stated that "finally misery will force the workers to the struggle". For "Martti" this expressed a trust in "primordial might", because in the declaration the "importance and necessity of the Party as an organiser and leader of the struggle of the masses was not pointed out".[118]

One interesting point in this muddle of concepts, is that there was also an antonym to all the above expressions. Marxist-Leninist "dialectics", we may say, required this, although the actors did not perhaps understand the matter in these terms. The antonym was "vanguardism" (*avangardism*). Kullervo Manner condemned biased emphasis of the role of the Communist Youth Movement in the history of the SKP as "vanguardism".[119]

---

[116] Manner to Malm, Dec. 30, 1932, MMC, pp. 119–120.

[117] Malm to Manner, Feb. 19, 1933, MMC, pp. 235–237.

[118] MPCC, July 8 – July 24, 1932. RGASPI, f. 516, op. 2, 1932, d. 3, ll. 52–53.

[119] An activist of the Communist Youth Movement, Inkeri Lehtinen, edited a history of the Communist Youth International, in which one A. Azarkin wrote that in Finland the said international organisation was able to "conquer" young people and revolutionise it so that they, assisted by the Comintern, were able to establish the Finnish Communist Party. (A. Azarkin, "KNI:n II kongressi Heinäkuun 9–23 päivinä 1921" in *KNI:n historia sen kongressien valossa*, p. 84.) Manner was concerned about the facts, which "went all wrong" (*vallan päin mäntyä*). He also said that there was much "vanguardism" in this history. (Manner to Malm, Dec. 6. – Dec. 8, 1932. MMC, p. 77.) One may consider a symptom of vanguardism in a statement by the underground Viipuri District Com-

We may now conclude. It seems that there were two basic instances of instinctiveness, elementariness etc.

1. Communist leaders could be in the state of instinctiveness etc., when they behaved erroneously, heretically and deviantly. The impulse to such behaviour comes invariably from the petty-bourgeoisie (examples (i), (ii) and (iii)). We may also consider case in which the source of influence would be the state of instinctiveness of the working masses. The theory of a labour aristocracy would, of course, produce such a case. One further instance might be leaders who are under the influence of the peasants. I have not found such cases in my material.

2. The working masses can be in a state of instinctiveness because, or at least mainly because, there is no vanguard or the vanguard is weak. Here there are four variations:

2a. There are no Communist leaders, or if there are, they allow things to proceed without leading the struggle of the masses. The vanguard is simply absent. We may call this a case of default. This kind of explanation occurred in example (ix).

2b. There are leaders, but they are themselves not proletarians, or at least have no proletarian background (example (v)). We may call this an ouvrierist variant.

2c. The leaders are there, but they are impure, corrupted and degenerate (examples (v–viii)). We may call this an opportunist variant.

2d. There is a more or less adequate vanguard, but the political situation is chaotic, for example after a defeat in a revolution (example (iv)). We may call this a situational variant.

All these cases were from the time prior to Stalin's letter, so that the Luxemburgist argument did not explicitly emerge. It seems that in the Finnish Party this argument – that elementarism etc. is specifically a Luxemburgist heresy – occurred only after Stalin's letter. G. Badia states that the term "Luxemburgism" first appeared in 1925,[120] but he does not say where and in what context.

Among the Finns in Russia there was one notable case in which the term Luxemburgism appeared before the Malm case. In February 1932 Pentti Lund (Uuno Väre), a stipendiary (*aspirant*) in the Lenin School, published in the newspaper *Vapaus*, which appeared in Leningrad, an article entitled "The events of the year 1918 under Bolshevist self-criticism". This Lund was a friend of Manner and Malm; we may indeed say that he belonged to the Malm and Manner Opposition. What is especially interesting here is that Lund said that his source of inspiration was Stalin's letter, but he dealt with Luxemburgism in a non-Stalinist way. In con-

---

mittee (issued probably in 1932) in which the Committee demanded that the *Eduskunta* "must soon leave its place to the Manner government of 1918". ("Martti" in the Plenum of the CC. MPCC, July 8–July 24, 1932. RGASPI, f. 516, op. 2, 1932, d. 3, l. 52.)

[120] G. Badia, "Luxemburgisme" in *Dictionnaire critique du marxisme*, pp. 534–535.

trast he saw Luxemburgism as an expression of instinctiveness and primordial might.

Lund claimed that the self-criticism concerning the role of the Social Democratic leaders of the People's Deputation had been highly inadequate and had been based solely on Kuusinen's old text of the revolution. Thus, Social Democratic theories had not been "exposed" to the "working masses". If one looks at the old criticism based on Stalin's letter, one notes a "marked deficiency": Lund wrote:[121]

> This is, for example, the case especially in the questions involving the influence of the theories of Kautskyism and Luxemburgism on the causes of the 1918 defeat. However, Kautskyan conciliation and vacillation, Luxemburgian confidence in instinctiveness and primordial mightiness, were most characteristic features of the Soc. Dem. Party, which was in the lead of the revolution. These features exerted a crucial influence then and still influence the whole progression of our struggle.

Lund's conclusion was that Kautskyism and Luxemburgism must be exposed to the masses because there were still strong remnants of them. The "Fascist coup" (i.e. the suppression of the Communist movement) in Finland in 1930 points this out as does "abandonment to primordial might and the coming of the [Russian] Red Army".[122]

Was Hanna Malm a "Luxemburgist"?

We have seen that Hanna Malm wrote in Finland in 1921 about factory councils and even about a conglomerate of these councils which should take over state power. Examples of factory councils in Germany had inspired her. At the time Malm was not – as far as I know – accused of "Luxemburgism", the word itself, moreover, if it was used, was not pejorative. Now, in 1932, times were different. Nonetheless, Hanna Malm did not, I assume, have in mind either Luxemburgist elementarism or Stalin's letter when in April 1932 she wrote a polemical article – which proved to be fateful for her – against Lyyli Latukka, the editor of *Neuvostonainen* ("Soviet Woman"), who had published in the journal her article "Situation in Fascist Finland". Here Latukka recounted the programme of the Lapua Movement, which included the "abolition of the right to vote".[123] Malm considered this misleading

---

[121] P[entti] L[u]nd, "V. 1918 tapahtumat Suomessa bolshevistisen itsekritiikin alaiseksi", *Vapaus*, Feb. 14, 1932.

[122] *Ibid.*

[123] Lyyli L[atukka], "Tilanne fasisti-Suomessa", *Neuvostonainen* 2, Jan. 1932, p. 6. In summer 1930, the Lapua Movement demanded a reduction in the number of the MPs (it had been 200 since 1907), a change in the electoral system to a British-style majority system and unequal vote, so that people who paid high taxes have more votes than people whose incomes are low (Reijo Perälä, *Lapuan liike ja sanan mahti*, p. 246). In addition, a demand that only a part of the MPs be elected by the

because universal suffrage had already been suppressed in 1930 when the "remnants of democracy" were removed from "revolutionary workers". She claimed that such talk of "suppressing universal suffrage" served only the "enemies", especially the Social Democrats, who agitated workers to "defend the 'present democratic state' against all who threaten its constitution". Because as far as Malm was concerned the Fascists were already in power in Finland, there was nothing to defend.[124] The worst point in Latukka's article was, however, her conclusion: the "Finnish workers are becoming more and more conscious of the policy of the bourgeoisie and the Social Fascists and are preparing themselves, under the leadership of the Communist Party, for the struggle".[125] Malm commented on this somewhat confusingly. The workers were not "preparing themselves" for the struggle because there was the Communist Party, which "explained" the "necessity" of the struggle of the workers against the leaders of the bourgeoisie and the Social Democrats. However[126]

> the Party cannot confine itself **solely to point out** this necessity, because the working masses have drifted into this struggle without the lead of the Comparty. It is the instinct of the exploited masses for the preservation of life of individuals, as well as the whole, which drives them in larger and smaller numbers onto the path of the necessity and incontrovertibleness of the struggle.

According to Malm, "nearly all labour disputes" in Finland had been "raised on workers' own initiative" and had therefore come about by "the instinct for the preservation of life". In addition, the "instinctive struggle" led on to the "aim", which is the "freeing of the workers from bearing the consequences of depression". This is, however, not enough; the workers should not only "prepare" themselves for the "struggles ahead". If this path were adopted, the result would be an "instinctive rush to and for whatever demand would at any given time concern the everyday life of the working masses". At the same time, "a part of the workers would well prepare for the armed struggle for the overthrow of the bourgeoisie". According to Malm, Latukka had stated correctly what was the "aim", now in the sense of the

---

people and the rest by employers, universities and the central state administration, was presented (Martti Ahti, *Kaappaus? : Suojeluskuntaselkkaus 1921 : fascismin aave 1927 : Mäntsälän kapina 1932*, p. 130.) The Lapua Movement did not demand the complete abolition of suffrage; it did however demand, for instance, that people who lived in poorhouses (as in old-age homes), or depended on full poor relief, should not have the right of vote. A British-type electoral system would realise a more "healthy situation" in the "party system" (*puolueolot*) (Arvo Kokko, *Lapuan laki : talonpoikaisliike Suomessa v. 1930*, vol. 1, p. 58).

[124] Hanna Malm, "Ei oikealle eikä vasemmalle", *Vapaus*, April 23, 1932.

[125] Lyyli L[atukka], "Tilanne fasisti-Suomessa", *Neuvostonainen*, 2, Jan. 1932, p. 6.

[126] Hanna Malm, "Ei oikealle eikä vasemmalle", *Vapaus*, April 23, 1932.

ultimate aim, the "overthrow of the capitalist system". But Malm reproached Latukka for not stating how this aim was to be attained: "But by what *path*, overcoming what obstacles would the workers attain this aim, to which also their instinctive struggle, in fact, leads."[127] This was, of course, a heretical statement: the "instinctive struggle" can lead to the overthrow of Capitalism.

Lyyli Latukka together with the editors of the *Vapaus* published two answers to Malm in the same issue in which her article was published. In both answers, the question of instincts occupied an important place. For Latukka it was a heresy to state that the workers could struggle without the direction of the Communist Party. It meant a "lowering of the [revolutionary] movement to the level of primordial might".[128] The editors of the paper claimed that the SKP had led the struggles and generally[129]

> the claim that the struggles of the workers in Finland had originated solely from the instinct of self-preservation was not and could not be, correct in the present era of Capitalism and Imperialism, neither in Finland, nor elsewhere.

Malm's article was intended for publication in *Neuvostonainen*. It was instead published in *Vapaus*, which was a much larger forum than the womens' journal. Why did Malm write her polemical article and why did she resort to the argument of instincts? One question is the language of Malm's letter. It is incorrect and confusing.[130] It is evident that Malm did not show the article to her husband Kullervo Manner, chairman of the SKP, because he would surely have corrected the obvious mistakes. But why did the editors of *Vapaus* publish the article without correcting the language? The language in Communist publications was, of course, not always particularly polished, but in any case, Malm's article was an exception in this regard. We do not, of course, know what happened behind the scenes. It is possible that Malm refused all suggestions to enhance the language. Nevertheless, it is also possible that the editors of *Vapaus* published the article in its confusing form precisely to discredit Malm. Perhaps for that very reason the article was published in *Vapaus* and not in *Neuvostonainen.*

---

[127] *Ibid.*

[128] Lyyli Latukka, "Toveri Hanna Malmin kirjoituksen johdosta", *Vapaus*, April 23, 1932.

[129] *Vapaus*, April 23, 1932.

[130] There is, for example, the following sentence: "But it is fact that in summer 1930 the bourgeoisie seized the remnants of democracy (vote and eligibility in parliamentary elections) for revolutionary workers and their organisations public freedom of action which the workers could have preserved for themselves as a result of their own everlasting struggle from earlier and also in the period after the Russian revolution of 1905." (Hanna Malm, "Ei oikealle eikä vasemmalle", *Vapaus*, April 23, 1932.) I have tried to translate this passage as literally as I can.

Why this article? We can only speculate. It seems that Latukka was not Malm's best friend.[131] In emigrant circumstances, personal sympathies and antipathies were important; without taking account of this factor, it would be impossible to understand the hair-splitting and continuous wrangles, often about the most trivial matters. Why, then, the argument of instinctiveness? My guess is that Malm as an independent-minded individual simply thought in this way. We do not – necessarily – need any explanation about conspiracies here. From her Moscow observation-tower Malm looked at what was going on in Finland; she had no possibilities of having any impact on events there. From the Communist point of view, the prospects were desolate: the extreme Right fêted, the Communists were almost non-existent.[132] Due to depression, the lot of the workers was harsh. However, there were isolated strikes and spontaneous demonstrations here and there. Why not think that precisely the "instinct for the preservation of life" was the motive force behind these tumblings among the workers?

Malm continued the polemic. She tried especially to purify herself from the sin of underestimating the role of the Party in the struggles of the workers. That "primordial might plays a role in the movements of workers" does not mean that the "Comparty and Revolutionary Organisations" should not work to transform these "primordial movements into a *conscious* movement" by "bringing elements of revolutionary consciousness to that primordial might" so that the "movement can rise to a *higher* political level, as Com. Lenin teaches us".[133] Her new article, however, did not absolve her. The editors of *Vapaus* gathered up her schismatical statements. She had underrated the Communist Party by arguing that, i) the working masses had "drifted" into the struggle without the Communist Party, ii) the "instinctive struggle of the workers also led to the aim" and iii) the "instinct for the preservation of life" could be a motivating force in the struggle. The editors stated that in her new article Malm wrote about instinctiveness "more appropriately", but did not admit any of her mistakes. She did not make any "Bolshevist criticism" of her-

---

[131] Malm to Manner, Feb. 19, 1933, MMC, p. 233. Malm says that one of her friends in the village of her deportation, Ukhta, who wrote for a small district newspaper, would be a better editor of *Neuvostonainen* than Latukka.

[132] Kullervo Manner wrote in summer 1931 that all campaigns the Communists tried to organise, namely on the Day of Unemployed, February 25 and on First of May, came to nothing. (K. Manner, "Tärkeimpien joukkokamppailujemme epäonnistumisen johdosta", *Proletaari*, 6, 1931, p. 10.

[133] Hanna Malm, "Vieläkin vaistonvaraisuudesta Suomen työläisten taisteluissa viime vuonna ja vähän muustakin", *Vapaus*, May 24, 1932. Malm had presented a similar argument in an article on the tasks of the Party in *Proletaari*, an underground journal of the Party. She stated in this article that one criterion of "Bolshevik skill to approach the masses" was that "although we place ourselves on the level of the masses, we do not remain on this level". The Communists were "before the masses" and "they illustrate, clarify and assure" to the masses the "inner laws of Capitalism" which the masses do not "right away understand". (Mutteri [Hanna Malm], "Puolueemme ja taistelu työväen elinehtojen puolesta", *Proletaari*, 1, 1931, p. 24.)

self.[134] This was a rather ominous estimation at the time. As far as I know this was the last time Malm had a possibility to publish any factional article in the Party press.

There cannot be an unambiguous answer to the question whether Malm was a "Luxemburgist" or not. She was not, and could not be, a "Luxemburgian", a straight follower of Rosa Luxemburg's doctrines. However, if we mean by "Luxemburgism" a vague conception of spontaneity etc., we can conclude that Malm used such vocabulary. In any case, she was a "Luxemburgist" only in parentheses.

Consequences of Malm's "Luxemburgism"

Malm's instinct article had an important place among the sins which the Plenum of the Central Committee dealt with in July 1932. The most authoritative was Kuusinen's condemnation. According to Kuusinen, Malm's article was confusing because she did not at all take "class boundaries" into account. The "instinct for the preservation of life", Kuusinen said, is common not only to all humans but also to animals. Kuusinen surmised that Manner had not read the article before it was published. Manner's reaction to this was the interjection "do not conspire" (*ei konspireerata*).[135] Of Malm's "enterprises", Kuusinen said, not very cordially, that one "should not to speak much of them, because Hanna is not really capable of discernment (*arvostelukykyinen*) in these subjects".[136] Toivo Antikainen declared that although Malm also wrote about the role of the Party, her "thesis of the instinct for life" denied the role of the Party.[137] Jukka Lehtosaari condemned Malm as a representative of the "theory of spontaneity".[138]

Another sin was Malm's speech in the Club of Estonians in the Lenin School where in January 1932 she argued that the leaders of the Finnish Revolution in 1918, including Manner, were traitors to the working-class. When she was reproached for this in the Plenum of the Central Committee, she declared in her defence the following:[139]

> At the beginning of the revolution I was set in the Department of the War Affairs. Difficult task. I had to struggle against a counter-revolutionary body of intellectuals, who were trying to get out of the country. Com. Haapalainen [Commander-in-Chief] had given me a standing order that nobody should be allowed to leave. I was constantly in dispute over this with Com. Sirola [People's Deputy of Foreign Af-

[134] "Eräitä huomautuksia tov. Malmin kirjoituksen johdosta", *Vapaus*, May 24, 1932.

[135] MPCC, July 6–24, 1932. RGASPI, f. 516, op. 2, 1932, d. 4, l. 359.

[136] *Ibid.*, l. 367.

[137] MPCC, July 6–24, 1932. RGASPI, f. 516, op. 2, 1932, d. 3, ll. 114–115.

[138] *Ibid.*, l. 58.

[139] *Ibid.*, l. 226.

> fairs]. Often gentlewomen came to me and appealed with tears to the cultivated Sirola, who treated them humanly and would let them go, but I, who am a workingwoman, do not. I have said that my proletarian class instinct aroused me to struggle against them. Was it wrong? It was not.

We shall discuss the long controversy over the nature of the revolution in 1918 below. However, this is an interesting ouvrierist *passus*, because it seems that Malm thought she was above the gentry in the Party, because she in her youth she had been a worker (a bookbinder) and thus had genuine "class instinct", something which educated could not have. It was immediately pointed out by various speakers that Malm had been a quarter of century out of physical work.[140] Malm's worst mistake was, however, to declare, as we have already seen that "if in the SKP it is not permissible to speak of the treachery [of 1918] because Com. Kuusinen was in the leadership of the Communist International, I, as a Communist, submit to that".[141] She was condemned by Vikentii Simanovich Michkevich-Kapsukas,[142] the representative of the Comintern in the SKP, who announced that Malm's statement was a "slander" of Kuusinen and the Comintern.[143]

Malm had now to condemn herself. She stated in writing that she had slandered Kuusinen, the Comintern and the lead of the SKP. It was "the most grave mistake" and "I condemn it as an inclination to Trotskyism".[144] Malm also announced that she accepted Kuusinen's "rectification" in the matter of instinctiveness.[145] This did not prevent her condemnation in public. Malm was reproached for "adulation of the instinctiveness of the masses". The representatives of this deviation did not do "serious work to raise the revolutionary spirit of the masses", but instead of doing "true Bolshevik mass work they went into high-sounding phrases".[146] From the resolution "On the work in the ideological front" one could read that "special attention" must be given to the[147]

---

140 Jukka Lehtosaari (MPCC, July 6–24, 1932. RGASPI, f. 516, op. 2, 1932, d. 4, l. 315) and Toivo Antikainen (*Ibid.*, l. 324).

141 MPCC, July 6–24, 1932. RGASPI, f. 516, op. 2, 1932, d. 3, l. 226.

142 This is Russified form of the name of the Lithuanian Communist leader Vintsas Mitskjavitshjus-Kapsukas. The Russified form was used in publications and documents of the SKP.

143 MPCC, July 6–24, 1932. RGASPI, f. 516, op. 2, 1932, d. 3, ll. 275–276.

144 Hanna Malm, Announcement of the Plenum of the CC of the SKP. MPCC, July 6–24, 1932. RGASPI, f. 516, op. 2, 1932, d. 4, ll. 277–278.

145 MPCC, July 6–24, 1932. RGASPI, f. 516, op. 2, 1932, d. 4, l. 390.

146 Iivo [Antti Hyvönen], "Suomen kommunistisen puolueen KK:n täysi-istunto", *Kommunisti*, Oct. 15, 1932, p. 884.

147 *Suomen Kommunistinen Puolue : puoluekokousten, konferenssien ja Keskuskomitean Plenumien päätöksiä : ensimmäinen kokoelma*, p. 409.

> "struggle against the worship of instinctiveness, be it either a Rightist opportunist defence of one's own inactivity and inefficiency [...] or 'Leftist' exaggeration of unprompted readiness for the struggle of the workers (for example Com. H. Malm's articles in *Vapaus*).

In November 1932, Malm was deported to Ukhta. There she tried to collect material to prove that leaders of the international Communist movement had also spoken of elementariness. She, for example, asked Kullervo Manner to send her the Finnish translation of excerpts of the journal *Kommunisticheskii Internatsional.*[148] One of these was from a speech by Dmitrii Zakharovich Manuilskii, who had stated that many Communist parties had to fight for the "lead of primordially mighty movements, not in such an organisational and political situation as we should like, but in such as history gives us".[149] Malm was excited when *Kommunisti* published Lenin's *Letter to Comrades,* described above.[150]

In November 1932, *Vapaus* published an article in which Malm – although her name was not mentioned – was accused of "Leftism". The "representatives" of this Leftist deviation "slander the Party about remaining behind and [when compared with] the radicalisation of the masses and revolutionary movements, supposedly 'originated from the instinct for the preservation of life,'" although this radicalisation was a "result of the tough and unyielding work of the Party among the masses".[151] Malm was now able to defend herself only in her private letters to Manner and in the meetings of the local organisations of the VKP(b) in Ukhta. She declared to Manner that economic strikes in Finland originated from the "instinct for the preservation of life", i.e. the "lack of bread". She wondered how leading Communists could assert that in all "primordially mighty" movements there was influence from the Communist Party. She posed the question why, then, were there not even instinctive movements in Finland. Her conclusion was that in Russia Finnish Communists overestimated the importance of the Party in Finland, in other words, they deceived people. Malm could not understand why and for whom this was done. She appealed to Manner to do something:[152]

> Listen now, my dear friend and colleague. One cannot pass over in silence this kind of presentation of affairs. You have the opportunity and duty seize upon such. Silence is just rotten Liberalism.

---

[148] Malm to Manner, Nov. 25, 1932, MMC, p. 65.

[149] The excerpt was originally published in *Коммунистический Интернационал*, Sept. 30, 1932, pp. 28–29. Manner's translation is in Jukka Paastela and Hannu Rautkallio, "Viitteet" in MMC, p. 458.

[150] Hanna Malm to Kullervo Manner, Nov. 25, 1932, MMC, p. 65.

[151] R. S. (probably Rutu Salomaa pseudonym of Matti Janhunen), "Suomen proletariaatti Lokakuun opetuksia omaksumassa", *Vapaus*, Nov. 6, 1932.

[152] Malm to Manner, Dec. 16, 1932, MMC, pp. 99–100, quotation on p. 100.

Manner answered with a long speculation on the concepts. The "instinct for life" is the "most primitive impulse" in which there is no "influence of class consciousness". For example in many strikes there appear both "instinct for life" and "instinct for class". Manner actually, however, agreed with Malm as to the isolation of the Party in Finland. He related the Finnish case to that in Norway, of which it was said in the Scandinavian Secretariat of the Comintern that there reigns an "abstract-sectarian stance and practice".[153]

Manner could be outspoken and candid in this way in a private letter; in the Party he was solicitous and apprehensive: he tried, above all, to calm the situation and save Malm from further punishments and, ultimately, from expulsion.

The Confrontation over the Finnish Revolution

There was, as one would expect, much debate about why the 1918 revolution was a flop. In 1928, the Central Committee of the SKP accepted a resolution on this subject. It was claimed that the revolutionary situation during the general strike in November 1917 should have been taken into account. Workers, according to the document, opposed a halt to the strike in many towns. The reason why this revolutionary situation was neglected was the lack of a Bolshevik Party.[154] This was a mistake. The second mistake, now in the spring 1918, was the Swiss-type draft for a constitution for Red Finland. There was nothing about the dictatorship of the proletariat in the document.[155] Finally, nothing was created that would have resembled the Cheka in Soviet Russia. There were also no "revolutionary tribunals".[156]

The question why there was no Bolshevik Party in Finland during her "revolutionary situations" in 1917–1918, was widely discussed among émigré circles from the very beginning of the emigration. In 1928, the tenth anniversary of the Civil War, it was natural that theses were published and meetings were organised. What is important is the overall impression of the document: it was relatively modest, if not analytical. The reference to the Cheka was the most "radical" point in the text.

The "betrayal theory" was very likely Hanna Malm's creation.[157] It was, however, Kullervo Manner who firstly presented it in the prestigious forum of the Foreign

---

153 Manner to Malm, Dec. 30, 1932, MMC, pp. 120–121.

154 Suomen Kommunistisen Puolueen Keskuskomitean teesit Suomen vallankumouksesta 1918 (Theses about the Finnish revolution by the CC of the SKP). Published in *Kommunisti* 1/1929 under the title "Suomen Työväen vallankumous v. 1918", thesis 15, p. 14.

155 *Ibid.*, thesis 15, p. 14.

156 *Ibid.*, thesis 29, p. 19.

157 KK:n Plenumin [1932] poliittisen valiokunnan työjaoston luonnos päätöslauselmaksi Hanna Malmin puolueenvastaisen työn ryhmäkuntaisuudesta ja sen kannattamisesta toveri Mannerin taholta. (A draft of the working section of the political committee of Plenum [1932] of the CC [of

Bureau of the SKP in Moscow. He had five points on what the leaders of the Finnish revolution (including Manner himself) should have done in 1918.

i) There were Right, Centre and Left (among the Red Guards); Manner, Kuusinen, Sirola etc. belonged to the Centre. It was that Centre which "salvaged" the unity of the Social Democratic Party.[158] According to Manner the threat of a split presented by the Right did not make the correct impact on the Centre. At this time,[159] it would have been a splendid occasion to split the Party. ii) The Party refused its "*Socialist* task" during the general strike of November 1917, although there was Lenin's letter in which it was suggested that the Social Democrats should take power. (At this point comes Kuusinen's note in the margin: "The letter was written after the general strike"). iii) It was a fateful mistake not to take power in November 1917. The initiative would have been in "our hands" and it should have been easy to split the Social Democratic Party. iv) The Finnish Right-Wing Social Democrats were helping the bourgeoisie "and we by our half-heartedness objectively helped the bourgeoisie". Now, faced with the capitulation in 1930, "I completely understood my mistake in 1918", Manner declared. v) Kuusinen had proclaimed that although there were many errors it was important that Social Democracy and the workers mobilised by that Party fought. They fought, Manner agreed, but this was not the point. The key question was how to fight and "we fought poorly", not energetically enough.[160]

The most important argument in the perspective of this present study is point (iv). In proclaiming that the Social Democrats during the Civil War "objectively" helped the bourgeoisie, Manner came close to the argument that Social Democratic leaders consciously betrayed the Finnish revolution. Even closer to this argument Manner seems to have come in a speech in the Club of Estonians in the Lenin School in March 1932. He had said there that the leaders did not betray out of "malice", but their weakness, half-heartedness, vacillation etc. meant that there was a betrayal. The Social Democrats cut off the general strike. The Social Democratic Party was guilty, not the working masses. Thus, it was an "outrageous falsification" on the part of Kuusinen, Manner muttered, to say that "the genius of revolt passed over the country [but we] did not mount upon its wings",[161] i.e. the leaders

---

the SKP] for a decision on Hanna Malm's factional anti–Party activity and its backing by Comrade Manner.) RGASPI, 516, op. 2, 1932, d. 11.

[158] This is not an accurate description of what happened. There were Rightist leaders – Väinö Tanner became most famous of them – who did not accept the rebellion and did not participate in it at all.

[159] It is difficult to know what time Manner was speaking of; it could be any time between November 1917 and February 1918.

[160] Minutes of the meeting of the Foreign Bureau of the SKP (hereafter abriged as MMFB), April 4, 1932. RGASPI, op. 516, op. 2, 1930, d. 1, ll. 12–43, with Kuusinen's remarks in the margin. The same document is located in RGASPI, op. 516, op. 2, 1932, d. 14, but without Kuusinen's remarks.

[161] O. W. Kuusinen, *The Finnish Revolution : a Self-Criticism*, p. 6.

did not have as their aim the dictatorship of the proletariat, whereas the working-class had.[162] (One may ask how the working-class could have the dictatorship of the proletariat as an aim, when the workers did not know what the dictatorship of the proletariat meant.)

There was a fiery debate over Malm and Manner and the "betrayal thesis" in the Plenum of the Central Committee of the SKP in July 1932. Jukka Lehtosaari, the editor of *Kommunisti*, told the Plenum that "Com. Manner had given up his betrayal thesis". However, Manner had, according to Lehtosaari, developed a new thesis according to which the struggle of the Emir of Afghanistan against imperialism is analogous with the situation in Finland in 1918;[163] there the leaders were also, like the Emir of Afghanistan, furthering the world revolution although they did not know it.[164]

Yrjö Sirola took the question of betrayal very seriously. In the 1932 Party Conference he, firstly, explained what kind of word Lenin has used when he wrote about betrayal. There had been betrayals in recent history, Sirola explicated. The behaviour of German Social Democracy in 1914 was treacherous; in Hungary, Social Democracy betrayed the working-class in 1919. But Finland? Sirola told the Plenum that he had enquired of Aleksander Shottman, who met Lenin at the end of 1917, what Lenin had said about the retreat of the Finnish Social Democrats in November 1917. Shottman had told Sirola that Lenin was very "angry". To Sirola's question "did he say that they betrayed, Shottman had said no, he did not say that, but angry he was". For Sirola the central question was the arming of the workers. In Germany after the First World War, the Social Democrats urged the workers to give up their arms and that was treacherous, but in Finland after the general strike in November 1917, the Social Democrats bade no such thing, on the contrary, the Party Congress in November decided that the workers should not give arms up they possessed to anybody.[165]

Before the Plenum was over Manner withdrew his betrayal thesis. One might guess how strong the pressure upon him was in the corridors.[166] It is likely that Sirola discussed the matter with Manner, because it was Sirola who after Manner's

---

162 Kullervo Manner, A speech in the club of Estonians in the Lenin School. RGASPI, f. 516, op. 2, 1932, d. 11, ll. 8–11.

163 I have not found any text in which Manner spoke about the Emir of Afghanistan. However, Manner did not deny the accusation.

164 Jukka Lehtosaari in the Plenum of the CC of the SKP. MPCC, June 8–24, 1932. RGASPI, f. 516, op. 2, 1932, d. 3, p. 64.

165 MPCC, June 8–24, 1932. RGASPI, f. 516, op. 2, 1932, d. 3, ll. 154.–158.

166 That did not happen only in the corridors, however. The representative of the Comintern, Michkevich-Kapsukas told the Congress that Manner's "mistake" was "grave" but he felt it would be a "great blow" to "lose" him. (RGASPI, f. 516, op 2, 1932, d. 3, ll. 275–276.

statement affirmed that Manner is "worthy of confidence".[167] What had Manner said? He proclaimed that there was no "betrayal" in Finland, but there were "single cases" which must be characterised as "treacherous". For example, during November 1917, when the general strike was ended, the leaders assured the masses that the next step would be a "Red government". According to Manner, the leaders did not themselves believe in such a government. In November, the Social Democrats had refused to do their "class duty". Among other fateful miscalculations were the preservation of the unity of the Social Democratic Party, the draft for a constitution for a democratic Finland etc. It was a fatal mistake to declare on November 28, 1917, that "societal order and power based on working-class ideology, however, cannot be realised at the moment alone in Finland [even] at the cost of the blood of the most heroic comrades". According to Manner, this was not a "deliberate" betrayal; there were only "elements of betrayal". Furthermore, there was according to Manner a Trotskyite idea of the impossibility of Socialism in one country. Moreover, the target of the November 28 declaration was not in fact Finland, it was Russia, Manner claimed.[168]

Social Democratic leaders (Manner, Kuusinen, Sirola etc.) certainly thought in November 1917 that Socialism was not possible in Russia alone. Outside Russia, there were few people who, at that time believed that the Bolshevik coup d'état could be something resembling some final stage in the turbulent development in Russia in 1917. Moreover, the Bolshevik leaders themselves at the time believed that the revolution in Germany was a necessary condition for the building of Socialism in Russia. However, Manner's reference to Trotskyism in this context was, of course, misleading. The question of world revolution contra Socialism in one country was simply not laid down in November 1917. Stalin presented his formulation of Socialism in one country for the first time in December 1924.[169] In 1932, however, it was quite agreeable to announce that in the past some erroneous political line had been Trotskyite. In 1932, people did not yet know that any kind of Trotskyite formulation in such a relatively remote past (in this case the doctrine of permanent revolution against which Stalin polemised in 1924) was already a horrible crime.

Overall, the thesis of betrayal was a very odd conception. As far as I know, the thesis never became public in Finland. However, had it become such, it would have been a gift to the Social Democrats. It seems that Kuusinen used this argument in the 1932 Plenum. The "Social Fascists" would say that yes, Kuusinen & Co betrayed you, the workers, in 1918. They "fooled" you when they led you onto revo-

[167] RGASPI, f. 516, op 2, 1932, d. 4, l. 404.

[168] RGASPI, f. 516, op 2, 1932, d. 4, ll. 397–404.

[169] Carr, *Socialism in One Country*, vol. 2, p. 30.

lution. Now you certainly believe that this was the aim of Manner, Kuusinen and Sirola. The same men are now leaders of the Communist Party. "The next time they will betray you so daintily, that you will not be aware of it".[170]

Hanna Malm's fate in the Plenum was grim. She was already in 1931 given a "serious reprimand" (*vakava muistutus*), not, however, a "severe warning" as Kuusinen had suggested in the meeting of the Foreign Bureau of the SKP.[171] Then, in the 1932 Plenum, she avowed that the betrayal theory had been wrong, "a 'Left' opportunist inclination".[172] Then there was her declaration on Kuusinen ("one should not speak about betrayal because Kuusinen was in a leading position in the Comintern", quoted above p. 311), which created much irritation. Kuusinen's reaction to Malm was the following:[173]

> One should not so much speak about Hanna's endeavours, because she is not really judicious in these [political] matters. Nevertheless, she is also in political matters close to Manner. It would be Com. Manner's duty to put some kind of stop to this carry-on of Hanna's. Such fear of espionage, questioning and such slander, as Com. Hanna uses, should be put to an end. One should give her a serious reprimand and warning, if she wishes to stay in the Party.

Malm was compelled (by Manner?) to make the following statement in the Plenum:[174]

> A statement like this means the slandering of the leadership of the C[ommunist] I[nternational] and also that of the leadership of the SKP. Coming from me, who have been a Party organiser from the beginning, this is the gravest mistake and I condemn it by its political character as an inclination towards Trotskyism. [...] Com. Mitzkevits [Michkevich-Kapsukas], quite rightly and justifiably criticised my statement and uncovered my error, helping me to see it and to abandon it. As to the betrayal "theory", it was Com. Y. Sirola who shook my opinion, which was not sure, by pointing out that the so-called Siltasaari group (Centre), which was in the Party leadership, did not *forbid* the arming of workers, but, on the contrary, did precisely

---

170 Notes on Kuusinen's speech on May 14, 1932, in the meeting of the Foreign Bureau of the SKP. RGASPI, f. 516, op. 2, 1932, d. 12, ll. 16–17. This is a secondary source, written in unknown hand. However, the argument against the "betrayal theory" is so obvious that it is not hard to believe that Kuusinen did present in the 1932 CC Plenum.

171 The decision was made by Manner, Sirola, Lehtosaari and Kuusinen. (MMFB, Oct. 11, 1931. RGASPI, f. 516, op. 2, 1931, d. 14.)

172 Malm's speech in the 1932 Plenum. MPCC, July 8–24, 1932. RGASPI, f. 516, op. 2, 1932, d. 4, l. 283.

173 MPCC, July 8–24. RGASPI, f. 516, op. 2, 1932, d. 4, l. 367.

174 Hanna Malm, Announcement to the Plenum of the CC of the SKP, July 14, 1932. RGASPI, f. 516, op. 2, 1932, d. 10. Italics in original.

> that, albeit feebly. The speech of Com. Mitzkevits has pointed out to me that the betrayal "theory" is wrong, eliminating even my latest vacillations in this question.

Kuusinen's remark was a plain threat against Malm and Manner. Kuusinen was, however, not the only personage in the Party leadership who had such thoughts about the relationship between Malm and Manner.[175] Malm was given "a serious reprimand and a severe warning".[176]

Verbal reprimands and warnings were, however, not enough for Kuusinen and his supporters. Although Malm had been not elected to the Central Committee in 1930, she had been some kind of clerk in the Foreign Bureau. On October 18, 1932, the Foreign Bureau decided, as proposed by Antikainen, to deport Malm to "mass work" in Karelia. Only Manner opposed this decision.[177] There can be no doubt that a key figure in this matter was Kuusinen. Malm asked to be put to her occupational work,[178] but the Foreign Bureau did not accept this request. Kuusinen's idea was obviously to separate Malm and Manner from each other.

Hanna Malm's Deportation to Ukhta, November 1932–September 1933

To be exact, Malm was to be deported to Karelia, not precisely to Ukhta. It was clear, however, that the actual location could not be the capital of Soviet Karelia, Petrozavodsk, but some village in which there were substantial numbers of Finnish émigrés, Karelian-speaking Karelians,[179] and / or Finnish-speaking Karelians.

---

[175] Malm's declarations in the Plenum were qualified by Toivo Antikainen as an indication of "outrageous political coarseness". He also stated that Malm "hates Kuusinen personally". Malm had stated in the Polish-Baltic Secretariat that the political line was not correct and Manner, on his part, has announced that there had not been a turning-point deep enough in the Party. (MPCC, July 8–24, 1932. RGASPI, f. 516, op. 2, 1932, d. 4, ll. 320–324.) Kalle Lepola said that Malm, when she said that talk of betrayal was not allowed because Kuusinen was a leader of the Comintern, laid such a rotten egg that is not to be endured". Malm, Lepola said, had now extended her "factional appearance openly against the Comintern". (MPCC, July 8–24, 1932. RGASPI, f. 516, op. 2, 1932, d. 3, l. 241.)

[176] Decision of the Plenum of the CC of the SKP, no date. RGASPI, f. 516, op. 2, 1932, d. 11, l. 3.

[177] MMFB, Oct. 18, 1932, RGASPI, f. 516, op. 2, 1932, d. 12.

[178] MMFB, Oct. 18, 1932, RGASPI, f. 516, op. 2, 1932, d. 12.

[179] Karelians meant in this context people who spoke the Karelian language. This language was in the latter 1930s developed as a literary language, written in Cyrillic. The aim was to suppress the use of Finnish totally. However, when after the Winter War there were, because of the new border, also Finns, the Finnish language was again accepted. Ironically, there were very few Finns who decided to remain there after the Moscow peace treaty of 1940. Virtually everyone, 450,000 people emigrated behind the new border. This was a surprise to the Soviets and difficult to explain in propaganda. (Kilin, *Suurvallan rajamaa*, p. 186.) Karelian was not used as a literary language after the war.

Malm went first to Petrozavodsk to discuss her destination. There she met Toivo Alavirta, an ancient MP (1916–1917), a Red refugee and now Party secretary of Ukhta District Committee,[180] who was interested in having Malm edit the broadcasts of a local radio, which was to commence activity on January 1, 1933.[181] She also edited a small weekly, *Punainen Uhtua* (Red Ukhta); she was, however, soon expulsed from these tasks because she reverted to her "betrayal thesis".

Ukhta (from 1935 Kalevala) meant at one and the same time the whole *raion* and a village which was its administrative centre. According to information obtained in 1933, there were 10,747 inhabitants in the *raion*, of whom 90 per cent were Finns or Karelians. Ukhta was known in Finland as an important source of traditional poetry, where the creator of *Kalevala*, Elias Lönnrot, collected poems.[182] The political history of Ukhta was not untypical of districts, close to the Finnish border. In July 1917 a meeting was organised, which decided to join Ukhta and some neighbouring municipalities to Finland. In March 1920, when the area was not yet under the control of the Bolshevik government, an all-Karelian meeting was organised about the future of the region. According to some sources – information about what happened there is scanty – the meeting declared Karelia an independent state and elected a six-member "government".[183] The Bolsheviks captured the *raion* in June 1920, and the "government" moved to Finland.[184] In the period 1918–1922 some 700 people moved from Ukhta to Finland and a part of the houses were left empty,[185] to be subsequently used by Finnish Red fugitives.

Soviet Karelia was one of laboratories of "indigenisation" (or "rooting", *коренизация*), realised in Soviet Russia / the Soviet Union in the 1920s. In Karelia, however, indigenisation meant the Fennicisation led by Edvard Gylling, Kustaa Rovio and other Red Finns rather than indigenous people. Troubles over Karelian nationality policy began in the autumn of 1932 with an OGPU[186] operation against what was seen as a "conspiracy of the Finnish General Staff". The Russian political elite proclaimed that there was a menace of Finnish nationalism, conspiracies or-

---

[180] Later Alavirta was a worker of a ski factory. In 1937 he was imprisoned and in 1939 accused for spying and condemned to a labour camp, where he perished in 1940. (Lahti-Argutina, *Olimme joukko vieras vaan*, p. 62.)

[181] Malm (in Petrozavodsk) to Manner (in Moscow), Nov. 23, 1932, MMC, p. 58.

[182] Eino Leskinen, "Uhtua" in *Otavan iso tietosanakirja*, vol. 9, p. 446.

[183] V. M. Holodkoskij, *Suomi ja Neuvosto-Venäjä 1918–1920*, p. 194. See also Toivo Nygård, *Suur-Suomi vai lähiheimolaisten auttaminen : aatteellinen heimotyö itsenäisessä Suomessa*, p. 58 and a detailed description in Stacy Churchill, *Itä-Karjalan kohtalo 1917–1922 : Itä-Karjalan itsehallintokysymys Suomen ja Neuvosto-Venäjän suhteissa 1917–1922*, pp.121–128

[184] Mauno Jääskeläinen, *Itä-Karjalan kysymys : kansallisen laajennusohjelman synty ja sen toteuttaminen Suomen ulkopolitiikassa vuosina 1918–1920*, p. 278.

[185] Toivo Nygård, *Itä-Karjalan pakolaiset 1917–1922*, pp. 74–75.

[186] Объединенное Государственное политическое Управление (State Political Administration).

ganised from Finland and, of course, the danger of "kulak influence".[187] Soviet Karelia was, as Sari Autio stresses, a periphery in a "mental sense" during the years 1928–1937. There was rapid industrialisation and Karelia was unable to establish a viable economy based on its main wealth, the forests.[188] Forced collectivisation led in Karelia as elsewhere, to severe shortages of foodstuffs, vegetables above all. As a result, especially lumbermen suffered from scurvy; according to one estimate in August 1932, one in ten woodcutters in Karelia had scurvy.[189] – In 1932, the question of nationalism was not yet strongly felt in Ukhta, but the food situation was grave.[190] The peasants lost every last spark of motivation to work efficiently under the new serfdom. This state of affairs was seen in the management of horses. According to Malm, the kolkhoz peasant, unlike free peasants before collectivisation, treated horses "barbarously".[191]

When Malm came to Ukhta, she was, in spite of her confession in Moscow, still under the devilish influence of the "betrayal thesis" and her struggle with this Devil was to continue up to 1935 when she was arrested and imprisoned. In December 1932 she found a statement by Vikentii Michkevich-Kapsukas, who had stated in the XIIth Plenum of the Comintern that there were in the SKP no longer "legalistic currents" such as had "strongly increased before the Fascist coup" in June 1930. The SKP had "come close to the masses and here and there managed to place itself in the lead of their struggle".[192] This, Malm thought, proved her thesis true, because the Party had led the masses only here and there and not everywhere. In her opinion, the leaders of the SKP had overestimated the influence of the Party in Finland. There was no instinctive movement, supposedly always led by the Party. The masses were simply silent. On the part of the leaders of the SKP, silence about facts was "treacherous" and "rotten Liberalism". She urged Manner to bring all this out in Moscow.[193]

On January 26, 1933, Malm became excited in a course of lectures in Ukhta. She asked for the floor and announced that Wilhelm Pieck, a German Communist chief, also one of most prestigious leaders of the Comintern, had stated in a Comintern meeting that Communists in Germany committed an error when they

---

187 Kangaspuro, "Russian Patriots and Red Fennomans", p. 40.

188 Sari Autio, "Soviet Karelian Forests in the Planned Economy of the Soviet Union, 1928–37" in *Rise and Fall of Soviet Karelia : People and Power*, p. 85.

189 Ol'ga A. Zakharova (Nikitina), "Peculiarities of Collectivization in Karelia" in *Rise and Fall of Soviet Karelia : People and Power*, p. 113.

190 Malm to Manner, Dec. 12, 1932, MMC, p. 72.

191 Malm to Manner, Feb. 7–8, 1933, MMC, pp. 214–215.

192 [Vikenti] Mitshkevitsh-Kapsukas, "Baltian maiden kommunististen puolueiden tilasta", *Kommunisti*, Nov. 15. 1932, p. 984.

193 Malm to Manner, Dec. 16–17, 1932, MMC, pp. 99–100.

failed to stage a coup immediately after the end of the First World War. He had further stated that the Communists "vacillated" and "made mistakes" in their struggle against Revisionist and Centrist elements, i.e. minions of Karl Kautsky.[194] Pieck's statements, she declared, supported the "betrayal thesis". She also dealt with the question of why there had been no Bolshevik Party in Finland in 1917 and during the Civil War.

For Malm it was fatal that in the meeting in which she made this agitated speech, there were not only Party members, but also non-Party people. She was, she wrote to Manner, branded as a "supporter of a counter-revolutionary gang". The next day a meeting of the Bureau of the District Committee of the Party, whose secretary was Alavirta, accepted a resolution against Malm. For Malm the decision contained an entirely "extraordinary" argument that an agreement existed between the Communist International and the SKP over the "betrayal thesis". According to the resolution Malm knew this and therefore her behaviour proved that she was an "anti-Party element".[195] – Manner was horrified when he read the letter. Although there was little information as to what had really happened in the meetings in Ukhta, there were, for Manner, "a series of mistakes", above all the "betrayal thesis" and its presentation in the way Malm had done it.[196] Manner referred to the thesis accepted by the Foreign Bureau of the SKP, in which the arguments were similar to those of Pieck referred to. No-one understood, it was argued, in 1917–1918,[197]

> the role of the Party in the proletarian revolution and therefore the revolution *lacked the leadership of the Party*. [...] Siltasaarian cadres had in spite of their opportunist Social Democracy grown up together with the large masses so closely that they did not wholly abandon the battle of the workers.

Manner knew Alavirta as a trustworthy comrade and when he read that he had condemned Malm, it increased Manner's fear that Malm had made "great mistakes". Manner, however, gave assurance that Malm was not "subjectively a hostile element" in the SKP. Manner said that he himself had also not been a subjectively hostile element in 1932, but objectively he had adopted a position (i.e. the "betrayal thesis"), which was "against the Party". "Dear Hanna, I cry, stop", he wrote to her. Manner was so nervous and depressed at the information in Malm's letter that he could not sleep at all the following night.[198] Malm, however, announced to

194 Wilhelm Pik [*sic*], "Saksan Kommunistinen Puolue 14-vuotias", *Punainen Karjala*, Jan. 9, 1933.

195 Malm to Manner, Jan. 31 – Feb. 1, 1933, MMC, pp. 205–206.

196 Manner to Malm, Feb. 9, 1933, MMC, p. 217.

197 "Thesiŝ of the Foreign Bureau of the SKP about the 15th anniversary of Finnish Revolution", *Kommunisti*, Jan. 30, 1933, p. 84.

198 Manner to Malm, Feb. 9, 1933, MMC, pp. 216–219; quotations on p. 219.

Manner that she had no insomnia problem.[199] Manner's position was simply wrong and she would defend her standpoint in the Control Commission system of the VKP(b) up to the Central Control Commission.[200]

Manner's anxiety grew and in the meeting of the Foreign Bureau he asked permission to meet Malm. He argued he could gain a hold over her and rid her of her "anti-Party standpoint". Manner explained that Malm's mistakes were only "objectively", not "subjectively" against the Party. The meeting authorised Manner's journey to Karelia. At the same time, the Bureau condemned Malm's behaviour in Ukhta as contrary to the decisions of the 1932 Plenum of the Central Committee.[201]

Meanwhile Malm's difficulties in Ukhta increased. The Party fraction of the Executive Committee of the Ukhta Soviet expelled Malm, and she was transferred to a new post as secretary of the council of the trade unions. She wrote to the Petrozavodsk Regional Committee an explanation comprising 25 pages.[202] When the couple met in Petrozavodsk on March 9–14, 1933, Manner was able to persuade Malm to give up her "betrayal theory" and to make a confession of her sins to the SKP and the VKP(b). Malm condemned herself as guilty of "Left-opportunist side-slidings" (*sivuliukumat*), open opposition to the decisions of the SKP and "outrageous slander of the leadership of the SKP and some of its members" as well as "offence to the statutes and mores" of the VKP(b).[203] The Moscow leaders of the SKP were, however, still disappointed because they did not believe that Malm's confessions were genuine. Manner urged Malm "soon to make it clear that in the practice" her confession was "fully true". He also told her that there had been "voices" in Moscow demanding that Malm be expelled from the SKP for some period.[204]

The Malm affair was the most important matter in a joint meeting of the three bureaus of the SKP, the Foreign Bureau (Moscow), the Leningrad Bureau and the Petrozavodsk Bureau. Toivo Antikainen accused Malm of giving arms into the hands of the "counter-revolutionaries" in a border district (Ukhta). Kuusinen was not very interested in Malm's declarations and writings, but he was, as earlier on, concerned over the influence of Malm on Manner. He demanded that Manner should publicly defend the line of the Central Committee. If private and Party matters were contradictory, one should cut out such private matters.[205] In April 1933, the

---

199 Malm to Manner, March 2, 1933, MMC, p. 248.

200 Malm to Manner, Feb. 10, 1933, MMC, p. 223.

201 MMFB, Feb. 14, 1933. RGASPI, f. 516, op. 2, 1933, d. 16.

202 Malm to Manner, March 2, 1933, MMC, pp. 254–256.

203 T. Antikainen, "Tov. Hanna Malmin puoluevastaisten esiintymisten johdosta", *Punainen Karjala*, June 1, 1933.

204 Manner to Malm, March 28, 1933, MMC, p. 262.

205 Minutes of the negotiation meeting of the Foreign Bureau, March 20–23. RGASPI, op. 2, 1933, d. 15, l. 16.

Foreign Bureau expelled Malm from the Party for one year. This meant that after one year Malm was entitled to make an appeal to rejoin the Party.[206]

In Ukhta Malm was yet again transferred to a new post. She became a "responsible secretary" of the local unit of the MOPR in Ukhta.[207] Her task was to organise "mass work" among forest workers. Although this might be seen as a punishment, Malm seemed to regard it as the interesting "mass work" she wanted to do. She claimed she could conjoin "international enlightenment" of the Ukhta "masses" and propagation of money collecting for the MOPR. Her task was to organise special MOPR fields, i.e. to clear entirely new land from which the crops should be handed over to the MOPR without recompense. This proposition was certainly not popular with Karelian peasants, most of whom only a few years ago had been compelled to give up private farming and to join kolkhozes. Malm also carried out propaganda among Ukhtan forest workers. In her addresses to log-floaters, Malm wrote to Manner, she had united explanations about forms of proletarian struggles in other countries. She lectured, for example, to forest workers about the hunger strike of Polish miners. She did not, however, forget domestic topics like how to fight against "kulaks" who "sabotaged" sowings. – At the same time the effects of forced collectivisation were experienced; according to Malm, people had no other foodstuffs but bread, salt and water.[208]

On June 1, 1933, *Vapaus* published an article signed by Toivo Antikainen in which Malm's confession was described as unsatisfactory: Malm's assurance to submit to Party discipline had not been clear enough. Moreover, Malm's explanation that her mistakes have been Leftist opportunism in character was not taken seriously in Moscow. Malm's political background was declared "petty-bourgeois, totally alien to Communists".[209] Malm's answer to this was to withdraw her confession, written on March 12, 1933. On May 26, 1933 she wrote a letter to the Karelian Control Commission of the Party criticising the standpoints she had taken in the previous letter of March 12.[210] Her decision was also an act of no-confidence to Manner. She hoped, however, that Manner would also adopt the same "course". Due to Malm's "new course", she was expelled also from the VKP(b). Like her expulsion from the SKP, this expulsion was not final: if Malm's behaviour were to change, she

---

206 Manner alone opposed this resolution in the Foreign Bureau. (MMFB, April 4, 1993, RGASPI, f. 516, op. 2, 1933, d. 16.

207 *Международная органзация помощи борьцам революции* – "The aid organisation of international revolutionary fighters" was an association which arranged help for imprisoned Communists outside the Soviet Union.

208 Malm to Manner April 22–24, 1933. MMC, p. 328.

209 T. Antikainen, "Tov. Hanna Malmin puoluevastaisten esiintymisten johdosta", *Punainen Karjala*, June 1, 1933.

210 Malm to Manner, June 6–7, 1933, MMC, pp. 393–394.

would be admitted again into the ranks of the Russian Party.[211] All this deepened Manner's despair. He commented on Malm's "needless quips" and her "rage", which were consequences of her "passionate nature".[212]

Malm's adventures in Karelia were from the point of view of the SKP serious. There had been an unwritten principle that the Finns should try to keep – as far as possible – their mutual quarrels to themselves; now Malm's writings to various Soviet and VKP(b) organs broke that silence. It was considered especially dangerous among Karelian Finnish leaders that she accused them of nationalism at a time when accusations of Finnish nationalism were being made by the Russians. In the Plenum of the Central Committee of the SKP Gylling had to defend his national policy. Gylling assured the participants that despite mistakes, the national policy in Karelia was based on correct principles.[213]

After the "Fascist coup" in Finland the Comintern trimmed down[214] its funding of the SKP. The Party had, however, "support groups" in the Soviet Union, especially in Karelia, which collected money for the Party. They acted partly secretly. It was an activity parallel with the VKP(b) and therefore potentially dangerous in a totalitarian society. The groups sometimes used cover names like study groups on the history of the Finnish revolution or cells of the MOPR. In Karelia, Edvard Gylling, leader of Soviet Karelia, and Kustaa Rovio, the highest Party official there, were members of the leading body of such a cell in Karelia, the Petrozavodsk Group. The group organisation was able to nominate a paid clerk, who was Otto Vilmi. In the end of 1933, there were 33 groups in Karelia and others in Leningrad and elsewhere in the Soviet Union. Their functions were extended to Karelia: they tried to help Finnish refugees who came to the Soviet Union due to high unemployment in Finland. Later membership in a supporting group was to constitute sufficient proof of "wreckership".[215]

Last Throes

While Malm was still in Ukhta, a new fragment of Lenin's writings concerning the Finnish revolution was found in the *Leninskii Sbornik*, vol. XI, which volume had already been published in 1929. (It was considered a scandal that the notes had

[211] Malm to Manner, June 8–9, 1933, MMC, p. 405.

[212] Manner to Malm, Aug. 11, 1933, MMC, p. 406.

[213] Markku Kangaspuro, *Neuvosto-Karjalan taistelu itsehallinnosta : nationalismi ja suomalaiset punaiset Neuvostoliiton vallankäytössä 1920–1939*, pp. 276–278.

[214] *Ibid.*, p. 276. Kangaspuro also writes that the Comintern ceased to fund the activities of SKP in the Soviet Union altogether (*ibid.*, p. 271). In 1933 Comintern curtailed its allowance to the SKP (*ibid.*, p. 273). Some funding continued, however. In 1938 the Comintern gave Tuominen, who was in Stocholm, 3,000 dollars using the Swedish CP leader Sven Linderoth as courier. (G. Dimitrov's diary, Dec. 13, 1938. Georgi Dimitroff, *Tagebücher 1933–1943*, p. 230.)

[215] Kangaspuro, *Neuvosto-Karjalan taistelu itsehallinnosta*, pp. 271–275 and p. 321.

been there for four years and nobody had found them.) Lenin had written in his notebook in January 1918 two notes, numbered 10 and 10 *bis*, possibly as an outline for a later article he never wrote. The notes read: "10. National chauvinism, amongst repressive and repressed. 10 *bis*: P[etty] b[our]g[e]ois parasitism and the betrayal of Finnish S[ocial] D[emocrac]y".[216] The implications of this note were discussed in a meeting in which Sirola was the main speaker. He explained that as to betrayal one might make five points. i) Väinö Tanner and other Right Social Democratic leaders had already betrayed the revolution at the time when it was under way; ii) the behaviour of the leadership of the SDP in November 1917 was wrong; iii) if one were to continue the same course as that of November, it could end in betrayal; iv) the "political halfness" of the People's Deputy and its "democratic programme" caused a situation in which a possibility of betrayal was "objectively" substantial; v) it is not, however, correct to describe the behaviour of the Social Democratic leaders during the revolution as treacherous, because they accepted and sponsored the arming of the workers. Nonetheless, the plan to organise free elections after the war was a "glaring mistake". It was imagined that after the revolution people would elect a Socialist majority to the new Parliament.[217] In addition, O. W. Kuusinen spoke of the Finnish Revolution. He thought that there was not enough "ferocity", "burning hate" and, of course, no "revolutionary vanguard". In the Russian Revolution there were many features regarded erroneously by the Finnish leaders as special Russian characteristics because "Russia itself was a speciality". Thus, for instance, Kuusinen proclaimed that "the GPU was unknown to us".[218]

Hanna Malm returned from Karelia to Moscow in September 1933. She was thus not away one year as decided by the Foreign Bureau of the SKP. Now, however, Malm was a member of neither the SKP nor the VKP(b). Manner and Malm had some Scandinavian friends who suggested that the Moscow Agrarian Institute could take Malm as a *referent* of Scandinavian affairs. The said institution was one unit in the Comintern's large organisation and therefore it was necessary to request a statement from the SKP on the suggestion. In its statement, the Foreign Bureau

---

[216] В. И. Ленин. *Из дневника публициста : (темы для разработки)*. Written between Dec. 24–28, 1917 / Jan. 6–10, 1918. *Ленинский сборник*, vol. XI, p. 8.

[217] Minutes of the First Common Negotiation Meeting of the Research Group of the Finnish Revolution, the History Departments the Regional Committees of Leningrad and Karelia, the Section of the Revolutionary History of the Karelian Scientific Research Institute and the Representatives of Other Institutes and Party Actives Doing Research on Revolutionary Movements in Finland, Karelia and in the District of Leningrad, on May 20–22, 1933, in Leningrad. RGASPI, f. 516, op. 2, 1933, d. 47, l. 81.

[218] Speech of Comrade Kuusinen in the XVth anniversary to celebrate the Finnish Revolution in a general municipal festival in Leningrad (no date), RGASPI, f. 522. op 1, d. 39. pp. 3–7. The theme of hate was, as we have seen, typical of Kuusinen.

announced that because Malm was a "non-Party person", it was not recommendable to place her in any Comintern post.[219] Similarly, Manner was prevented from becoming a teacher of the history of the Comintern in the Swedish Section of the Lenin School.[220]

In the autumn of 1933 Matti Stein (pseudonym of Hannes Mäkinen), who was in the 1930s a representative of the SKP in various Comintern organs, now on the platform of the International accused Manner of underestimating the leading role of the Party in the struggle for the "creation of Soviet Finland" and "exhorted" the Finnish workers to brawl for this aim. In his speech, Stein also branded Manner as a Right opportunist.[221] Manner naturally denied this charge.[222] In a meeting of the members of the Central Committee of the SKP in Russia, Finnish administrators in the Comintern and Profintern and teachers and stipendiaries in the Lenin School, the Manner case was a subject on which most speakers spoke. Manner himself argued that the most important problem of the Finnish Communists was that the Communists did not differentiate "clearly enough" from the Social Democrats.[223] (What else Manner possibly said in this Plenum is not known because the minutes of the meeting, as to Manner's presentations, are obviously not complete.)

The main prosecutor was, of course, Kuusinen. For him speaking of a "Social Democratic inheritance" was "hair-splitting".[224] Kuusinen could not yet say in an SKP forum whether there were plans inside the Comintern to change its political course substantively.[225] There were two courses in its formation; their dividing line was the attitude towards Social Democracy and Fascism. O. W. Kuusinen, Georgi Dimitrov and D. Z. Manuilskii were among those who demanded a change in tactics, while Bela Kun and Vilgelm Georgevich Knorin among others denounced Social Democracy as a main prop of the ruling class. Kuusinen, Dimitrov and Manuilskii condemned slogans like "Social Fascism" as schematic while Bela Kun and colleagues continued to use this slogan. Kuusinen *et al* could thus not argue about the character of Social Democracy; he and others planned behind the scenes

---

219 MMFB, Jan. 2, 1934, § 15. RGASPI, f. 516, op. 2, 1934, d. 19.

220 MMFB, Feb. 15, 1934, § 13. RGASPI, f. 516, op. 2, 1934, d. 19.

221 M. Stein, "Tilanteesta Suomessa : Suomen kommunistisen puolueen tilasta ja tehtävistä" (On the situation in Finland : of condition and tasks of the Finnish Communist Party). Speech in the Plenum of the Executive Council of the Comintern. Published in *Kommunisti*, Feb. 25, 1934, p. 91.

222 Statement by Kullervo Manner in the Plenum of the Executive Committeee of the Comintern, Dec. 11, 1933. KtS!, pp. 307–309. See also Kullervo Manner to D. Z. Manuilskii, V. G. Knorin and O. A. Piatnitski, March 31, 1934. KtS!, pp. 310–311.

223 Minutes of the meeting called by the Foreign Bureau of the SKP for the members of the CC in Russia, Finnish administrators in Comintern and Profintern and teachers and stipendiaries in the Lenin School, Feb. 1–8, 1934. RGASPI, f. 516, op. 2, 1934, d. 3, l. 29. (The page numbers of this document are those added to the document in the Archives.)

224 *Ibid.*, l. 37.

225 Liisa Linsiö, *Komintern ja Kuusinen*, pp. 59–77.

to abandon completely the slogan of "Social Fascism". Manuilskii warned against simplification and underestimation of the menace of Fascism.[226]

In the meeting, Kuusinen spoke of the imminence of the war. He argued that there were only a few months' time before the next war would be precipitated, now probably by Japan, joined later by Germany and England. Kuusinen stressed that in this regard one should not put Germany and England "against each other". He explained that the main task of the SKP was to explain to "starving" Finnish workers and peasants that salvation was near: the "watchword"[227] should be "unification of Soviet Karelia and Finland". For Kuusinen the situation was similar to that in 1918; now too a revolution could save the workers and a programme, written by Kuusinen in autumn 1918, *Kiireellisiä toimintaohjeita Suomen vallankumokselliselle työväelle ja sotaväelle* (Urgent action directives to Finnish revolutionary workers and soldiers)[228] should as soon as possible be rewritten and then sent to Finland in tens of thousands of copies and spread there as widely as possible. Manner, however, Kuusinen declared, had said nothing about what was to be done, what were the tasks of the SKP. He has only said, according to Kuusinen, that it was important for the Communist Party to take a stand on the question whether the human soul is immortal or mortal.[229]

It is difficult to explain why Kuusinen now, in a secret meeting, took up the subject of the imminence of war. In Soviet propaganda, this was a daily slogan and usually, in the first part of the 1930s, England was seen as the main enemy. Stalin and his OGPU staff extorted and arrested opposition leaders to make them confess their connections with the British and French governments and to tell their blackmailers imaginary stories about their preparation for war against the Soviet

---

226 E. H. Carr, *The Twilight of Comintern, 1930–1935*, pp. 126–128.

227 The word used in this context not only by Kuusinen but also by several other speakers, was *loosunki*, a Fennicisation of the German word *Losung*; in English "watchword", "password", or "slogan". This kind of wording was typical in émigré circles. No common Finnish worker could understand what *loosunki* might mean.

228 In this programme workers were given detailed advice on preparation for an armed uprising, sabotage included. One of its slogans was "electoral humbug to blazes!" Parliament should be abolished because by universal suffrage the bourgeoisie had been able to elect "enemies of the people" to the *Eduskunta*. All power would be taken into the "hands of the working-class" by forming councils of workers and revolutionary soldiers and thus "Socialist Council Power of Finland" (*Suomen sosialistinen Neuvostovalta*). The poor will have "almighty power", i.e. "dictatorship of the proletariat" which is not the "power of one person or an oligarchy of some small group". All property of "exploiters" would be expropriated, including "excessive housing rooms, household goods and clothes". (*Kiireellisiä toimintaohjeita Suomen vallankumoukselliselle työväelle ja sotaväelle : antanut Suom. Kommunistisen Puolueen Keskuskomitea*, pp. 3–5.)

229 Minutes of the meeting invited by the Foreign Bureau of the SKP for the members of the CC in Russia, Finnish administrators in the Comintern and Profintern and teachers and the stipendiaries in the Lenin School, Feb. 1–8, 1934. RGASPI, f. 516, op. 2, 1934, d. 3, ll. 37–38. – I have not succeeded in ascertaining what kind of debate took place over the human soul.

Union.[230] At the same time Stalin, in the XVIIth Congress of the VKP(b) in January 1934 spoke about non-aggressive pacts of the Soviet Union and Powers like Finland, Poland, France and Italy. He thought these pacts would further peace, but he did not mean that there was no threat of intervention by capitalist countries, England, above all, against the Soviet Union. There had been developments, which could lead towards a "new imperialist war". Stalin declared: "They who try to assault our country will meet such a shattering repulse that they will not wish in the future to poke their pig's snout into our Soviet vegetable garden. (Thunderous applause.)"[231]

One may point out that according to Bolshevism, wars may lead to revolutions. This was Kuusinen's position in the autumn of 1918; now even the vocabulary was the same, only the thesis of the popularisation of the Soviet Union was dissimilar. Kuusinen also proclaimed that he had no doubt that if the Party put all its forces to bear, "as the Bolsheviks do", Finnish workers would follow the Party.[232] The Politsecretariat of the Comintern condemned Manner declaring that there was an "opportunist underestimation of war among the SKP".[233] Kuusinen was undoubtedly behind this resolution.

Some speakers sought to point out that Manner was led by his wife, Malm. This was, in fact, a common opinion in this gathering and obviously not without grounds. A close minion of Kuusinen, Jukka Lehtosaari declared:[234]

> Manner has never personally tried to develop himself; he has only had occasional quotations. The lack of resistance has therefore been followed. Had he been a true Bolshevik, he would have resisted the anti-Party presentations of Hanna Malm and also helped her onto the correct path.

Manner's activities in late 1933 and in 1934 were no more judicious. He worsened his own situation when he entered into relations with Väinö Pukka, who was in Moscow after he had succeeded, in spite of the protests of the SKP, in joining the

---

230 Stalin to Com. Menzhinsky (head of the OGPU), probably in the autumn of 1932. Published in *Stalin's Letters to Molotov 1925–1936*, pp. 195–196.

231 И. В. Сталин, Отчетный доклад XVII съезду партии о работе ЦК ВКП(б), 26 января 1934 г. И. В. Сталин, *Сочинения*, vol. 13, p. 305.

232 Minutes of the meeting called by the Foreign Bureau of the SKP for the members of the CC in Russia, Finnish administrators in the Comintern and Profintern and teachers and stipendiaries in the Lenin School, Feb. 1–8, 1934. RGASPI, f. 516, op. 2, 1934, d. 3, l. 40.

233 Protokoll Nr. 220 der geschlossenen Sitzung des Politsekretariats am 11.5.1934., § 1 and appendix: Резолюция политсекретариата ИККИ о положении в КПФ и ее основных задачах, принята 11.5.1934 г. RGASPI, f. 495, op. 3, d. 415, l. 2. Also KtS!, p. 314.

234 Minutes of the meeting called by the Foreign Bureau of the SKP for the members of the CC in Russia, Finnish administrators in Comintern and Profintern and teachers and the stipendiaries in the Lenin School, Feb. 1–8, 1934. RGASPI, f. 516, op. 2, 1934, d. 3, l. 47.

VKP(b).[235] This enabled Kuusinen and his followers to create a conception "the Manner–Malm–Pukka Opposition" which was used against Manner.[236]

In spring 1934 the SKP nominated a commission, whose task was to prepare the sentence to be issued by the Comintern. Eino Rahja gave material concerning Malm and Manner to the authorities,[237] probably for this Comintern commission. The commission suggested that Manner should dissociate himself from "Hanna Malm's factionalism and Left Social Democratic ideology".[238] This was an offence to Manner because he had presented himself and Malm as personages who had striven to "heighten, sharpen and exacerbate the struggle against Social Democratism and its underestimation".[239] The Comintern set a "special commission" to investigate the Manner affair. Manner wrote a long memorandum to this commission in which he stated that the divergence of opinion between himself and Kuusinen concerned diverging assessments of the nature of *Siltasaarism*, which Manner translated into German as *Siltasaarianertum*.[240] Manner's explanations did not, however, convince the Commission. The Politsecretariat of the Executive Council of the Comintern decided on May 11, 1934 to transfer Manner from the SKP to the Comintern. Debates on history were decreed closed.[241]

In spring 1934 Manner made another attempt to support Malm and her ideas – since there was now no correspondence, we cannot know in what way. Malm was "conclusively" expelled from the VKP(b). The NKVD arrested Malm on March 14, 1935.[242] Manner was arrested on July 2, 1935. In addition, other Finns, branded (justifiably or not) as supporters of Manner were arrested. There were more or less fictitious charges. Kuusinen declared in 1948 that there was a conspiracy against him; it was, Kuusinen explained, the aim of Manner and his Opposition to murder him.[243] On November 9–12, 1935, the War Collegium of the Highest Court of the Soviet Union pronounced the sentence: both Manner and Malm were condemned

---

235 Kullervo Manner, An die spezielle Kommission des EKKI über Angelegenheiten der K. P. Finnlands, May 1, 1934. RGASPI, f. 516, op. 2, 1934, d. 20, l. 9.

236 Rentola, *Kenen joukoissa seisot?*, pp. 30–31.

237 Leo Laukki to O. W. Kuusinen, Feb. 14, 1937. KtS!, pp. 363–364.

238 An die Kommission der P. K. des EKKI für die finnischen Fragen : kurze Zusammenfassung des Inhalts des Resolutionsentwurfes der Kommission des ZK der F.K.P über den Faktionarismus der Genossen Malm und Manner, April 26, 1934. RGASPI, f. 516, op. 2, 1934, d. 20, l. 6.

239 Kullervo Manner, Lisähuomautuksia SKP:n KK:n helmikuun Plenumille Työjaoston esittämän päätösluonnoksen johdosta (Addtional notes to the Plenum of the CC in February on the resolution draft presented by the working section), Feb. 17, 1934. RGASPI, f. 15, op. 2, 1933, d. 1.

240 Kullervo Manner, An die spezielle Kommission des EKKI über Angelegenheiten der K. P. Finnlands, May 1, 1934. RGASPI, f. 516, op. 2, 1934, d. 20.

241 Hanna Malm's personal folder. RGASPI, f. 495, op. 269, d. 1791.

242 Manner tried to obtain an audience to Manuilskii, but did not succeed. He then wrote him a letter, in which he explained that he had tried to influence her, partly successfully, partly unsuccessfully. (Kullervo Manner to D. Z. Manuilskii, April 15, 1935. KtS!, pp. 325–326.)

243 О. В. Куусинен, *Автобиография*, May 4, 1948. RGASPI, f. 522, op. 2, d. 114.

to ten years' forced labour.[244] In 1936 Malm was able to write from her labour camp in Svir (in Finnish Syväri) in Eastern Karelia to the Foreign Bureau a letter in which she expressed anxiety at the fate of Manner and asked comrades to help her to gain release from the camp and return to political work.[245] This appeal proves that Malm even in the camp could not recognise the character of the society in which she lived. According to the official announcement, she drowned in the lake at the Solovetsk labour camp in 1938.[246] According to one rumour, she committed suicide by drowning herself in a brook.[247] Manner perished in January 1939.[248] Both Malm and Manner were posthumously rehabilitated in 1957.[249]

We may ask whether the Malm and Manner Opposition was in any way influential among the SKP. The answer is that it was significant among a certain small elite in Moscow. This elite consisted mostly of Finnish teachers in the Lenin School and other intellectuals. One of Manner's supporter was Väinö Rautio. He escaped to Russia in 1918, was a recruit in the Red Officer School, and then probably studied in the Sverdlov University and became a "Red Professor". He also studied in the Frunze War Academy. Rautio was a teacher in the Communist University of Western Minority Nationalities in Leningrad and in the Lenin School in Moscow.[250] At the Lenin School Rautio lectured on the old Finnish Social Democracy. According to Manner, he told his students that Finnish Social Democracy was "by essence" Menshevik and clearly in contradiction with Bolshevism. The Siltasaarians had the merit of going into the revolution with the workers. They did not, like Right-Wing Social Democrats, betray the revolution, but they remained Social Democrats and were therefore on the way of treacherous policy.[251] For Manner this kind of juxtaposition, was, of course, welcome.[252]

Another follower was Allan Wallenius, also a teacher in the Lenin School. His native language was Swedish, and he taught in the Scandinavian department of the School and was head of this department in 1934–1935.[253] He supported Rautio,

---

[244] This infomation comes from the Finnish Detective Central Police. Ek-Valpo I, PF 647, Kullervo Manner and PF 757, Hanna Malm, KA.

[245] Malm to the Finnish Section of the Comintern, April 18, 1936. The letter is only in Russian translation in the Archives. Minutes of the Foreign Bureau of the SKP, May 11, 1936. RGASPI, f. 516, op. 2, 1936, d. 1. It is published in Finnish in KtS!, pp. 344–345

[246] Нач. 2 отдела ухт-утемлага НКВД. Dec. 20, 1938. Signature: Dimakov. Lenin Museum, Tampere.

[247] Aino Kuusinen, *Jumala syöksee enkelinsä*, p. 224.

[248] В Прокуратуру СССР. Dec. 20, 1939. Place and signature unclear. Lenin Museum, Tampere.

[249] Lahti-Argutina, *Olimme joukko vieras vaan*, pp. 322–323.

[250] Ek-Valpo I, PF 1717, Väinö Rautio. KA.

[251] Manner to Malm, April 22–23, MMC, p. 315.

[252] Manner to Malm, May 2–3, 1933, MMC, pp. 343–344.

[253] Ek-Valpo I, PF 885, Allan Wallenius.

who had "found" the now famous Lenin fragment treating of the betrayal of Finnish Social Democracy. In the Central Committee Plenum in August 1933 Wallenius declared that he had "hated" Social Democracy in 1917 and 1918. He said it was impossible to "build a wall of China between Social Democracy in the autumn of 1917 and 1918". The Social Democratic leaders were one and the same "traitors" in 1917 as in 1918.[254] According to a letter which Arvo Tuominen, secretary of SKP, wrote to the Central Control Commission of the VKP(b) in 1937, Wallenius belonged for some time to Manner's "grouping" but cut his contacts with the grouping, which was, according to Tuominen, a positive step.[255]

Perhaps one most important follower of Manner was Pentti Lund. He studied first in the Communist University of Western Minority Nationalities, was then sent to take up underground work in Finland. He was among those few whom the Finnish police did not succeed in arresting in the last years of the 1920s. In May 1930, the Secretariat invited Lund to Moscow. In September 1931, he was nominated stipendiary to the Lenin School. He was expelled from the School in 1934 and imprisoned. According to the Finnish Detective Central Police, he was shot.[256]

Lund's speeches in various plenums were often somewhat confused. For instance, in the 1932 Plenum of the Central Committee, he attacked Rosa Luxemburg, who, according to Lund, preached the imminent decrepitude of Capitalism which would take place more or less automatically. This line, Lund explained, led to political passivity, because, if the decrepitude was inevitable in the near future, why do anything but await the collapse.[257] This, of course, was a rather curious interpretation of Luxemburg's position. In the same Plenum, Lund condemned his earlier betrayal thesis.[258] In the 1933 Plenum of the Central Committee of SKP he referred to Wallenius' thesis of the "wall of China" in a positive sense. As to the betrayal thesis, Lund was now able to declare that he "did not want to set himself against Lenin in this question",[259] a declaration surely annoying to the Kuusinen group.

At the 1934 Plenum Lund presented a written statement in which he opposed the decision to condemn Malm's and Manner's statements as "personal factionalism and petty-bourgeois errant aspirations" (*viistopyrinnöt*). Manner had had "much unclarity" in his analysis concerning the year 1918, but had, nevertheless seriously tried to seek out the basis of opportunism and to find means "whereby the influence of this ideology [of opportunism] could be thwarted and exposed to the work-

---

254 MPCC, Aug. 4–17, 1933, pp. 103–104. RGASPI, f. 516, op. 2, 1933, d. 2, ll. 103–104.

255 Arvo Tuominen to the Central Control Committee of the VKP(b), May 4, 1937, RGASPI, f. 516, op. 2, 1937, d. 5 (in Russian).

256 Ek-Valpo I, PF 1294, Uuno Väre, KA.

257 MPCC, July 8–24, 1932. RGASPI, f. 516, op. 2, 1932, d. 2, l. 137.

258 *Ibid.*

259 MPCC, Aug. 4–17, 1933. RGASPI, f. 516, op. 2, 1933, d. 2, l. 118.

ing masses so that one could on that ground develop [attacks] against Soc. Democracy".[260] Lund told the meeting that there had been arguments claiming that he, Lund, "supports Manner's thought for 'personal reasons'". He protested: "Do you think that one goes into such a game on personal grounds when one knows that you will beat me and possibly send me to Siberia?"[261] According to information received by the Detective Central Police, Lund was executed.[262]

The Malm and Manner Opposition did not differ from the Kuusinen group as to the final aim of the Finnish Communist Party, namely the joining of Finland to the Soviet Union. One sympathiser of this Opposition, Einari Laaksovirta, who wrote studies on the peasant problem in Finland, asserted that after the struggle for "partial demands" had been combined into the struggle against "chauvinism, intervention and war in general"[263] there would be, "to a certain degree", a struggle for Finland's "joining together with Soviet Karelia and the Soviet Union".[264] This orthodoxy did not shelter Laaksovirta; in the War Collegium he received the "highest punishment", i.e. execution.[265]

---

260 Minutes of the meeting called by the Foreign Bureau of the SKP for the members of the CC in Russia, Finnish administrators in the Comintern and Profintern and teachers and stipendiaries in the Lenin School, Feb. 1–8, 1934. RGASPI, f. 516, op. 2, 1934, d. 3, l. 63.

261 *Ibid.*, l. 69.

262 Ek-Valpo I, PF, Väre, Uuno.

263 N. Tähti [pseudonym of Laaksovirta], *Fasismi ja Suomen maaseutu*, pp. 126–127.

264 N. Tähti, *Luokkakerrostuminen Suomen maaseudulla ja proletariaatin liittolaiskysymys*, p. 75.

265 Rentola, *Kenen joukoissa seisot?*, p. 30.

X Conclusion: The Finnish "Congress of Victors" (1935)

One may term the VIth Congress of the SKP in 1935 a "Congress of Victors", in the same sense as the XVIIth Congress of the VPK(b), in 1934, was called in Party propaganda a "Congress of Victors". In this Congress, the speakers competed in extolling I. V. Stalin. However, some speakers eulogized Stalin so robustly and stalwartly that some of the delegates understood the glorification as irony and laughed.[1] There was also an opposition to him; in a more or less secret ballot on the new Central Committee about 300 out of 1,225, delegates came out against Stalin.[2] When we count also delegates without a vote, there were 1,966 representatives; of these 1,109 envoys were arrested on charges of "anti-revolutionary crimes", as Nikita Khrushchev put it in the XXth Congress of the Communist Party of the Soviet Union in 1956; of 139 members and candidate members of the Central Committee elected by this Congress, 98 were shot.[3] – In the XVIIIth Congress in 1939, nobody laughed at Stalin.

In the Finnish Congress, nobody laughed at Kuusinen. When he opened the Congress, he received "thunderous applause" and "tumultuous, prolonged applause". When Kuusinen proclaimed that "our Party is the VKP and our leader is Com. Stalin" his declaration let loose "applause and cheers"[4] and finally there was a standing ovation in honour of Kuusinen.

---

1 Oleg Khlevniouk, *Le cercle du Kremlin : Staline et le Bureau politique dans les années 30 : les jeux du pouvoir*, pp. 108–109.

2 Dmitri Volgogonov, *Staline : triumphe et tragédie*, pp. 148–150.

3 Nikita Khrushchev, Secret Speech, published in *Khrushchev remembers*, pp. 624–625.

4 Minutes of the VIth Congress of the SKP, Sept. 10–20, 1935. RGASPI, f. 516, op. 2, 1935, d. 1, l. 20.

The Murder Opposition preserved a certain solidarity in the Far East. They contacted each other regularly there. For some oppositionists it became possible to return to Finland, either legally or illegally. – I have no statistics, but many, perhaps even most affiliates of the Murder Opposition, wrote long confessions,[5] some published in *Vapaus* newspaper and were thereafter duly accepted for membership in the SKP. However, most membership candidates were not interested in the membership book of the SKP, but that of the VPK(b), which opened so many gates in Soviet totalitarian society.

Behind both the Murder Opposition and the Rahja Opposition were an exceptional situation, peculiar military discipline of the Red Army and the fact that there were, if not open mutinies against the leaders of the Finnish revolution, processes fairly close to this. That the Opposition in the International War School became the Murder Opposition is, of course, in the last analysis, a whim. The fate of this Opposition might have been different without the murders. The most obvious allegiance might have developed between the two "workers' oppositions" together with Malm and Manner Opposition and indeed there was some vague plans to organise such an alliance in 1935. According to Aleksander Vasten, who reported of the affair to the members of the Foreign Bureau, Eino Rahja had announced in an unofficial meeting (in which alcohol probably was more than enough consumed) that he had received a letter from Manner and there had been discussions concerning a "New Central Committee". According to Rahja, the possible new Central Committee could consist of Hanna Malm, Kullervo Manner, Väinö Pukka, Allan Höglund [Hägglund] and August Paasi – "and Eino Rahja", it was said. Then Rahja had proclaimed that he would never participate in same Central Committee with Pukka.[6] It seems that the Rahja Opposition and the Malm and Manner Opposition also had contacts in 1934 or 1935 with Mikko Kokko, a supporter of Rahja and a Chekist[7] (or perhaps now an ex-Chekist).[8] The alliances between oppositions were, of course, fantasies in the circumstances in which *прожеркка* (from the Russian word *proverka* or "checking", "examination") was regarded crucial and the most secret task of the organisation of the SKP.[9]

---

5 E.g. Allan Höglund [Hägglund] and August Paasi to the editors of *Vapaus*, June 17, 1934 (in Russian). RGASPI, f. 516, op. 2, 1934, d. 28.

6 Meeting of the members of the Foreign Bureau, July 6, 1935, in Petrozavodsk. RGASPI, f. 516, op. 2, 1935, d. 17. This meeting led to nothing, but an interesting detail was that Rahja rejected Pukka, but not Paasi; it was, as whe have seen, a group led by Paasi who actually made the murders. Perhaps Rahja's especially strong anti-intellectualism had a role here. That Pukka had been in Sverdlov University and was a Red Professor might had been too much for Eino, who lost his intelligent brother Jukka in the murders at the Kuusinen Club.

7 Rentola, *Kenen joukoissa seisot?*, p. 67.

8 MMFB, Dec. 12, 1935, *spravka* to the Leningrad Department of the NKVD. RGASPI, f. 516, op 2, 1935, d. 16, appendix 2.

9 Minutes of the "production negotiations" of the office staff of the SKP, July 2, 1936. Arvo Tuominen's speech. RGASPI, f. 516, op. 2, 1936, d. 3.

Väinö Pukka's ultimate success in the Soviet trade union movement created much *Angst* in the Central Committee of the SKP. He succeeded in his application to join the the Bolshevik Party and was not expelled in spite of the demands of the Foreign Bureau. In a meeting of this Bureau it was decided that the "Pukka case" should be brought before the Central Control Commission of the VKP(b) and his contacts with Manner "reported" so that he would be expelled from the VKP(b).[10] He was able to enjoy membership of the VKP(b) for only a couple of years and ended his days before a firing squad. – Pukka, however, was not only an ex-Murder Opposionist who built a remarkable career in Siberia. Several letters written by August Paasi to Lauri Sulander and Leander Krokfors (later Kajasuo) after they had moved to Finland – illegally – in 1926, have been preserved. Paasi was a *spetsi* in an agricultural production unit (probably either kolkhoz or sovkhoz) in Buryat-Mongolia. He boasted that the salary and other privileges were such that a *spetsi*, "who was furnished with the blood of a worker, hardly needs any better". In 1927, Paasi wrote to Sulander that he was preparing to take a holiday of three months with full salary and another three months for study in a "scientific testing institute".[11] In 1932, Paasi was able to study in the Institute of Red Professors in Moscow and after his studies, he rested in the Crimea.[12] Paasi's last preserved letter to Sulander is dated December 4(?), 1936.[13] It is probable that Paasi was arrested in the late 1930s; he most likely perished in a labour camp or was executed.

The Rahja Opposition had its base in the army and the Cheka / GPU / OGPU / NKVD. Rahja himself was an agent in the said organisation, for how long, however, remains unclear. Rahja and his group had also high ranking protectors in the army. Leo Laukki, who belonged to this Opposition, was an eccentric: he had somewhat wild plans, like Pukka, to become a famous scholar. He was undoubtedly an exceptionally intelligent person, but in the conditions of Soviet Russia / the Soviet Union, he had no possibility to develop his talents fully. – In the VIth Congress, the

---

10 MPCC, July 1–17, 1934, RGASPI, f. 516, op. 2, 1934, d. 1, l. 123.

11 August Paasi in "Back-Baykal" to Lauri Sulander in Finland, Oct. 10, 1927. Lauri Sulander's collection, People's Archives. (It is noteworthy that it was possible for Paasi to write and receive (although highly irregularly) letters to and from Sulander, who had gone to Finland without the permit of the Soviet authorities.)

12 Paasi to "Good Comrade" (Sulander), Nov. 2, 1932. Sulander's collection, Kansan arkisto.

13 Paasi in Buryat-Mongolia to Sulander in Finland, Dec. 4(?), 1936. Sulander's collection, Kansan arkisto. – It may be interesting to note that when Sulander sought acceptance as a member of the SKP after the Finnish-Russian War of 1941–1944, he had to write an explanation of his doings as a member of the Murder Opposition. In this clarification, Sulander declared, "I, however, dare still argue that in this organising [of murders] there had been no fingers or plots of the Okhrana". (Lauri Sulander to the Party Committee of the SKP and to the Control Commission of the Party dated Dec. 12, 1944. Sulander's collection, Kansan arkisto.) The correct year is probably 1947 because the Cadre Department of the SKP sent Sulander a letter in Dec. 16, 1947 asking for more information about his doings in Russia. (Hemming Lindholm, a functionary in the Cadre Department of the SKP to Sulander, Dec. 16, 1947. Sulander's collection, Kansan arkisto.)

affairs of sundry renegades were well presented. Eino Rahja's Opposition was termed the *pivnaia* (beer) opposition. Rahja survived under the protection of the NKVD until 1936, when, suffering for alcoholism and tuberculosis, he passed away. He was given the funerals of a Civil War hero and a protector of Lenin.[14]

The Kuusinen Opposition in 1919–1921 in Finland and Sweden, was obviously a grouping strictly tied to the contemporary situation in Finland immediately after the Civil War. – The intellectual vs. workers antagonism was manifest in the oppositions of the SKP. Two main leaders, Manner and Kuusinen (and a third, Sirola) had in Finland passed the matriculation examination, a rare thing at the time. Kuusinen was a "helpless doctrinist"; so was also Manner but Kuusinen surpassed Manner overwhelmingly in the composition of "dialectical" chains of reasoning.

As to the Malm and Manner[15] Opposition, Yrjö Sirola "confessed" in the 1935 Congress of the SKP that he had taken it too lightly, had underestimated this factor. Sirola praised Kuusinen perceiving this "damaging" Opposition in time; this was his "principal merit".[16] Antti Hyvönen, a future official historian of the SKP declared that "the working-class has lost Manner"; "his Bolshevik base did not endure".[17] Hyvönen, however, was perhaps the only delegate who expressed any kind of sympathy for Manner, albeit in an inquisitorial way. Hyvönen characterised Manner's actions as "self-torture", which meant that "Manner proffers his bottom and says, hit me, miserable sinner".[18] Before his imprisonment, Manner had been about one year in the service of the Comintern, looking after Latin American (!) affairs.[19] Nobody knows what he was thinking in the labour camp. Did he even then revalue his maxim, presented to Malm in 1933, honestly that is sure: "We do not possess ourselves, we are the labour force of the Party and therefore we do not decide our own fates and the extent and quality of our labour forces".[20] This was, and is, a maxim of totalitarianism.

---

14 Rentola, *Kenen joukoissa seisot?*, p. 31.

15 Manner was expelled from the SKP as late as December 1935. The Foreign Bureau decided on December 5, 1935, that "because Manner was a political leader and initiator in a such counter-revolutionary group, which had direct connection with the class enemy, the F[oreign] B[ureau] decides, unanimously, to expel Manner from SKP membership and submit the FB decision to the CC of the SKP for confirmation. (MMFB, Dec. 5, 1935, § 8. RGASPI, f. 516, op. 2, 1935, d. 16)

16 Minutes of the VIth Congress of the SKP, Sept. 10–20, 1935 RGASPI, f. 516, op. 2, 1935, d. 1, l. 20.

17 *Ibid.*, l. 114. (Cited also in Rentola, *Kenen joukoissa seisot?*, p. 31.)

18 Minutes of the VIth Congress of the SKP, Sept. 10–20, 1935. RGASPI, f. 516, 1935, d. 1, l. 112.

19 Rentola, *Kenen joukoissa seisot?*, p. 25.

20 Manner to Malm, Feb. 2, 1933, MMC, pp. 245–246. Such thinking was common. For example, when one Petrozavodskian Helmi Heikkilä, whose husband was arrested in 1938 – she said that mainly "drunkards and windbags" were *not* arrested –, and she was pregnant and lived in misery, wrote a polite letter to the SKP, in which she surmised that one person was "finally of little value when compared to the totality of a great cause" and apologized that she wrote of her own personal matters to the Party. (Agnes (Helmi Heikkilä) to the SKP, July 14. 1938. KtS!, pp. 375–376.)

Plate A. Eino Rahja (after 1924)

Source:
Nikolai Kondratjev, *Luotettava toveri*, picture in the beginning of the book.

Plate B. Toivo Antikainen in 1922

Source:
Uljas Vikström, *Toiska : kertomus Toivo Antikaisen elämästä*, appendix of pictures.

Sources

Unprinted Archive Material

Российский гоударственный архив социально-политической истории (Russian State Archives of Social and Political History, RGASPI), former *Российский Центр Хранения и Изучения Документов Новейшей Истории* (Russian Centre for the Preservation and Study of Documents of Contemporary History, RTsKhIDNI), Moscow.
Fond 5, V. I. Lenin's secretariat
Fond 17, Central Committee of the RKP(b) / VKP(b)
Fond 324, Zinov'ev, Grigorii Evseevich
Fond 495, Communist International
Fond 501, Petrograd Representative of the Communist International
Fond 516, Finnish Communist Party
Fond 518, Antikainen, Toivo
Fond 522, Kuusinen, Otto Vil'gelmovich
Fond 525, Sirola, Yrjö Elias

Центральный Государственный Архив Красной Армии (Central State Archives of the Red Army), Moscow.
Fond 6, Register Administration

Kansallisarkisto (National Arcives, KA), former *Valtionarkisto* (State Arcives, VA) Helsinki
Ek-Valpo (Detective Central Police / State Police).
Document folders on Finnish Communism,
II 6 1 b, Travels to the Soviet Union
III.A.3, Finnish Bureau of the SKP
XXXIII A 4 a, Forgery of 1000 *markkas* bank notes
XXXV A 1, Murders in the Kuusinen Club
XX D 3, Parliamentary elections in 1930

Personal folders
603, Kuusinen, Otto Wilhelm
2416, Laaksovirta, Einari
802, Myyryläinen, Janne
3699, Paasi, August
3895, Pylkkänen, Oskari
3896, Pylkkänen, Otto
1064, Rahja, Eino
2017, Rasi, Jalmari
1717, Rautio, Väinö
1279, Taimi, Adolf
1294, Väre, Uuno
3361, Vikstedt, Ernst
885, Wallenius, Allan
Personal cards
Hägglund, Allan Kaarlonpoika
Höglund, Allan
Rissanen, Valter Oskar

Kansan arkisto (People's Archives), Helsinki.
Lauri Sulander's collection.

Lenin Museum, Tampere.
Hanna Malm's and Kullervo Manner's death certifications.

Työväen arkisto (Workers' Archives), Helsinki.
Interview of Arvo Tuominen by V. O. Veilahti, February 20–21, 1954. Unpublished manuscript.
Minutes of the board of directors of Tampereen Työväen Sanomalehti Oy, 1910.

Newspapers

Helsingin Sanomat, Helsinki, 1919, 1923, 1935.
Iltalehti, Helsinki, 1924, 1925.
Liekki, Helsinki 1927.
Правда, Moscow, 1923.
Punainen Karjala, Petrozavodsk, 1933, 1936.
Punasotilas, Petrograd, 1920.
Savon Työ, Kuopio, 1924.
Suomen Sosialidemokraatti, Helsinki, 1922, 1927, 1929, 1930.
Suomen Työläinen, Helsinki, 1921.
Suomen Työmies, Helsinki, 1921–1922.
Työ, Viipuri, 1929.
Työn Ääni, Vaasa, 1929.
Työväenjärjestöjen Tiedonantaja, Helsinki, 1924, 1927, 1930.
Uusi Suomi, Helsinki, 1929.
Wapaus / Vapaus, Petrograd / Leningrad, 1918, 1920, 1932, 1936.

Printed Primary Material, Contemporary Publications and Memoirs

Aatteet ja aseet. Helsinki: Tammi, 1967.

Asiantuntija (pseudonym), *Kommunismi ja Suomen Ammattijärjestö.* Helsinki: WSOY, 1929.

Azarkin, A., "KNI:n II kongressi Heinäkuun 9–23 päivinä 1921" in *KNI:n historia sen kongressien valossa.* Leningrad: Kirja, 1932.

Bebel, August, *Nainen ja sosialismi.* (Transl. by Yrjö Sirola.) Kotka: Kyminlaakson työväen sanomalehti- ja kirjapaino-osuuskunta, 1907.

Composition of Presiding Committee and commissions in *Workers of the World and Oppressed Peoples, Unite! : Proceedings and Documents of the Second Congress [of the Comintern], [July 19–August 7], 1920.* Vol. 2. (Ed. by John Riddell.) New York: Pathfinder Press, 1991.

de **Custine**, Adolphe, *La Russie en 1839.* Paris: Solin, 1990 [1843].

*The **Demands** of the Kronstadters,* published in *The Russian Revolution 1917–1921.* (Ed. by Ronald Kowalski.) London: Routledge, 1997.

Dimitroff, Georgi, *Tagebüchern 1933–1943.* (Ed. by Bernhard H. Bayerlein; transl. by Wladislaw Hedeler and Birgit Schliewenz.) Berlin: Aufbau-Verlag, 2000.

Eastman, Max, *Love and Revolution : My Journey Through an Epoch.* New York: Random House, 1964.

"**Eduskuntavaalit** vuonna 1924; 1927, 1929 / Élections au Parlement en 1925, 1927, 1929 " in *Suomen Tilastollinen Vuosikirja 1924 / Annuaire Statistique de Finlande 1924.* Helsinki: Tilastollinen Päätoimisto / Le Bureau Central de Statistique de Finlande, 1925, 1928 and 1929.

Eloranta, Voitto I., *Poika vallankumouksen jaloissa.* Helsinki: Otava, 2000.

Enckell, Carl, *Poliittiset muistelmani.* Vol. 1. Porvoo: WSOY, 1956.

***Ensimmäinen** kansainvälinen talonpoikain kokous : pidetty Moskovassa 1923 : selostuksia ja päätöksiä.* Stockholm: Frams Förlag, 1923.

[**Evä**, K. M.], *"Kosto Suomen köyhälistön pyöveleille".* S.l.e.a. [Pietari, 1918].

Evä, K. M., "Luokkasodan taistelutoimet luoteisella (pohjoisella) rintamalla" in *Punakaarti rintamalla : luokkasodan muistoja.* (Ed. by J. Lehtosaari.) Leningrad: Kirja, 1929.

[**Evä**, K. M.], *Työväen luokkadiktatuuri Suomeen! Tov. K. M. Evän luento työväen diktatuurin hallituskoneistosta Kommunistisilla agitaattorikursseilla Pietarissa 30 p. marrask. 1918.* Pietari: Suomalaisen Kommunistisen Puolueen Keskuskomitea, 1918.

Extracts of the speech of Timofei Sapronov in the ninth Party Conference, September 1920, published in *The Russian Revolution 1917–1921.* (Ed. by Ronald Kowalski.) London: Routledge, 1997.

Extracts of the Theses of the sixth Comintern Congress on the international situation and the tasks of the Communist International : from the Protocol of the Congress, August 29, 1928. Published in *The Communist International 1919–1943 : Documents,* vol. II, *1923–1928.* (Ed. by Jane Degras.) London: Oxford University Press, 1960.

Extracts of the Theses of the Tactics Adopted by the Fifth Comintern Congress. Published in *The Communist International 1919–1943: Documents.* Vol. II, *1923–1928.* (Ed. by Jane Degras.) London: Oxford University Press, 1960.

Extracts of the Theses on the Bolshevization of Communist Parties : adopted at the Fifth ECCI Plenum. Published in *The Communist International 1919–1943 : Documents.* Vol. II, *1923–1928.* (Ed. by Jane Degras.) London: Oxford University Press, 1960.

Extracts of The Theses on the Structure of Communist Parties and on the Methods and Content of their Work. Published in *The Communist International 1919–1943 : Documents.* Vol. 1, *1919–1922.* (Ed. by Jane Degras.) London: Oxford University Press, 1956.

***Finland** and Russia 1808–1920 : from Autonomy to Independence : a Selection of Documents.* (Ed. and transl. by D. G. Kirby.) London: Macmillan 1975.

Front, Hjalmar, *Kremlin kiertolaisia : muistelmia monivaiheisen elämän varrelta.* Forssa: Alea-Kirja, 1970.

Gromyko, Andrej, *Erinnerungen*. Internationale Ausgabe. (Transl. by Hermann Kusterer.) Düsseldorf: Econ Verlag, 1989.

Iivo [Antti Hyvönen], "Suomen kommunistisen puolueen KK:n täysi-istunto", *Kommunisti*, Oct. 15, 1932.

Jaakkola, N., P. Hyppönen, and V. Takala, *Leniniläisen vaiheen puolesta (tov. I. Lassyn Marxismin perusteiden arvostelua)*. Leningrad: Kirja, 1932.

Joint Plenum of the Central Committee and the Central Control Commission, 16–23 April, 1929. Published in *Resolutions and decisions of the Communist Party of the Soviet Union*. Vol. 2, *The Early Soviet Period: 1917–1929*. (Ed. by Richard Gregor.) Toronto: University of Toronto Press, 1974.

"**Kaatuneet** kommunaardit" in *Elokuun kommunaardit : kommunaardien muistojulkaisu : kommunismin puolesta kaatuneille elokuun 31 p:nä 1920 veriteon uhrien muistolle omistaa tämän julkaisun Suomen kommunistinen puolue*. Leningrad: S. K. P.:n K. K, 1926.

"***Kallis** toveri Stalin!*" : *Komintern ja Suomi*. (Ed. by Natalya Lebedeva, Kimmo Rentola, and Tauno Saarela.) Helsinki: Edita, 2002.

***Kansalaissota** dokumentteina*. (Ed. by Hannu Soikkanen.) Vols. 1 and 2. Helsinki: Tammi, 1967 and 1969.

***Kiireellisiä** toimintaohjeita Suomen vallankumoukselliselle työväelle ja sotaväelle : antanut Suom. Kommunistisen Puolueen Keskuskomitea*. Pietari 1919.

Kiisikinen, Aura, *Vuosikymmenien takaa : muistelmia*. Kolmas painos. Petroskoi: Karjalan ASNT:n valtion kustannusliike, 1960.

Kokko, Arvo, *Lapuan laki : talonpoikaisliike Suomessa v. 1930*. Vol. 1. Huopalahti: Tieto, 1930.

Kollontai, Alexandra, *Workers' Opposition*, published in *Selected Writings of Alexandra Kollontai*. (Transl. by Alix Holt.) London: Allison and Busby, 1977.

***Kommunistinen** vaalilippu : Suomen köyhälistölle, maan raatajille ja herravallan sortoa vihaaville sotilaille* in *Suomen Kommunistinen Puolue : puoluekokousten, konferenssien ja Keskuskomitean pleenumien päätöksiä : ensimmäinen kokoelma*. Leningrad: Kirja, 1935.

Kondratjev, Nikolai, *Luotettava toveri*. (Transl. by Tyyne Perttu.) Moskova: Edistys, s. a.

[**Krylenko**, N. V.], "Mitä vallankumouksellisen proletariaatin oikeus veriteosta sanoi", in *Elokuun kommunaardit : kommunaardien muistojulkaisu : kommunismin puolesta kaatuneille elokuun 31 p:nä 1920 veriteon uhrien muistolle omistaa tämän julkaisun Suomen kommunistinen puolue*. Leningrad: S. K. P.:n K. K, 1926.

Kulo, K. L., "Puolustimme Tamperetta" in *Luokkasodan muisto*. Helsinki: Kansankulttuuri, 1947.

Kuusinen, O. V. (W.), see also Sotamies, Usko.

Kuusinen, O. V., "Fasistiliikettä suomalaisten vallankumouspakolaisten keskuudessa Neuvosto-Venäjällä" in *Elokuun kommunaardit : kommunaardien muistojulkaisu : kommunismin puolesta kaatuneille elokuun 31 p:nä 1920 veriteon uhrien muistolle omistaa tämän julkaisun Suomen kommunistinen puolue*. Leningrad: S. K. P.:n K. K, 1926.

Kuusinen, O. W., *Sinovjevin historiallinen valhe* (Trotskin-Sinovjevin oppositiota vastaan 1927 kirjoitettu kirjanen). Published in O. W. Kuusinen, *Kommunistisen internationalen ja sen osastojen tehtävistä : puheita ja kirjoituksia*. Leningrad: Kirja, 1932.

Kuusinen, O. W., "Suomen porvariston johtajille", *Viesti*, March 24, 1920, in Otto V. Kuusinen and Yrjö Sirola, *Suomen työväen tulikoe : kirjoitelmia Suomen luokkasodan jälkeisiltä ajoilta*. Amerikan suomal. sosialistiset kustannusliikkeet, s. l., 1923.

Kuusinen, O. W., "Suomen sosialidemokratian johtajille", *Sosialistinen Aikakauslehti*, April 16, 1920.

Kuusinen, O. W, *Suomen vallankumouksesta : itsekritiikkiä*. Pietari: Suomalaisen Kommunistisen Puolueen Keskuskomitea, 1918.

Kuusinen, O. W., "Uusi kausi ja käänne Kominternin politiikassa (Tov. Stalinin 50-vuotispäivän johdosta kirjoitettu artikkeli)" in O. W. Kuusinen, *Kommunistisen internationalen ja sen osastojen tehtävistä : puheita ja kirjoituksia*. Leningrad: Kirja, 1932.

Kuusinen, O. W., *The Finnish Revolution : a Self-Criticism*. London: The Workers' Socialist Federation, 1919.

Kuusinen, O. W., "Venäjän johdolla" in O. W. Kuusinen, *Valitut teokset (1918–1964)*. Moskova: Edistys, s. a.

Kuusinen, O. W., "Yhteenvedot VKP:ssa esiintyneestä oppositiosta" in O. W. Kuusinen, *Valitut teokset (1918–1964)*. Moskova: Edistys, s. a.

Laaksovirta, Einari, see Tähti, N.

Laukki, Leo, *Suuret orjataistelut : piirteitä vanhan-ajan työväenliikkeestä*. Fitchburg, Mass: Suom. sos. kust.-yhtiö, 1912.

Laukki, Leo, *Teolliseen yhteiskuntaan*. Duluth, Minn.: The Workers Socialist Pub. Co., 1917.

Laukki, Leo, *Venäjän vallankumous, bolshevismi ja soviettitasavalta*. Duluth, Minn.: Workers Socialist Publishing Company, 1919.

"The **Left** Communists on the Consequences of Peace Treaty with Germany", originally published in *Kommunist*, April 1918. Extracts published in *The Russian Revolution 1917–1921*. (Ed. by Ronald Kowalski.) London: Routledge, 1997.

Lenin, V. I., "Kirje tovereille", *Kommunisti*, Oct. 15, 1932.

Liebknecht, Karl, *Militarismi ja antimilitarismi erikoisesti kansainvälistä nuorisoliikettä silmälläpitäen*. (There is no mention about translator.) Tampere: Tampereen Työväen Kirjapaino, 1910.

Louhikko, E. K., *Teimme vallankumousta*. Helsinki: Suomen kirja, 1943.

Luhtakanta, Arvid (Emil Saarinen), *Suomen punakaarti*. Kulju: E. A. Täckman, 1938.

Lumivuokko, J., *Laillinen ammattiyhdistysliike vaiko vallankumous?* Pietari: Suomalaisen Kommunistisen Puolueen Keskuskomitea, 1919.

Lumivuokko, J., *Teollisen tuotannon järjestämisestä Työväen diktatuurin ensi asteilla Suomessa*. Pietari: Suomalaisen Kommunistisen Puolueen Keskuskomitea, 1919.

Luxemburg, Rosa, *Massenstreik, Partei und Gewerskchaften*. Published in Rosa Luxemburg, *Ausgewählte politische Schriften in drei Bänden*. Vol. 2. Frankfurt am Main: Marxistische Blätter, 1971.

Luxemburg, Rosa, *Unser Programm und die politische Situation*. Speech given in the founding Congress of the German Communist Party, December 31, 1918. Published in *Die Gründung der KPD : Protokoll und Materialen des Gründungsparteitages der Kommunistischen Partei Deutschlands 1918/1919*. Berlin: Dietzz Verlag, 1993.

"**Maanviljelystyöväen** keskimääräiset palkat vuosina 1914–1923 / Salaires moyens d'ouvriers agricoles 1914–1923" in *Suomen Tilastollinen Vuosikirja 1924 / Annuaire Statistique de Finlande 1924*. Helsinki: Tilastollinen Päätoimisto / Le Bureau Central de Statistique de Finlande, 1925.

Machiavelli, Niccolò, *The Discourses* [*on the First Ten Books of Titus Livius*]. (Ed. with an introduction by Bernard Crick using the translation of Leslie J. Walker, S.J. with revisions by Brian Richardson.) London: Penguin Books, 1974.

Mäkinen, Hannes, see M. Stein.

Malm, Hanna, see Mutteri.

Manifesti Eduskunnan hajoittamisesta heinäkuun 18/31 päivänä 1917 ja uusien vaalien toimittamisesta, *Suomen Suuriruhtinaanmaan Asetuskokoelma* N:o 50, 1917. Published in *Suomen kansanedustuslaitoksen historia*. Vol. XII. Helsinki: Eduskunnan historiakomitea, 1982.

Manner, K., "Tärkeimpien joukkokamppailujemme epäonnistumisen johdosta", *Proletaari*, 6, 1931.

Manner, Kullervo and Hanna Malm, *Rakas kallis toveri : Kullervo Mannerin ja Hanna Malmin kirjeenvaihtoa 1932–33*. (Ed. by Jukka Paastela and Hannu Rautkallio). Porvoo: WSOY, 1997.

Manner, Olga, "Verilöylyssä" in *Elokuun kommunaardit : kommunaardien muistojulkaisu : kommunismin puolesta kaatuneille elokuun 31 p:nä 1920 veriteon uhrien muistolle omistaa tämän julkaisun Suomen kommunistinen puolue*. Leningrad: S. K. P.:n K. K, 1926.

Mitshkevitsh-Kapsukas [Vikentii], "Baltian maiden kommunististen puolueiden tilasta", *Kommunisti*, Nov. 15. 1932.

Mitä tahtoo Suomalainen Kommunistinen Puolue? : Selostuksia Moskovan neuvottelukokouksista elok. 25 p. – syysk. 5. p. 1918. Stockholm: Framis Förlag, 1918.

[**Molotov**, V. M.], *Molotov Remembers : Inside Kremlin Politics : Conversations with Felix Chuev.* (Ed. by Albert Reis.) Chicago: Ivan R. Dee, 1993 [1991].

Mutteri [Hanna Malm], "Puolueemme ja taistelu työväen elinehtojen puolesta", *Proletaari*, 1, 1931.

***On** the Syndicalist and Anarchist Deviation in Our Party*. Published in *Resolutions and decisions of the Communist Party of the Soviet Union.* Vol. 2, *The Early Soviet Period: 1917–1929.* (Ed. by Richard Gregor.) Toronto: University of Toronto Press, 1974.

Osinski, N., *Sosialismin rakentaminen : yleiset tehtävät : tuotannon järjestäminen.* Pietari: V.K.P:n Suomalaisten Järjestöjen Keskus-Toimisto, 1920.

Palomeri, R. (pseudonym of Raoul Palmgren), *30-luvun kuvat.* Helsinki: Tammi, 1953.

***Pöytäkirja** Suomen Sosialidemokratisen Nuorisoliiton II:sta edustajakokouksesta Vaasassa 6–8 p. kesäk. 1908.* Vaasa: Vapaan Sanan kirjapaino, 1908.

Preliminary list of delegates in *Workers of the World and Oppressed Peoples, Unite! : Proceedings and Documents of the Second Congress [of the Comintern].* Vol. 2. (Ed. by John Riddell.) New York: Pathfinder Press, 1991

Presidentin valitsijamiesten vaalit vuonna 1925 / Èlections des électeurs du président en 1925 in *Suomen Tilastollinen Vuosikirja 1925 / Annuaire Statistique de Finlande 1926.* Helsinki: Tilastollinen Päätoimisto / Le Bureau Central de Statistique de Finlande, 1925.

***Proceedings** and Documents of the Second Congress*, see *Workers of the World and Oppressed Peoples, Unite! : Proceedings and Documents of the Second Congress [of the Comintern].*

[**Relander**, Lauri Kristian], *Presidentin päiväkirja.* Vol. 1, *Lauri Kristian Relanderin muistiinpanot vuosilta 1925–1927.* (Ed. by Eino Jutikkala.) Helsinki: Weilin + Göös, 1927.

Report of the Executive Committee, July 6, 1920 in *Workers of the World and Oppressed Peoples, Unite! : Proceedings and Documents of the Second Congress [of the Comintern], [July 19–August 7], 1920.* Vol. 1. (Ed. by John Riddell.) New York: Pathfinder Press, 1991.

Rahja, Jukka, "Kämärä" in *Punakaarti rintamalla : luokkasodan muistoja.* Leningrad: Kirja, 1929.

Rantanen, S. Hj., *Kuljin SKP:n tietä.* Toinen painos. Helsinki: Otava.

Saarinen, Emil, see Luhtakanta, Arvid.

***Saksan** Spartacus : omistettu Karl Liebknechtin ja Rosa Luxemburgin muistolle.* Pietari: Suomalaisten Kommunistien Sarjajulkaisu no 45, 1919.

Šaljapin, Fjodor, *Šaljapin* in Maxim Gorki and Fjodor Šaljapin, *Šaljapin.* (Transl. by Seppo and Päivi Heikinheimo.) Porvoo: WSOY, 1987.

Salmi, Väinö, *Pakolaisena Itä-Karjalassa eli Neljätoista vuotta sosialismia rakentamassa. Muistelmien II osa vuosilta 1927–1929.* Helsinki: Akateeminen kustannusliike, 1970.

Salmi, Väinö, *Punaisen sirpin Karjala : suomalaisten kommunistien kohtaloita Neuvostoliitossa. Muistelmia ja vastamuistelmia suomalaisten kommunistien kohtaloista Neuvosto-Karjalassa.* Jyväskylä: Alea-kirja, 1976.

Sinovjev, G., "Mielettömyyttä ja rikosta", a speech hold in the common meeting of Finnish Party organisations, Sept. 17, 1920, published in *Elokuun kommunaardit : kommunaardien muistojulkaisu : kommunismin puolesta kaatuneille elokuun 31 p:nä 1920 veriteon uhrien muistolle omistaa tämän julkaisun Suomen kommunistinen puolue.* Leningrad: S. K. P.:n K. K, 1926.

Sirola, Yrjö, *«Isänmaa on vaarassa – aseisiin!» : Puhe pidetty suomalaisille puna-armeijalaisille Moskovassa heinäkuulla 1918.* Pietari: Suomalaisen Kommunistisen Puolueen Keskuskomitea, 1918.

[**Sirola**, Yrjö], *Kunnia Lokakuun Vallankumouksen Sankareille! : Puhe, jonka tov. YRJÖ SIROLA piti Pietarin Suomalaisten työläisten vallankumousjuhlassa 8 p:nä marrask. 1918.* Pietari: Suomalaisten Kommunistisen Puolueen Keskuskomitea, 1918.

S[irola], Y[rjö], "Suomen työväen v:n 1918 vallankumouksen johto bolshevikkien luxemburgilaisena arvostelijana – käytännössä", *Kommunisti*, January 1932.

Sirola, Yrjö, "Ulkoasiain valtuutettuna vallankumoushallituksessa : muistelmia ja mietteitä" in *Suomen luokkasota : historiaa ja muistelmia.* (Ed. by A. Halonen.) Superior, Wis.: Amerikan Suom. Sos. Kustannusliikkeiden Liitto, 1928.

Sotamies, Usko (O. W. Kuusinen), "Kirje vasemmistososialismista ja kommunismista", *Sosialistinen Aikakauslehti*, Oct. 10, 1919.

Sotamies, Usko, (O. W. Kuusinen), "Valkoinen hallitusmuoto", *Sosialistinen Aikakauslehti*, Aug. 1, 1919.

[**Stalin** I. V.], *Stalin's Letters to Molotov 1925–1936.* (Ed. by Lars T. Lih, Oleg V. Naumov and Oleg V. Khlevniuk; transl. by Catherine A Fitzpatrick.) New Haven: Yale University Press, 1995.

Stalin, J. V., "Muutamista bolshevismin historian kysymyksistä", *Kommunisti*, November, 1931.

Stein, M. (Hannes Mäkinen), "Tilanteesta Suomessa : Suomen kommunistisen puolueen tilasta ja tehtävistä", *Kommunisti*, Feb. 25, 1934.

Steinberg, I. V., *In the Workshop of the Revolution.* New York: Rinnehart, 1953.

Sundström, Cay, "Barbusse ja 'ajatuksen internationaali'", *Kirjallisuuslehti*, July 15, 1935.

Suomen kansanvaltuuskunnan ehdotus Suomen valtiosäännöksi : esitetty pääneuvostolle tarkastettavaksi ja päätettäväksi yleistä kansanäänestystä varten. Helsinki: Suomen kansanvaltuuskunta, 1918.

Suomen Kommunistisen Puolueen Keskuskomitean teesit Suomen vallankumouksesta 1918, published in *Kommunisti* 1/1929 under the title "Suomen Työväen vallankumous v. 1918".

Suomen Sosialidemokratisen Puolueen yhdeksännen puoluekokouksen pöytäkirja : kokous pidetty Helsingissä kesäkuun 15–18 p:nä 1917. Turku: Sosialistin Kirjapaino-osuuskunta, 1918.

Suomen sosialistisen työväenpuolueen ohjelma. (Hyväksytty puolueen perustavassa kokouksessa Helsingissä 15.5.1920.) Published in Olavi Borg, *Suomen puolueet ja puolueohjelmat 1880–1964.* Porvoo: WSOY, 1965.

Suomen valtiollinen tila ja puolueen lähimmät tehtävät. Published in *Suomen Kommunistinen Puolue : puoluekokousten, konferenssien ja Keskuskomitean Plenumien päätöksiä : ensimmäinen kokoelma.* Leningrad: Kirja, 1935.

Tähti, N. (Einari Laaksovirta), *Fasismi ja Suomen maaseutu.* Leningrad: Kirja, 1935.

Tähti, N. (Einari Laaksovirta), *Luokkakerrostuminen Suomen maaseudulla ja proletariaatin liittolaiskysymys.* Leningrad: Kirja, 1934.

Taimi, Adolf, *Sivuja eletystä.* Petroskoi 1954.

Tanner, Väinö, *Kahden maailmansodan välissä : muistelmia 20- ja 30-luvuilta.* Helsinki: Tammi. 1966.

Tanner, Väinö, *Kuinka se oikein tapahtui : vuosi 1918 esivaiheineen ja jälkiselvittelyineen.* Helsinki: Tammi, 1957.

Theses on the role and structure of the Communist Party before and after the taking of power by the proletariat, in *Workers of the World and Oppressed Peoples, Unite! : Proceedings and Documents of the Second Congress [of the Comintern], [July 19–August 7], 1920*, vol. 1. (Ed. by John Riddell.) New York: Pathfinder Press, 1991.

Toiset valtiopäivät 1917 : pöytäkirjat. Helsinki: Valtioneuvosto, 1918.

Toiset valtiopäivät 1929 : pöytäkirjat. Helsinki: Valtioneuvosto, 1930.

Trotsky, Léon, *Défense du marxisme : U.R.S.S., marxisme et bureaucratie.* (Transl. by Denis Berger, Jean-Jacques Marie, Katya Dorey and G. Volochine.) Paris: Etudes et documentations internationales, 1976.

Trotsky, Leon, "Hands off Rosa Luxemburg", *The Militant*, Aug. 6 and 13, 1932. Published in (Lev Trotskii), *Writings of Leon Trotsky.* (1932, ed. by George Breitman and Sarah Lovell.) New York: Pathfinder Press, 1973.

Trotsky, Leon, *Literature and Revolution.* (Transl. by Rose Strunsky.) Ann Arbor: The University of Michigan Press, 1971 [1924].

Trotsky, Leon, *My Life : an Attempt at an Autobiography.* (The name of the translator is not mentioned.) Harmondsworth: Penguin Books, 1984 [1929].

Trotsky, Leon, *The New Course.* (Transl. by Max Shachtman.) In Leon Trotskii, *The New Course* and Max Shachtman, *The Struggle for the New Course.* Ann Arbor: The University of Michigan Press, 1965 [1923].

Valtiopäivät 1921, liitteet I–VIII. Helsinki: Valtioneuvosto 1921.

Tuominen, Arvo, *The Bells of the Kremlin : an Experience in Communism*. (Ed. by Piltti Heiskanen, transl. by Lily Leino.) Hanover, N.H.: University Press of New England.

Tuominen, Arvo, *Kremlin kellot : muistelmia vuosilta 1933–1939*. 2. painos. Helsinki: Tammi, 1956.

Tuominen, Arvo, *Maan päällä ja alla : muistelmia vuosilta 1921–1933*. Neljäs painos. Helsinki: Tammi, 1958.

Tuominen, Arvo, *Sirpin ja vasaran tie : muistelmia*. Neljäs painos. Helsinki: Tammi, 1956.

Valtiopäivät 1930 : pöytäkirjat. Helsinki: Valtioneuvosto, 1930.

Wallenius, Allan, "O. W. Kuusinen", *Sosialistinen Aikakauslehti,* March 1, 1920.

Wilkuna Kyösti, *Kahdeksan kuukautta Shpalernajassa.* Helsinki: Kustannusosakeyhtiö Kirja, 1917.

Workers of the World and Oppressed Peoples, Unite!* : *Proceedings and Documents of the Second Congress [of the Comintern], [July 19–August 7], 1920. Vols. 1 and 2. (Ed. by John Riddell.) New York: Pathfinder Press, 1991.

Wuolijoki, Hella, *Und ich war nicht Gefangene : Memoiren und Skizzen*. (Ed. by Richard Semrau, transl. by Regine Pirschel.) Rostock: Hinstorff, 1987.

Zinov'ev, G., see Sinovjev, G.

Ylimääräiset valtiopäivät 1918 : pöytäkirjat. Helsinki: Valtioneuvosto, 1918.

Printed Primary Material in Russian

Note:
"PSS" refers to Lenin's Collected works. (В. И. Ленин, В. И., *Полное собрание сочнений*. Издание пятое. Москва: Государственное издательство, 1976–1978.)
Stalin's Collected works (И. В. Сталин, *Сочинения*) were published in 1948–1951 in Moscow by Государственное издательство политической литературы.

Бухарин, Н., *Программа коммунистов (большевиков)*. Петроград: Издание Петроградского Совета Рабочних и Красноарм. Депутатов, 1919.

Зиновьев, Г, *Беспартийный или коммунист : речь т. Зиновьева на собрании, в театре Речкина на Московской заставой*. Москва: Государтственное издателъство, 1919.

Ленин, В. И., *Государство и революция : учение марксизма о государстве и задачи пролетариата в революции*. PSS, vol. 33.

Ленин, В. И., Заключительное слово перед закрытием съезда 18 (31) января. Третий всероссийский съезд советов рабочих, солдатских и крестьянских депутатов. PSS, vol. 35.

Ленин, В. И. Заключительное слово по отчету ЦК РКП(б) 9 марта [1921]. PSS, vol. 43.

Ленин, В. И., *Из дневника публициста : (темы для разработки)*. Written in January 1918. published in *Ленинский сборник*. Vol. XI. (Ed. by N. I. Buharin, V. M. Molotov, and M. A. Saveleva.) Москва: Институт Ленина при Ц. К. В. К. П. (б.), MCMXXIX. Nendeln, Liechtenstein: Kraus Reprint, 1966.

Ленин, В. И., "Как В. Засулич убивает ликвидаторство", *Просвещение*, September, 1913. PSS, vol. 19.

Ленин, В. И., О профессиональных союзах, о текущем моменте и об ошибках т. Троцкого : речь на соединенном заседании делегатов VIII съезда советов, членов ВЦСПС и МГСПС – членов РКП(б) до декабря 1920 г. PSS, vol. 32.

Ленин, В. И., Отчет о политической деятельности ЦК РКП(б) 8 марта [1921]. (Speech in the Xth Congress of the RKP(b)). PSS, vol. 43.

Ленин, В. И., "Письмо к товарищам", *Рабочий Путь*, Oct. 19, 20 and 21 (Nov. 1, 2, and 3). PSS, vol. 34.

Ленин, В. И., Политический отчет центрального комитета РКП(б) 27 марта 1922. PSS, vol. 45.

Ленин, В. И., "Политический шантаж", *Пролетарий*, Aug. 24 / Sept. 6, 1917. PSS, vol. 34.

Ленин, В. И., *Пролетарская революция и ренегат Каутский*. PSS, vol. 37.

Ленин, *Что делать? : наболевшие вопросы нашего движения*. PSS, vol. 6.

Петерс, "Воспоминания о работе в ВЧК в первый год революции", *Пролетарская революция*, 10 (33), Октябрь 1924.

Постановление Политбюро о конспирации, May 16, 1929 in *Сталинское Политбюро в 30-е годы : Сборник документов*. Москва: Аиро – XX, 1995.

Слуцкий, А., "Большевики о германской с.-д. в период ее предвоенного кризиса", *Пролетарская революция*, July 6, 1930.

Сталин, И. В., Заключительное слово по политическому отчету центрального комитета, 23 декабря, [1925]. И. В. Сталин, *Сочинения*, vol. 7.

Сталин, И. В., "К международному положению". *Большевик*, Sept. 20, 1924. И. В. Сталин, *Сочинения*, vol. 6.

Сталин, И. В., Международное положение и оборона СССР : речь 1 августа. И. В. Сталин, *Сочинения*, vol. 10.

Сталин, И. В., Об основах ленинизма : Лекции читанные в Свердлосвском университете (1924). И. В. Сталин, *Сочинения*, vol. 6.

Сталин, И. В., *Октябрьская революция и тактика русских коммунистов : предисловие к книге "На путях к Октябрю"*. И. В. Сталин, *Сочинения*, vol. 6.

Сталин, И. В., О независимости Финляндии : доклад на заседании ВЦИК 22 декабря 1917 г. (Газетный отччм), *Правда*, Dec. 23, 1917. И. В. Сталин, *Сочинения*, vol. 4.

Сталин, И. В., "О некоторых вопросах истории большевизма : писмо о редакцию 'Пролетарская Революция'", *Пролетарская Революция*, 6/1931. И. В. Сталин, *Сочинения*, vol. 13.

Сталин, И. В., "Ответ Олехновичу и Аристову : по поводу письма о редакцию журнала 'Пролетарская Революция' 'О некоторых вопросах истории большевизма'", *Большевик*, Aug. 30, 1932 (dated January 25, 1932), И. В. Сталин, *Сочинения*, vol. 13.

Сталин, И. В., Отчетный доклад XVII съезду партии о работе ЦК ВКП(б), 26 января 1934 г. И. В. Сталин, *Сочинения*, vol. 13.

Сталин, Отчетный доклад ЦК, 27 июля, 1917 г. in И. В. Сталин, *Сочинения*, vol. 3.

Сталин, И. В., По поводу смерти Ленина : речь на II Всесоюзном съезде Советов, 26 января 1924 г. И. В. Сталин, *Сочинения*, vol. 6.

Сталин, И. В., Речь на съезде финляндской социал-демократической рабочей партии в Гельсингфорсе, 14 ноября 1917 г., *Правда*, Nov. 16, 1917. И. В. Сталин, *Сочинения*, vol. 4.

Ялава, Г. Э., "'Кочегар' паровоза № 293" in *Воспоминания о Владимире Ильиче Ленине*. Vol. 1. Москва: Государственное изательство политической литературы, 1956.

Secondary Literature

Aaltonen, Olavi, "Kullervo Akilles Manner" in *Tiennäyttäjät : Suomen työväenliikkeen merkkimiehiä Ursinista Tanneriin*. Helsinki: Tammi, 1967.

Abeshaus, G. and Protasov, *Puoluetiedon kirja : oppikirja kaupunkien supistettuja puoluekouluja varten : valtion oppineiden komitean tieteellispoliittisen jaoston hyväksymä*. Vol. 1. Leningrad: Kirja, 1926.

Abraham, Richard, *Rosa Luxemburg : a Life for the International*. Oxford: Berg, 1989 .

Ahola, Tero, *Leo Laukki Amerikan suomalaisessa työväenliikkeessä*. Unprinted master's thesis in political history. Library of the Faculty of Social Sciences, University of Helsinki, 1973.

Ahti, Martti, *Kaappaus? Suojeluskuntaselkkaus 1921 : fascismin aave 1927 : Mäntsälän kapina 1932.* Helsinki: Otava, 1990.

Ahtokari, Reijo, *Pirtua, pirtua.... : kieltolaki Suomessa 1.6.1919–5.4.1932.* Porvoo: WSOY, 1972.

Ala-Kapee, Pirjo and Marjaana Valkonen, *Yhdessä elämä turvalliseksi : SAK:laisen ammattiyhdistysliikkeen kehitys vuoteen 1930.* Helsinki: Suomen ammattiliittojen keskusjärjestö, 1982.

Alapuro, Risto, *State and Revolution in Finland.* Berkeley: University of California Press, 1988.

Alapuro, Risto, *Suomen synty paikallisena ilmönä 1890–1933.* Helsinki: Hanki ja jää, 1994.

Arendt, Hannah, *The Origins of Totalitarianism.* New edition with added prefaces. New York: Harcourt Brace Jovanovich, 1973.

Aristotle, *The Politics.* (Ed. by Stephen Everson; there is no mention of the traslator.) Cambridge: the Cambridge University Press, 1988.

Arter David, *Politics and Policy-Making in Finland.* Brighton: Wheatsheaf Books, 1987.

Autio, Sari, "Soviet Karelian Forests in the Planned Economy of the Soviet Union, 1928–37" in *Rise and Fall of Soviet Karelia : People and Power.* (Ed. by Antti Laine and Mikko Ylikangas.) Helsinki: Kikimora Publications, 2002.

Basso, Lelio, *Rosa Luxemburg : a Reappraisal.* (Transl. by Douglas Parmée.) London: Andre Deutsch, 1975 [1967].

Berdyaev, Nicolas, *The Origin of Russian Communism.* (Transl. by R. M. French.) Manchester: Geoffrey Bles, 1937.

Bettelheim, Charles, *Les luttes des classes en URSS.* Vol. 1, *Première période 1917–1923.* Vol. 2, *Deuxième période 1923–1930.* Paris: Seuil | Maspero, 1974 and 1977.

Boll, Friedhelm, "Scheidemann, Philipp" in *Lexikon des Sozialismus.* (Ed. by Thomas Meyer, etc.) Köln: Bund, 1986.

Borg, Olavi, *Suomen puolueideologiat : periaateohjelmien sisältöanalyyttinen vertailu sekä katsaus niiden historialliseen taustaan ja syntyprosessiin.* Porvoo: WSOY, 1965.

Borg, Olavi and Risto Sänkiaho, "Demokratia jälleen koetuksella – pulakauden kautta punamultaan" in *Suomalaisten tarina.* Vol. 2, *Etsijäin aika.* (Ed. by Jaakko Itälä.) Helsinki: Kirjayhtymä 1993.

Borkenau, Franz, "Zur Soziologie des Fascismus", *Archiv für Sozialwisswnschaft und Sozialpolitik.* Februar 1933. Published in *Theorien über den Fascismus.* (Ed. by Ernst Nolte.) Königstein/Ts.: Verlagsgruppe Athenäum, Hain, Scriptor, Hanstein, 1979.

Boukovsky, Vladimir, *Jugement à Moscou: Un dissident dans les archives du Kremlin.* (Transl. by Louis Martinez.) Paris: Robert Laffont, 1995.

Braunthal, Julius, *History of the International.* Vols. 1, *1864–1914* & 2, *1914–1943.* (Transl. by John Clark.) London: Nelson, 1966 &1967.

Bronner, Stephen Erik, *Rosa Luxemburg : a Revolutionary for Our Times.* New York: Columbia University Press, 1987,

Broué, Pierre, *Histoire de l'Internationale communiste 1919–1943.* Paris: Fayard, 1997.

Brucker, Gene, *Florentine Politics and Society 1343–1378.* Princeton: Princeton University Press, 1962.

Brucker, Gene, *The Civic World of Early Renaissance Florence.* Princeton: Princeton University Press, 1977.

Burrowes, Robert, "Totalitarianism : the Revised Standard Version", in *Between Totalitarianism and Pluralism.* (Ed. by Alexander Dallin.) New York: Garland, 1992 [1969].

Calvez, Jean-Yves, *La pensée de Karl Marx.* Edition revue et abrégée. Paris: Editions du Seuil, 1970.

Carr, Edward Hallet and R. W. Davies, *Foundation of a Planned Economy.* Vol. 1. Harmondsworth: Penguin Books, 1974 [1969].

Carr, Edward Hallet, *Foundations of a Planned Economy 1926–1929.* Vol. 2. Harmondsworth: Penguin Books, 1976 [1971].

Carr, Edward Hallet, *Socialism in One Country 1924–1926.* Vols. 1–2. Harmondsworth: Penguin Books, 1970 [1958, 1959].

Carr, Edward Hallet, *The Bolshevik Revolution 1917–1923*. Vols. 1–3. Harmodsworth: Penguin Books, 1972 and 1973 [1950, 1952, 1953].

Carr, Edward Hallet, *The Interregnum 1923–1924*. Harmondsworth: Penguin Books, 1969 [1954]

Carr, E[dward] H[allet], *The Twilight of Comintern, 1930–1935*. London: Macmillan, 1982.

Carrère d'Enchausse, Hélène,*Victorieuse Russie*. Paris: Fayard, 1992.

Caute, David, *The Fellow-Travellers : a Postscript to the Enlightenment*. London: Quartet Books, 1977.

Chamberlin, William Henry, *The Russian Revolution 1917–1921*. Vol. 2. New York: Macmillan, 1960 [1935]

Churchill, Stacy, *Itä-Karjalan kohtalo 1917–1922 : Itä-Karjalan itsehallintokysymys Suomen ja Neuvosto-Venäjän suhteissa 1917–1922*. (Transl. by Katariina Churchill.) Porvoo: WSOY, 1970.

Churchward, L. G., *The Soviet* Intelligentsia : *an Essay on the social structure and roles of Soviet intellectuals during the 1960s*. London: Routledge and Kegan Paul, 1973

Claudin, Fernando, *The Communist Movement : From Comintern to Cominform*. Harmondsworth: Penguin Books, 1975.

Clements, Barbara Evans, *Bolshevik Feminist : the Life of Alexandra Kollontai*. Bloomington: Indiana University Press, 1979.

Cohen, Stephen F., "Bolshevism and Stalinism" in *Stalinism : Essays in Historical Interpretation*. (Ed. by Robert C. Tucker) New York: W. W. Norton, 1977.

Cohen, Stephen F., *Bukharin and the Bolshevik Revolution : a Political Biography*, 1888–1938. Oxford: Oxford University Press, 1980 [1971].

Cohen, Stephen F., *Rethinging the Soviet Experience : Politics and History Since 1917*. New York: Oxford University Press, 1986 [1985].

Courtine-Denamy, Sylvie, *Hannah Arendt*. Paris: Belfond, 1994.

Courtois, Stéphane, "Comprendre la tragédie communiste", *Le Monde*, Dec. 20, 1997.

Courtois, Stéphane, "Les crimes du communisme" and "Pourquoi?" in Stéphane Courtois, Nicolas Werth, Jean-Louis Panné, Andrzej Paczkowski, Karle Bartosek and Jean-Louis Margolin in collaboration with Rémi Kauffer, Pierre Rigoulot, Pascal Fontaine, Yves Santamaria and Sylvain Boulouque, *Le livre noir du communisme : crimes, terreur et répression*. Paris: Robert Laffont, 1997.

[**Courtois**, Stéphane], "Der rote Holocaust : Interview mit dem französichen Historiker Stéphane Courtois, dem Herausgeber des 'Schwarzbuches' ", *Die Zeit*, Nov. 21, 1997.

Dähn, Horst, *Rätedemokratische Modelle : Studien zur Rätediskussion in Deutschland 1918–1919*. Meissenheim am Glan: Anton Hain, 1975.

Daniels, Robert Vincent, *The Conscience of the Revolution : Communist Opposition in Soviet Russia*. Cambridge, Mass.: Harvard University Press, 1960.

Danielson-Kalmari, J. R., *La question des îles d'Aland de 1914 à 1920*. Helsinki: Imprimerie du gouvernement, 1921.

Davenport, T. R H., *South Africa. A Modern History*. Fourth Edition. Houndmills: Macmillan, 1991.

Davis, Mary, *Sylvia Pankhurst : a Life in Radical Politics*. London: Pluto Press, 1999.

DeFronzo, James, *Revolutions and Revolutionary Movements*. Boulder: Westview Press, 1996.

Deutscher, Isaac, *Stalin : a Political Biography*. Revised edition. Harmondsworth: Penguin Books, 1972 [1966].

Deutscher, Isaac, *The Prophet Armed : Trotsky: 1879–1921*. London: Oxford University Press, 1970 [1954].

Deutscher, Isaac, *The Prophet Unarmed : Trotsky: 1921–1929*. London: Oxford University Press, 1970 [1959].

Dobb, Maurice, *Soviet Economic Development since 1917*. Sixth revised edition. London: Routledge & Kegan Paul, 1972 [1966].

Durkheim, Émile, *The Elementary Forms of the Religious Life*. (Transl. by Joseph Ward Swain.) London: George Allen & Unwin, 1976 [1915].

Duverger, Maurice, *Les orangers du lac Balaton*. Paris: Seuil, 1980.

Duverger, Maurice, *Les partis politiques*. Paris: Armand Colin, 1976 [1951].

Eerola, Jari and Jouni Eerola, *Henkilötappiot Suomen sisällissodassa 1918*. Turenki: Jaarli, 1998.

Ehrnrooth, Jari, *Sanan vallassa, vihan voimalla : sosialistiset vallankumousopit ja niiden vaikutus Suomen työväenliikkeessä 1905–1914*. Helsinki: Suomen Historiallinen Seura, 1992.

Engels, Friedrich, Letter to Eduard Bernstein, Feb. 27–March 1, 1883. Published in Karl Marx and Friedrich Engels, *Werke*. Vol. 35. Berlin: Dietz Verlag, 1967.

Engels, Friedrich, Letter to Karl Marx, Feb. 12, 1851, in Karl Marx and Frederick Engels, *Collected Works*. Karl Marx and Frederick Engels, *Collected Works*. Vol. 38. Moscow: Progress Publishers, 1982.

Faisod, Merle, *How Russia is Ruled*. Second edition. Cambridge, Mass.: Harvard University Press, 1963.

Farnsworth, Beatrice, *Alexandra Kollontai : Socialism, Feminism, and the Bolshevik Revolution*. Stanford: Stanford University Press, 1980.

Faye, Jean Pierre, *Théorie du récit : introduction aux langages totalitaires : critique de la raison de l'économie narrative*. Paris: Hermann, 1972.

Fejtö, François, *L'Héritage de Lénine : introduction à l'histoire du communisme mondial*. Nouvelle édition revue et augmentée. Paris: Librairie Générale Française, 1977.

Fischer, Ruth, *Stalin und die deutsche Kommunismus*. Vol. 1, *Von der Entstehung des deutschen Kommunismus bis 1924*. Vol. 2, *Die Bolschewisierung des deutschen Kommunismus ab 1925*. Berlin: Dietz Verlag, 1991.

Fitzpatrick, Sheila, "New Perspectives on Stalinism" in *Stalin and Stalinism*. (Ed. by Alexander Dallin and Bertrand M. Patenaude.) New York: Garland, 1992 [1986].

Fowkes, Ben, *Communism in Germany under the Weimar Republic*. London: Macmillan, 1984.

Freeland, Richard M., *The Truman Doctrine and the Origins of McCarthyism : Foreign Policy, Domestic Politics and International Security 1946–1948*. New York: Alfred A. Knopf, 1972.

Friedrich, Carl Joachim, *Man and His Government : an Empirical Theory of Politics*. New York: McGraw-Hill, 1963.

Friedrich, Carl J. and Zbigbiew K. Brezezinski, *Totalitarian Dictatorship and Autocracy*. Second edition, revised by Carl J. Friedrich. Cambridge, Mass.: Harvard University Press, 1965.

Frölich, Paul, *Rosa Luxemburg : Ideas in Action*. (Transl. By Joanna Hoornweg.) London: Pluto Press, 1972 [1939].

Gellner, Ernest, *Nations and Nationalism*. Oxford: Blackwell, 1983.

Getty, J. Arch, "Party and Purge in Smolensk: 1933–1937" in *Between Totalitarianism and Pluralism*. (Ed. by Alexander Dallin.) New York: Garlan, 1992 [1983].

Getty, J. Arch, "State, Society, and Superstition" in *Stalin and Stalinism*. (Ed. by Alexander Dallin and Bertrand M. Patenaude.) New York: Garland, 1992 [1986].

Getty, J. Arch, *Origins of the Great Purges : the Soviet Communist Party Reconsidered, 1933–1938*. New York: Cambridge University Press, 1985.

Getzler, Israel, *Kronstadt 1917–192 : the Fate of A Soviet Democracy*. Cambridge: Cambridge University Press, 1983.

Gill, Graeme, *Stalinism*. London: Macmillan 1990.

Gill, Graeme, *The Origins of the Stalinist Political System*. Cambridge: Cambridge University Press, 1990.

Gleason, Abbot, "'Totalitarianism' in 1984" in *Between Totalitarianism and Pluralism*. (Ed. by Alexander Dallin.) New York: Garlan, 1992 [1984].

"**Glossary**" in *Workers of the World and Oppressed Peoples, Unite! : Proceedings and Documents of the Second Congress [of the Comintern]*. Vols. 1–2. (Ed. by John Riddell.) New York: Pathfinder Press, 1991.

Glucksmann, André, *Les maîtres penseurs*. Paris: Bernard Grasset, 1977.

Golomstock, Igor, "Problems in the Study of Stalinist Culture" in *The Culture of the Stalin Period*. (Ed. by Hans Günther.) London: Macmillan, 1990.

Gramsci, Antonio, *Selections from the Prison Notebooks*. (Ed. and transl. by Quintin Hoare and Geoffrey Nowell Smith.) London: Lawrence and Wishart, 1971.

Gregor, Richard, "Introduction" in *Resolutions and decisions of the Communist Party of the Soviet Union*. Vol. 2, *The Early Soviet Period: 1917–1929*. (Ed. by Richard Gregor.) Toronto: University of Toronto Press, 1974.

Haapala, Pertti, *Kun yhteiskunta hajosi : Suomi 1914–1920*. Helsinki: Painatuskeskus, 1995.

Haikara, Kalevi, *Bertold Brechtin aika, elämä ja tuotanto*. Helsinki: Art House, 1992.

Hakalehto, Ilkka, *Suomen kommunistinen puolue ja sen vaikutus poliittiseen ja ammatilliseen työväenliikkeeseen 1918–1928*. Porvoo: WSOY, 1966.

Hakovirta, Harto, *The World Refugee Problem*. Tampere Hillside, 1991.

Haslam, Jonathan, "Political Opposition to Stalin and the Origins of the Terror in Russia, 1932–1936" in *Between Totalitarianism and Pluralism*. (Ed. by Alexander Dallin.) New York: Garlan, 1992 [1986].

Hatch, John B., "Labor Struggles in Moscow, 1921–1925" in *Russia in the Era of NEP : Explorations in Soviet Society, and Culture*. (Ed. by Sheila Fitzpatrick, Alexander Rabinowitch and Richard Stites.) Bloomington: Indiana University Press, 1991.

Haupt, Georges and Jean-Jacques Marie, *Les bolchéviks par eux-mêmes*. Paris: François Maspero, 1969.

Heikkilä, Jouko, *Kansallista luokkapolitiikkaa : sosiaalidemokraatit ja Suomen autonomian puolustus 1905–1917*. Helsinki: Suomen historiallinen seura, 1993.

Held, David, *Models of Democracy*. Second edition. Cambridge: polity Press, 1996.

Heller, Agnes, "An Imaginary Preface to the 1984 Edition of Hannah Arendt's *The Origins of Totalitarianism*" in Ferenc Fehér and Agnes Heller, *Eastern Left, Western Left*. Cambridge: Polity Press, 1987.

Hirvikallio, Paavo, *Tasavallan presidentin vaalit Suomessa 1919–1950*. Helsinki, no mention about publisher (academic dissertation), 1958.

Hitler, Adolf, *Mein Kampf*. Vol. 1, *Eine Abrechnung*. München: Zentralverlag der NSDAP. Frz. Eher Nachf., 1941 [1925].

Hobsbawn, Eric, *Age of Extremes : the Short Twentieth Century 1914–1991*. London: Abacus, 1995.

Hodgson, John H., *Communism in Finland : A History and Interpretation*. Princeton: Princeton University Press, 1967.

Hodgson, John H., *Otto Wille Kuusinen : poliittinen elämäkerta*. Helsinki: Tammi, 1975.

Holodkovskij, V.M., *Suomi ja Neuvosto-Venäjä 1918–1920*. (Transl. by Marja-Leena Jaakkola.) Helsinki: Tammi, 1975.

Holt, Alix, "Translator's note" in *Selected Writings of Alexandra Kollontai*. London: Allison and Busby, 1977.

Huldén, Anders, *Kuningasseikkailu Suomessa*. (Transl. by Ritva Lassila.) Helsinki: Kirjayhtymä, 1988.

Immonen, Kari, *Ryssästä saa puhua… : Neuvostoliitto suomalaisessa julkisuudessa ja kirjat julkisuuden muotona 1918–39*. Helsinki: Otava, 1987.

Jakobson, Max, *Finnish neutrality : a Study of Finnish Foreign Policy Since the Second World War*. London: Hugh Evelyn, 1968.

Jansson, Jan-Magnus, "Eduskunnan hajotukset" in *Suomen kansanedustuslaitoksen historia*. Vol XII. Helsinki: Eduskunnan historiakomitea, 1982.

Jaroslawski, Jan, *Soziologie der kommunistischen Partei*. (Transl. by Edda Werfel.) Frankfurt: Campus, 1978.

Jarreau, Patrick, "Nouvelle controverse sur le caractère criminel du communisme", *Le Monde*, Dec. 20, 1997.

Jussila, Osmo, *Nationalismi ja vallankumous venäläis-suomalaisissa suhteissa 1899–1914*. Helsinki: Suomen Historiallinen Seura, 1979.

Jussila, Osmo, *Terijoen hallitus 1939–1940*. Porvoo: WSOY, 1994.

Jutikkala, Eino, "Finland Becomes an Autonomous State" and "Independent Finland" in Eino Jutikkala with Kauko Pirinen, *A History of Finland*. (Transl. by Paul Sjöblom.) Helsinki: WSOY, 1995.

Järvinen, Lauri, *Kalajoen työväenliikkeen historia.* Kalajoki: Kalajoen työväen historiatoimikunta, 1986.

Jääskeläinen, Mauno, *Itä-Karjalan kysymys : kansallisen laajennusohjelman synty ja sen toteuttaminen Suomen ulkopolitiikassa vuosina 1918–1920.* Porvoo: WSOY, 1961.

Kagarlitsky, Boris, *Thinking Reed : Intellectuals and the Soviet State : 1917 to the Present.* (Transl. by Brian Pearce.) London: Verso, 1988.

Kairamo, Aimo, *Ponnistuksien kautta vapauteen : Sosialidemokraatisen nuorisoliikkeen historia.* Vol 1, *1906–1922.* (Ed. by Harri Kivenmaa.) Helsinki: Sosialidemokraattisen Nuorison Keskusliitto & Nuorten Puolesta Keskusliitto, 1986.

Kangaspuro, Markku, "Läskikapina – SKP:n vallankumousyritys 1922", *Historiallinen aikakauskirja* 4/1998.

Kangaspuro, Markku, *Neuvosto-Karjalan taistelu itsehallinnosta : nationalismi ja suomalaiset punaiset Neuvostoliiton vallankäytössä.* Helsinki: Suomalaisen Kirjallisuuden Seura, 2000.

Kangaspuro, Markku, "Russian Patriots and Red Fennomans" in *Rise and Fall of Soviet Karelia.* (Ed. by Antti Laine and Mikko Ylikangas.) Helsinki: Kikimora Publications, 2002.

Karemaa, Outi, *Vihollisia, vainoojia, syöpäläisiä : venäläisviha Suomessa 1917–1923.* Helsinki: Suomen Historiallinen Seura, 1998.

Karsten, Rafael, *A Totalitarian State of the Past : the Civilization of the Inca Empire in Ancient Peru.* Helsingfors: Societas Scientarum Fennica, 1949.

Kasekamp, Andres, *The Radical Right in Interwar Estonia.* London: Macmillan, 2000.

Kenez, Peter, *The Birth of the Propaganda State : Soviet Methods of Mass Mobilization 1917–1929.* Cambridge: Cambridge University Press, 1985.

Ketola, Eino, *Kansalliseen kansanvaltaan : Suomen itsenäisyys, sosialidemokraatit ja Venäjän vallankumous 1917.* Helsinki: Tammi, 1987.

Ketonen, Oiva, *Kansakunta murroksessa : kesä 1918 ja sen taustaa.* Porvoo: WSOY, 1983.

Kettunen, Pauli, *Poliittinen liike ja sosiaalinen kollektiivisuus : tutkimus sosialidemokratiasta ja ammattiyhdistysliikkeestä Suomessa 1918–1930.* Helsinki: Suomen Historiallinen Seura, 1986.

Khlevniouk, Oleg, *Le cercle du Kremlin : Staline et le Bureau politique dans les années 30 : les jeux du pouvoir.* (Transl. by Pierre Forgues and Nicholas Werth.) Paris: Seuil, 1996.

Khrushchev, Nikita, *Secret Speech* [of 1956]. Published in *Khrushchev remembers.* Boston: Little, Brown and Company, 1970.

Kilin, Juri, *Suurvallan rajamaa: Neuvosto-Karjala Neuvostoliiton politiikassa 1920–1941.* (Transl. by Robert Kolomainen and Ari Hepoaho.) Rovaniemi: Pohjois-Suomen historiallinen yhdistys, 2001.

Knight, Amy, *Beria : Stalin's First Liutenant.* Princeton: Princeton University Press, 1993.

Kock, W. J. de, "The Anglo-Boer War, 1899–1902" in C. F J. Müller (ed.), *Five Hundred Years : a History of South Africa.* Third revised edition. Pretoria: Academica, 1981.

Kolakowski, Leszek, "Totalitarianism and the Virtue of the Lie", in *1984 Revisited : Totalitarianism in Our Century.* (Ed. by Irving Howe.) New York: Harper & Row, 1983.

Kolakowski, Leszek, *Main Currents of Marxism : its Origin, Growth, and Dissolution.* Vol. 3, *The Breakdown.* (Transl. by P. S. Falla.) Oxford: Claredon Press, 1978.

Kosiek, Rolf, *Historikerstreit und Geschichtsrevision.* Tübingen: Grabert, 1987.

Kossolapow, Richard, "Zur Herausbildung des kommunistischen Charakters der Arbeit im realen Sozialismus", *Marx-Engels-Jahrbuch* 3, 1980.

Kujala, Antti, *Vallankumous ja kansanllinen itsemääräämisoikeus : Venäjän sosialistiset puolueet ja suomalainen radikalismi vuosisadan alussa.* Helsinki: Suomen historiallinen seura, 1989.

"**Kustantajan** alkusana" in Nuori Otto Ville Kuusinen 1881–1920. Jyväskylä: K. J. Gummerus, 1970.

Köhler, Joachim, *Wagners Hitler : der Prophet und sein Vollstrecker.* München: Karl Blessing, 1997.

Lackman, Matti, *Jahvetti Moilanen – Läskikapinan johtaja : poliittinen elämäkerta (1881–1938).* Scripta Historica XX. Oulu: Oulun historiaseura, 1993.

Lackman, Matti. "Kommunistien salainen toiminta Kainuussa (1918–1944)" in Reijo Heikkinen and Matti Lackman, *Korpikansan kintereillä : Kainuun työväenliikkeen historia*. Kajaani: Kainuun työväenliikkeen historiatoimikunta, 1986.

Lackman, Matti, *Kommunistien salainen toiminta Tornionjokilaaksossa 1918–1939*. Oulu: Pohjoinen, 1991.

Lackman, "Mihin katosi Jalmari Rasi?" in *Turun historiallinen arkisto*, vol. 37. Turku: Turun historiallinen yhdistys, 1982

Lackman, Matti, "Mikä kaatoi Kullervo Mannerin?", *Historiallinen Aikakauskirja* 3/1981.

Lackman, Matti, "Mitalin toinen puoli" in Lacman, *Jääkärimuistelmia*. Helsinki: Otava, 1994.

Lackman, Matti, *Suomen vai Saksan puolesta? : jääkäriliikkeen ja jääkäripataljoona 27:n (1915–1918) synty, luonne, mielialojen vaihteluita sekä sisäisiä kriisejä sekä niiden heijastuksia itsenäisen Suomen ensi vuosiin saakka*. Helsinki: Otava 2000.

Lackman, Matti, *Taistelu talonpojasta : Suomen Kommunistisen Puolueen suhde talonpoikaiskysymykseen ja talonpoikaisliikkeeseen 1918–1939*. Oulu: Pohjoinen, 1991.

Lackman, Matti and Tuulia Sirviö, "Etsivä keskuspoliisi : 'valkoisen Suomen' turvallisuuspoliisi (1919–1937" in *Isänmaan puolesta : Suojelupoliisi 50 vuotta*. (Ed. by Matti Simola and Tuulia Sirviö.) Jyväskylä: Gummerus, 1999.

Lahti-Argutina, Eila, *Olimme joukko vieras vain : venäjänsuomalaiset vainouhrit Neuvostoliitossa 1930-luvun alusta 1950-luvun alkuun*. Turku: Siirtolaisinstituutti, 2001.

Laine, Antti, *Suur-Suomen kahdet kasvot : Itä-Karjalan siviiliväestön asema suomalaisessa miehityshallinnossa 1941–1944*. Helsinki: Otava, 1982.

Laing, Dave, *The Marxist Theory of Art*. Sussex: The Harvester Press, 1978.

Lappalainen, Jussi, T., *Itsenäisen Suomen synty*. Neljäs, korjattu painos. Jyväskylä: 1985.

Lauerma, Matti, *Kuninkaallinen Preussin jääkäripataljoona 27: vaiheet ja vaikutus*. Porvoo: WSOY, 1966.

Laqueur, Walter, *Stalin: The Glasnost Revelations*. London: Hyman, 1990.

Lefort, Claude, *The Political Forms of Modern Society : Bureaucracy, Democracy, Totalitarianism*. (Ed. by John B. Thompson.) Cambridge: Polity Press, 1984.

Leggett, George, *The Cheka: Lenin's Political Police : the All-Russian Extraordinary Commission for Combating Counter-Revolution and Sabotage (December 1917 to February 1922)*. Oxford: Claredon Press, 1981.

Leskinen, Eino, "Uhtua" in *Otavan iso tietosanakirja*, vol. 9. Helsinki: Otava, s.a.

Liebman, Marcel, *Le Léninisme sous Lénine*. Vol. 2, *L'épreuve du pouvoir*. Paris; Seuil, 1973.

Lih, Las T. "Introduction" in *Stalin's Letters to Molotov 1925–1936*. (Ed. Lars T. Lih, Oleg V. Naumov and Oleg V. Khlevniuk.) New Haven: Yale University Press, 1995.

Linsiö, Liisa, *Komintern ja Kuusinen*. Helsinki: Kursiivi, 1978.

Linz, Juan J., "Totalitarian and Authoritarian Regimes" in *Handbook of Political Science*. (Ed. by Fred, I. Greenstein and Nelson W. Polsby.) Vol. III. Reading, Mass.: Addison-Wesley, 1975.

Lukács, Georg, *History and Class Consciousness : Studies in Marxist Dialectics*. (Transl. by Rodney Livingston.) Cambridge, Mass.: The MIT Press, 1972.

Majander, Mikko, "The Soviet view on Social Democracy : From Lenin to the End on the Stalin Era", in *Communism : National & International*. (Ed. by Tauno Saarela and Kimmo Rentola.) Helsinki: Suomen Historiallinen Seura, 1998.

Malia, Martin, *The Soviet Tragedy : a History of Socialism in Russia. 1917–1991*. New York: The Free Press, 1994.

Manninen, Ohto, "Taistelevat osapuolet" in *Itsenäistymisen vuodet 1917–1920*. Vol. 2, *Taistelu vallasta*. Helsinki: Painatuskeskus, 1993.

Manninen, Turo, *Vapaustaistelu, kansalaissota ja kapina : taistelun luonne valkoisten sotapropagandassa vuonna 1918*. Jyväskylä: Studia historica Jyväskyläensia 24, 1982.

Marcou, Lily, "Tardive querelle d'Allemands", *Le Monde*, Nov. 14, 1997.

Margolin, Jean-Louis "'Historien, militant ou procureur?'", *Le Monde*, Nov. 9–10, 1997.

Margolin, Jean-Louis and Nicolas Werth, "Communisme : retour à l'histoire", *Le Monde*, Nov. 14, 1997.

Marjomäki, Heikki, "Translated Communism : Remarks on 'Politics Translated' in the Finnish Communist Movement during the 1920s and 1930s" in *Communism National & International*. (Ed. by Tauno Sarela and Kimmo Rentola.) Helsinki: Suomen Historiallinen Seura, 1998.

Marks, Shula, "Southern and Central Africa, 1852–1910" in *The Cambridge History of Africa*. Vol. 6, *From 1870 to 1905*. Cambridge: Cambridge University Press, 1985.

Marx, Karl, Letter to Wilhelm Liebknecht, Feb. 11, 1878. Published in Karl Marx and Friedrich Engels, *Werke*. Vol. 34. Berlin: Dietz Verlag, 1967.

Marx, Karl and Friedrich Engels, Letter to August Bebel, Wilhelm Liebknecht, Wilhelm Bracke etc. Sept. 17–18, 1879, published in Karl Marx and Friedrich Engels, *Werke*. Vol. 34. Berlin: Dietz Verlag, 1967.

Marx, Karl and Frederick Engels, *The German Ideology*. Published in Karl Marx and Friedrich Engels, *Collected Works*. Vol. 5. Moscow: Progress Publishers, 1976.

May, Derwent, *Hannah Arendt*. Harmondsworth: Penguin Books, 1992.

Medvedev, Roy A., *Let History Judge : the Origins and Consequences of Stalinism*. New York: Macmillan, 1971.

Medvedev, Roy A., *On Socialist Democracy*. (Ed. by Ellen de Kadt.) London: Macmillan, 1975.

Medvedev, Zhores, *Soviet Agriculture*. New York: W. W. Norton, 1987.

Menuhin, Yehudi, *Unfinished Journey*. London: Futura, 1978.

Mink, Georges and Jean-Charles Szurek, "Pour une analyse complexe du communisme", *Le Monde*, Nov. 27, 1997.

Moore, Barrington, Jr., *Social Origins of Dictatorship and Democracy : Lord and Peasant in the Making of the Modern World*. Harmondsworth: Penguin Books, 1984 [1966].

Morin, Edgar, "The Anti-totalitarian Revolution" in *Between Totalitarianism and Postmodernity : a Thesis Eleven Reader*. (Ed. by Peter Beilharz, Gillian Robinson and John Rundell.) Cambridge, Mass.: The MIT Press, 1992.

Mtschedlow, Michail, "Das Problem des Allgemeinmenschlichen und Klassenmäßigen im Marxismus-Leninismus", *Marx-Engels-Jahrbuch* 2, 1979.

Murray, Oswyn, *Early Greece*. Second edition. London: Fontana Press, 1993.

Nevalainen, Pekka, "Inkerinmaan levottomuudet ja Suomen rajarauha 1919–1920" in *Kahden Karjalan välillä : kahden Riikin riitamaalla*. Joensuu: Joensuun yliopiston humanistinen tiedekunta, 1994.

Nevalainen, Pekka, *Punaisen myrskyn suomalaiset : suomalaisten paot ja paluumuutot idästä 1917–1939*. Helsinki: Suomalaisen Kirjallisuuden Seura, 2002.

Nevalainen, Pekka, *Rautaa Inkerin rajoilla : Inkerin kansalliset kamppailut ja Suomi 1918–1920*. Helsinki: Suomen Historiallinen Seura, 1996.

Nolte, Ernst "Between Myth and Revisionism? The Third Reuch un the Perspective of the 1980s" in H. W Koch (ed.), Aspects of the Third Reich. Houndmills: Macmillan, 1985.

Nolte, Ernst, "Vergangenheit, die nicht vergehen will : eine Rede, die Geschrieben, aber nicht gehalten werden konnte", *Frankfurter Allgemeine Zeitung* June 6, 1987. Published in *"Historikerstreit" : die Dokumentation der Kontroverse um die Einzigartigkeit der nationalsozialistischen Judenvernichtug*. München: Piper, 1987.

Nygård, Toivo, *Itä-Karjalan pakolaiset 1917–1922*. Jyväskylä: Jyväskylän yliopisto, 1980.

Nygård, Toivo, *Suur-Suomi vai lähiheimolaisten auttaminen : aatteellinen heimotyö itsenäisessä Suomessa*. Helsinki: Otava, 1978.

Okihito, Gary (essay) and Joan Myers (photographs), *Whispered Silences : Japanese Americans and World War II*. Seattle: University of Washington Press, 1996.

Paakkanen, Martti, "Kyläräätälin poika" in *Nuori Otto Ville Kuusinen 1881–1920*. Jyväskylä: K. J. Gummerus, 1970.

Paasivirta, Juhani, *Finland and Europe : the early years of independence 1917–1939*. Helsinki: Suomen Historiallinen Seura, 1988.

Paastela, Jukka "Miten poliittinen teko on selitettävissä? – Kuusisen klubin murhiin johtaneista tekijöistä" in *Vaalit valta ja vaikuttaminen : juhlakirja Olavi Borgin 60-vuotispäiväksi*. Tampere: Tampere University Press, 1995.

Paastela, Jukka, "Käsite totalitarismi Neuvostoliiton / Venäjän tutkimuksen perspektiivistä tarkasteltuna" in *Politiikan paikat*. (Ed. by Pertti Lappalainen.) Studia Politica Tamperensis 2, 1997.

Paastela, Jukka, "Kommunismin musta kirja: historioitsijakiista à la française", *Historiallinen aikakauskirja* 4/1998.

Paastela, Jukka, *Marx's and Engels' concepts of the parties and political organizations of the working class*. Acta Universitatis Tamperensis ser A vol 199. Tampere, 1985.

Paastela, Jukka and Hannu Rautkallio, "Johdanto : Hanna Malmin ja Kullervo Mannerin elämä ja toiminta" and "Viitteet" in Kullervo Manner and Hanna Malm, *Rakas kallis toveri : Kullervo Mannerin ja Hanna Malmin kirjeenvaihtoa 1932–33*. (Ed. by Jukka Paastela and Hannu Rautkallio). Porvoo: WSOY, 1997.

Paavolainen, Jaakko, *Poliittiset väkivaltaisuudet Suomessa 1918*. Vol. 1, *"Punainen terrori"*, 1967.

Paavolainen, Jaakko, *Vankileirit Suomessa 1918*. Helsinki: Tammi, 1970.

Palmgren, Raoul, *Joukkosydän : vanhan työväenliikkeemme kaunokirjallisuus*. Vol. II. Porvoo: WSOY, 1966.

Parmanen, Eino I., *Taistelujen kirja : kuvauksia itsenäisyystaistelumme vaiheista sortovuosina*. Vol. IV, *Suurlakko ja sitä lähinnä seurannut aika*. Porvoo: WSOY, 1941.

Parsons, Robert, "Georgians" in *The Nationalities Question in the Soviet Union*. (Ed. by Graham Smith.) London: Longman, 1990.

Perälä, Reijo, *Lapuan liike ja sanan mahti*. Rovaniemi: Pohjois-Suomen Historiallinen Yhdistys, 1998

Piilonen, Juhani, "Yhteinen vihollinen yhdistää 1908–1917" in *Lenin ja Suomi*. Vol. 1. Helsinki: Opetusministeriö, 1987.

Pipes, Richard, *Russia under the Bolshevik Regime*. New York: Vintage Book, 1995.

Pipes, Richard, *Russia under the Old Regime*. London: Penguin Books, 1990 [1974].

Pipes, Richard, *The Russian Revolution 1899–1919*. London: Fontana Press, 1990.

Plato, *The Republic*. (Transl. by Richard W. Sterling and William C. Scott.) New York: W.W. Norton, 1985.

Plutarch, *On Sparta*. (Transl. by Richard J. A. Talbert.) London: Penguin Books, 1988.

Polvinen, Tuomo, *Venäjän vallankumous ja Suomi 1917–1920*. Vol. 1, *helmikuu 1917–toukokuu 1918*; vol. 2, *toukokuu 1918 – joulukuu 1920*. Porvoo: WSOY, 1967 and 1971.

Poulantzas, Nicos, *Fascism and Dictatorship : the Third International and the Problem of Fascism*. (Transl. by Judith White.) London: NLB, 1974.

Puntila, L. A., *Histoire politique de la Finlande de 1809 à 1955*. (Transl. by Jean-Louis Perret.) Neuchâtel: Éditions de la Baconnière, 1966.

Rasila, Viljo, *Kansalaissodan sosiaalinen tausta*. Helsinki: Tammi, 1968.

Raun, Toivo U., *Estonia and the Estonians*. Second edition. Stanford: Hoover Institution Press, 1991.

Rautkallio, Hannu, *Suuri viha : Stalinin suomalaiset uhrit 1930-luvulla*. Porvoo: WSOY, 1955.

Renkama, Jukka, "Kuusinen ja neuvostovaltion käsitteen uudistaminen vuosina 1957–1961" in *O. W. Kuusinen neuvostoideologina* (forthcoming).

Rentola, Kimmo, *Kenen joukoissa seisot? : suomalainen kommunismi ja sota 1937–1945*. Porvoo: WSOY, 1993.

Rentola, Kimmo, "Finnish Communism, O. W. Kuusinen, and Their Two Native Countries" in *Communism National & International*. (Ed. by Tauno Sarela and Kimmo Rentola.) Helsinki: Suomen Historiallinen Seura, 1998.

The ***research*** *project on War Victims in Finland 1914–1922 : a brief introduction*. A leaflet published by the Finnish Prime Minister's Office, s. a. [2001 or 2002].

Rigby, T. H., "Politics in the Mono-organizational Society" in *Between Totalitarianism and Pluralism*. (Ed. by Alexander Dallin.) New York: Garland, 1992 [1969].

Rigby, T. H., "Stalinism and Mono-Organizational Society" in *Stalinism : Essays in Historical Interpretation*. (Ed. by Robert C. Tucker.) New York: W. W. Norton, 1977.

Rigby, T. H., *The Changing Soviet System : Mono-organisational Socialism from its Origins to Gorbachev's Restructuring*. Aldershot: Edward Elgar, 1990.

Rinta-Tassi, Osmo, "Kuusinen vallankumousvuosina" in *Nuori Otto Ville Kuusinen 1881–1920*. (Ed. by Vesa Salminen.) Jyväskylä: K. J. Gummerus, 1970.

Rinta-Tassi, Osmo, *Kansanvaltuuskunta punaisen Suomen hallituksena*. Helsinki: Opetusministeriö, 1986.

Ropert, André, *La misère et la gloire : histoire culturelle du monde russe de l'an mil à nos jours*. Paris: Armand Colin, 1992.

Rosenfeldt, Nils-Erik, *Knowledge and Power : the Role of Stalin's Secret Chancellery in the Soviet System of Government*. Copenhagen: Rosenkilde and Bakker, 1978.

Saarela, Tauno, *Suomalaisen kommunismin synty 1918–1923*. Helsinki: KSL, 1996.

Saarela, Tauno, "Tuhatmarkkasia, miljoonia ruplia, dollareita : SKP:n tilinpäätös 1920-luvulta" in *...vaikka voissa paistais? : Venäjän rooli Suomessa*. Festschrift for professor Osmo Jussila on March 14, 1988. (Ed. by Jorma Selovuori.) Porvoo: WSOY, 1998.

Saarela, Tauno, "Tusindmarksedler, millioner af rubler, dollars... : FKP's regnskap i 1920'erne" in *Guldet fra Moskva : Finansieringen af de nordiske kommunistpartier 1917–1990*. (Ed. by Morten Thing; transl. by Søren Sørensen.) Viby J.: Forum, 2001.

Salkola, Marja-Leena, *Työväenkaartien synty ja kehitys punakaartiksi*. Vol. 2. Helsinki: Opetusministeriö, 1985.

Salminen, Vesa, "Estetiikan opiskelijasta poliitikoksi vuosina 1900–1906" in *Nuori Otto Ville Kuusinen 1881–1920*. Jyväskylä: K. J. Gummerus, 1970.

Salminen, Vesa, "Laillisuuden esitaistelija vai oman edun tavoittelija – Kuusinen ja toinen sortokausi" in *Nuori Otto Ville Kuusinen 1881–1920*. (Ed. by Vesa Salminen.) Jyväskylä: K. J. Gummerus, 1910.

Salomaa, Erkki, "Usko Sotamies – O. W. Kuusinen" in *Tiennäyttäjät : Suomen työväenliikkeen merkkimiehiä Ursinista Tanneriin*. (Ed. by Hannu Soikkanen.) Vol. 3. Helsinki: Tammi, 1968.

Salomaa, Erkki, "Yrjö Sirola" in *Tiennäyttäjät*. (Ed. by Hannu Soikkanen.) Vol. 1. Helsinki: Tammi, 1967.

Salomaa, Erkki, *Viaporin kapina : 60 tuntia vallankumousta*. Helsinki: Kansankulttuuri, 1965.

Salomaa, Erkki, *Yrjö Sirola : Sosialistinen humanisti*. Helsinki: Kansankulttuuri, 1966.

Salomaa, Markku, *Punaupseerit*. Porvoo: WSOY, 1992.

Sariola, Sakari, *Amerikan kultalaan : Amerikansuomalaisten siirtolaisten sosiaalihistoriaa*. Helsinki: Tammi, 1982.

Schapiro, Leonard, *The Communist Party of the Soviet Union*. London: Methuen, 1970.

Schapiro, Leonard, *The Origin of the Communist Autocracy : Political Opposition in the Soviet State : First Phase 1917–1922*. New York: Praeger, 1965 [1955].

Schapiro, Leonard, *Totalitarianism*. London: Macmillan, 1972.

Service, Robert. *Lenin : A Biography*. London: Macmillan, 2000.

Shane, Scott, *Dismantling Utopia : How Information Ended the Soviet Union*. Chigaco: Ivan R. Dee, 1994.

Schejnis, Sinowi, *Alexandra Kollontai : das Leben einer ungewöhnlichen Frau : Biografie*. Berlin: Neues Leben, 1987.

Seppälä, Helge, *Suomi miehittäjänä 1941–1944*. Helsinki: SN-kirjat, 1989.

Singleton, Fred, *A Short History of Finland*. Cambridge: Cambridge University Press, 1989.

Skilling, H. Gordon, "Interest Groups and Communist Politics" in *Between Totalitarianism and Pluralism*. (Ed. by Alexander Dallin.) New York: Garlan, 1992 [1966].

Skocpol, Theda, *States and Social Revolutions : a Comparative Analysis of France, Russia, and China.* Cambridge, Mass.: Cambridge University Press, 1979.

Smith, Hedrick, *The Russians.* Revised edition. New York: Ballantine Books, 1984.

Soikkanen, Hannu, "Johdanto suurlakkoa koskeviin asiakirjoihin" in *Kansalaissota dokumentteina.* Vol. 1. Helsinki: Tammi, 1967.

Soikkanen, Hannu, "Miksi revisionismi ei saanut kannatusta Suomen vanhassa työväenliikkeessä?" in *Oman ajan historia ja politiikan tutkimus. Helsinki:* Otava, 1967.

Soikkanen, Hannu, *Kohti kansanvaltaa.* Vol. 1, *1899–1937.* Helsinki: Suomen Sosialidemokraattinen Puolue – Puoluetoimikunta, 1975.

Soikkanen, Hannu, *Luovutetun Karjalan työväenliikkeen historia.* Helsinki: Tammi, 1970.

Soikkanen, Hannu, *Sosialismin tulo Suomeen : ensimmäisiin yksikamarisen eduskunnan vaaleihin asti.* Porvoo: WSOY, 1961.

Solzhenitsyn, Aleksandr, *The Gulag Archipelago 1918–1956 : an Experiment in Literary Investigation.* Vols. I – II. (Transl. by Thomas P. Whitney.) London: Collins & Harvill, 1973.

Soper, Steven Paul, *Totalitarianism: A Conceptual Approach.* Boston: University Press of America, 1985.

Sulkanen, Elis, *Amerikan Työväenliikkeen historia.* Fitchburg, Mass.: Amerikan Suomalainen Kansanvallan Liitto ja Raivaaja Publishing Company. 1951.

Suomen työväenliikkeen historia. (Ed. by Lauri Haataja, Seppo Hentilä, Jorma Kalela, and Jussi Turtola. – There are nine authors but it is not specified who is written what part of the text.) Helsinki: Työväen Sivistysliitto, 1976.

Sworakowski, Wirold S., "International Communist Front Organizations" in *World Communism : a Handbook 1918–1965.* Stanford, California: Hoover Instution, 1973.

"**Teknisiä** selityksiä" in*"Kallis toveri Stalin!" : Komintern ja Suomi.* (Ed. by Natalya Lebedeva, Kimmo Rentola, and Tauno Saarela.) Helsinki: Edita, 2002.

Tucker, Robert C., "Does Big Brother Really Exists?" in *1984 Revisited : Totalitarianism in Our Century.* (Ed. by Irving Howe.) New York: Perennial Library, 1984.

Turchetti, Mario, *Tyrannie et tyrannicide de l'Antiquite à nos jours.* Paris: Presses Universitaire de France, 2001.

Ulam, Adam B., *In the Name of People: Prophets and Conspirators in Prerevolutionary Russia.* New York: The Viking Press, 1977.

Unger, Aryeh I., *The Totalitarian Party : Party and People in Nazi Germany and Soviet Russia.* Cambridge: Cambridge University Press, 1974.

Uola, Mikko, *"Seinää vasten vain!": Poliittisen väkivallan motiivit Suomessa 1917–18.* Helsinki: Otava, 1998.

Upton, A. F., "The Communist Party of Finland" in A. F. Upton with contributions by Peter P. Rohde and A. Sparring, *Communism in Scandinavia and Finland: Politics of Opportunity.* New York: Anchor Books, 1973.

Upton, Anthony, *The Finnish Revolution 1917–1918.* Minneapolis: University of Minnesota Press, 1980.

Vaksberg, Arkadi, *Alexandra Kollontaï.* (Transl. by Dimitri Sesemann.) Paris: Fayard, 1996.

Vallinharju, Maarit, "Elvira Willman-Eloranta : ihanteellinen sosialisti" in *Tiennäyttäjät.* Vol. 1. Helsinki: Tammi, 1967.

Vares, Vesa, *Kuninkaan tekijät : suomalainen monarkia 1917–1919 : myytti ja todellisuus.* Porvoo: WSOY, 1998.

Venturi, Franco, *Roots of Revolution : a History of Populist and Socialist Movement Movements in Nineteenth Century Russia.* (Transl. by Francis Haskell.) New York: Knopf, 1960.

Vettenniemi, Erkki, *Surviving the Soviet Meat Grinder : the Politics of Finnish Gulag memoirs.* Helsinki: Kikimora Publications, 2001.

Vikström, Uljas, *Toiska : kertomus Toivo Antikaisen elämästä.* Petroskoi: Karjala-Kustantamo, 1975.

Volgogonov, Dimitri, *Le vrai Lénine : d'après les archives secrètes soviétiques.* (Transl. by Serge Quadruppani and Dimitri Sesenann.) Paris: Robert Laffont, 1995.

Volgogonov, Dimitri, *Staline : triumphe et tragédie*. (Transl. by Yvan Mignot.) Paris: Flammarion, 1991.

Volgogonov, Dmitrii, *Trotsky : the Eternal Revolutionary*. (Transl. and ed. by Harold Shukman.) New York: The Free Press, 1996.

Voslensky, Michael S., *Das Geheime wird offenbar : Moskauer Archive erzählen 1917–1991*. (Transl. by Kurt Baudisch.) München: Langen Müller, 1995.

Voslensky, Michael, *Nomenklatura : die herrschende Klasse der Sowjetunion*. Aktualisierte und erweiterte Ausgabe. (Transl. by Elisabeth Neuhoff and Adele Kleinert.) München: Edition Molden, 1984.

Wasastjerna, Hans R., *Minnesotan suomalaisten historia*. Duluth, Minn.: Minnesotan suomalais-amerikkalainen historiallinen seura, 1957.

Watson, David, *Arendt*. London: Fontana Press, 1992.

Weber, Max, *Wirtschaft und Gesellschaft : Grundriss der verstehenden Soziologie*. Zweiter halbband. Tübingen: J. C. B. Mohr, 1946 [1919].

Weeks, Albert L., *The First Bolshevik : a Political Biography of Peter Tkatchev*. New York: New York University Press, 1969.

Wieviorka, Annette, "Stéphane Courtois en un combat douteux", *Le Monde*, Nov. 27, 1997.

Wittfogel, Karl A., *Oriental Despotism : a Comparative Study of Total Power*. New York: Vintage Book, 1981 [1957].

Wuorinen, John H., *A History of Finland*. New York: Columbia University Press, 1965

Ylikangas, Heikki, "Miten sisällissodasta tehtiin vapaussota", *Helsingin Sanomat*, January 27, 1998.

Ylikangas, Heikki, *Tie Tampereelle : dokumentoitu kuvaus Tampereen antautumiseen johtaneista sotatapahtumista Suomen sisällissodassa 1918*. Porvoo: WSOY, 1993.

Ylikangas, Heikki, "Vuoden 1918 vaikutus historiatieteessä" in *Vaikea totuus : vuosi 1918 ja kansallinen tiede*. (Ed. by Heikki Ylikangas.) Helsinki: Suomalaisen kirjallisuuden seura, 1993.

Zakharova (Nikitina), Ol'ga A., "Peculiarities of Collectivization in Karelia" in *Rise and Fall of Soviet Karelia : People and Power*. (Ed. by Antti Laine and Mikko Ylikangas.) Helsinki: Kikimora Publications, 2002.

Secondary Literature in Russian

Большой *энциклопедический словарь*. Vols. 1 and 2. Москва: Советская энциклопедия, 1991.

Власть *и оппозиция : российский политический процесс XX столетия*. (Written by a collective of ten authors.) Москва: Росспэн, 1995.

Зарубин, В. Н., *Большой театр : первые постановки опер на русской сцене* 1825–1993. Москва: Эллис Лак, 1994.

История *всесоюзной коммунистической партии (большевиков) : краткий курс*. (Ed. by editorial commission of the CC of the VKP(b). Accepted by the CC of the VKP(b) in 1938.) S. l. Государственное изательство политической литературы, 1940.

Ключевский, В. О., *Русская история : полный курс лекций в трех книгах*. Vol. 3. Москва: "Мысль", 1993.

Коронен, М. М., *В. И. Ленин и Финляндия*. Ленинград: Лениниздат. 1977.

Коронен, М. М., *Финские интернационалисты в борьбе за власть советов*. Ленинград: Лениниздат, 1969.

Смагина, С. М., "Советский политический режим в условиях нэпа : Ликвидация небольшевистских партий и организаций" in *Политические партии России в контесте ее истории*. Ростов-на-Дону: Феникс, 1998.

List of Pseudonyms

In this list only pseudonyms (or "Party names"), pen names and alternative names of the Finns that appear in the text or in footnotes are mentioned. Most SKP leaders in Russia used their original names. For more complete catalogues of pseudonyms, see Tauno Saarela, *Suomalaisen kommunismin synty 1918–1923*, pp. 506–507 and Kimmo Rentola, *Kenen joukoissa seisot? : suomalainen kommunismi ja sota 1937–1945*, pp. 671–673.

Pseudonym / later name	**Original name**
Agnes	Helmi Heikkilä
Father (*Isä*)	Otto Wille Kuusinen
Iivo	Antti Hyvönen
L. – A.	Leonard Leopold Lindquist
Lammela	Esa Hölttä
Laukki, Leo	Leonard Leopold Lindquist
Laukki-Tiura, Leo	Leonard Leopold Lindquist
Lund, Pentti	Uuno Väre
Luoma, Iikka	Väinö Ruusunen
Kajasuo, M. L.	Matthias Leander Krogfors
Kurutin	Leonard Leopold Lindquist
Matero, Juuso	Frans Johan (Janne) Myyryläinen
Moilanen, Jahvetti	Frans Johan (Janne) Myyryläinen
Moses	Jaakko Kivi
Mutteri	Hanna Malm
Paasi, August (Aku)	August Pyy
Railo, Valter	Oskar Toivola
Railo-Rissanen, Valter	Oskar Toivola
Rissanen, Eino Valdemar	Oskar Toivola
Rissanen, Heino Voldemar	Oskar Toivola
Rissanen, Valter	Oskar Toivola
Salminen, Jalmari	Hjalmar Eklund
Salomaa, Rutu	Matti Janhunen
Sotamies, Usko	Otto Wille Kuusinen
Stein, Matti	Hannes Mäkinen
Taimi,Adolf	Adolf Vasten
Tähti, N.	Einari Laaksovirta
Tiura, Leo	Leonard Leopold Lindquist

Index

Figures written after page numbers by $_{\text{subscript}}$ indicate footnotes and names written in *italics* present-day scholars and other authors.

KIKIMORA PUBLICATIONS

Series A

Temkina, Anna (1997): Russia in Transition: The Case of New Collective Actors and New Collective Actions. ISBN 951-45-7843-0

Mustonen, Peter (1998): Sobstvennaia ego imperatorskogo velichestva kantseliariia v mekhanizme vlastvovaniia instituta samoderzhca 1812–1858. ISBN 951-45-8074-5

3 Rosenholm, Arja (1999): Gendering Awakening : Femininity and the Russian Woman Question of the 1860s. ISBN 951-45-8892-4

4 Lonkila, Markku (I 999): Social Networks in Post-Soviet Russia: Continuity and Change in the Everyday Life of St. Petersburg Teachers. ISBN 951-45-891 I-4

5 Hanhinen, Sari (2001): Social Problems in Transition. Perceptions of Influential Groups in Estonia, Russia and Finland. ISBN 951-45-9867-9

6 Vettenniemi, Erkki (2001): Surviving the Soviet Meat Grinder: The Politics of Finnish Gulag Memoirs. ISBN 951-45-9868-7

7 Hellenberg, Timo (2002): Challenging Disasters : Natural Disaster Reduction in the Context of Intergovernmental Relations. ISBN 952-10-0741-9.

Series B

Granberg, Leo (ed.) (1998): The Snowbelt: Studies on the European North in Transition. ISBN 951-45-8253-5

Sutela, Pekka (1998): The Road to the Russian Market Economy: Selected Essays 1993–1998. ISBN 951-45-8409-0

4 Törnroos, Jan-Åke and Nieminen, Jarmo (eds.) (1999): Business Entry in Eastern Europe: A Network and Learning Approach with Case Studies. ISBN 951-45-8860-6

5 Miklossy, Katalin (toim.) (1999): Syitä ja seurauksia: Jugoslavian hajoaminen ja seuraaja-valtioiden nykytilanne. ISBN 951-45-8861-4

Vinnikov, Aleksandr: Tsena svobody. ISBN 5-89739-002-9

Lebina, N.B.: Povsednevnaia zhizn′ sovetskogo goroda: Normy i anomalii 1920 i 1930 godov. ISBN 5-87516-133-7, 5-87940-004-0

8 Lejins, Atis (ed.) (1999): Baltic Security Prospects at the Turn of the 21th Century. ISBN 951-45-9067-8

9 Komulainen, Tuomas and Korhonen, Iikka (eds.) (2000): Russian Crisis and Its Effects. ISBN 951-45-9100-3

10 Salminen, Ari ja Temmes, Markku (2000): Transitioteoriaa etsimässä. ISBN 951-45-9238-7

11 Yanitsky, Oleg (2000): Russian Greens in a Risk Society: A Structural Analysis. ISBN 951-45-9226-3

12 Vihavainen,Timo ja Takala, Irina (toim.) (2000): Yhtä suurta perhettä: Bolsevikkien kansallisuuspolitiikka Luoteis-Venäjällä 1920-1950-luvuilla. ISBN 951-45-9275-1

13 Oittinen, Vesa (ed.) (2000): Evald Ilyenkov's Philosophy Revisited. ISBN 951-45-9263-8

14 Tolonen, Juha and Topornin, Boris (eds.) (2000): Legal Foundations of Russian Economy. ISBN 951-45-9276-X

15 Kotiranta, Matti (ed.) (2000): Religious Transition in Russia. ISBN 951-45-9447-9

16 Kangaspuro, Markku (ed.) (2000): Russia: More different than most. ISBN 951-45-9423-1

17 Massa, Ilmo and Tynkkynen,Veli-Pekka (eds.) (2001): The Struggle for Russian Environmental Policy. ISBN 951-45-9574-2

18 Liljeström, Marianne, Rosenholm, Arja and Savkina, Irina (eds.) (2000): Models of Self: Russian Women's Autobiographical Texts. ISBN 951-45-9575-0

19 Kivinen, Markku (2002): Progress and Chaos: Russia as a Challenge for Sociological Imagination. ISBN 951-45-9636-6

20 Nordenstreng, Kaarle, Vartanova, Elena and Zassoursky, Yassen (eds.) (2001, 2002): Russian Media Challenge. ISBN 951-45-9689-6

21 Nystén-Haarala, Soili (2001): Russian Law in Transition : Law and Institutional Change. ISBN 951-45-9902-0

22 Ihanus, Juhani (2001): Swaddling, Shame and Society : On Psychohistory and Russia. ISBN 952-10-0098-8

23 Snellman, Hanna (2001): Khants' Time. ISBN 951-45-9997-7

24 Laine, Antti and Ylikangas, Mikko (eds.) (2001): Rise and Fall of Soviet Karelia : People and Power. ISBN 952-10-0099-6

25 Kivinen, Markku and Pynnöniemi, Katri (eds.) (2002): Beyond the Garden Ring : Dimensions of Russian Regionalism. ISBN 952-10-0544-0

26 Medijainen, Eero and Made, Vahur (eds.) (2002): Estonian Foreign Policy at the Cross-Roads. ISBN 952-10-0754-0

27 Paastela, Jukka (2003): Finnish Communism under Soviet Totalitarianism : Oppositions within the Finnish Communist Party in Soviet Russia 1918–1935. ISBN 952-10-0755-9

Orders:
Aleksanteri Institute
PO. Box 4, Fin-00014 University of Helsinki
Telephone +358-9-191 24175
Telefax +358-9-191 23822
E-mail: kikimora-publications@helsinki.fi
www.kikimora-publications.com